The Official VisiBroker™ for Java™ Handbook

Michael McCaffery
Bill Scott

A Division of Macmillan Computer Publishing
201 West 103rd St., Indianapolis, Indiana 46290 USA

THE OFFICIAL VISIBROKER™ FOR JAVA™ HANDBOOK

Copyright © 1999 by Sams Publishing

All rights reserved. No part of this book shall be reproduced, stored in a retrieval system, or transmitted by any means, electronic, mechanical, photocopying, recording, or otherwise, without written permission from the publisher. No patent liability is assumed with respect to the use of the information contained herein. Although every precaution has been taken in the preparation of this book, the publisher and authors assume no responsibility for errors or omissions. Neither is any liability assumed for damages resulting from the use of the information contained herein.

International Standard Book Number: 0-672-31451-7

Library of Congress Catalog Card Number: 98-87216

Printed in the United States of America

First Printing: March, 1999

00 99   4 3 2 1

Trademarks

All terms mentioned in this book that are known to be trademarks or service marks have been appropriately capitalized. Sams Publishing cannot attest to the accuracy of this information. Use of a term in this book should not be regarded as affecting the validity of any trademark or service mark. Java is a trademark of Sun Microsystems, Inc. VisiBroker is a trademark of Inprise Corporation.

Warning and Disclaimer

Every effort has been made to make this book as complete and as accurate as possible, but no warranty or fitness is implied. The information provided is on an "as is" basis. The authors and the publisher shall have neither liability nor responsibility to any person or entity with respect to any loss or damages arising from the information contained in this book or from the use of the CD or programs accompanying it.

EXECUTIVE EDITOR
Tracy Dunkelberger

ACQUISITIONS EDITOR
Ron Gallagher
Aolly Allender

DEVELOPMENT EDITOR
Jeff Durham

MANAGING EDITOR
Jodi Jensen

PROJECT EDITOR
Heather Talbot

COPY EDITOR
Rhonda Tinch-Mize

INDEXER
Erika Millen

PROOFREADERS
Eddie Lushbaugh
Betsy Brown

TECHNICAL EDITOR
Inprise

SOFTWARE DEVELOPMENT SPECIALIST
Andrea Duvall

TEAM COORDINATOR
Michelle Newcomb

INTERIOR DESIGN
Anne Jones

COVER DESIGN
Anne Jones

LAYOUT TECHNICIAN
Susan Geiselman

OVERVIEW

	Introduction 1
1	Introduction to CORBA and VisiBroker for Java 3
2	Introduction to IDL 19
3	IDL to Java Language Mapping 35
4	Advanced IDL and the idl2java Compiler 81
5	Server Essentials 113
6	The Smart Agent 139
7	Using Factories and IORs 167
8	The Common Object Services (COS) Naming Service 185
9	The URLNaming Service 201
10	Applets and the GateKeeper 211
11	Caffeine 239
12	Dynamic VisiBroker 257
13	Interface Repository 293
14	DynAnys 317
15	Object Activation Daemon and Object Activators 345
16	Smart Stubs, Callbacks, and Object Wrappers 361
17	Event Handlers and Principal Authentication 383
18	Understanding the GIOP Protocol and Message Interceptors 411
19	Location Service and Smart Agent Triggers 447
20	The COS Event Service 463
21	Monitoring and Debugging 483
	Index 496

CONTENTS

INTRODUCTION   **1**

1 INTRODUCTION TO CORBA AND VISIBROKER FOR JAVA   **3**
    Let's Start at the Very Beginning… 4
    The CORBA Communication Model 5
        Client and Object Implementation 6
        Static Stubs and Skeletons 7
        The Dynamic Invocation Interface and Dynamic Skeleton
            Interface (DII and DSI) 8
        Object Adapter 9
        ORB Interface 10
    VisiBroker for Java Details 10
        Smart Agent 10
        Smart Binding 10
        Thread and Connection Management 10
        URL Naming 11
        GateKeeper 11
        Caffeine Compilers 11
        Object Activation Daemon 11
        Smart Stubs 12
        Event Handlers 12
        Interceptors 12
        Location Service 12
        Object Request Debugger 12
    VisiBroker Common Object Services 13
        VisiBroker Naming Service 13
        VisiBroker Events Service 13
    Install VisiBroker for Java 13
        Basic System Requirements 13
    After Installation 14
    A Review of the VisiBroker Installation 15
    Summary 16

2 INTRODUCTION TO IDL   **19**
    Background 20
    Comments 21
    Names, Reserved Names, and Reserved Words 22
        Modules and Name Scoping 24
        Interfaces 28
        Forward Declarations 29

	Constants	30
	Attributes	31
	Operations	32
	Summary	34

3 IDL to Java Language Mapping   35

Passing Direction and the Holder Class	36
Basic Data Type Mapping	37
Boolean	38
char	38
wchar	38
octet	38
string	39
wstring	39
short	39
unsigned short	39
long	40
unsigned long	40
long long	40
unsigned long long	40
double	40
Data Passing Example Using Basic Types	40
Constructed Data Types	45
Enum	45
Union	47
Structures	53
Typedef	55
Sequences	56
Arrays	57
Parameter Passing Example Using Constructed Types	58
IDL Specific Data Types	62
Anys	62
Context	75
Summary	79

4 Advanced IDL and the idl2java Compiler   81

IDL Interface Inheritance	82
Inheritance in Java	82
Interface Inheritance	83
Interface Inheritance in IDL	84
Interface Inheritance Through IDL to Java Mapping	85
Exceptions	88
System Exceptions	88

User-defined Exceptions 92
The VisiBroker IDL to Java Compiler 94
    IDL Preprocessor 94
    idl2java Code Generated 98
    Code Suppression Options 103
The idl2java Generated Files 103
    `<IDL Interface Name>.java` 104
    `<Type Name>Holder.java` 104
    `<IDL Type Name>Helper.java` 105
    `_st_<IDL Interface Name>.java` 107
    `<IDL Interface Name>ImplBase.java` 108
    `<IDL Interface Name>Operations.java and #tie#`
        `<IDL Interface Name>.java` 109
    `_example_<IDL Interface Name>.java` 110
Summary 110

5 SERVER ESSENTIALS   113

The ORB 114
The BOA 116
    Generation and Mapping of Object References to Their
        Implementations 116
    Registrations of Implementations 118
Built-in Threading Models for VisiBroker Servers 119
    Thread-per-Session 121
    Thread Pool 121
    Connection Management 123
Developing Server Objects 124
    Developing Server Objects with the Skeleton Approach 124
    Developing Server Objects by Using the `Tie` Delegation
        Approach 126
The `Tie` Mechanism 128
Core Operations for All Server Objects 132
A Full Review of Implementing a Server Object 134
Summary 137

6 THE SMART AGENT   139

How Does a Client Find the Server? 140
The VisiBroker Smart Agent 142
Smart Agents 146
    Smart Agent to Smart Agent Communication 147
    Communication Between Server Objects and the Smart Agent 148
    Using Persistent Objects with Smart Agents 150
Communication Between Clients and Smart Agents 154

   `bind(org.omg.CORBA.ORB orb)` 155
   `bind(org.omg.CORBA.ORB orb, java.lang.String name)` 156
   `bind(org.omg.CORBA.ORB orb, java.lang.String name,`
    `java.lang.String host,`
    `org.omg.CORBA.BindOptions options)` 156
  Client Connections 158
  Automatic Smart Binding by Clients 160
  Smart Agents and Multiple Environments 161
  Smart Agents and Different Networks 162
  Understanding Smart Agents, IORs, and DNS Lookups 163
  Smart Agents and Multi-Homed Hosts 163
  Turning Off Smart Agents Broadcast 164
  From Within a Client Applet 165
 Summary 166

7   Using Factories and IORs   167
 The Factory Pattern Explained 168
 IORs 168
 How to Use IORs Without the Smart Agent 171
 How to Implement a Factory Server Object 176
 Summary 184

8   The Common Object Services (COS) Naming Service   185
 COS Naming Service Background 186
 Obtaining an Initial Context 187
 Binding and Resolving: Operations That Change the Naming
  Structure 191
   `NameComponent` 192
   `Name` 193
 Navigating the Name Structure 196
 Summary 199

9   The URLNaming Service   201
 URLNaming IDL 202
  How a Server Registers with the Web Server 203
  Exceptions 205
 How a Client Locates a Server 205
  Approach One—Using the `bind()` Method 206
  Approach Two—Using
   `resolve_initial_references()` and `narrow()` 208
 Summary 209

10   Applets and the GateKeeper   211
 Applet Overview 212
 The Sandbox Problem 212
 GateKeeper Overview 213

  A Sandbox Proxy 213
  An HTTP Tunneling Proxy 214
  A Lightweight HTTPd for Testing 216
 An Inside Look at a VisiBroker Applet 217
  Applet HTML Settings and Configurations 222
  Starting the GateKeeper 224
  The gkconfig Tool 224
  Chaining GateKeepers 232
  Java Applications and Firewalls 232
  Security Considerations with the GateKeeper 232
 Signed Applets and Alternative Download Strategies 233
  Making a Netscape Pre-install 234
  Using Netcaster 238
 Summary 238

11   CAFFEINE   239

 Why Caffeine? 240
 Understanding the java2iiop Compiler 241
  Options for java2iiop 243
 Understanding the java2idl Compiler 244
  Options for java2idl 245
 Java to IDL Language Mapping 246
 Extensible Structs 247
  An Example of Extensible Structs 248
  Using Extensible Structs Directly in IDL 252
 Exceptions 253
 Summary 255

12   DYNAMIC VISIBROKER   257

 Uses for the Dynamic Features 258
 A Review of DII Types and Terms 258
  Context 258
  Any, TypeCodes, and TCKind 259
  NamedValues 262
  NVList 263
  Environment 265
 The Dynamic Invocation Interface 265
  Getting the Server Object Reference 266
  Create a Request Object 267
  Send the Request 273
  Handling Return Types 279
  Exceptions 280
  The idl2java Shortcut 280
 The Dynamic Skeleton Interface 282

	Steps Needed to Use the DSI	283
	The idl2java Shortcut for DSI	288
	Summary	291
13	**INTERFACE REPOSITORY**	**293**
	The Interface Repository Structure	294
	Interface Repository Types	295
	`Repository`	295
	`ModuleDef`	296
	`InterfaceDef`	296
	Definition Kind	300
	Using the Interface Repository Objects	301
	A Sample DII Client That Uses the Interface Repository	305
	Summary	316
14	**DynAnys**	**317**
	A Review of `Anys` and `TypeCodes`	318
	`TypeCodes` Revisited	325
	`DynAnys`	327
	`DynAny` Types	327
	Creating `DynAnys` and `DynAny` Types	327
	The `DynAny` Interface	328
	A `DynAny` Example	333
	Summary	343
15	**OBJECT ACTIVATION DAEMON AND OBJECT ACTIVATORS**	**345**
	Object Activation Daemon for Java	346
	Using the oadj	347
	Using Service Activators	354
	Summary	360
16	**SMART STUBS, CALLBACKS, AND OBJECT WRAPPERS**	**361**
	Smart Stubs	362
	Creating Smart Stubs	362
	Using Smart Stubs on the Client	364
	Summary of Smart Stubs	366
	Callbacks	366
	Implementing Callbacks	367
	Object Wrappers	372
	Typed Object Wrappers	373
	Untyped Object Wrappers	378
	Combining Typed and Untyped Object Wrappers	382
	Summary	382

17   Event Handlers and Principal Authentication   383

- The Principal 384
  - Obtaining the Principal 385
  - An Example Using the Principal 386
- Server-side Event Handlers 390
  - `bind(in ConnectionInfo, in Principal, in CORBA::Object)` 394
  - `unbind(in ConnectionInfo, in Principal, in CORBA::Object)` 395
  - `client_aborted(in ConnectionInfo, in org.omg.CORBA.Object)` 396
  - `pre_method(in ConnectionInfo, in org.omg.CORBA.Principal, in String operation_name, in org.omg.CORBA.Object)` 397
  - `post_method(in ConnectionInfo, in org.omg.CORBA.Principal, in String operation_name, in org.omg.CORBA.Object)` 398
- Client-side Event Handlers 399
- `HandlerRegistry` 401
- Summary 410

18   Understanding the GIOP Protocol and Message Interceptors   411

- GIOP and IIOP 412
  - The `Request` Message 414
  - The `Reply` Message 416
  - The `CancelRequest` Message 417
  - The `LocateRequest` Message 418
  - The `LocateReply` Message 419
  - The `CloseConnection` Message 420
- Interceptors 420
  - Bind Interceptors 420
  - Client Interceptors 425
  - Server Interceptors 429
  - Interceptor Factories 434
  - Chaining Interceptors 437
  - The `ServiceInit` Class 441
  - Installing Interceptors and Interceptor Factories 444
- Summary 444

19   Location Service and Smart Agent Triggers   447

- Location Service and Smart Agents 448
- Methods for Querying the Smart Agent 450
- Methods for Using Smart Agent Triggers 451
- Starting the Location Service 454

Obtaining a Reference to the Location Service 454
A Sample Load Balancer 455
Summary 462

20 THE COS EVENT SERVICE   463

Event Basics 464
The COS Event API 466
    `PushConsumer` 467
    `PushSupplier` 468
    `PullSupplier` 468
    `PullConsumer` 468
    `CosEventChannelAdmin` 468
Events and the `Any` Type 471
Implementing with the `Push` Model 471
Implementing with the `Pull` Model 476
Starting the Event Service 481
Summary 481

21 MONITORING AND DEBUGGING   483

Introduction to the VisiBroker Management API 484
The ORB Management Interface 484
    Attributes 485
    Server Interface 486
    Adapter Interface 491
The VisiBroker Graphical Debugger 493
    Using the Debugger 493
    Starting the Debugger 493
    Options on the Debugger 494
Summary 495

INDEX 496

ABOUT THE AUTHORS

Michael McCaffery is currently the partner marketing manager at Persistence Software in San Mateo, California. His work is to provide technical account management to Peristence's various industry partners, including writing whitepapers and integration documentation, and developing prototypes. He is also involved in market research and competitive analysis in the areas of distributed computing and application servers.

Prior to his work at Persistence, Michael spent several years with Visigenic Software (purchased in 1997 by Borland International, forming Inprise Corporation), makers of the VisiBroker for Java product. While at Visigenic, Michael spent time in various capacities. He started as a senior systems engineer working with strategic customers and partners on VisiBroker applications. He spent time developing and conducting training courses in both VisiBroker for C++ and VisiBroker for Java, as well as developing sales training material. He spent time working in Visigenic's European facilities in Paris and London, working in sales, sales support, training, and consulting, all in the areas of VisiBroker for C++ and Java. He finally returned to Visigenic in San Mateo to spend time working with the Professional Services Organization as a senior consultant, working on projects with several major investment banks and telecommunications firms.

Michael started his software career in Boston at Open Environment Corporation (another company purchased by Borland International, in 1994), a very early company in the space of "3-Tier" Client/Server computing, remote procedure calls, and DCE. He spent time in various roles within OEC, working in technical support, consulting, training, and account management. He was involved with the opening of two field offices, in Dallas and Tokyo.

Michael holds a bachelor's degree in business administration, with a concentration in Management Information Systems from Boston University. He currently resides in San Francisco and can often be found quoting lines from "The Simpsons," listening and dancing to excessively loud house music, and attempting to stay in shape by playing hoops with friends. He loves reading email and can be reached at michaelm@persistence.com.

Bill Scott works for BEA WebXpress (formerly WebLogic), where he is an architectural consultant for various Web- and Java-based technologies. His current area of focus is integrating Internet applications with new and existing enterprise systems. Prior to WebLogic, Bill spent several years with Open Horizon, working with Message-Oriented Middlewares and other various distributed computing technologies.

Bill holds engineering degrees from Boston University (bachelor's) and Lehigh University (master's). He currently lives and works in San Francisco.

ACKNOWLEDGMENTS

I have spent a great deal of time thinking about this section of the book throughout this rather long process. Many people played a very important role in keeping me from becoming totally overwhelmed by this whole process, in one capacity or another. I will attempt to highlight each of these people here and give my sincere thanks.

First and foremost, I want to extend my sincerest thanks to Bill Scott, my co-author. I have no problem saying I would not have been able to produce the caliber of work I set out to write had he not been my partner. His engineering mind and Java knowledge became invaluable resources to me as this work was coming together. Simply put, Bill made this a much better book, and for that I am very grateful. I also thank Bill for his utterly angry, sarcastic sense of humor, which kept me laughing hysterically on many a Saturday afternoon as I was writing. You are the best Grumpus, I hope you never change…

I would like to extend my deepest thanks and warm regards to everyone at Sams Publishing for their help throughout this process. I would like to highlight Ron Gallagher, my acquisitions editor, who held my hand through the entire experience and always had time to provide assistance. I'd also like to thank Jeff Durham for his diligence in pushing the editing process through so quickly.

Other thanks go to several of my old colleagues at Inprise Corporation. I would like to thank Erin Hoffmann and Vishy Kasaravalli who did my technical editing. I would like to thank Dale Lampson and Andreas Vogel, for being great friends and mentors and for ultimately giving me the idea to pursue this writing project. I would also like to thank all the original folks from PostModern Computing who taught me everything I know about CORBA today. Thus, a major thanks to Jens Christensen, Neguine Navab, Prasad Mokkapati, Alain Demour, Jon Goldberg, Nikhyl Singhal, and especially Jonathan Weedon. To Jonathan, I know I was a pain in the early days, but I appreciate all the time you took to teach me…

On a more personal note, I would like to thank all my lunatic friends that kept me smiling and sane throughout my "summer of writing." So major thanks to Jay "Let's make it a banner evening" Schlesinger, "The long arm of the law" D.A. McGoo, Eric "Why do you hate KFC?" Spence, Lena Mah, G-Love, "Sassy" Brian Ledbetter, "Naisty" Joeboo Christ, Ralph the Monkey, Girly Bearly, Ted Vilalba, Sara "smills" Mills, Karen Crowley, September "I love Dink" Reynolds, Shea "I'll meet you there" Byrnes, Laura "I love Droopy" Pesavento, Kristen "Freedom!" Chae, Patricia "I only do brakes" De La Torre, Katie "Ms. Woolery" Belding, Andrew Strickman and Reading Maley and the entire lunatic fringe of 151 Alma Street in SF (hey, the music sounds better with all of you), Victoria "Thursday at Micks" Griggs and the guys at Twofish Software, the entire "21st Amendment" crew in Boston, and my favorite email pal, Thuy Pham. I must also thank my wonderful sister, Julie, for always having positive words of encouragement for me. I'm sure I forgot someone here, so if I did, I will thank you for not reminding me that I forgot your name on this list.

I must highlight the one individual who spent months and months continually trying to convince me that I had vague talent as a writer, Robyn Moss. To Robyn, I will always be thankful to you for the confidence and encouragement you always gave me to write. You helped me overcome my own writing insecurities to ultimately take on this project. I know this was not the type of book you had in mind for me to write, but it is a start. Thanks so much, Robyn.

And last but certainly not least, a special acknowledgment to Wendy Tacquard for being a constant source of encouragement, support, and smiles when my energy towards this project was at its lowest. Wendy, you have become an unbelievable source of inspiration to me, I feel very lucky and thankful to have you in my life.

—*Michael McCaffery*

I'd like to thank my parents who gave me encouragement throughout the writing of this book (sorry about the Thanksgiving spent doing revisions, Mom). I'd also like to thank McCaf for putting this whole thing together.

—*Bill Scott*

TELL US WHAT YOU THINK!

As the reader of this book, *you* are our most important critic and commentator. We value your opinion and want to know what we're doing right, what we could do better, what areas you'd like to see us publish in, and any other words of wisdom you're willing to pass our way.

As the Executive Editor for the Advanced Programming and Distributed Architectures Team at Sams Publishing, I welcome your comments. You can fax, email, or write me directly to let me know what you did or didn't like about this book—as well as what we can do to make our books stronger.

Please note that I cannot help you with technical problems related to the topic of this book, and that due to the high volume of mail I receive, I might not be able to reply to every message.

When you write, please be sure to include this book's title and authors as well as your name and phone or fax number. I will carefully review your comments and share them with the authors and editors who worked on the book.

Fax:		317-581-4770
Email:		programming@mcp.com
Mail:		Tracy Dunkelberger, Executive Editor
		Advanced Programming and Distributed Architectures
		Sams Publishing
		201 West 103rd Street
		Indianapolis, IN 46290 USA

INTRODUCTION

Over the past year, there has been a significant increase in the number of software development groups looking at building distributed object oriented applications with Java and CORBA. VisiBroker for Java was the first all Java-based CORBA implementation when first introduced in early 1996, and it has continued to be the market leader in this area.

The purpose of this book is to be your own personal training tool on how to quickly and effectively build distributed applications using VisiBroker for Java. It doesn't take the approach many other Java or CORBA books take; spending half the book discussing design methodologies for building n-tier applications, and then discussing the CORBA standard at a high level. This book doesn't attempt to force any particular development methodology; there are plenty to choose from and that can be an exercise for the readers. Nor does this book attempt to be CORBA neutral; rather, this book is specifically focused on how to use the Inprise CORBA implementation, VisiBroker for Java. Within the text, we will attempt to clearly identify which features are CORBA compliant and which ones are specific VisiBroker add-value features. However, the goal and focus of this book is to give you all the tools necessary to quickly become a proficient VisiBroker for Java programmer.

This text attempts to be unique in that it is the only book on VisiBroker for Java written in a tutorial format. By following through each chapter, you will build a strong foundation for the basic skills needed to write VisiBroker for Java Clients, Applets, and Servers. The latter sections provide comprehensive code samples on how to most effectively use the advanced features within VisiBroker.

This book will teach you everything you need to know in order to start using VisiBroker for Java quickly and effectively. The design of the text is to model an actual VisiBroker training course: building chapter by chapter so that at the end you will have been exposed to all aspects of the product and will be able to immediately make use of VisiBroker for Java in your current and upcoming projects.

Who Should Read This Book

This book doesn't assume any prior knowledge of CORBA or distributed architectures. It requires only a working knowledge of the Java programming language and basic object-oriented development principles. The text doesn't spend any time discussing Java syntax.

2

INTRODUCTION TO CORBA AND VISIBROKER FOR JAVA

CHAPTER 1

IN THIS CHAPTER

- LET'S START AT THE VERY BEGINNING... *4*
- THE CORBA COMMUNICATION MODEL *5*
- VISIBROKER FOR JAVA DETAILS *10*
- VISIBROKER COMMON OBJECT SERVICES *13*
- INSTALL VISIBROKER FOR JAVA *13*
- AFTER INSTALLATION *14*
- A REVIEW OF THE VISIBROKER INSTALLATION *15*

Welcome to The Official VisiBroker for Java Handbook! This book will serve as your own personal VisiBroker tutor. It starts off with the basics and builds each chapter upon the skills and techniques from the chapter before, so you will learn how to quickly and effectively make use of the VisiBroker for Java development and deployment capabilities. This book requires only that you are proficient in the Java programming language. That's it! We will carefully guide you through the rest. This book covers in thorough detail

- CORBA fundamentals
- How to install and configure VisiBroker
- IDL to Java language mapping
- Location Strategies with VisiBroker
- VisiBroker and the WWW
- VisiBroker and Caffeine
- Advanced VisiBroker development
- Distributed design patterns using VisiBroker

LET'S START AT THE VERY BEGINNING...

This story begins in 1989 when a non-profit group called the Object Management Group (OMG) was formed. The goal of this group was to come up with unified distributed object standards. The OMG realized that object-oriented (OO) development was becoming the preferred development paradigm for virtually all software development. Unfortunately, there were no industry-wide standards for how to make different platforms, different languages, or different software products work together. Hence, in October of 1991 the OMG introduced the first version of the Common Object Request Broker Architecture (CORBA) specification. The key thing to understand here is that the OMG does not provide code or even software. They simply design and approve common standards and leave it up to industry vendors to implement these standards. CORBA was designed to be the middleware glue allowing different languages to implement objects on different platforms and having the CORBA Object Request Broker (ORB) provide the seamless communication between them. The CORBA ORB is shown in Figure 1.1.

As shown in Figure 1.1, the idea behind CORBA is to shield the developer from any of the low-level complexities of having one program communicate via a network to a program on another physical host. It is the responsibility of the Object Request Broker (ORB) to establish the remote communication with distributed objects and handle all network interaction in passing data between objects. We will explain how the ORB does this throughout the remainder of this book.

Because CORBA is nothing more than a specification, various vendors can implement the CORBA specification with a fair amount of latitude. By defining CORBA as a specification only, you should realize that it was not created as a software product. Rather, it was merely a document outlining all the various interfaces that an ORB must support. How these interfaces were implemented and on which platforms they were implemented was completely left up to the vendors. Early versions of the CORBA specification did not discuss interoperability between ORB implementations. Various vendors were implementing the standard CORBA interfaces thereby making their products CORBA compliant, but at the wire level there was no mandatory protocol specified for these different vendors to communicate with each other. This lack of interoperability presented early challenges for CORBA and was a major factor with why CORBA was not widely accepted in its early versions. However, in August 1996 the OMG introduced CORBA 2.0, featuring the mandatory interoperable Internet Inter-ORB Protocol (IIOP) protocol. Finally, the true promise of interoperable objects across languages, platforms, and vendors was a reality.

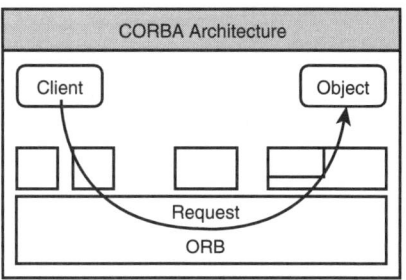

FIGURE 1.1
The role of CORBA is to provide the low-level communication for a Client to communicate to a remote Server Object.

Today, the OMG is thriving with offices in several countries and over 700 members from virtually every major industry. More information on the OMG can be obtained from the OMG Web site at http://www.omg.org.

THE CORBA COMMUNICATION MODEL

As of this writing, the CORBA specification is currently in its 2.2 version and outlines each of the items depicted in Figure 1.2.

As we have seen from Figure 1.1, the ORB itself is responsible for the location of the remote object, the preparation of the data to be passed, and the direct communication with the network to pass the data. The ORB itself is simply the software bus that moves messages from one object to another. Software bus in this context is intended to mean that the ORB is responsible for the transport of messages between objects. The tremendous value of this software bus is that it can move messages between objects that are written in different languages on different hardware platforms implemented by different vendors. This opens a significant number of opportunities in the software world for interoperability and truly open systems.

FIGURE 1.2
The OMG CORBA Architecture and each of its respective components.

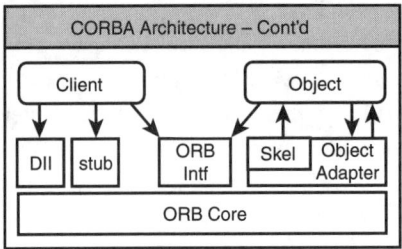

The CORBA model shown in Figure 1.2 highlights the core components of the CORBA architecture. We will touch on these briefly here and will cover them in more detail in later chapters as we discuss the VisiBroker implementation of these components.

Client and Object Implementation

We've established that CORBA has defined how to call from one machine in language A to another application on a different machine in language B. This is only part of the puzzle. For example, we have yet to discuss how the programs on machine A find machine B.

Finding objects in the system, known as location, is resolved automatically by the ORB. Chapters 6–9 show various techniques the ORB uses to resolve the location issue. The second issue of what the remote objects look like is handled by the Interface Definition Language (IDL). Now, we expect to hear the moans and groans, "Oh I need to use Java and learn a whole new programming language too?"

The answer is no. Please understand, IDL is not a programming language; it is a descriptive language to describe the interfaces being implemented by the remote objects. The entire design of CORBA is based on the separation of interface from implementation. This is how different languages can communicate so easily via CORBA.

IDL is covered in great detail over the next three chapters, Chapters 2–4, but we cover the broad strokes right now so you can put it into context. IDL is used to simply define what the remote objects look like. As such, the syntax of IDL is very similar to that of a C++ header file. Within IDL, you define the name of the interface, the names of each of the attributes and methods, the arguments for each of the methods, and the return type. For example, take a look at Listing 1.1.

LISTING 1.1 A SAMPLE IDL FILE

```
//IDL

interface someInterfaceName
{
```

```
    short testShorts(in short shortVal,
          inout short inoutShort,
          out short outShort);
};
```

In the preceding IDL, we define an interface called `someInterfaceName` with a single method called `testShort`. We see the `testShort` method returns a short data type and takes three arguments. Notice that for each of the three arguments, it is required to specify the direction of the argument. CORBA IDL has three possible directions, in, inout, and out. Thus, in the preceding `testShort` method, we pass in a short value, we pass in a short value that we expect to be returned, and then we pass a reference to a short value that we expect to be returned.

Do not worry too much about syntax here, the purpose of Listing 1.1 is to give you a feel for what an IDL interface description looks like. You should notice that we have not mentioned anything regarding implementation, language, or location of where this object will reside. We are simply describing the object. Therefore, at this point the client developer can work independently of the server developer because he has the interface and method definitions of the remote object. The client developer knows he will be calling an object called `someInterfaceName` and calling a method `testShort` passing in three short values and getting one short passed as a return value. Similarly, the server developer can implement this same interface several different ways in several different languages on several different hosts. As long as the implementation supports the interface definition as defined by the IDL, the server implementation can change without requiring any changes on the client.

Static Stubs and Skeletons

The way the IDL bridges the gap between client implementation and server implementation is through the generation of static stubs and skeletons. A stub is a client-side Java source file that implements a local proxy object. The client interacts directly with the client stub. It is the responsibility of the client stub to make the invocation to the actual Server Object implementation. A skeleton refers to the server-side Java source that the Server Object Implementation registers with. The skeleton's responsibility is to receive requests and dispatch these requests as appropriate to the Server Object implementations.

After an IDL file is written, it is passed to an IDL compiler that creates source code for both the client and the server.

The OMG has specified official language mappings for IDL to Java, C, C++, Smalltalk, and COBOL. Thus, the IDL compiler supplied by the vendor does the work of appropriately mapping the IDL definitions to their appropriate Java types. The full IDL to Java language mapping is discussed in great detail in the next three chapters.

The client compiles in the stub source files and the server implementation compiles in the server skeleton files. The purpose of the stub is to create a local proxy object that the client communicates with. However, the proxy implementation does not perform the actual operations. Rather, the proxy simply packages up the arguments and performs the necessary marshalling for network communication.

FIGURE 1.3
The process of creating Client Stubs and Server Skeletons from an IDL file.

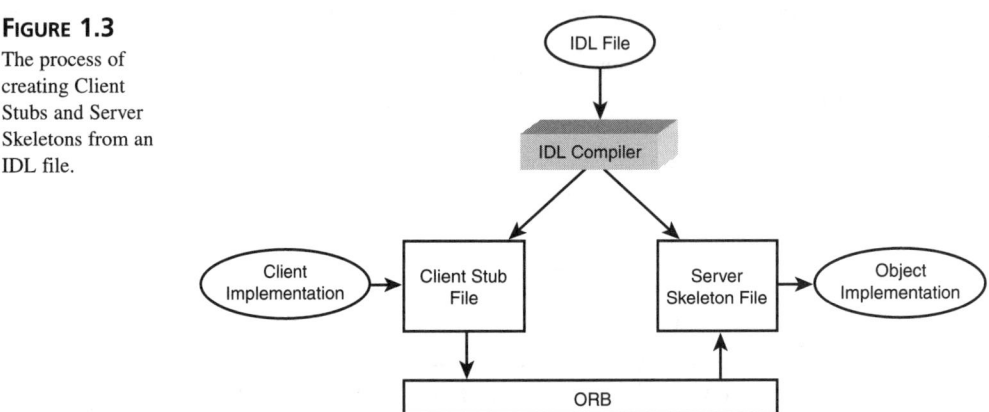

The Dynamic Invocation Interface and Dynamic Skeleton Interface (DII and DSI)

These features are the exact opposite of the static approach we just discussed. Static stubs and skeletons must be generated at build time and compiled in with your source code. With the DII and DSI, it is not necessary to use IDL to generate static stubs and skeletons. Rather, the DII allows clients an interface by which they can dynamically query the ORB's Interface Repository for available objects and construct method requests on-the-fly. The Interface Repository is a standard CORBA component, a container of CORBA interfaces that are implemented by servers in the current environment. Similarly, the server object does not need to be compiled in with a static skeleton to receive requests. The DSI automatically enables new objects to receive requests without having inherited from the IDL generated skeleton.

Figure 1.4 demonstrates the typical sequence of events when using the DII. The client first contacts the Interface Repository to find out which objects are available. The Interface Repository contains meta-data describing the objects available. In fact, the IR contains the same information specified in IDL. Thus, from using the Interface Repository Application Programming Interface (API), the client can determine what interfaces are available, and what their methods, parameters, and return types are. After the client has gathered all this information, it can dynamically create a method request using the DII. When the request hits the wire, the server object receives the request having no knowledge of whether the Client was built with static stubs or with the DII interface.

FIGURE 1.4
Clients can be constructed to dynamically create requests to Server Objects. This is commonly done using the Interface Repository

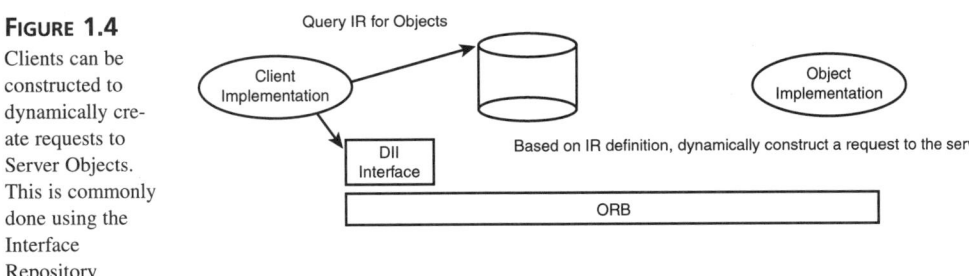

The DII and DSI are covered in more detail in Chapter 12.

Object Adapter

The Object Adapter(OA) is the main way by which Object Implementations access services via the ORB. The OA serves the following several important functions for the Object Implementation:

- Generation and Mapping of Object References to their Implementations

    When an object is created, the OA is responsible for creating a unique Internet Object Reference (IOR). Other objects use an object's IOR to locate and establish communication with it. Communication can be either a TCP/IP socket connection for objects on separate hosts, or some type of inter-process communication for objects on the same host. This implementation is left up to the vendor.

- Registrations of Implementations

    When objects are created, they must register with the OA. The OA keeps a table of all registrations and creates a unique IOR identifier for each object registered.

- Activation and Deactivation of Object Implementations

    It is possible for the Object Implementations to register policies under which the OA activates new instances and deactivates existing instances. The OA keeps an internal reference count of activated instances; when the reference count has been reduced to zero, the instance is destroyed.

    Another CORBA component that is used in the activation process is the Implementation Repository. Similar to the Interface Repository, it is a persistent storage mechanism. However, rather than containing interface information, it contains objects with all the information needed for the OA to activate object implementations. Thus, a reference to the actual implementation is contained in the Implementation Repository for future activation. This is discussed in detail in Chapter 13.

- Method invocation

When the ORB on the server side receives calls, they are passed to the OA for dispatching to the appropriate object. Because the OA is involved with the creation of each object, it keeps a table of all available object implementations and handles the up-call to these objects when method calls are received.

The use of the Object Adapter is introduced in Chapter 5.

ORB Interface

There is a well-defined API directly into the ORB bus layer. This API is used primarily by the stubs and skeletons as well as the DII and DSI. Unless you plan on writing your own ORB, you will only need to use a few of these. This Interface is examined in detail in Chapter 5.

Now that we have established some basic CORBA fundamentals, it is time to take a look at VisiBroker for Java itself.

VISIBROKER FOR JAVA DETAILS

VisiBroker for Java was the first all Java implementation of the CORBA 2.0 specification. Further, it was the first Java ORB to natively support IIOP, providing instant interoperability right out of the box. It fully supports all the core functionality described in the preceding as well as many value-added features.

Smart Agent

The Smart Agent is a VisiBroker extension providing an easy way to obtain server object references. It is a dynamic, distributed directory service providing load balancing and fault tolerance. It is a fundamental part of the VisiBroker architecture because it provides VisiBroker with the features of automatic object location, load balancing, high availability, and failover recovery. It is discussed in detail in Chapter 6.

Smart Binding

VisiBroker internally uses the most effective communication possible based on the location of the remote object. If a client and object implementation are in the same process on the same physical host, VisiBroker communicates via direct Java methods, bypassing the ORB marshalling and IIOP transport. This is discussed further, along with various binding options, in Chapter 5.

Thread and Connection Management

VisiBroker for Java implements two different threading models, saving developers significant time and effort. VisiBroker provides either a thread-per-session model or a thread-pool session. In addition to the threading models, VisiBroker has built-in Connection Management.

Connection Management enables Servers to recycle existing connections for maximum performance, scalability, and throughput. These advanced features are already built into the product and require no extra programming; developers need only set the parameters they like. Using these features is discussed in Chapter 5.

URL Naming

We will teach you an alternative to the Smart Agents in Chapter 6 called the URLNaming feature, which allows you to obtain remote object references via URL addresses. This is a great way to obtain remote references for object implementations from other CORBA vendors. This technique is explained in Chapter 9.

GateKeeper

The GateKeeper is a very important part of the VisiBroker for Java Internet architecture. The GateKeeper is a lightweight HTTP daemon written in Java. It serves several purposes. It enables Internet applications to work beyond the Java Sandbox by acting as a global proxy on the Web server, which enables communication from applets to hosts that are not the applet code base. The GateKeeper also enables IIOP communication through corporate firewalls by supporting HTTP Tunneling. When IIOP communication is not allowed, the VisiBroker runtime automatically wraps the IIOP packet into an HTTP packet for standard Internet communication through the firewall. The GateKeeper then unwraps this HTTP packet and forwards the IIOP packet to the appropriate object implementation. Finally, because the GateKeeper is a light-weight httpd, it is a very useful tool for testing applets without a full-blown enterprise Web server.

The GateKeeper is explained in Chapter 10.

Caffeine Compilers

Because you are already familiar with Java, we assume you would like to continue to work exclusively with Java while still writing CORBA applications. Well, you are in luck because VisiBroker has several compilers that let you define your remote object implementations in your favorite language, Java! No IDL here. We show you how in Chapter 11.

Object Activation Daemon

VisiBroker provides an all Java daemon that can be used to automatically start object implementations for you. It works in conjunction with the Implementation Repository to provide a guaranteed mechanism to start objects on demand. Further, it provides a very easy to use command-line interface to register, unregister, and list objects stored in the Implementation Repository that can be started by the Object Activation Daemon. The Object Activation Daemon is discussed in Chapter 15.

Smart Stubs

One common concern with distributed architectures is that of potentially unnecessary remote method invocations. The Smart Stubs prevent this by allowing you to write logic that determines whether a remote invocation is actually necessary. We will show you how to maximize the benefit of Smart Stubs by making the best use of local caches and how to obtain automatic updates from servers, thereby eliminating the need for remote invocations. These techniques are covered in Chapter 16.

Event Handlers

For debugging and auditing purposes, it is often times important to know what the behavior of the ORB is when certain events occur. By implementing the Event Handler interfaces, you will be able to write your own custom logic for what the ORB does when these events occur. Chapter 17 discusses how to implement these interfaces.

Interceptors

Perhaps the most powerful feature within the ORB, Interceptors allow developers to intercept ORB method invocations at various points on both the client and the server side. It allows the interceptors to read and write to the data buffers being passed. Be careful! If you are not careful with these, you can have many errors that will be hard to detect. Not to worry though, we will show you how to get a handle on these Interceptors safely. This is covered in Chapter 18.

Location Service

The Location Service provides an API into the VisiBroker Smart Agents. It allows querying of all the implementations registered with various Smart Agents throughout the entire local network. This is very useful for writing custom load balancing for servers. It also includes a trigger mechanism with the Smart Agents, whereby Agents can send asynchronous notification if certain object implementations have either been started or have been shutdown. This is the focus of Chapter 19.

Object Request Debugger

VisiBroker provides an easy to use graphical debugger to trace operation failures at the critical points of communication from client to object implementation. It works similar to standard debuggers allowing users to set breakpoints and identify values of important variables. Its usage is discussed in Chapter 21.

VISIBROKER COMMON OBJECT SERVICES

Whereas the CORBA specification outlines only the major components discussed in the earlier section, the OMG has put forth several additional separate specifications for common services needed for building enterprise applications. Covering all these services is beyond the scope of this text. However, we will focus in on the two Common Object Services that VisiBroker for Java supports: Naming and Events.

VisiBroker Naming Service

The Naming Service provides a CORBA compliant alternative from our value-added Smart Agent for locating remote object references. Its design is very different from that of either the VisiBroker Smart Agent or the URL Naming Service, built in a tree structure to provide large-scale directory assistance. In fact, the Smart Agent and Naming Service can actually be augmented for a very scalable global directory solution. This strategy is discussed in Chapter 8.

VisiBroker Events Service

The Events Service is a distributed notification system that complements VisiBroker's remote method invocation architecture. The role of the Event Service is to de-couple communication between client and object implementation. It provides a mechanism whereby clients and object do not communicate directly with each other as in the typical CORBA model; rather, they each communicate to the event channel. It then performs the operation of queuing these messages and sending them to the appropriate object. VisiBroker's implementation allows for either a push or a pull model. The VisiBroker Event Service is covered in Chapter 20.

INSTALL VISIBROKER FOR JAVA

Now that we have highlighted many of the features of VisiBroker, it is time to install and configure it on your machine. Enclosed in the book is a CD-ROM with an installation of the ORB, as well as a directory structure with all the code samples used throughout the text. Alternatively, you can go to the Inprise Web site at `http://www.inprise.com` and download a free 60-day evaluation copy. In either case, there are a few things to point out.

Basic System Requirements

Regardless of the system that is running VisiBroker for Java, you must have an installation of the Java Developer Kit (JDK). All examples in this text were built using the standard JDK available from JavaSoft (`www.javasoft.com`). However, you are free to use any Java Integrated Development Environment (IDE) that includes its own JDK and Java runtime environment. The version of the JDK must be 1.1 or greater. For the hardware requirements of each particular operating system, please consult the Inprise Web site.

TABLE 1.1 VISIBROKER DISK SPACE REQUIREMENTS

Disk Space Requirements for Installation of VisiBroker for Java: VisiBroker Package	Amount of Free Disk Space Needed
VisiBroker for Java 3.2 Developer Package	15MB
VisiBroker for Java 3.2 Runtime Package	10MB
VisiBroker Naming Service 3.2 Developer Package	1/2MB
VisiBroker Naming Service 3.2 Runtime Package	1/2MB
VisiBroker Event Service 3.2 Developer Package	1/2MB
VisiBroker Naming Service 3.2 Runtime Package	1/2MB
VisiBroker GateKeeper 3.2 Runtime and Configuration Package	1/2MB

For specific questions concerning the actual installation of VisiBroker for Java, please consult the The VisiBroker for Java Installation and Administration Guide available at www.inprise.com.

AFTER INSTALLATION

After VisiBroker for Java is installed on your system, there are a few environment variables that must be set in order to get you on your way.

If you are installing on Windows, the local registry is updated accordingly. Any registry settings made during installation can be overridden by using the appropriate command-line arguments. Under UNIX, the necessary environment variables are added to the vbroker.sh or vbro-ker.csh shell script file that is generated by VisiBroker during installation.

The three key environment variables that must be set are

- PATH
- CLASSPATH
- VISIBROKER_ADM

PATH should include

1. Directory with your project files
2. Your JDK/bin directory
3. Your VisiBroker/bin directory

CLASSPATH should include

1. Directory with your project files
2. Your JDK/lib/classes.zip
3. Optionally, you can explicitly include each of the Java Archive files (JARs) that are located in the VisiBroker/lib directory. This is not required because VisiBroker provides utilities that will automatically append the necessary jar files for you.

VISIBROKER_ADM should include

1. The directory where you want to store your configuration information on the Interface Repository, Object Activation Daemon, and Smart Agent.

A REVIEW OF THE VISIBROKER INSTALLATION

Let's do a quick review of the installation of VisiBroker for Java and outline which tools you will be using. We will breakdown the tools into two categories: development and deployment. Development tools (see Table 1.2) are those which assist in actually writing either Clients or Server Objects. Deployment tools (see Table 1.3)are those which are needed to actually run the developed Clients and Server Objects.

TABLE 1.2 BREAKDOWN OF EACH OF THE VISIBROKER FOR JAVA DEVELOPMENT TOOLS AND THEIR PURPOSE

Development Tools	Description
idl2java	This will likely be the most commonly used tool of the bunch. It is the IDL to Java language compiler that generates your stubs and skeletons.
idl2ir	This tool populates your IDL file into the Interface Repository. This allows clients using the DII an ability to browse the interfaces of available objects and dynamically build requests to them.
java2idl	One of the Caffeine tools that allows you the ability to define your object interfaces in Java rather than IDL. Alternatively, it allows you to take existing Java interface files and generate IDL files from them.
java2iiop	The second of the Caffeine tools allowing you to completely bypass the step of defining your interfaces in IDL. Using this tool, you define your server interfaces as Java interfaces, compile into bytecode, and then java2iiop creates VisiBroker stubs and skeletons from the bytecode.

TABLE 1.3 BREAKDOWN OF EACH OF THE VISIBROKER FOR JAVA DEPLOYMENT TOOLS AND THEIR PURPOSE

Deployment Tools	Description
osagent	The Smart Agent Directory Service.
locserv	Starts a Location Service. The Location Service provides an API to the Smart Agents running on your network.
irep	Starts an Interface Repository.
oadj	Starts an Object Activation Daemon (OAD).
oadutil	Provides an ability to list, register, and unregister all object implementations within the Implementation Repository and recognized by the OAD.
osfind	A simple command-line management tool that gives you a quick overview of all your currently running VisiBroker processes. It lists all Smart Agents running in your network, all OADs running in your network, as well as all object implementations running. For each item, osfind returns the host and ports on which it is currently running.
gatekeeper	Starts the GateKeeper.
gkconfig	A graphical utility designed to easily create GateKeeper configuration files.

Now you have an understanding of where the CORBA standard came from and what its core components are. In the preceding table, we also highlighted all the add value features that VisiBroker offers and those beyond the CORBA specification. For the remaining chapters, we will take an in-depth look at each of these features, so you can immediately take advantage of them and start building mission critical distributed applications right away.

SUMMARY

We have seen from Chapter 1 that the Common Object Request Broker Architecture (CORBA) is not software itself; rather, it is merely a specification of standard interfaces for distributed object computing. The focus of this book is not necessarily on the CORBA spec, but rather on the Inprise implementation of this spec: VisiBroker for Java.

CORBA outlines an architecture for allowing distributed objects to communicate with each other regardless of location, language, or hardware. The ORB handles all data translations and network communication in an effort to shield the developer from worrying about low-level details. Developers can work at a much higher level, defining their object implementations with a descriptive language known as IDL. Beyond this point, VisiBroker for Java provides the necessary tools to make the necessary direct calls into the ORB runtime libraries, which then handle all network communication.

CORBA also provides a dynamic interface, (DII), that does not require clients to have pre-compiled stubs linked into their application. Rather, a client has the ability to browse the network to find new object implementations and then use the Interface Repository to get the necessary object meta-data in order to dynamically create a remote method invocation. Similarly, object implementations have the ability to receive requests from clients without the need for a statically pre-compiled skeleton, (DSI).

18

INTRODUCTION TO IDL

CHAPTER 2

IN THIS CHAPTER

- BACKGROUND *20*
- COMMENTS *21*
- NAMES, RESERVED NAMES, AND RESERVED WORDS *22*

We mentioned in Chapter 1 that one of the critical components of CORBA development is the Interface Definition Language (IDL). We also tried to emphasize that IDL is not another programming language; it is actually designed to work a level above the programming language. IDL is a purely descriptive language designed to describe the object implementations that are being developed. The focus of Chapters 2–4 is on learning all the various constructs within the IDL language and how to use the VisiBroker for Java IDL compiler, idl2java.

This chapter begins with a discussion of the basics of IDL. We will introduce its syntax and reserved words. We will then discuss the various constructs of IDL, as well as the data types supported by IDL. Two more advanced topics to the IDL syntax, interface inheritance and exceptions, are saved for Chapter 4 after we have built a solid foundation of IDL knowledge.

BACKGROUND

Before we launch right into all the constructs of IDL, it is important to understand why IDL is really necessary. As we just mentioned, IDL is designed to work at a level above the actual implementation programming language. This is because CORBA was not designed with any one particular programming language in mind. This would be completely contrary to everything the Object Management Group (OMG) was trying to establish in the way of language and hardware independence. Thus, CORBA wanted to be as open and flexible to as many different programming languages as possible. However, the OMG realized that in order to achieve this goal, they must agree on some common definitions within IDL without regard for what languages IDL might be mapped to. Take a look at the steps taken when using IDL, as shown in Figure 2.1.

FIGURE 2.1
VisiBroker development steps.

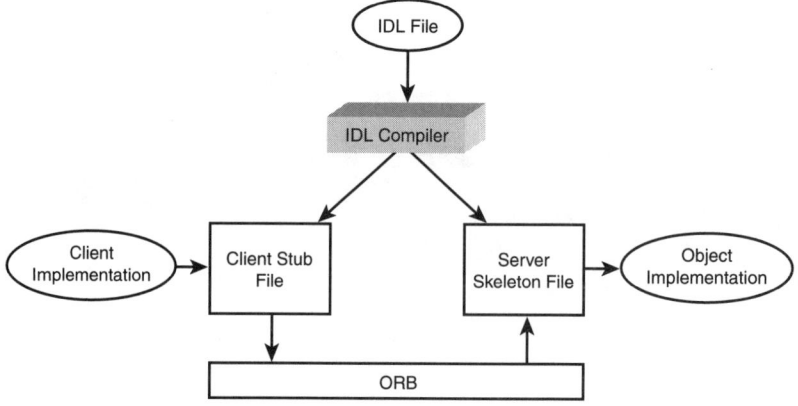

1. Using any text editor you like, write an IDL file.
2. Run VisiBroker's IDL compiler called idl2java.
3. You now see client stub source files and server skeleton files being generated. These files are generated for a specific programming language, Java.

The previous steps use the VisiBroker IDL compiler that is designed for the Java language, meaning that it creates stub and skeleton files in the Java programming language. Thus, you see that the idl2java language compiler does a mapping. It takes all the interface definitions and data-type declarations in the IDL file and creates the appropriate Java data types from this.

The OMG has defined specifications for several such language mappings. In addition to a Java language mapping, there are currently official language mappings to C, C++, Smalltalk, Ada, and COBOL. Looking at the wide variety of languages, you see that it includes object-oriented languages such as C++, Java, and Smalltalk as well as procedural languages such as C and COBOL that have no notion of objects. It also includes languages that are compiled, as well as languages that are interpreted. It is important to note that the CORBA architecture itself is an object-oriented architecture, despite its support of several non–object-oriented development languages. Because of the many differences between all these languages, IDL has to be a level above each programming language, and must support a common set of data structures and definitions that are completely independent of the programming language with which the stub and skeleton files will be generated. As such, IDL supports data types that might not be supported by some of the languages. For example, IDL supports C style enumerations and unions, yet COBOL and Java have no built-in understanding of these types. This does not matter because the IDL compiler maps these definitions into constructed types that each respective language understands. This capability is crucial to writing cross-language applications. When writing applications that involve Java clients communicating to C or C++ servers, it is absolutely necessary for the Java client to understand how to use the C data types when they are passed as parameters. The IDL-generated stubs and skeletons handle this translation for you automatically.

Now that you understand why IDL is important, you will learn the syntax. The remainder of this chapter provides demonstrations of each aspect of the IDL language. It is important to develop solid IDL skills because almost all VisiBroker development discussed throughout this book relies on IDL to some level.

COMMENTS

Because we will be showing you lots of IDL code throughout this chapter, we start with the most important way to convey information in code—comments. IDL supports both C and C++ style comments, as shown in Listing 2.1.

LISTING 2.1 COMMENTS IN IDL

```
/**
 * A C style IDL comment
 */
// A C++ style IDL comment.
```

NAMES, RESERVED NAMES, AND RESERVED WORDS

Before you start typing anything, you need to know which keywords are off-limits, or otherwise reserved, and which ones are safe to use. Take a look at the rules.

Unless there is a name collision, anything you type in IDL as a name or identifier is mapped exactly to Java names and identifiers of the exact same name with no change whatsoever. If, however, there is a collision (that is, you attempt to define one of your data types with a Java reserved word), idl2java resolves the name collision by inserting an underscore(_) to the name you declared in the IDL. In addition to Java reserved words, the preceding rules apply to IDL reserved words as well. It is generally good programming practice to avoid using either Java reserved words or IDL reserved words to describe your identifier. An example is shown in Listing 2.2.

LISTING 2.2 BASIC LANGUAGE MAPPING FROM IDL TO JAVA

```
// IDL
interface abstract
{
};
```

maps to

```
// _abstract.java
public interface _abstract extends org.omg.CORBA.Object {
}
```

When you try to use a Java keyword in your IDL, a name collision occurs when running idl2java. The idl2java compiler is unable to create a Java interface that is the same name as a Java keyword, so it automatically resolves this error by adding an underscore character to the interface name.

> **NOTE**
>
> Although the idl2java handles this name conflict automatically, you should be careful not to use any programming language keywords in writing your IDL. It is a poor programming practice, which generates code that is very hard to understand.

There is also a possibility for name collision with the many files that are generated by idl2java as well. For the idl used in Listing 2.2, the following files are generated:

```
_abstract.java
abstractHolder.java
abstractHelper.java
_st_abstract.java
_abstractImplBase.java
abstractOperations.java
_tie_abstract.java
_example_abstract.java
```

At this point, it is not important to worry about what each file does, we will introduce these generated files in Chapter 3. However, it is important to focus on the names of the generated files in order to avoid possible name conflicts. For every interface declared in IDL, you will get a generated `Helper`, `Holder`, and `Operations` class. This is another possible naming collision situation where an interface name that has any of the above suffixes is used.

```
// IDL
interface testOperations
{
};
```

generates the following files

```
testOperations.java
testOperationsHolder.java
testOperationsHelper.java
_st_testOperations.java
_testOperationsImplBase.java
testOperationsOperations.java
```

> **NOTE**
>
> Notice in Listing 2.3 that to avoid name collision, the standard `Operations` suffix is appended to the interface name.

LISTING 2.3 FILES GENERATED BY THE IDL COMPILER

```
_tie_testOperations.java
_example_testOperations.java
```

Again, don't be concerned yet with the significance of all these files. The important thing to understand here is what the rules are in case of a name collision. A full listing of the Java reserved words that ensure a name collision and cause an underscore (_) to be inserted are found in Table 2.1.

TABLE 2.1 ALL JAVA RESERVED WORDS THAT CAUSE NAME COLLISIONS WITHIN IDL

abstract	finally	public
boolean	float	return
break	for	short
byte	goto	static
case	if	super
catch	implements	switch
char	import	synchronized
class	instanceof	this
const	int	throw
continue	interface	throws
default	long	transient
do	native	try
double	new	void
else	package	volatile
extends	private	while
final	protected	

Modules and Name Scoping

IDL provides the notion of a module for the purpose of name scoping to prevent name clashing of IDL identifiers. A module is a logical namespace for grouping related interfaces. Thus, any IDL identifiers that are contained in one module might be totally redefined in another module with the exact same names without any problem. The IDL module corresponds to a defined namespace, making a logical mapping to a Java package. Take a look at an example in Listing 2.4.

LISTING 2.4 THE SAME INTERFACE NAME DEFINED IN TWO SEPARATE MODULES

```
// IDL
module A
{
    interface test
    {
    };
};

module B
{
```

```
        interface test
        {
        };
    };
};
```

LISTING 2.5 FILES GENERATED FROM THE IDL DEFINED IN LISTING 2.4

```
A      ↵ Notice a new directory is created in the filesystem to hold all of
                 the elements of the package.
A\test.java
A\testHolder.java
A\testHelper.java
A\_st_test.java
A\_testImplBase.java
A\testOperations.java
A\_tie_test.java
A\_example_test.java
B      ↵ A new directory is created for the new module.  Notice that the files
                 being created for this directory are exactly identical to the files
           listed above.  However, they contain different scoped names because
           the classes are contained in different packages.
B\test.java
B\testHolder.java
B\testHelper.java
B\_st_test.java
B\_testImplBase.java
B\testOperations.java
B\_tie_test.java
B\_example_test.java
```

The fully scoped names for the interfaces defined in Listing 2.4 are A.test and B.test, respectively.

It is also possible to have nested modules. The IDL used in Listing 2.4 has changed, as shown in Listing 2.6.

LISTING 2.6 EXAMPLE OF NESTED MODULES

```
// IDL
module A
{
    module B
    {
        module C
        {
            interface test
            {
            };
        };
    };
};
```

The IDL in Listing 2.6 generates the files shown in Listing 2.7.

LISTING 2.7 FILES GENERATED FROM THE IDL IN LISTING 2.6

```
A          ↵ Creation of top level module directory
A\B        ↵ Creation of the second module directory
A\B\C      ↵ Creation of the third module directory
A\B\C\test.java
A\B\C\testHolder.java
A\B\C\testHelper.java
A\B\C\_st_test.java
A\B\C\_testImplBase.java
A\B\C\testOperations.java
A\B\C\_tie_test.java
A\B\C\_example_test.java
```

So for the IDL example in Listing 2.6, the fully scoped name for the interface test is A.B.C.test.

The interface test is generated as shown in Listing 2.8.

LISTING 2.8 THE GENERATED INTERFACE FROM THE IDL DEFINING NESTED MODULES

```
package A.B.C;
public interface test extends org.omg.CORBA.Object {
}
```

It is also possible to take nested modules and redefine the same interface. See the IDL example in Listing 2.9.

LISTING 2.9 SAMPLE IDL CONTAINING NESTED MODULES WITH THE SAME INTERFACE NAME DEFINED IN EACH MODULE

```
// IDL
module A
{
    module B
    {
        module C
        {
            interface test
            {
            };
        };

        interface test
        {
        };
    };
```

```
    interface test
    {
    };
};
```

This creates the files found in Listing 2.10.

LISTING 2.10   FILES GENERATED FROM THE IDL IN LISTING 2.9

```
A                           ↵ Top level module
A\B                     ↵ Second level module, sub module of A
A\B\C                     ↵ Third level of module, sub module of B
A\B\C\test.java              ↵ Interface test, with full scope of A.B.C.test
A\B\C\testHolder.java
A\B\C\testHelper.java
A\B\C\_st_test.java
A\B\C\_testImplBase.java
A\B\C\testOperations.java
A\B\C\_tie_test.java
A\B\C\_example_test.java
A\B\test.java                ↵ Interface test, with full scope of A.B.test
A\B\testHolder.java
A\B\testHelper.java
A\B\_st_test.java
A\B\_testImplBase.java
A\B\testOperations.java
A\B\_tie_test.java
A\B\_example_test.java
A\test.java                  ↵ Interface test, with full scope of A.test
A\testHolder.java
A\testHelper.java
A\_st_test.java
A\_testImplBase.java
A\testOperations.java
A\_tie_test.java
A\_example_test.java
```

> **NOTE**
>
> Because the Java language relies on name scoping with packages more than other languages supported by CORBA, it is possible to alter the module-to-package mapping when generating classes from IDL. This -idl2package flag is a feature of the VisiBroker idl2java compiler and is covered in Chapter 3.

Using modules is not required; however, you should be very cautious when not using modules because all the files will be generated into your current working directory, making it confusing as to which source files are yours and which ones have been generated for you automatically.

When a module is not used, all operations and data structures are mapped to the Java default package as shown in Listing 2.11.

LISTING 2.11 AN EXAMPLE OF AN IDL DEFINITION NOT USING A MODULE

```
// IDL
interface test
{
};
```

> **NOTE**
>
> In the Java language, any class not defined to be in a package is said to be in the *default package*. The default package, although not named, is a valid package. Classes generally should not be placed in the default package unless there are special circumstances (such as the main entry point to an application).

Because the IDL in Listing 2.11 is not within a module declaration, the generated files are written into the current working directory and are in the default Java package, shown in Listing 12.12.

LISTING 2.12 GENERATED FILES FROM THE IDL DEFINITION IN LISTING 2.11

```
test.java
testHolder.java
testHelper.java
_st_test.java
_testImplBase.java
testOperations.java
_tie_test.java
_example_test.java
```

By looking at the generated test.java from the IDL definition in Listing 2.11, you see Listing 2.13.

LISTING 2.13 GENERATED INTERFACE FROM IDL IN LISTING 2.12

```
public interface test extends org.omg.CORBA.Object {
}
```

The fully scoped name for this interface is test; notice that there is no package declaration.

Interfaces

Interfaces have been mentioned in some of the previous examples but have never been fully defined. Interfaces are the most critical part of IDL because they define all the available operations of a given server object. It is through this interface that clients know what methods a given object implementation supports, as well as the exact signatures of those methods. As long as the interface does not change, the actual implementation of that interface can change without any impact to the client code.

An IDL interface maps to a public Java interface of the exact same name. This Java interface is implemented by the generated client stub as well as the server skeleton. If you use the test interface discussed in the previous example, you see the generation of the Java interface, as shown in Listing 2.14.

LISTING 2.14 AN IDL INTERFACE

```
// IDL
interface test
{
};
```

When the IDL in Listing 2.14 is parsed and compiled by the idl2java compiler, it creates a public interface of the exact same name which extends `org.omg.CORBA.Object`, the base interface for any CORBA Object Implementation.

```
// Generated by idl2java
public interface test extends org.omg.CORBA.Object {
}
```

> Many systems such as CORBA use the term *compiler* to describe an application that generates code for the developer. Some people new to CORBA find this confusing because it does not compile code as a traditional compiler. It is therefore sometimes helpful to think of the idl2java application as being a *code generator*.

The IDL interface must declare and define all constants, attributes, operations, and exceptions defined in the IDL. The IDL interface, similar to a Java interface, declares these constants, attributes, operations, and exceptions, but will not define them. Each of these is discussed in the following sections.

Forward Declarations

Forward declarations are supported for IDL interfaces. An example of how this is done is shown in Listing 2.15.

LISTING 2.15 AN EXAMPLE OF USING FORWARD REFERENCING WITH IDL

```
// IDL
interface forward;

interface test
{
    void pass_ref_to_server(in forward forwardObj);
};

interface forward
{
};
```

In the IDL in Listing 2.15, notice that the test interface makes use of another interface called forward before the forward interface has even been defined. This is perfectly legal because an initial forward declaration has been created. The IDL compiler allows this as long as the definition of the forward interface appears somewhere within the IDL file.

> **CAUTION**
>
> Only interfaces are allowed to be forward declared. No other IDL data type is allowed to be forward declared.

Constants

An IDL constant can be mapped in two slightly different ways, depending on how they are defined within the IDL. The mapping differs depending on whether the constant is declared within an IDL interface or outside an IDL interface. We will show you both ways in the following sections.

Constant Within an Interface

In the following example, I'll illustrate this constant that occurs within the interface itself. I will also show what the IDL will generate.

LISTING 2.16 AN EXAMPLE OF AN IDL CONSTANT DEFINED WITHIN AN INTERFACE

```
// IDL

interface testConstant
{
    const float pi = 3.14;
};
```

The IDL in Listing 2.16 generates the interface shown in Listing 2.17.

LISTING 2.17 Generated Interface from the IDL Defined in Listing 2.16

```
public interface testConstant extends org.omg.CORBA.Object {
  final public static float pi = (float) 3.14;
}
```

So you see that when a constant is declared within an interface, it simply becomes a public class variable.

Constants Declared Outside of an Interface

Unlike our last example, now we will illustrate how to declare a constant outside of an interface. This is demonstrated in Listing 2.18.

LISTING 2.18 An Example of an IDL Constant Defined Outside of an IDL Interface

```
//IDL
const float pi = 3.14;
```

The IDL in Listing 2.18 generates the interface shown in Listing 2.19.

LISTING 2.19 Generated Interface from the IDL Defined in Listing 2.18

```
public interface pi {
  final public static float value = (float) 3.14;
}
```

Notice the difference in the mapping. Here, a public Java interface of the exact same name as the constant variable is generated with a final static variable called `value`. In this mapping, it is actually the `value` variable that holds the value of the IDL declared constant.

> **CAUTION**
>
> If you want to define some constants to be used throughout your system, but don't want to tie them to a particular interface or many small interfaces, you can collect all constants and define them on a single interface called <systemName>Constants.

Attributes

An attribute is defined in IDL as a means to create `accessor` and `modifier` methods within the Server Implementation.

> **NOTE**
>
> Said in Java terms, *accessors* refer to the get methods, and *modifiers* refer to the set methods. It should be noted, however, that the IDL to Java mapping doesn't follow the Java naming conventions of accessors and modifiers.

Take a look at an IDL definition in Listing 2.20.

LISTING 2.20 AN EXAMPLE OF DEFINING ATTRIBUTES WITHIN IDL

```
// IDL
interface testAttributes
{
    attribute              long read_write_attr;
    readonly attribute     long read_only_attr;
};
```

The IDL in Listing 2.20 generates the interface shown in Listing 2.21.

LISTING 2.21 GENERATED INTERFACE FROM THE IDL IN LISTING 2.20

```
public interface testAttributes extends org.omg.CORBA.Object
{
public void read_write_attr(int read_write_attr );         // accessor method
public int read_write_attr();                              // modifier method

public int read_only_attr();                    //only an accessor method is
//created because it was defined as //"readonly".
}
```

Notice that for our standard attribute definition, `read_write_attr`, two methods are generated for the Java interface, an `accessor` and a `modifier` method. These are typically set up to allow access to an Object Implementation's private data members. As such, by declaring `read only attr` as read-only, our generated interface has only an accessor method generated.

Operations

IDL operations are the definitions of the methods implemented by the Object Implementation. Each operation must have the following characteristics:

- A unique name. Seen in the preceding section on modules. If multiple modules are used, an operation can be defined differently in multiple modules while keeping the same name. However, within the same scope, each operation name must be unique.

> **NOTE**
>
> It is not possible to overload methods in IDL as is the case in Java. This was a decision made by the OMG because operation names are used by both static stubs as well as the Dynamic Invocation Interface.

- A return type. This can be either a primitive type, a complex type, or even another interface. We discuss these types in Chapter 3.
- The method parameters, their type, and their direction. We further discuss passing direction when we discuss data types. For now, you should know that the possible directions are in (client to server), out (server to client) and inout (from client to server and back again).

An example of how operations look in IDL is shown in Listing 2.22.

LISTING 2.22 AN EXAMPLE OF AN OPERATION, OR METHOD DECLARATION WITHIN AN IDL INTERFACE

```
// IDL
interface test
{
      long   testLong(in long inLong,
                      inout long inoutLong,
                      out long outLong);
};
```

So you see in Listing 2.22 that you have an operation called `testLong` that has a return type of `long` and has three parameters, all of which are `long` values as well. Notice that each parameter has a type and a direction.

> **NOTE**
>
> Some Java developers might find out and inout parameters odd in the Java language that does not support pointers. In normal Java, it isn't possible to pass a primitive value to another method and have that method modify the passing object's primitive value. This is because Java only passes primitives by copy. We discuss how this is done in Java through the use of generated classes in Chapter 3.

Oneway

There is one qualifier an IDL developer can place on an operation—oneway. The default behavior of an operation is that the client initiates the remote call and then blocks until a response is sent from the server. However, this behavior can be modified by using the IDL keyword oneway. This causes the remote call to be made and control to immediately be returned back to the client; the request doesn't wait for a response. There are two issues to be aware of when making use of the oneway call.

1. You must specify the return type to be of type void.
2. The oneway operation cannot raise a user-defined exception.

So, make the sample operation you just saw a oneway method as shown in Listing 2.23.

LISTING 2.23 AN EXAMPLE OF A *Oneway* OPERATION WITHIN AN IDL INTERFACE

```
// IDL
interface test
{
        oneway void testLong(    in long inLong,
                                 inout long inoutLong,
                                 out long outLong);
};
```

Notice that the only changes made were adding the oneway keyword and changing the return type from a long to a void.

SUMMARY

Chapter 2 introduced many new terms. In fact, it introduced an entirely new description language called IDL. We began with a discussion that IDL is the way CORBA enables objects to have interfaces declared in a language-neutral manner. We then discussed the syntax of IDL from how operations are declared to how modules can be used for scoping.

Over the next few chapters, we will build on this foundation to develop more complex IDL interfaces and ultimately learn how to use the VisiBroker idl2java compiler to compile these IDL interfaces.

IDL TO JAVA LANGUAGE MAPPING

CHAPTER 3

IN THIS CHAPTER

- PASSING DIRECTION AND THE HOLDER CLASS 36
- BASIC DATA TYPE MAPPING 37
- DATA PASSING EXAMPLE USING BASIC TYPES 40
- CONSTRUCTED DATA TYPES 45
- PARAMETER PASSING EXAMPLE USING CONSTRUCTED TYPES 58
- IDL SPECIFIC DATA TYPES 62

In Chapter 2 we discussed the principals of Interface Definition Language (IDL), and how it maps into the Java language. We saw data types being defined in IDL, but didn't mention which types are supported and how they are passed. We will now discuss the IDL data types. Before listing all the different types, we will first discuss how they are passed from client to implementation using parameter direction and holders.

After discussing direction, we will then discuss the various data types in IDL. The types fall into three categories: basic, constructed, and IDL specific. The basic types are those that map to Java primitives types (and the Java String, which is a special case). Constructed types are those types that encapsulate one or more primitive types or other constructed types. They are data types found natively in other languages supported by CORBA and must be constructed as objects in the Java mapping to provide similar functionality. The final types are the IDL-specific types. These are data types that don't exist natively in other languages. Like constructed types, they appear in the Java language as Java classes.

PASSING DIRECTION AND THE HOLDER CLASS

Before discussing the various data types supported by IDL, we will first revisit the concept of passing direction introduced briefly in Chapter 2. A passing direction must be declared for each parameter in an IDL operation. The passing direction indicates whether the implementation object can modify the value of the passed parameters during a remote method call. The possible directions are

1. `in`—This parameter is declared and initialized on the client and then sent to the server object. It isn't returned to the client. To the Java-only developer, this is the expected behavior.

2. `out`—This parameter is declared on the client, but not initialized. It is then sent to the server where it is initialized and modified and sent back to the client. Said in other terms, the parameter is declared on the client but sent to the server to receive a value.

3. `inout`—This parameter is declared and initialized on the client. It is sent to the server where it is modified and returned back to the client. It is the combination of the `in` and `out` behaviors.

> **TIP**
>
> Java developers often use the terms *server* and *implementation* interchangeably. Later in this book, you will begin to see the difference when you see interface inheritance and other server-side techniques. For now, you might consider the terms as meaning "the object that is providing the implementation of the calls from the stub."

`Inout` and `out` parameters have implications in the Java language that don't have the concept of pointers. Because Java doesn't have pointers (and readers might not be familiar with their use), we won't discuss this problem in terms of pointers. Instead, we will examine the situation in terms of observer behavior.

If a client makes a call to an implementation with an `inout` parameter of type long (a Java `int`, as you'll learn shortly), IDL says it is possible for the server to change that value. The implication is that after the method call, the client's local int variable has changed! This isn't possible in the Java language because primitive types are passed by value (copy).

The IDL to Java mapping solves this problem by creating the concept of a Holder class. A Holder class is a simple wrapper around instances of data types to allow implementations to change the values of passed parameters This is accomplished by creating a Holder class for each data type in IDL. The *Holder* classes follow the naming convention `<Type Name>Holder`.

The Holder class has a single data member called value. The programmer is asked to place any `out` or `inout` variables into the Holder (by setting the value of value) before the method call and retrieve those values from the Holder after the call.

There is one Holder class for each type, so the value data member is correctly typed. For those data types defined in IDL (basic and IDL types), these Holders are in the `org.omg.CORBA` package. For user-defined types, the Holders are generated by the idl2java code generator.

BASIC DATA TYPE MAPPING

Table 3.1 shows how the primitive IDL types are mapped to basic Java types.

TABLE 3.1 THE IDL TO JAVA LANGUAGE MAPPING FOR THE PRIMITIVE IDL TYPES

IDL Type	Java Type	Possible Exception
Boolean	Boolean	
char	char	`CORBA::DATA_CONVERSION`
wchar	char	
octet	byte	
string	`java.lang.String`	`CORBA::MARSHAL`
		`CORBA::DATA_CONVERSION`
wstring	`java.lang.String`	`CORBA::MARSHAL`
short	short	
unsigned short	short	
long	int	

continues

TABLE 3.1   CONTINUED

IDL Type	Java Type	Possible Exception
unsigned long	int	
long long	long	
unsigned long long	long	
float	float	
double	double	

We will now discuss each of these IDL data types in detail.

> **NOTE**
>
> For the wchar (Wide Character) and wstring (Wide String), Unicode is used on the wire for support of International double byte character sets.

Boolean

This first data type we'll introduce is quite easy because IDL defines a type Boolean that has the same characteristics of a Java language Boolean, representing either the value `True` or the value `False`. IDL has constants for TRUE and FALSE that map to the Java Boolean `True` and `False`.

char

An IDL char is an 8-bit quantity, whereas a Java char is a 16-bit unsigned Unicode character. IDL characters are represented using the ISO-Latin-1 (8859.1) character set. The VisiBroker for Java handles this conversion during the marshaling of parameters for method invocation. To ensure type safety, it verifies the value of the char against the validity range of the ISO character set. If it falls outside of that range, a `CORBA::DATA_CONVERSION` exception is thrown.

wchar

An IDL wchar is a 16-bit quantity mapping directly to a standard Java char, which too is 16 bits.

octet

An IDL octet is an 8-bit quantity to represent a raw byte stream. It maps directly to a Java byte.

string

An IDL string maps directly to a `java.lang.String`. Within IDL, it is legal to declare a string with or without a maximum length. If a maximum length is specified within the IDL and either the client or server overwrites data to the buffer, a `CORBA::MARSHAL` exception is raised during the marshaling of the string in either the stub or the skeleton.

> **NOTE**
>
> Strings are immutable objects in the Java language. After a string is created, the string object itself cannot be changed (there is no set method on a string). IDL allows the developer to define a string as an in, inout, or out parameter. What are the implications for Java Strings when they are used as inout parameters?
>
> If strings are treated as if they were primitive types, the out String is reassigned to the original reference that was used before the call. This is much the same as with a long, short, or other primitive type. This technique leverages the Holder to hold the reassignment over the network. However, in the Java Language, strings are objects, not primitives. If strings are treated as objects, the Holder is supposed to carry the SAME object back and forth between remote calls. If the same instance is transported, it should be impossible to change. Strictly speaking, the inout parameter can never carry back a changed object because that class of object can never be changed. Using the Holder to reassign the String reference is misusing the Holder to workaround the rules of the language.
>
> What we have here is a subtle conflict between the rules of IDL and the rules of the Java Language. It is up to you, the developer, to interpret this situation on a case-by-case basis.

wstring

The IDL wstring type is very similar to a normal IDL string in its mapping. It too is mapped to a `java.lang.String`. Further, a bounded wstring raises a `CORBA::MARSHAL` exception if the number of characters written to the buffer exceeds the maximum number declared in the IDL.

short

An IDL short is a 16-bit value with a range of –2 (to the 15th power) to 2 (to the 15th power minus 1). It maps directly to a Java short, which is also 16 bits and has an identical range.

unsigned short

Dealing with unsigned IDL types causes some new considerations in the mapping because the Java language doesn't support unsigned types. The problem lies in the ranges, an IDL unsigned short is a 16-bit value between the range of 0–2(to the 16th power minus 1) while a Java short range goes only to 2(to the 15th power minus 1). Thus the developer is responsible for correctly handling unsigned values.

long

An IDL long is a 32-bit value with a range of –2(to the 31st power) to 2(to the 31st power minus 1). It maps directly to a Java int that is also 32 bits and has an identical range.

unsigned long

An IDL unsigned long is similar to the IDL long in that they both map to a 32-bit Java int. However, as with the unsigned short, the problem lies in the range. The range of the IDL unsigned long is 0–2(to the 32nd power minus 1), whereas a Java int has a range of 0–2(to the 31st power minus 1). A conversion routine similar to that for the unsigned short should be used with the unsigned long.

long long

An IDL long long is a 64-bit value with a range of –2 (to the 63rd power) to 2 (to the 63rd power minus 1). It maps directly to a Java long that is also 64 bits and has an identical range.

unsigned long long

An IDL unsigned long long is similar to the IDL long long in that they both map to a 64-bit Java int. However, as with the unsigned short, the problem lies in the range. The range of the IDL unsigned long is 0–2 (to the 64th power minus 1), whereas a Java int has a range of 0–2 (to the 63rd power minus 1). A conversion routine similar to that for the unsigned short should be used with the unsigned long long.

double

An IDL double maps directly to a Java double.

DATA PASSING EXAMPLE USING BASIC TYPES

Although the different basic data types represent String, Numerical, and Boolean values, the data passing rules for each are the same. When the direction of the parameter is in, the value is passed directly. When the type being passed has an inout or out direction, the Holder class must be used. We will now walk through a full example of passing three IDL long values (remember—an IDL long is a Java int) to an implementation. The IDL shown in Listing 3.1 defines an interface with a single operation—testLong. testLong accepts in, inout, and out parameters.

LISTING 3.1 THE IDL THAT DEFINES AN INTERFACE WITH A SINGLE OPERATION INTERFACE
LongTest

```
{
  long testLong(
    in long inLongVal,
    inout long inoutLongVal,
    out long outLongVal);
};
```

A client to this interface can pass the `in` value without concern for how it will be manipulated by the implementation because it isn't expected to be returned. For the `inout` and `out` parameters, the Holder class must be used. Because long is a standard IDL type, the Holder class is in the Java package `org.omg.CORBA`. Listing 3.2 shows a client for the IDL in Listing 3.1. Do not be too concerned with the initialization code because we will cover this in Chapter 5.

> **NOTE**
>
> The examples in this chapter are the first real examples you've seen so far. It might be observed that the classes are in packages, but the IDL isn't in a module. We will introduce further how you can control the mapping of modules to packages for your generated classes when we discuss the idl2package flag on the idl2java compiler in Chapter 4.

LISTING 3.2 CLIENT TO IDL SHOWN IN LISTING 3.1

```
package chapter3.longType;

/*
 * Client to test the passing of long types, showing the
 * use of in/inout/out parameters and Holders
 *
 * Note that the IDL type long maps to the Java int
 */
public class Client
{
  public static void main(String[] args)
  {
    try
    {
      //Initialize the ORB
      org.omg.CORBA.ORB orb = org.omg.CORBA.ORB.init();
```

continues

LISTING 3.2 CONTINUED

```java
        //Bind to the Implementation
        chapter3.longType.generated.LongTest longTest =
          chapter3.longType.generated.LongTestHelper.bind(orb, "Long Sample");


        //Initialize the three parameters
        //  Create the int for the in value
        int inLongVal = 5;

        // Create the holder for the inout value
        org.omg.CORBA.IntHolder inoutLongVal =
          new org.omg.CORBA.IntHolder(5);

        // Create the holder for the out value
        org.omg.CORBA.IntHolder outLongVal =
          new org.omg.CORBA.IntHolder();


        //For the purposes of observation, let's set the value on the
        //out parameter.  Note that on the server, this value is lost.
        outLongVal.value = 5;

        //For observation, print out the parameters
        //before making the call
        System.out.println("About to call testLong() method\n" +
          "\tin parameter" + inLongVal + "\n" +
          "\tinout parameter " + inoutLongVal.value + "\n" +
          "\tout parameter " + outLongVal.value);

        //Call the remote method with the in, inout, and out parameters
        int returnValue = longTest.testLong(
          inLongVal,
          inoutLongVal,
          outLongVal);

        //For observation, print out the parameters after making the call
        System.out.println("After calling testLong() method\n" +
          "\tin parameter" + inLongVal + "\n" +
          "\tinout parameter " + inoutLongVal.value + "\n" +
          "\tout parameter " + outLongVal.value);
      }
      catch(org.omg.CORBA.SystemException ex)
      {
        ex.printStackTrace();
      }
    }
}
```

In Listing 3.2, the calling client uses the `IntHolder` for the inout and out parameters. It should be noted that the int holder (the Java type) rather than the long holder was used. Listing 3.3 completes this example by showing the implementation of this code.

LISTING 3.3 IMPLEMENTATION OF IDL SHOWN IN LISTING 3.1

```java
package chapter3.longType;

/*
 * Server to test the passing of long types, showing the
 * use of in/inout/out parameters and Holders
 *
 * Note that the IDL type long maps to the Java int
 */

public class LongTestImpl extends chapter3.longType.generated._LongTestImplBase
{

  //Constructor for transient object
  public LongTestImpl()
  {
  }

  //Constructor for persistent object
  public LongTestImpl(String name)
  {
    super(name);
  }

  public int testLong(
    int inLongVal,
    org.omg.CORBA.IntHolder inoutLongVal,
    org.omg.CORBA.IntHolder outLongVal)
  {
    //For observation, print out the parameters
    //before as passed to this method
    System.out.println("Beginning testLong() method\n" +
      "\tin parameter" + inLongVal + "\n" +
      "\tinout parameter " + inoutLongVal.value + "\n" +
      "\tout parameter " + outLongVal.value);

    //Change the value of the in parameter.  Note that
    //this is done to show that this new value is
    //NOT carried back to the client
    inLongVal = 6;

    //Change value of inout parameter
    inoutLongVal.value = 6;
```

continues

LISTING 3.3 CONTINUED

```java
    //Set value of the out parameter
    outLongVal.value = 6;

    //For observation, print out the parameters
    //before the return
    System.out.println("About to return from testLong() method\n" +
      "\tin parameter" + inLongVal + "\n" +
      "\tinout parameter " + inoutLongVal.value + "\n" +
      "\tout parameter " + outLongVal.value);

    return 0;
  }

  //Put registration code here in a main for convenience
  public static void main(String[] args)
  {
    try
    {
      // Initialize the ORB.
      org.omg.CORBA.ORB orb = org.omg.CORBA.ORB.init();

      // Initialize the BOA.
      org.omg.CORBA.BOA boa = orb.BOA_init();

      // Create the RequestReply objects.
      LongTestImpl longTest=
      new LongTestImpl("Long Sample");

      // Export the newly create object.
      boa.obj_is_ready(longTest);

      System.out.println(longTest + " is ready.");

      // Wait for incoming requests
      boa.impl_is_ready();
    }
    catch(org.omg.CORBA.SystemException ex)
    {
      ex.printStackTrace();
    }
  }
}
```

The server implementation looks much like the client, except the `IntHolders` have already been initialized. When the previous code is run, you will observe that no value was received at the server for the `out` parameter, and the int `inout` value on the client has been changed by the value set on the server.

CONSTRUCTED DATA TYPES

In addition to the basic data types previously discussed, IDL also defines some constructed data types. These data types will seem familiar to anyone who has programmed in C. They include data types such as structs and unions, and are native to some languages supported by CORBA. Although Java doesn't natively have such types, they are constructed as objects through the IDL to Java mapping.

Enum

An Enumeration (or enum, for short) is a complex type that IDL inherited from languages like C. For those Java programmers who haven't worked in a language that has the concept of an enum, we will briefly explain its use.

An *enum* is a list of named constants, which can be compared as integers. It is useful to make your code more readable and error free, while supporting conditional computation based on numerical values rather than strings. For example, an auto rental application might support either compact, luxury, or sport cars. Communication between objects in this system would have to convey the car of choice. As many programmers know, using string compares is an expensive operation in conditional code. Performing conditional code based on number values is much faster, but can lead to programming errors. For example, a class with a method public void setCarType(in carType) forces the calling application to know that the int value for a compact is 1, for a luxury car you use 2, and so on. Someone could accidentally pass an out-of-range value, and such errors are only detected at runtime.

Enums solve this problem by creating constants corresponding to each valid type. The constants are given human-readable names, so the programmer can intuitively read through his code and understand the meaning. Enums also map an integer value to each of these constant objects, so conditional coding techniques such as case/switch can be employed.

An IDL enumeration (see Listing 3.4) has identical syntax to a standard C enumeration.

LISTING 3.4 AN EXAMPLE OF AN IDL ENUMERATION

```
// IDL
interface CarRental
{
    enum CarTypes{compact, luxury, sport};
};
```

An IDL enumeration is mapped directly to a public Java final class of the exact same name. Each enumeration element is mapped to two separate static data members:

- One static data member is a Java int with an inserted underscore (_) attached to the name given in IDL. Thus for the IDL shown in Listing 3.4, you get what's shown in Listing 3.5.

LISTING 3.5 A PORTION OF THE GENERATED CLASS FOR THE IDL ENUM

```
final public class CarType
{
    final public static int __compact = 0;
    final public static int __luxury = 1;
    final public static int __sport = 2;
    ...
    }
```

- A static member that has the same name as the IDL enum label represents each of the enum's possible values. The type of the member is of Enum. That is, the class has static members corresponding to instances of the class (something some Java programmers might not know was legal). Continuing in the same generated code from Listing 3.5 you see what's shown in Listing 3.6.

LISTING 3.6 A PORTION OF THE GENERATED CLASS FOR THE IDL ENUM DECLARED IN LISTING 3.4

```
final public class CarType
{
  final public static int __compact = 0;
  final public static int __luxury = 1;
  final public static int __sport = 2;
  final public static CarType compact = new CarType(_compact);
  final public static CarType luxury = new CarType(_luxury);
  final public static CarType sport = new CarType(_sport);
  ...
}
```

Given an enum and the structure described in Listing 3.4, you now need a way to get the value that the enum is holding. This is done through the generated value() method. The signature is as follows:

```
public int value();
```

Similarly, after you have the int value of a given enum, there must be a way to return an instance of an enum of that type. This is achieved through the static from_int() method, as follows:

```
public static myEnum from_int(int $value);
```

Thus, to obtain an enum, use the static method `from_int(...)` passing one of the possible enum values, shown Listing 3.7.

LISTING 3.7 AN EXAMPLE OF HOW TO DEFINE AN IDL ENUMERATION WITHIN YOUR JAVA CODE

```
CarType  selectedCar =      CarType.from_int(CarType._sport);
```

For the enum declaration shown in Listing 3.7, you get the following:

CarType is the class name.
selectedCar is an instance of the CarType Class.

The instance is returned from using the static method `from_int(...)`, passing one of the three possible enum values. If you attempt to pass in a value that isn't specified in the enum declaration, a `CORBA.BAD_PARAM` exception is thrown.

After you have an enum instance, you can obtain the actual value through the `value()` method. Using the enum declared in Listing 3.7, we will demonstrate the `value()` method, as follows:

```
selectedCar.value();
```

This line returns the ordinal value of the enum. From here you will need to use either an if/then block or a switch statement to indicate exactly which value the enum is representing. Using the enum we've discussed so far, we will examine a possible section of code from a Car Rental application shown in Listing 3.8.

LISTING 3.8 A POSSIBLE SECTION OF CODE FROM A CAR RENTAL APPLICATION

```
public void setCarType(CarType selectedCar)
{
  switch(selectedCar.value())
  {
    case CarType._compact:
        //perform conditional code here
    case CarType._luxury:
        //perform conditional code here
    case CarType._sport:
        //perform conditional code here
  }
  ...
//Rest of method
}
```

Union

In other languages, a union is a type that can be treated as several types while occupying the same address in memory. Of course, such direct manipulation of memory isn't possible in Java, so the concept of a union must become an object with similar behavior. Unlike some of the other constructed types, a union doesn't seem to be of great value in Java. We must not forget, however, that CORBA is a cross language system.

Similar to an enum, an IDL union looks very similar to a standard C union declaration. As an example, we will use a union that holds a numerical value that can be accessed as both an IDL float and long, as shown in Listing 3.9.

LISTING 3.9 AN EXAMPLE OF AN IDL UNION

```
// IDL
enum NumberType {whole, real};

union myUnion switch(NumberType)
{
        case whole:
                long whole_value;
        case real:
                float float_value;
};
```

A union is declared with an enum indicating all the possible variants that the discriminator can represent. This enum is passed in as the switch argument, and is used as the unique discriminator for the union. Thus, in Listing 3.9, the myUnion structure can either be a whole number, in which myUnion actually holds a long value. Otherwise, the myUnion structure holds a float value.

An IDL union is mapped to a final Java class with the following:

*) Same name as the IDL identifier
final public class myUnion {....}

Unless there is a name collision, in which case the standard rules apply. For example, we will change the IDL in Listing 3.9 to cause a name collision to occur, as shown in Listing 3.10.

LISTING 3.10 AN EXAMPLE DEMONSTRATING A NAME COLLISION WITH AN IDL UNION

```
// IDL
enum NumberType {whole, real};

union abstract switch(NumberType)
{
        case whole:
            long whole_value;
        case real:
            float float_value;
};
```

As described in Chapter 2 with regard to name collision, the abstract title for the union has an underscore (_) inserted to generate the following:

```
final public class _abstract{....}
*)    A default constructor.

public myUnion() {  }


*)    An accessor method for the union's discriminator,
*)    appropriately named discriminator()

final public class myUnion
{
private NumberType _disc;

public NumberType discriminator()
{
return _disc;
}
.....
}
```

This is an important method to understand when working with unions because this returns the enum indicating which value the union is holding. As you saw in the previous section on enums, after given an enum, it is possible to find out the value of the enum by using the value() method. Moving ahead, we will refer to the range of values contained in the enum as the *discriminant* because it is the value returned to us from the *discriminator*.

*)   An accessor and modifier method for each possible branch within the union.

For the IDL listed in Listing 3.10, the following accessor/modifier methods are created:

```
public int whole_value() {....}        // Our "accessor" methods
public float float_value() {....}

public void whole_value(int value) {.....}     // Our "modifier" methods
public void float_value(float value) {.....}
```

Notice that the methods are overloaded with the same name as the union field specified in the IDL file. As always, the standard name collision rules apply to these fields.

However, the generated methods are slightly different if one variant corresponds to more than one union field. Notice the slight change to the IDL, originally shown in Listing 3.9, in Listing 3.11.

LISTING 3.11 A MODIFICATION OF THE IDL IN LISTING 3.10, TO DEMONSTRATE HOW TO HANDLE A SINGLE VARIANT CORRESPONDING TO MULTIPLE UNION FIELDS

```
// IDL
enum NumberType {whole, real};

union myUnion switch(NumberType)
{
        case whole:
                float float_value;
        case real:
                float float_value;
};
```

Now, a new method is generated in the `myUnion` class in addition to the standard accessor and modifier you saw previously, as follows:

```
// Same accessor method as before
public float float_value() {...}

// Same modifier method as before
public void float_value(float value) {....}

public void float_value(NumberType disc, float value) {...}
```

This method is generated so we can tell the `float_value()` method which discriminant (whole or real) we want to store the value as.

```
*) A "default" method will be generated if needed.
```

As with C style unions, it is possible to use the default keyword and syntax within an IDL union. Take a look again at the example from Listing 3.9.

```
// IDL
enum NumberType {whole, real};

union myUnion switch(NumberType)
{
        case whole:
                long whole_value;
        case real:
                float float_value;
};
```

In Listing 3.9, no `default()` method will be generated because the case labels within the union declaration cover every possible value for the discriminant. Furthermore, it is illegal IDL syntax to attempt to put a default case label inside the union when the union already covers every possible case. This is shown in Listing 3.12.

LISTING 3.12 AN IDL UNION EXAMPLE THAT INCORRECTLY USES THE DEFAULT DECLARATION

```
// IDL
enum NumberType {whole, real};

union myUnion switch(NumberType)
{
        case whole:
                long whole_value;
        case real:
                float float_value;
        default:
                float float_value;
};
```

This is illegal IDL syntax and won't correctly compile if you attempt to run it. You will see the following error message:

`Error: idl2java Unable to assign value for default label`

The `default()` method is generated if you don't specify a case statement for every possible discriminant or use the default keyword syntax within the IDL. See Listing 3.13 to see the original enum from Listing 3.9 expanded, yet we have only two case labels set up within the union. Listing 3.14 shows the creation of a `default()` Accessor Method.

LISTING 3.13 AN IDL UNION EXAMPLE DEMONSTRATING WHEN A `default()` ACCESSOR METHOD IS GENERATED

```
// IDL
enum NumberType {whole, real, imaginary, decimals, fractions};

union myUnion switch(NumberType)
{
        case whole:
                long whole_value;
        case real:
                float float_value;
};
```

LISTING 3.14 GENERATED CLASS FROM THE IDL DEFINED IN LISTING 3.13 DEMONSTRATING A `default()` ACCESSOR METHOD BEING CREATED

```
    The following is generated within the myUnion class:

final public class myUnion
{
        private NumberType _disc;
```

continues

LISTING 3.14 CONTINUED

```
        private NumberType _defdisc = NumberType.fractions;

        public void _default()
        {
                disc = _defdisc;
                object = null;
        }
        .......
}
```

In Listing 3.14 you see that a `default()` method is generated and one of the discriminant types that isn't used in the union case statement is automatically assigned to the default value. However, if you want to set the default value, you must use the default keyword within the IDL as shown in Listing 3.15.

LISTING 3.15 AN IDL UNION EXAMPLE DEMONSTRATING WHEN A `default()` MODIFIER METHOD WILL BE GENERATED

```
// IDL
enum NumberType {whole, real, imaginary, fractions, decimals};

union myUnion switch(NumberType)
{
        case whole:
                long whole_value;
        case real:
                float float_value;
        default:
                short default_value;
};
```

Notice that in the IDL in Listing 3.15, we specify a default value. This causes the IDL to generate accessor and modifier methods just like other case statements. This allows you to modify the default value at any time. See the generated code in the `myUnion` class in Listing 3.16.

LISTING 3.16 GENERATED CLASS FROM THE IDL DEFINED IN LISTING 3.15 DEMONSTRATING A `default()` MODIFIER METHOD BEING CREATED

```
final public class myUnion
{
        private java.lang.Object _object;
        private NumberType _disc;
        private NumberType _defdisc = NumberType.fractions;
        public short default_value() {...}
        public void default_value(short value) {...}
        ....
}
```

So you see that a default is automatically assigned, but you now have a modifier method by which to change this value.

Structures

A structure (or struct) is another type found in C and C++. For the Java programmer, a struct should be easy to understand if it is compared to an Object. In fact, a struct is the precursor to an Object.

A struct is a data type made up of one or more other types in a grouping. In Java terms, it would be a class with one or more public data members. Unlike an object, a struct can only hold data and not define behavior. Therefore, a struct has no methods to access or manipulate its data. A struct in IDL is defined as is shown in Listing 3.17.

LISTING 3.17 AN EXAMPLE OF AN IDL STRUCT

```
// IDL
struct myStruct
{
        long longVal;
        short shortVal;
    string stringVal;
};
```

From the IDL in Listing 3.17, myStruct is mapped to a final Java class of the exact same name with the characteristics shown in Listing 3.18.

LISTING 3.18 GENERATED myStruct CLASS FROM THE IDL IN LISTING 3.17

```
*)      The generated class will have one public instance variable for each
*)      field defined in the struct.  Thus, for our struct shown in Listing 3.17
*)      we see the following generated:

final public class myStruct
{
        public int longVal;
        public short shortVal;
        public java.lang.String stringVal;
        ......
}
```

You see from the generated code in Listing 3.18 that for each of the fields defined in the IDL struct (`longVal`, `shortVal`, and `stringVal`) there is a public instance variable of the exact same name.

> **TIP**
>
> Because the notion of a struct is a procedural programming precursor to an object, just think of structs as objects without any methods because that is exactly what they are mapped to.

The Two Types of Constructors for Structs

In addition to creating instance variables to represent each field in the struct, two constructors are provided. Each is discussed in the following:

1. A default constructor

    ```
    final public class myStruct
    {
    public myStruct()
    {
    }
    }
    ```

The purpose of this constructor is for creating an instance of the `myStruct` class and using the default values for each of the variables. These default values will either be null (for Objects) or zero (for numerical Java primitives).

> **CAUTION**
>
> It is important to note that a Java null is only legal for representing null CORBA object references. For any other data structure, it must be initialized before passing or you will encounter a `NullPointerException`. This is especially true for strings. In order to pass a blank string, a string must be initialized to be of length zero. In our example, setting `stringVal` to null causes a `NullPointerException`.

So if you were to create an instance of `myStruct` for passing as an argument, you would need to following the steps shown in Listing 3.19.

LISTING 3.19 AN EXAMPLE OF HOW TO INSTANTIATE A `struct` OBJECT AND INITIALIZE THE STRING WITHIN THE `struct`

```
myStruct structVar = new myStruct();     // Uses the null constructor
structVar.stringVal = "";                // Initialize a zero length string
```

Note that the numeric types need not be initialized because these will be set to zero. At this point, the `structVar` can be passed as an argument in a method invocation without throwing a `NullPointerException`.

These default values can be easily modified at any point after construction simply by directly accessing the public instance variables.

2. A constructor designed to take arguments for initializing each instance variable in the class, shown in Listing 3.20.

LISTING 3.20   THE SECOND CONSTRUCTOR GENERATED FOR THE IDL struct

```
public myStruct(int longVal, short shortVal,  java.lang.String stringVal)
{
       this.longVal = longVal;
       this.shortVal = shortVal;
       this.stringVal = stringVal;
}
```

This constructor simply fills in a default value for every instance variable based on the values passed into the constructor. Similar to the null constructor, it is perfectly legal to change these instance variables at any point by directly accessing the instance variables themselves.

> **NOTE**
>
> Passing a null value for anything other than a CORBA Object Reference is an illegal operation because some languages cannot support a null string. The concept of a null value is really specific to the C, C++, and Java languages. Because the CORBA specification was designed to support multiple, very different languages, it had to support only the most common set of features.
>
> There is an ORB runtime flag (`-DORBnullString`) that allows null strings to be passed. It should be noted that this ORB flag is an add value and is not CORBA compliant. It is designed specifically for those who are not concerned with interoperability or compliance to the CORBA specification.

Typedef

The purpose of the typedef is to create an alias for existing datatypes. The IDL typdef construct is slightly tricky because Java has no such construct available. The rules regarding typedefs are different depending on what type of data is being typedefed. For primitive IDL Types, an example is shown in Listing 3.21.

LISTING 3.21 AN IDL EXAMPLE DEMONSTRATING A TYPEDEF OF A PRIMITIVE DATA TYPE

```
// IDL
typedef long            mylong;
```

In this particular case, the typedef is meaningless and any other IDL constructs that reference the mylong type are automatically mapped to an original long type itself, not an aliased mylong type. However, the IDL compiler still generates an appropriate Helper class for this type. For Complex IDL Types, an example is shown in Listing 3.22.

LISTING 3.22 AN IDL EXAMPLE DEMONSTRATING A TYPEDEF OF A COMPLEX DATA TYPE

```
// IDL
struct myStruct
{
    long longVal;
    short shortVal;
    string stringVal;
};
```

```
typedef myStruct aliasName;
```

In the preceding IDL, you see that a complex type is being aliased. In this case, the typedef is mapped to either a simple IDL type or to the user-defined IDL type being aliased. Similar to the behavior for the simple types, a Helper class is generated.

The exception to note is the behavior when typedefing IDL arrays and sequences. In this case, both a Helper and a Holder class are generated based on the aliased name in the IDL.

Sequences

An IDL sequence can be defined in one of two ways, either bounded or unbounded. Both are mapped to Java arrays as shown in Listing 3.23.

LISTING 3.23 AN IDL EXAMPLE DEMONSTRATING HOW TO DEFINE BOTH A BOUNDED AND AN UNBOUNDED SEQUENCE

```
// IDL
typedef sequence<long, 20>      long_bounded_seq;
typedef sequence<long>          long_unbounded_seq;
```

Unlike with the previous complex data structures we have examined, the declarations for sequences won't generate a new class that must be used. You simply declare the sequences as Java arrays, passing them size values as a subscript operator [ ]. Thus, the two sequences shown in Listing 3.23 would be declared in Java as shown in Listing 3.24.

LISTING 3.24 EXAMPLE OF HOW TO CREATE BOTH BOUNDED AND UNBOUNDED SEQUENCES

```
// Client code
int[ ] long_bounded_seq = new int[20];
// Bounded Sequences can be any length
// up to the bound limit
// specified in the IDL.  If this bound
// is exceeded at any point a CORBA::BAD_PARAM
//exception will be raised.

int[ ] long_unbounded_seq = new int[50];
// Unbounded Sequences can be initialized
//  with any length.
```

At this point, both types of sequences are accessed using the exact same subscript notation as a Java array.

> **NOTE**
>
> You might question why IDL sequences are not mapped to Java Vectors. The OMG decided against Vectors because they are untyped. When the OMG was considering mapping options, they thought it was more important to have type safety than to provide the dynamic growing and shrinking capability defined by IDL sequences.

Arrays

IDL arrays map directly to Java arrays. Further, the syntax for using arrays is virtually identical to that of the syntax for bounded sequences you saw in the last section. This is shown in Listing 3.25.

LISTING 3.25 AN EXAMPLE OF CREATING SINGLE- AND MULTI-DIMENSIONAL ARRAYS WITHIN IDL

```
// IDL
typedef long            longArray[10];
typedef long            multi_dim_longArray[10][10];
```

IDL arrays are similar to bounded sequences in that both must be declared with an upper bound for the maximum size of the Java array at IDL compile time. However, IDL arrays differ from bounded sequences in the following two ways:

- IDL arrays might be multi-dimensional: Sequences are one-dimensional
- Bounded sequences can have any length up to the bound limit, not necessarily the maximum length defined in the IDL. Arrays must have a length equal to the bound.

Array declaration examples are shown in Listing 3.26.

LISTING 3.26 AN EXAMPLE OF HOW TO DECLARE AN IDL ARRAY WITHIN YOUR JAVA CODE

```
// Client code

int[ ] longArray = new int[10];
int[ ] [ ] multi_dim_longArray = new int[5][10];
```

Notice the syntax is identical to that of sequences because both IDL types are represented as Java arrays.

PARAMETER PASSING EXAMPLE USING CONSTRUCTED TYPES

The constructed types just discussed are somewhat different from each other, but the passing rules are the same for each. Like the basic types, a Holder class must be used for `inout` and `out` parameters. To demonstrate the passing rules for constructed types, we will use a struct. The IDL shown in Listing 3.27 defines an interface with a single operation—`testStruct`. `testStruct` accepts in, inout, and out parameters.

LISTING 3.27 IDL FOR INTERFACE ACCEPTING in, inout, AND out STRUCT VALUES

```
struct BasicStruct
  {
    long   longVal;
    string stringVal;
  };

  interface StructTest
  {
    long testStruct(
      in BasicStruct inBasicStruct,
      inout BasicStruct inoutBasicStruct,
      out BasicStruct outBasicStruct);
  };
```

The client to an implementation of the IDL in Listing 3.27 can pass the `in` value without assistance, but must use a Holder for the `inout` and `out` values. Unlike the basic type example, the Holder is generated for the user-defined struct. This generation takes place when the idl2java generator is run (we'll further discuss this and other generated files in Chapter 4). The name of the generated Holder is *<packageName>*`BasicStructHolder.class`. Listing 3.28 shows a client calling the implementation using these generated Holders.

LISTING 3.28   CLIENT CALLING IMPLEMENTATION OF IDL IN StructTest INTERFACE DEFINED IN LISTING 3.27

```
package chapter3.structType;
/*
 * Client to test the passing of structs types, showing the
 * use of in/inout/out parameters and Holders
 *
 * Note that the IDL type Struct maps to a generated Java class
 */
public class Client
{
  public static void main(String[] args)
  {
    try
    {
      //Initialize the ORB
      org.omg.CORBA.ORB orb = org.omg.CORBA.ORB.init();

      //Bind to the Implementation
      chapter3.structType.generated.StructTest structTest =
        chapter3.structType.generated.StructTestHelper.bind
        ➥(orb, "Struct Sample");


      //Initialize the three parameters
      //  create the in parameter
      chapter3.structType.generated.BasicStruct inBasicStruct =
        new chapter3.structType.generated.BasicStruct(5, "fromClient");

      //  Create the holder for the inout value.  For simplicity, reuse
      //   the struct created for the in parameter
      chapter3.structType.generated.BasicStructHolder inoutBasicStruct =
        new chapter3.structType.generated.BasicStructHolder(inBasicStruct);

      //  Create the holder for the out value
      chapter3.structType.generated.BasicStructHolder outBasicStruct =
        new chapter3.structType.generated.BasicStructHolder();


      //For the purposes of observation, let's set the value on the
      //out parameter.  Note that on the server, this value is lost.
      outBasicStruct.value = new chapter3.structType.generated.BasicStruct
        ➥(5, "fromClient");

      //Print the values before calling the remote method
      System.out.println("\n\nBefore method testStruct()\n\tin parameter
        ➥longVal " +
        inBasicStruct.longVal +
```

continues

LISTING 3.28 CONTINUED

```
          " and stringVal " + inBasicStruct.stringVal +
          "\n\tinout parameter longVal " + inoutBasicStruct.value.longVal +
          " and stringVal " + inoutBasicStruct.value.stringVal +
          "\n\tout parameter longVal " + outBasicStruct.value.longVal +
          " and stringVal " + outBasicStruct.value.stringVal);

      //Call the remote method with the in, inout, and out parameters
      int returnValue = structTest.testStruct(inBasicStruct,
        inoutBasicStruct,
        outBasicStruct);

      //Print out the values after calling remote method
      System.out.println("\n\n\nAfter method testStruct()\n\tin parameter
➥longVal " +
        inBasicStruct.longVal +
        " and stringVal " + inBasicStruct.stringVal +
        "\n\tinout parameter longVal " + inoutBasicStruct.value.longVal +
        " and stringVal " + inoutBasicStruct.value.stringVal +
        "\n\tout parameter longVal " + outBasicStruct.value.longVal +
        " and stringVal " + outBasicStruct.value.stringVal);
    }
    catch(org.omg.CORBA.SystemException ex)
    {
      ex.printStackTrace();
    }
  }
}
```

The client shown in Listing 3.27 uses the `BasicStructHolder` for the inout and out parameters. The server appears much like the client except the holder classes do not need to be recreated. An example implementation is shown in Listing 3.29.

LISTING 3.29 IMPLEMENTATION OF `StructTest` INTERFACE AS DEFINED IN LISTING 3.27

```
package chapter3.structType;
/*
 * Server to test the passing of structs types, showing the
 * use of in/inout/out parameters and Holders
 *
 * Note that the IDL type Struct maps to a generated Java class
 */
public class StructTestImpl extends
➥chapter3.structType.generated._StructTestImplBase
{

  //Constructor for transient object
  public StructTestImpl()
```

```java
{
}

//Constructor for persistent object
public StructTestImpl(String name)
{
  super(name);
}

public int testStruct(chapter3.structType.generated.BasicStruct
➥inBasicStruct,
  chapter3.structType.generated.BasicStructHolder inoutBasicStruct,
  chapter3.structType.generated.BasicStructHolder outBasicStruct)
{
  //For demonstration, print out the passed values.  Note the values
  //of the out parameter is null so we just show this
  System.out.println("\n\nBegin method testStruct()\n\tin parameter longVal
➥" +
    inBasicStruct.longVal +
    " and stringVal " + inBasicStruct.stringVal +
    "\n\tinout parameter longVal " + inoutBasicStruct.value.longVal +
    " and stringVal " + inoutBasicStruct.value.stringVal +
    "\n\tout parameter " + outBasicStruct.value);

  //Change the value of the in parameter.  Note that
  //this is done to show that this new value is
  //NOT carried back to the client
  inBasicStruct.longVal = 6;
  inBasicStruct.stringVal = "fromServer";

  //Change value of inout parameter
  inoutBasicStruct.value.longVal = 6;
  inoutBasicStruct.value.stringVal = "fromServer";

  //Set value of the out parameter
  outBasicStruct.value =
    new chapter3.structType.generated.BasicStruct(6, "fromServer");

  //For demonstration, print out the values being returned
  System.out.println("\n\n\nEnd method testStruct()\n\tin parameter longVal
➥" +
    inBasicStruct.longVal +
    " and stringVal " + inBasicStruct.stringVal +
    "\n\tinout parameter longVal " + inoutBasicStruct.value.longVal +
    " and stringVal " + inoutBasicStruct.value.stringVal +
    "\n\tout parameter longVal " + outBasicStruct.value.longVal +
    " and stringVal " + outBasicStruct.value.stringVal);

  return 0;
}
```

continues

Listing 3.29 CONTINUED

```java
//Put registration code here in a main for convenience
public static void main(String[] args)
{
  try
  {
    // Initialize the ORB.
    org.omg.CORBA.ORB orb = org.omg.CORBA.ORB.init();

    // Initialize the BOA.
    org.omg.CORBA.BOA boa = orb.BOA_init();

    // Create the RequestReply objects.
    StructTestImpl structTest=
    new StructTestImpl("Struct Sample");

    // Export the newly create object.
    boa.obj_is_ready(structTest);

    System.out.println(structTest + " is ready.");

    // Wait for incoming requests
    boa.impl_is_ready();
  }
  catch(org.omg.CORBA.SystemException ex)
  {
    ex.printStackTrace();
  }
}
}
```

IDL SPECIFIC DATA TYPES

Unlike the constructed types, IDL has defined types not found in any language supported by CORBA. We will introduce two of these types, the `Any` and the `Context`.

Anys

An IDL `Any` is designed to be able to hold any single value, whether it is a basic data type, a user constructed data type, or another `Any`. It is the wildcard container for a single value of any primitive, OMG type, or user-defined type. The IDL `Any` is mapped to an `org.omg.CORBA.Any` class. An `Any` can be thought of as a container for any type. Items are placed into and out of the `Any` through operations known as insertions and extractions.

Although an `Any` can hold any type, it is programmatically used differently depending on whether the data type is a standard CORBA type or not. By standard IDL type, we are referring to the basic types (int, long, Boolean), and those types are already defined in the standard

CORBA package. These include `Any`, `Principal`, and `TypeCode`, as well as a few others. The distinction is needed because of how `Any`s are used. There are typed methods on the `Any` class such as public void `insert_long` (long value) and public int `extract_long()`. Because the parameters and returns are typed on the method signatures, the OMG needed a different approach to support user defined types.

For user-defined types (such as a struct, an enumeration, or another interface), a generated Helper class is used for insertion and extraction. Like the holder, the helper is created by the idl2java compiler (we will cover all these generated classes in Chapter 4). Helper classes have two static methods that follow the pattern public static `<type>` extract (`Any anAny`) and public static void insert (`Any anAny, <type> anInstance`) where `anInstance` is an instance of the user-defined type. If the insertion or extraction methods are given a mismatched type, a `CORBA::BAD_OPERATION` exception is likely to occur.

Although somewhat special in the sense that they are a wildcard type, `Any`s follow the same pattern of using the holder class for `in` and `inout` parameters. We will now go through two examples of using `Any`s to pass values. In the first example, we will use a basic type that leverages the types `insert` and `extract` methods on the `Any` class. In the second example, we will examine using the `Any` with a user-defined type.

Example Using `extract` and `insert` Methods on `Any` Class

Listing 3.30 shows the IDL for an interface `PrimitiveTestAny` that uses an `Any` to pass a primitive value from client to implementation.

LISTING 3.30 IDL FOR INTERFACE WITH OPERATION USING THE `Any` TYPE TO PASS PRIMITIVE VALUES

```
// IDL
interface PrimitiveAnyTest
{
  long testPrimitiveAny(
    in Any inPrimitiveAny,
    inout Any inoutPrimitiveAny,
    out Any outPrimitiveAny);
};
```

In this example, we want to use the `Any` to pass IDL long values in the `testPrimitiveAny` operation. The client must create `Any` values to hold the long type. Because the method signature also defines `inout` and `out` parameters, we need to use a holder for the `Any`. Listing 3.31 shows a client to an implementation of the `PrimitiveAnyTest`. Note that Listing 3.31 is a working implementation and uses some constructs we haven't yet discussed like transient objects and a call to bind. We will cover these operations in the upcoming chapters.

LISTING 3.31 CLIENT TO IMPLEMENTATION OF PrimitiveAnyTest

```java
package chapter4.primitiveAny;

/* This sample demonstrates using the CORBA Any
 * type to pass primitive types between the client
 * and server.  Note that there is one
 * more level of objects to notice when
 * dealing with inout/out Anys.
 *
 *    AnyHolder
 *       |
 *       |
 *      Any
 *       |
 *       |
 * member of Any
 *
 * We will use the IDL type long, aka the Java type Int
 */
public class Client
{
  public static void main(String[] args)
  {
    try
    {
      //Initialize the ORB
      org.omg.CORBA.ORB orb = org.omg.CORBA.ORB.init();

      //Bind to the Implementation
      chapter4.primitiveAny.generated.PrimitiveAnyTest primitiveAnyTest =
        chapter4.primitiveAny.generated.PrimitiveAnyTestHelper.bind
          (orb, "PrimitiveAny Sample");


      //////////////////////////////////////////////////////
      //   Begin Parameter Initialization
      //
      //   Create the in value
      int inLongVal = 5;
      //   Create the in Any
      org.omg.CORBA.Any inPrimitiveAny = orb.create_Any();
      //   Pack the inLongVal into the Any
      inPrimitiveAny.insert_long(inLongVal);
      //   Create the inAnyHolder, passing the in Any into the
      //   constructor
      org.omg.CORBA.AnyHolder inPrimitiveAnyHolder =
        new org.omg.CORBA.AnyHolder(inPrimitiveAny);

      //   Create the inout value
      int inoutLongVal = 5;
      //   Create the inout Any
```

```
org.omg.CORBA.Any inoutPrimitiveAny = orb.create_Any();
// Pack the inoutLongVal into the Any
inoutPrimitiveAny.insert_long(inoutLongVal);
// Create the inoutAnyHolder, passing the inout Any into the
// constructor
org.omg.CORBA.AnyHolder inoutPrimitiveAnyHolder =
  new org.omg.CORBA.AnyHolder(inoutPrimitiveAny);

// Create the outAnyHolder
org.omg.CORBA.AnyHolder outPrimitiveAnyHolder =
  new org.omg.CORBA.AnyHolder();
//
// End Parameter Initialization
//////////////////////////////////////////////////////


//For demonstration purposes, print the values
//before calling the remote method
System.out.println("\n\nBefore method testPrimitiveAny()\n" +
  "\tin parameter " + inLongVal + "\n" +
  "\tinout parameter " + inoutLongVal);

//Call remote method
int returnValue = primitiveAnyTest.testPrimitiveAny(
  inPrimitiveAny,
  inoutPrimitiveAnyHolder,
  outPrimitiveAnyHolder);


//////////////////////////////////////////////////////
// Begin Parameter Extraction
//
//Retrieve the inoutPrimitiveAny from the
//holder
inoutPrimitiveAny = inoutPrimitiveAnyHolder.value;
//Retrieve the inoutLongVal from the Any
inoutLongVal = inoutPrimitiveAny.extract_long();

//Retrieve the outPrimitiveAny from the holder
org.omg.CORBA.Any outPrimitiveAny = outPrimitiveAnyHolder.value;
//Retrieve the outLongVal from the Any
int outLongVal = outPrimitiveAny.extract_long();
//
// End Parameter Extraction
//////////////////////////////////////////////////////


//For demonstration purposes, print out the values
//after calling remote method
System.out.println("\n\nAfter calling method testPrimitiveAny()\n" +
```

continues

LISTING 3.31 CONTINUED

```
          "\tinout parameter " + inoutLongVal + "\n" +
          "\tout parameter " + outLongVal);
    }
    catch(org.omg.CORBA.SystemException ex)
    {
      ex.printStackTrace();
    }
  }
}
```

Listing 3.31 uses a method on an ORB object to create the Any object. After the Any object was created, we used the insert and extract methods directly on the Any method to get our long values into and out of the Any. For the inout and out values, we also leveraged the AnyHolder class, as observed with primitive types.

Listing 3.32 shows the server implementation of the PrimitiveAnyTest object. There is no new code introduced in this listing because the holder pattern remains the same as does the use of the insert and extract methods directly on the Any class.

LISTING 3.32 SERVER IMPLEMENTATION OF THE PrimitiveAnyTest OBJECT

```
package chapter3.primitiveAny;

/* This sample demonstrates using the CORBA Any
 * type to pass primitive types between the client
 * and server.  Note that there is one
 * more level of objects to notice when
 * dealing with inout/out Anys.
 *
 *       AnyHolder
 *          |
 *         Any
 *          |
 * member of Any
 *
 * We will use the IDL type long, aka the Java type Int
 */
public class PrimitiveAnyTestImpl extends
⮕chapter3.primitiveAny.generated._PrimitiveAnyTestImplBase
{

    //Constructor for transient object
    public PrimitiveAnyTestImpl()
    {
    }
```

```java
//Constructor for persistent object
public PrimitiveAnyTestImpl(String name)
{
  super(name);
}

public int testPrimitiveAny(
  org.omg.CORBA.Any inPrimitiveAny,
  org.omg.CORBA.AnyHolder inoutPrimitiveAnyHolder,
  org.omg.CORBA.AnyHolder outPrimitiveAnyHolder)
{
  /////////////////////////////////////////////////////
  //   Begin Parameter Extraction
  //
  //Extract the inLongVal from the Any
  int inLongVal = inPrimitiveAny.extract_long();

  //Extract the inout Any from the holder
  org.omg.CORBA.Any inoutPrimitiveAny = inoutPrimitiveAnyHolder.value;
  //Extract the inoutLongVal from the Any
  int inoutLongVal = inoutPrimitiveAny.extract_long();
  //
  //   End Parameter Extraction
  /////////////////////////////////////////////////////


  //For demonstration, print out the passed values.
  System.out.println("\n\nBeginning method testPrimitiveAny()\n" +
    "\tin parameter " + inLongVal + "\n" +
    "\tinout parameter " + inoutLongVal);

  /////////////////////////////////////////////////////
  //   Begin Setting values for Return
  //
  //Set the value on the inoutLongVal
  inoutLongVal = 6;
  //Insert this inoutLongVal into the Any
  inoutPrimitiveAny.insert_long(inoutLongVal);


  //We must create a outLongVal to add into the
  //Any to be passed back to the client.
  int outLongVal = 6;
  //Create a new Any to be put into the outAnyHolder.  Note that
  //we create this by calling to the org.omg.CORBA.ORB accessed
  //through our inherited _orb() method
  org.omg.CORBA.Any outPrimitiveAny = _orb().create_Any();
  //Assign the outPrimitiveAny to the outPrimitiveAnyHolder
  outPrimitiveAnyHolder.value = outPrimitiveAny;
```

continues

LISTING 3.32 CONTINUED

```java
        //Insert the new outLongVal into the out Any.
        outPrimitiveAny.insert_long(outLongVal);
        //
        // End Setting values for Return
        /////////////////////////////////////////////////////////


        //For demonstration, print out the values being returned
        System.out.println("\n\nAbout to exit method testPrimitiveAny()\n" +
          "\tinout parameter " + inoutLongVal + "\n" +
          "\tout parameter " + outLongVal);

        return 0;
    }

    //Put registration code here in a main for convenience
    public static void main(String[] args)
    {
      try
      {
        // Initialize the ORB.
        org.omg.CORBA.ORB orb = org.omg.CORBA.ORB.init();

        // Initialize the BOA.
        org.omg.CORBA.BOA boa = orb.BOA_init();

        // Create the RequestReply objects.
        PrimitiveAnyTestImpl primitiveAnyTest=
        new PrimitiveAnyTestImpl("PrimitiveAny Sample");

        // Export the newly create object.
        boa.obj_is_ready(primitiveAnyTest);

        System.out.println(primitiveAnyTest + " is ready.");

        // Wait for incoming requests
        boa.impl_is_ready();
      }
      catch(org.omg.CORBA.SystemException ex)
      {
        ex.printStackTrace();
      }
    }
}
```

Example Using `extract` and `insert` Methods with the Generated Helper Classes

In the previous example, we showed the use of the Any class with known types. We will now show how the CORBA's Any can be used with user-defined types.

When idl2java is run on a user created IDL file, many classes are generated in support of user-defined types. We've already discussed the Holder class as a mechanism for supporting `inout` and `out` parameters. Another generated class is the Helper class. The helper provides many useful methods including the `insert` and `extract` static methods (we will discuss more of the helper's functionality in Chapter 4).

Our example defines an operation on an interface that accepts `in`, `inout`, and `out` parameters of type Any. Although not shown in the interface, we will be using the Anys to hold a struct. Because the struct is a user-defined type, the example uses the Helper class to perform the insertion and extraction operations. Listing 3.33 shows the IDL for our example.

LISTING 3.33 IDL FOR THE `ComplexAnyTest` INTERFACE SUPPORTING AN OPERATION USING `Any`S TO PASS COMPLEX DATA TYPES

```
struct BasicStruct
  {
    long    longVal;
    string  stringVal;
  };

  interface ComplexAnyTest
  {
    long testComplexAny(
      in Any inComplexAny,
      inout Any inoutComplexAny,
      out Any outComplexAny);
  };
```

Listing 3.34 shows the client to an implementation of `ComplexAnyTest`. Most of the code in Listing 3.34 has been seen before. We use the Holder to pass `inout` and `out` parameters to the implementation. Pay special attention to the use of the Helper class to insert and extract our `BasicStruct` type into the Any.

LISTING 3.34 CLIENT TO `ComplexAnyTest` IMPLEMENTATION USING HELPER CLASS TO `insert` AND `extract` VALUES FROM AN Any

```
package chapter3.complexAny;

/* This sample demonstrates using the CORBA Any
```

continues

LISTING 3.34 CONTINUED

```
 * type to pass complex types between the client
 * and server.  Note that there is one
 * more level of objects to notice when
 * dealing with inout/out Anys.
 *
 *    AnyHolder
 *        |
 *        |
 *       Any
 *        |
 *        |
 * member of Any
 */
public class Client
{
   public static void main(String[] args)
   {
     try
     {
       //Initialize the ORB
       org.omg.CORBA.ORB orb = org.omg.CORBA.ORB.init();

       //Bind to the Implementation
       chapter3.complexAny.generated.ComplexAnyTest complexAnyTest =
         chapter3.complexAny.generated.ComplexAnyTestHelper.bind
         ➥(orb, "ComplexAny Sample");


       //////////////////////////////////////////////////////
       //  Begin Parameter Initialization
       //
       //  Create the in BasicStruct
       chapter3.complexAny.generated.BasicStruct inBasicStruct =
         new chapter3.complexAny.generated.BasicStruct(5, "fromClient");
       //  Create the in Any
       org.omg.CORBA.Any inComplexAny = orb.create_Any();
       //  Pack the BasicStruct into the Any
       //  using the BasicStructHelper
       chapter3.complexAny.generated.BasicStructHelper.insert
       ➥(inComplexAny, inBasicStruct);
       //  Create the inAnyHolder, passing the in Any into the
       //  constructor
       org.omg.CORBA.AnyHolder inComplexAnyHolder =
         new org.omg.CORBA.AnyHolder(inComplexAny);

       //  Create the inout BasicStruct
       chapter3.complexAny.generated.BasicStruct inoutBasicStruct =
         new chapter3.complexAny.generated.BasicStruct(5, "fromClient");
       //  Create the inout Any
       org.omg.CORBA.Any inoutComplexAny = orb.create_Any();
```

```
//  Pack the BasicStruct into the Any
//  using the BasicStructHelper
chapter3.complexAny.generated.BasicStructHelper.insert
➥(inoutComplexAny, inoutBasicStruct);
//  Create the inoutAnyHolder, passing the inout Any into the
//  constructor
org.omg.CORBA.AnyHolder inoutComplexAnyHolder =
  new org.omg.CORBA.AnyHolder(inoutComplexAny);

//  Create the outAnyHolder
org.omg.CORBA.AnyHolder outComplexAnyHolder =
  new org.omg.CORBA.AnyHolder();
//
//  End Parameter Initialization
////////////////////////////////////////////////////////


//For demonstration purposes, print the values
//before calling the remote method
System.out.println("\n\nBefore method testComplexAny()\n" +
  "\tin parameter's struct's longVal " + inBasicStruct.longVal +
  " and stringVal " + inBasicStruct.stringVal + "\n" +
  "\tinout parameter's struct's  longVal " + inoutBasicStruct.longVal +
  " and stringVal " + inoutBasicStruct.stringVal);

//Call remote method
int returnValue = complexAnyTest.testComplexAny(
  inComplexAny,
  inoutComplexAnyHolder,
  outComplexAnyHolder);


////////////////////////////////////////////////////////
//  Begin Parameter Extraction
//
//Retrieve the inoutComplexAny from the
//holder
inoutComplexAny = inoutComplexAnyHolder.value;
//Retrieve the inout struct from the
//Any using the BasicStructHelper
inoutBasicStruct =
  chapter3.complexAny.generated.BasicStructHelper.extract
  ➥(inoutComplexAny);

//Retrieve the outComplexAny from the holder
org.omg.CORBA.Any outComplexAny = outComplexAnyHolder.value;
//Retrieve the out struct from the
//Any using the BasicStructHelper
chapter3.complexAny.generated.BasicStruct outBasicStruct =
  chapter3.complexAny.generated.BasicStructHelper.extract(outComplexAny);
```

continues

LISTING 3.34 CONTINUED

```
      //
      //  End Parameter Extraction
      //////////////////////////////////////////////////////


      //For demonstration purposes, print out the values
      //after calling remote method
      System.out.println("\n\nAfter calling testComplexAny() method\n" +
        "\tinout parameter's struct's longVal " + inoutBasicStruct.longVal +
        " and stringVal " + inoutBasicStruct.stringVal + "\n" +
        "\tout parameter's struct's  longVal " + outBasicStruct.longVal +
        " and stringVal " + outBasicStruct.stringVal);
    }
    catch(org.omg.CORBA.SystemException ex)
    {
      ex.printStackTrace();
    }
  }
}
```

Listing 3.34 shows the use of the Helper class to insert and extract from the Any. This is required because the `insert` and `extract` operations must be typed. The server implementation shown in Listing 3.35 uses the same approach to using the helper to perform insertions and extractions.

> **NOTE**
>
> At this point you might be wondering how the generated classes can read/write from an Any. The generated classes use special input/output streams to decompose the objects into primitive types, so they can be marshaled and packed for the remote call.

LISTING 3.35 SERVER IMPLEMENTATION

```
package chapter3.complexAny;

/* This sample demonstrates using the CORBA Any
 * type to pass complex types between the client
 * and server.  Note that there is one
 * more level of objects to notice when
 * dealing with inout/out Anys.
 *
 *    AnyHolder
 *
```

```
 *         Any
 *          |
 * member of Any
 */
public class ComplexAnyTestImpl extends
➥chapter3.complexAny.generated._ComplexAnyTestImplBase
{

   //Constructor for transient object
   public ComplexAnyTestImpl()
   {
   }

   //Constructor for persistent object
   public ComplexAnyTestImpl(String name)
   {
      super(name);
   }

   public int testComplexAny(
     org.omg.CORBA.Any inComplexAny,
     org.omg.CORBA.AnyHolder inoutComplexAnyHolder,
     org.omg.CORBA.AnyHolder outComplexAnyHolder)
   {
     /////////////////////////////////////////////////////
     //  Begin Parameter Extraction
     //
     //Extract the in BasicStruct from the Any using
     //the BasicStructHelper
     chapter3.complexAny.generated.BasicStruct inBasicStruct =
        chapter3.complexAny.generated.BasicStructHelper.extract(inComplexAny);

     //Extract the inout Any from the holder
     org.omg.CORBA.Any inoutComplexAny = inoutComplexAnyHolder.value;
     //Extract the inout struct from the Any
     //using the BasicStructHelper
     chapter3.complexAny.generated.BasicStruct inoutBasicStruct =
        chapter3.complexAny.generated.BasicStructHelper.extract(inoutComplexAny);
     //
     //  End Parameter Extraction
     /////////////////////////////////////////////////////


     //For demonstration, print out the passed values.
     System.out.println("\n\nBegin method testComplexAny()\n" +
       "\tin parameter's struct's longVal " + inBasicStruct.longVal +
       " and stringVal " + inBasicStruct.stringVal +
       "\n\tinout parameter's struct's longVal " + inoutBasicStruct.longVal +
       " and stringVal " + inoutBasicStruct.stringVal);
```

continues

LISTING 3.35 CONTINUED

```java
        //////////////////////////////////////////////////////
        //   Begin Setting values for Return
        //
        //Set the value on the inout parameter
        inoutBasicStruct.longVal = 6;
        inoutBasicStruct.stringVal = "fromServer";
        //Insert this modified Struct into the Any
        chapter3.complexAny.generated.BasicStructHelper.insert
➥(inoutComplexAny, inoutBasicStruct);


        //We must create a new BasicStruct to add into the
        //Any to be passed back to the client.
        chapter3.complexAny.generated.BasicStruct outBasicStruct =
          new chapter3.complexAny.generated.BasicStruct(6, "fromServer");

        //Create a new Any to be put into the outAnyHolder.  Note that
        //we create this by calling to the org.omg.CORBA.ORB accessed
        //through our inherited _orb() method
        org.omg.CORBA.Any outComplexAny = _orb().create_Any();
        //Assign the outComplexAny to the outComplexAnyHolder
        outComplexAnyHolder.value = outComplexAny;
        //Insert the new Struct into the out Any.  This is
        //done using the static insert() method on the
        //generated BasicStructHelper
        chapter3.complexAny.generated.BasicStructHelper.insert
➥(outComplexAny, outBasicStruct);
        //
        //   End Setting values for Return
        //////////////////////////////////////////////////////


        //For demonstration, print out the values being returned
        System.out.println("\n\nAbout to exit method testComplexAny()" +
          "\n\tinout parameter's struct's longVal " + inoutBasicStruct.longVal +
          " and stringVal " + inoutBasicStruct.stringVal +
          "\n\tout parameter's struct's longVal " + outBasicStruct.longVal +
          " and stringVal " + outBasicStruct.stringVal);

      return 0;
    }

    //Put registration code here in a main for convenience
    public static void main(String[] args)
    {
      try
      {
        // Initialize the ORB.
        org.omg.CORBA.ORB orb = org.omg.CORBA.ORB.init();
```

```
    // Initialize the BOA.
    org.omg.CORBA.BOA boa = orb.BOA_init();

    // Create the object
    ComplexAnyTestImpl complexAnyTest=
    new ComplexAnyTestImpl("ComplexAny Sample");

    // Export the newly create object.
    boa.obj_is_ready(complexAnyTest);

    System.out.println(complexAnyTest + " is ready.");

    // Wait for incoming requests
    boa.impl_is_ready();
    }
    catch(org.omg.CORBA.SystemException ex)
    {
      ex.printStackTrace();
    }
  }
}
```

Context

An IDL Context provides a mechanism to pass a mapping of string names on the client side to string values on the server side. These mappings are passed as a Context object that becomes another parameter to the method invocation. We will take a look at how to define this in Listing 3.36, and the code is generated in Listing 3.37.

LISTING 3.36 AN EXAMPLE DEMONSTRATING HOW TO SET A CONTEXT VALUE WITHIN IDL

```
interface LongTest
{
        long testLong(in long inLong,
                    inout long inoutLong,
                    out long outLong)
                    context("MyUsername", "MyPassword");
};
```

This IDL generates the interface shown in Listing 3.37.

LISTING 3.37 GENERATED CODE FROM THE IDL

```
public interface LongTest extends org.omg.CORBA.Object
{
        public int testLong(int inLong,
                         org.omg.CORBA.IntHolder inoutLong,
```

continues

LISTING 3.37 CONTINUED

```
                            org.omg.CORBA.IntHolder outLong,
                            org.omg.CORBA.Context _context);
};
```

Notice the extra parameter that has been added. A Context object provides a very powerful capability of packaging mappings of strings once that can be reused in multiple operations. However, caution must be used with Contexts because there is no type safety involved. As such, Contexts are one of the least used features in IDL.

The Context Object is defined in Listing 3.38.

LISTING 3.38 THE org.omg.CORBA.Context CLASS DEFINITION

```
public abstract synchronized class org.omg.CORBA.Context extends
➥java.lang.Object
{
        public abstract java.lang.String context_name();
        public abstract org.omg.CORBA.Context parent();
        public abstract void set_one_value(java.lang.String, org.omg.CORBA.Any);
        public abstract void set_values(org.omg.CORBA.NVList);
        public abstract org.omg.CORBA.NVList get_values(java.lang.String, int,
                java.lang.String);
        public abstract void delete_values(java.lang.String);
        public abstract org.omg.CORBA.Context create_child(java.lang.String);
        public org.omg.CORBA.Context();
}
```

We will go into more detail on this class in Chapter 12 when we discuss the dynamic aspects of VisiBroker. Listing 3.39 is an example of how to pass string values in the Context object from Client to Server with the IDL.

LISTING 3.39 A FULL EXAMPLE DEMONSTRATING HOW TO USE AN IDL CONTEXT OBJECT TO PASS STRINGS TO THE SERVER

The Client:

```
// A segment of Client.java

// A local ref to the proxy, this example does not show how to obtain this
// reference, this will be discussed in Chapter 6.
LongTest longTest;

// Set up the Context object to be passed to the Server
org.omg.CORBA.Context context = orb.get_default_context();

org.omg.CORBA.Any context_value_auth = orb.create_Any();
```

```
context_value_auth.insert_string("scott");
context.set_one_value("MyUsername", context_value_auth);

org.omg.CORBA.Any context_value_name = orb.create_Any();
context_value_name.insert_string("tiger");
context.set_one_value("MyPassword", context_value_name);

// Initialize the three parameters
// Create the int for the in value
int inLongVal = 5;

// Create the holder and initialize the inout value
org.omg.CORBA.IntHolder inoutLongVal = new org.omg.CORBA.IntHolder(5);

// Create the holder for the out value. Notice that the outHolder is not
// initialized to any value.  Any value put in the outHolder will not be
// sent across the wire.  If a value needs to be passed, it should be sent as
// an "inout" parameter.
org.omg.CORBA.IntHolder outLongVal = new org.omg.CORBA.IntHolder();

//For the purposes of observation, let's set the value on the
//out parameter.  Note that on the server, this value is lost.
outLongVal.value = 5;

//For observation, print out the parameters before making the call
System.out.println("About to call testLong() method\n" +
"\tin parameter" + inLongVal + "\n" +
"\tinout parameter " + inoutLongVal.value + "\n" +
"\tout parameter " + outLongVal.value);

//Call the remote method with the in, inout, and out parameters and the context
int returnValue = longTest.testLong(inLongVal, inoutLongVal, outLongVal,
➥context);

//For observation, print out the parameters after making the call
System.out.println("After calling testLong() method\n" +
"\tin parameter" + inLongVal + "\n" +
"\tinout parameter " + inoutLongVal.value + "\n" +
"\tout parameter " + outLongVal.value);
```

Segment of the `LongTestImpl` object:

```
public int testLong(int inLongVal,
                    org.omg.CORBA.IntHolder inoutLongVal,
                    org.omg.CORBA.IntHolder outLongVal,
                    org.omg.CORBA.Context _context)
{
        // Look at context information
        org.omg.CORBA.NVList list = _context.get_values(null, 0, "My*");
        int end = list.count();
```

continues

LISTING 3.39 CONTINUED

```
        for (int i = 0; i < end; i++)
        {
                try
                {
                        org.omg.CORBA.NamedValue item = list.item(i);
                        org.omg.CORBA.Any val = item.value();
                        String string_val = val.extract_string();
                        System.out.println("Context value for " + item.name() + " is "
           ↪+ string_val);
                }
                catch (org.omg.CORBA.Bounds e)
                {
                        System.out.println("Context is *** unknown ***" );
                        System.out.println;
                }
        }

        //For observation, print out the parameters
        //before as passed to this method
        System.out.println("Beginning testLong() method\n" +
        "\tin parameter" + inLongVal + "\n" +
        "\tinout parameter " + inoutLongVal.value + "\n" +
        "\tout parameter " + outLongVal.value);

        //Change the value of the in parameter.  Note that
        //this is done to show that this new value is
        //NOT carried back to the client
        inLongVal = 6;

        //Change value of inout parameter
        inoutLongVal.value = 6;

        //Set value of the out parameter
        outLongVal.value = 6;

        //For observation, print out the parameters before the return
        System.out.println("About to return from testLong() method\n" +
        "\tin parameter" + inLongVal + "\n" +
        "\tinout parameter " + inoutLongVal.value + "\n" +
        "\tout parameter " + outLongVal.value);

        return 0;
}
```

SUMMARY

In this chapter we continued our discussion of how to write IDL. In Chapter 2, we provided a high-level overview of why the IDL language is necessary, and you started to learn how the primitive data types are represented in IDL. In this chapter we expanded upon this foundation for you to try to understand how to define your own constructed types within IDL. These constructed types can contain any of the primitive types discussed in Chapter 2, or any of the more complex constructed types discussed in this chapter.

The types discussed in this chapter include enums, unions, structures, typedefs, sequences, arrays, Anys, and Contexts. After reading the chapter, you have likely recognized that each of these constructed types follow the same semantics as to how they are passed as arguments. All are passed by value as in arguments. However, for inout and out arguments the constructed types must be passed in their respective Holder wrapper classes. These Holder objects contain the value of the constructed type and provide a pass-by-reference capability. An inout Holder object must be initialized, an out Holder object does not. As you are developing your complex applications, the examples in this chapter should provide you an adequate guide for how to pass these constructed types in any direction.

ADVANCED IDL AND THE IDL2JAVA COMPILER

CHAPTER 4

IN THIS CHAPTER

- **IDL INTERFACE INHERITANCE** *82*
- **EXCEPTIONS** *88*
- **THE VISIBROKER IDL TO JAVA COMPILER** *94*
- **THE IDL2JAVA GENERATED FILES** *103*

This is our final chapter dedicated to the understanding of Interface Definition Language (IDL). The focus in this chapter is on some advanced IDL concepts as well as how to use the VisiBroker IDL compiler, idl2java, in order to convert the IDL you develop into usable Java code.

In the previous chapter, we analyzed how to make use of all the IDL primitive types as well as how to define data structures using the IDL constructed types. We introduced the concept of direction (in, inout, and out parameters) and showed that the holder class is used to facilitate features found in CORBA but not natively in Java.

Today we will begin with the last two previously uncovered IDL topics—Interface Inheritance and Exceptions. We will then explore the idl2java compiler in greater detail, as well as those files it produces.

IDL INTERFACE INHERITANCE

In discussing IDL interface inheritance, we will start with a discussion of interface and implementation inheritance in the Java language. We will then discuss what inheritance means in IDL. With these topics introduced, we will discuss interface and implementation inheritance with the IDL to Java mapping.

Inheritance in Java

Inheritance is the ability for a class or interface to extend a previously created class or interface. The most common example in Java is *class inheritance*. A graphical user interface (GUI) programmer wishing to change the sizing behavior of a button can extend java.awt.Button and override the reshape(...) method. Extending the button class is an example of using class inheritance. Less well known in the Java world are the rules behind *interface inheritance*.

As you recall, there are two types of object definitions in Java. The first is a class. A *class* defines a collection of method signatures and member variables. A class can implement one or more interfaces, and extend at most one parent class. An abstract class is like a regular class except it might declare one or more abstract methods. An abstract method is a method declaration without definition. It is the responsibility of the subclass to implement any abstract methods inherited from the parent. An abstract class cannot directly be instantiated, but must be extended for use. The second object definition in Java is an interface. An *interface* can only declare abstract methods and static final constants. No implementations are permitted in interfaces. We will now examine the inheritance rules for interfaces, as well as a design pattern to work around the lack of multiple class inheritance in the Java Language.

Interface Inheritance

Because Interfaces in Java define no implementations on method signatures, the rules against multiple inheritance are relaxed. Consider the interface declarations in Listing 4.1.

LISTING 4.1 JAVA CODE SHOWING MULTIPLE INTERFACE EXTENSION

```
public interface OneInterface
{
  public void fooOne();
}

public interface TwoInterface
{
  public void fooTwo();
}

public interface MyInterface extends OneInterface, AnotherInterface
{
}
```

We will examine the interface declaration to analyze how we were able to extend more than one interface. An interface is just a series of method signatures. By implementing an interface, a class declares, "I will implement all methods declared on the interface(s) I implement." When an interface implements one or more parent interfaces, the Java syntax reads extends. In the code shown in Listing 4.1, `MyInterface` simply inherits the methods declared on `OneInterface` and `TwoInterface`. A valid class that implements `MyInterface` would appear as shown in Listing 4.2.

LISTING 4.2 A CLASS THAT IMPLEMENTS MyInterface FROM LISTING 4.1

```
public class MyClass extends MyParent  implements MyInterface
{
  public void fooOne()
  {
    //do something
  }

  public void fooTwo()
  {
    //do something else
  }
}
```

As we can see in Listing 4.2, multiple inheritance of interfaces is permitted because it is still up to the concrete class (implementer) to define those methods declared on any interfaces it implements. The last point to make on this topic is the strong type safety this brings us in Java. `MyClass` is said to be of type `MyInterface`. We can pass an instance of `MyClass` to a method that only knows about objects of `MyInterface`. Examine the passing of an object of type `MyClass` in Listing 4.3.

LISTING 4.3 PASSING AN OBJECT AS THE TYPE OF AN INTERFACE IT IMPLEMENTS

```
{
.........
//within a method

    MyClass myClass = new MyClass();
    doSomething(myClass);
}

public void doSomething(MyInterface anInterface)
{
  anInterface.fooOne();
}
```

We did not have to do any casting to pass `myClass` to the `doSomething` method. In Java, every object can be passed as its type (`MyClass`), the type of all interfaces implemented (`MyInterface`, `OneInterface`, `TwoInterface`), or the type of its parent (`MyParent`).

Interface Inheritance in IDL

So far we have discussed inheritance in Java. Because IDL stands for Interface Definition Language, we should hope that the rules for interface inheritance in Java apply in IDL. Fortunately, they do.

The syntax for inheritance in IDL is similar to C++ with the semicolon : indicating inheritance. If you are inheriting from an interface that is in another scope, you must indicate the full scope via the :: notation. Leading ::indicates that it is the absolute path (scoped from the top-level module) for the particular interface. The IDL in Listing 4.4 shows the definition for two interfaces, one without a parent and one using inheritance.

LISTING 4.4 INTERFACE INHERITANCE IN IDL

```
interface Interface1
{
  string doSomething();
};

interface Interface2 : Interface1
{
  string doSomethingElse();
};
```

In the definitions in Listing 4.4, `Interface2` extends `Interface1`. Interpreted from left to right, the declaration for `Interface2` reads "this is the definition for an interface named `Interface2` that extends `Interface1`." As in the Java language, an interface can also have several ancestors. Consider the definitions shown in Listing 4.5.

LISTING 4.5 MULTIPLE INTERFACE INHERITANCE IN IDL

```
interface ParentInterface1
{
  string doParent1Method();
};

interface ParentInterface2
{
  string doParent2Method();
};

interface ChildInterface : ParentInterface1, ParentInterface2
{
  string doChildMethod();
};
```

In Listing 4.5, `ChildInterface` extends from both `ParentInterface1` and `ParentInterface2`. It should be expected that any object implementing `ChildInterface` will implement both `doParent1Method()` and `doParent2Method()`.

Interface Inheritance Through IDL to Java Mapping

We have discussed the rules for interface inheritance in Java and IDL. Fortunately, they map rather well. Listing 4.6 shows the result of running the IDL file in Listing 4.11 through the idl2java compiler.

LISTING 4.6 CODE GENERATED FROM IDL CONTAINING AN INTERFACE INHERITED FROM TWO OTHER INTERFACES

```
public interface ParentInterface1 extends org.omg.CORBA.Object
{
  public java.lang.String doParent1Method();
}

public interface ParentInterface2 extends org.omg.CORBA.Object
{
  public java.lang.String doParent2Method();
}
```

continues

LISTING 4.6   CONTINUED

```
public interface ChildInterface extends ParentInterface1, ParentInterface2
{
  public java.lang.String doChildMethod();
}
```

The generated interfaces read just like their corresponding IDL definitions. Note that in both Java and IDL, you do not re-declare inherited methods in an interface definition, and there is no way to override an abstract method. Thus, Listing 4.7 would not be valid.

LISTING 4.7   INVALID IMPLEMENTATION OF `ChildInterface`

```
public class MyBrokenClass implements ChildInterface
{
  public java.lang.String doChildMethod()
  {
    return "Some String";
  }
}
```

Listing 4.7 would not compile because the interface `ChildInterface` defines three methods. A valid implementation of the `ChildInterface` is shown in Listing 4.8.

LISTING 4.8   VALID IMPLEMENTATION OF Child Interface

```
public class ChildInterfaceImpl implements ChildInterface
{
  public java.lang.String doParent1Method()
  {
    return "Some String";
  }

  public java.lang.String doParent2Method()
  {
    return "Some String";
  }

  public java.lang.String doChildMethod()
  {
    return "Some String";
  }
}
```

> ### AN ASIDE ON NAMING CONVENTIONS
>
> In the previous example, you might have noticed that the interface defined contained the word Interface. Many programmers (the authors included) would not use such a convention in practice, but it gets the point across for our examples.
>
> This raises the greater issue of coding conventions when programming CORBA applications in Java. The authors of the Java Programming Language defined the following naming conventions for Java:
>
> *Classes or Interfaces*—The names for Classes and Interfaces in Java should be nouns, using mixed case. The first letter of each internal word should be capitalized. Examples include `NullPointerException` and `MouseListener`.
>
> *Methods or Variable Members*—The convention for methods or variables is again a mixed-case name, with the first letter of the first word in lowercase. Examples include `setSize(int, int)` and `openNewDocument()`.
>
> In a Java-only world, following these conventions is easy. Because this is a Java book, we've tried to follow those conventions in our IDL naming. When you start your first collaborative Java/CORBA application, you might not get so lucky. Your IDL might be written by Smalltalk, C++, or even C programmers, who do not have the same naming conventions. In addition, there are some conventions for IDL itself such as the underscore "_" to separate internal words in a compound word.

The inheritance relationship defined in IDL is preserved during the transformation into Java code. The class `ChildInterfaceImpl` is of Java type `Parent1Interface` and `Parent2Interface`. Listing 4.9 demonstrates the polymorphism of our implementation.

LISTING 4.9 POLYMORPHISM OF AN OBJECT IMPLEMENTING SEVERAL INTERFACES DERIVED FROM IDL

```
{
.........
//Within some method

  org.omg.CORBA.ORB orb = org.omg.CORBA.ORB.init();

  //Bind to the Implementation
  ChildInterface child = ChildInterfaceHelper.bind(orb, "Inheritance Sample");

  //Operate on the returned instance.  To demonstrate
  //how interfaces are inherited, we will call three methods
```

continues

LISTING 4.9 CONTINUED

```
    //Call method that only knows about Parent1.
    //Note that there is no casting necessary
    useParent1Interface(child);

    //Call method that knows about the child
    useChildInterface(child);
}

//Method that knows how to act on an
//object that implements ChildInterface
public static void useChildInterface(ChildInterface child)
{
  System.out.println(child.doParent1Method());
  System.out.println(child.doParent2Method());
  System.out.println(child.doChildMethod());
}

//Method that does not know about the child class,
//and can only act on a class that implements
//the ParentInterface1 interface
public static void useParent1Interface(ParentInterface1 parent)
{
  System.out.println(parent.doParent1Method());
}
```

No cast is required to pass an object of type `ChildInterface` to a method that knows only of `ParentInterface1`.

EXCEPTIONS

Exceptions are discussed in two categories: System Exceptions and User Exceptions. System Exceptions are those exceptions thrown by VisiBroker itself as well as any of the VisiBroker generated code. Programmers must be aware of these exceptions and the ramifications when the exceptions are thrown within their application code; however, they need not be concerned with these exceptions when designing their IDL. The other type of exceptions we will be discussing are User Exceptions. System exceptions typically reflect errors at the infrastructure level, and User Exceptions reflect errors at application level. User Exceptions must be defined within the IDL.

System Exceptions

When programming against any API in Java, you need to be aware of any possible runtime exceptions that could be thrown. For example, when making database calls, the database could be down, thus you should receive a specific exception indicating the reason for the failure.

Another example is when you overwrite the end of an array, you will receive an `ArrayIndexOutOfBounds` exception, indicating exactly what the reason for the failure is. VisiBroker for Java is designed to automatically propagate a finite number of predefined CORBA System Exceptions for situations such as these. For errors that are likely to occur within a specific application, specific User Exceptions should be defined to handle these conditions.

Without even having to see the code, think about what could go wrong when programming in CORBA. One obvious example is a network failure. CORBA has defined various security systems, which a user could violate and thus receive an exception. Some of the more advanced concepts like the Dynamic Invocation Interface (DII), discussed in Chapter 12, leave opportunities for programming errors that are detected only at runtime. CORBA has created a list of these possible exceptions and defined them to be System Exceptions. A list of these exceptions is shown in Table 4.1 with a brief description of the reason for their being raised.

TABLE 4.1 A FULL BREAKDOWN OF EACH OF THE PREDEFINED CORBA SYSTEM EXCEPTIONS AND A BRIEF DESCRIPTION OF THEIR CAUSE

Exception Class Name	Description
BAD_CONTEXT	Error processing the Context Object
BAD_INV_ORDER	Routine invocations out of order
BAD_OPERATION	Invalid Operation
BAD_PARAM	An invalid parameter was passed
BAD_TYPECODE	Invalid TypeCode
COMM_FAILURE	Communication failure
DATA_CONVERSION	Data Conversion error
FREE_MEM	Unable to free memory
IMP_LIMIT	Implementation limit violated
INITIALIZE	ORB initialization failure
INTERNAL	An ORB internal error
INTF_REPOS	Error with Interface Repository
INV_FLAG	Invalid flag was specified
INV_INDENT	Invalid identifier syntax
INV_OBJREF	Invalid object reference specified
MARSHAL	Error marshaling parameters or return code
NO_IMPLEMENT	Operation Implementation not available

continues

TABLE 4.1 CONTINUED

Exception Class Name	Description
NO_MEMORY	Dynamic memory allocation failure
NO_PERMISSION	No permission for attempted operation
NO_RESOURCES	Insufficient system resources to process request
NO_RESPONSE	Response to request is not yet available
OBJ_ADAPTER	Failure detected by object adapter
OBJ_NOT_EXIST	Object is not available
PERSIST_STORE	Persistent Storage failure
TRANSIENT	Transient failure
UNKNOWN	Unknown exception

Table 4.1 lists the standard system exceptions defined by the OMG. These can be thrown at any point within either your Client or Server application on any of your IDL defined operations. For brevity, we did not list the full package name of the exceptions. Fortunately, all system exceptions are in the same package, the org.omg.CORBA package. Therefore from the previous table we can see that an exception thrown when a user has violated a security constraint would be of type org.omg.CORBA.NO_PERMISSION.

It is worthwhile to note the inheritance hierarchy of the system exceptions so as a programmer you can choose to catch the parent class of some exceptions rather than the individual classes. This hierarchy is shown in Figure 4.1.

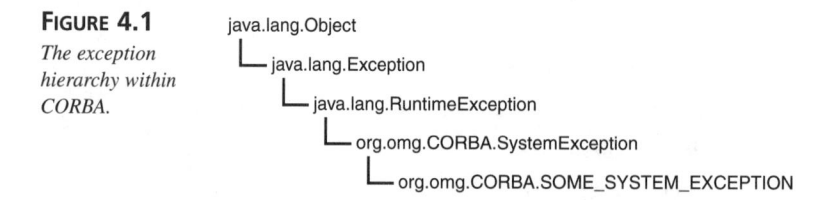

FIGURE 4.1

The exception hierarchy within CORBA.

```
java.lang.Object
  └─ java.lang.Exception
       └─ java.lang.RuntimeException
            └─ org.omg.CORBA.SystemException
                 └─ org.omg.CORBA.SOME_SYSTEM_EXCEPTION
```

An experienced Java programmer will quickly notice that all system exceptions descend from java.lang.RuntimeException. For those who are newer to Java, a runtime exception is an exception that doesn't have to be declared by a method for that method to throw the exception. For example, NullPointerException and ArrayIndexOutOfBounds are runtime exceptions. Operations on an array don't declare that they throw such an exception, so the programmer doesn't have to catch them to have their code compile. A programmer can write and compile code against an API that throws runtime exceptions without having to catch any specific exception.

> ### WHY ARE SYSTEM EXCEPTIONS RUNTIME EXCEPTIONS?
>
> The reasoning behind this is that runtime exceptions could be thrown by generated classes derived from user-defined IDL. Consider a simple application where the client code is calling into a stub. After a few successful calls the network connection is lost. On the next method call, the stub cannot fulfill the request and must throw an exception.
>
> There are many things that can go wrong with network-centric CORBA programming (network problems, security issues, and so on). If the IDL developer had to always declare each problem that could go wrong with each call, he would always declare each method to throw the 26 exceptions defined by the OMG. These exceptions wouldn't be of the programmer's doing: they would have occurred in the ORB layer. Because the IDL does not define the methods to throw exceptions, the corresponding Java should not add extra exceptions. This would cause confusion between the IDL and Javadoc as sources of documentation. It was therefore decided that stubs can throw runtime exceptions. It is important to be aware that System Exceptions can occur and code accordingly.

Because the system exceptions are runtime exceptions, the two code samples shown in Listing 4.10 are valid.

LISTING 4.10   TWO VALID CALLS TO METHOD THAT THROWS A RUNTIME EXCEPTION

```
//obtain a remote reference from the ORB.  We will assume
//that this is assigned to a member variable
//called myRemoteReference
public void method1()
{
  myRemoteReference.doSomething();
}

public void method2()
{
  try
  {
    myRemoteReferenceReference.doSomething();
  }
  catch(org.omg.CORBA.SystemException ex)
  {
  //tell user that there was a problem and take action
  }
}
```

Both of the previous methods are valid from a Java perspective and would compile. However, `method1()` is vulnerable to runtime exceptions because it didn't catch any of the possible runtime exceptions.

> **CAUTION**
>
> When programming with VisiBroker, always be aware that each call into a remote reference can throw runtime exceptions. Uncaught, these will propagate to the top of the current thread, causing a stack dump.

User-defined Exceptions

In the previous section, we discussed those exceptions thrown by the ORB as well as VisiBroker-generated code. When writing VisiBroker code, you need to be aware of the standard CORBA System Exceptions. However, as a programmer you will likely need to create application specific exceptions to indicate application specific failures. For example, say that you are creating the IDL for a data-entry application. You might declare a method to set the phone number. Being a seasoned developer, you know that people don't always type correct information into text boxes, so some server-side field validation is required. If they type an invalid phone number, you will likely declare that the method throws an `InvalidPhoneNumberFormat` exception.

Before you can declare that your Java code throws an exception, you must first declare that exception in IDL and indicate that your method raises that exception. The IDL in Listing 4.11 shows the declaration of an exception and the declaration of a method that raises such an exception.

LISTING 4.11 IDL SHOWING USER-DEFINED EXCEPTION AND METHOD THAT RAISES THIS EXCEPTION

```
module chapter4
{
  exception UserException1
  {
  string reason;
  };

  interface ExceptionTest
  {
    void throwAUserException()
      raises(UserException1);
  };
};
```

There are several things to note from the syntax. The first is that the exception is declared with the keyword exception. An exception can have several attributes. When a particular method wishes to throw an exception, it uses the keyword raises. If the exception is not within the same scope as the interface, you must define the path (using the :: syntax discussed in the previous section on Inheritance) to the IDL definition of the exception.

After you have defined the IDL for your exception and a method that throws that exception, you must run the file through idl2java. Several files are generated from the IDL in Listing 4.11, including the .java file for the exception. The generated .java file for your exception is shown in Listing 4.12.

LISTING 4.12 GENERATED CLASS FOR YOUR USER EXCEPTION DEFINED IN LISTING 4.11

```
final public class UserException1 extends org.omg.CORBA.UserException {
  public java.lang.String reason;
  public UserException1() {
  }
  public UserException1(
    java.lang.String reason
  ) {
    this.reason = reason;
  }
  public java.lang.String toString() {
    org.omg.CORBA.Any any = org.omg.CORBA.ORB.init().create_any();
    chapter4.UserException1Helper.insert(any, this);
    return any.toString();
  }
}
```

As you probably guessed, the attributes of the exception from IDL become public members of the Java exception. You'll note that the generated code extends from org.omg.CORBA.UserException. Unlike the System Exceptions, User Exceptions are not runtime exceptions. Therefore, User Exceptions must be caught by the application in order to compile. Note that all User Exceptions subclass the org.omg.CORBA.UserException class, and are generated as final classes.

After running our example IDL file through the idl2java compiler, we also produced a Java interface for the ExceptionTest object. The .java file for this interface is shown in Listing 4.13.

LISTING 4.13 GENERATED JAVA INTERFACE FOR IDL INTERFACE DECLARED TO RAISE AN EXCEPTION

```
public interface ExceptionTest extends org.omg.CORBA.Object
{
  public void throwAUserException()
    throws chapter4.generated.UserException1;
}
```

Observe that the interface declares that the Java exception `UserException1` is thrown. Any code written calling this operation must catch this exception. Listing 4.14 shows the implementation of the `ExceptionTest` object we defined in the IDL shown in Listing 4.11.

LISTING 4.14 SEGMENT OF SERVER IMPLEMENTATION DERIVED FROM IDL IS LISTING 4.11

```
//Implement method that throws our user-defined exception
public void throwAUserException() throws UserException1
{
  if(true) //This conditional code is for the compiler only
  {
        UserException1 ex = new UserException1();
        ex.reason = "This is the reason from the server";
        throw ex;
  }
}
```

In the method `throwAUserException`, we simply threw a new exception. The VisiBroker infrastructure takes care of marshaling the exception and throwing it back at the calling client on the other side of the network.

THE VISIBROKER IDL TO JAVA COMPILER

Now that we have showed you how all the constructs in IDL are mapped to Java, we will take a look at how the actual VisiBroker IDL compiler, idl2java, works.

IDL Preprocessor

The first thing to note is that idl2java is an IDL compiler that also contains its own fully functional preprocessor. The IDL preprocessor is similar to the C++ preprocessor in functionality and syntax. As such, your IDL can contain many of the same preprocessor directives as traditional C++ header files. For the reader unfamiliar with C++, a list of the preprocessor directives are as follows.

#include

It is legal to #include another IDL file for reference in your IDL file. It has the effect of substituting all text found in the included file into your IDL file at the point of the #include tag. This is much more efficient than redefining interfaces or maintaining single large IDL files. This #include directive is treated exactly the same as it is in C++. An example using the #include tag is shown in Listing 4.15.

LISTING 4.15 SAMPLE IDL FILE 2 USING #include TO INCLUDE CONTENTS OF FILE 1

```
// IDL File #1
// A.idl
//
module A
{
    interface test
    {
    };
};
// IDL File #2
#include "A.idl"

module B
{
    interface test
    {
    };
};
```

Now, with this syntax, the idl2java compiler gives you the option of whether to generate code for the included files or not. Given the two previous idl files, if you type

```
prompt> idl2java B.idl

B\test.java
B\testHolder.java
B\testHelper.java
B\_st_test.java
B\_testImplBase.java
B\_testOperations.java
B\_tie_test.java
B\_example_test.java
```

This only generates files for B.idl, not any of the include files. However, if you use the -incl_files flag to the preprocessor, files are generated for the contents of both module A and module B, as shown in the following:

```
prompt> idl2java -incl_files_code B.idl
```

This option generates code for all the included files as well. If inclusion of multiple IDL files is important for your development, the following preprocessor directives should be considered:

```
#ifndef
#define
#endif
```

These three are useful for preventing multiple inclusion of IDL files within large projects. The syntax is as follows:

```
#ifndef <SOME UNIQUE NAME>
#define <SOME UNIQUE NAME>

    <IDL>

#endif
```

The advantage of this directive is that you won't include the same IDL in multiple files if it has already been included once. This saves time in compilation of large projects.

#pragma Prefix

The `#pragma` prefix directive can be used as a means to add a string value to the Repository ID of the interfaces within an IDL file. We will discuss the `#pragma` prefix in relation to the IDL shown in Listing 4.16.

LISTING 4.16 IDL FILE FOR WHICH WE WILL USE THE #pragma PREFIX

```
module A
{
    interface test
    {
    };
};
```

The IDL in Listing 4.16 produces the following Repository ID for the interface:

`"IDL:A/test:1.0"`

Repository IDs will be covered in more detail later. However, for now notice that the module name is listed first, followed by a backslash with the interface name. Now, take a look at what happens when we add a `#pragma` prefix to our IDL as shown in Listing 4.17.

LISTING 4.17 IDL FILE USING THE #pragma PREFIX

```
#pragma prefix "book.example"

module A
```

```
{
    interface test
    {
    };
};
```

The following is the Repository ID for the interface in Listing 4.17:

`"IDL:book.example/A/test:1.0"`

The Repository ID can be retrieved by calling `_ids( )` on the client stub. Here, you see that our `#pragma` prefix string has been inserted into our existing interface definition. This allows for another namespace convention without having to use modules and packages. Other supported preprocessor directives are as follows:

```
#if
#ifdef
#elif
#else
#define
#undef
#defined
#error
```

When using the idl2java compiler, several options can be passed to the pre-processor. They are as listed in Table 4.2.

TABLE 4.2 IDL2JAVA COMMAND OPTIONS

Command Option	Purpose
-C	Keep IDL comments when the Java code is generated. The default is that IDL comments won't appear in the generated Java code.
-H	Prints the fully qualified paths of include files.
-P	Turns off line number tags in the preprocessed code.
-d	Preprocessor debugging.
-D*name*	Add definition for macro *name*.
-D*name* =*definition*	Defines a macro with the given value. An example: `#define pi=3.14` could be passed as `-Dpi=3.14`.
-U *name*	Undefine the defined macro *name*.
-I directory	Passes the full or relative path to the directory holding `#include` files. This is used when the preprocessor is searching for the included files.

idl2java Code Generated

In order to use idl2java, you must make sure that your CLASSPATH has

- The directory with your project files.

You also must have your PATH appropriately set to include

- Your JDK\bin directory.
- Your vbroker\bin directory.

Now that you can successfully run the idl2java command, we will see the various options you can use.

So far we've discussed the preprocessor within the idl2java compiler. We will now discuss those options that, when used, are directives for the code generation portion of idl2java.

-package

`-package <name>` Generate code into the package name specified. As with the behavior of the *module*, the package name corresponds to a directory on the file system. If the directory doesn't exist, the idl2java compiler creates one. If one has already been created, idl2java updates the existing files as needed.

Thus far, you have seen that if you want to group similar interfaces into a package, include them into an IDL module. However, if you are writing cross-language applications between C++ and Java, extensive use of module can make for some very tricky programming on the C++ side. The reason is that in the IDL to C++ language mapping, a module is mapped to either a C++ namespace or a nested class. Because C++ namespaces are not widely supported among most C++ compilers, the module is typically mapped to a nested class. Several layers of modules that are easily referenced with import statements in Java cause extremely long type names in C++ that make for very hard to follow code. The `-package` option is an excellent alternative in this situation. Take a look at the following:

```
// IDL
module A
{
interface test
{
};
};
```

You already know (from Chapter 2) that this generates your code into a package called A that is contained in a directory on your file system called A. This generation produces

```
A
A\test.java
A\testHolder.java
```

```
A\testHelper.java
A\_st_test.java
A\_testImplBase.java
A\testOperations.java
A\_tie_test.java
A\_example_test.java
```

Now, try this without a module definition in your IDL:

```
// IDL
interface test
{
};
```

Using the -package option as follows

```
prompt> idl2java -package A A.idl
```

generates the following files

```
A
A\test.java
A\testHolder.java
A\testHelper.java
A\_st_test.java
A\_testImplBase.java
A\testOperations.java
A\_tie_test.java
A\_example_test.java
```

Nested packages follow the exact same syntax as the preceding does.

```
// IDL
interface test
{
};
prompt> idl2java -package A.B.C A.idl
```

generates the following

```
A
A\B
A\B\C
A\B\C\test.java
A\B\C\testHolder.java
A\B\C\testHelper.java
A\B\C\_st_test.java
A\B\C\_testImplBase.java
A\B\C\testOperations.java
A\B\C\_tie_test.java
A\B\C\_example_test.java
```

Notice that this creates the necessary directories and nested packages for us automatically.

-idl2package

The `-idl2package <idl> <package>` option puts all definitions within the scope of the IDL into a specific package.

It is different from the previous `-package` option, in that it actually replaces the module definition in the IDL with a fully qualified package name. This is useful when working between C++ and Java. It is problematic to have many multiple modules in IDL when using C++ because this generates nested classes. To overcome this, you need only define a single module in IDL and the resulting package in Java can be as long as you want. Think of it as a preprocessor macro substitution. The syntax is as follows:

```
// IDL
module A
{
  interface test
  {
  };
};
```

Notice that here we have defined a module A. However, we would like to have this code generated into a nested package of `A.B.C`. The `-idl2package` option performs this substitution and ensures the proper package qualification for the specified modules. In our example, we want to swap module A for the fully qualified module `A.B.C`.

```
prompt> idl2java -idl2package ::A A.B.C A.idl
```

This produces the following files:

```
A
A\B
A\B\C
A\B\C\test.java
A\B\C\testHolder.java
A\B\C\testHelper.java
A\B\C\_st_test.java
A\B\C\_testImplBase.java
A\B\C\testOperations.java
A\B\C\_tie_test.java
A\B\C\_example_test.java
```

-root_dir

`-root_dir <directory name>`

This places all the generated files into the specified directory instead of the current working directory. For package declarations that generate their own directories, they will all be generated off this root directory specified.

-version

`-version`

This flag returns the version of VisiBroker for Java.

```
prompt>idl2java -version
VisiBroker Developer for Java [03.02.02.C1.01]  (MAY 01 1998 16:45:39)
Java: Version 1.1.5 from Sun Microsystems Inc.
OS:   Windows 95 version 4.0; CPU: x86
```

-verbose

`-verbose`

This flag turns `-verbose` mode on for extra debugging information.

-portable

`-portable`

This flag generates `-portable` stubs using the DII. We will show you how handy this option is when we discuss the DII in Chapter 12. The generated stub file with this option is not `_st_someInterfaceName.java`, rather it is `portable_stub_someInterfaceName.java`.

-strict

`-strict`

This flag generates stubs and skeletons that can be used with any CORBA 2.0-compliant ORB. Thus, it doesn't generate any of the VisiBroker specific extensions or methods.

Using this option is the same as setting

```
-portable
-no_toString
-no_bind
```

-smart_proxy

`-smart_proxy`

This flag generates special Helper classes for use with the Smart Stub feature. This will be discussed in detail in Chapter 14, "DynAnys."

-obj_wrapper

`-obj_wrapper`

This flag generates special stubs, skeletons, and helper classes for use with the Object Wrapper classes. This feature will be discussed in detail in Chapter 18, "Understanding the GIOP Protocol and Message Interceptors."

-incl_files

`-incl_files_code`

This flag generates code for the `#include` IDL files. These files are referenced but not compiled without this option. This option is discussed in the previous section on the idl2java preprocessor.

-all_serializable

`-all_serializable`

This flag makes the following IDL types implement `java.io.Serializable`:

- structs
- estructs (part of the Caffeine tools, discussed in Chapter 11)
- exceptions
- unions
- enums

-serializable <idl_file>

`-serializable <idl_file>`

For the given IDL file passed as an argument, the preceding data types implement `java.io.Serializable`.

-map_keyword

`-map_keyword <keyword> <mapping>`

In an effort to prevent name clashes, you can provide a keyword and mapping so that if an IDL identifier clashes with the given keyword, it is automatically mapped to the mapping value.

-deprecated

`-deprecated_skel`

This flag generates the Server skeleton with the deprecated naming convention of `_sk_someInterfaceName.java` instead of `_someInterfaceNameImplBase.java`.

Code Suppression Options

For more efficient code generation of a large number of IDL files, there are several code suppression options available (shown in Table 4.3). The idea here is to minimize the generation of code in order to produce only what your application requires.

TABLE 4.3   CODE SUPPRESSION COMMAND-LINE OPTIONS

Command Option	Purpose
`-no_stub`	Suppress generation of the client stub.
`-no_skel`	Suppress generation of the server skeleton.
`-no_tie`	Suppress generation of the `_tie` class and `Operations` class.
`-no_comments`	Suppress generation of comments.
`-no_examples`	Suppress generation of the `_example` class.
`-no_bind`	Suppress generation of the `bind( )` methods in the generated Helper class.
`-no_toString`	Suppress generation of the `toString( )` methods.

THE IDL2JAVA GENERATED FILES

You have seen several generated files because we began our discussion of IDL in Chapter 2, "Introduction to IDL." Now we will explore what each generated file is for. Throughout this discussion, we refer to the IDL file shown in Listing 4.18.

LISTING 4.18   A SAMPLE IDL INTERFACE

```
// IDL
interface test
{
};
```

If we take this very simple IDL and run it through idl2java, you will see the following generated files:

```
test.java
testHolder.java
testHelper.java
_st_test.java
_testImplBase.java
testOperations.java
_tie_test.java
_example_test.java
```

We will now examine each generated file in more detail in the following sections. Each section includes a listing of the generated file from the IDL in Listing 4.18, followed by an explanation. Some of the files, like the helper and holder, you've already seen in our previous discussions. Other files will be new to you, and will be further discussed as we introduce more advanced topics in the chapters to come.

<IDL Interface Name>.java

The simplest of the generated files is the Java interface generated for each IDL interface. Listing 4.19 shows the Java interface for the simple IDL.

LISTING 4.19 GENERATED INTERFACE FOR THE IDL DEFINED IN LISTING 4.18

```java
// test.java
public interface test extends org.omg.CORBA.Object {
}
```

This is the direct mapping of the IDL interface definition to the appropriate Java interface. This interface is then implemented by both the client stub and the server skeleton. The generated interfaces always extend from `org.omg.CORBA.Object`, the base interface for all CORBA objects.

<Type Name>Holder.java

Each type defined in IDL has a corresponding `<Type Name>Holder` class generated. There was one type (an interface) defined in the sample IDL. The holder for this interface is shown in Listing 4.20.

LISTING 4.20 GENERATED HOLDER CLASS FOR THE IDL DEFINED IN LISTING 4.18

```java
// IDL      testHolder.java
final public class testHolder implements org.omg.CORBA.portable.Streamable {
  public test value;
  public testHolder() {
  }
  public testHolder(test value) {
    this.value = value;
  }
  public void _read(org.omg.CORBA.portable.InputStream input) {
    value = testHelper.read(input);
  }
  public void _write(org.omg.CORBA.portable.OutputStream output) {
    testHelper.write(output, value);
```

```
  }
  public org.omg.CORBA.TypeCode _type() {
    return testHelper.type();
  }
}
```

We discussed the purpose of the holder classes in Chapter 3 when we introduced the passing rules for IDL types. As discussed in Chapter 3, "IDL to Java Language Mapping," the holder provides a technique for Java types to be passed by reference from client to implementation. This is accomplished by having the holder act as a container for types before and after method calls with inout and out parameters.

<IDL Type Name>Helper java

For each user-defined type, a helper class is also created by idl2java. We discussed the helper classes in Chapter 3 when we discussed the Any type. An example of such a helper for our test interface is shown in Listing 4.21.

LISTING 4.21 GENERATED HELPER CLASS FOR THE IDL DEFINED IN LISTING 4.18

```
// testHelper.java

abstract public class testHelper {
  public static test narrow(org.omg.CORBA.Object object) {
    return narrow(object, false);
  }
  private static test narrow(org.omg.CORBA.Object object, Boolean is_a) {
    if(object == null) {
      return null;
    }
    if(object instanceof test) {
      return (test) object;
    }
    if(is_a || object._is_a(id())) {
      _st_test result = (_st_test)new _st_test();
      ((org.omg.CORBA.portable.ObjectImpl) result)._set_delegate
        (((org.omg.CORBA.portable.ObjectImpl) object)._get_delegate());
      ((org.omg.CORBA.portable.ObjectImpl) result._this())._set_delegate
        (((org.omg.CORBA.portable.ObjectImpl) object)._get_delegate());
      return (test) result._this();
    }
    return null;
  }
  public static test bind(org.omg.CORBA.ORB orb) {
    return bind(orb, null, null, null);
  }
```

continues

LISTING 4.21 CONTINUED

```java
  public static test bind(org.omg.CORBA.ORB orb, java.lang.String name) {
    return bind(orb, name, null, null);
  }
  public static test bind(org.omg.CORBA.ORB orb, java.lang.String name,
➥java.lang.String host, org.omg.CORBA.BindOptions options) {
    return narrow(orb.bind(id(), name, host, options), true);
  }
  private static org.omg.CORBA.ORB _orb() {
    return org.omg.CORBA.ORB.init();
  }
  public static test read(org.omg.CORBA.portable.InputStream _input) {
    return testHelper.narrow(_input.read_Object(), true);
  }
  public static void write
➥(org.omg.CORBA.portable.OutputStream _output, test value) {
    _output.write_Object(value);
  }
  public static void insert(org.omg.CORBA.Any any, test value) {
    org.omg.CORBA.portable.OutputStream output = any.create_output_stream();
    write(output, value);
    any.read_value(output.create_input_stream(), type());
  }
  public static test extract(org.omg.CORBA.Any any) {
    if(!any.type().equal(type())) {
      throw new org.omg.CORBA.BAD_TYPECODE();
    }
    return read(any.create_input_stream());
  }
  private static org.omg.CORBA.TypeCode _type;
  public static org.omg.CORBA.TypeCode type() {
    if(_type == null) {
      _type = _orb().create_interface_tc(id(), "test");
    }
    return _type;
  }
  public static java.lang.String id() {
    return "IDL:test:1.0";
  }
}
```

The Helper class is an abstract class with various static methods for the generated Java interface. There are a few methods that you will make heavy use of, so it is important to understand their significance.

narrow( )

Remember how we said that any interface declared in IDL extends from the CORBA base class org.omg.CORBA.Object? Well, because of this, the narrow( ) method allows you to take an `org.omg.CORBA.Object` and narrow, or downcast, this to an object reference of the appropriate interface. In this example, this would narrow to an object implementing the test interface. Note that the `narrow( )` method should be used instead of the Java construct for casting because of internal ORB requirements.

bind( )

We see three signatures for this overloaded operation. The `bind(...)` operation is a VisiBroker for Java proprietary extension allowing dynamic communication to the VisiBroker for Java Directory Service, the Smart Agent. This method isn't part of the CORBA standard. The use of `bind(...)` and the various binding options are discussed in detail in Chapter 6, "The Smart Agent."

insert( ) and extract( )

The methods `insert( )` and `extract( )` are used to write the object implementing this interface to and from a CORBA `Any` type. This is discussed in Chapter 3.

type( )

The method `type( )` is for creating `Typecodes` for use with the `Any` type. `Typecodes` are used by some of the more dynamic features of CORBA. `Typecodes` are discussed in Chapter 6.

id( )

The method `id( )` returns the Repository ID for the given interface. The syntax for the Repository ID is as follows:

1. `IDL:` is at the beginning of the string.
2. Replace all non-leading instances of `::` with `/`. This is to indicate the package path to the Server class.
3. Add `:1.0` to the end of the string.

Thus, for the IDL example in Listing 4.18, the Repository ID is

- `IDL:test:1.0`

The significance of the Repository and Repository IDs is discussed in more detail in Chapter 12, "Dynamic VisiBroker."

st_<IDL Interface Name>.java

In Chapter 1, "Introduction to CORBA and VisiBroker for Java," we briefly discussed the role of the client stub. It is a Java class that is generated from our IDL definition to provide the Client application a proxy to the actual Object Implementation. It is this proxy object within the Client Stub that is responsible for passing data to and receiving data from the actual remote Implementation. Listing 4.22 shows the generated stub for our test interface.

LISTING 4.22 GENERATED CLIENT STUB FOR THE IDL DEFINED IN LISTING 4.18

```
public class _st_test extends org.omg.CORBA.portable.ObjectImpl implements
➥test {
  protected test _wrapper = null;
  public test _this() {
    return this;
  }
  public java.lang.String[] _ids() {
    return __ids;
  }
  private static java.lang.String[] __ids = {
    "IDL:test:1.0"
  };
}
```

The client stub represents the client-side proxy object for the server-side object, implementing the IDL-defined Interface. When the client application obtains a remote reference to the server object and calls methods, communication with the implementation is facilitated via the stub. Because this local proxy implements the same interface as the remote server object, it accepts all method calls from the client, performs all the necessary marshaling of data, and then sends the data to the remote object implementation.

<IDL Interface Name>ImplBase.java

This file, <IDL Interface Name>ImplBase, is the server-side skeleton for the interface. The Server Skeleton is a Java source file that is generated from idl2java. Its purpose is to listen for incoming requests and to pass these requests to the appropriate object implementation. The skeleton is the other half of the remoting system. The stub wraps calls from the client into a network-ready package. At the other side of this call is the skeleton who unwraps the package and passes the call on to the implementation. The skeleton for our example IDL is shown in Listing 4.23.

LISTING 4.23 GENERATED SERVER SKELETON FOR THE IDL DEFINED IN LISTING 4.18

```
abstract public class _testImplBase extends
➥org.omg.CORBA.portable.Skeleton implements test {
  protected test _wrapper = null;
  public test _this() {
    return this;
  }
```

```
  protected _testImplBase(java.lang.String name) {
    super(name);
  }
  public _testImplBase() {
  }
  public java.lang.String[] _ids() {
    return __ids;
  }
  private static java.lang.String[] __ids = {
    "IDL:test:1.0"
  };
  public org.omg.CORBA.portable.MethodPointer[] _methods() {
    org.omg.CORBA.portable.MethodPointer[] methods = {
    };
    return methods;
  }
  public Boolean _execute(org.omg.CORBA.portable.MethodPointer method,
    org.omg.CORBA.portable.InputStream input,
    org.omg.CORBA.portable.OutputStream output) {
    switch(method.interface_id) {
    case 0: {
      return _testImplBase._execute(_this(), method.method_id, input, output);
    }
    }
    throw new org.omg.CORBA.MARSHAL();
  }
  public static Boolean _execute(test _self, int _method_id,
    org.omg.CORBA.portable.InputStream _input,
    org.omg.CORBA.portable.OutputStream _output) {
    switch(_method_id) {
    }
    throw new org.omg.CORBA.MARSHAL();
  }
}
```

This is the Server side skeleton class that allows calls from the ORB runtime classes to be propagated up to the Server Object Implementation. Every server that implements the IDL interface must extend the server skeleton file.

<IDL Interface Name>Operations.java and #tie#<IDL Interface Name>.java

What if your server implementation is already extending from another Java class? This presents a problem because the Java language doesn't allow for multiple implementation inheritance, only multiple interface inheritance. The generated operations and _tie files provide a way around this issue through the use of delegation. Delegation and the tie class are discussed in more detail in Chapter 5, "Server Essentials."

example<IDL Interface Name>.java

The _example file is provided as a useful shell for implementing your server implementation. Listing 4.24 shows the _example file for our test interface.

LISTING 4.24 GENERATED example IMPLEMENTATION FROM THE IDL DEFINED IN LISTING 4.18

```
public class _example_test extends _testImplBase
{
        // Notice it extends the skeleton

        /** Construct a persistently named object. */
        public _example_test(java.lang.String name)
        {
                // The two types of constructors
                // are automatically created for
                // you.
                super(name);
        }

        /** Construct a transient object. */
        public _example_test()
        {
                super();
        }

// Method signatures would all be listed here
}
```

Listing 4.24 shows that the example file is a shell of the implementation. If there were operations defined in the interface, we would see the methods listed with empty brackets making it extremely easy to simply add the functionality. You see that it automatically creates constructors for both a persistent and transient object implementations. Do not worry about the significance of these two different constructors because they are discussed in detail in Chapter 6, "The Smart Agent."

SUMMARY

Chapter 4 concludes our discussion of the IDL language. We looked at the advanced IDL topics of Exceptions and Inheritance. We then explained the idl2java application in detail. We concluded with a summary of the files generated by the idl2java compiler.

Exception Handling falls into one of two categories in CORBA. The first of those exceptions are CORBA System Exceptions, a finite list of predefined errors thrown by the ORB infrastructure. These exceptions all extend from org.omg.CORBA.SystemException and are thrown as Java Runtime Exceptions. Although not enforceable at compile time, it is a good idea to always catch these exceptions.

The second category of Exception discussed is User Exceptions. These are likely required for any type of robust business application where there are cases when the calling code violates some type of business rule. To create your own exceptions, you must first define the exception in IDL. When the corresponding Java code is generated, you'll have a final class that descends from org.omg.CORBA.UserException. Any IDL method that raises a User Exception is mapped into a Java interface that throws a corresponding Java exception. A server implementation of such an interface can therefore throw the exception, and the ORB runtime ensures that it reaches the calling client.

IDL does support the notion of Interface Inheritance, not Implementation Inheritance. IDL allows developers to declare interfaces as ancestors of interfaces. Fortunately, the rules for interface inheritance follow those for IDL, which are:

- An interface might extend one or more ancestor interfaces.
- When generating Java code from IDL, Java Interfaces are generated for each interface defined in IDL. Any interfaces inheriting from ancestor interfaces in IDL have the same lineage in Java.
- Generated code on the client (remember from Chapter 2, "Introduction to IDL," they're called stubs) that implements an interface also implements all ancestors of that interface.

Finally, the chapter discusses the various options that can be used when using the VisiBroker for Java IDL compiler, idl2java. This tool is used in virtually every chapter for the rest of this book, so you will probably find yourself referring back to this chapter quite often.

SERVER ESSENTIALS

CHAPTER 5

IN THIS CHAPTER

- THE ORB *114*
- THE BOA *116*
- BUILT-IN THREADING MODELS FOR VISIBROKER SERVERS *119*
- DEVELOPING SERVER OBJECTS *124*
- THE TIE MECHANISM *128*
- CORE OPERATIONS FOR ALL SERVER OBJECTS *132*
- A FULL REVIEW OF IMPLEMENTING A SERVER OBJECT *134*

You have spent the past three chapters learning how to define your Server Objects in IDL. This chapter teaches you everything you need to know about actually implementing a VisiBroker Server Object. We will start with a discussion of how Server Objects identify themselves to the Object Request Broker (ORB) environment and how they receive and process requests. In understanding how requests are received by Server Objects, we will explain the internal threading and connection management of VisiBroker. We will then present two different approaches to developing Server Objects, using Skeleton Inheritance and using the `Tie` delegation method. This chapter examines each of these steps in great detail through a variety of code listings.

THE ORB

The first step that must be taken when building any VisiBroker Server is to perform some ORB initialization. This is achieved by getting a reference to the ORB object. An example of obtaining such a reference to the ORB is shown in Listing 5.1.

LISTING 5.1 AN EXAMPLE OF HOW TO INITIALIZE THE ORB BY USING ITS DEFAULT PROPERTIES

```
}
public static void main(String[] args)
{
        // Initialize the ORB
        org.omg.CORBA.ORB orb = org.omg.CORBA.ORB.init();
}
```

The ORB reference obtained in Listing 5.1 provides you a reference to the ORB interface using the default ORB initialization options. If you would like to set your own options for the ORB (we discuss such options later in this chapter), these can be passed in as a `java.util.Properties` object. Passing options to the ORB is shown in Listing 5.2.

LISTING 5.2 AN EXAMPLE OF HOW TO INITIALIZE THE ORB BY SETTING YOUR OWN VALUES FOR CERTAIN ORB PROPERTIES

```
public static void main(String[] args)
{
        java.util.Properties props = new java.util.Properties();
        props.put("ORBdebug", "true");
        org.omg.CORBA.ORB orb = org.omg.CORBA.ORB.init(args, props);
}
```

Alternatively, you can pass ORB options to your VisiBroker Server at the command line when it is started. The following is an example of how to start a VisiBroker Server called Server with command-line options being passed to the ORB initialization.

```
prompt> vbj -DORBdebug=true Server
```

or

```
prompt>vbj Server -ORBdebug true
```

> **NOTE**
>
> VisiBroker for Java can be built using any compliant Java bytecode compiler and invoked with any Java compliant interpreter. However, you will notice that VisiBroker provides a couple of useful utilities for compiling and running your applications.
>
> - **vbjc**—This is a utility for compiling your VisiBroker applications. It adds all the necessary VisiBroker JAR files to your CLASSPATH and then invokes the JDK javac compiler. It isn't a Java compiler itself.
> - **vbj**—A utility for invoking your VisiBroker Java applications. Similar to vbjc, it is basically your systems standard Java compiler with the CLASSPATH for VisiBroker inserted.

If your ORB options are passed on the command line using the *-<property> <value>* notation, your ORB initialization code should be changed to use the method call shown in Listing 5.3.

LISTING 5.3   AN EXAMPLE OF HOW TO ENABLE THE ORB TO BE INITIALIZED WITH COMMAND-LINE ARGUMENTS

```
public static void main(String[] args)
{
        org.omg.CORBA.ORB orb = org.omg.CORBA.ORB.init(args, null);
}
```

If there are other application specific command-line arguments within the String[] shown in Listing 5.3, the ORB.init() simply ignores these. A full listing of the ORB options is discussed in Chapter 21.

We have just discussed the first required initialization step that all VisiBroker Server Objects must perform, the ORB initialization. Next, we will take a look at the second required initialization step, the BOA initialization.

THE BOA

The Basic Object Adapter (BOA) is the mechanism by which VisiBroker Servers receive requests via the ORB. In order to use the BOA, a reference to the BOA must be obtained. This is done through calling `BOA_init()` on the ORB reference as shown in Listing 5.4.

LISTING 5.4 AN EXAMPLE OF HOW TO INITIALIZE THE BOA

```
public static void main(String[] args)
{
        // Initialize the ORB
        org.omg.CORBA.ORB orb = org.omg.CORBA.ORB.init();
        org.omg.CORBA.BOA boa = orb.BOA_init();

}
```

The BOA provides several key functions for the VisiBroker Server that we explain in the following section.

Generation and Mapping of Object References to Their Implementations

When an object is created, the Object Adapter (OA) is responsible for creating a unique Interoperable Object Reference (IOR). An object's IOR is used by other objects to locate and establish communication with it. The IOR of an object implementation is the unique identifier of an object implementation, providing all the information necessary for another CORBA process to locate and communicate with it. Take a look at what information is contained within an IOR.

First, you will see what an IOR looks like:

```
IOR:000000000000001c49444c3a42616e6b2f4163636f756e744d616e6167657273a312e
➥30000000000100000000000005400010000000000d3230372e39322e38372e35320000
➥042b0000003800504d43000000000000001c49444c3a42616e6b2f4163636f756e7461
➥6e6167657273a312e30000000000c42616e6b4d616e6167657200
```

The ORB knows how to interpret this IOR. The ORB translates the preceding sequence of unreadable bytes to the following:

```
Interoperable Object Reference:
  Type ID: IDL:Bank/AccountManager:1.0
  Contains 1 profile.
```

```
Profile 0-IIOP Profile:
  version: 1.0
  host: 207.92.87.52
  port: 1067
  Object Key: PersistentId[repId=IDL:Bank/AccountManager:1.0,
↪objectName=BankManager]
```

From this breakdown, you can tell quite a bit about the object implementation you are trying to connect with. We will examine this in more detail.

> **TIP**
>
> The IOR breakdown from a sequence of characters to a human-readable summary can be obtained by passing any IOR string to the VisiBroker utility printIOR. This can be done as follows
>
> ```
> prompt>    printIOR <some IOR string here>
> ```

Understanding the Elements of a CORBA IOR

Type ID: `IDL:Bank/AccountManager:1.0` refers to the Repository ID. This was discussed briefly in Chapter 2. Remember that from the syntax of this string, you can see that you have an interface called AccountManager nested within a module called Bank. Following the scoped name is a version number. At present, VisiBroker for Java does not support the modification of this version string.

Next, you see an IIOP profile.

```
....
Profile 0-IIOP Profile:
....
```

Remember from Chapter 1 that IIOP stands for Internet Inter-ORB protocol. IIOP is the implementation of the General Inter-ORB protocol for TCP/IP networks. IIOP is the wire protocol outlined in the CORBA 2.0 specification for interoperability with other vendor ORBs. CORBA 2.0 ORBs were not required to naturally support this protocol. However they were required to provide some type of bridging support for this protocol in order to have interoperability with other ORB vendors. The designers of VisiBroker felt it was unnecessary to maintain proprietary protocols and made IIOP the only available protocol with VisiBroker. VisiBroker supports IIOP as its only natural protocol. When looking at an IOR from a VisiBroker for Java object, it becomes evident that only an IIOP profile will be supported.

Looking at the IIOP profile, it should start to become clear how the ORB runtime uses this information to locate the remote object. The ORB is able to recognize that the remote object is located at the remote host and remote port listed. At this point, the client runtime knows exactly where the remote object is located and opens a network connection directly to that remote socket.

Registrations of Implementations

When objects are created, they must register with the BOA. The OA keeps a table of all registrations and creates a unique IOR identifier for each object registered. This is done with the call to the BOA shown in Listing 5.5, passing in the Server Object as the only argument.

LISTING 5.5 AN EXAMPLE OF HOW TO REGISTER YOUR SERVER OBJECT WITH THE BOA

```
public static void main(String[] args)
{
        // Initialize the ORB
        org.omg.CORBA.ORB orb = org.omg.CORBA.ORB.init();
        org.omg.CORBA.BOA boa = orb.BOA_init();

        MyObject objRef = new MyObject();
        boa.obj_is_ready(objRef);

}
```

The `obj_is_ready()` call will be discussed in further detail later in this chapter and when we discuss Smart Agents in Chapter 6.

Activation and Deactivation of Object Implementations

Object Implementations can register themselves with the BOA such that the BOA can activate new instances and deactivate existing instances. The BOA keeps an internal reference count of activated instances; when the reference count has been reduced to zero, the instance is destroyed and left to be garbage collected. Object Activation is the key focus in Chapter 15.

Method Invocation

When calls are received by the ORB on the server side, they are passed to the BOA for dispatching to the appropriate object. Because the BOA is involved with the creation of each object, it keeps a table of all available object implementations and handles the "up-call" to these objects when method calls are received.

The server calls the `impl_is_ready()` method on the BOA in order to wait for requests from Clients. When `impl_is_ready()` is called, the Server runs indefinitely until it is explicitly shut down, as shown in Listing 5.6.

LISTING 5.6 AN EXAMPLE OF HOW TO PREPARE YOUR SERVER OBJECT TO BEGIN TO RECEIVE REQUESTS FROM CLIENTS

```java
public static void main(String[] args)
{
        // Initialize the ORB
        org.omg.CORBA.ORB orb = org.omg.CORBA.ORB.init();

        // Initialize the BOA
        org.omg.CORBA.BOA boa = orb.BOA_init();

        // Create the new Server Object
        MyObject objRef = new MyObject();

        // Register the newly created object with the BOA
        boa.obj_is_ready(objRef);

        // Wait for incoming requests
        boa.impl_is_ready();
}
```

We have just discussed each of the necessary steps in order to initialize the ORB and the BOA. Further, you saw how to register your Server Objects with the BOA such that they will be able to receive requests from Clients.

BUILT-IN THREADING MODELS FOR VISIBROKER SERVERS

As we continue to create the groundwork for building your first CORBA application, it is important to discuss some of the implementation within VisiBroker. The purpose of this section is to provide an in-depth understanding of how VisiBroker supports threading. Because the Java environment itself is multi-threaded, VisiBroker for Java is multi-threaded. VisiBroker for Java offers two different built-in thread models that you can take advantage of without having to write any threading code, the Thread-per-Session model and the Thread Pooling model. This section discusses these two models in detail.

> **NOTE**
>
> Because of the inherent multi-threading built into VisiBroker for Java, you must always program your VisiBroker Server Objects to be thread safe.

In the last section, you took a look at how to initialize the BOA using the default settings, the `BOA_init()` call. When the call to `BOA_init()` is made, the ORB runtime creates a new listener thread that sits on a randomly selected port. It also initializes the ORB to the appropriate threading model. This is done by passing either the string `TSession` or `TPool` as the first argument to the `BOA_init()`. If no argument is passed, the ORB uses `TPool` as the default. Examples of initializing the BOA with the two threading modes is shown in Listing 5.7.

LISTING 5.7 AN EXAMPLE OF HOW TO INITIALIZE THE BOA WITH A SPECIFIC THREAD POLICY

```
org.omg.CORBA.ORB orb = org.omg.CORBA.ORB.init();
org.omg.CORBA.BOA boa = orb.BOA_init("TSession", null);
```

or

```
org.omg.CORBA.ORB orb = org.omg.CORBA.ORB.init();
org.omg.CORBA.BOA boa = orb.BOA_init("TPool", null);
```

It is possible to start the BOA on a specific IP address (if a multi-homed host is used) or on a specific port for communication. This is done by creating a `java.util.Properties` object to be passed as a second argument to the `BOA_init()` call. Using properties to set the host/port information while initializing the BOA is shown in Listing 5.8.

LISTING 5.8 AN EXAMPLE OF HOW TO INITIALIZE THE BOA WITH SPECIFIC PARAMETER SETTINGS

```
....
java.util.Properties boaProperties = new java.util.Properties();
// for a multi-homed host
boaProperties.put("OAipAddr", "207.92.87.52");
// or alternatively you can put a valid hostname for this argument
// boaProperties.put("OAipAddr", "host1");
boaProperties.put("OAport", "8899");

org.omg.CORBA.BOA boa = orb.BOA_init("TPool", boaProperties);
.....
```

These options can also be set on the command line as follows:

```
vbj -DOAipAddr=207.92.87.52 Server
```

Or

```
vbj Server -OaipAddr 207.92.87.520
```

We just showed that the host/port information can be set during initialization with the BOA. A complete listing of such BOA options is discussed in Chapter 21.

At this point, you have learned how to set up your Object Adapter to listen for incoming requests on either a random port or the port specified in the Java Properties. We have also instructed the VisiBroker runtime to create a listener thread to do nothing but listen for incoming requests and dispatch them, based on the threading model set during the BOA initialization. This process is shown in Figure 5.1. It is important to note that regardless of the number of objects created within a given server process, there is a single listener thread for each BOA handle you have. Thus you can create multiple BOA instances, perhaps one using Thread-per-Session and one using Thread Pooling. In this scenario, each new BOA instance results in a new listener thread being created.

FIGURE 5.1
The default listener thread is created within the `BOA_init()` *call.*

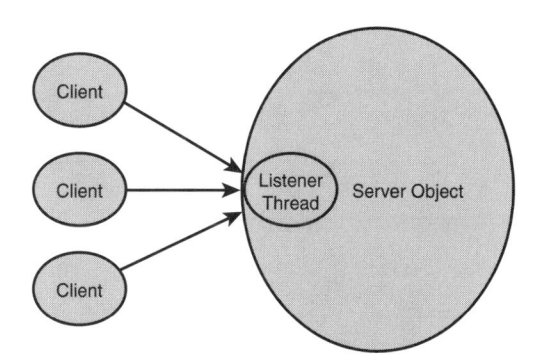

When a Server does a BOA_init(), a listener thread is created that will listen for incoming requests and dispatch them based on the selected thread model.

Thread-per-Session

The Thread-per-Session model is designed to designate new worker threads per each client connection. In this model, every time a new Client connects to the Server Object the listener thread accepts the connection and spawns a new worker thread to handle the dedicated connection to the Server Object. This is shown in Figure 5.2. When the Client disconnects from the Server Object, the worker thread is completed.

Thread Pool

In this model, threads are not issued on a per-connection basis, rather on a per-method basis. Each time a call is made into the Server process, the listener thread won't create a new thread to last the lifetime of the connection as with the session model. Instead, it looks to use an existing, unused thread in a Thread Pool. The Thread Pool is a collection of already started threads waiting to drive code based on user requests. The thread retrieved from the pool performs the requested operation and returns to the Thread Pool for future requests. This is shown in Figure 5.3.

FIGURE 5.2

The Thread-per-Session model, creating a new Server thread to handle the dedicated connection to the Client.

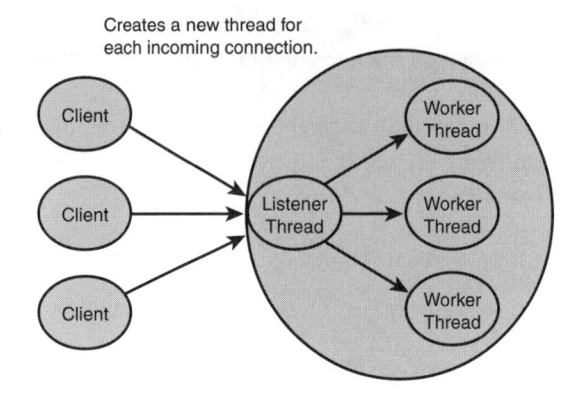

Creates a new thread for each incoming connection.

In thread-per-session, the listener thread will create a new thread to handle the work for each individual connection.

FIGURE 5.3

The Thread Pooling model, reusing available threads only for the duration of the method request.

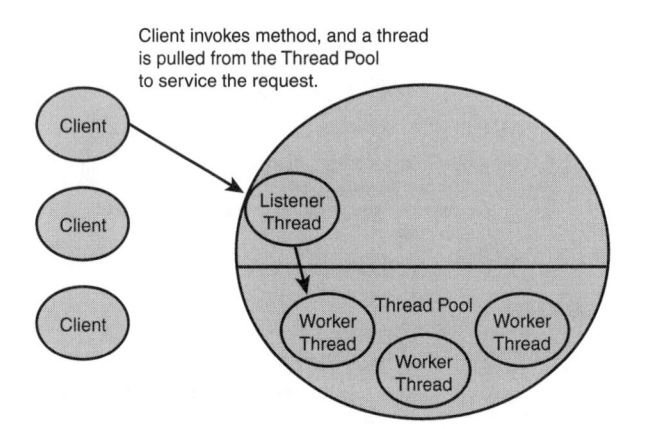

Client invokes method, and a thread is pulled from the Thread Pool to service the request.

In the thread pool model, for each method request that comes in, the listener thread will pull a thread out of the thread pool to service the request. After the request is finished, the thread is returned to the pool for future use.

There are several important parameters that can be set upon startup to have better control over the size and behavior of the Thread Pool. They are

    OAthreadMax

    OAthreadMin

    OAthreadIdleTime

When a Server Object is started, the ORB continually creates new threads to handle each incoming connection. However, when new ones are created the old ones are not destroyed, rather they are passed back into the Thread Pool for future use. Threads are dynamically created until the `OAthreadMax` is hit or until the system won't enable any more threads. After the Thread Pool is completely filled, the ORB continually reuses these existing threads. This enhances performance by avoiding the penalty of having to continually create and destroy worker threads. If all available worker threads are being used, the listener thread blocks until a thread has been freed up and is available for processing.

> **TIP**
>
> Unless some specific concurrency behaviors are desired, the pool model of threading is the most efficient in terms of resource usage.

In addition to understanding the built-in threading behaviors of VisiBroker, it is also important to understand how VisiBroker for Java manages socket connections. VisiBroker has a sophisticated connection management capability for maximizing throughput to VisiBroker for Java Server Objects. This is discussed in the next section.

Connection Management

Connection management is a built-in feature to give the ORB control over how many active connections any given Server Object can have active at any given time. A common problem with CORBA applications is that connections to a Server Object are constantly created and destroyed, but the resources are never cleaned up. This results in an otherwise available Server Object unable to accept any new connections because it doesn't have any available socket connections. They are simply unable to clean out the disconnected sockets fast enough, or all the available socket connections are being consumed by Clients. The built-in connection management within VisiBroker for Java is designed to provide an automated mechanism for managing server-side socket connections to provide maximum scalability.

> **CAUTION**
>
> On UNIX systems, it is possible for your process to run out of file descriptors with too many connected clients. In some cases, this number is as low as 64. Note that this is not an inherent problem in VisiBroker, but rather an issue with your UNIX system configuration. Before using UNIX systems, make sure your file descriptor limit is high enough to handle the number of connections your server is expecting.

The design of the server side connection management is very similar to that of Web Servers. A Web Server must be very efficient in its use of socket connections in order to enable the greatest number of browser clients to access the site. To do this, it is common for the Web Server to disconnect active connections and require clients to re-connect when they actually click on a hyperlink. The implementation of VisiBroker connection management is very similar. A Server Object has a limited number of socket connections that might be established. When this limit has reached its maximum capacity, the Server Object can no longer accept any new connections. However, with VisiBroker connection management, when this limit has been reached, the ORB automatically disconnects the connection that has been idle for the longest period of time. However, it won't disconnect any active clients. If the connection management recognizes that all available sockets are being actively used, it blocks until a client request has finished and the server socket becomes idle again. The ORB cleans up the socket resources of this connection to enable the new connection to come through immediately. This ensures that socket connections are managed and cleaned up immediately to be reused for new incoming connections.

Now that we have explained how VisiBroker internally manages threads and connections, it is time to examine how to write the server implementations themselves.

DEVELOPING SERVER OBJECTS

Our discussion of server essentials has so far introduced how the programmer or administrator communicates connection and threading properties to the VisiBroker runtime. We have yet to introduce how you actually define your server code. We will now discuss how to create the server implementations using two techniques: skeleton inheritance and the `Tie` approach.

Developing Servers Objects with the Skeleton Approach

One approach to developing your Server Objects is to have your Object Implementation extend from the IDL generated server skeleton file. Listing 5.9 shows an example IDL file containing an interface, `MyInterface`, that we will be using throughout this discussion.

LISTING 5.9 A SAMPLE IDL INTERFACE

The IDL:
```
// IDL
interface MyInterface
{
};
```

When you run the IDL in Listing 5.9 through the idl2java compiler, you get the following list of files generated:

```
MyInterface.java
MyInterfaceHolder.java
```

```
MyInterfaceHelper.java
_st_MyInterface.java
_MyInterfaceImplBase.java
MyInterfaceOperations.java
_tie_MyInterface.java
_example_MyInterface.java
```

Looking at the object model in Figure 5.4, you can see the relationship between the various generated files and the core ORB interfaces.

FIGURE 5.4
The class hierarchy within VisiBroker when developing with the generated skeleton class.

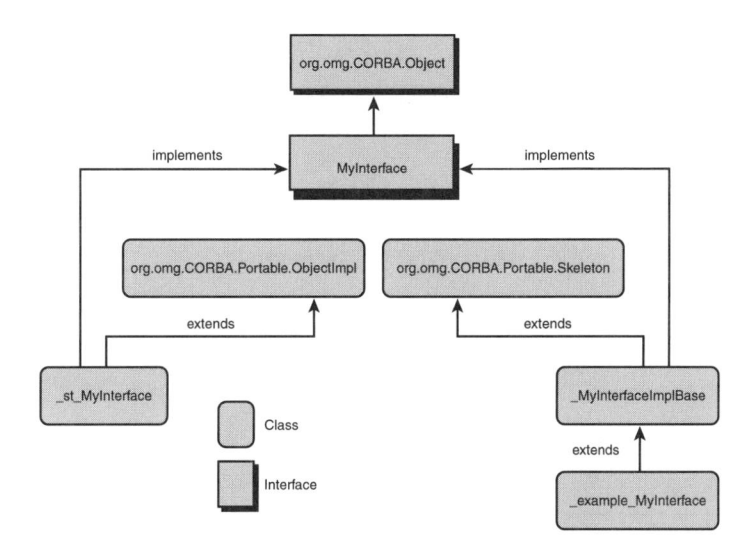

We see that using our Implementation of the `MyInterface` interface, `MyInterfaceImpl`, inherits the implementation of the `_MyInterfaceImplBase` skeleton class. This is demonstrated in the code shown in Listing 5.10.

LISTING 5.10 AN EXAMPLE OF HOW TO DEFINE YOUR IMPLEMENTATION CLASS IF YOU ARE IMPLEMENTING WITH THE SKELETON INHERITANCE APPROACH

```
public class _MyInterfaceImpl extends _MyInterfaceImplBase {
    .........
}
```

Listing 5.10 shows the implementation of the `MyInterface` interface. In order to instantiate this object, you need to follow the programmatic initialization steps described earlier in the chapter. The initialization and registration of your server is shown in Listing 5.11.

LISTING 5.11 A FULL EXAMPLE OF HOW TO INSTANTIATE YOUR SERVER OBJECT, REGISTER IT WITH THE ORB AND BOA, AND HAVE IT WAIT FOR INCOMING REQUESTS

```
public static void main(String[] args)
{
    try
    {
        // Initialize the ORB.
        org.omg.CORBA.ORB orb = org.omg.CORBA.ORB.init();

        // Initialize the BOA.
        org.omg.CORBA.BOA boa = orb.BOA_init();

        //Create an instance of the MyInterfaceImpl object
        MyInterfaceImpl objRef = new _MyInterfaceImpl();

        // Export the newly create object.
        boa.obj_is_ready(objRef);

        System.out.println(objRef + " is ready.");

        // Wait for incoming requests
        boa.impl_is_ready();
    }
    catch(org.omg.CORBA.SystemException ex)
    {
        ex.printStackTrace();
    }
}
```

The only possible problem with the skeleton approach is that, because of Java language restrictions, it is only possible to inherit from one implementation. As such, any VisiBroker Servers you create that use the Skeleton Inheritance approach will be unable to inherit from any other classes. This doesn't prevent the class from implementing other interfaces, it only prevents the class from extending any other classes.

Developing Server Objects by Using the Tie Delegation Approach

As you just learned in our discussion of the skeleton approach to implementing our server, the skeleton approach requires your server to inherit from a special base class. If it is undesirable to descend from this base class because of other programming requirements of your server, you can use the Tie approach to server implementation.

There are many such cases throughout the Java API where the programmer must use class inheritance. In the java.io package, new input streams must descend from java.io.InputStream or one of its children. If the programmer wants to create a new stream and have that stream extend from some other class, he is stuck.

In Java, one mechanism for working around the lack of multiple inheritance is through the use of delegation. Delegation is the pattern of having a class defer implementation of one or more methods to a second class through a known interface. We can see an example of delegation with the class `java.awt.Thread`. Consider the case of someone who wants to write a simple timer in Java as shown in Listing 5.12.

LISTING 5.12 A SIMPLE TIMER CLASS

```java
public class MyTimer extends Thread
{
    public MyTimer()
    {
        start();
    }

    int count = 0;

    public void run
    {
        while(true)
        {
            sleep(500);
            System.out.println(++count);
        }
    }
}
```

This simple class extends thread and overrides the `run()` method. It prints an ever increasing number to the console every half second. Consider now the example of a programmer who wants to encapsulate this timing functionality into a GUI widget. If she wants a text area to print the count, she must descend from `java.awt.TextArea`. However, if she wants the functionality of a Thread, she must extend from `java.lang.Thread`. Thus, it is becoming apparent that the lack of multiple class inheritance in Java can cause problems.

The way around this is through delegation and the `java.lang.Runnable interface`. You can create a class that fulfills the requirements of your timer as shown in Listing 5.13.

LISTING 5.13 USING THE RUNNABLE INTERFACE TO DELEGATE

```java
public class TimerTextArea extends java.awt.TextArea implements Runnable
{
    public TimerTextArea()
    {
        super();
        Thread t = new Thread(this);
```

continues

LISTING 5.13 CONTINUED

```
            t.start();
        }

        int count = 0;
        public void run()
        {
                setText(++count + "");
        }
}
```

The class `java.lang.Thread` treats objects of type `Runnable` as delegates for the `run()` method. If a thread is constructed with a `Runnable` object, all the functionality of the thread is intact, except the implementation of the `run()` method is passed off to the object of type `Runnable`. This deferring of implementation to another object of a known interface is an example of delegation.

THE `Tie` MECHANISM

We have alluded to a problem that might arise if you want your server implementation to descend from a class other than the generated `_XXXXImplBase` class. We then discussed the delegation pattern as a way to work around multiple inheritance for Java's Thread class. We will now discuss the `Tie` mechanism, which is the realization of delegation in the generated VisiBroker classes.

Assume that you have the IDL shown in Listing 5.14.

LISTING 5.14 IDL FOR A SIMPLE INTERFACE TO SHOW THE `Tie` MECHANISM

```
interface Test
{
    long add(in long aNumber,
             in long anotherNumber);
};
```

Running the idl2java program on the IDL in Listing 5.14 file produces the following .java files:

```
Test.java
TestHolder.java
TestHelper.java
_st_Test.java
_TestImplBase.java
TestOperations.java
_tie_Test.java
_example_Test.java
```

We discussed the purpose of each of these files in Chapter 4. We will quickly review what you have learned about each generated file in Table 5.1.

TABLE 5.1 IDL GENERATED FILES

Name of File	Purpose of File
`Test.java`	This is the Java interface definition of our IDL interface. The important thing to note about this interface is that it extends from the base CORBA interface: `org.omg.CORBA.Object`. The `Test.java` interface is implemented by both the Client Stub, `_st_Test.java`, and the Server Skeleton, `_TestImplBase.java`.
`TestHolder.java`	This is the wrapper class for passing the Test Interface as an `inout` or an `out` argument.
`TestHelper.java`	An abstract class providing many useful static methods for connecting to VisiBroker's Smart Agent, providing type-safe downcasts using `narrow()`, as well as several methods for inserting and extracting the Test interface into and out of a CORBA Any type.
`_st_Test.java`	The Client Stub. This implements the `Test.java` interface and acts as a local proxy object for the client to communicate with. The Client Stub is responsible for marshalling the parameters and passing the data across the wire to the Server Object.
`_TestImplBase.java`	The Server Skeleton. Implements the `Test.java` interface and passes requests from the ORB to the Object Implementation.
`_example_Test.java`	An empty shell of a Test Object Implementation. It creates an Object Implementation that uses Skeleton Inheritance and provides all the necessary signatures for all the operations defined in the IDL interface. This handy utility is used to generate Object shells so that all you have to do is go back and write the logic within the braces to implement the operations within the object.

We will now discuss the last two generated files, the `_tie_Test.java` and `TestOperations.java` files.

> **NOTE**
>
> Occasionally, we use the term *business methods* in the text to refer to those methods on an object defined in the IDL. Although all IDL derived methods might not be
>
> *continues*

> relevant to a company's business (such as findAllLargeAccounts() or calculateReturn()), we have introduced the term to distinguish between those methods on an object relevant to the ORB (such as bind()) to those relevant to the cross-language object. You can think of business methods as meaning those methods defined on the original IDL that was compiled and turned into a Java interface.

These files combine to allow the developer to delegate the business methods to an Object that doesn't descend from a generated class. _tie_InterfaceName (we will now refer to this simply as the tie class for short) looks very similar to the ImplBase class except that it is not abstract. In fact, it descends from the ImplBase class and implements all the business methods. The tie class requires an object of type InterfaceNameOperations (we will refer to such a class simply as the operations class for short) as a parameter in both its constructors. We will discuss the significance of these constructors in the next chapter. The tie class can be directly instantiated, and implements all the necessary, generated methods required by the ORB. For all business methods, the tie defers, or *delegates*, the calls directly to those of the same signature in the operations class.

Thus, here are the final two IDL generated files referenced in Table 5.1:

_tie_*InterfaceName*.java	A descendent of _*InterfaceName*ImplBase that defers implementation of all IDL defined methods to a delegate. The delegate implements the interface *InterfaceName*Operations.
*InterfaceName*Operations	The interface that defines the Java signatures for all IDL defined methods. It is used in conjunction with the _tie_*InterfaceName* class to implement delegation through the Tie mechanism.

To use the Tie mechanism, you must provide an implementation of the business methods in a class that implements the operations interface. The class diagram for the Tie delegation is shown in Figure 5.5.

We will walk through an example with the Test interface you used in Chapter 4 during the discussion of the generated files. To use the Tie mechanism, first provide the delegate that implements the operations interface, shown in Listing 5.15.

LISTING 5.15 SERVER IMPLEMENTATION OF BUSINESS METHODS USING THE Tie MECHANISM

```
public class TestDelegate extends SomeBaseClass implements TestOperations
{
        //Because we are not descending from a generated
        //base, we do not need a transient and named
        //constructor.  In such a case, the default
```

```
        //constructor in implicit


        //This is the only business method defined in the IDL, and the
        //only signature we must implement from the
        // TestOperations interface
        public int add(int aNumber, int anotherNumber)
        {
                return aNumber + anotherNumber;
        }

}
```

FIGURE 5.5
The class hierarchy within VisiBroker when developing with the delegation Tie *approach.*

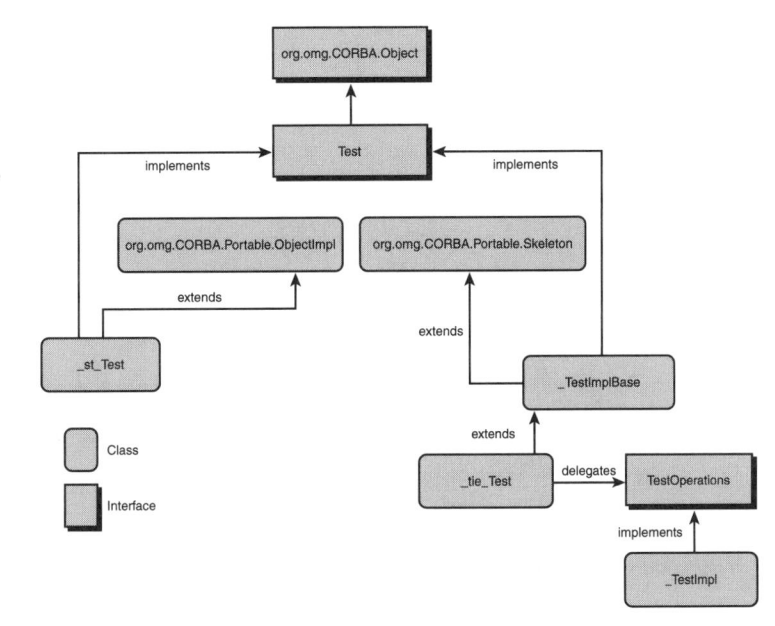

Note that the code in Listing 5.15 represents your Server, but descends from a non-generated base class. You need to implement the business methods and retain any instance members relevant to those methods. When you have defined your delegate, you still need to initialize the BOA and register your server with the BOA. This is done by invoking operations on the generated tie class. Listing 5.16 shows creating and binding of your server.

LISTING 5.16 CREATING AND BINDING SERVER IMPLEMENTATION WITH THE Tie MECHANISM

```
""""""public static void main(String[] args)
{
        try
        {
```

continues

LISTING 5.16 CONTINUED

```
            // Initialize the ORB.
            org.omg.CORBA.ORB orb = org.omg.CORBA.ORB.init();

            // Initialize the BOA.
            org.omg.CORBA.BOA boa = orb.BOA_init();

            // Create our delegate
            TestDelegate delegate = new TestDelegate();

            //Create the Tie, passing our object that implements the "operations"
            //interface - the delegate
            tie_Test tie = new _tie_Test(delegate, "Tie Sample1");

            // Export the newly create object.
            boa.obj_is_ready(tie);

            System.out.println(tie + " is ready.");

            // Wait for incoming requests
            boa.impl_is_ready();
        }
        catch(org.omg.CORBA.SystemException ex)
        {
            ex.printStackTrace();
        }
}
```

Did Listing 5.16 look familiar? It should because it is almost the same as operations without using the `Tie` mechanism. The only differences are that we are not binding the user-written code, but rather the generated `Tie` code.

CORE OPERATIONS FOR ALL SERVER OBJECTS

Because all Server Objects ultimately extend from the base CORBA interface `org.omg.CORBA.Object`, take a look at the operations that can be called on all Server Objects:

```
public interface org.omg.CORBA.Object extends java.lang.Object {
    public abstract boolean _is_a(java.lang.String);
    public abstract boolean _is_equivalent(org.omg.CORBA.Object);
    public abstract boolean _non_existent();
    public abstract int _hash(int);
    public abstract org.omg.CORBA.ORB _orb();
    public abstract org.omg.CORBA.BOA _boa();
    public abstract java.lang.String _object_name();
    public abstract java.lang.String _repository_id();
    public abstract boolean _is_local();
    public abstract boolean _is_remote();
    public abstract boolean _is_bound();
```

```
    public abstract boolean _is_persistent();
.........
}
```

This is not a full listing of all the available methods on the org.omg.CORBA.Object interface. However, the methods that have been omitted are covered later in the text when relevant. Quickly examine each of the methods listed in Table 5.2.

TABLE 5.2 METHODS AVAILABLE ON ALL VISIBROKER SERVER OBJECTS

Methods on the org.omg.CORBA.Object Interface	Purpose of Method
_is_a(String)	Determines whether the Server implements the specified interface name passed in as an argument.
_is_equivalent (Object)	Returns true or false for whether two objects both implement the same interface.
_non_existent()	Attempts to ping the Server Object to determine whether it is available for Client connections. Returns true if the Server is available, or false if the Server is occupied.
_hash(int)	Computes a hash value for the Server Object, with the value being passed in as the maximum possible value. Thus, the hash is between 0 and the maximum value.
_orb()	Returns the current reference to the ORB.
_boa()	Returns the current reference to the BOA.
_object_name()	Returns the name of the Server Object instance. If the Server Object is Transient(which we discuss in Chapter 6) it is unnamed and a null is returned.
_repository_id()	Returns the Repository ID for the Server Object. For more information on the syntax of the Repository ID, refer back to Chapter 2.
_is_local()	Returns true if the Server implementation is in the local Java Virtual Machine (JVM).
_is_remote()	Returns true if the Server implementation is in a remote JVM.
_is_bound()	Returns true if there is currently an open TCP connection to the Server Object.
_is_persistent()	Returns true if the Server Object is a Persistent Object. Persistent Objects are discussed in more detail in Chapter 6.

A FULL REVIEW OF IMPLEMENTING A SERVER OBJECT

Now, we'll review each of the development steps discussed in the first five chapters. We discussed in Chapters 2–4 how to define your Server Objects in IDL. In this chapter, we have shown all the steps necessary to create your Server Object Implementations and register these with the ORB and the BOA. This section walks you through a full development example.

1. Write the IDL. For this example, we will pick a somewhat complex system based on concepts you've learned in Chapters 2–5, a struct called `BasicStruct` and an interface that accepts an array of `BasicStruct` objects. The IDL file for this example is shown in Listing 5.17.

LISTING 5.17 A SAMPLE IDL DEMONSTRATING COMPLEX IDL TYPES

```
module Example
{
    struct BasicStruct
    {
        long    longVal;
        string  stringVal;
    };

    typedef BasicStruct    BasicStructArray[2];

    interface ArrayOfComplexTest
    {
            long testArrayOfComplex(
            in BasicStructArray inBasicStructArray,
            inout BasicStructArray inoutBasicStructArray,
            out BasicStructArray outBasicStructArray);
    };
};
```

2. Write the Object Implementation and Server main. When you have defined your Server interface, it is time to write your Java implementation of the Server Object.

```
package ExampleImpl;
```

It is good programming practice to put your code in its own separate Java package, away from the IDL generated files that are put in a package with the name specified in the module command.

```
/*
 * Server to test the passing of arrays of complex types, showing the
 * use of in/inout/out parameters and Holders
 *
 * Note that IDL fixed sequences map to Java arrays
 */
```

Notice that your implementation inherits from the generated server skeleton, which is the name of your interface with the suffix ImplBase attached.

```
public class ArrayOfComplexTestImpl extends Example._ArrayOfComplexTestImplBase
{
```

The significance of the Transient and Persistent constructor is discussed in Chapter 6.

```
//Constructor for transient object
    public ArrayOfComplexTestImpl()
    {
    }

    //Constructor for persistent object
    public ArrayOfComplexTestImpl(String name)
    {
        super(name);
    }
```

Now it is time to implement your method. If you are at all confused by this method declaration, look in the generated _example_ java file discussed in Chapter 4. It is a pre-built shell of a Server Object implementation. This is a great way to verify that you have all the right values for your arguments, especially all those tricky Holder classes.

```
    public int testArrayOfComplex(Example.BasicStruct[] inBasicStructArray,
Example.BasicStructArrayHolder inoutBasicStructArray,
            Example.BasicStructArrayHolder outBasicStructArray)
    {
        //Print the parameters as passed
        System.out.println("Beginning method testArrayOfComplex\n" +
            "\tin param " + inBasicStructArray + "\n" +
            "\tinout param " + inoutBasicStructArray.value + "\n" +
            "\tout param " + outBasicStructArray.value);

        //Change the values in the inout array
        inoutBasicStructArray.value[0].longVal = 6;
        inoutBasicStructArray.value[0].stringVal = "fromServer";
        inoutBasicStructArray.value[1].longVal = 6;
        inoutBasicStructArray.value[1].stringVal = "fromServer";

        //Create a new array for the out value then assign values
        outBasicStructArray.value =
            new chapter2.arrayOfComplex.generated.BasicStruct[2];
        outBasicStructArray.value[0]=
            new chapter2.arrayOfComplex.generated.BasicStruct(6, "fromServer");
        outBasicStructArray.value[1]=
            new chapter2.arrayOfComplex.generated.BasicStruct(6, "fromServer");
```

```
//Print the parameters as returned
System.out.println("Before returning from method testArrayOfComplex\n" +
    "\tin param " + inBasicStructArray + "\n" +
    "\tinout param " + inoutBasicStructArray.value + "\n" +
    "\tout param " + outBasicStructArray.value);

    return 0;
}
```

It is possible to separate your Server mainline from your Server Object Implementations; however, because this example has only one Implementation, it is just as easy to include it in the same file.

```
//Put registration code here in a main for convenience
public static void main(String[] args)
{
    try
    {
```

The first thing to do 'is to get a handle on the ORB and initialize, as shown in the following:

```
// Initialize the ORB.
org.omg.CORBA.ORB orb = org.omg.CORBA.ORB.init();
```

Now, it is time to initialize the local Basic Object Adapter. This is critical because it is the BOA initialization that creates the first listener thread. As discussed earlier in the chapter, the BOA is the component that takes the method requests from the ORB and does the distribution to the appropriate server object. Further, it handles the dispatching of requests to the worker threads depending on what type of threading model is being used. If you want to change the default threading model to Thread-per-Session, this must be passed to the BOA_init() call. All variables with regard to threading are passed in to the BOA_init() method.

```
// Initialize the BOA.
org.omg.CORBA.BOA boa = orb.BOA_init();
```

Time to create an object instance.

```
// Create the ArrayOfComplexTestImpl object.
ArrayOfComplexTestImpl arrayOfComplexTest =
    new ArrayOfComplexTestImpl("ArrayOfComplex Sample");
```

You need to make this instance known to the BOA, so you can start receiving method requests. The BOA keeps an internal reference count on the number of object implementations registered with it.

```
// Export the newly create object.
boa.obj_is_ready(arrayOfComplexTest);

System.out.println(arrayOfComplexTest + " is ready.");
```

Finally, with this method, the BOA and ORB wait for incoming requests off the wire. This call sits in a continuous event loop waiting for incoming calls.

```
        // Wait for incoming requests
        boa.impl_is_ready();
    }
```

Here you will catch a Java Exception such that you can catch either CORBA System Exceptions or User Exceptions. If this is unclear, refer back to Chapter 4's discussion on Exception Handling.

```
catch(java.lang.Exception ex)
        {
            ex.printStackTrace();
        }
    }
}
```

3. Compile the Server. Here you can use any Java 1.1+ bytecode compiler you like. We offer vbjc, which is a utility that effectively adds all the necessary VisiBroker jar files to your local CLASSPATH and then compiles your Server Object.

```
prompt> vbjc ExampleImpl/ArrayOfComplexTestImpl.java
```

4. Run your Server. This should be done using the vbj utility that comes with VisiBroker for Java. The vbj utility starts the local Java interpreter. In this example, we use the VisiBroker Smart Agent Directory Service in order to enable the Client and Server to locate each other. This is the focus of Chapter 6.

```
prompt> osagent
prompt> vbj ExampleImpl/ArrayOfComplexTestImpl
```

That's it! Now you have created your first Server implementation that is running and waiting for Clients to make invocations on it. This will be our focus in Chapter 6 as you learn how to write Clients and how those Clients connect to the Server Objects.

SUMMARY

This chapter covers everything you need to know to start developing VisiBroker Server Objects. We started with an overview of the CORBA ORB interface. Getting a reference to the local ORB is the first step in any Server development. From this reference, you are able to obtain a reference to the Basic Object Adapter (BOA).

The BOA serves several purposes. It generates the unique Interoperable Object Reference (IOR) that identifies the Server Object and provides the necessary host and port information for a Client to establish a connection with it. The BOA also keeps a registration table of all the objects started and dispatches requests to the appropriate objects as calls come in from the ORB.

The BOA is responsible for the initialization of the internal threading within VisiBroker. VisiBroker offers two types of thread models, Thread-per-Session and Thread Pooling. In Thread-per-Session, a new thread is created for each new Client connection to the Server Object. When the Client disconnects, the thread is destroyed. In Thread Pooling, every request that is dispatched to the Server Object obtains an existing thread from a pool of available threads to service the operation. When the operation has finished, the thread returns to the pool to be made available for other operations.

Object implementations can be written in one of two ways, using Skeleton inheritance and `Tie` delegation. Skeleton inheritance involves having your Object Implementation extend or inherit from the Skeleton Class. This is the easier approach, but is somewhat limiting because the Java language only enables single class inheritance. Thus, if you require your Server Object to extend from another class skeleton, inheritance cannot be used.

The `Tie` mechanism is a straightforward implementation of delegation. It provides the developer with a means to implement the methods defined in IDL on a Java class that does not descend from generated code. Two `Tie` files are created by running idl2Java on your IDL. The first is a `_tie_InterfaceName` class that provides the concrete implementation of the server implementation. At runtime, it delegates the implementation of business methods to a delegate class through a well-known interface, the second generated file, `InterfaceNameOperations` interface.

THE SMART AGENT

CHAPTER 6

IN THIS CHAPTER

- HOW DOES A CLIENT FIND THE SERVER? 140
- THE VISIBROKER SMART AGENT 142
- SMART AGENTS 146
- COMMUNICATION BETWEEN CLIENTS AND SMART AGENTS 148

The previous few chapters have been devoted to teaching you the syntax necessary to define your Object Implementations in IDL and implement them in Java through the IDL to Java mapping. We emphasized that Interface Definition Language (IDL) is important because it defines all the attributes and operations of the remote implementation. A client developer doesn't need to be concerned with the implementation or location of the remote object because the client only codes against the Java interface generated from the IDL.

IDL doesn't, however, cover any concept of where the remote object is located or how to connect to it. IDL doesn't address what a client program needs to do in order to locate the remote object. This concept hasn't been introduced yet because IDL syntax doesn't discuss object location. This would violate the role of IDL, to simply describe the interface. Issues, such as location of the remote object and how to connect to the remote object, are the responsibility of the application.

Over the next few chapters, we will show you four different strategies on how to handle the issue of remote object location. In this chapter, we will focus exclusively on the Smart Agent Directory Service, a non-CORBA compliant VisiBroker extension.

HOW DOES A CLIENT FIND THE SERVER?

The CORBA specification itself doesn't mandate any particular type of convention for locating remote objects. The specification simply discusses how an object implementation makes itself available to start receiving invocations and how it creates a unique reference for itself, the Interoperable Object Reference (IOR). The IOR of an object implementation is the unique identifier of an object implementation, providing all the information necessary for another CORBA process to locate and communicate with it. An IOR can be seen in Listing 6.1.

LISTING 6.1 AN IOR

```
IOR:000000000000001c49444c3a42616e6b2f4163636f756e744d616e6167657273a312
e30000000000010000000000000054000100000000000d3230372e39322e38372e353200
00042b0000003800504d43000000000000001c49444c3a42616e6b2f4163636f756e744
d616e6167657273a312e30000000000c42616e6b4d616e6167657200
```

Does the series of characters in Listing 6.1 make any sense to you? We doubt it. However, it makes no difference whether you understand it or not because any ORB knows how to interpret this IOR. Although the character string in Listing 6.1 looks meaningless to the human eye, it contains all the information the ORB needs in order to locate the object the IOR references. Because the information stored in an IOR is in a standardized format, any CORBA ORB can understand it. The ORB translates the preceding sequence of unreadable bytes to the information shown in Listing 6.2.

LISTING 6.2 INFORMATION CONTAINED IN AN IOR

```
Interoperable Object Reference:
Type ID: IDL:Bank/AccountManager:1.0
Contains 1 profile.
Profile 0-IIOP Profile:
version: 1.0
host: 207.92.87.52
port: 1067
Object Key: PersistentId
➥[repId=IDL:Bank/AccountManager:1.0,objectName=BankManager]
```

To the reader, the contents of Listing 6.2 makes more sense than Listing 6.1. From this breakdown, you can tell quite a bit about the object implementation that you are trying to connect with. We will examine this in more detail...

Type ID: `IDL:Bank/AccountManager:1.0` refers to the Repository ID. This is discussed briefly in Chapter 4. From the syntax of this string, you can see that an interface called `AccountManager` is nested within a module called Bank. Following the scoped name is a version number. At present, VisiBroker for Java doesn't support the modification of this version string. Thus, this should not be of concern to the reader for now.

Next, you see the following IIOP profile:

```
....
version: 1.0
host: 207.92.87.52
port: 1067
....
```

Looking at the IIOP profile, it should start to become clear how the ORB runtime uses this information to locate the remote object. The key pieces of data for this are the remote host name and port number. At this point, the client runtime knows where the remote object is located when this information is passed to a client.

So far we have discussed the translation of IORs, but haven't mentioned yet any strategies for how client code obtains the IOR. This problem of how to find the initial entry into a self-navigable system is often referred to as *bootstrapping*. This is where the CORBA specification does not make any requirements. The CORBA specification itself does not mandate any one particular way for a client to obtain a server object's IOR. There is, however, a Common Object Services specification for a Naming Service, which does speak to this issue in great detail. The CORBA Naming Service is the focus of Chapter 8. In this chapter, we will examine an alternative approach to allow clients to find servers: The VisiBroker Smart Agent.

THE VISIBROKER SMART AGENT

Because the original CORBA 2.0 specification didn't require that CORBA vendors handle the bootstrapping issue, the issue of how a client can obtain the server IOR, VisiBroker developers created their own proprietary Directory Service called the Smart Agent. The Smart Agent provides a dynamic, distributed directory service. A simple overview of how the Smart Agent works is as follows:

1. A Smart Agent is started on the network.
2. A Server Object is started and registers its location information (the information contained in the IOR) with the Smart Agent.
3. A Client is started and calls the Smart Agent requesting the location information of the Server Object.
4. The ORB instantiates a local proxy object, or stub, which has the necessary IOR details of the real Server Object. The Client is returned to a local reference to the stub that handles all the data marshaling and network communication to the actual Server Object implementation.

> **NOTE**
>
> The VisiBroker Smart Agent is written in C++ and is therefore platform dependent. In fact, the Smart Agent is the same for both the C++ and Java product. It was never ported to Java in the early releases of VisiBroker for Java because early versions of the JavaSoft JDK didn't support Unreliable Datagram Protocol (UDP) broadcasts, a technology that you will soon learn is fundamental to the Smart Agent.

In trying to understand the behavior and dynamics of the Smart Agent, think of this process as analogous to the process of using the local 411 directory assistance for calling an old friend. Review the following sequence of steps:

1. You have the name of your old friend Ralph whom you would like to call.
2. You do not have Ralph's number, but you do have the number to directory assistance, 411.
3. You call 411, providing the operator with the name of your friend, and the operator provides you with the direct phone number of your friend.
4. If Ralph's phone number is not listed in that local area, the operator can contact other operators and do a larger search in surrounding areas.

5. After you receive the direct phone number, you call your friend directly and don't call 411 directory assistance again.

Now the behavior of the VisiBroker Smart Agent, as well as a VisiBroker Client and Server Object, is virtually identical to this telephone example. The person trying to make the call is similar to the client, he knows who he wants to contact but doesn't have the contact information. The server is similar to the old friend whose phone number is registered with directory assistance. The directory assistance service is similar to the Smart Agent, able to provide contact information so the first party can have a conversation with the second. We will now go through the same sequence with clients and servers.

1. A client process knows the name of the remote server it would like to talk to from the IDL compiled stub. However, the client has no idea where this implementation is. The IDL for this interface is shown in Listing 6.3.

LISTING 6.3 AN IDL INTERFACE, ANALOGOUS TO KNOWING THE NAME OF THE FRIEND YOU WANT TO CALL, BUT NOT KNOWING WHAT HIS DIRECT NUMBER IS

```
// IDL
interface test
{
};
```

We spent Chapters 2–4 looking at the role of IDL. Figure 6.1 shows how the written IDL is run through the idl2java compiler to generate the Client stub and the Server Skeleton.

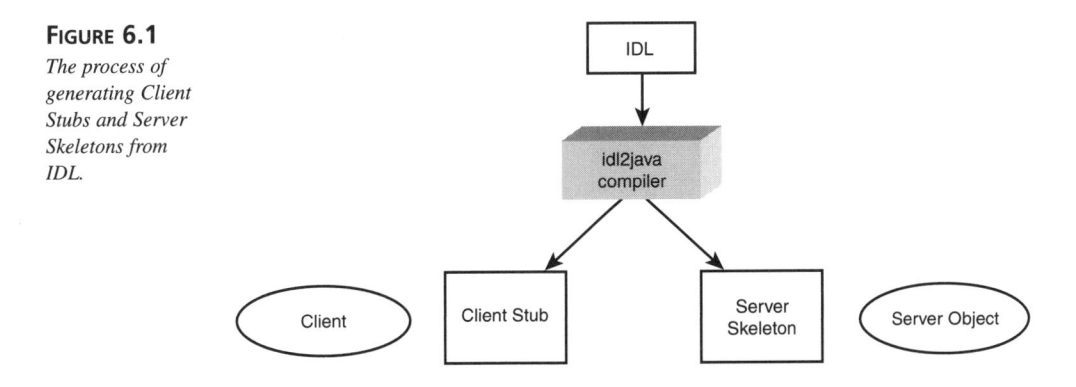

FIGURE 6.1
The process of generating Client Stubs and Server Skeletons from IDL.

Simply generating a Client Stub still doesn't provide the Client with the information it needs to locate the remote Object Implementation. You must now examine how the Client Stub locates the remote Server Object.

2. Because the Client has no idea where on the network to find the Server Object, it must use a directory service. For VisiBroker, this is the Smart Agent. The Client locates an available Smart Agent by sending a UDP broadcast across the network on the port specified by the OSAGENT_PORT environment variable. Although the Client doesn't have the exact location information of a Smart Agent, the broadcast returns the necessary socket information of a Smart Agent to communicate directly with. This is shown in Figures 6.2 and 6.3.

FIGURE 6.2
How a Client locates a Smart Agent. Client sends out a UDP broadcast on the OSAGENT_PORT in order to find a Server Object.

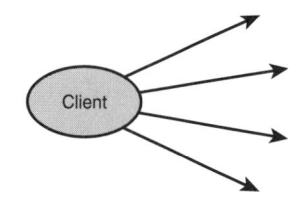

FIGURE 6.3
An Agent replies to the Client. An available Smart Agent responds to the Client, providing its host information to establish UDP point-to-point communication.

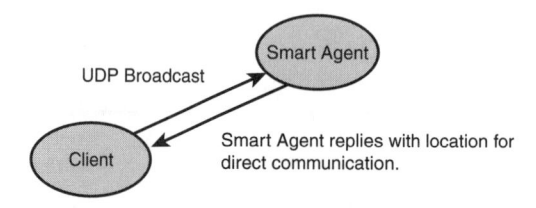

Analogous to calling 411 to ask Directory Assistance if they have a listing for the name of your friend.

3. An available Smart Agent responds. At this point, the Client asks the Smart Agent Directory Service for the location information of the Server Object it wants to connect with. The Smart Agent returns the Server Object location details, a client-side proxy object is instantiated, and the local proxy reference is returned to the Client. This is shown in Figure 6.4.

> **NOTE**
>
> Once the Client has the location of a Smart Agent, the Client requests the IOR of the particular Server Object. The Smart Agent looks up the IOR information in its local table. The Smart Agent keeps its table in local memory.

FIGURE 6.4
It does not write any information to disk.

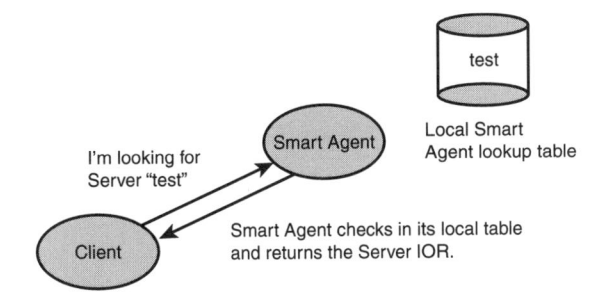

[Figure 6.4: Client asks Smart Agent "I'm looking for Server 'test'". Smart Agent checks in its local table and returns the Server IOR. Local Smart Agent lookup table contains "test".]

Analogous to making the call to Directory Assistance requesting the phone number of your friend. You provide the Directory Assistance with the name of your friend and they perform the necessary look up on the name and return your friend's direct number.

4. If the Smart Agent that the Client initially connects with does not have the location information for the Server Object requested, the Smart Agent sends a message to the other Smart Agents on the network to see if they have the location information. If another Smart Agent has the location information, it is returned directly to the Client, as shown in Figure 6.5.

FIGURE 6.5
Smart Agent interacts with other Smart Agents if they don't have a Server listing

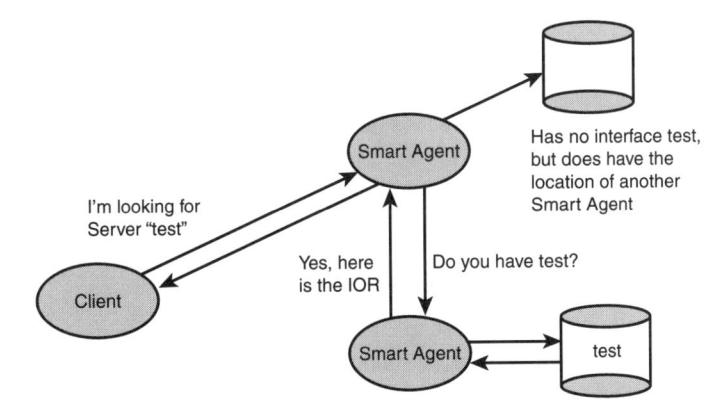

[Figure 6.5: Client asks Smart Agent "I'm looking for Server 'test'". First Smart Agent has no interface test, but does have the location of another Smart Agent. It asks second Smart Agent "Do you have test?" which has test. Response "Yes, here is the IOR" returned to Client.]

In Figure 6.5, Smart Agent checks in its local table. If this Smart Agent does not have the location of the requested Server Object, the Smart Agent will initiate a UDP broadcast to other Smart Agents in order to get the Server IOR back to the Client.

Analogous to the situation where your friend's phone number is not listed in that local area, prompting the operator to contact other operators and do a larger search in surrounding areas.

5. After the Server Object location information has been returned to the Client, the Client doesn't call the Smart Agent again; rather, the Client initiates a call directly to the Server Object via the local proxy (shown in Figure 6.6).

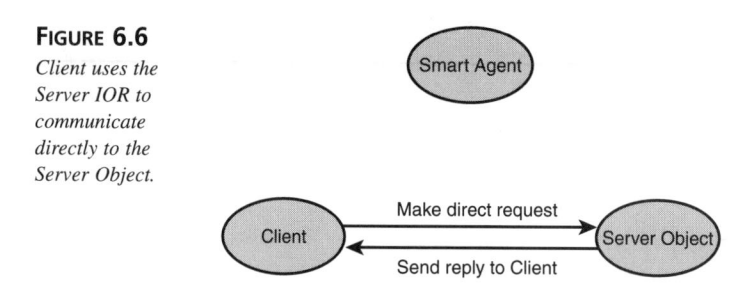

FIGURE 6.6
Client uses the Server IOR to communicate directly to the Server Object.

Analogous to receiving the direct phone number and making the call to your friend directly, and not having to call 411 directory assistance again.

SMART AGENTS

Smart Agents were designed as very lightweight processes that provide very quick and efficient lookups to large numbers of concurrent clients. As part of this design, the Smart Agents maintain their table of server listings in local memory (never writing to the hard disk).

It isn't necessary to run a Smart Agent on every host, nor is it necessary to run the Smart Agent on the same host as your server object implementations. The default behavior is as follows:

1. Start a Smart Agent on some host on the subnet. The default listen port is 14000, but this can be overridden by setting the `OSAGENT_PORT` environment variable to whatever value you choose. The osagent itself is started by typing the following on the command line:

    ```
    prompt> osagent
    ```

    Alternatively, on Windows 95 and Windows NT, a startup icon is available that simply needs to be double-clicked. Note that if you want to start the Smart Agent from a command line on Win32, you must use the -C flag as follows:

    ```
    prompt> osagent -C
    ```

2. The first thing the Smart Agent does upon startup is make a UDP broadcast on a given port number. The broadcast is done either to port 14,000 or whatever value was set in the `OSAGENT_PORT` environment variable, as shown in Figure 6.7.

> **NOTE**
>
> The default behavior of the Smart Agent requires NO administration or configuration files whatsoever. Because of the dynamic UDP functionality, the Smart Agents automatically find other Smart Agents on the same subnet.

FIGURE 6.7
Upon startup, the Smart Agent will initiate a UDP broadcast on the OSAGENT_PORT *in order to get a list of all the available Smart Agents on the network.*

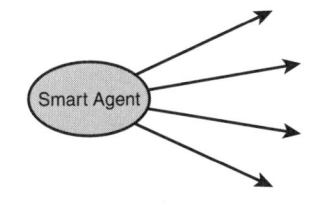

Smart Agent to Smart Agent Communication

If there is more than one Smart Agent alive on the network, the Smart Agents exchange their location information. Within the local dictionary of each Smart Agent, the location of the other Smart Agent is kept for future reference. After the Smart Agent has communicated with the other Smart Agents on the network, it waits for incoming requests from both Clients as well as Object Implementations, as shown in Figure 6.8.

FIGURE 6.8
A Smart Agent communicates with other Smart Agents if it cannot find a Server listing in its local data table.

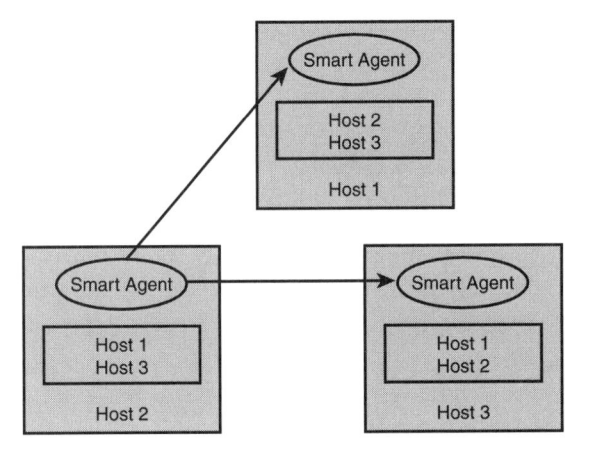

> **NOTE**
>
> Notice that after each Smart Agent starts up, it does a UDP broadcast to get the location information for each of the other Smart Agents. This information is kept in its local lookup table.

Smart Agents don't replicate the information they maintain in their internal tables. This is in an effort to keep the Smart Agents as lightweight and efficient as possible. Thus, Smart Agents each maintain their own internal listing of available Server Object. Any given Smart Agent's internal listing is going to be different from every other Smart Agent listing of available Server Objects because each Server Object registers with one Smart Agent at most. Each Smart Agent has a subset of the available Server Objects. The only exception to this is if the Server Object detects that the Smart Agent it has registered with has crashed. This is covered in the next section.

If a request comes into a Smart Agent that it doesn't have a listing for, the Smart Agent contacts each of the other Smart Agents it has listed in its internal table asking if they have a registration for the requested Server Object. If the requested Server Object is registered with another Smart Agent, the Smart Agents communicate with each other to pass the Server Object IOR back to the Client.

> **NOTE**
>
> The original Smart Agent, however, doesn't add this Server Object to its internal table because it is being maintained by another Smart Agent. The Smart Agents don't replicate any Server information with each other.

Communication Between Server Objects and the Smart Agent

After at least one Smart Agent has been started on your network, it's time for your Server Objects to register their binding information with the Smart Agent. However, only certain types of VisiBroker Servers register with the Smart Agent. We will examine the two different types of VisiBroker Server Objects.

Persistent Versus Transient Objects

VisiBroker has two types of objects, `persistent` and `transient`. `Persistent` Objects are those which are started with a specific instance name and are registered with the Smart Agent. An example of registering a `Persistent` Object is shown in Listing 6.4.

LISTING 6.4 EXAMPLE OF HOW TO INSTANTIATE A `Persistent` OBJECT BY USING THE IDL FROM LISTING 6.3

```
// Segment of Server.java for Persistent Objects
public class Server
{
public static void main(String[] args)
```

```
{
try
{
// Initialize the ORB.
org.omg.CORBA.ORB orb = org.omg.CORBA.ORB.init();

// Initialize the BOA.
org.omg.CORBA.BOA boa = orb.BOA_init();

// Create a Persistent Object
Test test=new TestImpl(""Specific Instance Name"");
// Export the newly create object to the Smart
// Agent
boa.obj_is_ready(test);
// Wait for incoming requests
boa.impl_is_ready();
        }
catch(org.omg.CORBA.SystemException e) {}
    }
}
```

The Server Object Implementation is created with a specific instance name to identify a unique instance of the test interface. When this object reference is passed to the obj_is_ready() call, the VisiBroker runtime makes the necessary UDP broadcast to locate and register with a Smart Agent.

Transient Objects are started without a specific instance name and aren't registered with the Smart Agent. Transient Objects tend to be lighter weight because they don't maintain the ongoing communication with the Smart Agent. The drawback with Transient Objects is that you must come up with your own mechanism for getting the Transient Object's IOR back to the Client. The only way any Client is ever able to communicate with a Transient Object is if the Client is explicitly passed the Transient IOR. The creation of a transient object is shown in Listing 6.5

LISTING 6.5 EXAMPLE OF HOW TO INSTANTIATE A Transient OBJECT BY USING THE IDL FROM LISTING 6.3

```
// Segment of Server.java for Transient Objects
public class Server
{
public static void main(String[] args)
{

try
{
// Initialize the ORB.
```

continues

LISTING 6.5 CONTINUED

```
org.omg.CORBA.ORB orb = org.omg.CORBA.ORB.init();

// Initialize the BOA.
org.omg.CORBA.BOA boa = orb.BOA_init();

// Create a Transient Object
Test test = new TestImpl();
//Export the newly created object.  This will
//register the object instance with the
//BOA for incoming requests, however the ORB will
//not make the UDP call to  the Smart Agent.
boa.obj_is_ready(test);
// Wait for incoming requests
boa.impl_is_ready();
            }
catch(org.omg.CORBA.SystemException e) {}
        }
}
```

`Transient` Objects are typically seen when designing a Callback pattern. You will see explicit details on how to do this in chapter 16.

Using `Persistent` Objects with Smart Agents

A Server Object starts by finding a Smart Agent. Similar to the UDP broadcast done by the Smart Agent to locate other Smart Agents, the broadcast done by the Server is done on the `OSAGENT_PORT` value as shown in Figure 6.8. The first available Smart Agent on the network responds to the Server Object via a direct message The Agent replies to the Server Object's broadcast by providing the Server Object with its host and port information, so the Server can communicate directly with the Smart Agent. The Server Object then messages the Smart Agent in order to pass the Smart Agent its unique IOR, as depicted in Figure 6.9. Figure 6.10 shows how the Smart Agent maintains an internal table of these Server registrations.

> **NOTE**
>
> Similar to startup of the Smart Agent, the Server Object does a UDP broadcast at startup in order to locate an available Smart Agent. After a Smart Agent is located, the Smart Agent and the Server Object establish a UDP peer-to-peer communication so the Server Object can pass its IOR and binding information to the Smart Agent.

FIGURE 6.9
How Server Objects locate Smart Agents.

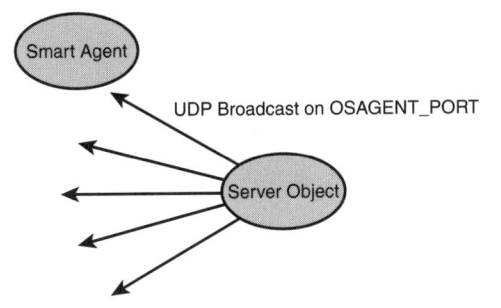

NOTE

The Server Object registers its IOR information with the Smart Agent for Client lookup.

FIGURE 6.10
Smart Agent keeps a listing of Server locations.

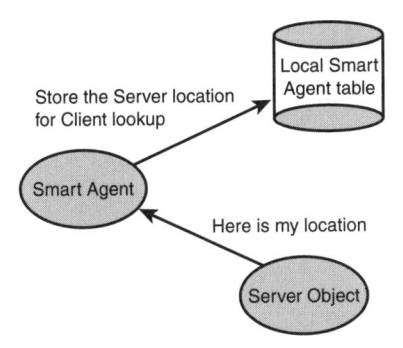

When the Server Object has successfully registered with the Smart Agent, the Server Object is ready to begin receiving requests from any Clients who obtain its unique IOR. After this initial registration, however, communication between the Smart Agent and the Server Object doesn't end. Every 120 seconds after the Server Object has registered with the Smart Agent, the Server Object sends a UDP message to the Smart Agent, effectively asking, Are You Alive?. This message (sometimes called a *ping*) is shown in Figure 6.11. The purpose of this communication is twofold.

NOTE

This heartbeat call made by the Server to verify that the Smart Agent is still running is made every 120 seconds. This is a hard-coded interval that cannot be changed. It was the decision of Inprise engineering not to make this a configurable parameter.

FIGURE 6.11

Every 120 seconds, the Server Object initiates an Are You Alive? *message to make sure the Smart Agent is still running.*

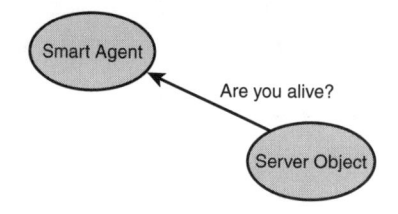

Some possible sequence of events around the heartbeats are as follows:

1. Server asks Smart Agent Are You Alive?

    This Server initiated ping enables the Server Object to determine if the Smart Agent it had initially registered with is still alive. If this Smart Agent has crashed, there is no way for any new Clients to find this Server Object, as shown in Figure 6.12.

FIGURE 6.12

If the Server Object sends its Are You Alive? *and realizes the Smart Agent has crashed, it can no longer be reached by any new Clients. Thus, it needs to do another UDP broadcast to register with a new Smart Agent.*

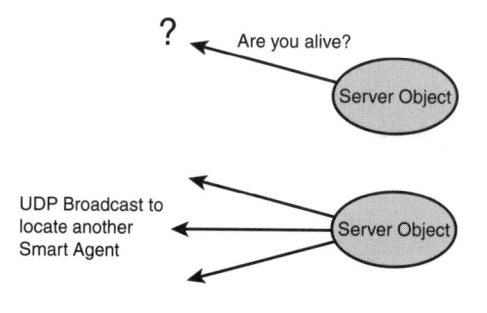

> **NOTE**
>
> If a Smart Agent crashes, this has no impact on any existing Clients that might already contain the IOR to the Server Object. They are able to continue their communication directly with the Server Object without any impact. This is because a Client only communicates with the Smart Agent in an effort to get the IOR of a Server Object. After this IOR has been returned, the Client communicates directly with the Server Object. A failure of the Smart Agent only impacts new Clients who are attempting to obtain the Server Object IOR for the first time.

At this point, the Server Object is stranded. Clients who don't already have the Server Object IOR are unable to find it despite the fact the Server Object is still running and available to receive requests. In an effort to prevent this situation, the Server Object performs the periodic ping, asking the Smart Agent `Are You Alive?`. If the Smart Agent is alive, the Server Object continues on with its normal operations. If, however, the Smart Agent has gone down, the Server Object performs another UDP broadcast to find another available Smart Agent somewhere on the network. This UDP broadcast is identical to the broadcast done upon startup, done merely as a mechanism to receive the contact information for an available Smart Agent. The Server Object follows the same steps of initiating communication with the new Smart Agent in order to register its IOR.

2. The Smart Agent makes the assumption that the Server Object has crashed.

The Smart Agent maintains an internal table of Server registrations, as well as other Smart Agent locations. For each Server Object that is registered with the Smart Agent, the Smart Agent knows to expect the `Are You Alive?` message within a certain time interval. If the Smart Agent notices that the interval has been exceeded and a certain Server Object in its internal table has not initiated the `Are You Alive?` call, the Smart Agent marks this Server's registration in the table as suspect. The Smart Agent continues to wait for the Server message for one more interval. If the Server Object has still failed to check in, the Smart Agent initiates a ping to the Server Object itself. At this point, the Server Object can determine if it is simply under a heavy load and unable to make the `Are You Alive?` call, or more important if the Server Object has crashed. This is important because the Smart Agent can now update its internal Server table and remove this Server's IOR. This ensures that when a Client obtains a Server Object's IOR from the Smart Agent, the IOR is valid and the Server Object is alive and ready to receive requests.

The significance of the heartbeat is shown in Figures 6.13 and 6.14. If the 120 second interval expires and the Smart Agent notices that the Server Object has not checked in, it gets a little suspicious. The Smart Agent marks the Server Object as suspect in its local table and waits for an additional 120 second time interval. At this point, if the Server Object hasn't checked in, the Smart Agent initiates a ping directly to the address of the Server Object in order to verify that it is running.

FIGURE 6.13
Smart Agent notices that the Server has not sent its message, so it checks to see if the Server is still running.

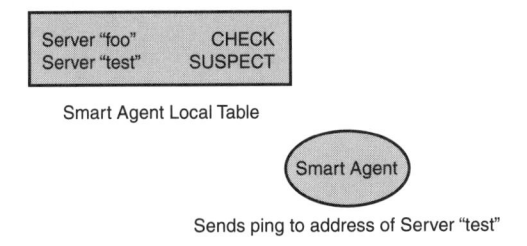

| Server "foo" | CHECK |
| Server "test" | SUSPECT |

Smart Agent Local Table

Smart Agent

Sends ping to address of Server "test"

?
Server "test" has crashed

FIGURE 6.14
Smart Agent removes the entry for the Server that has crashed.

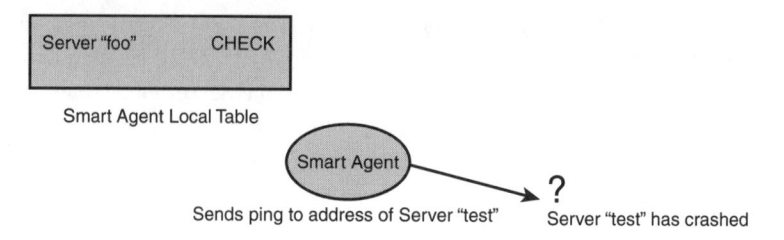

Server "foo"   CHECK

Smart Agent Local Table

Smart Agent

Sends ping to address of Server "test"   ?   Server "test" has crashed

COMMUNICATION BETWEEN CLIENTS AND SMART AGENTS

The Client uses the Smart Agent in order to get the IOR of a Server Object. We discussed the importance of this IOR at the beginning of the section—it contains the necessary host and port number information for the Client to establish a direct IIOP connection with the Server Object. Similar to the Server Object, the Client sends out a broadcast to locate and communicate with a Smart Agent. This UDP broadcast is performed when the Client makes use of the static `bind(...)` call defined in the generated Helper class. If the word Helper isn't ringing a bell, you might want to skip back to Chapter 4 and review the roles of the generated files from the IDL compiler. We'll take a closer look at this `bind(...)` call in relation to the example IDL file shown in Listing 6.6.

LISTING 6.6 A SAMPLE IDL

```
// IDL
interface Test
{
};
```

As you saw in Chapters 2–4, running this file through the idl2java compiler generates many files. Now, take a look at a segment of the generated testHelper.java from the IDL as shown in Listing 6.7.

LISTING 6.7 SEGMENT OF THE GENERATED HELPER CLASS SHOWING THE DIFFERENT SIGNATURES FOR bind()

```
public static Test bind(org.omg.CORBA.ORB orb)
{
......
}
public static Test bind(org.omg.CORBA.ORB orb, java.lang.String name)
{
```

```
     ......
}
public static Test bind(org.omg.CORBA.ORB orb, java.lang.String name,
↪java.lang.String host, org.omg.CORBA.BindOptions options)
{
     .....
}
```

In Listing 6.7 there are three different signatures for the `bind(...)` method. We will examine the role of each signature in the following sections.

bind(org.omg.CORBA.ORB orb)

This signature is used when the Client wants to bind to any instance of the given interface on any host. This method performs the same UDP broadcast to locate a Smart Agent. After a Smart Agent has responded, the Client communicates with the Agent via the bind method. In this example, the Client is requesting that the Smart Agent respond with an IOR of any available instance of the interface test running on any host. The ORB uses this IOR in instantiating the local client proxy (stub) to be returned to the Client.

Server Load Balancing

One of the functions of the Smart Agent is round-robin load balancing for replicated object instances. If a Client connects to a Smart Agent that has registrations of more than one instance of a given interface, the Smart Agent returns the first instance. Immediately upon returning that instance to the Client, the Smart Agent moves this instance to the bottom of its internal table such that the next Client that makes a request to the Smart Agent for an instance of the same interface gets a different reference. This load balancing is depicted in Figure 6.15. With this method signature, it makes no difference what the actual Server Object instance names are, the Client wants any reference available.

FIGURE 6.15
Smart Agent returns the first instance listed in its lookup table.

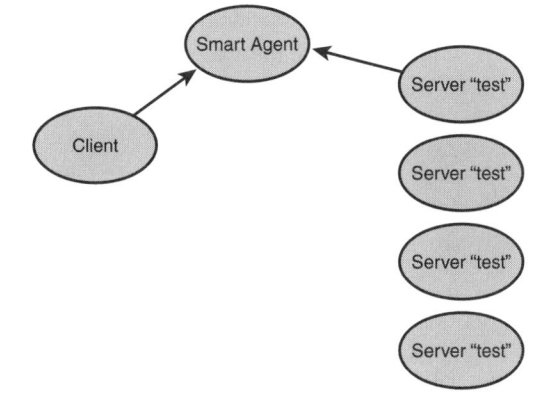

For more advanced load balancing capabilities, Chapter 17 discusses how to make use of the Location Service API. This is essentially the API into the Smart Agents, allowing you to write your own code to see each of the registered objects and perform your own load balancing.

`bind(org.omg.CORBA.ORB orb, java.lang.String name)`

This signature follows the same sequence steps of UDP broadcast as previously discussed in order to get a reference to an available Smart Agent. Using this method, the Client is requesting that the Smart Agent return only an instance of the interface test with the given instance name. The Client doesn't care which host these instances reside on.

Server Load Balancing

The Smart Agent load balancing with this method is slightly different from that of the first `bind()` signature. With this signature, the Client wants a specific instance of the interface. Here the Smart Agent performs the load balancing only on the instances of the interface that have the instance name specified in the second argument.

`bind(org.omg.CORBA.ORB orb, java.lang.String name, java.lang.String host, org.omg.CORBA.BindOptions options)`

This signature follows the same sequence of UDP broadcast as previously discussed in order to get a reference to an available Smart Agent. Using this method, the Client is requesting that the Smart Agent return only an instance of the test interface with the given instance name residing on a specific machine. Note that this method can be used with either the host name or options passed with a `null` value. This has the effect of letting the VisiBroker runtime choose default values for these parameters.

Server Load Balancing

The Smart Agent load balancing with this method is identical to the behavior described in the second signature, except it adds one more element to the search criteria: the hostname. With this method, the Smart Agent performs the object look up and load balancing on specific instances of a given interface residing on a specific host.

The final option is to set specific `BindOptions`. The `BindOptions` is an Object that has two public member variables of type Boolean that might be set and passed to the ORB. The members are `defer_bind` and `enable_rebinds`. We will take a closer look at these two flags in the following sections.

Defer Bind

Under normal semantics of the bind call, a connection is established to the Server Object during the bind call. However, if you make `defer_bind` true, the bind call itself won't actually set up the connection to the Server Object. Rather, the IOR is returned to the client, but the actual connection to the Server Object won't take place until the first method invocation takes place. The default value of this flag is false.

Enable Rebind

Under normal semantics of a Client call to a Server Object, if for whatever reason the connection is dropped, the default behavior is for the Client to attempt to rebind automatically to the Server Object. This is transparent to the Client and no special coding is required. If you are dealing with stateless Server Objects, having this option set to true is a very beneficial option. If any communication failure occurs, the VisiBroker runtime automatically catches it and attempts to rebind to the Server Object. If rebinding to that particular implementation continues to be unsuccessful, the runtime actually makes a call to the Smart Agent to find another implementation of that interface and attempts to connect with that Server Object instance. All this is totally transparent to the Client. If your client and server have conversational state, this option should be turned off. Alternatively, we will discuss some advanced workarounds later in the book when we discuss Event Handlers and Interceptors.

> **NOTE**
>
> Throughout this book and in discussions of distributed systems, the term *state* is often used, along with the related terms stateless and stateful. It should be noted that there are two kinds of state relevant to discussions in this book.
>
> *Persistent state* refers to the state of an object between invocations. An object representing your bank account is represented in the database, and thus has a persistent record. Any remote object that performs complex mathematical calculations doesn't itself represent a business entity. Thus it has no persistent state.
>
> *Conversational state* refers to the state of a series of remote method calls. If a client is communicating with a remote object with several `set()` methods, the client hopes that any calls to the `get()` methods return the same properties previously initialized with the `set()` method. When a client and server have a one-to-one relationship, they are said to have conversational state. If the client is making a series of calls to a remote object where each call is a discrete operation and there is no record of the client's previous calls on the server, the client and server are said to have no conversational state.
>
> Client/server relationships that have no conversational state are inherently easier to scale and load balance.

> **NOTE**
>
> The `bind(...)` call isn't CORBA compliant and is a VisiBroker specific extension. As such, it isn't possible to use this functionality with another vendor's CORBA ORB. Other vendors cannot have their Server Objects registering with the Smart Agent, nor can they have their Clients call `bind(...)` to our Smart Agent. Coincidentally, Iona's Orbix, another leading CORBA 2.0 implementation, also provides a `bind(...)` method within their product. These methods are completely proprietary and cannot be used to have a VisiBroker object talk to an Orbix Object. This must be done through explicit manipulation of IORs, which is covered in Chapter 7.

Client Connections

The first time a `bind(...)` is done, a new TCP/IP connection is established from the Client to the Server Object. From this point forward, any other `bind()` calls from this Client to any other interfaces within the same Server Process will multiplex over the same TCP connection. Listings 6.8, 6.9, and 6.10 show the IDL, client, and server of a system highlighting this socket multiplexing.

LISTING 6.8 AN IDL EXAMPLE TO DEMONSTRATE A CLIENT MAKING MULTIPLE bind() CALLS

```
// IDL
interface TestOne
{
};

interface TestTwo
{
};
```

LISTING 6.9 A SERVER INSTANTIATING TWO DIFFERENT OBJECTS

```
// Segment of Server.java
public class Server
{
public static void main(String[] args) {
try {
// Initialize the ORB.
org.omg.CORBA.ORB orb = org.omg.CORBA.ORB.init();
// Initialize the BOA.
org.omg.CORBA.BOA boa = orb.BOA_init();

// Create two objects
```

```
TestOne   testOne= new TestOneImpl(""Test Interface#1"");
TestTwo testTwo= new TestTwoImpl("Test Interface#2");j
// Export the newly create object.
boa.obj_is_ready(testOne);
boa.obj_is_ready(testTwo);
// Wait for incoming requests
boa.impl_is_ready();
    }
catch(...)

    }
}
```

LISTING 6.10 EXAMPLE OF A CLIENT ISSUING MULTIPLE bind CALLS TO SEPARATE SERVER OBJECTS

```
// Segment of Client.java
public class Client
{
public static void main(String[] args)
{

// Initialize the ORB.
org.omg.CORBA.ORB orb = org.omg.CORBA.ORB.init();
TestOne testOne = TestOneHelper.bind(orb, "Test Interface#1");
TestTwo testTwo= TestTwoHelper.bind(orb, "Test Interface#2");
    .............
}
```

Listing 6.10 shows a single Server process that is supporting two different objects with two separate interfaces. Now a client binding to multiple object implementations is actually done over the same TCP/IP connection, as shown in Figure 6.16. If the objects were to reside in two physically separate processes, the second bind(...) call would result in a second TCP connection being established. This same behavior is observed regardless of whether an IOR is returned via the Smart Agent or any other directory mechanism.

FIGURE 6.16
Multiple bind() *calls to the same Server process multiplex over the same single TCP/IP connection. It does not matter that the* bind() *calls are to completely separate objects.*

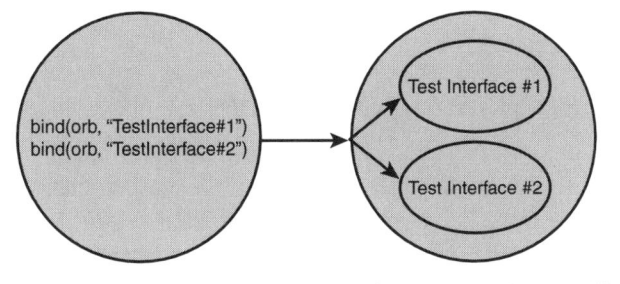

However, the difference between using `bind(...)` and obtaining the IOR from another mechanism is that the `bind(...)` causes a thread to be started by the orb. A separate thread is created to communicate with the agent. The only way to prevent this thread is to avoid the use of the `bind(...)` call.

If you require a separate connection to the same Server, this is done using `_clone( )`. The `_clone( )` operation actually makes a copy of the existing local proxy object and establishes a new TCP connection to the Server. Assume that the same Server from Listing 6.9 and the Client from Listing 6.10 could be modified to establish a second connection. The code for this modification is shown in Listing 6.11 and depicted in Figure 6.17.

LISTING 6.11 A `_clone()` FORCES A NEW TCP CONNECTION TO BE ESTABLISHED

```
// Segment of Client.java
// Bind to our interface creating the first TCP connection.
TestOne testOne = TestOneHelper.bind(orb, "" Test Interface#1");
// Let's set up a clone of the previous connection.  A copy is made and
// returned as a top level org.omg.CORBA.Object.
org.omg.CORBA.Object obj = testOne._clone();

// Because we have our ultimate base class, we narrow down to the
// appropriate interface type.// This operation will create our new
// TCP connection for methods invoked on this proxy
TestOne testOne clone_testOne = TestOneHelper.narrow(obj);
         . . . . . . . . . .
```

FIGURE 6.17
Unlike the bind(...) calls, a _clone() call forces a new TCP connection to be established.

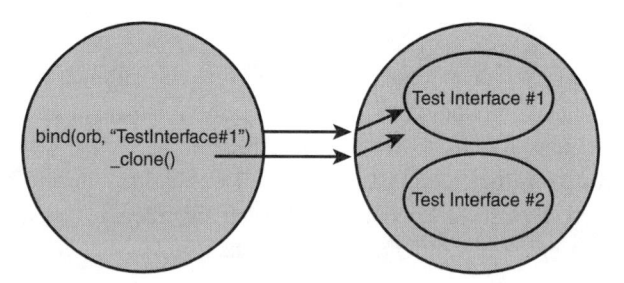

bind(orb, "TestInterface#1")
_clone()

Test Interface #1

Test Interface #2

Single Server Process that has 2 different Objects running.

Automatic Smart Binding by Clients

We have discussed the process by which a Client receives an IOR from the Smart Agent. After the IOR is received by the Client, the ORB decides what the most efficient binding mechanism is. The ORB checks to see if the Server Object reference returned is in the same process as the Client. If so, the ORB returns the actual Server Object reference to the Client instead of the proxy object. At this point, the Client communicates to the Server Object via direct Java methods and doesn't go through the ORB marshaling and TCP sockets. This Smart Binding is done automatically.

> **NOTE**
>
> You just learned that if the client and server are in the same process, the ORB returns a direct reference. This saves a great deal of overhead, but could create a subtle problem if you have not thought of this case while developing your implementation.
>
> When objects are passed by value across the network, the other side of the wire has a copy. A poorly written program might take advantage of this fact and begin to make changes on the passed object. In the case where client and server share the same address space, objects are not implicitly copied. Thus, different behavior is observed in the network versus local cases. To prevent such problems, copies of passed objects should always be made if they are to be changed, regardless of the client/server proximity.

Smart Agents and Multiple Environments

Because of the broadcast mechanism built into the Smart Agent, it is possible to set up multiple VisiBroker environments on the same host. These multiple environments can be referred to as *domains*. The idea here is that you can have both development and production environments on the same machines without interference between them. This is all handled via the OSAGENT_PORT variable. Starting multiple Smart Agents on a given host can only be done by setting separate OSAGENT_PORT variables, as depicted in Figure 6.18.

FIGURE 6.18
It is possible to keep production environments and development environments on the same machines.

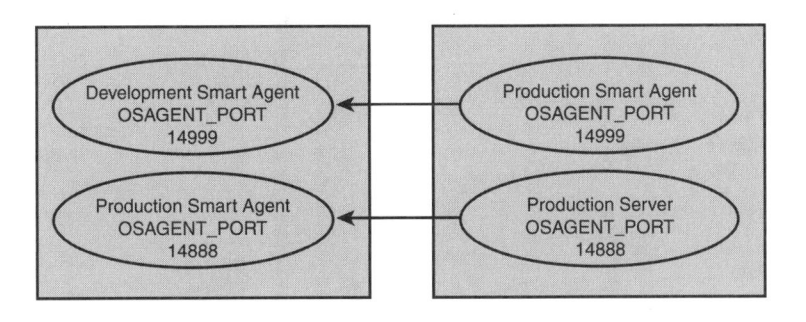

> **NOTE**
>
> It is possible to keep both environments on the same machines, because you can control which Server Objects and which Clients use which Smart Agents by the OSAGENT_PORT environment variable. As long as you are consistent with your OSAGENT_PORT, you will not run the risk of mixing environments.

Smart Agents and Different Networks

Thus far, we have talked about the UDP broadcast behavior of the Smart Agent. This UDP broadcast works fine in a local network environment, but often UDP doesn't work across subnets. In these situations, we are forced to set up a local configuration file called the *agentaddr* file. The purpose of this file is to list the IP addresses of the remote Smart Agents in order to set up a direct point-to-point communication.

The format of the agentaddr is simply a list of IP addresses as shown in Listing 6.12. A depiction of the two agents in this file is shown in Figure 6.19.

LISTING 6.12 EXAMPLE OF A SMART AGENT AGENTADDR FILE

```
204.179.98.5
204.179.98.6
```

The default location for this file is set by the environment variable VBROKER_ADM. This can be overridden by use of the OSAGENT_ADDR_FILE environment variable.

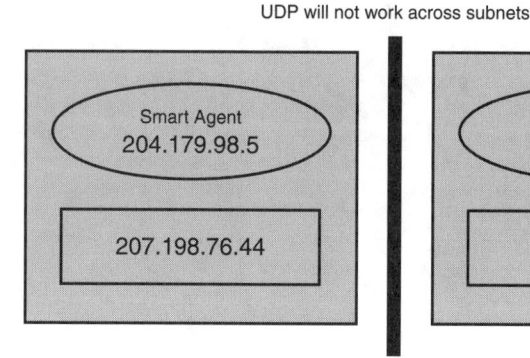

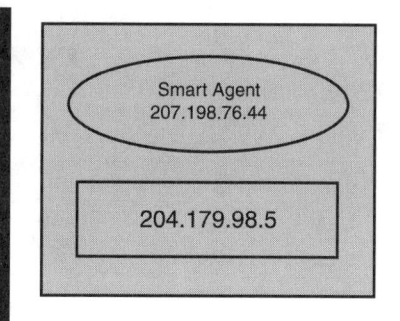

FIGURE 6.19

Because Smart Agents cannot send UDP across firewalls and subnets, the agentaddr is used to establish TCP connections to remote Smart Agents.

UDP will not work across subnets

Smart Agent 204.179.98.5

207.198.76.44

Smart Agent 207.198.76.44

204.179.98.5

Understanding Smart Agents, IORs, and DNS Look Ups

Entries listed in the agentaddr file must be in the form of an IP address, not a hostname, so a domain name service (DNS) look up isn't needed to locate a remote Smart Agent. This is important because the standard socket information contained in Server IORs is the IP address rather than the hostname. Thus, full communication to Smart Agents as well as Server Objects can be done without the requirement of having DNS installed in your environment.

To prevent DNS name look ups, you should do the following:

1. Define VBROKER_ADM to point to the adm directory of your VisiBroker installation.
2. Create the file $VBROKER_ADM/agentaddr with the IP address of any remote Smart Agents.
3. Define the OSAGENT_ADDR_FILE to be $VBROKER_ADM/agentaddr.
4. Start Server Objects with the option -OAipAddr={IPaddress}, where {IPaddress} is the IP address of the host the service is being started on.
5. Start the local client.

Smart Agents and Multi-Homed Hosts

It is possible to have a Smart Agent startup on a multi-homed host, a host that has multiple IP address interfaces. Because the two popular platforms for VisiBroker, WinNT, and UNIX are different, we will discuss the multi-homing for these platforms separately.

UNIX Hosts

For a UNIX implementation of the Smart Agent, this configuration is done automatically. The Smart Agent dynamically recognizes each interface and sets itself up to listen on each interface for incoming requests. However, you can explicitly list each interface name in a localaddr file that the ORB looks for, by default, in the directory specified by the VBROKER_ADM environment variable. If you would like to override this location, you can set the OSAGENT_LOCAL_FILE environment variable. The localaddr file is in the format found in Listing 6.13.

LISTING 6.13 EXAMPLE OF A LOCAL ADDR FILE FOR MULTI-HOMED UNIX MACHINES

```
<IP Address> <Subnet Mask> <Broadcast Address>
# Lines with a # sign are comments
#
# localaddr file for a multi-homed host
207.92.87.52    255.255.255.0    207.92.87.255
204.179.98.4    255.255.255.0    204.179.98.255
```

The preceding information should be identical to the following output returned from the UNIX command:

```
prompt> ifconfig -a
```

Windows NT Hosts

On a multi-homed Windows host, this configuration isn't done automatically. The administrator is required to set up a localaddr file. The syntax of this file is identical to that of the localaddr file previously described. The information for the localaddr file on Windows NT can be obtained through the following command:

```
prompt> ipconfig
```

Turning Off Smart Agents Broadcast

Although a lot of the more dynamic UDP features of the Smart Agent are advantageous, it is sometimes beneficial to have more control over which Smart Agents certain implementations will connect with. This can be done in two different ways:

- Environment variable OSAGENT_ADDR

    You have already seen the OSAGENT_PORT environment variable which overrides the default port number that the Smart Agent is listening on. This environment variable works the exact same way, except it is the default address the ORB tries to locate a Smart Agent on. If a Smart Agent is not found at this specified address, the ORB reverts back to its default UDP broadcast mechanism in order to communicate with any available Smart Agent.

- Runtime parameters

    There are two runtime parameters that might be used to designate both Smart Agent address and Smart Agent port number. They are

    ORBagentAddr

    ORBagentPort

> **NOTE**
>
> It is important to note that these command-line arguments override the Environment variables previously mentioned.
>
> The usage of these arguments is as follows:
>
> From the command line
>
> ```
> prompt> vbj -DORBagentAddr=207.92.87.52 Server
> prompt> vbj Server -ORBagentAddr=207.92.87.52
> ```

Modifying these parameters within your code is done by creating a Java properties object and filling it with the appropriate arguments as shown in Listing 6.14. This object must then be passed into the `ORB.init()` method at the beginning of either your Client or Server Object.

LISTING 6.14 HOW TO OVERRIDE THE DEFAULT ORB PROPERTIES FOR THE SMART AGENT IP ADDRESS AND PORT NUMBER

```
// Segment from either Client.java or Server.java
......
java.util.Properties orbProperties = new java.util.Properties();
orbProperties.put("ORBagentAddr", "207.92.87.52");
orbProperties.put("ORBagentPort", "18890");
org,omg.CORBA.ORB orb = org.omg.CORBA.ORB.init(args, props);
....
```

Thus, from the code in Listing 6.14, the process bypasses the use of UDP broadcast and attempts to open a direct communication with the Smart Agent at the host and port specified. A UDP broadcast occurs only if the direct communication to the Smart Agent specified fails.

From Within a Client Applet

In order to modify the ORB parameters directly in your HTML instead of the applet code, please refer to Listing 6.15. Listing 6.15 sets the same parameters programmatically set in Listing 6.14.

LISTING 6.15 HOW TO MODIFY THE DEFAULT ORB PARAMETERS FOR SMART AGENT ADDRESS AND PORT NUMBER FROM THE CLIENT APPLET HTML

```
<param name=ORBagentAddr value=207.92.87.52>
<param name=ORBagentPort value=18890>
```

The following reviews the steps taken by either a Client or Server Object when looking for a Smart Agent:

1. If the `-ORBagentaddr` option is used on the command line or passed to the `ORB.init()`, this address/port combination is immediately used to find a Smart Agent. The command-line arguments override the environment variables for setting `OSAGENT_ADDR` and `OSAGENT_PORT`.

2. If the `OSAGENT_ADDR` environment variable is set, this address is used immediately to communicate with a Smart Agent.

3. Prior to the UDP broadcast, a check is performed to see if the Smart Agent is running on the local host. This simply checks the port specified in the OSAGENT_PORT variable. This prevents having to do the broadcast if there is a Smart Agent on the local host.

4. A UDP broadcast on the local subnet tries to locate an available Smart Agent.

SUMMARY

The goal of this chapter is to provide a detailed explanation of the Smart Agent, the VisiBroker directory service. The focus of Chapters 2–5 is on how to define your Server Objects: This chapter shows one method of locating those objects and then making use of their methods on the client. We will continue this discussion of different Server location strategies throughout the next three chapters.

The Smart Agent is a dynamic, distributed directory service. It is dynamic because it uses automatic UDP broadcasts and can dynamically determine if Server Objects are available. Clients and Server Objects are able to dynamically locate Smart Agents without configuration files. Smart Agents are distributed because they share information across a network. Finally, they serve as critical directory services providing a way for Server Objects to register their location and a way for Clients to find those Server Objects.

USING FACTORIES AND IORS

CHAPTER 7

IN THIS CHAPTER

- **THE FACTORY PATTERN EXPLAINED** *168*
- **IORS** *168*
- **HOW TO USE IORS WITHOUT THE SMART AGENT** *171*
- **HOW TO IMPLEMENT A FACTORY SERVER OBJECT** *176*

Today is the second of our four-chapter look at different location strategies to obtain that initial Server Interoperable Object Reference (IOR). We spent the last chapter looking at the built-in directory service within VisiBroker, the Smart Agent. Although the Smart Agent has a number of important and useful features, it isn't CORBA compliant and might not be used in conjunction with other vendors' Object Request Brokers (ORBs). Today, we will take a look at a very common design pattern used for providing Clients a Server Object IOR, called a *factory*. Using the factory pattern can allow for interoperability with other vendors' ORBs.

THE FACTORY PATTERN EXPLAINED

A factory is nothing more than a Server Object that handles the task of creating and disposing of other Server Objects. The client connects to a Factory Server and requests a Server Object. Unlike the Smart Agent, the Factory Server creates a new instance of a Server Object and returns this IOR back to the Client. When the Client is ready to exit and no longer requires the use of this Server Object, the Client again contacts the Factory and tells it to dispose of the Server Object instance that the Client had been using.

The astute reader might notice that we still haven't solved the problem of locating the Factory Server. This is the problem of bootstrapping the system.

If you were to use the Smart Agent, you could call `bind()` to get that first reference to the Factory Server. However, this loses all interoperability if the Factory Server is written with another ORB vendor. To get around this, you have to use IORs directly. You will actually take the IOR of the Factory Server and write it to a file. The Client will then read this IOR from a file and use it to connect to the Factory Server.

IORS

Chapter 6 introduces the concept of an IOR. We will review quickly the role of the IOR because you will be making heavy use of it in this chapter. Although the IOR was introduced and used with the Smart Agent in Chapter 6, it was never explicitly manipulated in order to locate and communicate with remote Server Objects.

The IOR is effectively the lifeline of any Server Object within CORBA. It is the unique identifier of the Server Object and provides the critical binding information necessary for any other process to locate it and connect to it. In other words, it is the Server Object's way of saying "here is the interface I support, here is where you can find me, and here is how you talk to me." If other Clients and Servers have no means to obtain a given Server Object's IORs, it is effectively stranded. The Server Object might run forever, but if its IOR is not available to others, it will be impossible for any Client or Server Object to establish communication to it. This is the dilemma we discussed with regard to the Smart Agent as a reason behind the periodic "heartbeat" sent by Servers. A Server Object sends a "heartbeat" to the Smart Agent to ensure that it is running and that Clients have a means of obtaining the Server's IOR. If the Smart Agent fails, the Server Object is unable to be contacted by any new Clients.

Taking a look at a typical IOR, you can see it is represented as a String shown in Figure 7.1.

As discussed in Chapter 6, the sequence shown in Figure 7.1 is interpreted by the ORB as what is shown in Listing 7.1.

Figure 7.1
A typical IOR.

IOR:000000000000001c49444c3a42616e6b2f4163636f756e744d616e61
6765723a312e30000000000100000000000000054000100000000000d3230
372e39322e38372e35320000042b0000003800504d43000000000000001c
49444c3a42616e6b2f4163636f756e744d616e616765723a312e30000000
000c42616e6b4d616e6167657200

Listing 7.1 Information Contained in an IOR

```
Interoperable Object Reference:
  Type ID: IDL:Bank/AccountManager:1.0
  Contains 1 profile.
  Profile 0-IIOP Profile:
    version: 1.0
    host: 207.92.87.52
    port: 1067
ObjectKey: PersistentId
➥[repId=IDL:Bank/AccountManager:1.0,objectName=BankManager]
```

How can you put that long sequence of characters into some type of understandable format? In Chapter 5, we introduced a very useful tool for interpreting IORs called printIOR. It can be used by typing printIOR at the command line with the IOR string following it as depicted in Listing 7.2. Alternatively, you can simply insert this to a file containing an IOR file.

Listing 7.2 Using printIOR to Interpret an IOR

```
C:\>printIOR IOR:000000000000001c49444c3a42616e6b2f4163636f756e744d616e
616765723a312e30000000000100000000000000054000100000000000d3230372e39322e
➥38372e35320000042b0000003800504d43000000000000001c49444c3a42616e6b2f4163
➥636f756e744d616e
616765723a312e300000000000c42616e6b4d616e6167657200
Interoperable Object Reference:
  Type ID: IDL:Bank/AccountManager:1.0
  Contains 1 profile.
  Profile 0-IIOP Profile:
    version: 1.0
    host: 207.92.87.52
    port: 1067
    Object Key:
      ➥PersistentId[repId=IDL:Bank/AccountManager:1.0,
      ➥objectName=BankManager]
```

This tool is very useful when doing work between vendors. It is a useful way of looking at IORs generated from other ORBs. Furthermore, this tool indicates whether or not the IOR is IIOP compliant. Listing 7.3 shows the program printIOR being used with an IOR from Hewlett-Packard's ORB Plus product.

LISTING 7.3 PRINTIOR USED AGAINST AN IOR FROM HP

```
C:\>printIOR IOR:000000000000000E49444C3A48656C6C6F3A312E30000000000000
0200000001000000820000000000000006000000A0000000231000000081040000000
➥008534F413A312E30000000000B00000025353961333236366652D663438662D37316366
➥2D313762322D306631393338666130303030300000000000000C000000010000000081
➥04002000000000810400300000001231352E32352E35362E3235303B3130353500000000
➥0000000000004E000100000000000D31352E32352E35362E3235300000041F000000324
➥8503A534F413A312E30003100353961333236366652D66
3438662D373163662D313762322D306631393338666130303030300
```

```
Interoperable Object Reference:
  Type ID: IDL:Hello:1.0
  Contains 2 profiles.
  Profile 0-Unknown profile:
struct TaggedProfile{unsigned long tag=1;sequence<octet> profile_data=
➥{130 bytes: (0)(0)(0)(0)(0)(0)(0)(6)(0)(0)(0)(10)(0)(0)(0)(2)[1](0)(0)
➥(0)(8)(16)[@](0)(0)(0)(0)(8)[S][0][A][:][1][.][0](0)(0)(0)(0)(11)(0)(0)
➥(0)[%][5][9][a][3][2][6][6][e][-][f][4][8][f][-][7][1][c][f][-][1][7]
➥[b][2][-][0][f][1][1][9][3][8][f][a][0][0][0][0](0)(0)(0)(0)(0)(0)(12)
➥(0)(0)(0)(1)(0)(0)(0)(0)(8)(16)[@](2)...};;}
  Profile 1-IIOP Profile:
    version: 1.0
    host: 15.25.56.250
    port: 1055
    Object Key: ForeignId[object_key={50 bytes: [H][P][:][S][0][A][:][1]
    ➥[.][0](0)[1](0)[5][9][a][3][2][6][6][e][-][f][4][8][f][-][7][1][c]
    ➥[f][-][1][7][b][2][-][0][f][1][1][9][3][8][f][a][0][0][0][0](0)}]
```

Notice that the IOR in Listing 7.3 looks slightly different from the one generated by VisiBroker. With the HP IOR, notice that it supports two profiles. This is perfectly acceptable and very common among many ORB vendors. The purpose of the various profiles is to list the supported protocols within that particular ORB. In this case, you see that HP ORB Plus has its own internal protocol available (which VisiBroker obviously cannot understand) and it supports IIOP. Notice that the IIOP profiles are identical, and as such will enable the two ORBs to communicate. As mentioned previously, VisiBroker for Java supports only Internet Inter-ORB Protocol (IIOP) and only indicates one profile in its IORs.

When we discussed IORs with regard to the Smart Agent in Chapter 6, recall that you didn't really need to concern yourself too much with the contents of the IOR. This is because when using the Smart Agent and the `bind(...)` method, you don't need to take any extra steps on the returned IOR. However, if you decide not to use the Smart Agent because of a multi-vendor environment, you need to take extra steps in order to use the location information stored in the IOR. This is the focus of the next section.

HOW TO USE IORS WITHOUT THE SMART AGENT

In the last chapter, we spoke at great length about how to use the Smart Agent as a mechanism for obtaining Server IORs. The focus of this chapter, however, is to look at how to obtain IORs from your own factory mechanism. You will use the Factory to create objects, as well as destroy these objects when they are no longer required. The role of the create operation is to actually instantiate a new object instance. In contrast, the role of the destroy operation is to remove the object instance from the ORB and have it marked for garbage collection. We discuss the design of such a factory shortly, but first you must figure out a way for your Client to obtain that initial reference to the Factory. This requires a couple of very useful methods on the ORB itself. They are

```
Object string_to_object(in java.lang.string);
java.lang.string object_to_string(in Object);
```

These methods are referred to as *stringifying* an object reference or *objectifying* an IOR string. The sequence of steps for using these is as follows:

1. Create the Server Object as you did in Chapter 5, except you stringify your newly created object and write it to a file. The IDL, Implementation, and Server referenced in this sequence are shown in Listing 7.4.

LISTING 7.4   IDL AND SERVER FOR YOUR OBJECT TO OBTAIN IOR

```
// IDL
interface Test
{
long testMethod();
};


// TestImpl.java

public class TestImpl extends _TestImplBase
{
    // Constructor for a Persistent Server Object
      public TestImpl(java.lang.String name)
{
            super(name);
      }

    // Constructor for a Transient Server Object
```

continues

LISTING 7.4 CONTINUED

```java
    public TestImpl()
{
        super();
    }

    public int testMethod()
{
            return 0;
        }
}


public class Server
 {
     public static void main(String[] args)
{

    try
{

                // Initialize the ORB.
                org.omg.CORBA.ORB orb = org.omg.CORBA.ORB.init();

                // Initialize the BOA.
                org.omg.CORBA.BOA boa = orb.BOA_init();

                // Create the Test object.
                TestImpl test=new TestImpl("Test");

                // Export the newly create object.
                boa.obj_is_ready(test);

                // Stringify the IOR and write it to a file
    String IOR = new String (orb.object_to_string(obj));                          ❶

                try{
                  FileWriter f = new FileWriter("IOR_File");
                  f.write(IOR);
                  f.flush();
                  f.close();
                }
                  catch (IOException e)
{
                     System.out.println("some IO exception");
                     System.out.println(e.getMessage());
                     return ;
                }

                System.out.println(test + " is ready.");
```

```
                // Wait for incoming requests
                boa.impl_is_ready();
            }
            catch(org.omg.CORBA.SystemException e)
    {
                System.err.println(e);
            }
        }
}
```

❶ Here we stringify our IOR. This creates the IOR syntax seen in the examples at the beginning of the chapter.

Now, see what happens when you execute this Server. Because you don't want to rely on the Smart Agent, you have to start your Server Object with a special command-line option to turn off the Unreliable Datagram Protocol (UDP) broadcast to the Smart Agent. This option is `ORBdisableLocator`, which you need to set to `true` as shown in Listing 7.5.

LISTING 7.5 STARTING SERVER WITHOUT SMART AGENT

```
C:\TEMP>java -DORBdisableLocator=true Server
TestImpl[Server,oid=PersistentId[repId=IDL:test:1.0,objectName=Test]] is ready.
```

Now because you have stringified your IOR, you need to look in the `IOR_File` that was created for you. Here you see the following:

IOR:000000000000000d49444c3a746573743a312e30000000000000000
➥100000000000000410001000000000000d3230372e39322e38372e353200
➥0004480000002500504d43000000000000000d49444c3a746573743a312
➥e3000000000000000055465737400

Listing 7.5 shows the starting of your server. To verify that the server has been started correctly and that the IOR is valid, Listing 7.6 shows printIOR being run on the IOR from Listing 7.5.

NOTE

So far you've seen the `-DsomeName=SomeValue` used in some of the examples in this book. For those who are not familiar with this notation, it is a way of setting Java Environment Variables within the Java Virtual Machine (JVM). The syntax is

`java [-Dname=value] className [arguments to the class]`

This is a standard JVM mechanism and should not be considered a proprietary property of VBJ.

LISTING 7.6 PRINTIOR RUN AGAINST YOUR OWN SERVER

```
C:\TEMP>printIOR IOR:000000000000000d49444c3a746573743a312e30000000000
↪00000010000000000000004100010000000000d3230372e39322e38372e35320000044
↪80000002500504d43000000000000000d49444c3a746573743a312e300000000000000
↪0055465737400
Interoperable Object Reference:
  Type ID: IDL:test:1.0
  Contains 1 profile.
  Profile 0-IIOP Profile:
    version: 1.0
    host: 207.92.87.52
    port: 1096
Object Key: PersistentId[repId=IDL:test:1.0,objectName=Test]
```

So far you have successfully created a Server Object, stringified the IOR, and written the IOR to a local file. We will now explain how a client can take advantage of the IOR to locate an Object without the Smart Agent.

2. On the Client side, you will read the stringified IOR from the local file, objectify the IOR string, and make invocations on the remote Server Object. The client code is shown in Listing 7.7.

LISTING 7.7 CLIENT CODE

```
// Client.java

import java.lang.*;
import java.io.*;

public class Client
{
    public static void main(String[] args)
    {

        // Initialize the ORB.
            org.omg.CORBA.ORB orb = org.omg.CORBA.ORB.init();

        String IOR = new String();
        try
        {
        DataInput d =
        ↪new DataInputStream(new FileInputStream("IOR_File"));
        System.out.println("Found IOR from IOR_File");
        IOR=d.readLine();
            }
            catch (IOException e)
        {
            System.out.println("IO exception");
            System.out.println(e.getMessage());
```

```
            return;
        }

        System.out.println("IOR_File read successfully");
        System.out.println(IOR);
```

```
             org.omg.CORBA.Object  obj = orb.string_to_object(IOR);
             if (obj == null)
                     System.out.println("null obj reference");

             System.out.println("object reference converted");
             System.out.flush();
```
— ❶

```
             Test test=TestHelper.narrow(obj);
```
— ❷

```
             int return_value = test.testMethod();
    System.out.println ("Returned from  testMethod with
a return value of " + return_value);

        }
}
```
— ❸

❶ Notice that here you do the exact opposite operation of what was done on the Server side. Here you are constructing your local proxy object from the stringified IOR.

❷ Because the proxy returned to the Client is of type `org.omg.CORBA.Object`, you need to narrow this to the appropriate type.

❸ Now you have a local proxy that you use in the exact same manner as if you obtained the reference from the Smart Agent.

Listing 7.8 shows the execution of the client code. Note that you are able to read the stringified IOR, print it to the screen, and then reference the remote object.

LISTING 7.8 EXECUTION OF CLIENT PROGRAM USING IORS

```
C:\>java -DORBdisableLocator=true Client
Found IOR from IOR_File
IOR_File read successfully
IOR:000000000000000d49444c3a546573743a312e30000000000000000001000000000000
 ➥0041000100000000000d3230372e39322e38372e3532000004590000002500504d430000
 ➥00000000000d49444c3a546573743a312e3000000000000000000055465737400
object reference converted
Returned from  testMethod with a return value of 0
```

Listing 7.8 shows that you have successfully built a VisiBroker application without the Smart Agent, having built your own bootstrapping mechanism for obtaining the Server Object reference. At this point, how to manipulate IORs directly should be fairly straightforward, except you are probably questioning how to make use of this model in a large enterprise system. This is a valid concern because building an entire system around the passing of strings in files is not the best design. It is for this reason that you want to absolutely minimize the amount of stringifying you do, so you only rely on this approach to get over the bootstrapping hurdle in order to get that first IOR. At this point, a much better design is to implement a Factory Object that creates Server Objects for the Client and explicitly hands back IORs for the Client's use. This model allows for a scalable approach to starting and stopping many Server Objects, while only requiring the Client to read a stringified IOR initially to obtain the reference to the Factory Server.

HOW TO IMPLEMENT A FACTORY SERVER OBJECT

There are many different ways to design a Factory interface. We will focus on the two critical operations we want the Factory Server to implement: creation and deletion of objects. We will modify our earlier example to have it create and delete Server Objects. The modified IDL is shown in Listing 7.9.

LISTING 7.9 IDL FOR A FACTORY SERVER

```
// IDL
interface TransientObj
{
    long        transMethod(in string message);
};

interface Factory
{
TransientObj    createObject();
    long        deleteObject(in TransientObj proxy);
};
```

Here you need to define two interfaces, your Factory interface that is responsible for both creation and deletion of your TransientObj interfaces.

> The name of your TransientObj interface is not a coincidence. This example uses TransientObj as the name to demonstrate that because you won't be making use of the Smart Agent, you want the Factory Server to create Transient Objects, not Persistent Objects. Transient Objects use less resources because they won't make use of the UDP mechanism.

The Implementation of your Transient Object and your Factory Server is shown in Listing 7.10.

LISTING 7.10   OBJECT AND FACTORY SERVER FOR OUR EXAMPLE

```
// TransientObj implementation

public class TransientObjImpl extends _TransientObjImplBase
{
        // Only a Transient constructor                                     ❶
        public TransientObjImpl()
    {
            super();
    }

        public int transMethod(java.lang.String message)
        {
            System.out.println(message);
            return 1;
        }
}
// Factory Server implementation

public class FactoryImpl extends _FactoryImplBase
{
      // Persistent constructor
      public FactoryImpl(java.lang.String name)
    {
            super(name);
    }

      // Transient constructor
      public FactoryImpl()
    {
            super();
    }

    public transientObj createObject()
      {
        transientObjImpl newObj = new transientObjImpl();
        _boa().obj_is_ready(newObj);                                        ❷
        System.out.println("TransientObj has been created");
        return (newObj);
      }
```

continues

LISTING 7.10   CONTINUED

```
      public int deleteObject(transientObj proxy)
      {
        _boa().deactivate_obj(proxy);
        System.out.println("TransientObj has been deleted");
        return 1;
      }
}
// Server.java

import java.io.*;
import java.io.DataInput.*;

public class Server
{
      public static void main(String[] args)
    {

          try
      {
                // Initialize the ORB.
                org.omg.CORBA.ORB orb = org.omg.CORBA.ORB.init();

                // Initialize the BOA.
                org.omg.CORBA.BOA boa = orb.BOA_init();

                // Create the RequestReply objects.
                FactoryImpl factory=new FactoryImpl("Factory");

                // Export the newly create object.
                boa.obj_is_ready(factory);

            // Stringify the IOR and write it to a file
            // Optional Upcast
            org.omg.CORBA.Object obj = (org.omg.CORBA.Object) factory;
            String IOR = new String (orb.object_to_string(obj));
        try
            {
              FileWriter f = new FileWriter("IOR_File");
              f.write(IOR);
              f.flush();
              f.close();
            }
              catch (IOException e)
            {
                System.out.println("some IO exception");
                System.out.println(e.getMessage());
                return ;
            }
```

❸

```
                System.out.println(factory + " is ready.");

                // Wait for incoming requests
                boa.impl_is_ready();
            }
            catch(org.omg.CORBA.SystemException e)
    {
                System.err.println(e);
            }
        }
}
```

- ❶ Notice in this example that we do not define a Persistent constructor.

- ❷ This is the operation the Client calls to create a new instance of the `TransientObj` object. Here we will create a new instance as a Transient Object. Remember that passing an instance name to the Object constructor creates a `Persistent` Object, and passing nothing to the constructor creates a `Transient` Object. After the Object has been created, the IOR is returned to the Client.

- ❸ This operation is responsible for removing the `transientObj` from memory. We will call `deactivate_obj` to remove the object from the BOA registration. At this point, it is ready to be system garbage collected and can no longer be called by any Clients.

You should notice that the Server implementation in Listing 7.10 is virtually identical to the Server implementation you first looked at. It is important to see that there is only a small change in the Server main that needs to be made, but a change isn't needed in the Object implementation itself. Thus, stringify the IOR of the Factory Server for your Client to connect with. After this point, all new Server Objects will be created and destroyed by the Factory. Take a look at the Client shown in Listing 7.11.

LISTING 7.11 CLIENT USING THE FACTORY SERVER

```java
// Client.java

import java.lang.*;
import java.io.*;

public class Client
{
    public static void main(String[] args)
    {
        // Initialize the ORB.
            org.omg.CORBA.ORB orb = org.omg.CORBA.ORB.init();

        String IOR = new String();
        try
        {
```

continues

LISTING 7.11 CONTINUED

```
            DataInput d = new DataInputStream(new FileInputStream("IOR_File"));
            System.out.println("Found IOR from IOR_File");
            IOR=d.readLine();
              }
             catch (IOException e)
       {
        System.out.println("IO exception");
        System.out.println(e.getMessage());
        return ;
       }

            System.out.println("IOR_File read successfully");
        System.out.println(IOR);

            org.omg.CORBA.Object  obj = orb.string_to_object(IOR);
            if (obj == null)
                System.out.println("null obj reference");

            System.out.println("object reference converted");
            System.out.flush();

        Factory factory=FactoryHelper.narrow(obj);
```

```
            System.out.println("About to call factory for a new object");    ──❶
            transientObj local_proxy = factory.createObject();
```

```
            local_proxy.transMethod("Calling the Transient Object             ──❷
            ↪using ref from Factory");
```

```
            System.out.println ("About to delete the object");
            int return_value = factory.deleteObject(local_proxy);
        System.out.println ("Returned from factory_delete with a              ──❸
        ↪return value of " + return_value);

            return;
        }
    }
```

❶ Now you will make the call on the Factory to create an instance of your `transientObj` object. The Factory creates this object and returns the IOR to the Client. You are able to use the `transientObj` reference just as if you had received it via the `bind()` operation.

❷ Invoke a method on the Object reference returned from the Factory Server.

❸ Now that the Client no longer needs to use the Server Object, it makes the call to the Factory Server to remove the transientObj instance and have it garbage collected by the Java Virtual Machine.

> **NOTE**
>
> Those of you familiar with the advantages of the Java language might not like having to explicitly dispose of an object reference. Isn't this what garbage collection is for?
>
> The problem here is that this is a *distributed* garbage collection problem; the other side of the wire might be C++, which doesn't support automatic garbage collection. However, someone who is being quite clever might decide to subclass some of the generated code and have the stub release itself in its `finalize()` method.
>
> According to the Java language specification, an object can count on its `finalize()` method being called before the object is destroyed by the garbage collector. At first glance, this might appear to be a great place to call the factory's destroy method. There are several problems with this. The first is that the user can't know what internal parts of an ORB might also have a reference to the object. If some of the ORB code is holding on to the object, it will never be garbage collected although the user's client code is finished with the reference. A second problem is that the Java language spec says nothing about *when* the `finalize()` method is called. It might happen immediately after the last reference is lost, or it might never happen. A third problem with this approach is that the socket infrastructure required to tell the factory to release the transient object might be released *before* the stub. In such a case, the `finalize()` method has no way of contacting the server.

> **NOTE**
>
> Those of you familiar with VisiBroker for C++ might have noticed that upon creation of your `TransientObj`, you didn't have to perform a `_duplicate()` on the object reference before you went out of scope. Further, you might have noticed we have not called a `_release()` after the `deactivate_obj()` call.
>
> The `_duplicate` and `_release` methods are not used by VBJ. They were added to the Java language to provide support for user-defined mechanisms for distributed reference counting, but the IDL to Java language mapping specification explicitly states that they can be no-ops, which they are in VisiBroker for Java.

Now it is time to start the Server Object following the same syntax as the first example. You will use the same -DORBdisableLocator=true flag to turn off the use of the Smart Agent. The Factory Server writes its stringified IOR to a file that is read by the Client as shown in Listing 7.12.

LISTING 7.12 SYNTAX FOR USING THE ñDORBdisableLocator FLAG TO DISABLE USE OF THE SMART AGENT DIRECTORY SERVICE

```
C:\>java -DORBdisableLocator=true Server
FactoryImpl[Server,oid=PersistentId[repId=IDL:Factory:1.0,objectName=Factory]]
➥is ready.
TransientObj has been created
Calling the Transient Object using ref from Factory
TransientObj has been deleted

C:\>java -DORBdisableLocator=true Client
Found IOR from IOR_File
IOR_File read successfully
IOR:000000000000001049444c3a466163746f72793a312e30000000000100000000000
➥000440001000000000000d3230372e39322e38372e3532000004aa0000002800504d4300
➥000000000000104944
4c3a466163746f72793a312e30000000000008466163746f727900
object reference converted
About to call factory for a new object
About to delete the object
Returned from factory_delete with a return value of 1
```

Figures 7.2–7.5 review the sequence of steps in this example. Figure 7.2 reviews the process of the Server stringifying its IOR and writing it to a file. At this point, the Client reads this stringified IOR and performs the appropriate method to objectify this reference such that the Client can contact the Factory Server directly. In Figure 7.3, you see that the Client doesn't look for a remote reference to the transientObj implementation from the Smart Agent. Rather, the Client uses the IOR of the Factory in order to call the create() method to create a new transientObj instance. The IOR of this newly created instance is now returned to the Client, which it uses for all future invocations on the transientObj Implementation as shown in Figure 7.4. When the Client no longer needs its reference to the transientObj implementation, the Client invokes the destroy() method on the Factory as shown in Figure 7.5. At this point, the transientObj instance is removed from the BOA registration and is marked for garbage collection within the JVM.

FIGURE 7.2
Series of steps taken when explicitly using IORs and Factories.

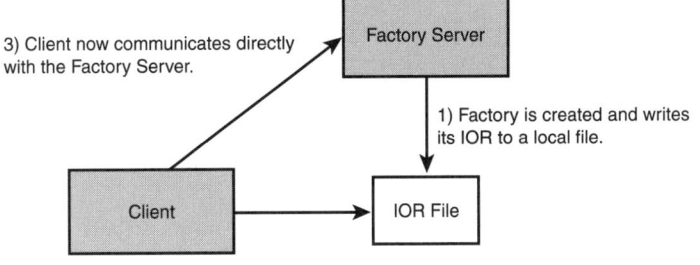

3) Client now communicates directly with the Factory Server.

1) Factory is created and writes its IOR to a local file.

2) Client reads the IOR string from the File and constructs the local proxy to the Factory Server.

FIGURE 7.3
Factory provides an interface to create and destroy new Transient Servers.

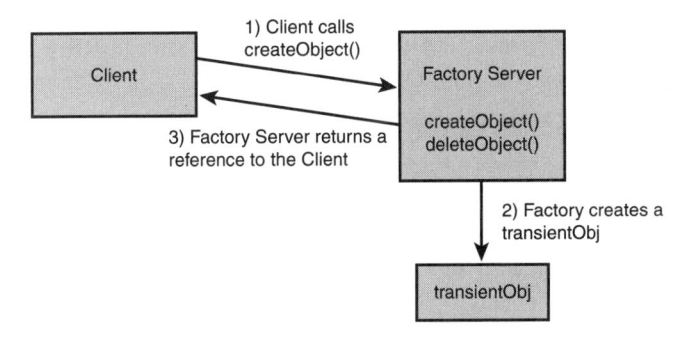

1) Client calls createObject()

3) Factory Server returns a reference to the Client

2) Factory creates a transientObj

FIGURE 7.4
Client uses the IOR returned from the `create()` *operation and contacts the Transient Server directly.*

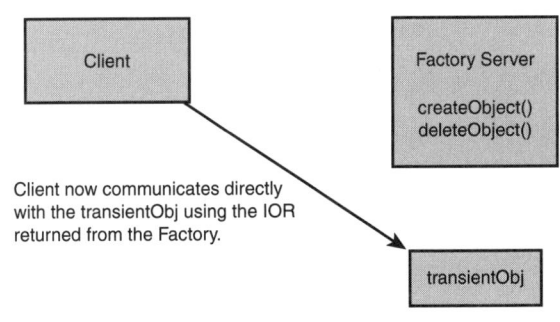

Client now communicates directly with the transientObj using the IOR returned from the Factory.

FIGURE 7.5
When the Client no longer wants the connection to the Transient Server, it calls `destroy()` *on the Factory.*

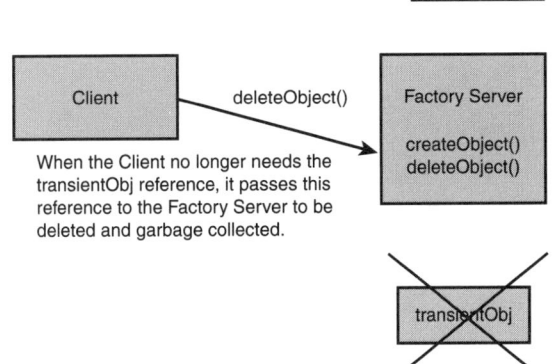

deleteObject()

When the Client no longer needs the transientObj reference, it passes this reference to the Factory Server to be deleted and garbage collected.

SUMMARY

In the preceding chapter, we discussed the usage of the VisiBroker proprietary directory service known as the Smart Agent. The main purpose of the Smart Agent is for Clients to locate the Server Objects they want to connect with. In this chapter, we focused on a CORBA-compliant mechanism for locating and creating Server Objects. We discussed the following two critical operations on the `org.omg.CORBA.ORB` interface:

```
string_to_object()
object_to_string()
```

These two operations give both Clients and Server Objects the capability to make use of IORs directly without any other type of Directory Service. Further, these are the operations that must be used if you are mixing Clients and Server Objects from different ORB vendors. A very useful tool for analyzing IORs is the printIOR utility.

The Factory design pattern is very useful in the CORBA architecture for creating and deleting objects for the Clients. It serves as a location mechanism for Clients. The Clients use some type of bootstrapping mechanism (thus far you have seen the Smart Agent and reading stringified IORs from a file) to obtain an IOR to a Factory Server. At this point, all Client communication is done through the Factory Server. The Factory Server creates and deletes object references for the Client on demand.

THE COMMON OBJECT SERVICES (COS) NAMING SERVICE

CHAPTER

8

IN THIS CHAPTER

- COS NAMING SERVICE BACKGROUND *186*
- OBTAINING AN INITIAL CONTEXT *187*
- BINDING AND RESOLVING: OPERATIONS THAT CHANGE THE NAMING STRUCTURE *191*
- NAVIGATING THE NAME STRUCTURE *196*

This is the third chapter devoted to looking at different strategies for Clients to locate the Services they want. In Chapter 6, we discussed the Visigenic proprietary Smart Agent. In Chapter 7, we looked at how to manipulate IORs directly and how to make use of the Factory design pattern to provide a scalable way for Clients to obtain the Server IORs they require. The focus of Chapter 8 is to introduce the first of the Common Object Services (COS), the COS Naming Service. The Naming Service provides a standard approach to naming and finding various object references in your distributed system. We will begin with a discussion of the principals behind a name service. We will then present the main entry point for this service, followed by a discussion of the major operations on the Naming Service.

COS NAMING SERVICE BACKGROUND

Before launching into a discussion of how to program for the COS Naming Service, we will first provide some background on the concept of a Naming Service. We aren't going to get too theoretical, but a short examination of the principals behind naming is appropriate.

In its most basic form, a Naming Service provides a mechanism for associating objects with a logical name within a searchable structure. A good place to start our model of a Naming Service is with a familiar structure, a file system. A file system provides a logical hierarchy of nodes (directories) that the user can traverse to find leaves (files) or other nodes (subdirectories). This concept of a tree with nodes and leaves provides a good starting point, but we will discuss some key differences between a file system and a Naming Service.

A file system contains files as leaves hanging off of the nodes. The files are referenced by the file's name (such as autoexec.bat or MyApplet.class). Therefore, the object (the file) is referenced by a property of that object (the file's name). In a Naming Service, the name of the object is a logical concept, and is not a property of the object. When you place a file into a directory, the file system places that file's name into the file system. For instance, the act of creating a file in a file system both instantiates that file and binds it to a name. However, with the Naming Service, the user has more control over this act of placing names into the tree. This act of associating a name with an object is called *binding*. When you place a file in a file system, the binding is implicit. With a Naming Service, the binding operation is explicit. There is one level of indirection between the object and its representation in the tree (the name).

In the file system, there are directories that contain 0 or more entities, which can be either files or subdirectories. This concept is generalized in the Naming Service to be a *context*. A context has a name, and might contain 0 or more bindings. Those bindings can represent the association of a name and a user-defined object or a name and another context. This pattern of contexts containing objects and other contexts bound into the Naming Service by name creates the entire naming system.

The COS Naming Service implements the functionality of associating objects with names in an organized structure. It defines interfaces to describe names and interfaces to represent the contexts associated with each node. Unlike a file system, the COS Naming Service holds references to remote objects available anywhere on the network. As with the other COS services, the Naming Service is just another object defined by its IDL. The difference between a COS service and a user-defined IDL interface is that the IDL for the Naming Service has been described by the OMG, so any vendor's implementation of that service exports the same interface.

We will discuss the COS Naming Service as a collection of operations that fall into the following three categories.

1. Obtaining an initial Naming Service Context.
2. Binding and Resolving: Operations that change the Naming Service.
3. Navigating the Naming Service.

As you previously learned, all operations on the a naming structure take place on various contexts. We will thus start with a discussion of how to acquire an initial context for the Naming Service. When we have the initial context, we will discuss those operations that change the naming structure. We will conclude with a discussion of those operations that navigate the structure.

> **HOW IS THIS REALLY DIFFERENT FROM THE ROLE OF THE SMART AGENT?**
>
> As we discuss the Naming Service in more detail, you will see that it is very different from the Smart Agent. They are similar in that they can both be used to obtain IORs to Server Objects; however, the implementation of each is very different. The Smart Agent operates on a peer-to-peer basis: There is no hierarchy of Smart Agents, and each is a peer to the other. The Naming Service is designed to be grouped into logical hierarchies. The Naming Service writes all its information to the local file system for recovery in case of a system crash. The Smart Agent never writes anything to disk and uses the Server heartbeat to handle situations in which the Smart Agent crashes. All the rebinding capabilities and load balancing built into the Smart Agent aren't part of the Naming Service.

OBTAINING AN INITIAL CONTEXT

By now you should realize that obtaining the initial context (bootstrapping) is the toughest thing to do. You learned in Chapter 3 how the Smart Agent and the `bind()` operation handle this. In the previous chapter, we looked more closely at direct usage of IORs. Because the

COS Naming Service is just another object in your system, either approach applies to acquiring a reference to the Naming Service. However, the Naming Service is represented as a structure of `NamingContexts`. The challenge at this point is determining which of the contexts is at the root of the structure.

When the Object Management Group (OMG) defined the COS Naming Service, they didn't define a way to describe an uppermost context. This uppermost context is similar to the root of a file system.

Although not defined by the OMG, VisiBroker for Java provides a mechanism for specifying a root context. This root context is created when you startup the VisiBroker Extended Naming Service. The VisiBroker Extended Naming Service implements the interface defined by the COS Naming Service, but provides the additional functionality of allowing the administrator to create and name an initial context. The command line for starting the VisiBroker Extended Naming Service is shown in the following:

```
prompt>\ java -DORBservices=CosNaming
➥com.visigenic.vbroker.services.CosNaming.ExtFactory Chapter5Root
➥chapter8RootLog
```

The first argument to the Java application

`com.visigenic.vbroker.services.CosNaming.ExtFactory`

is the name of the initial context. In this case, we have named the initial context `Chapter8Root`.

When the Naming Service has been started, the client program must obtain a reference to the Naming Service by finding the initial context. This is done using the methods on the Object Request Broker (ORB) found in Listing 8.1.

LISTING 8.1 METHODS ON THE ORB INTERFACE FOR BOOTSTRAPPING COS SERVICES

```
// PIDL interface for getting initial object references
module CORBA
{
interface ORB
{
typedef string ObjectId;
typedef sequence <ObjectId> ObjectIdList;
exception InvalidName {};

ObjectIdList list_initial_services ();
Object resolve_initial_references (in ObjectId identifier)
raises (InvalidName);
}
}
```

We will take a closer look at two of the operations available on the ORB interface as they relate to the Naming Service.

`resolve_initial_references(...)`

This operation, `resolve_initial_references(...)`, was designed in an effort to provide a portable mechanism to obtain references to various well-defined ORB services. The list of all the available services within the ORB that can be obtained via `resolve_initial_references(...)` can be obtained through a call to `list_initial_services(...)`.

`list_initial_services()`

This method returns a list of the well-known services to the ORB. It can be used in conjunction with `resolve_initial_references(...)`. An example of using `list_initial_services(...)` is shown in Listing 8.2.

LISTING 8.2 EXAMPLE OF HOW TO USE THE `list_initial_services()` CALL

```
// Code segment demonstrating how to view all the services currently available
// to the ORB
......
org.omg.CORBA.ORB orb = org.omg.CORBA.ORB.init(args,null);
String svces[];
svces = orb.list_initial_services();

int i;
int numofsvces = svces.length;
System.out.println("Number of services: " + numofsvces);
for (i = 0; i < svces.length; i++)
{
    System.out.println("Service name " + (i+1) + ": " +
        svces[1]);
}
......
```

The code found in Listing 8.2 produces the following output found in Listing 8.3.

LISTING 8.3 OUTPUT OF CODE FROM LISTING 8.2, OUTPUTTING INITIAL REFERENCES AVAILABLE THROUGH THE ORB

```
Number of services: 7
Service name 1: ChainClientInterceptorFactory
Service name 2: ChainServerUntypedObjectWrapperFactory
Service name 3: ChainServerInterceptorFactory
Service name 4: URLNamingResolver
Service name 5: ChainClientUntypedObjectWrapperFactory
Service name 6: HandlerRegistry
Service name 7: ChainBindInterceptor
```

Looking at the output in Listing 8.3, you should be asking yourself "Well if those are all the services available, why isn't the COS Naming Service listed?" Excellent observation! Certain additional services are installed at the startup of particular Clients and Server Objects. This is what is done with the `-DORBservices` command-line option. Recall the Naming Service startup line we mentioned previously:

```
prompt>   java -DORBservices=CosNaming
↪com.visigenic.vbroker.services.CosNaming.ExtFactory Chapter5Root
↪chapter5RootLog
```

Notice that here we specify `-DORBservices=CosNaming`, which installs `CosNaming` as one of the available services that can be contacted through `resolve_initial_references()`.

The code in Listing 8.4 shows a client program resolving an initial reference to the `NameService`. We will soon discuss the attributes of the `NamingContext` object, so just examine the code for how this object was obtained. Note that for simplicity, we have chosen to show the case using the Smart Agent and to avoid IORs.

LISTING 8.4   CLIENT RESOLVING REFERENCE TO NAMING SERVICE

```
// Segment of Client.java

//Obtain a reference to the Naming Service
org.omg.CORBA.Object obj = orb.resolve_initial_references("NameService");

//Narrow this reference to be a naming context,
//our root entry point into this name space
org.omg.CosNaming.NamingContext initialContext =
    org.omg.CosNaming.NamingContextHelper.narrow(obj);
```

Notice in Listing 8.4 that `resolve_initial_references(...)` returns a reference to your base interface within CORBA, `org.omg.CORBA.Object`. Because this is the base interface for all interfaces in CORBA, you must downcast to the `NamingContext` interface. This downcasting is done through the `narrow()` operation.

> **NOTE**
>
> `resolve_initial_references(...)` is a bootstrapping mechanism to well-known services by VisiBroker. The `resolve_initial_references()` only returns a reference to well-defined services offered as part of the ORB core classes. This includes CORBA-compliant components such as the COS Naming Service and the Interface Repository, as well as VisiBroker specific add-ons such as the URLNaming Service. Later when we discuss Interceptors, we will talk about how you can make your own Server Objects available via `resolve_initial_references()`.

BINDING AND RESOLVING: OPERATIONS THAT CHANGE THE NAMING STRUCTURE

Listing 8.4 shows a client program obtaining a reference to an object of type `NamingContext`. Most of the runtime operations on the Naming Service take place on `NamingContext` objects, where the user binds and resolves objects. These are the operations on a single node in the naming structure. To start this discussion, we will look at part of the IDL for the `COSNaming` module associated with those operations that change the naming structure shown in Listing 8.5. Note that one member of this `NamingContext` interface, `list()`, will be covered in our discussion of Name Service navigation although it is shown in Listing 8.5.

LISTING 8.5 PARTIAL IDL FOR COS NAMING SERVICE

```
// IDL for COSNaming Service

module CosNaming {

  typedef string Istring;

  struct NameComponent {
    Istring id;
    Istring kind;
  };

  typedef sequence<NameComponent> Name;

  interface NamingContext {

    enum NotFoundReason {
      missing_node,
      not_context,
      not_object
    };

    exception NotFound {
      NotFoundReason why;
      Name rest_of_name;
    };

    exception CannotProceed {
      NamingContext cxt;
      Name rest_of_name;
    };

    exception InvalidName {
    };
```

continues

LISTING 8.5 CONTINUED

```
    exception AlreadyBound {
    };

    exception NotEmpty {
    };

    void bind(in Name n, in Object obj)
      raises(NotFound, CannotProceed, InvalidName, AlreadyBound);

    void rebind(in Name n, in Object obj)
      raises(NotFound, CannotProceed, InvalidName);

    void bind_context(in Name n, in NamingContext nc)
      raises(NotFound, CannotProceed, InvalidName, AlreadyBound);

    void rebind_context(in Name n, in NamingContext nc)
      raises(NotFound, CannotProceed, InvalidName);

    Object resolve(in Name n)
      raises(NotFound, CannotProceed, InvalidName);

    void unbind(in Name n)
      raises(NotFound, CannotProceed, InvalidName);

    NamingContext new_context();

    NamingContext bind_new_context(in Name n)
      raises(NotFound, CannotProceed, InvalidName, AlreadyBound);

    void destroy()
      raises(NotEmpty);

    void list(in unsigned long how_many,
        out BindingList bl,
        out BindingIterator bi);

};
```

Now, we will discuss two of the complex members in the module.

NameComponent

The first is the NameComponent. In our file system analogy, this is simply an atomic name (such as autoexec.bat). The NameComponent has two members: The id is used for name resolution, and the kind is an additional member to associate more complex attributes with the object. Because the name should use logical conventions (PittsburgInventoryPlant) the type is a field that can hold additional, system-specific information about which class of object is held (`PlantBrowserService`, or `SynchronizedService`). A rough analogy in the file system world is the 8.3 convention from the FAT file system on MS-DOS. The file's name is the 8 characters preceding the dot (.). The three characters following the dot indicate to the operating system what type of file it is (for example, .bat or .ini).

Name

The second member of the COS Naming module we should discuss is the Name. A Name is a sequence of `NameComponents`. Because you learned in Chapter 2 that a sequence maps to a Java Array, it is an array of `NameComponents`. The reason for this array can again be found in the file system analogy. In a file system, if the user wants to refer to a file that is NOT in the current directory, he must provide the path to the file (c:\winnt\system32\someLibrary.dll). Note that although you think of this as a single string, it is really a compound name consisting of atomic names (c, winnt, system32, and someLibrary) and a separator character (\ on Microsoft systems). Because the COS Naming `NameComponent` isn't simply a string, the assembly of a compound name from several objects cannot be accomplished by a single character. The Naming Service handles this problem by defining that any compound name is expressed as an array of `NameComponents`.

Now that we've discussed the Name and `NameComponent`, we will examine in detail the methods available on the `NamingContext` interface.

- **bind**—The operation that associates a name with a CORBA object reference. It takes an Object and a Name. As we previously discussed, the Name can be a compound name or simply a name you want bound in the current context. If the user wants to bind the Object to the current context, the Name array should be of length 1.

> **NOTE**
>
> "Wait a second! I thought you said `bind()` was a Visigenic proprietary method for the Smart Agent?"
>
> Yes, you are correct. We have two very different `bind()` operations that serve very different purposes. As mentioned in Chapter 4, the VisiBroker `bind()` operation that is a static method on the generated `Helper` classes is a Visigenic specific extension exclusively for communication with the Smart Agent. However, COS Naming also introduces a `bind()` method that is for the Server Objects to register their context information with the Naming Service. So be careful that you are aware of what each `bind()` operation does.

- **rebind**—Analogous to bind except that there is no exception thrown if an object is already bound with the same name. In the case of such a collision, the existing object under that name is replaced. Note that unless there is a chance two systems are using the same context (a poor design choice) the `rebind` call is a simpler way to bind objects into the tree.
- **bind_context**—As the name implies, this call places a `NamingContext` into the naming structure. Note that a `NamingContext` is obtained through a factory call on an existing `NamingContext` (see the following).
- **rebind_context**—As with simple objects, the `rebind_context` method places a `NamingContext` into the tree, silently replacing any existing `NamingContext` that might already exist.

> **CAUTION**
>
> Unlike the simple file system you have been using to build your model of the Naming Service, there are no rules about binding a single object of `NamingContext` under several Names. UNIX file systems have a similar concept with soft links; however, these are recognizable as such (a soft link is a different object from a real subdirectory). With a Naming Service, there is no logical real `NamingContext` and other links. Although a powerful concept, the user of the system should be conscious of the possible side effects of binding `NamingContexts` under several names. Binding `NamingContext` A into B and B into A causes any program designed to "walk the structure" to go into an endless cycle.

- **resolve**—This method is the act of retrieving a previously bound object from the Naming Structure. This is a straightforward operation that throws exceptions if the object isn't found. Note that this method must be generic, and therefore returns the base class `org.omg.CORBA.Object`. The returned object must then be converted to the target type using the `narrow()` call on the Object's helper class.
- **unbind**—This method removes the object and its associated `NameComponent` from the Naming Structure.
- **new_context**—Because the OMG wants to keep the COS Naming Service portable, the construction of `NamingContext` objects is left to the vendor. Therefore, all new `NamingConventions` are created through this factory method. Note that although this `NamingContext` was obtained from an existing `NamingContext`, it is not implicitly bound.
- **bind_new_context**—Analogous to `rebind`, this method is a convenience to provide the programmer with a shortcut to two frequent operations, `new_context()` and `bind_context()`. In a single call, a new `NamingContext` is created and bound. The newly created `NamingContext` is returned for further operations.

- **destroy**—The call to `destroy` is the actual removal of a `NamingContext` as a valid object reference. It is a different operation from `unbind` that simply disassociates an existing, valid `NamingContext` from a location in the Naming structure.

Listing 8.6 shows the acquisition and use of an initial `NamingContext`. It is a continuation of Listing 8.5, which demonstrated how the `NamingContext initialContext` was obtained. With the initial context, an array of `NameComponents` are assembled and used in the call to rebind the object.

LISTING 8.6 CLIENT USING INITIAL CONTEXT TO BIND OBJECT

```
//Create the naming component to label
//our object when we bind
org.omg.CosNaming.NameComponent[] implNameComponentArray =
    new org.omg.CosNaming.NameComponent[1];
implNameComponentArray[0] =
    new org.omg.CosNaming.NameComponent();

//   Create the id.  This will be used for resolution
implNameComponentArray[0].id = "PhiladelphiaWarehouse";

//   Create the kind.  This is informational only
implNameComponentArray[0].kind = "WarehouseService";

// Use the rebind call.  This should be the default bind method used
// unless the presence/absence of an implementation
// is valuable data
initialContext.rebind(implNameComponentArray, warehouseObject);
........
```

Listing 8.6 shows the binding of the `warehouseObject` into the Naming structure. Listing 8.7 shows a different client resolving the same object reference from the Naming Service.

LISTING 8.7 CLIENT RESOLVING OBJECT REFERENCE WITH COS NAMING SERVICE

```
org.omg.CosNaming.NameComponent[] implNameComponentArray =
    new org.omg.CosNaming.NameComponent[1];
implNameComponentArray[0] = new org.omg.CosNaming.NameComponent();

//   Create the id.  This will be used for resolution
implNameComponentArray[0].id = " PhiladelphiaWarehouse ";

//   Create the kind.  This is informational only
implNameComponentArray[0].kind = " WarehouseService ";

//Resolve the object from the tree.  Note it is returned
//only as a base object
```

continues

Listing 8.7   continued

```
org.omg.CORBA.Object rawObject =
➥initialContext.resolve(implNameComponentArray);
//Narrow the object reference using the generated helper class
com.yoyodyne.WarehouseService philadelphiaWarehouse =
      com.yoyodyne.WarehouseServiceHelper.narrow(rawObject);
```

NAVIGATING THE NAME STRUCTURE

In the previous section, we discussed those operations around manipulating contexts and bindings within the name structure. Another essential element of a naming system is the ability to query the structure for its existing, bound objects. You've already seen one such method for doing this on the `NamingContext` interface, `list()`. Listing 8.8 shows more of the `CosNaming` module covering those operations and objects responsible for navigation.

Listing 8.8   COS Naming IDL

```
// COS Naming IDL

enum BindingType {
    nobject,
    ncontext
  };

struct Binding {
    Name binding_name;
    BindingType binding_type;
  };

typedef sequence<Binding> BindingList;


interface BindingIterator {

    boolean next_one(out Binding b);

    boolean next_n(in unsigned long how_many,
          out BindingList b);

    void destroy();


  };
```

As with the previous section, we will first examine the complex members shown in the IDL in Listing 8.8. The first is an enumeration called `BindingType`. A binding type defines the common syntax for differentiating child `NamingContexts` from regular Objects in a given

`NamingContext` (remember, you can put both Objects and `NamingContexts` into your naming structure). The next member to note is the struct Binding. As you might have guessed, a Binding represents the record in the naming structure for each bound object. It contains the Name representing each bound Object, as well as the `BindingType` indicating whether the Binding refers to a `NamingContext` or a leaf Object. The last member is a `BindingList`. As you know by now, this unbounded sequence maps to a Java array of Binding objects.

In addition to the structs, enumerations, and sequences discussed previously, there is also an interface for a `BindingIterator` object. One question you might have is, why do I have both a `BindingList` and a `BindingIterator`? Both constructs (the Iterator pattern and the array) provide a mechanism to go through each member of a list. The reason is that some systems use the `NamingContext` very differently.

Imagine a naming system implemented with the Naming Service that has many nodes, with each node having few bound objects. A diagram of such a naming structure is shown in Figure 8.1.

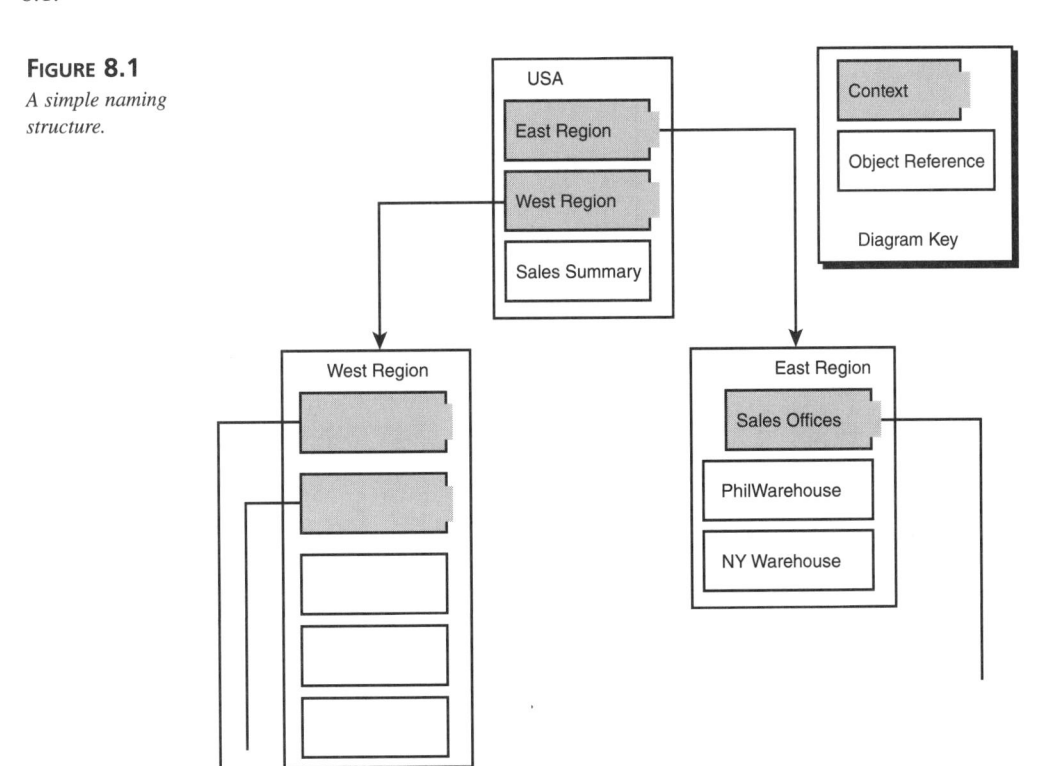

FIGURE 8.1
A simple naming structure.

In order to examine the contents of the East Region Context, we could simply list out all Objects on the node and look for one of interest. Because this is a small structure, it's not inefficient to move all information over the network to the client machine for scanning. Now imagine the naming structure shown in Figure 8.2.

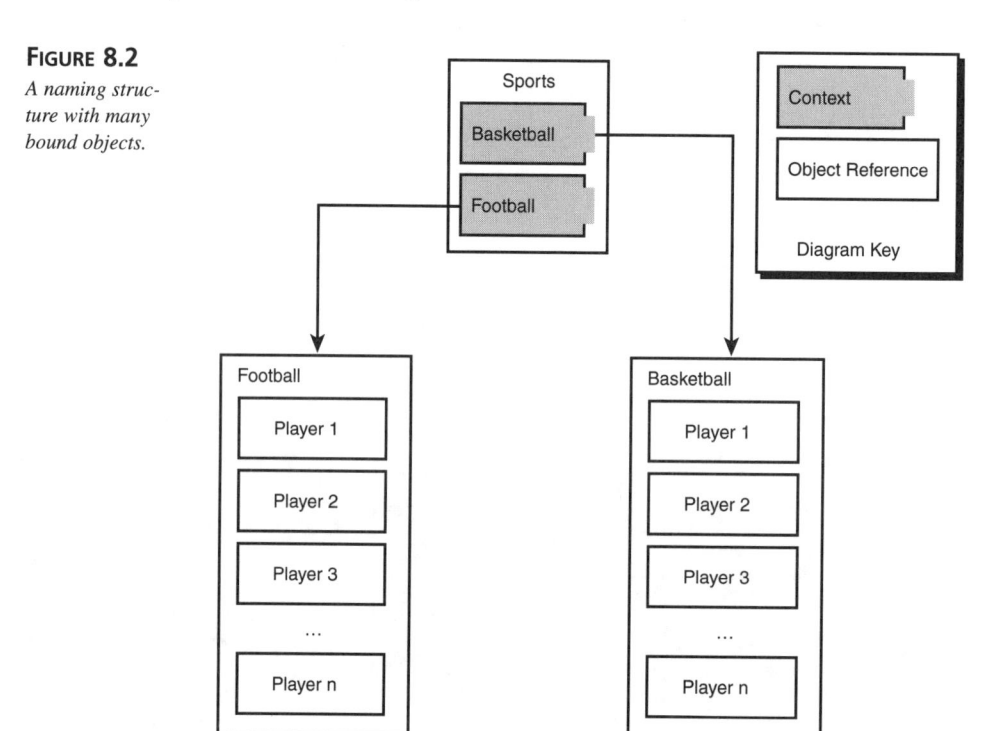

FIGURE 8.2
A naming structure with many bound objects.

If a client program wanted to inspect the contents of the Players node, a list of hundreds of NBA players would have to be moved across the network. This isn't an efficient use of resources, especially if the client program was looking for one of the first names that was returned!

The `list(...)` member of the `NamingContext` interface leverages both the array and iterator to enable the client program to choose the best approach for scanning the contents of a `NamingContext`. Looking at Listing 8.9, you can see that the client program has the option of returning every item in the initial request or following up through the iterator for more Bindings. Note also that this supports using RDBMS-like storage mechanisms to implement the naming structure, where counting the number of rows is often quite expensive. Listing 8.9 shows the use of the `list(...)` call, and then the iteration through the `BindingIterator`.

LISTING 8.9   USING THE LIST ITERATOR WITH THE NAMING SERVICE

```
//Create the holder for the out BindingList
org.omg.CosNaming.BindingListHolder bindingListHolder =
new org.omg.CosNaming.BindingListHolder();

//Create the holder for the out BindingIterator
org.omg.CosNaming.BindingIteratorHolder bindingIteratorHolder =
    new org.omg.CosNaming.BindingIteratorHolder();

//capture the bindings for the current context with
//the list(...) call.  Note that we have arbitrarily
//chosen to list 20 objects.
targetContext.list(
    20,
    bindingListHolder,
    bindingIteratorHolder);

...
//Assume more than 20 returned

while(bindingIteratorHolder.value.next_one(bindingHolder))
{
    //Get the binding
binding = bindingHolder.value;
//Act on the binding...
}
```

In Listing 8.9, the client program first went through the array contained in the `bindingListHolder`. When this was examined, there could be more bindings contained in the `bindingIterator`. Both the `next_one(...)` and `next_n(...)` methods fill the out values with Binding objects. The client can continue to call these methods until the call to next returns false.

SUMMARY

The COS Naming Service provides a simple way to label object references for others to find. It provides mechanisms for binding and resolving objects, as well as APIs for browsing an existing structure.

When using the COS Naming Service, you should first remember that the initial reference to the Naming Service is a `NamingContext`. This first context is necessary because the entire naming structure consists of interconnected `NamingContexts` and bound object references. Binding, unbinding, and resolving operations take place on `NamingContext` objects for both other contexts and objects. Examining the contents of a naming structure programmatically takes place through `BindingList` and `BindingIterator` objects obtained through the `list()` call on the `NamingContext`.

THE URLNAMING SERVICE

CHAPTER

9

IN THIS CHAPTER

- URLNAMING IDL *202*
- HOW A CLIENT LOCATES A SERVER *205*

Chapter 9 completes our discussion on different location strategies for Clients to find Server Objects by discussing the URLNaming Service. Before we dive right into the URLNaming Service, we will quickly review the location strategies we have already introduced.

- The VisiBroker Smart Agent

    A proprietary directory solution that provides built-in location registration for Server Objects, Server load balancing, fault-tolerance and automatic rebinding. This is the focus in Chapter 6.

- Factories and IORs

    A general design pattern that can be easily implemented to serve as a Server Object "generator". The bootstrapping issue can be resolved through stringifying the Factory IOR and explicitly providing this to the Client. This is the focus in Chapter 7.

- The COS Naming Service

    The OMG compliant Naming Service. It provides a tree-like hierarchical directory structure that associates Server Object references with names. It can be used to enable Server lookups even in multi-vendor environments. This is the focus of Chapter 8.

The URLNaming Service allows you to use any commercial Web Server as a Directory Service for retrieving Server IORs. The only requirement is that the Web Server/firewall enables HTTP PUT commands. A Server Object passes its IOR to the Web Server for storage and a Client contacts the Web Server requesting the specific IOR.

URLNAMING IDL

Take a look at the URLNaming IDL shown in Listing 9.1.

LISTING 9.1 URLNaming Service IDL

```
// URLNaming IDL

module URLNaming
{
    exception InvalidURL();
    exception CommFailure();
    exception ReqFailure();
    exception AlreadyExists();

    interface Resolver
    {
        Object locate(in string url_s)
raises (InvalidURL, CommFailure, ReqFailure);
        void register_url(in string url_s, in Object obj)
            raises(InvalidURL, CommFailure, ReqFailure, AlreadyExists);
        void force_register_url(in string url_s, in Object obj)
```

```
            raises(InvalidURL, CommFailure, ReqFailure);
    };
};
```

Notice that Listing 9.1 implements user-defined exceptions in the URLNaming IDL as we discussed in Chapter 4. We will focus on the Resolver interface and how this is used as a Web-based Directory Service.

The URLNaming Service is actually a very handy way for Server Objects to write their stringified IORs to a central location (that is, any commercial Web Server), and to provide a standard mechanism for a Client to obtain that stringified IOR via a standard URL address. If the notion of stringified IORs is not making sense, take a few minutes and refer to Chapter 7.

How a Server Registers with the Web Server

Both the Client and Server Object use the Resolver interface to register and obtain an IOR. In order to use the Resolver interface, the Server Object must first obtain a reference to a Resolver object. We will show the steps a server must implement to register its IOR in the URLNaming Service by using a single example throughout this section.

The first step in placing the server's IOR into the URLNaming Service is to obtain a reference to the Resolver implementation. This is done using the resolve_initial_references(...) call introduced in Chapter 8. An example using resolve_initial_references(...) to find the Resolver is shown in Listing 9.2.

LISTING 9.2 USING resolve_initial_references() TO GET THE INITIAL REFERENCE TO THE URLNAMING SERVICE

```
// Segment of Server.java

.......
// Obtain the initial reference to the Resolver
org.omg.CORBA.Object rawResolver =  orb.resolve_initial_references
➥("URLNamingResolver");

//Convert the Object to a Resolver through the use of the Helper call narrow()
com.visigenic.vbroker.URLNaming.Resolver resolver =
➥com.visigenic.vbroker.URLNaming.ResolverHelper.narrow(rawResolver);
.....
```

As mentioned in Chapter 8, the method resolve_initial_references(...) returns a reference to your base interface within CORBA, org.omg.CORBA.Object, and must downcast to the Resolver interface. This now provides you a reference to the local URLNaming Resolver interface.

After a reference to the Resolver has been obtained, it is time to use the methods within the Resolver interface to tell your Resolver instance where the Web Server is located and copy your Server IOR to a specific directory on the Web Server. This sequence is shown in Listing 9.3. Note that we are presuming all servers are running on the same machine in Listing 9.3. Using this example in a system of different machines would simply require changing the value of thisIP to be the IP of a different machine.

LISTING 9.3 USING THE URLNAMING METHODS TO REGISTER THE SERVER

```
// Segment of Server.java

// Create the Object implementation we want to bind
WebNamingTestImpl webNamingTestImpl =
         new  WebNamingTestImpl("WebNamingTestName");

// Export the newly created object.

boa.obj_is_ready(webNamingTestImpl);


// Before we assemble the URL for our registration, we need to determine the IP
// address of this machine
java.net.InetAddress localAddress = java.net.InetAddress.getLocalHost();
String thisIP = localAddress.getHostAddress();

// Force this server into the resolver's IOR file.  Before doing this, we must
// assemble the URL. Use the default port 15000.
// The final URL will look something like
// http://127.0.0.1:15000/webNamingTest.ior
String url = "http://" + thisIP + ":15000/webNamingTest.ior";


resolver.force_register_url(url, webNamingTestImpl);

System.out.println("Registered with URL " + url);

// Wait for incoming requests
boa.impl_is_ready();
.....
```

The first few steps in Listing 9.3 should seem familiar to the way you bootstrapped your initial COS Naming Service reference in the previous chapter. You are following the same steps that you have in the past few chapters for creating and registering your Server Object with the ORB.

In Listing 9.3, we demonstrate the use of force_register_url(...) to put your URL into the URLNaming Service. The use of the force_register_url(...) call overwrites any existing registrations and avoids the AlreadyExists exception from being thrown. If you don't want any

IORs to be overwritten, you should make use of the `register_url(...)` method instead. In either case, both methods take the same arguments and perform the same operations.

One more aspect to note with the URLNaming Service code in Listing 9.3 is the lack of IOR string code. If you recall our previous discussion of IORs in Chapter 4, that chapter's listings show several lines of code in order to stringify an IOR. The stringifying of IORs is handled automatically by the registration methods on the resolver.

> **NOTE**
>
> An alternative to writing your code with fully qualified package names when using URLNaming would be to include the following import statement at the beginning of your code:
>
>   import com.visigenic.vbroker.URLNaming.*;

Exceptions

We will discuss what errors cause the four URLNaming exceptions to be thrown. The following list illustrates these exceptions:

- **InvalidURL**—The URL passed to either the `bind()` operation or to the Resolver methods doesn't represent a valid WWW address.
- **CommFailure**—There is a problem with the network connection to the Web Server, and communication cannot be established.
- **ReqFailure**—The IOR file requested as part of the URL string in either the `bind()` call or the `Resolver.locate()` call isn't there.
- **AlreadyExists**—Thrown when the Server Object attempts to call `register_url(...)` with an IOR that is already being stored by the Web Server. If you require the ability to overwrite an exiting IOR being held in the Web Server, you should use `force_register_url(...)` instead. Using this method prevents this exception from being thrown.

HOW A CLIENT LOCATES A SERVER

The previous section discusses how a server's IOR gets into the Resolver. Now we will discuss how a client gets those IORs from the Resolver. The first question you should be asking is "How will the Client obtain a reference to the Server Resolver?" Great question! You have obviously been paying attention throughout our discussion of the various location strategies. We will review what you have seen thus far:

- **`bind()`**

    A bootstrapping means used in order to call the Smart Agent for a Server IOR.

- **`resolve_initial_references()` and `narrow()`**

    We first saw this bootstrapping mechanism in Chapter 8 when working with the COSNaming Service. As mentioned, this is a standard method on the ORB interface used to return the initial reference of well-defined services to the ORB.

- **`string_to_object()` and `narrow()`**

    A bootstrapping mechanism used when working directly with IORs from other vendors or using some type of user-defined directory service. This is the focus of Chapter 7 and isn't discussed in this section.

A Client that uses the URLNaming Service can implement one of the two following approaches.

Approach One—Using the `bind()` Method

1. It is possible to use one of the `bind(...)` methods on the server interface's generated Helper class to get the IOR from the URLNaming Service. If you don't recall the generated helper class, review Chapter 4. The `bind(...)` signature that takes a String name as the second argument can be used to bypass normal communication to the Smart Agent and go directly to the URL address of the Server IOR. The signature for this is as follows:

    ```
    public static <interface name> bind(org.omg.CORBA.ORB orb,
                                        ↪java.lang.String name);
    ```

The ORB investigates the string passed to see whether it follows the standard URL syntax. If so, communication bypasses the Smart Agent and goes directly to the URL specified in the String. If the URL passed is not valid, the InvalidURL() exception is thrown.

An example of a Client using this bind method is shown in Listing 9.4.

LISTING 9.4 CLIENT USING BIND(ORB, STRING) METHOD TO OBTAIN SERVER REFERENCE THROUGH URLNAMING TECHNIQUE

```
// WebNaming IDL

module chapter9WebNaming
{
    interface WebNamingTest
    {
        long add(in long aNumber,
            in long anotherNumber);
    };
};

package chapter9;
```

```java
/*
 * This class demonstrates the use bind() within WebNaming to
 * locate objects.
 */
public class Client
{

public static void main(String[] args)
    {
        try
        {
            //Initialize the ORB
            org.omg.CORBA.ORB orb = org.omg.CORBA.ORB.init();

            //Before we assemble the URL for our object,
            //we need to determine the IP address of this
            //machine
            java.net.InetAddress localAddress =
                java.net.InetAddress.getLocalHost();

            String thisIP = localAddress.getHostAddress();

            //Assemble the URL for our object.  Note that except for
            //the IP, we have hard-coded the URL to make this sample
            //simple.
            String url = "http://" + thisIP + ":15000/webNamingTest.ior";

            // Bind to the object using the Helper
            chapter9.generated.WebNamingTest webNamingTest =
                    ↳chapter9.generated.WebNamingTestHelper.bind(orb, url);
//For verification this worked, execute against the method
            System.out.println("Using the remote object, 1 plus 1 is: " +
                webNamingTest.add(1, 1));

        }
        catch(Exception ex)
        {
            ex.printStackTrace();
        }
    }
}
```

Notice that this Client example is virtually identical to all the examples you looked at in Chapter 6 with the Smart Agent. Why? Well, because all you needed to find your Server IOR is the bind(ORB, String) call. Nothing in this code distinguishes whether this particular example is using the Smart Agent or the URLNaming other than the different signature of the bind(...) method.

Approach Two—Using `resolve_initial_references()` and `narrow()`

The previous approach to finding a server implementation uses the helper class' bind(ORB, String) method. It relies on the fact that the VisiBroker runtime recognizes a URL as the String in the `bind(...)` call, and uses the URLNaming Service implicitly. The next approach we will discuss is a more explicit use of the Resolver interface. This approach implements the `resolve_initial_references(...)` to obtain a Resolver reference, and then uses the `Resolver.locate` method.

Listing 9.5 shows a client using `resolve_initial_references(...)` to obtain a reference to the Resolver, and the `locate(...)` method on the resolver to locate the server implementation.

LISTING 9.5 USING THE RESOLVER TO LOCATE SERVER IMPLEMENTATIONS

```
package chapter9;
/*
 * This class demonstrates the use of  the Resolver.locate() within WebNaming
 * to locate objects.
 */
public class Client
{
    public static void main(String[] args)
    {
        try
        {
            //Initialize the ORB
            org.omg.CORBA.ORB orb = org.omg.CORBA.ORB.init();

            //Obtain the initial reference to the Resolver
            org.omg.CORBA.Object rawResolver =
                orb.resolve_initial_references("URLNamingResolver");

            //Convert the Object to a Resolver through
            //the use of the Helper call narrow()
            com.visigenic.vbroker.URLNaming.Resolver resolver = com.
            ➥visigenic.vbroker.URLNaming.ResolverHelper.narrow(rawResolver);


            //Before we assemble the URL for our object,
            //we need to determine the IP address of this
            //machine
            java.net.InetAddress localAddress =
                java.net.InetAddress.getLocalHost();

            String thisIP = localAddress.getHostAddress();

            //Assemble the URL for our object.  Note that except for
```

```
            //the IP, we have hard-coded the URL to make this sample
            //simple.
            String url = "http://" + thisIP + ":15000/webNamingTest.ior";

            //Obtain a raw reference to our object
            org.omg.CORBA.Object rawWebNamingTest =
resolver.locate(url);
//Narrow the object using the helper
            chapter6.generated.WebNamingTest webNamingTest = chapter6.
            ↪generated.WebNamingTestHelper.narrow(rawWebNamingTest);
//For verification this worked, execute against the method
            System.out.println("Using the remote object, 1 plus 1 is: " +
                webNamingTest.add(1, 1));

        }
        catch(Exception ex)
        {
            ex.printStackTrace();
        }
    }
}
```

Listing 9.5 shows several steps. The first is obtaining a reference to the Resolver through the `resolve_intital_references(...)` call on the ORB. Next, a URL is assembled for the target server implementation. Note that, as with our discussion of URL registration, localhost is used for demonstration purposes only. Next, we used the `locate(...)` method on the Resolver to find the target implementation. This step is analogous to the `string_to_object()` call used in Chapter 7 when reading a stringified IOR out of a file and converting it into a CORBA base object. Using `locate(...)` is a much better approach because you can obtain this IOR from any well-known URL instead of having to rely on a local file.

When you have a reference to the CORBA base `interface org.omg.CORBA.Object`, you must use `narrow()` to downcast to the appropriate type as you did in Chapter 7. Downcasting was the final step in Listing 9.3 before you were able to use your obtained reference.

SUMMARY

We have now completed the last topic in our four chapter discussion of location strategies, the URLNaming Service. If you have been paying close attention to the discussion and the code segments, you should recognize the similarities between the URLNaming approach and what you saw in Chapter 4 when you wrote your IORs to a file and had the Client read the IORs from a file in order to communicate. URLNaming works effectively the same way, except it provides a standard interface that automatically stores the Server IOR to a file in a Web Server's directory path. This approach enables Clients to obtain this IOR from anywhere by simply specifying the Web Server URL.

Similar to the COS Naming Service, the `resolve_initial_references()` method must be used in order to bootstrap the URLNaming Service. This provides a reference to the URLNaming Resolver object. This object has two methods for Server Objects to register their IOR, `register_url()` and `force_register_url()`. Both methods work the same way, except `force_register_url()` overwrites the IOR file if it is already stored in the Web Server.

A Client communicates with the URLNaming Service through one of two mechanisms, using a special version of the `bind()` method, or using the `locate()` method on the Resolver object.

APPLETS AND THE GATEKEEPER

CHAPTER

10

IN THIS CHAPTER

- APPLET OVERVIEW *212*
- THE SANDBOX PROBLEM *212*
- GATEKEEPER OVERVIEW *213*
- AN INSIDE LOOK AT A VISIBROKER APPLET *217*
- SIGNED APPLETS AND ALTERNATIVE DOWNLOAD STRATEGIES *233*

In all the examples you have examined up through Chapter 9, you have worked only with Java application clients rather than Java applet clients. In this chapter, we will focus on how Clients need to be designed differently if they are to be used in browsers instead of run as standalone Java applications.

APPLET OVERVIEW

It is outside the scope of this text to discuss the details of Applet development, and it isn't necessary that you have extensive experience with Applets because VisiBroker doesn't make heavy use of applet-specific features. This text does, however, assume that you have a basic knowledge of the differences between Java Applets and Java Applications. In this section we will cover some of the issues that must be addressed when developing VisiBroker applications with Applet Clients instead of Application Clients.

THE SANDBOX PROBLEM

The notion of a *Sandbox* refers to the constrained execution environment setup when Applets are run on a client machine. Applets are downloaded from a Web Server and loaded into memory on the Client host machine. In an effort to protect the Client host machine from potentially harmful or malicious Applets, the Sandbox security model provides restrictions on what the Applet can do after it has been downloaded onto the Client machine. A few of the key restrictions are presented as follows:

- Applet cannot access the local hard drive. This doesn't present a major setback as far as VisiBroker is concerned because all the VisiBroker classes can be downloaded over the Web.

- Applets cannot open network communication (a socket) with any other host machine other than the *codebase* machine (that is, the host from which the Applet was downloaded). This is a restriction for the normal behavior of a VisiBroker client. One of the major benefits of VisiBroker is that processing can be performed by multiple objects on multiple physical hosts to provide scalability. The Sandbox restriction eliminates this benefit by requiring that all communication by the Applet can only be to one machine.

- Applets cannot use UDP broadcasts. This clearly presents a problem because this eliminates the Applet's capability to communicate with the Smart Agent to locate any Server Objects. Fortunately, the VisiBroker runtime compensates for this as you will soon see.

- Applets cannot accept incoming communication. This prevents a VisiBroker applet from being able to host any object implementations, such as standard Callback objects. *Callback objects* are objects created in the Client process space and invoked by Servers. Callback Objects are the focus of Chapter 16, "Smart Stubs, Callbacks, and Object Wrappers."

Given these hurdles, how does VisiBroker support applets? The answer is through the VisiBroker GateKeeper.

GATEKEEPER OVERVIEW

The GateKeeper serves three main purposes:

- A Sandbox Proxy
- An HTTP Tunneling Proxy
- A lightweight HTTP Daemon for testing

A Sandbox Proxy

Because a Java Applet cannot communicate with any host machines other than the one from which it is downloaded, the GateKeeper serves as a proxy object to facilitate communication to other hosts. Thus, it serves as a call forwarder to the actual Server Objects. The relationship between the Internet, GateKeeper, Applet, and Server Objects is shown in Figure 10.1.

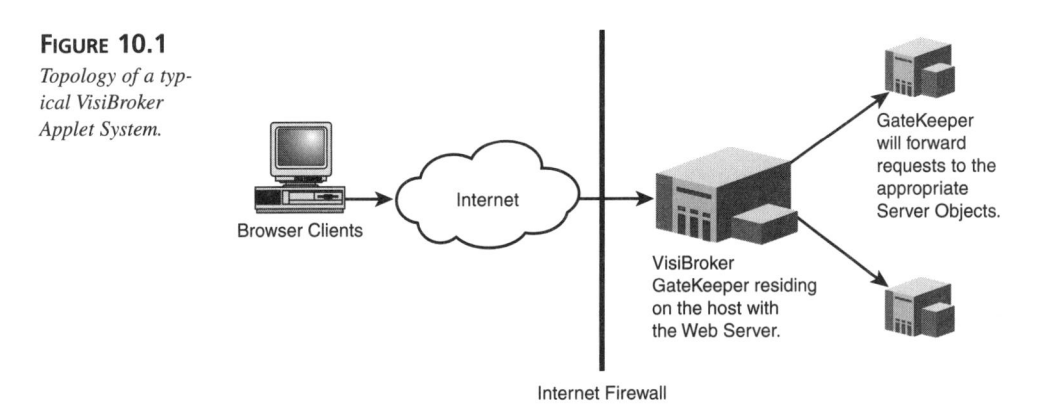

FIGURE 10.1
Topology of a typical VisiBroker Applet System.

The Applet opens a communication session with the GateKeeper, at which point the GateKeeper acts as a universal client. The GateKeeper then takes on the responsibility of performing the UDP broadcast to the Smart Agent to locate the appropriate Server Object requested by the Client. At this point the GateKeeper creates a forwarder object internally to act as the Client. In other words, the Applet communicates to the forwarder that in turn contacts the Smart Agent and ultimately contacts the Server Object. Results are passed back to the forwarder object, which sends the results back to the Applet.

The same forwarder model is also applied in cases of Applet Callback objects. In this situation, the Applet creates a local object and passes this object reference to the Server Object. As this is passed through the GateKeeper, the GateKeeper creates a forwarder object for the Callback to be made and passes to the actual Server Object an object reference to the internal forwarder object. In this model, the Server Object then initiates the Callback, which is made directly to the GateKeeper forwarder object that forwards this back to the Applet. An example is shown in Figure 10.2.

FIGURE 10.2
The GateKeeper as viewed from inside and outside the firewall.

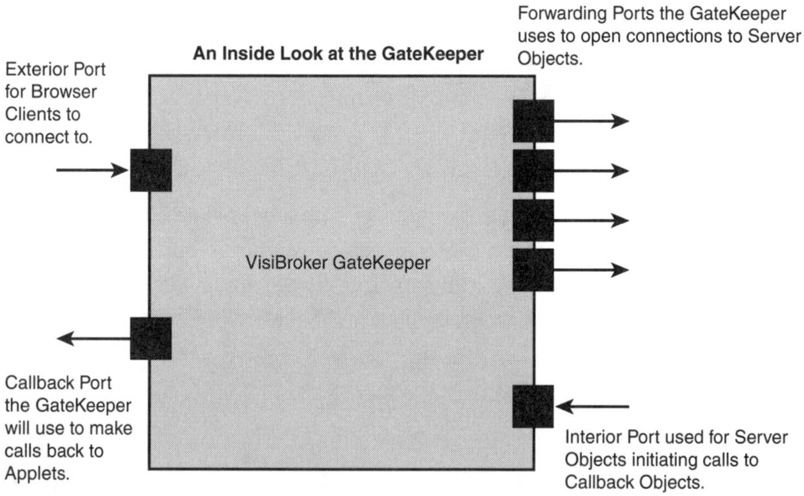

An Inside Look at the GateKeeper

Exterior Port for Browser Clients to connect to.

VisiBroker GateKeeper

Callback Port the GateKeeper will use to make calls back to Applets.

Forwarding Ports the GateKeeper uses to open connections to Server Objects.

Interior Port used for Server Objects initiating calls to Callback Objects.

An HTTP Tunneling Proxy

VisiBroker Applet clients communicate in exactly the same manner as other VisiBroker Clients, using the Internet Inter-ORB Protocol (IIOP) protocol. However, in situations where firewalls are involved, IIOP might not be a suitable protocol. IIOP is not a widely accepted protocol for Client and Server-side firewalls. Specifically, client-side firewalls typically only enable outgoing communication to be that of HTTP. In these situations, a VisiBroker IIOP call is rejected by the firewall as shown in Figure 10.3.

If the VisiBroker client notices that a request was returned because the firewall wouldn't let this protocol pass, VisiBroker performs Hypertext Transfer Protocol (HTTP) Tunneling. HTTP Tunneling refers to the process of taking the information contained in an IIOP packet and transferring this information into an HTTP packet. Then the HTTP packet is sent and passes through to the GateKeeper. The GateKeeper then unpacks this HTTP packet request and re-creates the original IIOP packet, which is then forwarded to the appropriate Server Object. The tunneling process is shown graphically in Figures 10.4 and 10.5.

FIGURE 10.3
Applet's IIOP request rejected by a firewall.

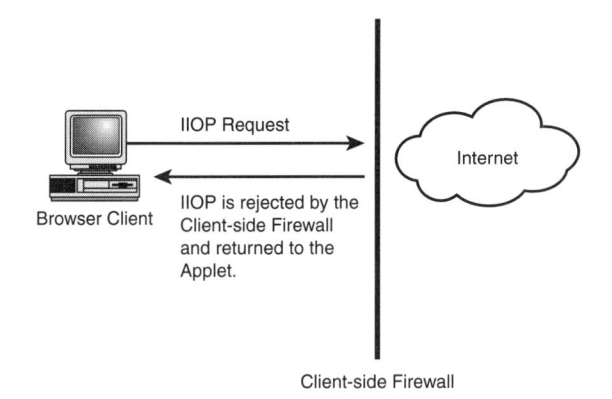

FIGURE 10.4
Applet Client contacting GateKeeper through IIOP tunneling.

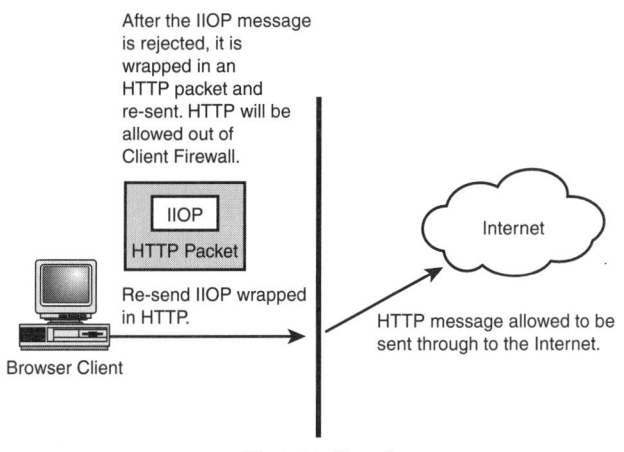

FIGURE 10.5
Applet Client tunneling through both a Client- and Server-side firewall.

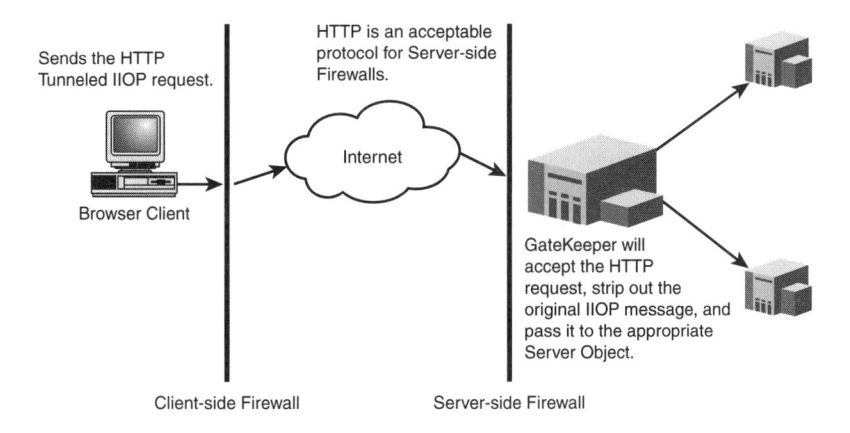

A Lightweight HTTPd for Testing

The GateKeeper is a Java HTTP Daemon (that is, Web Server) useful for delivering Applets without requiring a full-blown Web Server. Although not a Web Server for production, it is very useful to have a small, contained system on a single computer for testing. Using the GateKeeper as a testing platform is shown in Figure 10.6.

FIGURE 10.6
Using the GateKeeper as a test Web Server.

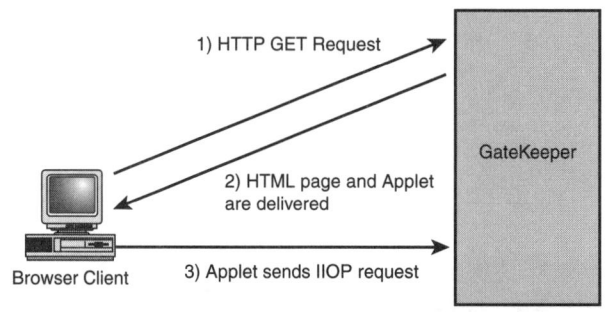

1) HTTP GET Request
2) HTML page and Applet are delivered
3) Applet sends IIOP request

Browser Client — GateKeeper

The GateKeeper has basic Web server capabilities and can be used to deliver HTML pages for testing purposes.

One question you might have at this point is "How are all the VisiBroker runtime classes installed on the browser for the Applet to use?" All the classes are downloaded dynamically when the Applet itself is downloaded. Thus, notice that it takes a longer time to get your first Applet up and running. However, your browser caches the Object Request Broker (ORB) classes and all future Applet initializations will happen much more rapidly. VisiBroker for Java has been repackaged in such a way that only the minimum number of classes are downloaded to the browser Client. An alternative strategy to this installation is discussed later in the section "Signed Applets and Alternative Download Strategies."

> **NOTE**
>
> The GateKeeper wasn't designed to be a production caliber Web Server and shouldn't be used as such. It is meant to work as a complement to your Web Server, performing the call forwarding and HTTP tunneling as previously described. However, for testing applets during development, the GateKeeper can serve to be a very handy HTTP Server to deliver your Hypertext Markup Language (HTML) page and Applet. The GateKeeper doesn't support all the features and functionality of a normal commercial Web Server.

AN INSIDE LOOK AT A VISIBROKER APPLET

Writing Applet Clients requires some additional steps that are not required with normal Java Application Clients. It is beyond the scope of this text to discuss all the differences between a Java Application and Java Applet. However, we do want to focus on how VisiBroker-related code will be different between an applet and an application. The difference can be found in the way the ORB is initialized. When initializing the ORB for an Applet Client, you must pass the Applet as the first argument to the `ORB.init()` method. The second argument is of type java.util.Properties to hold any additional parameter settings for the ORB. The initialization code for an Applet as a VisiBroker Client is shown in Listing 10.1.

LISTING 10.1 INITIALIZING A JAVA APPLET AS VISIBROKER CLIENT

```
// Segment of ClientApplet.java

public class ClientApplet extends java.applet.Applet implements ActionListener
{
    .......
org.omg.CORBA.ORB orb = org.omg.CORBA.ORB.init(this, null);
    .......
}
```

We will now present a full applet, which calls an Object derived from the Interface Definition Language(IDL) shown in Listing 10.2. We will then walk through a few aspects of the applet and discuss differences between applets and normal VisiBroker client applications.

LISTING 10.2 IDL FOR OUR APPLET APPLICATION

```
module chapter10AppletGateKeeper
{
    interface Adder
    {
       long add(
           in long aLong,
           in long anotherLong);
    };
};
```

In this example, we will examine the steps required for an applet to invoke an object implementation through the Web. Because there are several steps involved in setting up the entire applet -> GateKeeper -> implementation system, our server object has been made deliberately simple—it adds two numbers and returns the sum. The code for our simple server implementation is shown in Listing 10.3. Note that there are no new registration and implementation techniques shown in Listing 10.3.

LISTING 10.3 SERVER USED IN YOUR APPLET APPLICATION

```
package chapter10;

/*
 * Server to test locating an object through
 * the GateKeeper and an applet
 */
public class AdderImpl
extends chapter10.generated._AdderImplBase
{

    //Constructor for transient object
    public AdderImpl()
    {
    }

    //Constructor for persistent object
    public AdderImpl(String name)
    {
        super(name);
    }

    public int add(int aNumber, int anotherNumber)
    {
        return aNumber + anotherNumber;
    }
}
```

We will now examine the Applet client as shown in the following code listings. The key thing to remember here is the only VisiBroker change that must be made to make an Application Client into an Applet Client is to modify the `ORB.init()` method. You must pass the Applet itself as the first argument to the `ORB.init()` call. Notice that all other changes in the following pertain to the Applet GUI graphics and the Applet Event model.

```
package chapter10;
import java.awt.*;
import java.awt.event.*;

/**
 * A simple applet to demonstrate using VisiBroker
 * with the GateKeeper and applets.  Note that this
 * class does not handle user input problems very well.
 * This is because this is intended to be a simple example,
 * not an exercise in GUI programming.
 */
public class ClientApplet
extends java.applet.Applet
{
```

Applets and the GateKeeper
Chapter 10

An applet must extend from `java.applet.Applet`. This is required by the Applet specification, and VisiBroker doesn't alter this requirement.

```
//Some members for the GUI behavior
    protected TextField numberTF1 = null;
    protected TextField numberTF2 = null;
    protected Button button = null;
    protected TextArea consoleTA = null;
    protected Label sumLabel = null;

    //Reference to our remote reference
    protected chapter10.generated.Adder adder = null;


public void init()
```

An applet uses an `init()` method as the beginning point of execution.

```
{

            //Initialize our GUI elements
        numberTF1 = new TextField();
        numberTF2 = new TextField();
        button = new Button("Sum -->");
        sumLabel = new Label("0");
        consoleTA = new TextArea("", 5, 10,
            TextArea.SCROLLBARS_VERTICAL_ONLY);

        //Lay-out our GUI
        setLayout(new BorderLayout(5,5));
        Panel centerPanel = new Panel(
            new GridLayout(3,2));
        centerPanel.add(new Label("First Number"));
        centerPanel.add(numberTF1);
        centerPanel.add(new Label("Second Number"));
        centerPanel.add(numberTF2);
        centerPanel.add(button);
        centerPanel.add(sumLabel);
        add(centerPanel, BorderLayout.CENTER);
        add(consoleTA, BorderLayout.SOUTH);
        add(new Label("Add Two Numbers!"), BorderLayout.NORTH);

        button.addActionListener(new MyActionListener());
            try
{
```

Now it is time to initialize the ORB: Remember that the Applet itself must be the first argument to the initialization call.

```
org.omg.CORBA.ORB orb =
            org.omg.CORBA.ORB.init(this, null);
        adder = chapter10.generated.AdderHelper.bind(orb, "Adder");
```

```java
            consoleTA.append("Successfully initialized our remote reference");
        }
        catch(Exception ex)
        {
            consoleTA.append(ex.toString());
        }


    }
    //Inner class for simple GUI action
    class MyActionListener implements ActionListener
    {
        public void actionPerformed(ActionEvent event)
        {
            try
            {
                //Call our remote reference
                int theSum = adder.add(
                    readNumber(numberTF1),
                    readNumber(numberTF2));
                sumLabel.setText("" + theSum);
            }
            catch(Exception ex)
            {
                consoleTA.append(ex.toString());
            }

        }
        private int readNumber(TextField tf)
        {
            int ret = 0;
            try
            {
                ret = Integer.parseInt(tf.getText());
            }
            catch(Exception ex)
            {
                consoleTA.append(ex.toString());
            }
            return ret;
        }
    }

}
```

The preceding listing shows the Applet code to invoke our Adder implementation over the Web. Most of the code is applet-specific. (Because an Applet is a graphical object, we had to include some GUI code.) The VisiBroker-specific lines, the initialization of the ORB, were slightly different from the examples from Chapters 1–9 in that the applet was passed as an argument to the initialization method. Now, the final item needed to complete this example system is the HTML page that hosts the Applet. The .html page is shown in Listing 10.4. Note that we are using the applet param tag to pass information into the applet from the Web page.

LISTING 10.4 HTML PAGE FOR A VISIBROKER APPLET

```
<h1> Day 10 Client Applet </h1>
<hr>
<center>
    <applet code=chapter10.ClientApplet.class width=200 height=200>
    <param name=org.omg.CORBA.ORBClass value=com.visigenic.vbroker.orb.ORB>
    </applet>
</center>
<hr>
```

Listing 10.4 uses the applet parameter `org.omg.CORBA.ORBClass`. We will discuss each of the possible HTML parameters in detail in the next section. You can see the results in Figure 10.7. Figure 10.8 serves as a review for the steps that have just occurred.

FIGURE 10.7
Applet in Browser.

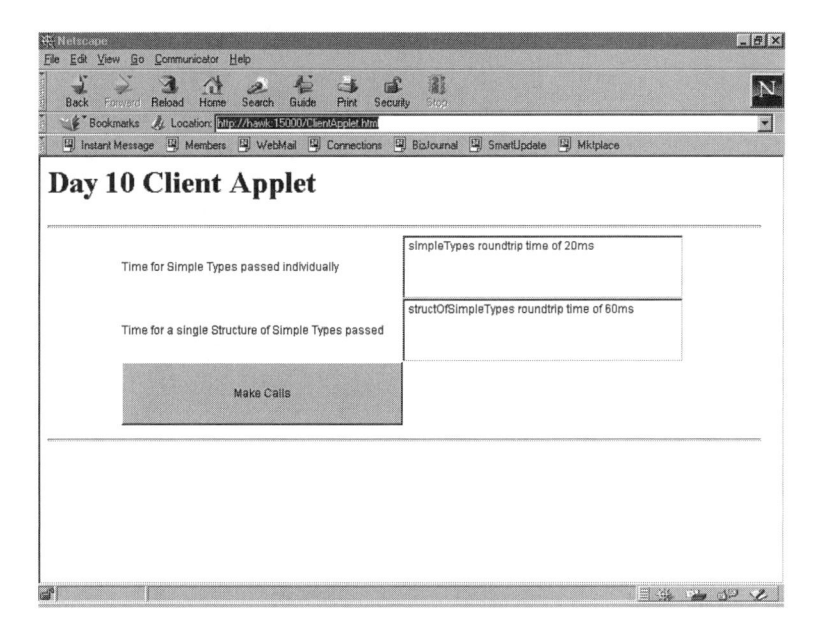

FIGURE 10.8
Client using GateKeeper and VisiBroker ORB to communicate across the Internet.

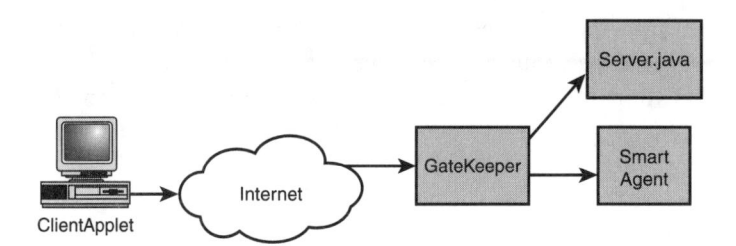

Client requests Applet from the GateKeeper. The Applet and all the base VisiBroker classes are downloaded to the Browser. The Applet then calls bind(), the Gatekeeper calls the Smart Agent to locate the Server Object. This Server IOR is then kept by the GateKeeper and a Forwarding Object is set up to pass requests from the Applet to the Server Object.

Applet HTML Settings and Configurations

The following sections detail some of the parameters that can be passed in the HTML that have an impact on the operation of the Applet and the GateKeeper.

ORBgatekeeperIOR

This parameter expects a full uniform resource locator(URL) string to the GateKeeper Interoperable Object Reference (IOR) file. When the GateKeeper is started, it automatically writes its IOR to a local file. If you are downloading your Applet from a normal Web Server but then want your Applet to communicate through the GateKeeper, this parameter must be set. This enables your Applet to get the GateKeeper IOR, and from what you learned about IORs in Chapter 7, "Using Factories and IORs," you know that this IOR contains the host or port information necessary to establish a network connection to the GateKeeper.

org.omg.CORBA.ORBClass

This parameter is specifically for Netscape Browsers 4.0 or greater that are currently bundling an older version of VisiBroker for Java (version 2.5). The older version is the default version used unless this parameter is set to the following:

```
com.visigenic.vbroker.orb.ORB
```

Setting this forces the Applet to download the ORB classes that are known to the Web Server, which will likely be the latest version of VisiBroker for Java.

This is only necessary if you are using Netscape 4.0 or greater and want the latest version of ORB to be downloaded into the browser. Unless features in the latest version are absent in version 2.5, you want to avoid this because it drastically increases download time.

USE_ORB_LOCATOR

If you plan to deploy an Applet Client built with the older VisiBroker 2.5 that is bundled into Netscape, you must set this parameter equal to true.

This is only necessary if you are using Netscape 4.0 or greater and want to use the older version 2.5 of VisiBroker for Java that is currently bundled into the browser. If you plan to use the older 2.5 version, you must run the GateKeeper in backward compatibility mode. This can be set up using the gkconfig tool, which is discussed shortly when we discuss the GateKeeper.

ORBdisableLocator

Setting this parameter to true disables the Applet from using the GateKeeper and the Smart Agent. This is necessary if you plan on creating a VisiBroker for Java Client that communicates to another vendor's Server Object. The default value is false.

If this option is set to true, there are certain issues to be aware of:

- The `bind()` call on the ORB Object won't work because it expects to use the Smart Agent.
- The VisiBroker runtime components can only communicate to Server IORs that are on the codebase machine (that is, the machine the Web Server is located on).
- Only client-side functionality is available to the Applet. This means that setting call-back objects within the Applet won't be permitted.

ORBalwaysProxy

The default behavior of a VisiBroker Applet Client is to attempt to make a normal `bind(...)` call to locate a Smart Agent (just like Client Applications do!) However, if the Web Server is on a remote host, which it typically is, such a `bind(...)` call isn't allowed because an Applet is restricted from making a UDP broadcast. When the ORB recognizes this, it immediately makes the call to the GateKeeper to set up a Call Forwarder Object.

This option is designed for situations in which the GateKeeper and Server Objects all reside on a single host. Setting this option to true requires that all communication be routed through the GateKeeper. If this option is set to false, the first call is made to the GateKeeper in order to talk to the Smart Agent to get the Server binding information, and all subsequent calls are made directly by the Applet to the Server Objects without going through the GateKeeper. This is perfectly legal as long as the Server Objects and the GateKeeper are all on the same host with the Web Server (that is, the machine from which the Applet was delivered). The default is false.

ORBalwaysTunnel

Setting this parameter to true causes the ORB to automatically perform HTTP Tunneling for all communication. In this case, the ORB never attempts to make a normal IIOP call, it sends all requests as IIOP wrapped in HTTP. This should be used in situations where you know there is a Client-side firewall that blocks the IIOP communication. Only set this option if necessary because HTTP tunneling has an impact on performance. The default value for ORBalwaysTunnel is false.

ORBdisableGatekeeperCallbacks

This parameter disables the GateKeeper's capability to host Callback Objects for Applet Clients. The default is false, which means CallBacks are enabled unless this is set to true.

> **NOTE**
>
> It should be noted that it isn't possible to have Callbacks with HTTP Tunneling, it is simply not a supported feature. Callbacks via HTTP tunneling don't represent a good technical solution because HTTP is a stateless protocol, only initiated from the client. Thus, it isn't possible to support Callbacks reliably because the Client or any HTTP proxy Server in the middle could decide to drop the HTTP connection, providing no way for the Server to reconnect. When ORBalwaysTunnel is set to true, this option is automatically true.

For a full list of all available ORB options that might be set here in the HTML, refer to Chapter 21 for the full list of read and write options for the ORB and BOA.

Starting the GateKeeper

First, we will discuss how the GateKeeper is started.

prompt> GateKeeper

The GateKeeper script that is provided with VisiBroker adds the following to the CLASS-PATH: vbjorb.jar, vbjapp.jar, and vbjgk.jar. In terms of the Jar packaging, vbjorb.jar is the minimal orb to run applets. However, applets using the GateKeeper will also require vbjgk.jar.

The previous prompt starts a GateKeeper with all the default settings. If you would like to modify any of the default settings, you must create a GateKeeper properties file and pass this as a command-line argument. VisiBroker version 3.2 and higher provides a graphical configuration tool for use with creating a GateKeeper properties file. It either appears as an item in the VisiBroker Program group, or can be invoked on the command line simply by calling:

prompt> gkconfig

This command launches the gkconfig graphical configuration tool, which is shown in Figure 10.9.

The gkconfig Tool

The purpose of this tool is to generate a GateKeeper properties file that the GateKeeper reads in at startup time. The GateKeeper properties file holds all the necessary configuration information for the GateKeeper. We will now discuss the functionality of the graphical gkconfig tool.

FIGURE 10.9
The opening palette for the gkconfig tool.

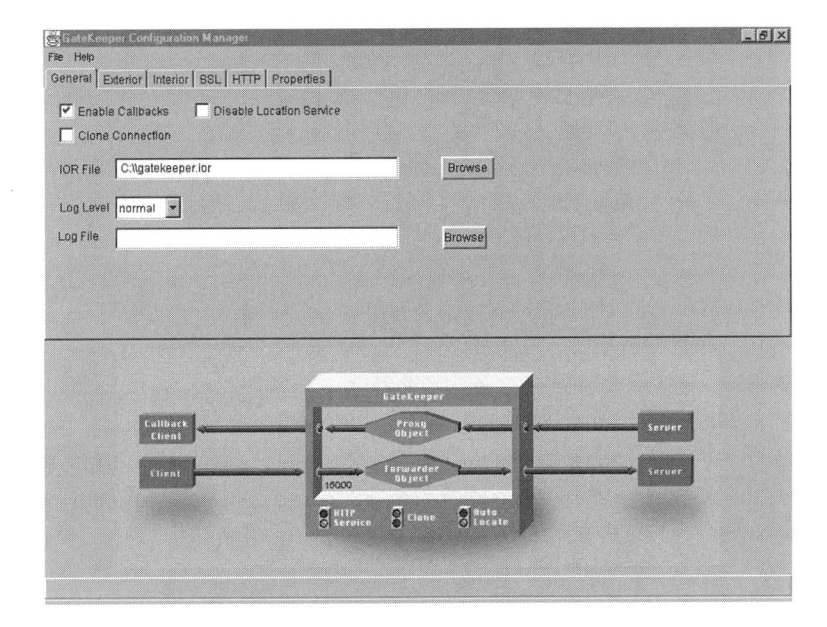

The General Tab

Notice that there are three check boxes at the top of the first form. They are

- Enable Callbacks—Clicking this option sets the GateKeeper property `enable_callbacks` equal to true. Notice that when you click this option, the Callback Client, Proxy Object, and Server in the picture at the bottom of Figure 10.9 are all greyed out.

- Disable Location Service—Clicking this option prevents the GateKeeper from being able to use the Smart Agent for Server Object lookups. The restrictions mentioned previously with regard to the Applet HTML `ORBdisableLocator` tag are the same when this option is set directly on the GateKeeper. When this option is set, notice that the Auto Locale light at the bottom of Figure 10.9 is set to red instead of green.

- Clone Connection—This option is for use exclusively when using the GateKeeper with the VisiBroker SSL product. It creates a separate connection to each Server Object for each Client. It should be used sparingly because it greatly reduces the overall number of new connections that the GateKeeper can support. When this option is set, the Clone light at the bottom of Figure 10.9 is green.

The following additional text fields might be filled out:

- IOR File—Allows you to browse to find an existing IOR file to use or allows you to simply type in the name of the new GateKeeper IOR file to be written. This IOR file is automatically generated when the GateKeeper is started.

> **NOTE**
>
> An equal sign (=) is an illegal character in the IOR File text field.

- Log Level—Allows you to set the output log debugging level to one of the following four different levels:

    quiet—Supresses all messages to standard output.

    warning—Only prints messages if an error occurs.

    normal—The default. Prints informational messages as well as errors when they occur.

    debug—Provides the most verbose setting, printing all informational messages, error messages, and internal debugging information.

- Log File—Allows you to capture all GateKeeper output to a file. You can either browse for an existing log file to overwrite or you can create a new one.

The Exterior Tab

The exterior tab is shown in Figure 10.10.

Here we must set the various IP address and port values that the GateKeeper makes use of.

Exterior Address and Exterior Port

This is the exterior socket on which the GateKeeper is listening for incoming requests from Applets.

In multi-homed environments, this must be the IP address where the Web Server is running.

The port can be any value between 0 and 65535.

The default port is 15000.

Exterior Proxy Address and Exterior Proxy Port

In situations where the GateKeeper is running behind a corporate firewall, it is often necessary to create a proxy that forwards requests to the GateKeeper. These values indicate the IP address and port number of the firewall, and are in the generated GateKeeper IOR instead of the actual IP address and port number. As requests are passed to this proxied IOR, the firewall provides a mechanism to forward the request to the GateKeeper.

FIGURE 10.10
The Exterior palette for the gkconfig tool.

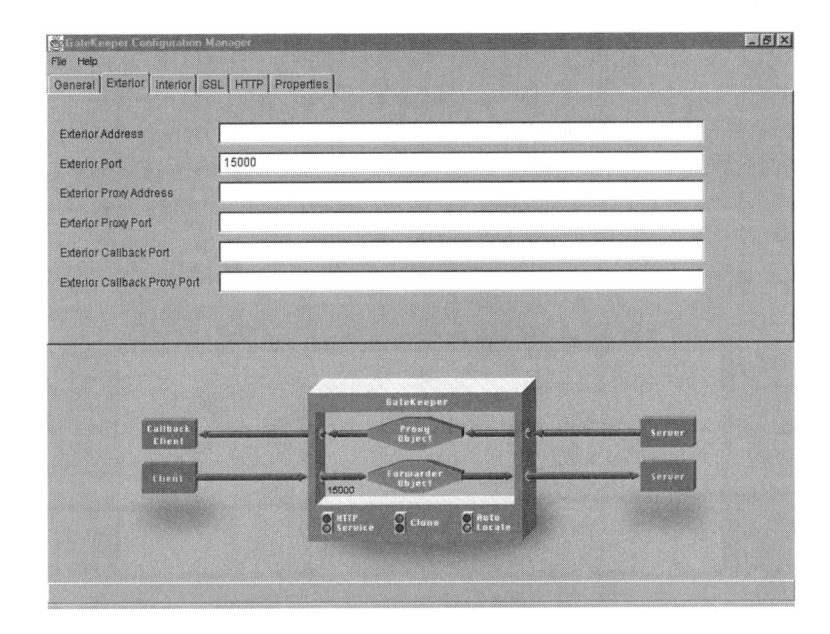

The defaults for these values are the Exterior Address and Exterior Port values.

Exterior Callback Port
The port on which the GateKeeper accepts incoming requests from Server Objects and initiates calls back to the Applet.

If this value isn't set, it is chosen at random by the operating system.

Exterior Callback Proxy Port
This proxy is used if multiple firewalls are involved and a proxy port must be established for Server Objects to communicate back to the GateKeeper.

The default value is the value set for the Exterior Callback Port.

The next tab is shown in Figure 10.11, which deals with the Interior Ports that must be set.

The Interior Tab
These values are necessary in the situation where the host on which the GateKeeper is running is a dual-homed host, having both an interior and exterior IP address. In order for messages to be forwarded between the two networks, both exterior and interior addresses and ports must be set.

FIGURE 10.11

The Interior palette for the gkconfig tool.

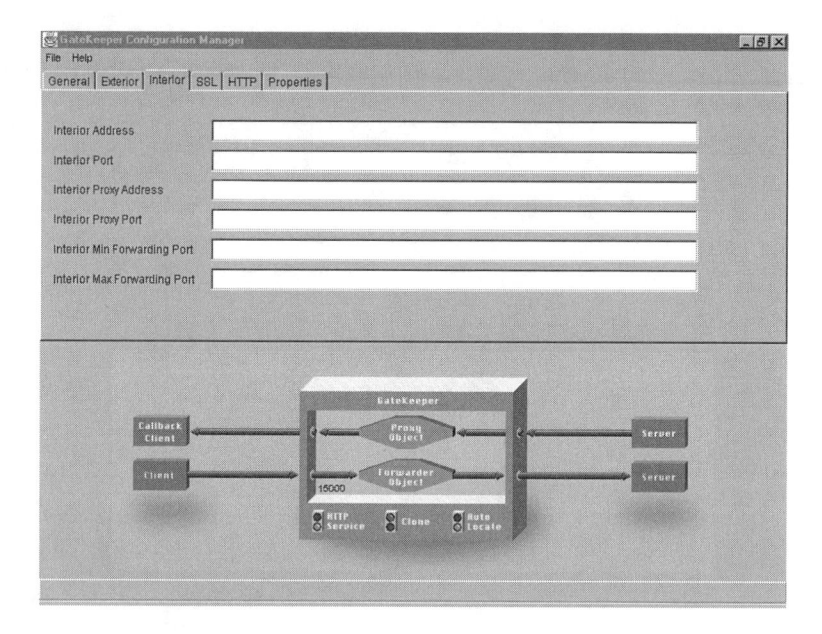

Interior Address and Interior Port

These are the IP address and port that are known to the inside network. When the GateKeeper receives a message to the Exterior Address and Port, the message is forwarded to this Interior Address and Port.

Interior Address and Interior Port are required if the GateKeeper is being used on a multi-homed host. Figure 10.12 shows the GateKeeper using multiple ports and addresses.

Interior Proxy Address and Interior Proxy Port

These are used if multiple firewalls are involved and a proxy must be established between the inside Server Objects and the interior GateKeeper Address and Port. When these values are set, you will notice a barrier set up between the GateKeeper and the Server Objects.

Min and Max Forwarding Ports

They enable a minimum and maximum number of ports to be opened for the purposes of forwarding requests to Server Objects.

The next tab shown in Figure 10.13 deals with the Secure Sockets Layer (SSL).

The SSL Tab

This tab deals with setting up the GateKeeper to work with the VisiBroker SSL product. With VisiBroker SSL, it is possible to have either an SSL connection from the Applet to the GateKeeper or from the GateKeeper to the Server Objects, or both. These settings are the top checkboxes. The remaining items deal with SSL specifics of the SSL certificate, Private Key and password.

FIGURE 10.12
An inside look at the multiple ports and addresses with which the GateKeeper can be configured.

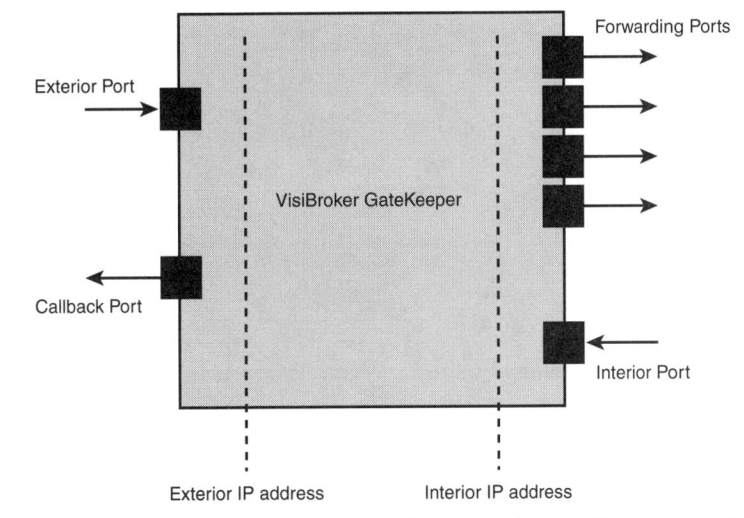

For a host with 2 IP addresses, it is necessary to set both internal and external IP addresses and por

FIGURE 10.13
The SSL palette for the gkconfig tool.

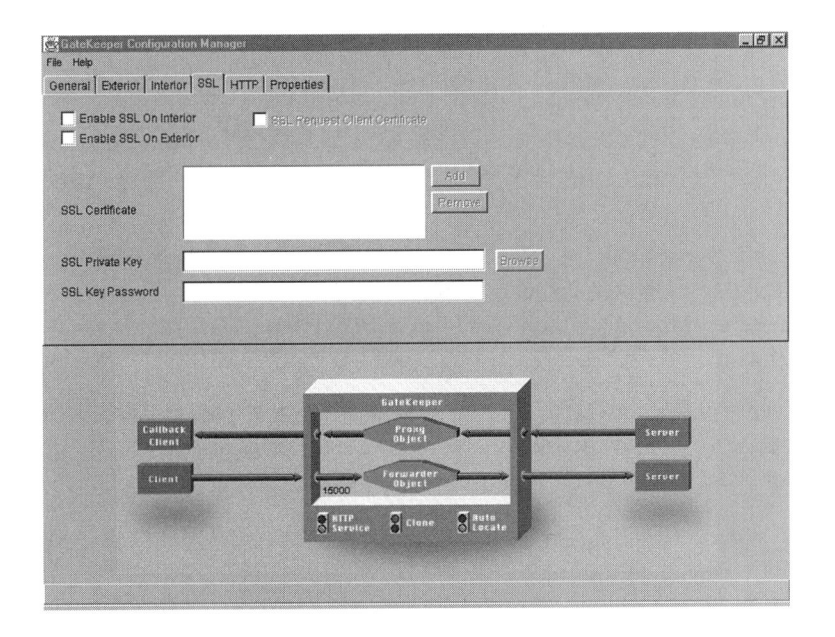

The HTTP Tab

The next tab, shown in Figure 10.14, deals with HTTP settings.

FIGURE 10.14
The HTTP palette for the gkconfig tool.

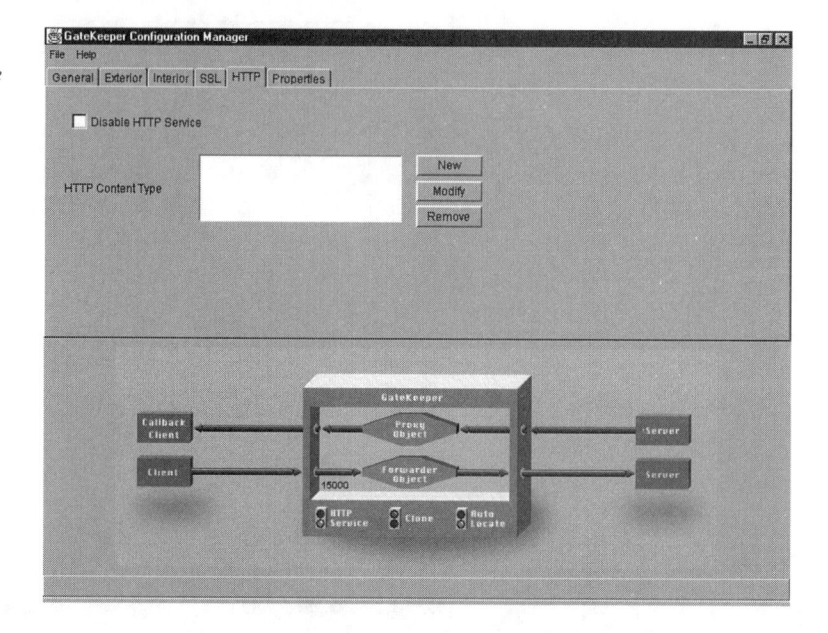

This tab allows you to disable the Web Server capability of the GateKeeper. If this is disabled, the GateKeeper only provides the Call Forwarding and HTTP Tunneling capabilities. If this is disabled, the HTTP Service light in the picture at the bottom of Figure 10.14 is switched to red.

If you choose to keep the HTTP Service enabled, you can add new HTTP types for the GateKeeper to support. As mentioned earlier, the GateKeeper is a lightweight HTTP Daemon that has support for only a limited number of HTTP types. This tab allows you to add new types and modify existing types.

GateKeeper implements the HTTP 1.0 spec plus the experimental Keep-Alive option. The Keep-Alive option is experimental because it is not part of official HTTP 1.1 spec. However, most browsers and JVMs provided support for this experimental Keep-Alive option before the HTTP 1.1 spec was adopted.

Persistent HTTP connection allows users to re-use a connection. HTTP 1.0 implementations with the Keep-Alive option that we currently use work in the following manner:

↳ Request1
↵ Response1

↳ Request2
↵ Response2

With the HTTP 1.1's persistent connection model, the following sequence is possible:

↳ Request1
↳ Request2
↵ Response1
↵ Response2

However, CORBA Servers have to keep the same response order as the request order, thus not providing any additional advantages over HTTP 1.0. The current GateKeeper is based on HTTP 1.0 specification and, therefore, doesn't support persistent HTTP 1.1 behavior.

The Properties Tab

The final tab in the gkconfig tool is the Properties tab shown in Figure 10.15.

FIGURE 10.15
The Properties palette for the gkconfig tool.

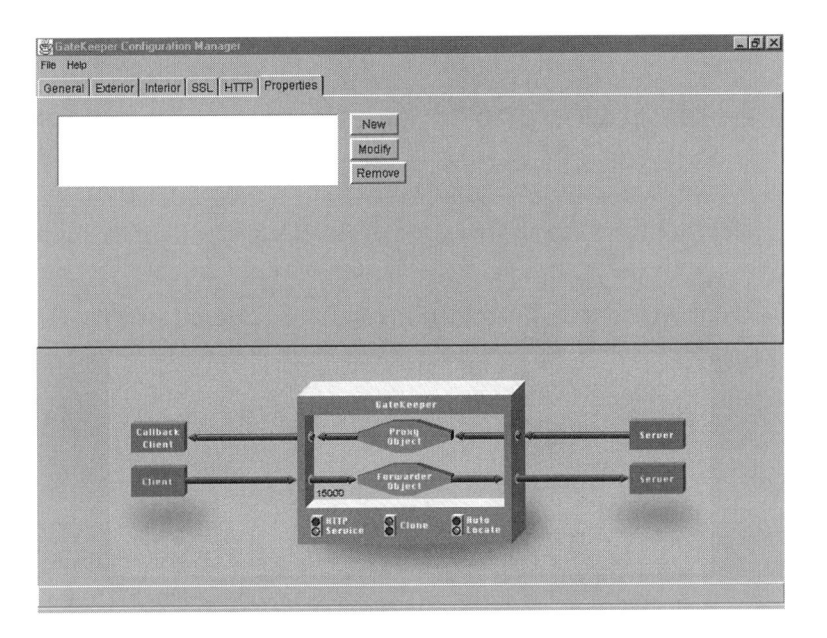

The final tab deals with setting up any additional properties for the GateKeeper. This can be any of the ORB or BOA options. For a comprehensive list of all the available ORB.init() options and BOA.init() options, refer to Chapter 21 and the listing of read/write options for the ORB and BOA.

This tab can also be used for initializing services such as The Naming Service or Interface Repository. It can also be used to initialize your own Services such as Interceptors, which are discussed later in the book.

Chaining GateKeepers

Certain firewall situations require a GateKeeper outside a firewall as well as a GateKeeper inside the firewall. This is often referred to as the DMZ by Firewall professionals. The following describes the configuration:

- The Client HTML and Applet are delivered by the external Web server.
- The Applet then uses the ORBgatekeeperIOR parameter to point to the external GateKeeper.
- The external GateKeeper is started with an ORBgatekeeperIOR parameter pointing to the internal GateKeeper.
- The internal GateKeeper must have an exterior port that is allowed to be called through the firewall.

Java Applications and Firewalls

One of the key benefits of the GateKeeper is its capability to enable IIOP traffic to pass through firewalls. Oftentimes this is necessary for Java Application Clients as well as Applets. Java Application Clients can also make use of the GateKeeper functionality by using the ORBgatekeeperIOR property. Thus, from the command line it is possible to run the following:

```
prompt> vbj -DORBgatekeeperIOR=http://somehostname:15000/gatekeeper.ior Client
```

This forces the Client to use the Call Forwarding mechanism of the GateKeeper to communicate with Server Objects and enables the Client to tunnel IIOP through firewalls.

> **NOTE**
>
> As stated before, HTTP Tunneling has an impact on performance. Use only when firewall policies mandate its use.

Security Considerations with the GateKeeper

It is important to understand how the GateKeeper doesn't compromise overall system security.

- The GateKeeper should never be run from a privileged root account or from a directory controlled by a privileged account. The GateKeeper startup directory only needs to contain the VisiBroker class files and the HTML files used to launch applets, all of which should be read-only.

- The GateKeeper accepts only IIOP and HTTP protocols on the ports that it specifies. The IIOP protocol won't enable write capabilities and only enables read access to the directory it was started in. The GateKeeper provides no mechanism to gain access to any directory other than the directory it was started in. A feature of the HTTP protocol is that a trusted machine could write a file into a directory at or below the initial GateKeeper startup directory. However, the GateKeeper doesn't provide a way for the file to be made executable. Thus, the file cannot damage the file system.

- It is recommended that you don't use the GateKeeper as your main Web Server. If you choose to do so anyway, there must not be any executable file at or below the GateKeeper startup directory that could be potentially harmful.

- Nothing below the GateKeeper startup directory should be in your PATH.

- To provide the maximum possible protection against any attack that might be devised to compromise a GateKeeper, it is recommended you create a VisiBroker group with a user for managing the GateKeeper and a user for running the GateKeeper.

- The manager account should own the JDK and VisiBroker environments and files; all of which should be set to rw-r--r-- (644) or lower permissions for files and rwxr-xr-x (755) for directories, except for the GateKeeper's startup directory that should be set to rwxr-wxr-x (775).

- The GateKeeper account needs to have privileges to run the JVM, to open socket connections, to write log and IOR files to the startup directory, and to read the classes and HTML files.

- Security consideration such as privacy, integrity, and authentication of data can be addressed by our VisiBroker SSL product.

SIGNED APPLETS AND ALTERNATIVE DOWNLOAD STRATEGIES

The use of the GateKeeper is one strategy to overcome the Java Sandbox security model. An alternative is to use *signed* applets; applets that are digitally signed to guarantee the true identity of the sender of the applet. A signed applet presents the user the option of whether he trusts the sender of the applet or not. After a signed applet has been loaded, it has special privileges that normal applets don't have. Signed applets can make calls to hosts other than the codebase machine, as well as have the capability to write to the local hard disk. Using signed applets enables a great deal of flexibility in your system design and alleviates the requirement of using the GateKeeper as a call forwarding mechanism.

Signed applets can also be very useful mechanisms to pre-install all the core VisiBroker components on your hard disk, so you don't pay the initial runtime penalty of having to download the VisiBroker runtime classes. The way this is done is different for every browser, but we will walk through an example of how this would be achieved in the Netscape environment. In order to work through this example, you must have a Class 3 Digital Signing Certificate and Private Key for Netscape. This can be obtained from Verisign, Inc. or any other security vendors.

> **NOTE**
>
> At the time of the writing of this book, the general state of public key infrastructures was still somewhat immature. If you are going to be attempting signed applets, be prepared for a lot of trial and error.

Making a Netscape Pre-install

The following steps are designed to walk you through the process of creating a digitally signed JAR file that installs all the necessary parts of your VisiBroker application automatically on the Client desktop. This prevents the need to download all the base VisiBroker classes the first time an applet is invoked.

1. Copy all the VisiBroker Jar files, any DLLs (if you are using VisiBroker SSL), and all applet classes into their own subdirectory using `test`.

2. Add an installation script to your `test` subdirectory. This is a JavaScript file that uses a Netscape Application Programming Interface(API) to write information to the local hard disk. Call this `install.js`. An example of such a script is shown in Listing 10.5.

LISTING 10.5 A NETSCAPE PRE-INSTALL SCRIPT

```
// Sample Installation script for our Netscape pre-install

// Conditional alert.
function cAlert (message)
{
    if (!this.silent)
            alert(message);
}

// Conditional confirm.
function cConfirm (message)
{
        if (this.silent)
                return true;
        else
```

```
                    return confirm(message);
}

// Variable indicating whether or not installation should proceed.
bInstall = true;


// Make sure Java is enabled before doing anything else.
if ( navigator.javaEnabled() ) {

    // Create a version object and a software update object
    vi = new netscape.softupdate.VersionInfo(4, 0, 0, 0);
    su = new netscape.softupdate.SoftwareUpdate
            (this, "Visigenic PreInstall");

      // Start the install process
      err = su.StartInstall
            ("java/", vi, netscape.softupdate.SoftwareUpdate.FULL_INSTALL);

      if (err == 0)
    {
            // Find the Java download directory on the user's machine
            JavaClassFolder = su.GetFolder("Netscape Java Classes");
        JavaBinFolder    = su.GetFolder("Netscape Java Bin");

            // Install the JAR archive. Unpack it and list where it goes
err = su.AddSubcomponent("preinstall JAR", vi, "myAppletClasses.jar",
    JavaClassFolder, "", this.force);
err = su.AddSubcomponent("preinstall JAR", vi, "vbj30ssl.jar",
    JavaClassFolder, "", this.force);
err = su.AddSubcomponent("preinstall JAR", vi, "vbjorb.jar",
    JavaClassFolder,"",this.force);
err = su.AddSubcomponent("preinstall JAR", vi, "vbj30ssl.dll",
    JavaBinFolder,"",this.force);
err = su.AddSubcomponent("preinstall JAR", vi, "vbrnissl.dll",
    JavaBinFolder,"",this.force);
       }

        // Unless there was a problem, move JAR archive to final location
        // and update the Client Version Registry
        if (err != 0)
              su.AbortInstall();
        else
    {
              su.FinalizeInstall();
cAlert("Installation complete. You must restart Communicator
          to use the new Java classes.");
       }
}
```

After this file has been created, put it in your test subdirectory. This is used by Netscape in order to correctly put the right components in the correct place on the hard disk. Full details on the Netscape Install JavaScript API can be found at *http://www.netscape.com*.

3. Use the Netscape signing tool to create a digitally signed Jar file that contains all the files you copied into the test subdirectory in step 1. For specific details on the syntax and options of the Netscape signing tool, refer to *http://developer1.netscape.com:80/docs/manuals/signedobj/signtool/index.htm*.

A sample Netscape signing script is as follows:

```
signtool ..... test
cd sign
zip -r0 ..\preinstall.jar *
cd ..
signtool -d. -v smartinstall.jar
```

The preceding script is analyzed in the line:

```
signtool ..... test
```

The Netscape signing tool is called signtool. Refer to the Netscape online documentation for instructions on its options. This can be found at *http://developer1.netscape.com:80/docs/manuals/signedobj/signtool/index.htm*. The test subdirectory contains all the files you are looking to install. In the line

```
zip -r0 ..\preinstall.jar *
```

Bundle up all the files in the test subdirectory and create a file called preinstall.jar. Finally, in the line

```
signtool -d. -v smartinstall.jar
```

Use the signtool utility to verify that preinstall.jar has been digitally signed.

4. Now you are ready to download this component into a Client browser. At this point, you must modify your HTML page to reflect the digitally signed Jar file. The modified HTML file is shown in Listing 10.6.

LISTING 10.6 HTML PAGE WITH PRE-INSTALL

```
<HTML>
<HEAD>
<SCRIPT LANGUAGE="JavaScript">

function startDownload(minVersion)
{
    var trigger = netscape.softupdate.Trigger;

        // Get the JIM version information
        version = trigger.GetVersionInfo("/java");

            // Installed by JIM, let JIM take care of version checking
```

```
                if (version != null)
                    return trigger.ConditionalSoftwareUpdate("http://walkabout/
                            preinstall.jar","/java",
                            new netscape.softupdate.VersionInfo(minVersion, 0, 0, 0),
                            trigger.DEFAULT_MODE);

        // No version of VisiBroker is currently installed on this machine,
            // so start the download
            else
                    return trigger.StartSoftwareUpdate
                            ("http://walkabout/preinstall.jar", trigger.DEFAULT_MODE);

    }


    function download ()
    {
        if ( navigator.javaEnabled() )
        {
            trigger = netscape.softupdate.Trigger;
               if ( trigger.UpdateEnabled() )
               {
                   if (navigator.platform == "Win32")
                   {
                                startDownload (0); //Install any version.
                          }
                    else alert("This pre-install only runs on Windows NT/95.");
                  }
             else alert("Enable Netscape SmartUpdate
                                before running this script.");
           }
         else alert("Enable Netscape Java before running this script.");
    }

    </SCRIPT>
    </HEAD>

    <BODY>

    <H1>VisiBroker Pre-Install Page</H1>
    <P>This page is a demonstration of how to create a digitally
    signed Jar file that will pre-install all VisiBroker components
    on the local hard disk, avoiding having to download all the runtime
    classes when starting up the Client Applet.</P>
    <CENTER><FORM METHOD="Post">
    <INPUT TYPE="button" VALUE="Pre-Install VisiBroker components Now!"
       onClick="download();">
    </FORM></CENTER>

       </BODY>
</HTML>
```

After the VisiBroker runtime classes and the Applet classes have been installed on the Client's hard disk, the Applet HTML can be modified to point to the local classes, so a download won't be necessary. A similar strategy can be used with Microsoft Internet Explorer browser through the use of digitally signed cabinet (CAB) files. For more information on how to create a pre-install with Microsoft, check out the following *http://www.microsoft.com*.

Using Netcaster

One option of pre-installing VisiBroker components is to use Netscape's Netcaster push capability. The use of Netcaster is beyond the scope of this text. Extensive details on this can be found at the following:

`ftp://ftp.visigenic.com/private/dev/vbj/netcaster.html`

SUMMARY

The focus of this chapter is to analyze how VisiBroker for Java works in Java-enabled browsers across the Internet. We discussed how there are many Java-specific changes that must be made to modify a Java Application Client into a Java Applet Client; however, there is only one VisiBroker change that must be made. The necessary change is to the `ORB.init()` signature, making sure to pass the Applet itself as the first argument. Otherwise, all changes that need to be made are Java related, having to do with painting an Applet GUI and adding the capability for the GUI to listen for events.

The key component to the VisiBroker for Java Internet Architecture is the GateKeeper. The GateKeeper serves the following three main purposes:

- Call Forwarding to workaround the Java Sandbox Security model.
- Provide HTTP Tunneling in situations where the Client Firewall won't enable IIOP packets through.
- Serve as a lightweight HTTP Daemon for testing purposes. It serves HTML pages and allows you to test Applets without having a real Web Server in your environment.

The GateKeeper provides a graphical tool called gkconfig that allows you to easily customize the GateKeeper based on your network environment. The GateKeeper is designed to handle a variety of firewall, router, and multi-homed host environments.

CAFFEINE

CHAPTER 11

IN THIS CHAPTER

- **WHY CAFFEINE?** *240*
- **UNDERSTANDING THE JAVA2IIOP COMPILER** *241*
- **UNDERSTANDING THE JAVA2IDL COMPILER** *244*
- **JAVA TO IDL LANGUAGE MAPPING** *246*
- **EXTENSIBLE STRUCTS** *247*
- **EXCEPTIONS** *253*

This chapter will be of particular interest to Java programmers who have worked with Java's Remote Method Invocation (RMI) package for distributed method invocation. VisiBroker's Caffeine tools and capabilities were designed to add RMI-like features to Common Object Remote Broker Architecture (CORBA). These features include the following:

- Defining all Server interfaces in Java, not Interface Definition Language (IDL). Caffeine provides a special compiler called java2iiop that generates standard VisiBroker stubs and skeletons from a Java interface rather than from an IDL interface.
- A compiler called java2idl, which takes a standard Java interface file and generates a CORBA-compliant IDL file. This IDL file can then be passed to any other IDL compiler to have CORBA stubs and skeletons generated.
- The ability to pass Java objects by value. VisiBroker offers a new IDL type designed for the purpose of passing a Java object by value called *extensible structs*. Extensible structs allow you to declare a Java object within IDL, and have the contents of this IDL serialized and passed by value.

WHY CAFFEINE?

The Caffeine compilers were designed specifically to allow Java developers to develop distributed CORBA applications while remaining in their familiar Java programming environment. Caffeine eliminates the need to have to learn IDL in order to define Server interfaces, allowing you to work directly with Java interfaces. For those of you who are working in a multi-language environment, the idea of the Caffeine compilers might not add as much value. If you recall our lengthy discussion of IDL in Chapters 2–4, remember the reason why CORBA uses IDL: to provide a layer of abstraction between the Object definitions and the actual programming language. The reasoning behind this abstraction is because CORBA must support multiple languages. As such, a higher-level descriptive language was needed to describe interfaces. IDL is language neutral and can be used to generate stubs and skeletons in several different programming languages.

For those programmers who will be working exclusively in Java, the requirement of using IDL can be a burden despite the aforementioned reasons. Java already has the notion of an interface. Why learn an entire additional language to define an interface when it can just as easily be defined directly in Java, right? Well, it's for this programming audience that Caffeine was designed. The goal behind the Caffeine compilers was to provide an easier transition for native Java developers to start developing VisiBroker applications. Using Caffeine, Java developers can maintain an all Java environment, never having to learn the mapping rules from IDL to Java.

A further benefit of staying in an all Java environment is that you can make use of native Java types and Java serialization. Because Caffeine allows developers to define interfaces in Java, native Java classes such as Hashtables and Vectors can be passed as VisiBroker arguments.

Because CORBA IDL is language independent, there is no way within IDL to represent native Java types.

One useful feature within Java is the ability to serialize objects and pass them by value. At the time this book was written, the latest CORBA specification didn't provide a standard mechanism to pass objects by value, only by reference. Caffeine provides an extension to the standard IDL, allowing you to define Java objects as extensible structs. When these extensible structs are marshaled for passing to the Server, they use Java serialization to pass the actual state of the object to the server rather than just a reference. Standard CORBA only supports pass by value for non-object types, making use of passing by reference for objects. You pass an object reference within your argument, not the object itself. IDL has no notion of passing objects by value.

> **NOTE**
>
> Some texts refer to serialization of an object as being the preservation of that object's state. Other texts simply use the terminology that serialization is "writing out the entire object". Both terms are describing the same action: preserving the data members of an object for later restoration.

UNDERSTANDING THE JAVA2IIOP COMPILER

The java2iiop compiler is responsible for reading Java interface files and generating standard VisiBroker stubs and skeletons. Unfortunately, it isn't possible to just take any existing Java interface file and pass it to java2iiop. There are a couple of Caffeine-specific requirements that must be part of the Java interface that is passed to java2iiop. These requirements are needed to ensure that the object implementations are ultimately derived from the root CORBA interface `org.omg.CORBA.Object`. All CORBA Objects must inherit from this interface, whether they are developed with Caffeine or with IDL. These are the following:

- The interface must be public
- The interface must inherit from `org.omg.CORBA.Object`

It is necessary for your interface to extend `org.omg.CORBA.Object` because this is the base interface for CORBA and it is necessary for the stubs and skeletons to follow this inheritance hierarchy.

Finally, although it is perfectly legal in Java, the java2iiop compiler doesn't support overloaded methods in the Java interfaces passed to it.

We will walk through the steps of using the java2iiop compiler on a simple Java interface. Figure 11.1 provides a nice overview of the development steps we will discuss.

FIGURE 11.1
The development steps of using the Caffeine compiler.

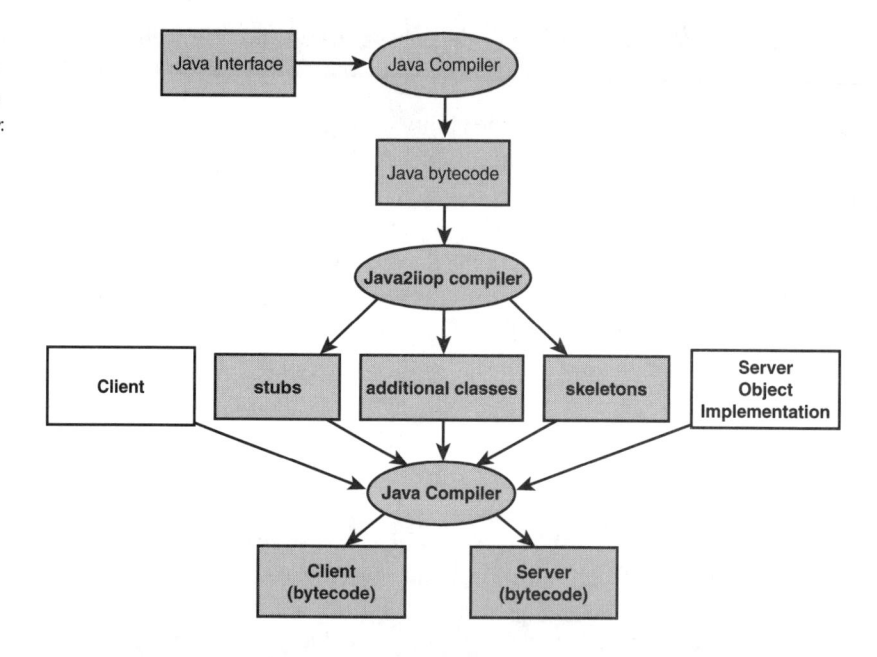

To begin developing with Caffeine, write a Java interface file. Listing 11.1 shows a simple Java interface that is public and inherits from the CORBA base interface `org.omg.CORBA.Object`.

LISTING 11.1 SAMPLE CAFFEINE INTERFACE

```java
package chapter11.primitive;

/**
 * A small interface to demonstrate the use of
 * Caffeine with a class using only primitive
 * types as parameters and returns.  Note that
 * we must extend CORBA object
 */

public interface Adder extends org.omg.CORBA.Object
{
    public int add(int anInt, int anotherInt);
}
```

1. The first step is to compile the Java interface from Listing 11.1. You can compile this using the vbjc utility:

    `C:\ >vbjc Adder.java`

    As mentioned previously, the vbjc utility isn't required for Java compilation. It is provided for convenience. VisiBroker for Java applications can be compiled using any standard Java bytecode compiler.

2. Next you need to set up two directories. The first one is called `chapter11`. Within the `chapter11` directory, set up a second directory called `primitive` to hold the contents of this package. There is notning special about `chapter11` and `primitive` other than they are part of the package name we are using. Then, copy the newly created `Adder.class` into the chapter11\primitive package directory. This is your input to the java2iiop compiler because it reads Java bytecode not Java source code.

> **NOTE**
>
> When using packages with Caffeine, you must explicitly create directories and subdirectories for your full package scope.

```
C:\ >mkdir chapter11
C:\ >mkdir chapter11\primitive
C:\ >copy Adder.class chapter11\primitive
        1 file(s) copied
C:\ >java2iiop chapter11\primitive\Adder.class
Creating: chapter11\primitive\AdderHolder.java
Creating: chapter11\primitive\AdderHelper.java
Creating: chapter11\primitive\_st_Adder.java
Creating: chapter11\primitive\_AdderImplBase.java
Creating: chapter11\primitive\AdderOperations.java
Creating: chapter11\primitive\_tie_Adder.java
Creating: chapter11\primitive\_example_Adder.java
```

Does this look familiar? It should! You have just created a new package and generated all the exact same VisiBroker stubs and skeletons for this package subdirectory as if you had written an IDL file and run the idl2java compiler instead. At this point, the Client and Server Object implementation are developed exactly as you have seen up until this point. Nothing special must be done to make use of the stubs and skeletons generated using the java2iiop compiler.

Options for java2iiop

The following is a list of command-line options that can be used with java2iiop.

- `-root_dir`—Places the generated files in the specified directory. The default is to write the files to the current working directory.
- `-strict`—Generates stubs and skeletons that can be run on any CORBA-compliant Object Request Broker (ORB). The default is to generate stubs and skeletons with VisiBroker specific extensions.

- `-smart_stub`—Generates the additional methods to implement Smart Stubs. You will learn more about these in chapter 16, "Smart Stubs, Callbacks, and Object Wrappers".
- `-version`—Displays the current version of VisiBroker for Java.
- `-portable`—Generates portable stubs using DII.
- `-wide`—Maps Strings and Characters to the IDL `wstring` and `wchar`.
- `-no_bind`—Suppresses generation of the VisiBroker specific `bind()` call. Remember that the `bind()` is necessary for communication to the Smart Agent.
- `-no_comments`—Suppresses the generation of comments in the stubs and skeletons.
- `-no_examples`—Suppresses the generation of example code.
- `-no_tie`—Suppresses the generation of the TIE interfaces and classes.
- `-W #`—Setting this to zero suppresses all warnings from the Java compiler.

We have just demonstrated how to generate VisiBroker stubs and skeletons without having to write a single line of IDL code. This is very advantageous to Java developers working in all Java environments. However, how could a developer in a mixed language (that is, C++ and Java) use the Caffeine compilers? For mixed environments, a second compiler, java2idl is provided. This compiler allows you to continue to develop your Server interfaces in Java. However, you will use java2idl to generate an IDL file representing the Java interface file. At this point, the IDL file can be used with VisiBroker for C++'s idl2cpp compiler to generate C++ client stubs. We will look at the java2idl compiler in greater detail in the next section.

UNDERSTANDING THE JAVA2IDL COMPILER

The purpose of the java2idl compiler is to generate an IDL file from our Java interface file. This is extremely useful when client stubs need to be generated for a language other than Java. The development process is the same as that of the Caffeine compiler.

1. Write an interface in Java adhering to the two rules mentioned earlier; the interface must be public, and it must inherit from `org.omg.CORBA.Object`.
2. Compile this Java interface in the same manner as described in the previous section, "Understanding the java2iiop Compiler."
3. Run this Java interface through java2idl to see what the IDL would like for this Java interface. Use the Java interface introduced in Listing 11.1 as an example and run this through the java2idl compiler as shown in Listing 11.2.

LISTING 11.2 IDL GENERATED FROM THE CAFFEINE INTERFACE DEFINED IN LISTING 11.1

```
C:\>java2idl chapter11.primitive.Adder
module chapter11
{
module primitive
```

```
    {
                interface Adder
    {
                    long add(in long arg0,in long arg1);
                };
            };
};
```

Is this what you expected? Compare this against one of the generated files found in Listing 11.3.

LISTING 11.3 SAMPLE IMPLEMENTATION SHELL GENERATED FROM THE JAVA2IIOP COMPILER OF THE CAFFEINE INTERFACE SHOWN IN LISTING 11.1

```
// The generated _example_Adderjava file that can
// be used as a shell for you to write your
// Server Object implementation.
// Notice how our Adder Java interface maps to this
// Implementation shell.

package chapter11\primitive;                     ──❶

public class _example_Adder extends chapter11.primitive._AdderImplBase
{
  /** Construct a persistently named object. */
  public _example_Adder(java.lang.String name)
{
    super(name);
}

  /** Construct a transient object. */
public _example_Adder()
{
    super();
}

public int add(int arg0, int arg1)
{
    // IMPLEMENT: Operation
    return 0;
  }
}
```

❶ The same package we declare in our Adder interface.

Options for java2idl

The following is a list of command-line options that can be used with java2idl.

- `-o some_filename`—Writes the java2idl output to the specified file.
- `-verbose`—Turns verbose output on, which prints a great deal of info on screen to assist in troubleshooting.
- `-version`—Displays the compiler version.
- `-wide`—Maps Strings and Characters to the IDL `wstring` and `wchar`.

JAVA TO IDL LANGUAGE MAPPING

You must do the opposite of what you did in Chapter 2 when you learned the mapping of IDL types to their respective Java types. It is important to understand how native Java type definitions are mapped to the appropriate CORBA IDL types for the generated stubs and skeletons. For each of the primitive types, the mapping is a direct reverse of the IDL to Java language mapping done in Chapters 2–4.

TABLE 11.1 THE JAVA TO IDL LANGUAGE MAPPING

Java Type	IDL/IIOP Type
package	module
Boolean	Boolean
char	char
byte	octet
java.lang.String	string
short	short
int	long
long	long long
float	float
double	double
org.omg.CORBA.Any	any
org.omg.CORBA.TypeCode	TypeCode
org.omg.CORBA.Principal	Principal
org.omg.CORBA.Object	Object

Okay, this seems pretty straightforward, but what about use of the native Java classes, such as Vectors, Dictionaries, and Hashtables mentioned earlier: How are these mapped to Internet Inter-ORB Protocol (IIOP) types?

We will now move on to discuss the mapping rules for the more complex Java classes and types and how they are mapped to IIOP types.

- **Interfaces**—Interfaces are treated in one of two ways:

    1. They are written to extend `org.omg.CORBA.Object` as shown in the first example. In this case, the interface follows the normal CORBA semantics and is passed by reference.

    2. They are not written to extend `org.omg.CORBA.Object`, in which case they will be mapped to VisiBroker IDL extensible structs and serialized.

- **Arrays**—Java arrays are automatically mapped to CORBA unbounded sequences.
- **Classes**—For any predefined Java classes or any user-created Java classes, four checks are done to determine how the class is passed across the wire. These checks are as follows:

    1. Is the class final?
    2. Is the class public?
    3. Does the class not use class inheritance?
    4. Are all the data members public?

If the answer to all four of the preceding questions is yes, the class is mapped to an IDL struct. However, if all the preceding criteria isn't met, the class is mapped to an extensible struct. This mapping process is demonstrated in Figure 11.2.

FIGURE 11.2
The criteria the java2iiop compiler uses to determine whether to map a Java class as a normal struct or an extensible struct.

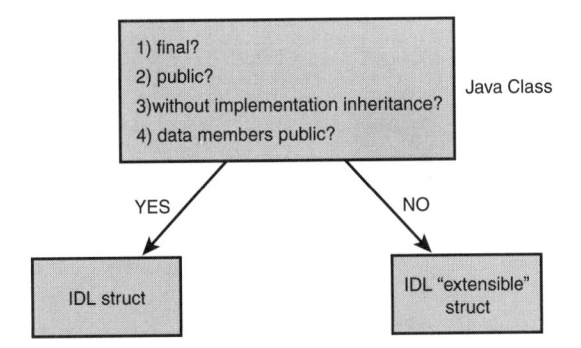

EXTENSIBLE STRUCTS

Extensible structs are VisiBroker-specific extensions designed to overcome CORBA's current lack of support for pass-by-value semantics. If you are concerned with designing an application with ORBs from multiple vendors, it is recommended that you don't use this feature.

In an all Java environment, it is common to write applications that make use of objects local to the Java Virtual Machine (JVM). Such local objects can include Java Hashtables and Java Vectors. Because Caffeine allows you to develop all your Server Object definitions in Java rather than IDL, it must take the responsibility for handling the passing of these local Java objects. Thus, VisiBroker must copy these objects across JVMs from the Client to the Server Object. This process is handled through the use of extensible structs.

Extensible structs are extensions of CORBA structs. The extensible struct allows the state of an object and all its parent objects to be written into a serial byte stream. In other words, VisiBroker writes all the fields of the object, including the base class and every derived class, to the extensible struct. Thus, the extensible struct can represent very complicated inheritance hierarchies, linked lists, or any other complex data structure. Extensible structs can make use of inheritance and can be self-referential. When writing information to the extensible struct, VisiBroker keeps a record of all pointers in order to properly reconstruct the object on the server side. These fields are written to the wire in the same IIOP buffers that normal requests are. The entire extensible struct is passed as an IDL octet sequence. The Client marshals the struct as a sequence of bytes; the Server Object unmarshals it and reconstructs the state of the object. Thus, the object arrives in exactly the same state with which it left the Client. The only requirement for types that are passed as extensible structs is that they must implement java.io.Serializable.

An Example of Extensible Structs

We will take a look at the Java interface in Listing 11.4 that makes use of extensible structs.

LISTING 11.4 AN EXAMPLE OF A COMPLEX CAFFEINE INTERFACE PASSING NATIVE JAVA TYPES

```
package chapter11.complex;

/**
 * A small class to demonstrate the use of
 * Caffeine with a class using complex passing
 * and return types.  Note that
 * we must extend CORBA object
 */
public interface HasAFrame  extends org.omg.CORBA.Object
{
    public java.awt.Frame getFrame();

    public void setFrame(java.awt.Frame frame);
}
```

```
C:\>vbjc HasAFrame.java
C:\ >java2iiop chapter11.complex.HasAFrame
Creating: HasAFrameHelper.java
Creating: HasAFrameHolder.java
Creating: _st_HasAFrame.java
Creating: _HasAFrameImplBase.java
Creating: HasAFrameOperations.java
Creating: _tie_HasAFrame.java
Creating: _example_HasAFrame.java
```

❶ To emphasize that extensible structs can handle complex objects, we have chosen to use an example with a very complex type—a Frame. Now, compile and generate the stubs and skeletons with java2iiop.

Examine what the IDL would look for in this Java interface using the java2idl tool as shown in Listing 11.5.

> **NOTE**
>
> You won't see the listing of files created when using java2iiop on Windows NT.

LISTING 11.5 THE IDL GENERATED FROM THE HasAFrame INTERFACE DEFINED IN LISTING 11.4

```
C:\>java2idl chapter11.complex.HasAFrame
module java
{
 module awt
 {
    extensible struct Component;
    extensible struct Container;
    extensible struct Window;
    extensible struct Frame;
};
};

module chapter11
{
  module complex
  {
     interface HasAFrame
  {
      ::java::awt::Frame getFrame();
      void setFrame(in ::java::awt::Frame arg0);
};
};
};
```

At this point, write your Server Implementation and Client just as you would normally do. A sample Server implementation is shown in Listings 11.6 and 11.7. A Sample Client is shown in Listing 11.8.

LISTING 11.6 THE IMPLEMENTATION OF THE HasAFrameImpl INTERFACE DEFINED IN LISTING 11.4

```java
package chapter11.complex;

/*
 * Server to test creating a Server
 * using Caffeine, passing complex
 * Java types.
 */
public class HasAFrameImpl extends chapter11.complex._HasAFrameImplBase
{
    private java.awt.Frame theFrame = null;

    //Constructor for transient object
    public HasAFrameImpl()
    {
        finishConstructor();
    }

    //Constructor for persistent object
    public HasAFrameImpl(String name)
    {
        super(name);
        finishConstructor();
    }

    private void finishConstructor()
    {
        theFrame = new java.awt.Frame("Isn't Caffeine Fun?");
        theFrame.add(new java.awt.Label("Please kill process " +
            "to close this window"));
    }

    public java.awt.Frame getFrame()
    {
        return theFrame;
    }

    public void setFrame(java.awt.Frame aFrame)
    {
        theFrame = aFrame;
    }

}
```

LISTING 11.7 THE IMPLEMENTATION OF THE SERVER MAINLINE INSTANTIATING A HasAFrameImpl OBJECT AS IMPLEMENTED IN LISTING 11.6

```java
package chapter11.complex;

/*
 * This class demonstrates creating client/server
 * using Caffeine, passing complex Java types
 */
public class Server
{
        public static void main(String[] args)
        {
            try
            {
                // Initialize the ORB.
                org.omg.CORBA.ORB orb = org.omg.CORBA.ORB.init();

                // Initialize the BOA.
                org.omg.CORBA.BOA boa = orb.BOA_init();

                // Create the Object implementation we
                // want to bind
                HasAFrameImpl haf = new HasAFrameImpl("HasAFrame");

                // Export the newly create object.
                boa.obj_is_ready(haf);

                System.out.println(haf + " is ready.");

                // Wait for incoming requests
                boa.impl_is_ready();
            }
            catch(org.omg.CORBA.SystemException ex)
            {
                ex.printStackTrace();
            }
            catch(Exception ex)
            {
                ex.printStackTrace();
```

LISTING 11.7   CONTINUED

```
            }
        }
}
```

LISTING 11.8   THE CLIENT THAT MAKES INVOCATIONS ON THE `HasAFrameImpl` SERVER SHOWN IN LISTINGS 11.6 AND 11.7

```java
package chapter11.complex;

/*
 * This class demonstrates using a Caffeine-created
 * server interface, passing and receiving complex types
 */

public class Client
{

    public static void main(String[] args)
    {
        try
        {
            //Initialize the ORB
            org.omg.CORBA.ORB orb = org.omg.CORBA.ORB.init();

            //Bind to the Implementation
            chapter11.complex.HasAFrame haf =
                chapter11.complex.HasAFrameHelper.bind(
                orb, "HasAFrame");

            //Call a method to make sure it works
            java.awt.Frame aFrame = haf.getFrame();
            aFrame.pack();
            aFrame.show();

        }
        catch(Exception ex)
        {
            ex.printStackTrace();
        }
    }
}
```

Using Extensible Structs Directly in IDL

Use of extensible structs isn't limited only to the java2iiop compiler. VisiBroker's idl2java compiler recognizes this extension and generates the exact same stubs and skeletons as java2iiop. However, you must use the following command-line argument if defining extensible structs in IDL:

```
C:\> idl2java -all_serializable test.idl
```

When the `-all_serializable` option is set, the generated classes for the following IDL data types implement `java.io.Serializable`:

- structs
- extensible structs
- exceptions
- unions
- enums

EXCEPTIONS

Including user exceptions within a Java interface requires that you create a separate Java interface for the exception. The only requirement is that the user exception interface inherits from org.omg.CORBA.UserException as demonstrated in Listing 11.9.

LISTING 11.9 AN IMPLEMENTATION OF A USER-DEFINED EXCEPTION THAT IS REFERENCED IN A CAFFEINE INTERFACE

```
// Except.java

package chapter11.complex;

import java.lang.*;

public class NO_WINDOW extends org.omg.CORBA.UserException{     ❶
    public String reason;

    public NO_WINDOW(String reason){
        this.reason = reason;
    }
}
```

❶ Must inherit from org.omg.CORBA.UserException

Using this exception within our previous Extensible Struct example from Listing 11.4 is shown in Listing 11.10.

LISTING 11.10 DEMONSTRATING HOW TO EXTEND THE CAFFEINE INTERFACE EXAMINED IN LISTING 11.4 TO THROW THE USER-DEFINED EXCEPTION THAT IS IMPLEMENTED IN LISTING 11.9

```
package chapter11.complex;

/**
 * A small class to demonstrate the use of
 * Caffeine with a class using complex passing
 * and return types.  Note that
 * we must extend CORBA object
 */

public interface HasAFrame  extends org.omg.CORBA.Object
{
    public java.awt.Frame getFrame() throws NO_WINDOW;

    public void setFrame(java.awt.Frame frame) throws NO_WINDOW;
}
```

Now, compile your new interfaces in Listings 11.9 and 11.10 as you did before.

LISTING 11.11 THE IDL THAT IS GENERATED FROM THE CAFFEINE INTERFACE SHOWN IN LISTING 11.10

```
C:\ >vbjc NO_WINDOW.java
C:\ >vbjc HasAFrame.java
C:\ >java2iiop chapter11.complex.HasAFrame
Creating: NO_WINDOWHolder.java
Creating: NO_WINDOWHelper.java
Updating: HasAFrameHolder.java
Updating: HasAFrameHelper.java
Updating: _st_HasAFrame.java
Updating: _HasAFrameImplBase.java
Updating: HasAFrameOperations.java
Updating: _tie_HasAFrame.java
Updating: _example_HasAFrame.java

C:\>java2idl chapter11.complex.HasAFrame

module java {
  module awt {
    extensible struct Component;
    extensible struct Container;
    extensible struct Window;
    extensible struct Frame;
```

```
    };
  };
module chapter11 {
  module complex {
    exception NO_WINDOW {
      string reason;
    };
    interface HasAFrame {
      ::java::awt::Frame getFrame(
      )
      raises(
         ::chapter11::complex::NO_WINDOW
      );
      void setFrame(
         in ::java::awt::Frame arg0
      )
      raises(
         ::chapter11::complex::NO_WINDOW
      );
    };
  };
};
```

❶ Here we see our UserException defined

❷ DL syntax we learned in Chapter 4 to "raise" a UserException.

At this point, use the UserException with exactly the same syntax implemented in Chapter 4 when we defined UserExceptions in our IDL.

SUMMARY

This chapter was probably a very exciting chapter for all the readers who will be working in an all Java environment. VisiBroker's Caffeine compilers, java2iiop and java2idl, allow you to define your Server Object interfaces in Java rather than IDL.

VisiBroker for Java has added an extension to the standard CORBA IDL called extensible structs. These are designed to enable objects to be passed by value. At this time, the CORBA standard doesn't have a specification for how objects are to be passed by value, CORBA only supports a pass by reference model. When objects are passed as arguments in a Java interface for the java2iiop compiler, the compiler checks four items in determining how to handle the object. The compiler checks the following:

- Is the class final?
- Is the class public?
- Does the class not make use of implementation inheritance?
- Are all the data members public?

If the answer to all four of these questions is yes, the object is mapped to an IDL struct; otherwise, it is mapped as an extensible struct. Extensible structs can also be defined directly in IDL by using the extensible keyword in front of the struct keyword. Extensible structs simply write the state of the object, as well as all parent objects, to an octet sequence that is then passed over the wire and reconstructed on the server side. It is through this mechanism that VisiBroker for Java enables native Java classes, such as Hashtables and Dictionaries, by value.

DYNAMIC VISIBROKER

CHAPTER

12

IN THIS CHAPTER

- USES FOR THE DYNAMIC FEATURES 258
- A REVIEW OF DII TYPES AND TERMS 258
- THE DYNAMIC INVOCATION INTERFACE 265
- THE DYNAMIC SKELETON INTERFACE 282

In this chapter, we will examine how to make use of VisiBroker in a dynamic environment, building Clients and Server Objects that won't make use of the Interface Definition Language (IDL) generated stubs and skeletons. Clients can make use of the Dynamic Invocation Interface (DII) to create an object proxy and create method invocations without having a `_st_XXX` class available. Further, Server Objects can make use of the Dynamic Skeleton Interface (DSI) such that they won't be required to inherit from the generated `XXXImplBase` class.

USES FOR THE DYNAMIC FEATURES

Before we examine the details of the Dynamic VisiBroker, we should probably discuss why this approach should be used. The DII and DSI capabilities of CORBA are primarily used by software vendors who are building tools and products on top of the Object Request Broker (ORB). The majority of end-user systems built using VisiBroker for Java will use the static stubs and skeletons generated from idl2java.

The dynamic approach provides a great deal of flexibility. Clients using DII aren't restricted to using Server Objects known at compile time, nor do they need to be recompiled if new Servers are introduced to the environment. Clients can be designed to poll the Interface Repository (as discussed in Chapter 13) in order to provide the user a list of available interfaces with which to connect.

Our discussion of the DII and DSI begins with an introduction to some of the common objects and techniques used in both the DII and DSI. We will then discuss how to code to the DII and DSI.

A REVIEW OF DII TYPES AND TERMS

Before we dive into the sequence of steps needed for using the DII, it is appropriate to introduce some new terms and data types that are important for developing with the DII. These include the Context and Environment classes, the `Any` and `TypeCodes`, as well as `NamedValues`. The use of these classes in the context of DII will be discussed when we discuss the steps for using DII.

Context

The Context type was introduced in Chapter 3, and is shown in IDL form in Listing 12.2. Its purpose is to represent a generic property list structure for Clients to pass to Server Objects. CORBA doesn't define how the contents of the Context object are to be structured. The structure of the Context object itself is that of a tree, whereby you start with a root Context object and can then add as many child Context objects as you like in any order. Listing 12.1 shows the method on the ORB interface used to create a Context.

LISTING 12.1 METHOD USED TO OBTAIN A DEFAULT CONTEXT OBJECT

```
package org.omg.CORBA;

abstract public class ORB{
    ....
    abstract public org.omg.CORBA.Context get_default_context();
    ....
}
```

LISTING 12.2 THE CONTEXT CLASS

```
// Context class
abstract public class Context
{
    public abstract java.lang.String context_name();
    public abstract org.omg.CORBA.Context parent();
    public abstract void set_one_value(java.lang.String, org.omg.CORBA.Any);
    public abstract void set_values(org.omg.CORBA.NVList);
    public abstract org.omg.CORBA.NVList get_values(java.lang.String, int,
java.lang.String);
    public abstract void delete_values(java.lang.String);
    public abstract org.omg.CORBA.Context create_child(java.lang.String);
    public org.omg.CORBA.Context();
}
```

Any, TypeCodes, and TCKind

We discussed the Any type in Chapter 3. As we learned in Chapter 4, the Any type can represent any IDL datatype, whether it is a CORBA primitive type, a CORBA complex type, or a user-defined type. The Any supports methods for the insertion and extraction of known Java types through methods defined on the interface. For user-defined types, insertion and extraction is handled by the helper classes generated by the idl2java compiler. If these terms don't seem familiar, review the section on Anys in Chapter 3.

During our discussion of the Any in Chapter 3, it was assumed that both the sender and receiver of the Any knew the type of the Any's payload at compile time. Knowing the Any's contents at compile time allows the developer to call the appropriate insert and extract methods on either the Any (for known types) or the helper (for user-defined types). In this chapter, we discuss how to create code that doesn't know about a method's argument types at compile type. The Any supports this situation through TypeCodes. Typecodes and their relation to the Any class are shown in Listing 12.3.

LISTING 12.3 A SUBSET OF THE Any CLASS

```
package org.omg.CORBA;

abstract public class Any {
    abstract public TypeCode type();
    abstract public void type(TypeCode type);
    abstract public void read_value(InputStream input, TypeCode type);
    abstract public void write_value(OutputStream output);
    abstract public boolean equal(Any value);
    ...
}
```

TypeCodes are used with Any types as a means of representing the type of argument or attribute being passed in the Any. All TypeCodes for the known IDL types are contained in the TCKind class, as shown in Listing 12.4. The TCKind is an enumeration representing all the possible TypeCodes for known IDL types.

TypeCodes are created in a similar manner to the Any type; however, there is a specific create method for each type of TypeCode. The TypeCode creation methods can be found on the ORB interface as highlighted in Listing 12.5.

LISTING 12.4 THE TCKind ENUMERATION THAT REPRESENTS EACH POSSIBLE TypeCode TYPE CONTAINED WITHIN AN Any

```
// IDL for TCKind
enum TCKind
{
        tk_null, tk_void, tk_short, tk_long, tk_ushort,
        tk_ulong, tk_float, tk_double, tk_Boolean, tk_char,
        tk_octet, tk_any, tk_TypeCode, tk_Principal, tk_objref,
        tk_struct, tk_union, tk_enum, tk_string, tk_sequence,
        tk_array, tk_alias, tk_except, tk_longlong, tk_ulonglong,
        tk_longdouble, tk_wchar, tk_wstring, tk_fixed
};
```

LISTING 12.5 METHODS ON THE ORB INTERFACE AVAILABLE FOR CREATING TypeCodes BASED ON THE TYPE

```
package org.omg.CORBA;

abstract public class ORB{
    ....
    public abstract org.omg.CORBA.TypeCode create_struct_tc(java.lang.String,
            java.lang.String, org.omg.CORBA.StructMember[]);
        public org.omg.CORBA.TypeCode create_estruct_tc(java.lang.String,
```

```
                java.lang.String, org.omg.CORBA.TypeCode,
                org.omg.CORBA.StructMember[]);
        public abstract org.omg.CORBA.TypeCode create_union_tc
            ↪(java.lang.String, java.lang.String,
                org.omg.CORBA.TypeCode, org.omg.CORBA.UnionMember[]);
        public abstract org.omg.CORBA.TypeCode create_enum_tc(java.lang.String,
                java.lang.String, java.lang.String[]);
        public abstract org.omg.CORBA.TypeCode create_alias_tc(java.lang.String,
                java.lang.String, org.omg.CORBA.TypeCode);
        public abstract org.omg.CORBA.TypeCode create_exception_tc
            ↪(java.lang.String, java.lang.String, org.omg.CORBA.StructMember[]);
        public abstract org.omg.CORBA.TypeCode create_interface_tc
            ↪(java.lang.String, java.lang.String);
        public abstract org.omg.CORBA.TypeCode create_string_tc(int);
        public abstract org.omg.CORBA.TypeCode create_wstring_tc(int);
        public abstract org.omg.CORBA.TypeCode create_sequence_tc(int,
                org.omg.CORBA.TypeCode);
        public abstract org.omg.CORBA.TypeCode create_recursive_sequence_tc
            ↪(int,int);
        public abstract org.omg.CORBA.TypeCode create_array_tc(int,
                org.omg.CORBA.TypeCode);
    ....
}
```

So if you remember the IDL mapping for enum types, you will recall that each element in the TCKind enum has an ordinal value uniquely identifying this particular datatype. For example, a TCKind of 0 represents a TCKind of null, meaning that the value within the Any is actually a null value. If you don't recall the details of using the Enum type, review Chapter 3.

Using the TCKind class works only for known CORBA types. For user-defined types, the TypeCode is taken care of by the generated Helper classes from idl2java. A sample IDL file is shown in Listing 12.6, and its corresponding generated helper class is shown in Listing 12.7.

LISTING 12.6 SAMPLE IDL INTERFACE TO DEMONSTRATE TypeCodes FOR USER-DEFINED TYPES

```
// Sample IDL
module DII
{
    interface LongTest
    {
        long testLong(
            in long inLongVal,
            inout long inoutLongVal,
            out long outLongVal);
    };
};
```

LISTING 12.7 SEGMENT OF THE HELPER CLASS GENERATED FOR THE IDL SHOWN IN LISTING 12.6; THIS CODE SEGMENT IS DESIGNED TO SHOW HOW UNIQUE TypeCodes ARE GENERATED FOR USER-DEFINED TYPES

```
// segment of LongTestHelper.java

....
private static org.omg.CORBA.TypeCode _type;
public static org.omg.CORBA.TypeCode type() {                    ──❶
    if(_type == null) {
      _type = _orb().create_interface_tc(id(), "LongTest");
    }
    return _type;
 }
....
```

❶ A unique TypeCode is generated for the LongTest interface.

Listing 12.7 shows that the generated helper class contains the method type() to return the TypeCode for a user-defined class.

NamedValueS

A NamedValue class holds a name and a value that represents either an input or an output argument for a DII method invocation. It is also used to represent a return value of a method request. The name is a string that represents the name of the parameter. The value is represented with an Any type. A NamedValue is obtained through a factory call to the ORB as shown in Listing 12.8.

LISTING 12.8 METHOD ON THE ORB INTERFACE USED TO CREATE A NamedValue OBJECT

```
package org.omg.CORBA;

abstract public class ORB{
    ....
public abstract org.omg.CORBA.NamedValue create_named_value
➥(java.lang.String name, Any value, int flags);
    ....
}
```

The NamedValue interface is shown in Listing 12.9.

LISTING 12.9 THE NamedValue INTERFACE

```
package org.omg.CORBA;

public interface NamedValue{
```

```java
    public java.lang.String name();
    public org.omg.CORBA.Any value();
    public int flags();
}
```

We will now examine each of the methods shown in detail.

- `name()`—Returns the name of this particular `NamedValue`.
- `value()`—Returns an `Any` type representing the value of the `NamedValue`.
- `flags()`—Returns one of the following based on the direction of the parameter:
    - ARG_IN
    - ARG_INOUT
    - ARG_OUT

The possible values for the flags are int values defined as constants in the CORBA IDL module. As you might recall from our discussion of the IDL to Java language mapping in Chapter 2, constants defined in a module but not within an interface are mapped to Java classes. The classes that hold the int values for ARG_IN, ARG_INOUT, and ARG_OUT are shown in Listing 12.10.

LISTING 12.10 THE THREE JAVA CLASSSES HOLDING THE STATIC ARG_IN, ARG_INOUT, AND ARG_OUT VALUES

```java
package org.omg.CORBA;

public final class ARG_IN{
    final public static int value = (int) 1;
}
package org.omg.CORBA;

public final class ARG_INOUT{
    final public static int value = (int) 3;
}
package org.omg.CORBA;

public final class ARG_OUT{
    final public static int value = (int) 2;
}
```

NVList

As you might have guessed from the name, the `NVList` is a class that contains a list of `NamedValue` objects. It also contains all the possible arguments for a given DII method invocation. The IDL interface for the NVList is shown in Listing 12.11. Like the other objects discussed so far in this section, a NVList is obtained through a factory call to the ORB. The methods for obtaining a NVList are shown in Listing 12.12.

LISTING 12.11 THE NVList INTERFACE

```
package org.omg.CORBA;

public interface NVList
{
    public int count();
    public void add(int flags);
    public void add_item(java.lang.String name, int flags);
    public void add_value(java.lang.String name, org.omg.CORBA.Any value,
            int flags);
    public org.omg.CORBA.NamedValue item(int index);
    public void remove(int index);
}
```

LISTING 12.12 METHODS ON THE ORB INTERFACE USED TO CREATE A NVList

```
package org.omg.CORBA;

abstract public class ORB{
    ....
public abstract org.omg.CORBA.NVList create_list(int);
public abstract org.omg.CORBA.NVList create_operation_list(
org.omg.CORBA.OperationDef);
    ....
}
```

We will now take a closer look at the methods defined on the NVList interface.

- count()—Returns the number of NamedValues in the NVList.
- add(...)—Adds a NamedValue without initializing the name or value. It initializes the parameter direction flag.
- add_item(...)—Adds a NamedValue to the list without initializing the value. It initializes the name and parameter direction flag.
- add_value(...)—Adds a NamedValue with the specified name, value, and parameter direction flag.
- item( )—Returns the specific NamedValue for the given index.
- remove( )—Removes the specific NamedValue for the given index.

Environment

The Environment interface is used exclusively to encapsulate exceptions being returned as part of DII invocations. This is necessary because exceptions alter the flow of control in a normal program by jumping to the enclosing catch block. Because a DII application is calling methods in an indirect, or constructed, manner we need an alternative way of checking for exceptions. The IDL for the Exception interface is shown in Listing 12.13. Environment objects are obtained through a factory call on the ORB interface as shown in Listing 12.14.

LISTING 12.13 THE ENVIRONMENT CLASS

```
abstract public class Environment
{
public abstract void exception(java.lang.Exception);
public abstract java.lang.Exception exception();
public abstract void clear();
public org.omg.CORBA.Environment();
}
```

LISTING 12.14 METHOD ON THE ORB INTERFACE TO CREATE AN ENVIRONMENT OBJECT

```
package org.omg.CORBA;

abstract public class ORB{
    ....
public abstract org.omg.CORBA.Environment create_environment();
....
}
```

By examining the interface shown in Listing 12.13, you can see that the Environment provides an accessor and modifier for an Exception, as well as a `clear()` method that clears the Environment of any Exception that might have been raised.

THE DYNAMIC INVOCATION INTERFACE

Until this chapter, all our development has used the many files generated from using idl2java. We will walk through the steps required to create clients that can invoke methods on remote implementations without any of the files produced by idl2java. Writing code to implement these dynamic invocation techniques uses the objects discussed in the previous section. This section begins with a discussion of how to dynamically obtain a reference to an implementation, and then discusses how to send and receive requests while accounting for possible exceptions.

Getting the Server Object Reference

As with our development using the static stubs and skeletons, the first step in a dynamic invocation is to obtain a reference to the Server Object. We spent Chapters 6–9 looking at different ways in which to obtain this initial reference. In Chapter 6, we focused on using the Smart Agent as a directory service for this purpose, introducing the static `bind()` method on the generated Helper class as a means for the Client to communicate with the Smart Agent. Today we will introduce a variation of the `bind(...)` method that might be used directly on the ORB itself without needing one of the generated Helper classes. However, any of the other methods discussed between Chapter 6 and 9 can be used to obtain the initial object reference.

A static `bind(...)` method exists on the ORB class that DII clients can use to get their initial object reference. It has the following signature:

```
public org.omg.CORBA.Object bind(java.lang.String    repository_id,
                java.lang.String object_name,
                java.lang.String host_name,
                org.omg.CORBA.BindOptions bind_options);
```

This signature is identical to the `bind(...)` method that is in the generated Helper classes with the exception of the first argument. We briefly discussed the notion of the Repository ID in Chapter 2 when we discussed IDL. The Repository ID represents a particular interface for which many implementations can exist. It takes the following format:

1. IDL: is always at the beginning of the string.
2. The fully scoped package name as indicated in the IDL, delimited with a /.
3. A :1.0 is added to the end of the string. This represents the major and minor version number of the interface. The current version of VisiBroker for Java doesn't support using multiple minor version numbers for versioning purposes. Binding will only be successful if there is an exact Repository ID match.

For example, take a look at the following IDL:

```
// IDL

module Example
{
    module Of
    {
        interface ArepositoryID
        {
        };
    };
};
```

The `ArepositoryID` interface is represented by the following `RepositoryID`:

`IDL:Example/Of/ArepositoryID:1.0`

Now that we discussed using the static `bind(...)` method on the ORB to dynamically obtain our object reference, we will discuss how to create a request.

Create a Request Object

After the initial Server Object reference is obtained, the Client must create a Request object. As the name implies, a Request object encapsulates a request (*method invocation* in Java terms) on an implementation. The interface for the Request class is shown in Listing 12.15.

LISTING 12.15 THE REQUEST CLASS

```
abstract public class org.omg.CORBA.Request
{
    public abstract org.omg.CORBA.Object target();
    public abstract java.lang.String operation();
    public abstract org.omg.CORBA.NVList arguments();
    public abstract org.omg.CORBA.NamedValue result();
    public abstract org.omg.CORBA.Environment env();
    public abstract org.omg.CORBA.ExceptionList exceptions();
    public abstract org.omg.CORBA.ContextList contexts();
    public abstract void ctx(org.omg.CORBA.Context);
    public abstract org.omg.CORBA.Context ctx();
    public abstract org.omg.CORBA.Any add_in_arg();
    public abstract org.omg.CORBA.Any add_named_in_arg(java.lang.String);
    public abstract org.omg.CORBA.Any add_inout_arg();
    public abstract org.omg.CORBA.Any add_named_inout_arg(java.lang.String);
    public abstract org.omg.CORBA.Any add_out_arg();
    public abstract org.omg.CORBA.Any add_named_out_arg(java.lang.String);
    public abstract void set_return_type(org.omg.CORBA.TypeCode);
    public abstract org.omg.CORBA.Any return_value();
    ....
    public org.omg.CORBA.Request();
}
```

A Request object is obtained through calls found on the `org.omg.CORBA.Object` interface. These calls on the Object class are shown in Listing 12.16.

LISTING 12.16 METHODS ON THE OBJECT INTERFACE AVAILABLE FOR CREATING REQUEST OBJECTS

```
package org.omg.CORBA;

public interface Object
{
    ...
    public org.omg.CORBA.Request _request(java.lang.String operation);
```

continues

LISTING 12.16 CONTINUED

```
    public org.omg.CORBA.Request _create_request(org.omg.CORBA.Context ctx,
                    java.lang.String operation,
                    org.omg.CORBA.NVList    arg_list,
                    org.omg.CORBA.NamedValue result);

    public org.omg.CORBA.Request _create_request(org.omg.CORBA.Context ctx,
                    java.lang.String operation,
                    org.omg.CORBA.NVList arg_list,
                    org.omg.CORBA.NamedValue result,
                    org.omg.CORBA.TypeCode[ ] exceptions,
                    java.lang.String[ ] contexts);
    ...
}
```

We will now examine the three different Request creation methods. `_request(...)` creates an empty Request object, having only an operation name. Simply creating a Request object with the appropriate operation name isn't enough to send to the Server Object.

Before the Request is passed, you must initialize all `in` and `inout` parameters, and have local variables available for the `out` parameters and return types. An example of how to use this call is shown in Listing 12.18, by invoking an implementation of the Interface shown in Listing 12.17.

LISTING 12.17 SAMPLE IDL INTERFACE TO DEMONSTRATE USE OF DII

```
// IDL

module DII
{
    interface LongTest
    {
        long testLong(
            in long inLongVal,
            inout long inoutLongVal,
            out long outLongVal);
    };
};
```

LISTING 12.18 SUBSET OF A DII CLIENT CREATING AN EMPTY REQUEST OBJECT AND SETTING THE ARGUMENTS AND RETURN VALUES EXPLICITLY

```
// Segment of Client.java

...
// Create a Request Object
```

```
org.omg.CORBA.Request request = longTest._request("testLong");

// Construct our "in" argument and initialize
org.omg.CORBA.Any inLongVal = request.add_in_arg();
inLongVal.insert_long(5);

// Construct an "inout" argument and initialize
org.omg.CORBA.Any inoutLongVal = request.add_inout_arg();
org.omg.CORBA.IntHolder inoutLongValHolder = new org.omg.CORBA.IntHolder(5);
inoutLongVal.insert_long(inoutLongValHolder.value);

// Construct an "out" argument
org.omg.CORBA.Any outLongVal = request.add_out_arg();
outLongVal.type(orb.get_primitive_tc(org.omg.CORBA.TCKind.tk_long));

// Set the return value
request.set_return_type(orb.get_primitive_tc(
    org.omg.CORBA.TCKind.tk_long));
```

Listing 12.18 shows an example of a client that used the simple _request(...) method to obtain a Request object. We will now take a look at an alternative approach to creating and populating a Request.

_create_request(...) is an overloaded method that provides two signatures for creating Request objects with all the necessary information to execute the operation. Passing all information in the Request creation call is a different approach from the _request() method that requires the user to explicitly set all Request parameters after creation. We will now take a closer look at each of the parameters in the _create_request(...) method. The parameters are

- ctx—This arepresents the implicit Context argument that can be appended to any method call by defining a Context object within the IDL. It can be left null if the application isn't using a Context object. For more details on how a Context is defined, refer to Chapter 3.
- operation—The name of the server method you want to invoke, such as testLong from our example.
- arg_list—A list of NamedValue objects that represent the arguments being passed to the method.
- result—A NamedValue object representing the result value from the method invocation.

We will take a look at how the Client looks using one of the _create_request() methods in Listing 12.19.

LISTING 12.19 A SUBSET OF A DII CLIENT USING THE _create_request() METHOD TO INVOKE AN IMPLEMENTATION OF THE INTERFACE SHOWN IN LISTING 12.17

```java
// segment of Client.java

....
//Declare a Context
org.omg.CORBA.Context ctx =  null;

//Create a NVList
org.omg.CORBA.NVList argList = orb.create_list(3);

// Create our "in" argument, initialize it, and add it to the argument
// list NVList
org.omg.CORBA.Any inLongVal = orb.create_any();
inLongVal.insert_long(5);
argList.add_value("inValue", inLongVal, org.omg.CORBA.ARG_IN.value);

// Create our "inout" argument, initialize it, and add it to the argument list
// NVList
org.omg.CORBA.Any inoutLongVal = orb.create_any();
org.omg.CORBA.IntHolder inoutLongValHolder = new org.omg.CORBA.IntHolder(5);
inoutLongVal.insert_long(inoutLongValHolder.value);
argList.add_value("inoutValue", inoutLongVal, org.omg.CORBA.ARG_INOUT.value);

// Create our "out" argument, and add it to the argument list NVList
org.omg.CORBA.Any outLongVal = orb.create_any();
outLongVal.type(orb.get_primitive_tc(org.omg.CORBA.TCKind.tk_long));
argList.add_value("outValue", outLongVal, org.omg.CORBA.ARG_OUT.value);

// Create our "return value" so it can be added to the resultSet NamedValue
org.omg.CORBA.Any returnVal = orb.create_any();
returnVal.type(orb.get_primitive_tc(org.omg.CORBA.TCKind.tk_long));

// Create a NamedValue to hold the return value.
org.omg.CORBA.NamedValue resultSet = orb.create_named_value("resultSet",
➥returnVal, org.omg.CORBA.ARG_OUT.value);

//Create a Request
org.omg.CORBA.Request request = longTest._create_request(ctx, "testLong",
➥argList, resultSet);
```

Careful examination of Listing 12.19 reveals that the Context object was left null. Listing 12.20 is a modified version of your simple IDL file that now uses a Context object.

LISTING 12.20 MODIFICATION OF THE IDL SHOWN IN LISTING 12.17 DEMONSTRATING THE USE OF PASSING CONTEXT OBJECTS

```
// IDL for Context example

module DII
{
      interface LongTest
      {
            long testLong(    in long inLongVal,
                  inout long inoutLongVal,
                  out long outLongVal)
                        context("MyUsername", "MyPassword");
      };
};
```

In Listing 12.20, we have added a Context with two values, MyUSerName and MyPassword to our already familiar LongTest interface. A client that uses the Context defined on LongTest is shown in Listing 12.21.

LISTING 12.21 MODIFICATION OF THE CLIENT CODE SHOWN IN LISTING 12.18 DEMONSTRATING HOW TO INITIALIZE A CONTEXT OBJECT AND PASS IT AS PART OF A DII REQUEST

```
The Client.java:

// segment of Client.java demonstrating how to pass a Context object in a DII
// Request

.....
//Create a Context
org.omg.CORBA.Context ctx =  orb.get_default_context();

// Create an Any for our first Context string, add it to the Context object
org.omg.CORBA.Any anyUsername = orb.create_any();
anyUsername.insert_string("ralph");
ctx.set_one_value("MyUsername", anyUsername);

// Create an Any for our second Context string, add it to the Context object
org.omg.CORBA.Any anyPasswd = orb.create_any();
anyPasswd.insert_string("monkey");
ctx.set_one_value("MyPassword", anyPasswd);

// Create a Request
org.omg.CORBA.Request request = longTest._create_request(ctx, "testLong",
➥argList, resultSet);
```

continues

LISTING 12.21 CONTINUED

```
// Create ContextList, which will hold our Context by adding our Context
// Strings
org.omg.CORBA.ContextList ctxlst=request.contexts();
ctxlst.add("MyUsername");
ctxlst.add("MyPassword");

// Make the invocation
request.invoke();
```

It is important to note that if a Context Object is being passed to the Server Object, the Server Object must be prepared to receive it. Listing 12.22 is an example Server Object for the Context-based Client shown in Listing 12.21.

LISTING 12.22 A SUBSET OF THE LongTestImpl SERVER OBJECT, DEMONSTRATING HOW A SERVER OBJECT RECEIVES A CONTEXT OBJECT PASSED FROM THE CLIENT

```
// segment of LongTestImpl.java demonstrating how to interpret a Context object

public int testLong(    int inLongVal,
                        org.omg.CORBA.IntHolder inoutLongVal,
                        org.omg.CORBA.IntHolder outLongVal,
                        org.omg.CORBA.Context _context)
{
     org.omg.CORBA.NVList nvList = _context.get_values(null ,0, "My*");

     for(int i=0; i < nvList.count(); i++)
     {
          try
          {
               org.omg.CORBA.NamedValue nv = nvList.item(i);
               System.out.println("For Context element:" + i + " the
                    name is: " + nv.name() + " and the
                    value is: " + nv.value());
          }
          catch (Exception ex)
          {
               ex.printStackTrace();
          }
     }
                //For observation, print out the parameters
                //before as passed to this method
                System.out.println("Begining testLong() method\n" +
                         "\tin parameter" + inLongVal + "\n" +
                         "\tinout parameter " + inoutLongVal.value +
                         "\n" +"\tout parameter " + outLongVal.value);

          //Change the value of the in parameter.  Note that
```

```
                //this is done to show that this new value is
                //NOT carried back to the client
                inLongVal = 6;

                //Change value of inout parameter
                inoutLongVal.value = 6;

                //Set value of the out parameter
                outLongVal.value = 6;

                //For observation, print out the parameters
                //before the return
                System.out.println("About to return from testLong()
                            method\n" +"\tin parameter" + inLongVal +
                            "\n" + "\tinout parameter " + inoutLongVal.value
                            + "\n" + "\tout parameter " + outLongVal.value);

                return 0;
        }
```

Now that we have discussed the approaches for creating a request, we will now examine how to send the request to a server implementation.

Send the Request

There are several different ways to send your Request Object to the Server. Listing 12.23 shows the methods on the Request class relevant to submitting the Request.

LISTING 12.23 A SUBSET OF THE REQUEST CLASS

```
abstract public class Request extends java.lang.Object
{
    ...
    public abstract void invoke();
    public abstract void send_oneway();
    public abstract void send_deferred();
    public abstract void get_response();
    public abstract Boolean poll_response();
    ....
}
```

We will now examine in detail each of the five methods shown in Listing 12.23.

- `invoke()`—Sends the method invocation and blocks until the method returns. It follows the same behavior as that of a normal two-way method call using an IDL stub.
- `send_oneway()`—Sends the method invocation as a *oneway* method, following normal oneway semantics. It won't block, it simply sends the request and doesn't wait for a response.

- **send_deferred()**—Sends the method invocation but doesn't block and wait for a response. It allows method invocations to be made asynchronously. Clients use the poll_response() and get_response() to get the return values when the method has completed.
- **get_response()**—Retrieves the return values from a method invocation that is issued with the send_deferred() method. Clients will first call poll_response() to determine whether the response has come back to the Client. When poll_response() comes back with a true, the Client calls get_response() to retrieve the results.
- **poll_response()**—Returns a Boolean value indicating whether the response from the send_deferred() method has returned.

Two approaches are leveraged with these five methods. The first two methods, invoke() and send_oneway(), reflect the normal blocking semantics of an invoke. The last three methods leverage an alternative approach where the client can send a request, and then poll for the response. We will examine an example of each, beginning with a client using the invoke() method as shown in Listing 12.24.

LISTING 12.24 A COMPLETE DII CLIENT FOR THE SAME IDL INTERFACE SHOWN IN LISTING 12.17, DEMONSTRATING THE USE OF THE invoke() METHOD TO ACTUALLY PASS THE REQUEST TO THE SERVER

```
// An example of the invoke() method in Client.java

public class Client
{
        public static void main(String[] args)
        {
                try
                {
                        //Initialize the ORB
                        org.omg.CORBA.ORB orb = org.omg.CORBA.ORB.init();

                        //Bind to the Implementation
                        org.omg.CORBA.Object longTest = orb.bind("IDL:DII/
                        ⇒LongTest:1.0", "LongTest", null, null);

                        // Create a Request Object
                        org.omg.CORBA.Request request = longTest._
                        ⇒request("testLong");

                        // Create and initialize our "in" argument
                        org.omg.CORBA.Any inLongVal = request.add_in_arg();
                        inLongVal.insert_long(5);

                        // Create and initialize our "inout" argument
```

```java
                    org.omg.CORBA.Any inoutLongVal = request.add_inout_arg();
                    org.omg.CORBA.IntHolder inoutLongValHolder = new org.
                    ➥omg.CORBA.IntHolder(5);
                    inoutLongVal.insert_long(inoutLongValHolder.value);

                    // Create our "out" argument
                    org.omg.CORBA.Any outLongVal = request.add_out_arg();
                    outLongVal.type(orb.get_primitive_tc(
                        org.omg.CORBA.TCKind.tk_long));

                    // Set the return value
                    request.set_return_type(orb.get_primitive_tc(
                        org.omg.CORBA.TCKind.tk_long));

                    // Make the invocation to the Server
                    request.invoke();

                    java.lang.Exception exception = request.env().exception();
                    if(exception != null)
                    {
                        throw (org.omg.CORBA.SystemException) exception;
                    }

                    int result = request.return_value().extract_long();

                    // Display the results
                    inoutLongValHolder.value = inoutLongVal.extract_long();
                    int outLong = outLongVal.extract_long();

                    //For observation, print out the parameters after making
                    ➥ the call
                    System.out.println("After calling testLong() method\n" +
                            "\tin parameter" + inLongVal.extract_long() +
                            ➥"\n" +
                            "\tinout parameter " + inoutLongValHolder.value +
                            "\n" + "\tout parameter " + outLong);
            }
            catch(org.omg.CORBA.SystemException ex)
            {
                    ex.printStackTrace();
            }
        }
    }
}
```

Listing 12.24 demonstrated the use of the `invoke()` call to reflect the normal, nonblocking semantics of a non-oneway call. Listing 12.25 shows a Client sending the same Request using the asynchronous `send_deferred()` approach.

LISTING 12.25 A CLIENT DEMONSTRATING THE USE OF THE send_deferred() AND get_response() METHODS FOR AN IMPLEMENTATION OF THE IDL SHOWN IN LISTING 12.17

```java
// Example of using the asynchronous send_deferred() call to the Server

public class Client
{
    public static void main(String[] args)
    {
        try
        {
            //Initialize the ORB
            org.omg.CORBA.ORB orb = org.omg.CORBA.ORB.init();

            //Bind to the Implementation
            org.omg.CORBA.Object longTest = orb.bind("IDL:DII/
            LongTest:1.0", "LongTest",null, null);

            // Create a Request Object
            org.omg.CORBA.Request request = longTest._request
            ("testLong");

            // Create and initialize our "in" argument
            org.omg.CORBA.Any inLongVal = request.add_in_arg();
            inLongVal.insert_long(5);

            // Create and initialize our "inout" argument
            org.omg.CORBA.Any inoutLongVal = request.add_inout_arg();
            org.omg.CORBA.IntHolder inoutLongValHolder =
            new org.omg.CORBA.IntHolder(5);
            inoutLongVal.insert_long(inoutLongValHolder.value);

            // Create and initialize our "out" argument
            org.omg.CORBA.Any outLongVal = request.add_out_arg();
            outLongVal.type(orb.get_primitive_tc(
                org.omg.CORBA.TCKind.tk_long));

            // Set the return value
            request.set_return_type(orb.get_primitive_tc(
                org.omg.CORBA.TCKind.tk_long));

            // Make asynchronous invocation to the Server
            try
            {
                request.send_deferred();
                System.out.println("Send deferred call is made");
            }
            catch(org.omg.CORBA.SystemException e)
            {
```

```
            System.out.println("Error while sending request...");
            System.out.println(e);
        }

        while (request.poll_response() == false)
        {
            try
            {
                System.out.println("Waiting for response");
                Thread.sleep(1000);
            }
            catch(Exception e)
            {
                System.out.println(e);
            }
        }

        try
{
    request.get_response();
}
catch(Exception except)
{
    except.printStackTrace();
}

java.lang.Exception exception = request.env().exception();
if(exception != null)
{
    throw (org.omg.CORBA.SystemException) exception;
}

int result = request.return_value().extract_long();

// Display the results
inoutLongValHolder.value = inoutLongVal.extract_long();
int outLong = outLongVal.extract_long();

//For observation, print out the parameters after making the call
System.out.println("After calling testLong() method\n" +
        "\tin parameter" + inLongVal.extract_long() + "\n" +
        "\tinout parameter " + inoutLongValHolder.value + "\n" +
        "\tout parameter " + outLong);
    }
    catch(org.omg.CORBA.SystemException ex)
    {
            ex.printStackTrace();
    }
        }
    }
}
```

Multiple Requests

The DII allows you to create an array of separate Request Objects that can all be sent to the Server Object at the same time. Multiple requests can be sent either one way or deferred.

In order to send multiple requests, take a look at Listing 12.26.

LISTING 12.26 METHODS ON THE ORB INTERFACE FOR SENDING MULTIPLE REQUESTS AT THE SAME TIME

```
package org.omg.CORBA;

abstract public class ORB
{
    ....
    abstract public void send_multiple_requests_oneway(Request reqs[ ]);
    abstract public void send_multiple_requests_deferred(Request reqs[ ]);
    ....
}
```

If multiple requests are sent in a deferred manner, two methods must be used to get the results from the Requests as shown in listing 12.27.

LISTING 12.27 METHODS ON THE ORB INTERFACE FOR OBTAINING THE RESULTS OF THE METHODS THAT ARE INVOKED AT THE SAME TIME

```
package org.omg.CORBA;

abstract public class ORB
{
    ....
    abstract public Boolean poll_next_response ( );
    abstract public org.omg.CORBA.Request get_next_response( );
    ....
}
```

The `poll_next_response()` method indicates whether a response has been received from any of the Request Objects. If a `True` value is returned, this indicates that at least one of the Request Objects has returned.

The `get_next_response()` method should be used to receive the response, after the `poll_next_response()` has returned a `True` value.

Handling Return Types

Now that we have created requests and sent them to the Server, we need to discuss how to interpret the response from the Server. Several methods must be used to set and handle a return type, depending on which approach you took in creating the Request.

If using the `_request()` method to create a Request Object, you need to implement the following steps to retrieve a return value. Note that for each step, we will include a snippet of code that demonstrates the use of appropriate methods.

1. Call set_return_type(TypeCode tc) on the Request Object. This requires that you make use of the TypeCode and TCKind classes in order to pass the appropriate TypeCode to the Request Object.

   ```
   request.set_return_type(orb.get_primitive_tc(org.omg.CORBA.TCKind.tk_long));
   ```

2. Obtain the return value by calling return_value() method on the Request Object. This method returns an Any type, so you will have to use the appropriate extraction technique, depending on whether the contexts are user defined or of known type.

   ```
   ....
       int result = request.return_value().extract_long();
   ....
   ```

Creating the Request using the `_request(...)` method on org.omg.CORBA.Object requires the steps listed previously to retrieve the response for the server. If using `_create_request()` to create a Request Object, you must follow a slightly different approach. We will now walk through this approach, showing example code for each step.

1. Create an Any value to hold the return value.

   ```
       ....
       org.omg.CORBA.Any returnVal = orb.create_any();
       ....
   ```

2. Initialize the Any with the appropriate Typecode, so the Any knows what type of value to expect.

   ```
       ...
       returnVal.type(orb.get_primitive_tc(org.omg.CORBA.TCKind.tk_long));
       ...
   ```

3. Because the `_create_request()` method holds the return value in its own specific NamedValue object, we must create a NamedValue as a holder and pass it to the `_create_request(...)` method.

   ```
       ...
       org.omg.CORBA.NamedValue resultSet = orb.create_named_value
       ("resultSet", returnVal, org.omg.CORBA.ARG_OUT.value);
       ...
       ....
   ```

```
        org.omg.CORBA.Request request =
        longTest._create_request(ctx, "testLong", argList, resultSet);
             ....
```

We have shown that, depending on your Request creation approach, retrieving the response follows one of two different approaches. The last topic we must cover in our discussion of DII is how to discover and handle error conditions—exceptions.

Exceptions

As we mentioned in our discussion of the Environment object, the Environment is used to pass exceptions when using DII calls. In order to learn of an exception within a DII Client, you must obtain the Environment Object from the Request Object and call `exception()` on the Environment to determine if an exception has occurred. Listing 12.28 shows a client using the Environment class to discover an exception.

LISTING 12.28 HOW TO CATCH EXCEPTIONS WITHIN A DII CLIENT

```
java.lang.Exception exception = request.env().exception();
if(exception != null)
{
        throw (org.omg.CORBA.SystemException) exception;
}
```

The idl2java Shortcut

At this point you might be thinking to yourself, "This DII stuff requires more coding than using the static stubs!" This is unfortunately true because we are reproducing a lot of the work the generated stubs do for us. We will now introduce a technique to cut down on some of this extra coding.

One of the most useful features of the idl2java compiler is the `-portable` option. Running the idl2java compiler with the `-portable` flag set generates a special portable stub that can be used to run your Client on any compliant CORBA ORB. However, it is also a wonderful shortcut to automatically generate your own DII client with only minimal coding on your part.

Listing 12.29 is the sample IDL introduced in Listing 12.17 that we have been using throughout this chapter.

LISTING 12.29—A SAMPLE IDL FILE TO DEMONSTRATE THE IDL2JAVA SHORTCUT FOR DII

```
module DII
{
    interface LongTest
    {
```

```
        long testLong(
            in long inLongVal,
            inout long inoutLongVal,
            out long outLongVal);
    };
};
```

Now, run this through your idl2java compiler with the `-portable` option set:

```
C:\>idl2java -portable longTest.idl
Traversing longTest.idl
Creating: DII
Creating: DII\LongTest.java
Creating: DII\LongTestHolder.java
Creating: DII\LongTestHelper.java
Creating: DII\_portable_stub_LongTest.java          ❶
Creating: DII\_LongTestImplBase.java
Creating: DII\LongTestOperations.java
Creating: DII\_tie_LongTest.java
Creating: DII\_example_LongTest.java
```

❶ Hmm....This looks new.

The `-portable_stub_LongTest.java` is going to provide us our shortcut code for DII clients. Listing 12.30 shows the generated source file for the portable stub.

LISTING 12.30 SPECIAL CLIENT CODE GENERATED FROM THE `-portable` OPTION ON THE IDL2JAVA COMPILER

```java
package DII;

public class _portable_stub_LongTest extends org.omg.CORBA.portable.ObjectImpl
 implements DII.LongTest {
  protected DII.LongTest _wrapper = null;
  public DII.LongTest _this() {
    return this;
  }
  public java.lang.String[] _ids() {
    return __ids;
  }
  private static java.lang.String[] __ids = {
    "IDL:DII/LongTest:1.0"
  };

  public int testLong(
    int inLongVal,
    org.omg.CORBA.IntHolder inoutLongVal,
    org.omg.CORBA.IntHolder outLongVal)
  {
      org.omg.CORBA.Request _request = this._request("testLong");
```

continues

LISTING 12.30 CONTINUED

```
    _request.set_return_type(_orb().get_primitive_tc
➥(org.omg.CORBA.TCKind.tk_long));
    org.omg.CORBA.Any $inLongVal = _request.add_in_arg();
    $inLongVal.insert_long(inLongVal);
    org.omg.CORBA.Any $inoutLongVal = _request.add_inout_arg();
    $inoutLongVal.insert_long(inoutLongVal.value);
    org.omg.CORBA.Any $outLongVal = _request.add_out_arg();
    $outLongVal.type(_orb().get_primitive_tc(org.omg.CORBA.TCKind.tk_long));
    _request.invoke();
    java.lang.Exception _exception = _request.env().exception();
    if(_exception != null) {
      throw (org.omg.CORBA.SystemException) _exception;
    }
    int _result;
    _result = _request.return_value().extract_long();
    inoutLongVal.value = $inoutLongVal.extract_long();
    outLongVal.value = $outLongVal.extract_long();
    return _result;
  }
}
```

Take a close look at the body of the `testLong()` method in Listing 12.30. You should notice that this code is exactly the same as the DII Client written by hand earlier in the chapter, and this was just generated automatically for us!

Typically, you will write your Clients using the DII because you won't know ahead of time what the IDL of the Server Objects will be. Most situations involving a DII Client have lookups to the Interface Repository in order to get the necessary interface information on the Server Objects. However, if you do know the IDL of the Server Objects you want to connect to at build time, the `-portable` option on the idl2java compiler is an invaluable shortcut to writing Clients.

This shortcut concludes our discussion of the DII. We will now introduce the logical "other half" to our dynamic clients, dynamic server objects through the Dynamic Skeleton Interface.

THE DYNAMIC SKELETON INTERFACE

The Dynamic Skeleton Interface (DSI) is very similar in design to the DII, except that it is used for Server Implementations instead of Clients. The DSI provides a generic mechanism to build Server Objects such that they aren't required to extend the generated Server Skeleton class, the XXXImplBase.java file that is generated, with the XXX representing the interface name. When using the DII, we noticed that we weren't required to make any modifications to the Server Object. A Server Object could handle either Clients built with static stubs or DII

Clients in the exact same fashion. The same is true for Server Objects implemented with the DSI; they can handle either Clients with static stubs or DII invokes.

Steps Needed to Use the DSI

Instead of having your Server implementations extending from the generated `ImplBase` skeleton class, the Server Object Implementation must extend the `org.omg.CORBA.DynamicImplementation` class. We will take a look at this class in Listing 12.31.

LISTING 12.31 THE `DynamicImplementation` CLASS

```
abstract public class org.omg.CORBA.DynamicImplementation extends
org.omg.CORBA.portable.ObjectImpl
{
        public abstract void invoke(org.omg.CORBA.ServerRequest);
        public org.omg.CORBA.DynamicImplementation();
        protected org.omg.CORBA.DynamicImplementation(java.lang.String,
            java.lang.String);
        protected org.omg.CORBA.DynamicImplementation(java.lang.String,
            java.lang.String[]);
        public java.lang.String _object_name();
        public java.lang.String _ids()[ ];
}
```

The key method to notice in Listing 12.31 is the `invoke(...)` method. This serves as the general method that the ORB calls when one of the methods on the Server Object is called. After `invoke(...)` is called, it is the responsibility of the Server Object to determine which method is being called, and then take the appropriate action. In order to understand how to use the `invoke(...)` method, we need to understand what the argument being passed in is. Listing 12.32 shows the methods on the `ServerRequest` object.

LISTING 12.32 THE `ServerRequest` CLASS

```
public abstract synchronized class org.omg.CORBA.ServerRequest extends
        java.lang.Object
{
    public abstract java.lang.String op_name();
    public abstract org.omg.CORBA.Context ctx();
    public abstract void params(org.omg.CORBA.NVList);
    public abstract void result(org.omg.CORBA.Any);
    public abstract void except(org.omg.CORBA.Any);
    public org.omg.CORBA.ServerRequest();
}
```

Thus, you can see that the `ServerRequest` object serves to handle all the information sent from the Client and all the information to be passed back to the Client. We will now take a closer look at each of the methods on the `ServerRequest` object.

> **NOTE**
>
> It is worth noting that the `ServerRequest` object has a rather misleading interface. `op_name()` and `ctx()` are accessors for the operation name and Context that were passed from the client. `result()` is essentialy a *set result* method to populate the result to send back to the client. The `params()` method looks similar to the `result()` method, except it is called to get rather than set information. When using the `ServerRequest` object, it is handy to think of the `params()` method as meaning "please populate the `NVList` that I am passing with the parameters sent by the calling client, and re-examine after I finish for any `inout` and `out` parameters".

- `op_name()`—Returns the name of the method that tells the Server Object which method the Client is trying to invoke.
- `ctx()`—Returns the Context passed from the Client.
- `params(...)`—A call into the `ServerRequest` object to populate a `NVList` with the parameters sent from the client. It also holds any `inout` and `out` parameters that should be sent back to the calling Holder objects.
- `result(...)`—Sets the return value to be sent to the client.
- `except(...)`—Sets an exception to be sent back to the calling client.

Now, we will demonstrate a Server Implementation that was implemented using the DSI shown in Listing 12.33. Note that this Server implementation is for the IDL from Listing 12.17 used throughout the chapter.

LISTING 12.33 A DSI SERVER FOR THE IDL SHOWN IN LISTING 12.17

```
// LongTestImpl.java

public class LongTestImpl extends org.omg.CORBA.DynamicImplementation
{
    LongTestImpl(java.lang.String name)
    {
        super(name, "IDL:DSI/LongTest:1.0");                    ❶
    }

    public void invoke(org.omg.CORBA.ServerRequest _request)
    {
```

```
if(!_request.op_name().equals("testLong"))                    ──❷
        {
            throw new org.omg.CORBA.BAD_OPERATION(_request.op_name());
        }

        // First,  create an empty NVList to hold the argument list
        org.omg.CORBA.NVList _params = _orb().create_list(0);

        // Next, create an Any for each parameter and add it to the NVList
        // Let's start with the "in" argument
        org.omg.CORBA.Any inAny = _orb().create_any();
        inAny.type(_orb().get_primitive_tc(org.omg.CORBA.TCKind.tk_long));
        params.add_value("inLongVal", inAny, org.omg.CORBA.ARG_IN.value);

        // Now the "inout" argument
        org.omg.CORBA.Any inoutAny = _orb().create_any();
        inoutAny.type(_orb().get_primitive_tc(org.omg.CORBA.TCKind.tk_long));
        params.add_value("inoutLongVal", inoutAny, org.omg.CORBA.ARG_INOUT.
➥value);

        // Now the "out" argument
        org.omg.CORBA.Any outAny = _orb().create_any();
        outAny.type(_orb().get_primitive_tc(org.omg.CORBA.TCKind.tk_long));
        params.add_value("outLongVal", outAny, org.omg.CORBA.ARG_OUT.value);

        // Pass in the params to be populated
        request.params(_params);

        // Now extract the "in" & "inout" parameters and create new values to send
        // back for "inout" and "out" parameters
        int inLongVal;
        inLongVal = inAny.extract_long();

        org.omg.CORBA.IntHolder inoutLongVal = new org.omg.CORBA.IntHolder();
        inoutLongVal.value = inoutAny.extract_long();

        org.omg.CORBA.IntHolder outLongVal = new org.omg.CORBA.IntHolder();

        // Make the actual invocation itself
        int _result = this.testLong(inLongVal,inoutLongVal,outLongVal);

        // Prepare the return value
        org.omg.CORBA.Any _resultAny = _orb().create_any();
        resultAny.insert_long(_result);
        request.result(_resultAny);

        inoutAny.insert_long(inoutLongVal.value);
        outAny.insert_long(outLongVal.value);
        return;
```

continues

LISTING 12.33 CONTINUED

```java
    }

    public int testLong(
        int inLongVal,
        org.omg.CORBA.IntHolder inoutLongVal,
        org.omg.CORBA.IntHolder outLongVal)
    {
        //For observation, print out the parameters
        //before as passed to this method
        System.out.println("Begining testLong() method\n" +
            "\tin parameter" + inLongVal + "\n" +
            "\tinout parameter " + inoutLongVal.value + "\n" +
            "\tout parameter " + outLongVal.value);

        //Change the value of the in parameter.  Note that
        //this is done to show that this new value is
        //NOT carried back to the client
        inLongVal = 6;

        //Change value of inout parameter
        inoutLongVal.value = 6;

        //Set value of the out parameter
        outLongVal.value = 6;

        //For observation, print out the parameters
        //before the return
        System.out.println("About to return from testLong() method\n" +
            "\tin parameter" + inLongVal + "\n" +
            "\tinout parameter " + inoutLongVal.value + "\n" +
            "\tout parameter " + outLongVal.value);

        return 0;
    }

    //Put registration code here in a main for convienence
    public static void main(String[] args)
    {
        try
        {
            // Initialize the ORB.
            org.omg.CORBA.ORB orb = org.omg.CORBA.ORB.init();

            // Initialize the BOA.
            org.omg.CORBA.BOA boa = orb.BOA_init();

            // Create the RequestReply objects.
            LongTestImpl longTest=
                new LongTestImpl("LongTest");
```

```
            // Export the newly create object.
            boa.obj_is_ready(longTest);

            System.out.println(longTest + " is ready.");

            // Wait for incoming requests
            boa.impl_is_ready();
        }
        catch(org.omg.CORBA.SystemException ex)
        {
            ex.printStackTrace();
        }
    }
}
```

- ❶ The second argument to the persistent DSI constructor is the Repository ID. If you forgot how these are constructed, refer to the earlier section on DII.
- ❷ Here we must check to see which of the Objects methods are being invoked. In this example it is easy because we are only implementing one method.

We will now review the steps that must be taken within the invoke( ) method in order to handle the parameters being passed to each of the methods. They are

1. Create a NamedValue List (NVList) so that you might construct a parameter list for the method. This will be used to retrieve any parameters sent from the client and to modify and inout or out parameters.

```
org.omg.CORBA.NVList _params = _orb().create_list(0);
```

2. Just as with your DII Clients, construct an Any object to hold the value of each parameter. Initialize the TypeCode of the Any as well as indicate the direction of the parameter (ARG_IN, ARG_INOUT, or ARG_OUT).

```
// First create the Any
org.omg.CORBA.Any inAny = _orb().create_any();

// Set the TypeCode
inAny.type(_orb().get_primitive_tc
        ↪(org.omg.CORBA.TCKind.tk_long));

// Add to the NVList setting the appropriate direction
params.add_value("inLongVal", inAny,
        org.omg.CORBA.ARG_IN.value);
```

3. Call the param() method on the ServerRequest to set the parameter list. Thus far you have only set up the appropriate space and structure for the incoming parameters; the call to param( ) actually populates the NVList that you pass in with the actual parameters. After the actual parameters are received, extract them for processing.

```
// Set the parameter list to be returned to the Client
request.params(_params);
```

```
            // Now extract the "in" & "inout" parameters and create
            // new values to send back for
            //"inout" and "out" parameters
            int inLongVal;
            inLongVal = inAny.extract_long();

            org.omg.CORBA.IntHolder inoutLongVal = new
                org.omg.CORBA.IntHolder();
            inoutLongVal.value = inoutAny.extract_long();

            org.omg.CORBA.IntHolder outLongVal = new
                org.omg.CORBA.IntHolder();

            // Make the actual invocation
            int _result = this.testLong(inLongVal,inoutLongVal,
                outLongVal);
```

4. Prepare the return value. This is done in a similar manner to the initialization needed by the in, inout, and out arguments.

```
            // Make the invocation, receiving a return value
            int _result = this.testLong(inLongVal,inoutLongVal,outLongVal);

            // Create an Any to hold the return value
            org.omg.CORBA.Any _resultAny = _orb().create_any();

            // Insert the return value into the Any
            resultAny.insert_long(_result);

            // Call _result() to set the return value to be passed
            // back to the Client.
            request.result(_resultAny);
```

This concludes our discussion of implementing a Server using the DSI. It should have looked very familiar because most of the techniques mirror the DII. As with the DII, there is also a shortcut you can take to build your dynamic server. We will now discuss this shortcut.

The idl2java Shortcut for DSI

As with the DII, the `-portable` option also automatically generates the majority of the DSI code you need to use to implement your dynamic Server. When using the `-portable` option on the idl2java compiler, the skeleton it creates actually already extends from the `DynamicImplementation` class. Thus, using the DSI skeleton allows you to run your Server Object on top of any CORBA-compliant ORB. Moreover, you will see that in this generated DSI skeleton is an implementation of the `invoke( )` method that you can make use of with very few changes.

Running our LongTest IDL file from Listing 12.17 through the idl2java compiler with the `-portable` flag produces a file _LongTestImplBase.

```
C:\>idl2java -portable longTest.idl
Traversing longTest.idl
Creating: DSI
Creating: DSI\LongTest.java
Creating: DSI\LongTestHolder.java
Creating: DSI\LongTestHelper.java
Creating: DSI\_portable_stub_LongTest.java
Creating: DSI\_LongTestImplBase.java
Creating: DSI\LongTestOperations.java
Creating: DSI\_tie_LongTest.java
Creating: DSI\_example_LongTest.java
```

Because we used the -portable flag, the _LongTestImplBase now supports dynamic invocation. Now, examine the _LongTestImplBase.java shown in Listing 12.34. It shows the Server skeleton generated for the IDL in Listing 12.17 using the -portable flag.

LISTING 12.34 THE -portable OPTION GENERATES A FULL IMPLEMENTATION OF THE invoke() METHOD THAT CAN BE USED IN YOUR DSI SERVER IMPLEMENTATION

```java
package DSI;

abstract public class _LongTestImplBase extends
        org.omg.CORBA.DynamicImplementation implements DSI.LongTest          ❶
{
protected DSI.LongTest _wrapper = null;

public DSI.LongTest _this()
{
        return this;
}

private java.lang.String _name;
public String _object_name()
{
        return _name;
}

protected _LongTestImplBase(java.lang.String name)
{
        name = name;
}

public _LongTestImplBase()
{
}

public java.lang.String[] _ids()
{
        return __ids;
```

continues

LISTING 12.34 CONTINUED

```
}

private static java.lang.String[ ] __ids =
{
        "IDL:DSI/LongTest:1.0"
};

private static java.util.Dictionary _methods = new java.util.Hashtable();
static {
__methods.put("testLong", new java.lang.Integer(0));
}

public void invoke(org.omg.CORBA.ServerRequest _request)                    ❷
{
        DSI.LongTest _self = this;
        java.lang.Object _method = _methods.get(_request.op_name());

        if(_method == null)
        {
                throw new org.omg.CORBA.BAD_OPERATION(_request.op_name());
        }

        int _method_id = ((java.lang.Integer) _method).intValue();
        switch(_method_id)
        {
            case 0:
            {
              org.omg.CORBA.NVList _params = _orb().create_list(0);
              org.omg.CORBA.Any $inLongVal = _orb().create_any();
              $inLongVal.type(_orb().get_primitive_tc
                  (org.omg.CORBA.TCKind.tk_long));
              _params.add_value("inLongVal", $inLongVal,
                  org.omg.CORBA.ARG_IN.value);
              org.omg.CORBA.Any $inoutLongVal = _orb().create_any();
              $inoutLongVal.type(_orb().get_primitive_tc(
                  org.omg.CORBA.TCKind.tk_long));
              _params.add_value("inoutLongVal", $inoutLongVal,
                  org.omg.CORBA.ARG_INOUT.value);
              org.omg.CORBA.Any $outLongVal = _orb().create_any();
              $outLongVal.type(_orb().get_primitive_tc
                  (org.omg.CORBA.TCKind.tk_long));
              _params.add_value("outLongVal", $outLongVal,
                  org.omg.CORBA.ARG_OUT.value);
              _request.params(_params);
              int inLongVal;
              inLongVal = $inLongVal.extract_long();
              org.omg.CORBA.IntHolder inoutLongVal = new
                  org.omg.CORBA.IntHolder();
              inoutLongVal.value = $inoutLongVal.extract_long();
```

```
                    org.omg.CORBA.IntHolder outLongVal = new
                        org.omg.CORBA.IntHolder();
                    int _result = _self.testLong
                        (inLongVal,inoutLongVal,outLongVal);
                    org.omg.CORBA.Any _resultAny = _orb().create_any();
                    _resultAny.insert_long(_result);
                    request.result(_resultAny);
                    $inoutLongVal.insert_long(inoutLongVal.value);
                    $outLongVal.insert_long(outLongVal.value);
                    return;
                }
            }
            throw new org.omg.CORBA.MARSHAL();
        }
    }
```

❶ Do you notice the difference here? Normal skeletons extend from `org.omg.CORBA.portable.Skeleton`. Thus, this implements a DSI Object that delegates method invocations up to our Server Object.

❷ Check this out! A full implementation of the `invoke()` method. Notice all the similarities between what you see here and the implementation that we first showed you.

Listing 12.34 should look familiar because it resembles most of the code created by hand in Listing 12.33.

SUMMARY

In this chapter, we introduced a completely new way to build Clients and Server Objects. Up until this point, you have spent all your time working with the static stubs and skeleton classes that are generated from the idl2java compiler. However, this chapter takes an in-depth look at how to build Clients and Server Objects without any prebuilt stubs, using the DII and the DSI instead. The DII allows Clients to dynamically build requests to Server Objects. The DSI allows Server Objects to receive invocations without needing to be extended from the IDL generated skeleton class.

Typically the DII and DSI are used by software vendors who want to build tools and products on top of a VisiBroker infrastructure. The DII and DSI provide a great deal of flexibility because they allow for new Server Objects to be introduced at any time and Clients can automatically communicate with them without having compiled in stubs. However, with that flexibility comes a price in the significant amount of code that must be written to implement DII Clients and DSI Servers. However, the idl2java compiler comes with an incredibly useful option `-portable` that generates the majority of the Client code needed in the `_portable_` file and the majority of the DSI code in the `_ImplBase` file. We highly encourage you to make the most of this option because it will save you a great deal of time and effort.

INTERFACE REPOSITORY

CHAPTER 13

IN THIS CHAPTER

- **THE INTERFACE REPOSITORY STRUCTURE** *294*
- **INTERFACE REPOSITORY TYPES** *295*
- **DEFINITION KIND** *300*

In this chapter, we continue our look at the dynamic features of VisiBroker. In Chapter 12, we examined the two dynamic interfaces in VisiBroker; the Dynamic Invocation Interface (DII) for Clients and the Dynamic Skeleton Interface (DSI) for Servers. The DII allows Clients to dynamically create requests to Server Objects even if the Clients were unaware of these interfaces at design time. In our discussion of the DII you saw how the DII interface is used; however, we didn't discuss how to discover these new Servers dynamically. We built DII Clients with the knowledge of the IDL of the Server Object. This chapter teaches you how to build a DII Client that can dynamically build a request to any Server Object.

In order to build a general DII Client, you will need the Interface Repository (IR). The Interface Repository is a database of Object Interfaces, not implementations. The purpose of this repository is to provide the interface descriptions of the Server Objects available to accept requests from Clients. Thus, using the Interface Repository, DII Clients can perform a lookup to see what Server Objects are available and then use the metadata contained in the Interface Repository to construct the request.

THE INTERFACE REPOSITORY STRUCTURE

The Interface Repository is structured in a hierarchy of container classes that contain all the interface metadata for Server Objects. The idea here is that the Interface Repository is built to hold all the type information in an Interface Definition Language (IDL) file. Because certain types are contained within other types, all IDL types fall into one of the following two categories:

- **Container**—An IDL type that can contain other types. For example, a module typically contains an interface within it. Thus, a specific type of Container for modules exists. IR objects that can contain other types implement the `org.omg.CORBA.Container` interface.

- **Contained**—An IDL type that cannot contain any other types; rather it can only be contained. For example, primitive data types such as strings and floats can be contained within modules, interfaces, and operations; however, they will never contain any other type. IR objects that can be contained within other objects implement the `org.omg.CORBA.Contained` interface.

All Container objects can be Contained as well. These objects implement both the `org.omg.CORBA.Container` interface as well as the `org.omg.CORBA.Contained` interface.

We will take a look at an example IDL in Listing 13.1 and see what type of hierarchy is created in the Interface Repository.

LISTING 13.1 SAMPLE IDL

```
module IR
{
        interface LongTest
```

```
    {
        long testLong(
                    in long inLongVal,
                    inout long inoutLongVal,
                    out long outLongVal);
    };
};
```

Within the Interface Repository, this resembles Figure 13.1.

FIGURE 13.1
The internal containment structure of the Interface Repository.

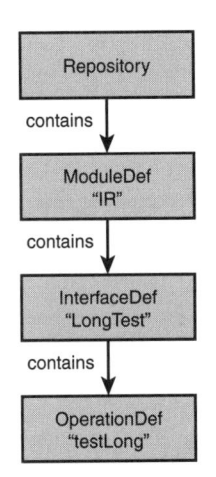

The Following is a top-down view of the Interface Repository structure. The Repository Object is the top-level Container. The Repository Object is a container of the ModuleDef container.

In our IDL, our "IR" module contains a single interface called "LongTest." Thus, our ModuleDef object is a container for an InterfaceDef object.

In our IDL, our "LongTest" interface defines one method called "testLong." Thus, our InterfaceDef is a container for an OperationDef object.

In the previous example, we introduced you to a few of the types of objects that can be stored in the Interface Repository. We will look at the complete list in the following section.

INTERFACE REPOSITORY TYPES

This section describes each of the types within the Interface Repository.

Repository

The `Repository` object is the top level object within the Interface Repository. This object serves as your root object with which you navigate through what is contained within the `Repository`. The `Repository` interface is shown in Listing 13.2.

LISTING 13.2 THE TOP LEVEL CONTAINER OF THE INTERFACE REPOSITORY, THE Repository INTERFACE

```
public interface org.omg.CORBA.Repository extends java.lang.Object
        implements org.omg.CORBA.Container
{
    public abstract org.omg.CORBA.Contained lookup_id(java.lang.String);
```

```
    public abstract org.omg.CORBA.PrimitiveDef get_primitive
        (org.omg.CORBA.PrimitiveKind);
    public abstract org.omg.CORBA.StringDef create_string(int);
    public abstract org.omg.CORBA.WstringDef create_wstring(int);
    public abstract org.omg.CORBA.SequenceDef create_sequence
        (int, org.omg.CORBA.IDLType);
    public abstract org.omg.CORBA.ArrayDef create_array
        (int, org.omg.CORBA.IDLType);
}
```

A Repository Object can be obtained through the `bind(...)` call, as shown in Listing 13.3.

LISTING 13.3 HOW TO BIND TO AN INTERFACE REPOSITORY

```
.....
//Initialize the ORB
org.omg.CORBA.ORB orb = org.omg.CORBA.ORB.init();

// Bind to the Interface Repository
org.omg.CORBA.Repository irep = org.omg.CORBA.RepositoryHelper.bind(orb);
.......
```

ModuleDef

The `ModuleDef` object represents an IDL module declaration. The `ModuleDef` object serves as a container for other `ModuleDef` objects, `InterfaceDef` objects, and basically any other IDL type that can be contained within a module.

InterfaceDef

The `InterfaceDef` object represents an IDL interface declaration. The `InterfaceDef` object serves as a container for the following:

- `AttributeDef` objects
- `OperationDef` objects
- `ConstantDef` objects
- `ExceptionDef` objects
- `StructDef` objects
- `UnionDef` objects
- `EnumDef` objects
- `AliasDef` objects
- `StringDef` objects
- `SequenceDef` objects

- `ArrayDef` objects
- `PrimitiveDef` objects

AttributeDef

The `AttributeDef` object represents an IDL attribute declaration. It implements the `org.omg.CORBA.Contained` interface and cannot contain any other objects.

OperationDef

The `OperationDef` object represents an IDL method declaration. This object contains information on the following:

- Parameters and their direction (`in`, `inout`, or `out`)
- The return value
- User-defined exceptions
- Contexts being passed

The `OperationDef` interface is shown in Listing 13.4.

LISTING 13.4 THE `OperationDef` INTERFACE

```
public interface org.omg.CORBA.OperationDef extends java.lang.Object
        implements org.omg.CORBA.Contained
{
    public abstract org.omg.CORBA.TypeCode result();                              ❶
    public abstract void result_def(org.omg.CORBA.IDLType);
    public abstract org.omg.CORBA.IDLType result_def();
    public abstract void params(org.omg.CORBA.ParameterDescription[]);
    public abstract org.omg.CORBA.ParameterDescription params()[];                ❷
    public abstract void mode(org.omg.CORBA.OperationMode);
    public abstract org.omg.CORBA.OperationMode mode();
    public abstract void contexts(java.lang.String[]);                            ❸
    public abstract java.lang.String contexts()[];
    public abstract void exceptions(org.omg.CORBA.ExceptionDef[]);
    public abstract org.omg.CORBA.ExceptionDef exceptions()[];                    ❹
}
```

❶ Returns the type of the return value
❷ Returns a list of the parameters
❸ Returns a list of contexts
❹ Returns a list of user exceptions

To visually understand the notion of how the structure of the Interface Repository is established, examine Figure 13.2.

FIGURE 13.2
Internal structure of the Interface Repository. The Repository is the outermost container, and it contains modules, which contain Interfaces, and so on.

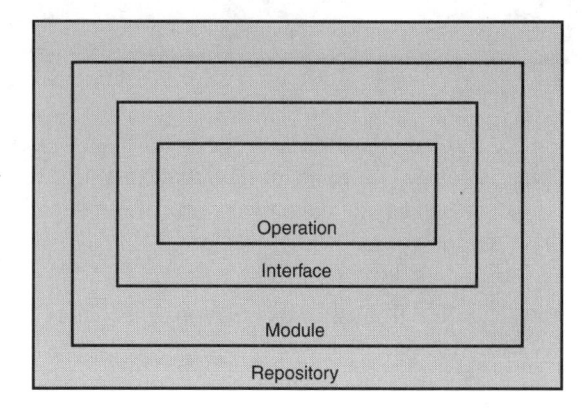

[Figure: nested rectangles labeled from innermost to outermost: Operation, Interface, Module, Repository]

ConstantDef

The `ConstantDef` object represents an IDL constant declaration. It implements the `org.omg.CORBA.Contained` interface and cannot contain any other objects.

ExceptionDef

The `ExceptionDef` object represents an IDL exception declaration. It implements both `org.omg.CORBA.Container` and `org.omg.CORBA.Contained`.

StructDef

The `StructDef` object represents an IDL structure declaration. It implements both `org.omg.CORBA.Container` and `org.omg.CORBA.Contained`.

UnionDef

The `UnionDef` object represents an IDL union declaration. It implements both `org.omg.CORBA.Container` and `org.omg.CORBA.Contained`.

EnumDef

The `EnumDef` object represents an IDL enum declaration. It implements `org.omg.CORBA.Contained`.

AliasDef

The `AliasDef` object represents an IDL typedef declaration. It implements `org.omg.CORBA.Contained`.

StringDef

The `StringDef` object represents an IDL bounded string declaration. It doesn't implement either `org.omg.CORBA.Container` or `org.omg.CORBA.Contained` because a string is a primitive CORBA type.

SequenceDef

The `SequenceDef` object represents an IDL sequence declaration. It doesn't implement either `org.omg.CORBA.Container` or `org.omg.CORBA.Contained` because an IDL sequence is always declared with a typedef declaration. We have already seen that the `AliasDef` implements `org.omg.CORBA.Contained`, so it isn't necessary for this object to do the same.

ArrayDef

The `ArrayDef` object represents an IDL array declaration. It doesn't implement either `org.omg.CORBA.Container` or `org.omg.CORBA.Contained` because an IDL array is always declared with a typedef declaration. We have already seen that the `AliasDef` implements `org.omg.CORBA.Contained`, so it isn't necessary for this object to do the same.

PrimitiveDef

The `PrimitiveDef` object represents a primitive IDL type. These types are as follows:

- `null`
- `void`
- `long`
- `ulong`
- `short`
- `ushort`
- `float`
- `double`
- `Boolean`
- `char`
- `octet`
- `any`
- `TypeCode`
- `Principal`
- `unbounded string`
- `objref`

Because primitive types are never declared outside of method declarations, typedefs, structs, and so on, there is no need for this interface to implement `org.omg.CORBA.Contained` or `org.omg.CORBA.Container`.

DEFINITION KIND

For each of the various objects described in the previous section, there is a specific constant that is defined to tell the Client what type of Object is within the Repository.

All Objects within the Interface Repository implement the `IRObject` interface as shown in Listing 13.5.

LISTING 13.5 THE IRObject INTERFACE

```
public interface interface org.omg.CORBA.IRObject extends java.lang.Object
      implements org.omg.CORBA.Object
{
    public abstract org.omg.CORBA.DefinitionKind def_kind();
    public abstract void destroy();
}
```

The def_kind( ) method returns the specific constant the Client needs to determine which type of IRObject was returned, whether it was a module or interface, and so on. Table 13.1 indicates the possible DefinitionKind values.

TABLE 13.1 UNDERSTANDING DefinitionKindS

DefinitionKind	Represents Constant
dk_none	Does not include anything; used in lookups
dk_any	All possible types; used in lookups
dk_Alias	An alias
dk_Array	An array
dk_Attribute	An attribute
dk_Constant	A constant
dk_Enum	An enum
dk_Estruct	A caffeine extended struct
dk_Exception	A user-defined exception
dk_Interface	An interface
dk_Module	A module
dk_Operation	A method
dk_Primitive	A primitive IDL type (char, short, and so on)
dk_Typedef	A typedef
dk_Union	A union

DefinitionKind	Represents Constant
dk_Repository	An Interface Repository
dk_Sequence	A sequence
dk_String	A string
dk_Struct	A struct
dk_Wstring	A Unicode wide string

So, how exactly would this be used?

After receiving the object reference to the Interface Repository, you need to obtain the object contained within the Interface Repository. This can be done as shown in Listing 13.6.

LISTING 13.6 HOW TO OBTAIN A REFERENCE TO THE INTERFACE REPOSITORY AND CHECK TO SEE WHAT IS CONTAINED THERE

```
org.omg.CORBA.Repository irep = org.omg.CORBA.RepositoryHelper.bind(orb);

org.omg.CORBA.Contained items[] = irep.contents
        (org.omg.CORBA.DefinitionKind.dk_all,true);
for (int i = 0; i < items.length; i++)
{
        switch (irep.def_kind().value())
        {
                case org.omg.CORBA.DefinitionKind._dk_Module:    .
                        System.out.println("Found a Module!    ..." );
                        break;
        }
}
```

Here you obtain your reference to the Interface Repository and create an array of what is contained within the outer Repository object. For each of these items, check its `DefinitionKind` value to determine what is contained in the Repository. In this simple example, check only to see whether the value is a module. A similar check should be performed against any other possible `DefinitionKind`.

Using the Interface Repository Objects

The following are the steps which must be taken in order to use the Interface Repository.

1. Obtain a `Repository` object by binding to the Interface Repository as shown in Listing 13.7.

LISTING 13.7 How to Bind to the Interface Repository

```
.....
//Initialize the ORB
org.omg.CORBA.ORB orb = org.omg.CORBA.ORB.init();

// Bind to the Interface Repository
org.omg.CORBA.Repository irep =
    org.omg.CORBA.RepositoryHelper.bind(orb);
.....
```

2. Determine what the first type of Container in the Interface Repository is, as shown in Listing 13.8.

LISTING 13.8 How to Determine the Initial Container Type in the Interface Repository

```
// Bind to the Interface Repository
org.omg.CORBA.Repository irep =
    org.omg.CORBA.RepositoryHelper.bind(orb);

org.omg.CORBA.Contained items[] = irep.contents
    (org.omg.CORBA.DefinitionKind.dk_all,true);




for (int i = 0; i < items.length; i++)
{
    switch (irep.def_kind().value())
    {
        case org.omg.CORBA.DefinitionKind._dk_Repository:     ──❶
            System.out.println("Found an IR..." );
            break;
        case org.omg.CORBA.DefinitionKind._dk_Module:         ──❷
            org.omg.CORBA.ModuleDef module =
                    org.omg.CORBA.ModuleDefHelper.narrow(irep);
            System.out.println
                    ("Found Module... " + module.name());
            break;
        case org.omg.CORBA.DefinitionKind._dk_Interface:      ──❸
            org.omg.CORBA.InterfaceDef iface =
                    org.omg.CORBA.InterfaceDefHelper.narrow(irep);
            System.out.println
                    ("Found Interface.... " + iface.name());
            break;
        case org.omg.CORBA.DefinitionKind._dk_Operation:      ──❹
            org.omg.CORBA.OperationDef op =
                    org.omg.CORBA.OperationDefHelper.narrow(irep);
            System.out.println
```

```
                            ("Found Operation.... " + op.name());
                   break;
               case org.omg.CORBA.DefinitionKind._dk_Exception:                    ─── ❺
                   org.omg.CORBA.ExceptionDef except =
                            org.omg.CORBA.ExceptionDefHelper.narrow(irep);
                   System.out.println
                            ("Found Exception.... " + except.name());
                   break;
               case org.omg.CORBA.DefinitionKind._dk_Attribute:                    ─── ❻
                   org.omg.CORBA.AttributeDef attr =
                            org.omg.CORBA.AttributeDefHelper.narrow(irep);
                   System.out.println
                            ("Found Attribute.... " + attr.name());
                   break;
               case org.omg.CORBA.DefinitionKind._dk_Constant:                     ─── ❼
                   org.omg.CORBA.ConstantDef cons =
                            org.omg.CORBA.ConstantDefHelper.narrow(irep);
                   System.out.println
                            ("Found Constant... " + cons.name());
                   break;
               default:
                   System.out.println
                            ("Unknown irep type (" + irep.def_kind() + ")");
                   break;
           }
    }
```

❶ Is it the base IR? This will be the case the very first time because the Repository Object is the outermost Container Object.

❷ Is it a Module?

❸ Is it an Interface?

❹ Is it a method call?

❺ Is it a user-defined exception?

❻ Is it an attribute?

❼ Is it a constant?

You'll notice that Listing 13.8 doesn't cover every possible type that could be found within the Interface Repository. We just discussed all the possible types that could be checked for; however, this listing only demonstrates a few. The types not shown in the previous listing will follow the exact same syntax.

Further, it should be noted that in Listing 13.8, the `contents()` method only reveals what is contained within one given container. In other words, the first time the code in Listing 13.8 executes, the contents of the Interface Repository reference is an outer `Repository` object. Thus, the only code that executes will be the case checking for `dk_Repository`.

To find out what is contained within the Repository, the contents( ) method must be called again. This recursive nature of checking contents( ) has to be done until the entire Interface Repository has been retrieved.

3. If there are method requests, a ParameterDescription array needs to be created. We will walk through specifically how this would be done. In order to create a ParameterDescription array, we must make use of the OperationDef interface. Review the OperationDef interface shown in Listing 13.9.

LISTING 13.9 THE OperationDef INTERFACE

```
public interface org.omg.CORBA.OperationDef extends java.lang.Object
 implements org.omg.CORBA.Contained
{
    public abstract org.omg.CORBA.TypeCode result();
    public abstract void result_def(org.omg.CORBA.IDLType);
    public abstract org.omg.CORBA.IDLType result_def();
    public abstract void params(org.omg.CORBA.ParameterDescription[]);
    public abstract org.omg.CORBA.ParameterDescription params()[];
    public abstract void mode(org.omg.CORBA.OperationMode);
    public abstract org.omg.CORBA.OperationMode mode();
    public abstract void contexts(java.lang.String[]);
    public abstract java.lang.String contexts()[];
    public abstract void exceptions(org.omg.CORBA.ExceptionDef[]);
    public abstract org.omg.CORBA.ExceptionDef exceptions()[];
}
```

The params() method returns an array of ParameterDescription objects. This represents all your in, inout, and out arguments. Take a look at the ParameterDescription class in Listing 13.10.

LISTING 13.10 THE ParameterDescription CLASS

```
public final synchronized class org.omg.CORBA.ParameterDescription extends
        java.lang.Object
{
    public java.lang.String name;
    public org.omg.CORBA.TypeCode type;
    public org.omg.CORBA.IDLType type_def;
    public org.omg.CORBA.ParameterMode mode;
    public org.omg.CORBA.ParameterDescription();
    public org.omg.CORBA.ParameterDescription(java.lang.String,
    org.omg.CORBA.TypeCode,org.omg.CORBA.IDLType,org.omg.CORBA.ParameterMode);
}
```

The name *variable* represents the name of the parameter.

The *type* represents the type of the parameter.

The *type_def* represents the IDL type of the parameter.

The *mode* represents the direction of the parameter. The `ParameterMode` class is as follows in Listing 13.11.

LISTING 13.11 THE ParameterMod*E* CLASS

```
public final synchronized class org.omg.CORBA.ParameterMode extends
      java.lang.Object
{
   public static final int _PARAM_IN;
   public static final int _PARAM_OUT;
   public static final int _PARAM_INOUT;
   public static final org.omg.CORBA.ParameterMode PARAM_IN;
   public static final org.omg.CORBA.ParameterMode PARAM_OUT;
   public static final org.omg.CORBA.ParameterMode PARAM_INOUT;
   public int value();
   public static org.omg.CORBA.ParameterMode from_int(int);
   static static {};
}
```

It can be seen that the `value()` method returns a constant representing one of the three types of parameters.

The `result( )` method on the `OperationDef` method returns the `TypeCode` representing the value for the return value. `TypeCodes` are discussed in detail in Chapter 12.

A Sample DII Client That Uses the Interface Repository

In all our DII examples in Chapter 12, we wrote our code with the knowledge of the interface we were connecting to. In this chapter, we will take the exact same IDL and Server, but we will connect to the Server only through analyzing the interface through the Interface Repository.

The IDL

We will start with the same IDL used throughout Chapter 12, which is shown in Listing 13.12.

LISTING 13.12 SAMPLE IDL TO REPRESENT THE INTERFACE STORED IN THE INTERFACE REPOSITORY

```
module IR
{
interface LongTest
    {
        long testLong(
            in long inLongVal,
```

continues

LISTING 13.12 CONTINUED

```
        inout long inoutLongVal,
        out long outLongVal);
   };
};
```

The DII Client Using the Interface Repository

Now we will modify our DII Client from Chapter 12, so the Client uses the Interface Repository to dynamically construct a request to the LongTest interface. The difference between this Client, as shown in Listing 13.3, and the Client from Chapter 12, is that in Chapter 12 we developed the Client knowing exactly what methods and arguments were in the LongTest interface. In this example, we will look up the LongTest interface in the Interface Repository and recursively walk through the Repository to read the Interface metadata. By recusively reading information from each container, the Client learns what methods and arguments are available on the LongTest interface. The sequence of events is shown in Figure 13.3.

FIGURE 13.3
The sequence of events our DII Client uses to dynamically create a request to the LongTest interface, based on the metadata in the Interface Repository.

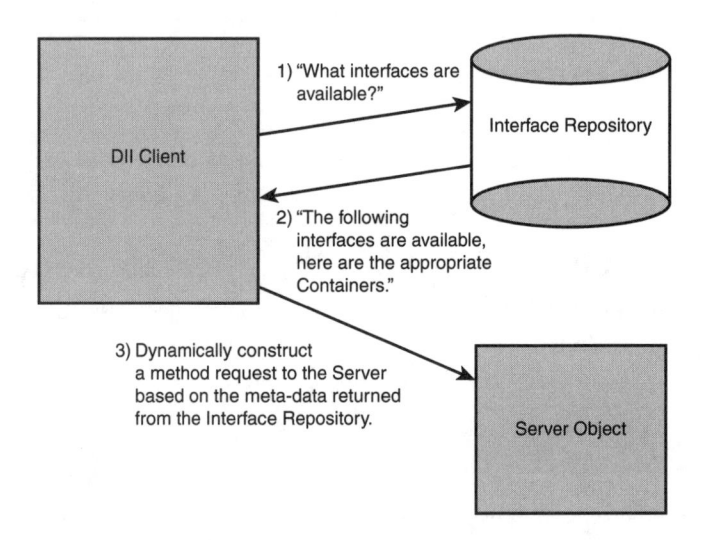

1) "What interfaces are available?"
2) "The following interfaces are available, here are the appropriate Containers."
3) Dynamically construct a method request to the Server based on the meta-data returned from the Interface Repository.

It should be noted that in this particular example the Client assumes all parameters are either of type short or type int. This was done for simplicity and would be extended in a real application, as shown in Listing 13.13.

LISTING 13.13 SAMPLE DII CLIENT DESIGNED TO PARSE THE INTERFACE REPOSITORY AND BUILD A REQUEST BASED ON THE METADATA CONTAINED IN THE INTERFACE REPOSITORY

```
package chapter13;
import java.util.*;
```

```java
/**
 * Class to test using the interface repository.  Note that to
 * use this app, you must start the interface repository (irep)
 * and add the IDL file containing our "TestLong" definition.  For
 * example
 *    prompt> irep -console aName src\chapter13\longTest.idl
 */
public class Client
{
    private Vector moduleNames    = new Vector();
    private Vector interfaceNames = new Vector();
    private Vector operationNames = new Vector();
    private Vector exceptionNames = new Vector();
    private Vector attributeNames = new Vector();
    private Vector constantNames  = new Vector();

      public Client()
      {
        try
        {
            //Initialize the ORB
            org.omg.CORBA.ORB orb = org.omg.CORBA.ORB.init();

            // Bind to the Interface Repository
            org.omg.CORBA.Repository irep =
                ➥org.omg.CORBA.RepositoryHelper.bind(orb);

            getContainerDetails(irep);

            // Construct the name of the object we are connecting
            // to based on the info we just got from the IR
            String moduleName = org.omg.CORBA.ModuleDefHelper.narrow
                ➥((org.omg.CORBA.Object) moduleNames.elementAt(0)).name();
            String interfaceName = org.omg.CORBA.InterfaceDefHelper.narrow
                (  (org.omg.CORBA.Object) interfaceNames.elementAt(0)).name();
            String obj_name = "IDL:"  +moduleName+  "/" +interfaceName+ ":1.0";

            //Bind to the Implementation
            org.omg.CORBA.Object objRef = orb.bind(obj_name, null, null, null);

            // Create a Request based on the first operation name
            String requestName = org.omg.CORBA.OperationDefHelper.narrow
                 (  (org.omg.CORBA.Object) operationNames.elementAt(0)).name();
            org.omg.CORBA.Request request = objRef._request(requestName);

            // Create the Parameter List
            org.omg.CORBA.ParameterDescription params[] =
                ➥org.omg.CORBA.OperationDefHelper.narrow
                 (  (org.omg.CORBA.Object) operationNames.elementAt(0)).params();
```

continues

LISTING 13.13   CONTINUED

```
                org.omg.CORBA.Any arguments[] =
                    ↪new org.omg.CORBA.Any[params.length];
                for(int i=0; i < params.length; i++)
                {
                    String argName = params[i].name;
                    switch (params[i].mode.value())
                    {
                        case org.omg.CORBA.ParameterMode._PARAM_IN:
                            System.out.println("in argument");
                            arguments[i] = request.add_in_arg();
                            switch (params[i].type.kind().value())
                            {
                                case org.omg.CORBA.TCKind._tk_short:
                                    System.out.println("short");
                                    arguments[i].insert_short( (short) 5);
                                    break;
                                case org.omg.CORBA.TCKind._tk_long:
                                    System.out.println("long");
                                    arguments[i].insert_long(5);
                                    break;
                                default:
                                    System.out.println("Unknown type kind
                                        ↪(" + params[i].type.kind() + ")");
                            }
                        break;

                        case org.omg.CORBA.ParameterMode._PARAM_INOUT:
                            System.out.println("inout argument");
                            arguments[i] = request.add_inout_arg();
                            switch (params[i].type.kind().value())
                            {
                                case org.omg.CORBA.TCKind._tk_short:
                                    System.out.println("short");
                                    org.omg.CORBA.ShortHolder
inoutShortValHolder =
                                        new org.omg.CORBA.ShortHolder(
(short) 5);

arguments[i].insert_short(inoutShortValHolder.value);
                                    break;
                                case org.omg.CORBA.TCKind._tk_long:
                                    System.out.println("long");
                                    org.omg.CORBA.IntHolder inoutLongValHolder
=
                                        new org.omg.CORBA.IntHolder(5);

arguments[i].insert_long(inoutLongValHolder.value);
                                    break;
                                default:
                                    System.out.println("Unknown type kind
```

```
                                            ➥(" + params[i].type.kind() + ")");
                        }
                        break;
                    case org.omg.CORBA.ParameterMode._PARAM_OUT:
                        System.out.println("out argument");
                        arguments[i] = request.add_out_arg();
                        switch (params[i].type.kind().value())
                        {
                                case org.omg.CORBA.TCKind._tk_short:
                                        System.out.println("short");
                                        arguments[i].type(orb.get_primitive_tc
                                            ➥(org.omg.CORBA.TCKind.tk_short));
                                        break;
                                case org.omg.CORBA.TCKind._tk_long:
                                        System.out.println("long");
                                        arguments[i].type(orb.get_primitive_tc
                                            ➥(org.omg.CORBA.TCKind.tk_long));
                                        break;
                                default:
                                        System.out.println("Unknown type kind
                                            ➥(" + params[i].type.kind() + ")");
                        }
                        break;

                    default:
                        System.out.println("Unknown mode");
            }
    }

    org.omg.CORBA.TypeCode returnTC = org.omg.CORBA.OperationDefHelper.narrow
        ( (org.omg.CORBA.Object) operationNames.elementAt(0)).result();

    switch (returnTC.kind().value())
    {
        case org.omg.CORBA.TCKind._tk_short:
                System.out.println("short");
                request.set_return_type(orb.get_primitive_tc
                    ➥(org.omg.CORBA.TCKind.tk_short));
                break;
        case org.omg.CORBA.TCKind._tk_long:
                System.out.println("long");
                request.set_return_type(orb.get_primitive_tc
                    ➥(org.omg.CORBA.TCKind.tk_long));
                break;
        default:
                System.out.println("Unknown type kind (" + returnTC.kind() +
")");
    }

    request.invoke();
```

continues

LISTING 13.13 CONTINUED

```java
            java.lang.Exception exception = request.env().exception();
            if(exception != null)
            {
                throw (org.omg.CORBA.SystemException) exception;
            }

            //For observation, print out the parameters after making the call
            System.out.println("After calling testLong() method\n" +
                "\treturn parameter" + request.return_value().toString());
        }
        catch(Exception ex)
        {
            ex.printStackTrace();
        }
    }
    public void getContentsOfContainer(
        org.omg.CORBA.Container container)
    {
        org.omg.CORBA.Contained items[] =
            container.contents(org.omg.CORBA.DefinitionKind.dk_all,true);
        for (int i = 0; i < items.length; i++)
        {
            getContainedDetails(items[i]);
        }
    }

    public void getContainerDetails(
        org.omg.CORBA.Container container)
    {
        switch (container.def_kind().value())
        {
            case org.omg.CORBA.DefinitionKind._dk_Repository:
                System.out.println("Found an IR..." );
                getContentsOfContainer(container);
                break;
            case org.omg.CORBA.DefinitionKind._dk_Module:
                org.omg.CORBA.ModuleDef module =
                    org.omg.CORBA.ModuleDefHelper.narrow(container);
                System.out.println("Found Module... " + module.name());
                moduleNames.addElement(module);
                getContentsOfContainer(module);
                break;
            case org.omg.CORBA.DefinitionKind._dk_Interface:
                org.omg.CORBA.InterfaceDef iface =
                    org.omg.CORBA.InterfaceDefHelper.narrow(container);
                System.out.println("Found Interface.... " + iface.name());
                interfaceNames.addElement(iface);
                getContentsOfContainer(iface);
                break;
            case org.omg.CORBA.DefinitionKind._dk_Operation:
```

```
                        org.omg.CORBA.OperationDef op =
                            org.omg.CORBA.OperationDefHelper.narrow(container);
                        System.out.println("Found Operation.... " + op.name());
                        operationNames.addElement(op);
                        break;
                    case org.omg.CORBA.DefinitionKind._dk_Exception:
                        org.omg.CORBA.ExceptionDef except =
                            org.omg.CORBA.ExceptionDefHelper.narrow(container);
                        System.out.println("Found Exception.... " + except.name());
                        exceptionNames.addElement(except);
                        getContentsOfContainer(except);
                        break;
                    case org.omg.CORBA.DefinitionKind._dk_Attribute:
                        org.omg.CORBA.AttributeDef attr =
                            org.omg.CORBA.AttributeDefHelper.narrow(container);
                        System.out.println("Found Attribute.... " + attr.name());
                        attributeNames.addElement(attr);
                        break;
                    case org.omg.CORBA.DefinitionKind._dk_Constant:
                        org.omg.CORBA.ConstantDef cons =
                            org.omg.CORBA.ConstantDefHelper.narrow(container);
                        System.out.println("Found Constant... " + cons.name());
                        exceptionNames.addElement(cons);
                        break;
                    default:
                        System.out.println("Unknown container type
                            ➥(" + container.def_kind() + ")");
                        break;
            }
        }

        public void getContainedDetails(org.omg.CORBA.Contained container)
        {
            switch (container.def_kind().value())
            {
                case org.omg.CORBA.DefinitionKind._dk_Module:
                    org.omg.CORBA.ModuleDef module =
                        org.omg.CORBA.ModuleDefHelper.narrow(container);
                    System.out.println("Found Module... " + module.name());
                    moduleNames.addElement(module);
                    getContentsOfContainer(module);
                    break;
                case org.omg.CORBA.DefinitionKind._dk_Interface:
                    org.omg.CORBA.InterfaceDef iface =
                        org.omg.CORBA.InterfaceDefHelper.narrow(container);
                    System.out.println("Found Interface.... " + iface.name());
                    interfaceNames.addElement(iface);
                    getContentsOfContainer(iface);
                    break;
                case org.omg.CORBA.DefinitionKind._dk_Operation:
```

continues

LISTING 13.13 CONTINUED

```
                    org.omg.CORBA.OperationDef op =
                        org.omg.CORBA.OperationDefHelper.narrow(container);
                    System.out.println("Found Operation.... " + op.name());
                    operationNames.addElement(op);
                    break;
                case org.omg.CORBA.DefinitionKind._dk_Exception:
                    org.omg.CORBA.ExceptionDef except =
                        org.omg.CORBA.ExceptionDefHelper.narrow(container);
                    System.out.println("Found Exception.... " + except.name());
                    exceptionNames.addElement(except);
                    getContentsOfContainer(except);
                    break;
                case org.omg.CORBA.DefinitionKind._dk_Attribute:
                    org.omg.CORBA.AttributeDef attr =
                        org.omg.CORBA.AttributeDefHelper.narrow(container);
                    System.out.println("Found Attribute.... " + attr.name());
                    attributeNames.addElement(attr);
                    break;
                case org.omg.CORBA.DefinitionKind._dk_Constant:
                    org.omg.CORBA.ConstantDef cons =
                        org.omg.CORBA.ConstantDefHelper.narrow(container);
                    System.out.println("Found Constant... " + cons.name());
                    exceptionNames.addElement(cons);
                    break;
                default:
                    System.out.println("Unknown container type
                            (" + container.def_kind() + ")");
                    break;
            }
        }
    }

    //Entry point.  All work done in constructor
    public static void main(String[] args)
    {
        new Client();
    }
}
```

Running the Interface Repository

Okay, so now that we have gone through all the code that you need to call the Interface Repository, how do you start it and populate your IDL into it? This can be done in one of two ways, either using the command-line utility `idl2ir` or using the Interface Repository GUI. However, before you can populate the Interface Repository, you must start the Interface Repository. To start the Interface Repository, use the following command.

```
prompt> irep [-console] IRname [file.idl]
```

The following list explains each of the `irep` command-line arguments in detail.

- `-console`—Directs the Interface Repository to run with a command-line interface; otherwise it presents a GUI.
- `IRname`—The instance name the Interface Repository starts with. Just as with other VisiBroker objects, this is the name in which it is registered with the Smart Agent. Clients can `bind( )` to specific instances by name.
- `File.idl`—A default IDL file to load into the IR when it starts up. If no filename is provided, you must use either the command-line interface or GUI interface to populate the IR.

After you have the Interface Repository running, you must populate it with interfaces. We will examine each of the two ways to add interfaces to the Interface Repository in the following section.

Populating the IR Through the Command Line

A command-line tool called `idl2ir` can be used to populate an IDL file into the IR. The `idl2ir` is actually a VisiBroker for Java (VBJ) Client that binds to the IR. You must keep a Smart Agent running while using this utility. The syntax for using `idl2ir` is as follows:

```
prompt> idl2ir [-ir IRname ] [-replace] file.idl
```

The following list explains each of the `idl2ir` command-line arguments in detail.

- `-ir IRname`—Directs the `idl2ir` client to the appropriate instance of the Interface Repository to bind to and populate. If this argument isn't used, `idl2ir` simply binds to the Interface Repository returned from the Smart Agent.
- `-replace`—Causes the `idl2ir` to overwrite an existing IDL entry of the same type.
- `file.idl`—Specifies the IDL file to be populated into the Interface Repository.

After entries are put into an Interface Repository, they cannot be removed. The only way to get around this is to stop the `irep` process and start another one.

Populating the IR Through the GUI

Figure 13.4 shows the graphical user interface (GUI) for the Interface Repository.

The Interface Repository GUI presents a rather simple GUI for adding and viewing IDL files. Take a closer look at the following menu options.

Under File, you have the following options:

- Load—Presents a dialog to load a given IDL file from the file system.

FIGURE 13.4

The Interface Repository GUI.

Very large IDL files with preprocessor directives should be loaded with `idl2ir` instead of the GUI. The `load` option on the `irep` GUI doesn't run the preprocessor, so it is limited in its ability to handle IDL directly.

- Save—Saves the IDL file within the Interface Repository under the same name as it was loaded.
- Save As—Saves the IDL file within the Interface Repository under a new name provided by the user.
- Exit—Shuts down the Interface Repository.

Under Language you have the following options:

- IDL—Displays the IR contents in IDL.
- C++—Displays the IR contents in C++. (This option is not currently implemented.)
- Java—Displays the IR contents in Java.

After loading the IDL file from Listing 13.12 into the Interface Repository, pressing the Lookup button presents the information shown in Figure 13.5.

Pressing the Java option under the Language menu item shows the Java version of the IDL, as shown in Figure 13.6.

FIGURE 13.5
The Interface Repository GUI listing the interfaces that are currently contained within it.

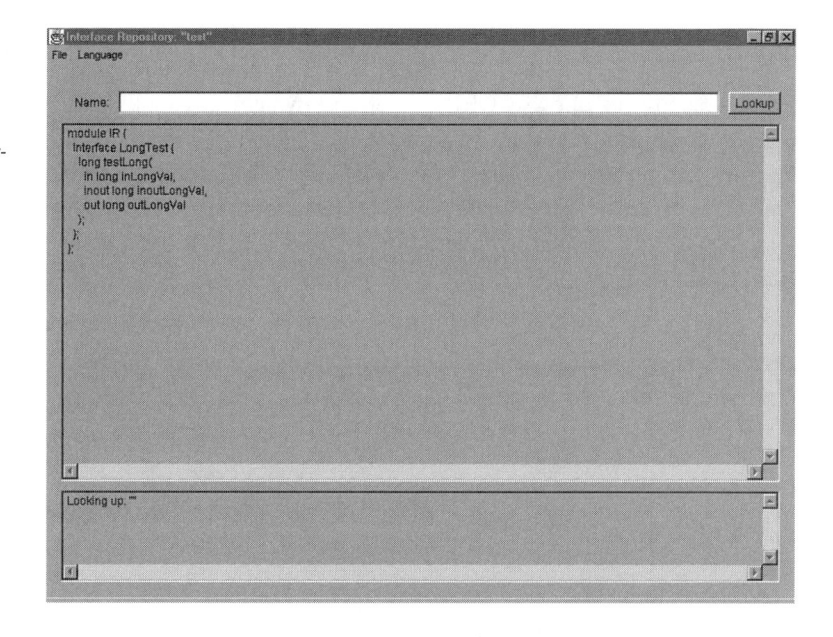

FIGURE 13.6
The Interface Repository GUI listing the Java version of the same IDL interface shown in Figure 13.5.

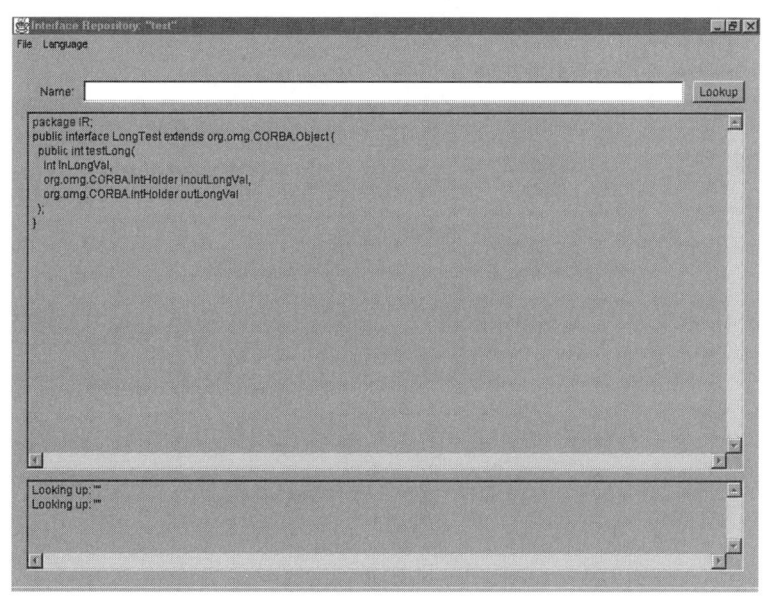

SUMMARY

The Interface Repository allows CORBA Clients to dynamically look up the interfaces of available Server Objects. It provides a hierarchy container structure to hold the contents of various IDL files. Clients can make use of the interfaces to the Interface Repository to get the necessary metadata on the Server Objects. Such metadata includes module names, interfaces names, method names, method signatures, and so on. Using this information, a Dynamic Invocation Client Request object can be constructed to call the given Server Object.

Using the Interface Repository alleviates the need for Clients to know about all the available Server Objects at design time. Rather, as Server Objects are instantiated with the skeleton inheritance or the DSI, their interfaces can be loaded into the Interface Repository. Clients can then perform lookups on the Interface Repository in order to get all the necessary information to make the method invocation.

DynAnyS

CHAPTER

14

IN THIS CHAPTER

- A REVIEW OF ANYS AND TYPECODES *318*
- DYNANYS *327*

In this chapter, we will finish our discussion of the Dynamic components within VisiBroker by discussing DynAnys. You can think of DynAnys in the same manner as you do normal Anys with one important exception. DynAnys provide a dynamic way to determine the type of a complex Any value without having any prior design-time or compile-time knowledge of the type contained within the Any. This chapter starts with a thorough review of the Any type and explains why a DynAny is important.

A REVIEW OF AnyS AND TypeCodeS

We will first review how we would make use of a complex Any if we knew about the Any at design time. If you are already comfortable with Anys and TypeCodes, you might want to skip ahead to our discussion of DynAnys and how they differ from the Any type.

We will start with the example in Listing 14.1 to review usage of the Any type.

LISTING 14.1 SAMPLE IDL TO DEMONSTRATE HOW TO DYNAMICALLY DETERMINE THE TYPE THROUGH DynAnyS

```
module DYNANY
{
  typedef sequence <short> myShortSequence;

    struct BasicStruct
    {
        myShortSequence seqVal;
        string     stringVal;
    };

    interface DynAnyTest
    {
        long testDynAny(
            in any inDynAny,
            inout any inoutDynAny,
            out any outDynAny);
    };
};
```

In the previous IDL, we define a complex data structure containing an unbounded sequence of short values and a single string value. If you have knowledge of this IDL when building your Server Object, you can easily make use of the `insert` and `extract` methods available on the generated Helper class. Look at the sample Server Object implementing this interface in Listing 14.2.

LISTING 14.2 A SERVER IMPLEMENTATION OF THE IDL INTERFACE

```java
public class DynAnyTestImpl extends DYNANY._DynAnyTestImplBase
{
    //Constructor for transient object
    public DynAnyTestImpl()
    {
    }

    //Constructor for persistent object
    public DynAnyTestImpl(String name)
    {
        super(name);
    }

    public int testDynAny(
        org.omg.CORBA.Any inDynAny,
        org.omg.CORBA.AnyHolder inoutDynAnyHolder,
        org.omg.CORBA.AnyHolder outDynAnyHolder)
    {

        //Extract the in BasicStruct from the Any using
        //the BasicStructHelper
        DYNANY.BasicStruct inBasicStruct =  DYNANY.BasicStructHelper.extract
            (inDynAny);

        //Extract the inout Any from the holder
        org.omg.CORBA.Any inoutDynAny = inoutDynAnyHolder.value;

        //Extract the inout struct from the Any
        //using the BasicStructHelper
        DYNANY.BasicStruct inoutBasicStruct = DYNANY.BasicStructHelper.extract
            (inoutDynAny);
        //
        //    End Parameter Extraction
        /////////////////////////////////////////////////////////

        for(int i=0; i< inoutBasicStruct.seqVal.length; i++)
        {
            System.out.println("Within the inout struct, the short seq value
                " + i + "is " + inoutBasicStruct.seqVal[i]);
        }

        //For demonstration, print out the passed values.
        System.out.println("\n\nBegin method testComplexAny()\n" +
            "\tin parameter's stringVal " + inBasicStruct.stringVal +
            "\n\tinout parameter's stringVal " + inoutBasicStruct.stringVal);
```

continues

LISTING 14.2 CONTINUED

```java
//Set the value on the inout parameter
inoutBasicStruct.seqVal[0] = 6;
inoutBasicStruct.seqVal[1] = 6;
inoutBasicStruct.seqVal[2] = 6;
inoutBasicStruct.stringVal = "fromServer";

//Insert this modified Struct into the Any
DYNANY.BasicStructHelper.insert(inoutDynAny, inoutBasicStruct);

short[] outShort = new short[3];
outShort[0] = 10;
outShort[1] = 11;
outShort[2] = 12;

//We must create a new BasicStruct to add into the
//any to be passed back to the client.
DYNANY.BasicStruct outBasicStruct = new DYNANY.BasicStruct
        (outShort, "fromServer");

//Create a new Any to be put into the outAnyHolder.  Note that
//we create this by calling to the org.omg.CORBA.ORB accessed
//through our inherited _orb() method
org.omg.CORBA.Any outDynAny = _orb().create_any();

//Assign the outComplexAny to the outComplexAnyHolder
outDynAnyHolder.value = outDynAny;

//Insert the new Struct into the out Any.  This is
//done using the static insert() method on the
//generated BasicStructHelper
DYNANY.BasicStructHelper.insert(outDynAny, outBasicStruct);
//
//    End Setting values for Return
/////////////////////////////////////////////////////////


//For demonstration, print-out the values being returned
System.out.println("\n\nAbout to exit method testComplexAny()" +
    "\n\tinout parameter's stringVal " + inoutBasicStruct.stringVal +
    "\n\tout parameter's stringVal " + outBasicStruct.stringVal);

for(int i=0; i< inoutBasicStruct.seqVal.length; i++)
{
        System.out.println("Within the inout struct, the short seq value
                " + i + "is " + inoutBasicStruct.seqVal[i]);
        System.out.println("Within the out struct, the short seq value
                " + i + "is " + outBasicStruct.seqVal[i]);
}
```

```
            return 0;

    }
```

The important lines to make note of are the lines that will extract the `BasicStruct` from the Any value as shown in Listing 14.3.

LISTING 14.3   HOW TO EXTRACT A STRUCT FROM AN Any

```
//Extract the in BasicStruct from the Any using
//the BasicStructHelper
DYNANY.BasicStruct inBasicStruct =  DYNANY.BasicStructHelper.extract
        (inDynAny);

//Extract the inout Any from the holder
org.omg.CORBA.Any inoutDynAny = inoutDynAnyHolder.value;

//Extract the inout struct from the Any
//using the BasicStructHelper
DYNANY.BasicStruct inoutBasicStruct = DYNANY.BasicStructHelper.extract
        (inoutDynAny);
```

The same sequence of steps is taken on the Client side to insert items into the Any as well. Take a look at this in Listing 14.4.

LISTING 14.4   A CLIENT PASSING DynAnyS TO THE SERVER IMPLEMENTATION SHOWN IN LISTING 14.2

```
public class Client
{
  public static void main(String[] args)
    {
        try
        {
            //Initialize the ORB
            org.omg.CORBA.ORB orb = org.omg.CORBA.ORB.init();

            //Bind to the Implementation
            DYNANY.DynAnyTest dynAnyTest = DYNANY.DynAnyTestHelper.bind
                    (orb, "DynAny Sample");

            short[] inShort = new short[3];
            inShort[0] = 0;
            inShort[1] = 1;
            inShort[2] = 2;
            DYNANY.BasicStruct inBasicStruct = new DYNANY.BasicStruct
                    (inShort, "fromClient");
```

continues

LISTING 14.4 CONTINUED

```
//      Create the in Any
org.omg.CORBA.Any inComplexAny = orb.create_any();

//      Pack the BasicStruct into the Any
//      using the BasicStructHelper
DYNANY.BasicStructHelper.insert(inComplexAny, inBasicStruct);

//      Create the inAnyHolder, passing the in Any into the
//      constructor
org.omg.CORBA.AnyHolder inComplexAnyHolder =
        new org.omg.CORBA.AnyHolder(inComplexAny);

short[] inoutShort = new short[3];
inoutShort[0] = 0;
inoutShort[1] = 1;
inoutShort[2] = 2;
//      Create the inout BasicStruct
DYNANY.BasicStruct inoutBasicStruct = new DYNANY.BasicStruct
        (inoutShort, "fromClient");

//      Create the inout Any
org.omg.CORBA.Any inoutComplexAny = orb.create_any();

//      Pack the BasicStruct into the Any
//      using the BasicStructHelper
DYNANY.BasicStructHelper.insert
        (inoutComplexAny, inoutBasicStruct);

//      Create the inoutAnyHolder, passing the inout Any into the
//      constructor
org.omg.CORBA.AnyHolder inoutComplexAnyHolder =
        new org.omg.CORBA.AnyHolder(inoutComplexAny);

//      Create the outAnyHolder
org.omg.CORBA.AnyHolder outComplexAnyHolder =
        new org.omg.CORBA.AnyHolder();

//Call remote method
int returnValue = dynAnyTest.testDynAny(
        inComplexAny,
        inoutComplexAnyHolder,
        outComplexAnyHolder);


///////////////////////////////////////////////////////
//      Begin Parameter Extraction
```

```java
            //
            //Retrieve the inoutComplexAny from the
            //holder
            inoutComplexAny = inoutComplexAnyHolder.value;

            //Retrieve the inout struct from the
            //Any using the BasicStructHelper
            inoutBasicStruct = DYNANY.BasicStructHelper.extract
                    (inoutComplexAny);

            //Retrieve the outComplexAny from the holder
            org.omg.CORBA.Any outComplexAny = outComplexAnyHolder.value;

            //Retrieve the out struct from the
            //Any using the BasicStructHelper
            DYNANY.BasicStruct outBasicStruct =
                    DYNANY.BasicStructHelper.extract(outComplexAny);

              for(int i=0; i< inoutBasicStruct.seqVal.length; i++)
              {
                    System.out.println("Within the inout struct,
                        the short seq value " + i +
                        "is " + inoutBasicStruct.seqVal[i]);
                    System.out.println("Within the out struct,
                        the short seq value " + i +
                        "is " + outBasicStruct.seqVal[i]);
              }

            //For demonstration purposes, print out the values
            //after calling remote method
            System.out.println("\n\nAfter calling testComplexAny()
                    method\n" + "\tinout parameter's stringVal " +
                    inoutBasicStruct.stringVal + "\n" +
                    "\tout parameter's stringVal " + outBasicStruct.stringVal);
        }
        catch(Exception ex)
        {
            ex.printStackTrace();
        }
    }
  }
}
```

In the Client in Listing 14.4, you first create your BasicStruct object, and then make use of the generated Helper class and the insert method to insert the BasicStruct into an Any. The lines of code in Listing 14.5 highlight this process.

LISTING 14.5 INSERTING AN IDL STRUCT INTO AN Any

```
short[] inShort = new short[3];
inShort[0] = 0;
inShort[1] = 1;
inShort[2] = 2;
DYNANY.BasicStruct inBasicStruct = new DYNANY.BasicStruct
        (inShort, "fromClient");

//     Create the in Any
org.omg.CORBA.Any inComplexAny = orb.create_any();

//     Pack the BasicStruct into the Any using the BasicStructHelper
DYNANY.BasicStructHelper.insert(inComplexAny, inBasicStruct);
```

Now examine the `insert` and `extract` methods from your generated Helper class to further understand how this type conversion is done automatically for you, shown in Listing 14.6.

LISTING 14.6 THE insert METHOD WITHIN THE IDL GENERATED HELPER CLASS

```
public static void insert(org.omg.CORBA.Any any, DYNANY.BasicStruct value) {
    org.omg.CORBA.portable.OutputStream output = any.create_output_stream();
    write(output, value);
    any.read_value(output.create_input_stream(), type());
  }
  public static DYNANY.BasicStruct extract(org.omg.CORBA.Any any) {
    if(!any.type().equal(type())) {
      throw new org.omg.CORBA.BAD_TYPECODE();
    }
    return read(any.create_input_stream());
  }
```

Thus far, you have been able to easily manipulate `Any`s containing complex types through the use of the Helper class and its `insert` and `extract` methods. Now, take a look at how you would make use of an `Any` value if you had no design-time knowledge of the `Any`. In other words, how would you be able to determine what type was contained in an `Any` if you didn't have the Helper extract method to help? If you have been paying attention to the previous chapters and think you can now stump the authors, we would expect your response to be, "Well, isn't that what the `TypeCode` value is for?" This finely assembled answer is only half correct as we explain over the next few sections. If you take another look at the `TCKind` class, the class that implements an IDL enumeration of all the possible types that can be contained in an `Any` is shown in Listing 14.7.

LISTING 14.7 THE TCKind ENUMERATION

```
enum TCKind
{
        tk_null, tk_void, tk_ushort, tk_ulong, tk_short, tk_long,
        tk_ushort, tk_ulong, tk_float, tk_double, tk_Boolean,
        tk_char, tk_octet, tk_any, tk_TypeCode, tk_Principal,
        tk_objref, tk_struct, tk_union, tk_enum, tk_string, tk_sequence,
        tk_array, tk_alias, tj_except, tk_longlong, tk_ulonglong,
        tk_longdouble, tk_wchar, tk_wstring, tk_fixed
};
```

So you see from the IDL definition of `TypeCodes` that the enumeration listed in Listing 14.7 only covers a finite number of possible values to be contained in the `Any`. This list doesn't cover the situation in our example in Listing 14.1 that has a struct containing a sequence and a string. At this point, I know you are probably asking the following question "Hold on a second, I thought this was the whole purpose of the TypeCode class and the various methods it provides specifically for this information?" Great observation; however, what the `TypeCode` class provides is not sufficient, and we will examine why in the next section.

TypeCodes Revisited

Use your IDL in Listing 14.1, which declares a struct that contains a sequence of short values and a single string value, and then take a look at Listing 14.8 to see what the `TypeCode` class offers that would allow you to interpret this type at runtime.

LISTING 14.8 THE TypeCode CLASS

```
public abstract synchronized class org.omg.CORBA.TypeCode extends
       java.lang.Object
{
    public abstract Boolean equal(org.omg.CORBA.TypeCode);
    public abstract org.omg.CORBA.TCKind kind();
    public abstract java.lang.String id();
    public abstract java.lang.String name();
    public abstract int member_count();
    public abstract java.lang.String member_name(int);
    public abstract org.omg.CORBA.TypeCode member_type(int);
    public abstract org.omg.CORBA.Any member_label(int);
    public abstract org.omg.CORBA.TypeCode discriminator_type();
    public abstract int default_index();
    public abstract int length();
    public abstract org.omg.CORBA.TypeCode content_type();
    public org.omg.CORBA.TypeCode();
}
```

The method for you to take special note of is the following:

```
public abstract int member_count();
```

This method is only available for the following types: structures, unions, enums, and exceptions. When a `TypeCode` is returned for one of the preceding types, this method is available to determine how many items are contained within their respective types.

For the IDL in Listing 14.1, the `TypeCode` for your `Any` would be a `tk_struct`, and when you called `member_count()` on that `TypeCode` it would return 2, one for the sequence of shorts, and one for the string.

```
public abstract String member_name(int index);
```

This method is only available for the following types: structures, unions, enums, and exceptions. When a `TypeCode` is returned for one of the preceding types, this method is available to reveal what the variable name is for the item.

For the IDL in Listing 14.1, you have just seen that using the `member_count()` method reveals a 2. Thus, if you call `member_name()` passing in an index of 0, you get back the String `seqVal`, the name of your sequence variable. When calling `member_name()` passing in an index of 1, you get back the String `stringVal`.

```
public abstract org.omg.CORBA.TypeCode member_type(int index);
```

This method is only available for the following types: structures, unions, and exceptions. When a `TypeCode` is returned for one of the preceding types, this method is available to reveal what the variable type is for the item.

For the IDL in Listing 14.1, you know that you have a `member_count` of 2. Thus, calling `member_type()` with an index of 0 returns a `tk_sequence` TypeCode. Calling `member_type()` with an index of 1 returns a `tk_string` TypeCode.

Without any use of your Helper class or any compile time knowledge, you have been able to determine that you have a struct containing two elements. You know that the first element is a sequence (further calls to the previous methods would reveal that you actually have a sequence of shorts) and a string. You know that the variable name of the sequence is `seqVal` and that the variable name of the string is `stringVal`. Now, what method do you use to get the values contained in this sequence and string within the `BasicStruct`? You have just found the heart of the problem. There is no such method available on the `TypeCode` class that gives you the *actual values* you want. It gives you all the necessary metadata, but there is no way for you to actually retrieve the values without use of the generated Helper class and its extract method, unless you make use of `DynAnys`.

DynAnyS

Dynamic Anys, or DynAnys, pick up where the TypeCode falls short. They provide the ability to create and interpret the values contained within an Any value without the need for the generated Helper insert and extract methods.

DynAny Types

DynAny objects are associated with data types in the same manner as normal Anys. For each DynAny type there is a specific TypeCode TCKind value. Take a look at Table 14.1.

TABLE 14.1 THE MAPPING OF DYNAMIC TYPES TO THEIR RESPECTIVE TCKind VALUES

Interface	TCKind Value	Contains
DynArray	_tk_array	An array
DynEnum	_tk_enum	An enum
DynSequence	_tk_sequence	A sequence
DynStruct	_tk_struct	A struct
DynUnion	_tk_union	A union

Creating DynAnys and DynAny Types

Creating DynAnys is very similar to creating normal Anys. We will make use of static methods on the org.omg.CORBA.ORB class. They are defined in Listing 14.9.

LISTING 14.9 THE METHODS ON THE ORB INTERFACE USED TO CREATE DYNAMIC AnyS

```
public abstract synchronized class org.omg.CORBA.ORB extends java.lang.Object
{
        static java.lang.Class class$org$omg$CORBA$ORB;
    ......
        public org.omg.CORBA.DynAny create_dyn_any(org.omg.CORBA.Any);
        public org.omg.CORBA.DynAny create_basic_dyn_any(org.omg.CORBA.TypeCode);
        public org.omg.CORBA.DynStruct create_dyn_struct(org.omg.CORBA.TypeCode);
        public org.omg.CORBA.DynSequence create_dyn_sequence
            (org.omg.CORBA.TypeCode);
        public org.omg.CORBA.DynArray create_dyn_array(org.omg.CORBA.TypeCode);
        public org.omg.CORBA.DynUnion create_dyn_union(org.omg.CORBA.TypeCode);
        public org.omg.CORBA.DynEnum create_dyn_enum(org.omg.CORBA.TypeCode);
    ......
        static java.lang.Class class$(java.lang.String);
        static static {};
}
```

Thus you see that there are two different methods for creating a `DynAny`. The first is

```
public org.omg.CORBA.DynAny create_dyn_any(org.omg.CORBA.Any value);
```

This signature creates a `DynAny` based on whatever value is contained in the `Any` that is passed in. The second method for creating a `DynAny` is

```
public org.omg.CORBA.DynAny create_basic_dyn_any(org.omg.CORBA.TypeCode type);
```

This signature creates a `DynAny` to hold a basic type based on the `TypeCode` value passed in.

You can create each of the `DynAny` types using the respective method for each type.

```
public org.omg.CORBA.DynStruct create_dyn_struct(org.omg.CORBA.TypeCode);
public org.omg.CORBA.DynSequence create_dyn_sequence(org.omg.CORBA.TypeCode);
public org.omg.CORBA.DynArray create_dyn_array(org.omg.CORBA.TypeCode);
public org.omg.CORBA.DynUnion create_dyn_union(org.omg.CORBA.TypeCode);
public org.omg.CORBA.DynEnum create_dyn_enum(org.omg.CORBA.TypeCode);
```

The DynAny Interface

Take a look at what operations a `DynAny` has that is useful for you so that you can understand the types and values contained within the `DynAny`. The `DynAny` interface is defined in Listing 14.10.

LISTING 14.10   THE DynAny INTERFACE

```
public interface org.omg.CORBA.DynAny extends java.lang.Object implements
       org.omg.CORBA.Object
{
        public abstract org.omg.CORBA.TypeCode type();
        public abstract void assign(org.omg.CORBA.DynAny);
        public abstract void from_any(org.omg.CORBA.Any);
        public abstract org.omg.CORBA.Any to_any();
        public abstract void destroy();
        public abstract org.omg.CORBA.DynAny copy();
        public abstract org.omg.CORBA.DynAny current_component();
        public abstract Boolean next();
        public abstract Boolean seek(int);
        public abstract void rewind();
        .........
}
```

Now, examine each of the `DynAny` methods in more detail.

```
public abstract org.omg.CORBA.TypeCode type();
```

Returns the `TypeCode` for the value contained within the `DynAny`.

```
public abstract void assign(org.omg.CORBA.DynAny);
```

Initializes the current DynAny with the DynAny value being passed in.

```
public abstract void from_any(org.omg.CORBA.Any);
```

Initializes the current DynAny with the Any value being passed in.

```
public abstract org.omg.CORBA.Any to_any();
```

Returns the value of the DynAny as an Any.

> It isn't possible to pass DynAny values as arguments; they might only be used locally by the process that created it. Attempting to do so causes a CORBA::NO_IMPLEMENT exception to be raised. As such, if you want to pass DynAnys as arguments, you must make use of the to_any() and from_any() methods in order to pass the DynAnys as normal Anys.
>
> A DynAny might not be stringified using the ORB.object_to_string() method either. Attempting to do so causes a CORBA::MARSHAL exception to be raised.
>
> The preceding rules apply equally to DynArrays, DynStructs, DynSequences, and DynEnums.

```
public abstract void destroy();
```

This operation destroys the current DynAny object.

```
public abstract org.omg.CORBA.DynAny copy();
```

Makes a copy of the current DynAny object and returns it.

```
public abstract org.omg.CORBA.DynAny current_component();
```

Returns the current component in this object. This is a slightly different implementation than how Anys are parsed through their TypeCodes. You saw earlier in this chapter that if you have an Any containing a struct, you must call member_count() to determine how many items are in the struct, and then increment the index in order to move from the first contained item to the next.

Using a DynAny, you need only call current_component() and it immediately returns the current item.

```
public abstract void rewind();
```

This rewinds the DynAny back to the first item it contains. In other words, it moves the DynAny offset back to the very first data element contained within the DynAny. When you looked at a normal Any, you had to first call member_count() on the Any's TypeCode to determine how many contained items there were. Then you simply moved from component to component by either incrementing or decrementing the index.

Using a DynAny makes this process much easier. A call to rewind() simply moves the DynAny offset to the very first item contained in the DynAny. Calling current_component() after rewind() therefore ensures that you have the first item contained in the DynAny.

```
public abstract Boolean next();
```

This moves the DynAny offset to the next component being contained in the DynAny. Calling next() and then calling current_component() retrieves the next component in the DynAny.

```
public abstract Boolean seek(int);
```

This advances the DynAny offset to the index passed in.

At this point, I expect a rather puzzled look on your face as you investigate the previous interface definition and try to figure out exactly how this Dynany interface gives you the value within the DynAny object. That is the whole point, right? I'm glad you are already thinking ahead. You are correct that we have not discussed the insertion and extraction capabilities of the DynAny interface. We will look at those now.

DynAny insertion methods:

```
public abstract void insert_Boolean(Boolean);
public abstract void insert_octet(byte);
public abstract void insert_char(char);
public abstract void insert_short(short);
public abstract void insert_ushort(short);
public abstract void insert_long(int);
public abstract void insert_ulong(int);
public abstract void insert_float(float);
public abstract void insert_double(double);
public abstract void insert_string(java.lang.String);
public abstract void insert_reference(org.omg.CORBA.Object);
public abstract void insert_typecode(org.omg.CORBA.TypeCode);
public abstract void insert_longlong(long);
public abstract void insert_ulonglong(long);
public abstract void insert_wchar(char);
public abstract void insert_wstring(java.lang.String);
public abstract void insert_any(org.omg.CORBA.Any);
```

DynAny extraction methods:

```
public abstract Boolean get_Boolean();
public abstract byte get_octet();
public abstract char get_char();
public abstract short get_short();
public abstract short get_ushort();
public abstract int get_long();
```

```
public abstract int get_ulong();
public abstract float get_float();
public abstract double get_double();
public abstract java.lang.String get_string();
public abstract org.omg.CORBA.Object get_reference();
public abstract org.omg.CORBA.TypeCode get_typecode();
public abstract long get_longlong();
public abstract long get_ulonglong();
public abstract char get_wchar();
public abstract java.lang.String get_wstring();
public abstract org.omg.CORBA.Any get_any();
```

Thus, insertion and extraction of primitive types is done in the same manner as with normal Anys. Over the next few sections, you will see how this is done with user constructed types.

DynArray Interface

A `DynArray` object can be created using the `ORB.create_dyn_array()`. After it has been created, there are two methods that can be used to get and set the values of the array, shown in Listing 14.11.

> The `DynArray`, `DynEnum`, `DynSequence`, `DynStruct`, and `DynUnion` interfaces each implement the `DynAny` interface described in the last section. As such, each of these objects provide each of the `DynAny` methods previously described.

LISTING 14.11 THE METHODS ON THE DynArray INTERFACE TO GET AND SET THE ELEMENTS WITHIN THE DynArray OBJECT

```
public interface org.omg.CORBA.DynArray extends java.lang.Object implements
      org.omg.CORBA.DynAny
{
    public abstract org.omg.CORBA.Any get_elements()[];
    public abstract void set_elements(org.omg.CORBA.Any[]);
}
```

DynEnum Interface

A `DynEnum` object can be created using the `ORB.create_dyn_enum()` call. This object provides two sets of methods for accessing and setting the value. The first two methods get and set based on a the enum's String representation. The second two methods get and set based on the enum's integer value. The `DynEnum` interface is shown in Listing 14.12.

LISTING 14.12 THE METHODS ON THE DynEnum INTERFACE USED TO SET AND GET THE VALUE WITHIN THE ENUMERATION IN EITHER ITS STRING FORM OR NUMERIC REPRESENTATION

```
public interface org.omg.CORBA.DynEnum extends java.lang.Object implements
        org.omg.CORBA.DynAny
{
    public abstract void value_as_string(java.lang.String);
    public abstract java.lang.String value_as_string();
    public abstract void value_as_ulong(int);
    public abstract int value_as_ulong();
}
```

DynSequence Interface

A `DynSequence` object can be created using the `ORB.create_dyn_sequence()` call. This object provides a two sets of accessor and modifier methods. The first set is to get and set the value of the elements within the sequence. The second is to get and set the value of the length of the sequence. The `DynSequence` interface is shown in Listing 14.13.

LISTING 14.13 THE METHODS ON THE DynSequence INTERFACE USED TO SET AND GET THE LENGTH AS WELL AS SET AND GET THE CONTENTS WITHIN THE SEQUENCE

```
public interface org.omg.CORBA.DynSequence extends java.lang.Object implements
        org.omg.CORBA.DynAny
{
    public abstract void length(int);
    public abstract int length();
    public abstract org.omg.CORBA.Any get_elements()[];
    public abstract void set_elements(org.omg.CORBA.Any[]);
}
```

DynStruct Interface

The `DynStruct` object can be created using the `ORB.create_dyn_struct()` call. This object provides accessor and modifier methods on the members of the structure. It also provides methods for getting the current component's variable name as well as its data type. The `DynStruct` interface is shown in Listing 14.14.

LISTING 14.14 THE METHODS ON THE DynStruct INTERFACE USED TO PROVIDE THE CONTENTS OF THE STRUCT

```
public interface org.omg.CORBA.DynStruct extends java.lang.Object implements
        org.omg.CORBA.DynAny
{
    public abstract java.lang.String current_member_name();
    public abstract org.omg.CORBA.TCKind current_member_kind();
```

```
    public abstract org.omg.CORBA.NameValuePair get_members()[];
    public abstract void set_members(org.omg.CORBA.NameValuePair[]);
}
```

DynUnion Interface

The `DynUnion` object can be created using the `ORB.create_dyn_union()` call. This object provides the same accessor and modifier methods for a standard union data type. The `DynUnion` interface is shown in Listing 14.15.

LISTING 14.15 THE METHODS ON THE DynUnion INTERFACE USED TO OBTAIN THE CONTENTS OF THE UNION

```
public interface org.omg.CORBA.DynUnion extends java.lang.Object implements
        org.omg.CORBA.DynAny
{
    public abstract void set_as_default(Boolean);
    public abstract Boolean set_as_default();
    public abstract org.omg.CORBA.DynAny discriminator();
    public abstract org.omg.CORBA.TCKind discriminator_kind();
    public abstract org.omg.CORBA.DynAny member();
    public abstract void member_name(java.lang.String);
    public abstract java.lang.String member_name();
    public abstract org.omg.CORBA.TCKind member_kind();
}
```

A DynAny Example

We will now revisit the example from the beginning of the chapter, renamed Listing 14.16 as shown in the following, and see how you can rewrite this example using `DynAnys` instead of normal Anys.

LISTING 14.16 SAMPLE IDL FROM BEGINNING OF CHAPTER, WHICH IS REPRINTED HERE FOR CONVENIENCE

The IDL:

```
module DYNANY
{
  typedef sequence <short> myShortSequence;

    struct BasicStruct
    {
        myShortSequence seqVal;
        string      stringVal;
    };
```

continues

LISTING 14.16 CONTINUED

```
    interface DynAnyTest
    {
        long testDynAny(
            in any inDynAny,
            inout any inoutDynAny,
            out any outDynAny);
    };
};
```

As you examine the sample DynAny client in Listing 14.17, pay attention to how this implementation is different from the normal Any Client shown at the beginning of the chapter. Notice that this example makes heavy use of recursion in order to get each data item contained in the DynAny. Further, when constructed types are found, recursion is used to go through each element of the constructed type. The key thing to note about the DynAny is that it allows you to retrieve the values of each data type as it is dynamically being discovered. This is not possible with normal Anys and TypeCodes.

LISTING 14.17 A SAMPLE CLIENT THAT MAKES USE OF THE IDL IN LISTING 14.16

```java
public class Client
{
  private static void getDynAnyValue(org.omg.CORBA.DynAny dynamicAny)
        throws Exception
  {
    boolean anotherElement;
    org.omg.CORBA.DynAny dAny;

    switch(dynamicAny.type().kind().value())
    {
      case org.omg.CORBA.TCKind._tk_null:
          System.out.println("Received a null within the Any");
          break;
      case org.omg.CORBA.TCKind._tk_any:
          System.out.println("Received an Any");
          break;
      case org.omg.CORBA.TCKind._tk_objref:
          System.out.println("Received an Obj ref");
          break;
      case org.omg.CORBA.TCKind._tk_short:
          short shortVal = dynamicAny.get_short();
          System.out.println("Received a short value of: " + shortVal);
          break;
      case org.omg.CORBA.TCKind._tk_long:
          long longVal = dynamicAny.get_long();
          System.out.println("Received a long value of: " + longVal);
          break;
```

```java
case org.omg.CORBA.TCKind._tk_string:
    java.lang.String stringVal = dynamicAny.get_string();
    System.out.println("Received a String value of: " + stringVal);
    break;
case org.omg.CORBA.TCKind._tk_struct:
    System.out.println("Struct");
    dynamicAny.rewind();
    anotherElement = true;

    while (anotherElement)
    {
      dAny = dynamicAny.current_component();
      getDynAnyValue(dAny);
      anotherElement = dynamicAny.next();
    }
    break;
case org.omg.CORBA.TCKind._tk_sequence:
    System.out.println("Sequence");
    dynamicAny.rewind();
    anotherElement = true;

    while (anotherElement)
    {
      dAny = dynamicAny.current_component();
      getDynAnyValue(dAny);
      anotherElement = dynamicAny.next();
    }
    break;
case org.omg.CORBA.TCKind._tk_array:
    System.out.println("Array");
    dynamicAny.rewind();
    anotherElement = true;

    while (anotherElement)
    {
      dAny = dynamicAny.current_component();
      getDynAnyValue(dAny);
      anotherElement = dynamicAny.next();
    }
    break;
case org.omg.CORBA.TCKind._tk_alias:
{
    System.out.println("Alias");
    dynamicAny.rewind();
    anotherElement = true;

    while (anotherElement)
    {
      dAny = dynamicAny.current_component();
```

continues

LISTING 14.17   CONTINUED

```java
                    getDynAnyValue(dAny);
                    anotherElement = dynamicAny.next();
                }
            }
            default:
                System.out.println("Did not understand the type contained within the
                        DynAny");
                System.out.println("The unknown int is: " +
                        dynamicAny.type().kind().value());

        }
    }

    public static void main(String[] args)
    {
        try
        {
                //Initialize the ORB
                org.omg.CORBA.ORB orb = org.omg.CORBA.ORB.init();

                //Bind to the Implementation
                DYNANY.DynAnyTest dynAnyTest = DYNANY.DynAnyTestHelper.bind
                        (orb, "DynAny Sample");

                // Create an "in" Dynamic Struct
                org.omg.CORBA.DynStruct inDynStruct = orb.create_dyn_struct
                        (DYNANY.BasicStructHelper.type());

                // Initialize the Dynamic Struct with data
                org.omg.CORBA.NameValuePair[] inNV =
                        new org.omg.CORBA.NameValuePair[2];

                org.omg.CORBA.Any inAnySeq = orb.create_any();
                short[] inSeqData = new short[3];
                inSeqData[0] = 0;
                inSeqData[1] = 1;
                inSeqData[2] = 2;
                DYNANY.myShortSequenceHelper.insert(inAnySeq, inSeqData);

                org.omg.CORBA.Any inAnyStr = orb.create_any();
                inAnyStr.insert_string("the IN string value....");

                inNV[0] = new org.omg.CORBA.NameValuePair("seqVal", inAnySeq);
                inNV[1] = new org.omg.CORBA.NameValuePair("stringVal", inAnyStr);

                inDynStruct.set_members(inNV);
                org.omg.CORBA.Any inDynAny = inDynStruct.to_any();

                // Create an "inout" DynStruct
```

```java
            org.omg.CORBA.DynStruct inoutDynStruct = orb.create_dyn_struct
                    (DYNANY.BasicStructHelper.type());

            // Initialize the Dynamic Struct with data
            org.omg.CORBA.NameValuePair [] inoutNV = new
                    org.omg.CORBA.NameValuePair[2];

            org.omg.CORBA.Any inoutAnySeq = orb.create_any();
            short inoutSeqData[] = new short[3];
            inoutSeqData[0] = 3;
            inoutSeqData[1] = 4;
            inoutSeqData[2] = 5;
            DYNANY.myShortSequenceHelper.insert(inoutAnySeq, inoutSeqData);

            org.omg.CORBA.Any inoutAnyStr = orb.create_any();
            inoutAnyStr.insert_string("the INOUT string value....");

            inoutNV[0] = new org.omg.CORBA.NameValuePair("seqVal", inoutAnySeq);
            inoutNV[1] = new org.omg.CORBA.NameValuePair("stringVal", inoutAnyStr);

            inoutDynStruct.set_members(inoutNV);
            org.omg.CORBA.AnyHolder inoutDynAnyHolder =
                    new org.omg.CORBA.AnyHolder(inoutDynStruct.to_any());


            // Create an "out" DynStruct
            org.omg.CORBA.DynStruct outDynStruct = orb.create_dyn_struct
                    (DYNANY.BasicStructHelper.type());
            // Initialize the Dynamic Struct with data
            org.omg.CORBA.NameValuePair [] outNV = new
                    org.omg.CORBA.NameValuePair[2];

            org.omg.CORBA.Any outAnySeq = orb.create_any();
            short outSeqData[] = new short[3];
            outSeqData[0] = 13;
            outSeqData[1] = 14;
            outSeqData[2] = 15;
            DYNANY.myShortSequenceHelper.insert(outAnySeq, outSeqData);

            org.omg.CORBA.Any outAnyStr = orb.create_any();
            outAnyStr.insert_string("Dummy OUT string value....");

            outNV[0] = new org.omg.CORBA.NameValuePair("seqVal", outAnySeq);
            outNV[1] = new org.omg.CORBA.NameValuePair("stringVal", outAnyStr);

            outDynStruct.set_members(outNV);
            org.omg.CORBA.AnyHolder outDynAnyHolder =
                    new org.omg.CORBA.AnyHolder(outDynStruct.to_any());

            //Call remote method
```

continues

LISTING 14.17   CONTINUED

```
            int returnValue = dynAnyTest.testDynAny(  inDynAny,
                    inoutDynAnyHolder,
                    outDynAnyHolder);

            System.out.println("Returned from remote method invocation,
                    checking values of out");
            System.out.println("Passing the out.....");
            getDynAnyValue(orb.create_dyn_any(outDynAnyHolder.value));


        }
        catch(Exception ex)
        {
            ex.printStackTrace();
        }
    }
}
```

You'll notice that this code looks very similar to the other dynamic code you have worked on for the past few chapters. Everything revolves around the TCKind value in order to determine the expected type. The key code to note in the previous example Client is the following:

```
case org.omg.CORBA.TCKind._tk_sequence:
        System.out.println("Sequence");
        dynamicAny.rewind();
        anotherElement = true;

        while (anotherElement)
        {
          dAny = dynamicAny.current_component();
          getDynAnyValue(dAny);
          anotherElement = dynamicAny.next();
        }
        break;
```

This is a perfect example of what must be done in checking for expected types from a DynAny. If the DynAny contains a complex type, you must parse through that type in order to determine how many layers of nested types are contained within one DynAny. Thus, in the previous example, if you see that you have a sequence, you must rewind() to the first element in the sequence and check what type the sequence contains. We will continue to check each element of the sequence to determine the type. The previous code works recursively in an effort to parse through each layer of the nested type.

You will also notice in Listing 14.18 that before any of the dynamic types are passed as arguments, they are converted to Anys.

Now we will examine the `DynAnyTestImpl` for the IDL in Listing 14.16. Because this Server Object accepts an `in` and `inout` `DynAny`, the code to parse through these `DynAnys` is virtually identical to the Client code shown in Listing 14.18. Again, recursion is used extensively in order to parse through each possible element within the `DynAny`.

LISTING 14.18 A SAMPLE SERVER IMPLEMENTATION FOR THE IDL IN LISTING 14.16

```java
public class DynAnyTestImpl extends DYNANY._DynAnyTestImplBase
{
    //Constructor for transient object
    public DynAnyTestImpl()
    {
    }

    //Constructor for persistent object
    public DynAnyTestImpl(String name)
    {
        super(name);
    }

    public int testDynAny(
        org.omg.CORBA.Any inDynAny,
        org.omg.CORBA.AnyHolder inoutDynAnyHolder,
        org.omg.CORBA.AnyHolder outDynAnyHolder)
    {
            // Get an ORB reference
            org.omg.CORBA.ORB orb = org.omg.CORBA.ORB.init();

        // Create a DynAny object
            org.omg.CORBA.DynAny inAny = orb.create_dyn_any(inDynAny);
            org.omg.CORBA.DynAny inoutAny = orb.create_dyn_any
                (inoutDynAnyHolder.value);

            try
            {
                getDynAnyValue(inAny);
                getDynAnyValue(inoutAny);

                // Create an "out" Dynamic Struct
                org.omg.CORBA.DynStruct outDynStruct = orb.create_dyn_struct
                    (DYNANY.BasicStructHelper.type());

                // Initialize the Dynamic Struct with data
                org.omg.CORBA.NameValuePair [] outNV = new
                    org.omg.CORBA.NameValuePair[2];

                org.omg.CORBA.Any outAnySeq = orb.create_any();
                short outSeqData[] = new short[3];
```

continues

LISTING 14.18   CONTINUED

```java
            outSeqData[0] = 9;
            outSeqData[1] = 10;
            outSeqData[2] = 11;
            DYNANY.myShortSequenceHelper.insert(outAnySeq, outSeqData);

            org.omg.CORBA.Any outAnyStr = orb.create_any();
            outAnyStr.insert_string("the OUT string value....");

            outNV[0] = new org.omg.CORBA.NameValuePair
                    ("seqVal", outAnySeq);
            outNV[1] = new org.omg.CORBA.NameValuePair
                    ("stringVal", outAnyStr);

            outDynStruct.set_members(outNV);
            outDynAnyHolder.value = outDynStruct.to_any();
        }
        catch(Exception ex)
        {
          ex.printStackTrace();
        }

    return 0;
  }

  private void getDynAnyValue(org.omg.CORBA.DynAny dynamicAny) throws Exception
  {
    Boolean anotherElement;
    org.omg.CORBA.DynAny dAny;

    switch(dynamicAny.type().kind().value())
    {
      case org.omg.CORBA.TCKind._tk_null:
          System.out.println("Received a null within the Any");
          break;
      case org.omg.CORBA.TCKind._tk_any:
          System.out.println("Received an Any");
          break;
      case org.omg.CORBA.TCKind._tk_objref:
          System.out.println("Received an Obj ref");
          break;
      case org.omg.CORBA.TCKind._tk_short:
          short shortVal = dynamicAny.get_short();
          System.out.println("Received a short value of: " + shortVal);
          break;
      case org.omg.CORBA.TCKind._tk_long:
          long longVal = dynamicAny.get_long();
          System.out.println("Received a long value of: " + longVal);
          break;
      case org.omg.CORBA.TCKind._tk_string:
```

```
        java.lang.String stringVal = dynamicAny.get_string();
        System.out.println("Received a String value of: " + stringVal);
        break;
    case org.omg.CORBA.TCKind._tk_struct:
        System.out.println("Struct");
        dynamicAny.rewind();
        anotherElement = true;

        while (anotherElement)
        {
          dAny = dynamicAny.current_component();
          getDynAnyValue(dAny);
          anotherElement = dynamicAny.next();
        }
        break;
    case org.omg.CORBA.TCKind._tk_sequence:
        System.out.println("Sequence");
        dynamicAny.rewind();
        anotherElement = true;

        while (anotherElement)
        {
          dAny = dynamicAny.current_component();
          getDynAnyValue(dAny);
          anotherElement = dynamicAny.next();
        }
        break;
    case org.omg.CORBA.TCKind._tk_array:
        System.out.println("Array");
        dynamicAny.rewind();
        anotherElement = true;

        while (anotherElement)
        {
          dAny = dynamicAny.current_component();
          getDynAnyValue(dAny);
          anotherElement = dynamicAny.next();
        }
        break;
    case org.omg.CORBA.TCKind._tk_alias:
    {
        System.out.println("Alias");
        dynamicAny.rewind();
        anotherElement = true;

        while (anotherElement)
        {
          dAny = dynamicAny.current_component();
          getDynAnyValue(dAny);
```

continues

LISTING 14.18   CONTINUED

```
                anotherElement = dynamicAny.next();
            }
        }
        default:
            System.out.println("Did not understand the type contained within the
                    DynAny");
            System.out.println("The unknown int is: " +
                    dynamicAny.type().kind().value());

        }
    }

    //Put registration code here in a main for convenience
    public static void main(String[] args)
    {
        try
        {
            // Initialize the ORB.
            org.omg.CORBA.ORB orb = org.omg.CORBA.ORB.init();

            // Initialize the BOA.
            org.omg.CORBA.BOA boa = orb.BOA_init();

            // Create the DynAnyTestImpl object.
            DynAnyTestImpl dynAnyTest=
            new DynAnyTestImpl("DynAny Sample");

            // Export the newly create object.
            boa.obj_is_ready(dynAnyTest);

            System.out.println(dynAnyTest + " is ready.");

            // Wait for incoming requests
            boa.impl_is_ready();
        }
        catch(org.omg.CORBA.SystemException ex)
        {
            ex.printStackTrace();
        }
    }
}
```

The example in Listing 14.18 wasn't designed to check for every possible primitive type contained within the structures being returned in the DynAny; this was done for simplicity. It should be clear, however, how to add checking for each of the types not checked in the getDynAnyValue() method.

SUMMARY

This chapter completed our discussion on the dynamic aspects of VisiBroker. We took an in-depth look at how to make use of DynAnys to be able to insert and extract the values within the Any without having any design-time or compile-time knowledge of what is contained in the Any.

Using normal Anys and TypeCodes, it is possible to find out a great deal about what is contained in the Any. You can find out the type, if it is complex, and you can find out how many elements are contained in it, their respective types and their respective variable names. However, the one thing you cannot access is the value contained in that Any. In order to do that, you must make use of the generated Helper class and the extract method.

DynAnys overcome this limitation by allowing Clients and Server Objects to insert and get values from an Any without having to use the Helper class.

It is important to remember that DynAnys, as well as the other dynamic complex objects, cannot be passed as arguments. If you want to pass their values as arguments, you must first convert the DynAny to a normal Any and pass it that way. It is not possible to do an ORB.object_to_string() on these dynamic types.

OBJECT ACTIVATION DAEMON AND OBJECT ACTIVATORS

CHAPTER

15

IN THIS CHAPTER

- OBJECT ACTIVATION DAEMON FOR JAVA *346*
- USING SERVICE ACTIVATOR *354*

In this chapter, we will look at a couple of different options VisiBroker provides for automatic Server Object activation. Up until this point, all our Server Object examples have been started manually at the command line and run continuously until they are explicitly shutdown. In large systems containing thousands of object implementations, this strategy can prove to be very inefficient. Thus, VisiBroker provides two different mechanisms to support on-demand activation. These two mechanisms are using the runtime Object Activation Daemon or the Activator interfaces. The goal of this chapter is to demonstrate how to use these two mechanisms for providing automatic activation to VisiBroker objects.

OBJECT ACTIVATION DAEMON FOR JAVA

VisiBroker provides an Object Activation Daemon (OAD) for Java, oadj, which is designed to provide automatic activation for Server Objects. The oadj works in conjunction with the CORBA Implementation Repository to start up object implementations on demand. The Implementation Repository is similar to the Interface Repository we discussed in Chapter 13. The Interface Repository is designed specifically to store information on VisiBroker interfaces, whereas the Implementation Repository is a database of the actual implementations themselves. The oadj relies on the information stored within the Implementation Repository in order to start Server Objects.

VisiBroker's Implementation Repository is implemented using flat files to store the necessary Server Object information.

The oadj is started by simply typing the following at the command line:

prompt> oadj [options]

The following list consists of oadj options:

- verbose—Turns verbose mode on
- version—Prints the version of VisiBroker for Java (VBJ), the Java Development Kit (JDK), and the Operating System (OS).
- path *path*—The directory containing the Implementation Repository. This option overrides the environment variable VBROKER_IMPL_PATH, which also points to the location of the Implementation Repository.
- filename *implementation_rep_filename*—The name of the Implementation Repository. This option overrides the environment variable VBROKER_IMPL_NAME, which sets the name of the Implementation Repository. If neither option is used, the default name for the Implementation Repository is impl_rep.
- timeout *# of seconds*—The OAD time-out. The default is 20 seconds, an infinite waiting period is indicated by a 0.
- kill—Kills spawned servers after they have been unregistered.

- `no_verify`—Turns off the check to make sure the Server Object registration is valid.

Several environment variables are needed when using the oadj. They are listed as follows:

- `VBROKER_ADM`—The default directory containing the Implementation Repository. The default is to write to the <VBROKER_ADM>/IMPL_DIR subdirectory.
- `VBROKER_IMPL_PATH`—Overrides the default `VBROKER_ADM` directory and specifies where the Implementation Repository is to be stored. This variable is overridden by the `-path` option to the oadj.
- `VBROKER_IMPL_NAME`—Specifies the name of the Implementation Repository. This variable is overridden by the `-filename` option to the oadj.

Using the oadj

Now that you have seen how to start the oadj and the relevant oadj environment variables, it is important to understand the runtime dynamics of how the oadj works.

In all the Client to Server Object communications you have seen in the previous chapters, you have in effect seen the same model. That model is as follows:

1. Start the Server Object. It registers with some Directory Service. This could be any of the four location strategies we discussed: Smart Agents, COS Naming Service, URL Naming Service, or simply passing Interoperable Object References (IOR) directly.
2. Start the Client. It uses one of the location mechanisms to retrieve the Server Object IOR.
3. The Client communicates directly to the Server Object.

This sequence of steps to instantiate a Server Object is different when using the oadj. When using the oadj, the communication model is as shown in Figure 15.1.

1. Start the Smart Agent.
2. Start the oadj. Because it is a CORBA Object, just like any other Server Object, it needs to register with the Smart Agent.
3. Register the Server Object with the oadj. This can be done either programmatically through the IDL interface to the oadj, or through using a command-line utility.
4. Start the Client. It attempts to locate the Server Object via the Start Agent. Because the Server Object itself isn't running, there is no registration for it in the Smart Agent's memory table. There is however, an entry for the oadj. Thus, when the request comes to the Smart Agent, the Smart Agent returns the reference of the OAD to the Client.

The client makes an invocation to the Server Object; however, this call actually goes to the oadj. The oadj then starts the Server Object and forwards the call to the newly spawned Server Object.

Figure 15.1
Sequence of steps for instantiating a Server Object when using the oadj for activation.

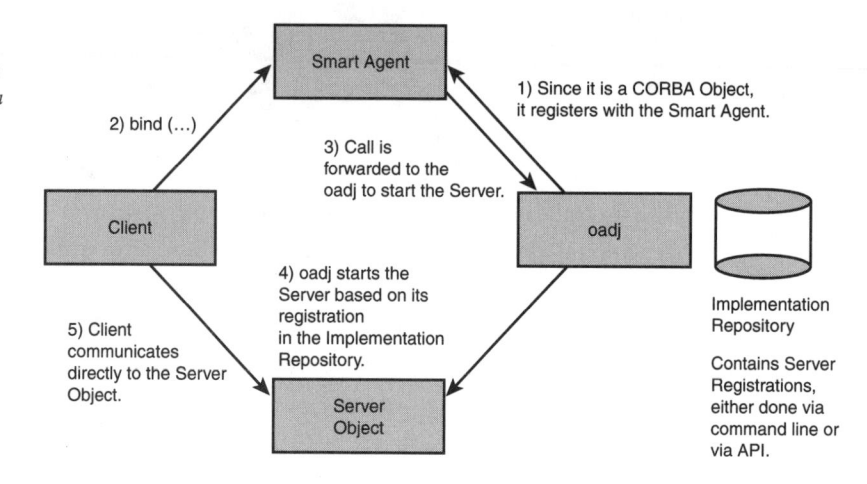

Activation Policies for the oadj

The oadj activates the Server Objects that are registered with it, based on its activation policy. The activation policy also indicates the lifespan and behavior of the Server Objects as well.

The CORBA specification defines four activation policies:

- Persistent Server
- Shared Server
- Unshared Server
- Server-per-method

The Persistent Server policy is actually what we have been using up until now. Within the VisiBroker context, any Server Object that is started manually outside of the oadj is created with the Persistent activation policy. This is true for Server Objects that are created as globally scoped objects or local transient objects. It isn't possible to have the oadj start a Server Object with the Persistent policy.

The Shared Server policy means that a single Server Object implementation is spawned and is shared by all Clients that attempt to `bind()` to it.

The Unshared Server policy means that every Client that attempts to bind to a Server Object causes the oadj to spawn a dedicated instance specifically for that Client. The Client maintains a connection to its own instance of the Server Object and is the only Client connected to that particular instance. Thus, the Server Object instance is around as long as the Client maintains a connection. After the Client drops the connection, the Server Object instance is marked for garbage collection.

The Server-per-method policy means that a Client receives a new instance of the Server Object for each method invocation. The Server Object instance exists for the duration of the method and then is marked for garbage collection after the method has completed. Each subsequent method invocation results in a new Server Object instance being created.

Registering with the oadj Interface Programmatically

The interface for the OAD is shown in Listing 15.1.

LISTING 15.1 THE OAD INTERFACE

```
public interface com.visigenic.vbroker.Activation.OAD extends
      java.lang.Object implements org.omg.CORBA.Object
{
        public abstract com.visigenic.vbroker.extension.CreationImplDef
            create_CreationImplDef();
        public abstract org.omg.CORBA.Object reg_implementation
            (com.visigenic.vbroker.extension.CreationImplDef);
        public abstract com.visigenic.vbroker.extension.CreationImplDef
            get_implementation(java.lang.String, java.lang.String);
        public abstract void change_implementation
            (com.visigenic.vbroker.extension.CreationImplDef,
            com.visigenic.vbroker.extension.CreationImplDef);
        public abstract void destroy_on_unregister(boolean);
        public abstract boolean destroy_on_unregister();
        public abstract void unreg_implementation(java.lang.String,
            java.lang.String);
        public abstract void unreg_interface(java.lang.String);
        public abstract void unregister_all();
        public abstract com.visigenic.vbroker.Activation.ImplementationStatus
            get_status(java.lang.String, java.lang.String);
        public abstract com.visigenic.vbroker.Activation.ImplementationStatus
            get_status_interface(java.lang.String)[];
        public abstract com.visigenic.vbroker.Activation.ImplementationStatus
            get_status_all()[];
        public abstract org.omg.CORBA.Object lookup_interface(java.lang.String,
            int);
        public abstract org.omg.CORBA.Object lookup_implementation
            (java.lang.String, java.lang.String, int);
        public abstract com.visigenic.vbroker.extension.CreationImplDef
            boa_activate_obj(org.omg.CORBA.Object, java.lang.String, int);
        public abstract void boa_deactivate_obj
            (org.omg.CORBA.Object, java.lang.String, int);
}
```

In order to register a Server Object with the oadj, you must make use of the `reg_implementation()` method as shown in Listing 15.1. This method takes a single argument of type `CreationImplDef`. This object is important as it contains all the necessary details for adding the Server Object into the Implementation Repository. A `CreationImplDef` object can be created using the `create_CreationImplDef()` method. Take a look at the `CreationImplDef` class in Listing 15.2.

LISTING 15.2 THE `CreationImplDef` CLASS

```
public abstract synchronized class com.visigenic.vbroker.extension.
        CreationImplDef extends org.omg.CORBA.ImplementationDef
{
    public abstract void repository_id(java.lang.String);
    public abstract java.lang.String repository_id();
    public abstract void object_name(java.lang.String);
    public abstract java.lang.String object_name();
    public abstract void id(byte[]);
    public abstract byte id()[];
    public abstract void path_name(java.lang.String);
    public abstract java.lang.String path_name();
    public abstract void activation_policy(
        com.visigenic.vbroker.extension.Policy);
    public abstract com.visigenic.vbroker.extension.Policy activation_policy();
    public abstract void args(java.lang.String[]);
    public abstract java.lang.String args()[];
    public abstract void env(java.lang.String[]);
    public abstract java.lang.String env()[];
    public com.visigenic.vbroker.extension.CreationImplDef();
}
```

This class contains accessor and modifier methods for the seven arguments that collectively make up an Implementation Repository entry. The four required attributes that must be set are

1. Repository ID—Identifies the interface that the given Server Object implements.
2. Object Name—The specific instance of the Server Object that is activated.
3. Path Names—The full path to the Server Object class file. It gives the oadj the ability to locate the Java class file that must be started.
4. Activation Policy—One of the three possible Activation Modes. This can be SHARED_SERVER, UNSHARED_SERVER, or SERVER_PER_METHOD. These policies are defined using the Policy class as shown in Listing 15.3.

LISTING 15.3 THE `Policy` CLASS, WHICH REPRESENTS THE ACTIVATION POLICY OF THE SERVER IMPLEMENTATION

```
public final synchronized class com.visigenic.vbroker.extension.Policy extends
java.lang.Object
{
    public static final int _SHARED_SERVER;
    public static final int _UNSHARED_SERVER;
```

```
    public static final int _SERVER_PER_METHOD;
    public static final com.visigenic.vbroker.extension.Policy SHARED_SERVER;
    public static final com.visigenic.vbroker.extension.Policy UNSHARED_SERVER;
    public static final com.visigenic.vbroker.extension.Policy
        SERVER_PER_METHOD;
    public int value();
    public static com.visigenic.vbroker.extension.Policy from_int(int);
    public java.lang.String toString();
    static static {};
}
```

The optional attributes that can be set as part of the Implementation Repository entry are

1. ReferenceData—Designed to serve as an application-specific identifier for the Server Object instance. The type of identifier that this is depends upon the application developer.
2. Command-line arguments—Any command-line arguments to the Server Object can be set here.
3. Environment flags—Any environment flags that need to be set for the Server Object can be set here.

Changing and Querying the oadj

After a Server Object has been registered with the oadj, it can be changed with the `change_implementation()` method.

The following methods are used for querying the oadj to determine the registrations within the Implementation Repository.

- `get_implementation()`—Returns the `CreationImplDef` object within the Implementation Repository for the given Server Object instance.
- `get_status()`—Returns the `ImplementationStatus` for a given Server Object instance.

Now, we will take a look at the `ImplementationStatus` class in Listing 15.4.

LISTING 15.4 THE ImplementationStatus CLASS

```
public final synchronized class com.visigenic.vbroker.Activation.
        ImplementationStatus extends java.lang.Object
{
    public com.visigenic.vbroker.extension.CreationImplDef impl;
    public com.visigenic.vbroker.Activation.ObjectStatus status[];
    public com.visigenic.vbroker.Activation.ImplementationStatus();
    public com.visigenic.vbroker.Activation.ImplementationStatus
        (com.visigenic.vbroker.extension.CreationImplDef,com.visigenic.vbroker.
```

continues

LISTING 15.4 CONTINUED

```
    Activation.ObjectStatus[]);
    public java.lang.String toString();
}
```

The `ImplementationStatus` object provides us the `ObjectStatus` as seen in Listing 15.5.

LISTING 15.5 THE ObjectStatus CLASS

```
public final synchronized class com.visigenic.vbroker.Activation.ObjectStatus
extends java.lang.Object
{
    public int unique_id;
    public com.visigenic.vbroker.Activation.State activation_state;
    public org.omg.CORBA.Object objRef;
    public com.visigenic.vbroker.Activation.ObjectStatus();
    public com.visigenic.vbroker.Activation.ObjectStatus
        (int,com.visigenic.vbroker.Activation.State,org.omg.CORBA.Object);
    public java.lang.String toString();
}
```

The important thing to note here is the `State` object as shown in Listing 15.6. This indicates whether the Server Object is active, inactive, or waiting for activation.

LISTING 15.6 THE State CLASS

```
public final synchronized class com.visigenic.vbroker.Activation.State extends
java.lang.Object
{
    public static final int _ACTIVE;
    public static final int _INACTIVE;
    public static final int _WAITING_FOR_ACTIVATION;
    public static final com.visigenic.vbroker.Activation.State ACTIVE;
    public static final com.visigenic.vbroker.Activation.State INACTIVE;
    public static final com.visigenic.vbroker.Activation.State
        WAITING_FOR_ACTIVATION;
    public int value();
    public static com.visigenic.vbroker.Activation.State from_int(int);
    public java.lang.String toString();
    static static {};
}
```

- `get_status_all()`—Returns an array of `ImplementationStatus` objects for all registered Server Object implementations.

- `get_status_interface()`—Returns an array of `ImplementationStatus` objects for a given Server Object interface.

UnRegistering a Server Object from the oadj

There are several methods available for unregistering a Server Object from the oadj and Implementation Repository. They are

- `unreg_implementation()`—Removes the given Server Object implementation from the Implementation Repository.
- `unreg_interface()`—Removes all Server Object implementations supporting a given interface from the Implementation Repository.
- `unregister_all()`—Unregisters all Server Object implementations.

For each of the previous methods, if the `destroy_on_unregister` attribute is set to true, the methods terminate all processes for the given interfaces.

Using the Command-line Utilities

Server Objects can be registered with the oadj through a command-line interface. A tool is provided called oadutil. The oadutil tool is used to provide the same functionality described in the previous methods. In order to use oadutil, simply type `oadutil` at the command line with a valid command as shown in the following.

```
C:\>oadutil
Usage:   oadutil {list | reg | unreg} [-options]
```

where valid commands are

```
list    List registered implementations in the OAD
reg     Register an implementation with the OAD
unreg   Unregister an implementation with the OAD.
```

When using the `reg` argument, the Repository ID or IDL name must be specified. Any of the following command-line arguments can be used with `reg` option:

```
Usage: oadutil reg {-required flags} [-options]
```

- -i interface_name -o object name
- -r repository_id -o object_name
- -s *service_name* (for registering Activators)
- -cpp filename_to_execute

    Applications registered with this option must be standalone C++ executables. The filename should include the full path to the executable.

- -java full_classname

    This option attempts to start the full_classname with the vbj command.

Optional `reg` arguments include

- -host *oad_hostname*—Specifies hostname on which the remote OAD is running.
- -verbose—Verbose mode prints debugging information to console.
- -version—Prints version information for oadutil.
- -d referenceData—Specifies reference data passed to spawned executable.
- -a arg1 -a arg2—Specifies command-line arguments for spawned executable.
- -e env1 -e env2—Specifies environment variables for spawned executable.
- -p {shared | unshared | per-method} (default: shared)—Specifies the activation policy of spawned objects.

> **NOTE**
>
> System settings won't be passed when using this option, and must be explicitly defined.

When using the `unreg` argument, the Repository ID or IDL name must be specified. Any of the following command-line arguments can be used with `unreg` option.

Usage: oadutil unreg {-required flags} [-options]

- -i interface_name -o object name
- -r repository_id -o object_name
- -s service_name (for service Activators)

Optional `unreg` arguments include

- Prints usage information.
- -host oad_hostname—Specifies hostname on which the remote OAD is running.
- -verbose—Verbose mode prints debugging information to console.
- -version—Prints version information for oadutil.

USING SERVICE ACTIVATORS

It is possible to have Server Objects activated on demand without use of the oadj, through the use of the Activator class. The Activator class is designed to register Server Objects with the ORB, and then automatically activate these objects when requests are made on these particular objects. Now, take a look at the Activator class in Listing 15.7.

LISTING 15.7 THE ACTIVATOR INTERFACE

```
public interface com.visigenic.vbroker.extension.Activator extends
java.lang.Object
{
    public abstract org.omg.CORBA.Object activate
        (org.omg.CORBA.ImplementationDef);
    public abstract void deactivate(org.omg.CORBA.Object,
        org.omg.CORBA.ImplementationDef);
}
```

To make use of the Activator interface, you must create your own class that implements the Activator class. Here you will register the Server Object implementation you want to be activated within the `activate()` method. You will also create an implementation of `deactivate()` that the ORB will automatically invoke when the Server Object is ready to be garbage collected.

We will walk through an example to demonstrate the use of the Activator class, starting with the sample IDL in Listing 15.8.

LISTING 15.8 SAMPLE IDL TO DEMONSTRATE HOW ACTIVATORS ARE USED

```
module ACTIVATE
{

  interface LongTest
    {
        long testLong(
            in long inLongVal,
            inout long inoutLongVal,
            out long outLongVal);
    };

  interface Register
  {
    LongTest register_obj(in string name);
  };

};
```

In order to have the Activator class activate your Server Object implementation, you must implement one general interface that will register your Server Object with the BOA, indicating that it will be activated by an Activator. When the BOA `obj_is_ready()` signature that accepts a Service Activator name is used, it won't actually make the Server Object ready for requests as it does by default. Rather, it simply indicates that the Server Object is activated by an Activator. Take a look at the implementation of this registration interface as shown in Listing 15.9.

LISTING 15.9 THE SERVER IMPLEMENTATION OF THE REGISTER INTERFACE AS DEFINED IN LISTING 15.8

```
public class RegImpl extends ACTIVATE._RegisterImplBase {

  public RegImpl(java.lang.String name)
  {
    super(name);
  }

  public RegImpl()
  {
    super();
  }

  public ACTIVATE.LongTest register_obj(java.lang.String name)
  {
      System.out.println("Creating:   " + name);
      ACTIVATE.LongTest obj = new LongTestImpl(name);
      int len = name.length();
      byte[] ref_data = new byte[len];
      name.getBytes(0, len-1, ref_data, 0);
      boa().obj_is_ready(obj, "MyService", ref_data);           ❶
      return obj;
  }
}
```

❶ This indicates the Server Object is to be started by an Activator.

This registration must be done before the Server Object can activate new objects. Within this registration Server Object, you will notice that it creates a new `LongTestImpl` object and registers this object with the BOA with a service name and a unique identifier represented by the Reference Data argument. Now, you must associate this registration with an Activator Implementation to actually instantiate the Server Object. Our sample Activator implementation is shown in Listing 15.10.

LISTING 15.10 AN IMPLEMENTATION OF YOUR CUSTOM ACTIVATOR CLASS, WHICH IMPLEMENTS THE VISIBROKER ACTIVATOR INTERFACE

```
import org.omg.CORBA.*;
import com.visigenic.vbroker.extension.*;

public class MyActivator implements Activator
{
    private static int _count;
    private org.omg.CORBA.BOA _boa;

    public MyActivator(org.omg.CORBA.BOA boa)
    {
        _boa = boa;
```

```
    }

    public org.omg.CORBA.Object activate(ImplementationDef impl)
    {
        System.out.println("Activator called " +  ++_count + " times");
        byte[] ref_data = ((ActivationImplDef) impl).id();
        LongTestImpl obj = new LongTestImpl(new String
                (ref_data, ref_data.length-1));
        boa.obj_is_ready(obj, "MyService", ref_data);
        return obj;
    }

    public void deactivate(org.omg.CORBA.Object obj, ImplementationDef impl)
    {
        System.out.println("Deactivator called");
        boa.deactivate_obj(obj);
        System.gc();
    }
}
```

Thus, when a call is made to the `testLong()` operation on the `LongTestImpl` object, the BOA invokes the `activate()` method on the Activator class shown previously.

The Server implementation code for the `RegImpl` object is found in Listing 15.11.

LISTING 15.11 THE SERVER MAINLINE FOR THE `RegImpl` OBJECT

```
public class Server
{
  public static void main(String[] args)
    {
        try
        {
                // Initialize the ORB.
                org.omg.CORBA.ORB orb = org.omg.CORBA.ORB.init();

                // Initialize the BOA.
                org.omg.CORBA.BOA boa = orb.BOA_init();

                ACTIVATE.Register reg = new RegImpl("Manager");

                boa.obj_is_ready(reg);

                // Wait for incoming requests
                boa.impl_is_ready("MyService", new MyActivator(boa));
        }
        catch(org.omg.CORBA.SystemException ex)
        {
                ex.printStackTrace();
        }
    }
}
```

The following steps must be taken to use the Activator described above:

1. Start the Server Object. This instantiates the `RegImpl` Server and initializes the class `MyActivator` with the BOA.
2. Create a Registration Client to register the `LongTestImpl` Server Object with the `MyActivator` class as shown in Listing 15.12.

LISTING 15.12 A SAMPLE CLIENT FOR THE REGISTER INTERFACE IDL DESCRIBED IN LISTING 15.8

```java
import java.io.*;

public class RegClient
{
    public static void main(String[] args)
    {
        try
        {
            //Initialize the ORB
            org.omg.CORBA.ORB orb = org.omg.CORBA.ORB.init();

            //Bind to the Implementation
            ACTIVATE.Register reg =
                    ACTIVATE.RegisterHelper.bind(orb, "Manager");

            // Call reg
            ACTIVATE.LongTest longTest =
                    reg.register_obj("NEW OBJECT");

                String ior = orb.object_to_string(longTest);
                FileWriter fileOut = new FileWriter("obj_ref.txt");
                fileOut.write(ior,0,ior.length());
                fileOut.close();
                System.out.println("Wrote the IOR to the file....");

        }
        catch(Exception ex)
        {
            ex.printStackTrace();
        }
    }
}
```

3. At this point, the Server must be restarted in order to recognize the registered Activators. It will now have the `LongTestImpl` Server Object Activator, represented by the `MyActivator` class, registered.
4. Start a Client for the `LongTestImpl` Server Object. A sample Client is shown in Listing 15.13. Notice that this Server Object is not running anywhere. The Activator class is

automatically invoked by the BOA when a call is made to `testLong()` on the `LongTestImpl` Object.

LISTING 15.13 A SAMPLE CLIENT FOR THE `LongTest` INTERFACE DESCRIBED IN LISTING 15.8; THE `LongTest` OBJECTS ARE ACTIVATED ON DEMAND

```
import java.io.*;

public class Client
{
    public static void main(String[] args)
    {
        try
        {
            //Initialize the ORB
            org.omg.CORBA.ORB orb = org.omg.CORBA.ORB.init();

            DataInputStream input =
                    new DataInputStream(new FileInputStream("obj_ref.txt"));
            String ior = input.readLine();
            org.omg.CORBA.Object object = orb.string_to_object(ior);
            ACTIVATE.LongTest longTest = ACTIVATE.LongTestHelper.narrow
                    (object);

            //Initialize the three parameters
            //    Create the int for the in value
            int inLongVal = 5;

            //    Create the holder for the inout value
            org.omg.CORBA.IntHolder inoutLongVal =
                new org.omg.CORBA.IntHolder(5);

            //    Create the holder for the out value
            org.omg.CORBA.IntHolder outLongVal =
                new org.omg.CORBA.IntHolder();


            //For the purposes of observation, let's set the value
            //on the out parameter.  Note that on the server, this
            //value is lost.
            outLongVal.value = 5;

            //For observation, print out the parameters
            //before making the call
            System.out.println("About to call testLong() method\n" +
                "\tin parameter" + inLongVal + "\n" +
                "\tinout parameter " + inoutLongVal.value + "\n" +
                "\tout parameter " + outLongVal.value);
```

continues

LISTING 15.13 CONTINUED

```
            //Call the remote method with the in, inout, and out
            //parameters
            int returnValue = longTest.testLong(
                inLongVal,
                inoutLongVal,
                outLongVal);

            //For observation, print out the parameters after making
            //the call
            System.out.println("After calling testLong() method\n" +
                "\tin parameter" + inLongVal + "\n" +
                "\tinout parameter " + inoutLongVal.value + "\n" +
                "\tout parameter " + outLongVal.value);
        }
        catch(Exception ex)
        {
            ex.printStackTrace();
        }
    }
}
```

Thus, we have just done a `string_to_object()` on a Server Object that was not even running! We registered the Server Object and an Activator with the BOA, and subsequent calls to the Server Object triggered the creation of the Server Object via the Activator.

SUMMARY

Today we examined an exciting new capability within VisiBroker for Java, the ability to start Server Objects on demand. We looked at two alternatives for starting Server Objects on demand, using the Object Activation Daemon or Activators.

The Object Activation Daemon is a CORBA object that uses information in the Implementation Repository in order to start Server Objects. Server Object Implementations can register with the oadj via the OAD API or through a VisiBroker utility called oadutil. When a Client attempts to connect to a Server Object registered to the oadj, the oadj spawns a new Server Object based on the Activation Policy designated and returns a reference to this new Server Object back to the Client. Server Object Activation Policies are shared server, unshared server, and server-per-method.

Activators provide a mechanism by which Server Objects can be registered with the BOA to be activated when operations on those Server Objects are called. As an association is created it calls a Service Name that links a particular Server Object implementation with an Activator implementation. After the Server Object has registered with the Activator, the Activator class automatically launches the Server Object when it is called.

SMART STUBS, CALLBACKS, AND OBJECT WRAPPERS

CHAPTER 16

IN THIS CHAPTER

- SMART STUBS *362*
- CALLBACKS *366*
- OBJECT WRAPPERS *372*

In this chapter we will be introducing three topics together—Smart Stubs, Callbacks, and Object Wrappers. Although three distinct technologies, they are being introduced at the same time because their combination results in a powerful technique for improving the performance and scalability of your VisiBroker applications. All techniques involve ORB-level programming on the client and are considered advanced topics. It should be noted that Callbacks are not a VisiBroker feature, but rather a common design pattern that nicely enhances the VisiBroker features of Smart Stubs and Object Wrappers.

We will first discuss Smart Stubs and Callbacks; then we will present techniques for using them together. We will then conclude with a discussion of Object Wrappers. Object Wrappers cover the same functionality as Smart Stubs but rely on different programming techniques. Like Smart Stubs, Object Wrappers have great synergy with Callbacks.

SMART STUBS

So far in this book, we haven't talked a lot about stubs. We explained what they are, where they live, and how they get created. In all these discussions, however, we have always taken for granted that the stub is an "automagically" generated black box of VisiBroker functionality. It represents the client-side of a remote object, and what happens between the stub and the actual implementation is the responsibility of the Object Request Broker (ORB).

After writing a few CORBA applications, you might start to get ideas about how this automatic code could be improved. For example, say you have a remote object that has an attribute Serial Number. Perhaps the serial number can only be set once, and from there, there is only a read accessor. After examining this situation for a few minutes, it might occur to you that there is no need to go to the server every time the client calls `getSerialNumber()`. After the first call, the serial number is on the client and doesn't change. One way to optimize this situation is to ask your client developers to cache the serial number locally and not call the stub each time they need this value. This isn't an elegant solution because you have now imposed coding restrictions on your clients. A nice solution would be to tell the stub to fetch the serial number from the server only once.

Smart Stubs were designed in order to place this type of intelligence into the stub used by the client developer (hence the name, Smart Stub). It is a mechanism for the server developer to push out some optimizations into the client's process without the client having to develop the code themselves.

Creating Smart Stubs

The process for creating Smart Stubs is quite straightforward. It is based on subclassing the generated stub. After you subclass the generated stub, you can choose to override the functionality of the business methods.

The process for creating a Smart Stub diverges from the process of creating a normal stub after you have created your IDL. To enable your client-side to leverage smart stubs, you must run the idl2java compiler with the -smart_stub flag. This flag adds another method to your generated _XXXXXXHelper class (we will discuss this when we talk about using Smart Stubs). Listing 16.1 shows the IDL for a small server interface, NumberSource, we will use to demonstrate Smart Stubs.

LISTING 16.1 IDL FOR SERVER TO BE USED WITH SMART STUB

```
//smartStub.idl
interface NumberSource
{
    long getTheNumber();
};
```

Note that unlike many of the previous examples, Listing 16.1 isn't simply a Test Server to highlight basic syntax. It is important to put this concept, Smart Stubs, in context. Our server is an object that the client will use to retrieve a number. The nature of the application is that the number won't change over the life of the client's session. It would therefore be unnecessary to continually go back to the server to retrieve the same information over subsequent calls. To generate the various stubs and skeletons as well as helper classes for the NumberSource object, you must type the following:

idl2java -smart_stub smartStub.idl

This enables the system to accommodate Smart Stubs. After you have generated your code, you now have the ability to alter the implementation of the stub. You do this by subclassing the stub itself (you will recall that the stub class has the name _st_<InterfaceName>.class). Listing 16.2 shows an example of the subclassed stub for the IDL defined in Listing 16.1.

LISTING 16.2 SMART STUB IMPLEMENTATION

```
public class SmartStub extends generated._st_NumberSource
{
    //The number that will be retrieved from the server
    //only once
    private int theNumber = 0;
    //Flag for our smart stub to know whether to use the local
    //"theNumber" value or go to the server
    private Boolean isNumberValid = false;

    //This is the business method we will override to make our
    //stub more efficient.
    public int getTheNumber()
    {
```

continues

LISTING 16.2 CONTINUED

```
        //Check if this is the first invocation.  If it is
        //we must go to the server for our value
        if(!isNumberValid)
        {
            //Note any call to "super" talks to the
            //"real" stub that talks to the server.  Here
            //we must ask the server for the number's value
            theNumber = super.getTheNumber();
            isNumberValid = true;
        }
        else
            System.out.println("use the local value ");
        return theNumber;
    }

}
```

Listing 16.2 shows the smart stub implementation overriding the stub's only business method—getTheNumber(). As stated previously, the characteristics of this server are such that the number won't change over the life of the client. The Smart Stub accommodates this by only hitting the network once. During the first call into the stub, a flag is checked to determine if the local number is valid. If it isn't, a call is made to the super class to retrieve the number. All subsequent calls into the stub results in a local method call.

> **TIP**
>
> When writing your Smart Stub, it is helpful to think of your super class as being the server. Any call you want to make to the server should be super.theMethod().

What code needs to be changed on the server? None. You have altered the behavior of your remote system at a level above the generated stub; thus the server continues to behave as expected.

Using Smart Stubs on the Client

In order for your clients to take advantage of your new Smart Stub, you must alter how your client sets up communication with the remote server. Recall how we indicated earlier that the -smart_stub flag created an extra method on your _NumberSourceHelper class. That allows you to tell the ORB to use an alternate stub to implement communication with the server. The method's signature reads setSmartStub(java.lang.Class stubClass). Listing 16.3 shows a client using this call to obtain a remote reference to the NumberSource server through your Smart Stub.

LISTING 16.3 CLIENT INVOCATION OF THE SERVER THROUGH A SMART STUB

```
public static void main(String[] args)
{
    try
    {
        //Initialize the ORB
        org.omg.CORBA.ORB orb = org.omg.CORBA.ORB.init();
        //call the static method to set our stub class
        generated.NumberSourceHelper.setStubClass(
            Class.forName("SmartStub"));

        //Bind to the Implementation
        generated.NumberSource numberSource =
            generated.NumberSourceHelper.bind(orb, NumberSource");
        //Call the method three times.  Note the printouts on client and server
        //will demonstrate that a network call was only used on the first
        //invocation
        for(int i = 0; i<3; i++)
            System.out.println("Calling our method returns " +
                numberSource.getTheNumber());

    }
    catch(Exception ex)
    {
        ex.printStackTrace();
    }
}
```

Compared with your normal client object resolutions, there is only once different call in Listings 16.3. You must tell the helper class to use your Smart Stub class as opposed to the default class.

> **TIP**
>
> When you need to reference a Java class (as with setting the Smart Stub) you have two choices. The more obvious is shown in Listings 16.3 that uses the static call on `java.lang.Class` to return a class object by its name. The lesser known technique for this is to use the class member on each class definition. The code in Listing 16.3 could have also been written
>
> `generated.NumberSourceHelper.setStubClass(SmartStub.class)`
>
> where we use the class member on the SmartStub class definition. The presence of this member isn't widely known.

Summary of Smart Stubs

Smart Stubs provide a mechanism for altering the behavior of generated stubs on the client. In the section just presented, we have justified their use for server attributes that won't change over the course of the client-server session.

Creating Smart Stubs is straightforward. When generating your VisiBroker classes from IDL, you must set the `-smart_stub` flag on the idl2java compiler. You can then sub class the stub and alter the behavior of the business methods. For the client to use the Smart Stub rather than the default, you must use the extra method `setSmartStub` on the generated helper classes.

At this point, it might already be obvious what the potential problem with heavy use of Smart Stubs is. How does the Smart Stub know if there is any change in the Server attribute value? Synchronization of the current value of the Server attribute with the current value within the Smart Stub must be addressed by the developer. There is nothing automatically built into the Smart Stubs to allow them to be notified of such changes in the Server. However, a good strategy for designing such a notification mechanism is to use Callbacks. In the next section, we will explain how Callbacks can be a great strategy to guarantee synchronization between the data in the Server and the data held in the Smart Stub.

CALLBACKS

So far in this chapter, we introduced Smart Stubs. Although it required a new flag to the idl2java compiler and an additional call to initialize server communication, it didn't introduce new syntax. Callbacks are a similar concept in that they don't introduce a new API or service. Rather, Callbacks leverage all our existing VisiBroker knowledge to create a new and powerful technique for dynamic client-server communication.

Every example we have given so far in this book involves the Client calling the Server. The Client is always the one to initiate a request and the Server is always the one to send a reply if one is expected. The exception to this communication is that of `oneway` method invocations that don't expect a reply from the Server. With respect to the Client, these operations are always synchronous—the call blocks until the server can respond. The method invocation on the Server can be thought of as happening on the Client's thread, where the remoted calls are simply inserted into the call path of the Client. It is the Client's thread (usually based on a user's interaction with a graphical user interface [GUI]) that is driving the system.

Callbacks allow us to view this situation in reverse. What if the server wants to drive? What if the client wants to sit back and just listen? Callbacks allow us to register Clients with Servers so the Server can call back the Clients when they want. Information flow from Server to Client doesn't always have to take place as the result of a synchronous call from Client to Server.

When would we want to use such a technique? Consider the business problem used to introduce Smart Stubs. There is a Server somewhere in the network that holds a number. When we discussed Smart Stubs, we said this number didn't change. Now assume that it does. If the number on the Server is changing and the Client always wants to know the latest number, the Client would have to engage in polling the Server. This amounts to a periodic call to the Server to essentially ask: "Has this value changed yet?" Polling techniques, although sometimes necessary, are usually inefficient. Many trips to the server might be wasted if the value hasn't changed, and polling can only approach real time as you increase the polling frequency to unreasonably high numbers (for example, is once every five seconds soon enough to learn the value of a stock has changed?).

> **NOTE**
>
> Callbacks and the Common Object Services (COS) have a great deal of overlap in functionality. We will be discussing the COS in Chapter 20. Until we get to Chapter 20, consider callbacks primarily in the scope of Smart Stubs and Object Wrappers.

Given our number Server example, we would want to give the ability for the Client to tell the Server, "let me know when and only when the value has changed". This is done through a Callback.

Implementing Callbacks

Unlike Smart Stubs, we are introducing no new methods or compiler flags for Callbacks. In fact, you already know how to implement Callbacks! Callbacks are simply taking the familiar client/server techniques and reversing them.

Before we begin discussing Callbacks, a word of caution. The terms Client and Server have always been synonymous with the program run by the human user and the daemon process hosting the implementation, respectively. With Callbacks, Client refers to the initiator of a call and a Server provides the role of responding to the call. The Client program acts as a client to one interface implementation, and provides the implementation of a second.

To begin implementing a Callback, we must first decide what information the Client program is interested in. This will be defined in IDL as an interface. For convenience of terms, we will call this a *listener* interface. We must also define the interface for the *source* of information. Such a source/listener relationship is shown in the IDL definition in Listing 16.4.

LISTING 16.4 IDL FOR CALLBACK SYSTEM

```
interface NumberListener
{
    void valueChanged(in long theValue);
};

interface NumberGenerator
{
    void addNumberListener(in Object aNumberListener);

    void removeNumberListener(in Object aNumberListener);
};
```

In Listing 16.4, the source of our information is the `NumberGenerator`, and the listener for this information is the `NumberListener`. Notice that the `NumberGenerator` has two methods that take an `in` parameter of type Object. These methods are for the registration and deregistration of Callbacks.

> **NOTE**
>
> The Callback pattern can be equated to the Observer/Observable pattern described in the popular book *Design Patterns* by Gama et al. Callbacks can also be observed in single JVM systems through the 1.1 AWT Event model. If an object is interested in an attribute of a `java.awt.Component`, that object can add itself as a listener to the component. Registering for these events requires the interested object to provide an object implementing a known interface for callback.

Listing 16.5 shows your Client, and Listing 16.6 shows your Server for the callback defined in Listing 16.4. We see in Listing 16.5 that the Client is creating a local CallBack object and passing this object reference to the Server in Listing 16.6. The Server simply invokes the `valueChanged()` method on this `CallBack` object reference when the value changes.

LISTING 16.5 CALLBACK CLIENT

```
public class Client
implements generated.NumberListenerOperations
{
    public Client()
    {
    }
```

```java
    public void valueChanged(int theValue)
    {
        System.out.println("Value Changed " + theValue);

    }
    public static void main(String[] args)
    {
        try
        {
            System.out.println("foo");
            //Initialize the ORB
            org.omg.CORBA.ORB orb = org.omg.CORBA.ORB.init();

            //Bind to the Implementation
            generated.NumberGenerator numberGenerator =
                generated.NumberGeneratorHelper.bind(orb, "NumberGenerator");

            System.out.println("Bound to remote number generator");

            //Create a new client.  This is the
            //implementation of the callback method
            Client client = new Client();

            //Bind the client as a callable object.  This
            //looks a lot like registering a server because it is
            org.omg.CORBA.BOA boa = orb.BOA_init();

            //Use the TIE mechanism to register the server.  Note
            //that the client (this class) implements the operations
            generated._tie_NumberListener tie =
                new generated._tie_NumberListener(client);


            boa.obj_is_ready(tie);

            //Add ourselves as a listener
            numberGenerator.addNumberListener(tie);

            //wait till someone hits return
            System.in.read();

        }
        catch(Exception ex)
        {
            ex.printStackTrace();
        }
    }
}
```

LISTING 16.6 CALLBACK SERVER

```
/*
 * Server used to highlight the use of callbacks.  Note that we have a
 * small inner-class to handle periodically changing a counter
 */
public class NumberGeneratorImpl
extends generated._NumberGeneratorImplBase
{
    java.util.Vector listeners = null;
    int theNumber = 0;

    //Constructor for transient object
    public NumberGeneratorImpl()
    {
        finishConstructor();
    }

    //Constructor for persistent object
    public NumberGeneratorImpl(String name)
    {
        super(name);
        finishConstructor();
    }

    private void finishConstructor()
    {
        listeners = new java.util.Vector();
        new NumberChanger().start();
    }

    public void addNumberListener(org.omg.CORBA.Object anObject)
    {
        System.out.println("Add number listener called for object: " +
            anObject.toString());
        //First, narrow the object to be of the NumberListener type
        generated.NumberListener aNumberListener =
            chapter16.callback.generated.NumberListenerHelper.narrow(anObject);

        //check if the objects exists.  It is unlikely that
        //the object could be bound but the implementation dead,
        //so soon yet we should still check.  This call is like
        //"ping"ing the object
        if(aNumberListener._non_existent())
        {
            //Object doesn't exist.  this is an invalid registration
            System.out.println("Object impl doesn't exist");
            return;
        }
        //Add to our list of listeners
        synchronized(listeners)
        {
            listeners.addElement(aNumberListener);
```

```
            System.out.println("Added listener to our list");
        }
    }
    public void removeNumberListener(org.omg.CORBA.Object aNumberListener)
    {

    }

    public void changeNumber(int newNumber)
    {
        System.out.println("Try to publish the change");
        theNumber = newNumber;
        try
        {
            synchronized(listeners)
            {
                java.util.Enumeration en = listeners.elements();
                while(en.hasMoreElements())
                {
                    generated.NumberListener listener =
                        (generated.NumberListener) en.nextElement();
                    //check if the listener is still valid
                    if(listener._non_existent())
                        continue;
                    //make the callback
                    listener.valueChanged(theNumber);
                }
            }
        }
        catch(Exception ex)
        {
            ex.printStackTrace();
        }
    }

    //Put registration code here in a main for convenience
    public static void main(String[] args)
    {
        try
        {
            // Initialize the ORB.
            org.omg.CORBA.ORB orb = org.omg.CORBA.ORB.init();

            // Initialize the BOA.
            org.omg.CORBA.BOA boa = orb.BOA_init();

            // Create the object.
            NumberGeneratorImpl generator =
            new NumberGeneratorImpl("NumberGenerator");
```

continues

LISTING 16.6 CONTINUED

```java
            // Export the newly create object.
            boa.obj_is_ready(generator);

            System.out.println(generator + " is ready.");

            // Wait for incoming requests
            boa.impl_is_ready();
        }
        catch(org.omg.CORBA.SystemException ex)
        {
            ex.printStackTrace();
        }
    }
}

class NumberChanger extends Thread
{
    int number = 0;
    public void run()
    {
        while(true)
        {
            try
            {
                sleep(1000);
                changeNumber(number++);
            }
            catch(Exception ex)
            {
                ex.printStackTrace();
            }
        }
    }
}
```

OBJECT WRAPPERS

In our discussion of Smart Stubs, we decided that they offer a convenient mechanism for altering the behavior of the code just below the calling application. Object Wrappers serve the same effect, but take a different approach.

> Before discussing Object Wrappers much further, we should address the issue of Object Wrappers versus Smart Stubs. Are they similar? Yes. In fact, you could argue

> that Object Wrappers provide a superset of the functionality provided by Smart Stubs. This section highlights the difference between Smart Stubs and Object Wrappers.

The Smart Stub allows a single developer to redefine the behavior of a Stub by subclassing the stub itself. Although the developer has total freedom to change the behavior of the stub, it must be done all at once. Object Wrappers take a different approach and do not re-implement the stub. Object Wrappers serve to insert themselves into the call stack around the stub. Choosing to insert one or more Object Wrappers around a stub is up to the application. The relative location of Object Wrappers in a typical application is shown in Figure 16.1.

FIGURE 16.1
Position of Object Wrapper within System.

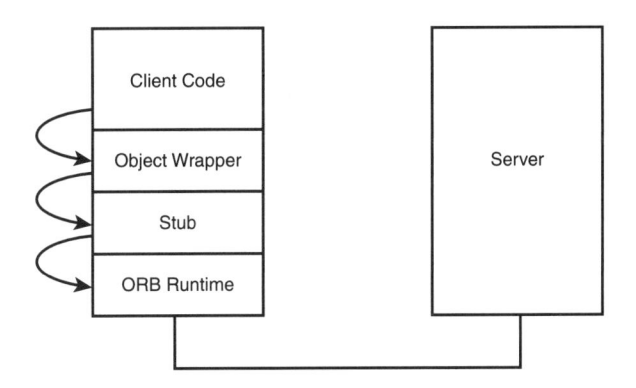

There should be one major feature in Figure 16.1 that appears different from our discussion of Smart Stubs, the presence of wrappers between the skeleton and implementation. We will shortly examine the use of positioning code between the skeleton and implementation, but we also must introduce the notion of *chaining*. Chaining is another feature of Object Wrappers that allows multiple object wrappers to be placed into the calling path or chained. Chaining is possible because Object Wrappers don't rely on solely subclassing the stubs and skeletons. Chained Object Wrappers are shown in Figure 16.2.

Object Wrappers come in two varieties: typed and untyped. The remainder of this of our Object Wrapper Discussion deals with these varieties separately; then we will discuss using them together.

Typed Object Wrappers

As their name implies, Typed Object Wrappers are designed to wrap around a particular interface. They have been written for a particular, user-defined Java type—an interface. Much like Smart Stubs, Typed Object Wrappers afford the developer the opportunity to alter the behavior of a remote call, perhaps choosing to cache information on the client. Unlike Smart Stubs, the same Object Wrappers can also be used on the Server.

FIGURE 16.2
Chained Object Wrappers.

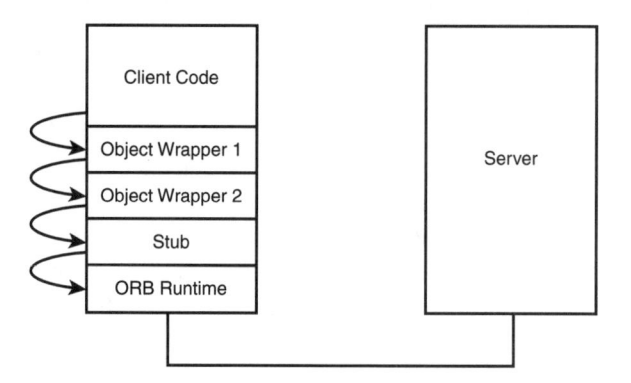

```
┌──────────────────┐        ┌──────────┐
│   Client Code    │        │          │
├──────────────────┤        │          │
│ Object Wrapper 1 │        │          │
├──────────────────┤        │  Server  │
│ Object Wrapper 2 │        │          │
├──────────────────┤        │          │
│      Stub        │        │          │
├──────────────────┤        │          │
│   ORB Runtime    │────────│          │
└──────────────────┘        └──────────┘
```

To understand how the same Typed Object Wrapper can be used on both Client and Server, consider for a moment the notion of a wrapper chain. We previously mentioned that one or more wrappers can be linked together on the Client and Server machines to create a chain of wrappers. Examining Figure 16.2 for a moment, you can imagine that each element in that chain must implement the same interface. The client initially called into the first wrapper, viewing that wrapper as being the remote object. That wrapper was then able to pass the call along to the next wrapper and then to the stub. Because we don't want to tightly couple one element of the chain to the other, the remote interface is the only knowledge each element has of the other.

To further our discussion, view the stub and skeleton as being a single unit. A call enters one side of the network then it pops out the other. The combination of the stub and skeleton is yet another member of our chain. In a normal system, the skeleton calls the Impl by delegating the skeleton methods into the implementation. How does a skeleton know about the Implementation? It knows by interface. We can leverage this interface-only relationship between implementation and skeleton and insert another element of our chain between skeleton and implementation.

Each member of the chain knows about the others by viewing them only through the remote interface. Listing 16.8 shows a sample `ObjectWrapper` for the IDL interface defined in Listing 16.7.

LISTING 16.7 SAMPLE IDL TO DEMONSTRATE TYPED OBJECT WRAPPERS

```
interface StringManipulator
{
    long countCharacters(in string aString);
```

```
        string toUpperCase(in string aString);
    };
```

LISTING 16.8 SAMPLE TYPED OBJECT WRAPPER FROM IDL IN LISTING 16.7

```java
/*
 * Implementation of our typed Object Wrapper.  Note that we will
 * override the business methods, but only use our implementation
 * to print to console
 */
public class SimpleTypedObjectWrapper
extends generated.StringManipulatorObjectWrapper
{
    public int countCharacters(String aString)
    {
        //Print a message to console so we can observe the order
        //of method calls
        System.out.println("ObjectWrapper Implementation of countCharacters()
                has been called");
        //Get the "real" result from our superclass, that calls
        //the stub (client) or Impl (server)
        return super.countCharacters(aString);
    }

    public String toUpperCase(String aString)
    {
        //Print a message to console so we can observe the order
        //of method calls
        System.out.println("ObjectWrapper Implementation of toUpperCase()
                has been called");
        //Get the "real" result from our superclass, that calls
        //the stub (client) or Impl (server)
        return super.toUpperCase(aString);
    }
}
```

Listings 16.8 shows a Typed Object Wrapper for the `StringManipulator` interface. One feature of this class that should catch the eye of the reader is the super class of the `SimpleTypedObjectWrapper` : `StringManipulatorObjectWrapper`. This is a class generated by VisiBroker's idl2java utility. Generation of this class is not automatic, and requires use of the -obj_wrapper flag to the compiler as is shown in the following.

prompt> idl2java -obj_wrapper typedWrapperExample.idl

We have asserted that the same object wrappers can be used on both Client and Server. Listing 16.9 shows the client code inserting the Object Wrapper into the chain.

LISTING 16.9 INSTALLING TYPED OBJECT WRAPPER ON CLIENT

```
public class Client
{
    public static void main(String[] args)
    {
        try
        {
            //Initialize the ORB
            org.omg.CORBA.ORB orb = org.omg.CORBA.ORB.init();

            //Add our typed object wrapper to the chain on the client.
            //Note that this is done through the Helper class for our
            //remoted object
            generated.StringManipulatorHelper.addClientObjectWrapperClass(
                orb, Class.forName("SimpleTypedObjectWrapper"));

            //Bind to the Implementation of our StringManipulator
            generated.StringManipulator stringManipulator =
                generated.StringManipulatorHelper.bind
                (orb, "StringManipulator");

            //Call the two methods to show the untyped wrapper being called
            String aString = "VisiBroker";
            System.out.println("Within client, about to call
                countCharacters() ");
            int length = stringManipulator.countCharacters(aString);
            System.out.println("Within client, just after calling
                countCharacters() ");

            System.out.println("Within client, about to call toUpperCase() ");
            String upper = stringManipulator.toUpperCase(aString);
            System.out.println("Within client, just after calling
                toUpperCase() ");

        }
        catch(Exception ex)
        {
            ex.printStackTrace();
        }
    }
}
```

In Listing 16.9, the application tells the ORB to add an Object Wrapper to the chain. This is done through a call to the generated Helper class, which is in contact with the ORB. The parameters to this call are the ORB reference itself and the *class* of the wrapper. The class is provided instead of an instance, so the ORB can call `class.newInstance()` for each remote reference obtained. If the calling client binds to two remote instances of our `StringManipulator`, two `ObjectWrappers` are created. Note that the wrapper must be installed before binding to any remote object. Registering a wrapper after binding won't retroactively insert the wrapper into already bound objects.

The process for installing an `ObjectWrapper` on the Server is almost the same except instead of calling `Helper.addClientObjectWrapperClass(...)`, the method `addServerObjectWrapperClass(...)` is invoked. Like on the Client, this must be called before remote objects are bound. Listing 16.10 shows the `StringManipulatorImpl` installing this typed Object Wrapper.

> **CAUTION**
>
> Since the ORB is creating new instances of your `ObjectWrapper` class, the class must support a default constructor (that is, one that takes no arguments)!

LISTING 16.10 INSTALLING TYPED OBJECT WRAPPER ON SERVER

```
//...
//Within Server Code
public static void main(String[] args)
{
    try
    {
        // Initialize the ORB.
        org.omg.CORBA.ORB orb = org.omg.CORBA.ORB.init();

        // Use the helper class to add our typed object wrapper
        enerated.StringManipulatorHelper.addServerObjectWrapperClass(
            orb, Class.forName("SimpleTypedObjectWrapper"));

        // Initialize the BOA.
        org.omg.CORBA.BOA boa = orb.BOA_init();

        // Create the object.  NOTE THIS CALL VERY CAREFULLY
        // We are actually using the object returned from the _this() call
        // to call "ready" with the BOA.  This is the Impl that has been
        // added to the chain
        generated.StringManipulator stringManipulator =
            new StringManipulatorImpl("StringManipulator")._this();

        // Export the newly create object.
        boa.obj_is_ready(stringManipulator);

        System.out.println(stringManipulator + " is ready.");
```

continues

LISTING 16.10 CONTINUED

```
            // Wait for incoming requests
            boa.impl_is_ready();
        }
        catch(Exception ex)
        {
            ex.printStackTrace();
        }
    }
}
```

One call in Listing 16.10 should receive close examination. As you are creating your `StringManipulatorImpl` and preparing to call the `obj_is_ready()` method, you are calling `_this()`. What's this for? It has to do with the nature of the Java Language and VisiBroker's implementation. The call to `_this()` registers a chained implementation with the BOA, ensuring that the Object Wrapper is called before the Implementation.

> **CAUTION**
>
> Failure to register the object returned by `_this()` results in difficult to identify runtime bugs. When using Object Wrappers on the Server, always remember to register `_this()`.

Untyped Object Wrappers

Like Typed Object Wrappers, Untyped Object Wrappers can be chained into the call order between Client and Implementation. Unlike Typed Object Wrappers, Untyped Object Wrappers don't implement the interface being remoted on each call. Instead, Untyped Object Wrappers implement a generic interface where methods are called as the request is being made and as the reply returns.

Untyped Object Wrappers all implement the same interface with two well-known methods. Listing 16.11 shows an Untyped Object Wrapper sample with the two mandatory methods.

LISTING 16.11 UNTYPED OBJECT WRAPPER

```
/*
 * Implementation of the UntypedObjectWrapper.  Because
 * this is a simple exercise, we will just print-out
 * the fact that each method has been called
 */
public class SimpleUntypedObjectWrapper
implements com.visigenic.vbroker.interceptor.UntypedObjectWrapper
```

```java
{
    //Method called before invoking any method on target
    //object.  Note that we do NOT have access to the
    //parameters on the remote object
    public void pre_method(String operation,
        org.omg.CORBA.Object target,
        com.visigenic.vbroker.interceptor.Closure closure)
    {
        //Our only job is to inform the console that we have been
        //called
        System.out.println("pre_method called for operation " +
            operation);
    }

    //Method called after method call from stub/impl has returned
    public void post_method(String operation,
        org.omg.CORBA.Object target,
        org.omg.CORBA.Environment environment,
        com.visigenic.vbroker.interceptor.Closure closure)
    {
        //remember our only job is to tell the console the remote
        //operation is complete
        System.out.print("post_method called for operation " +
            operation);

        //See if there were any exceptions thrown during the invoke
        Exception ex = environment.exception();
        if(ex == null)
            System.out.println(" There were no exceptions thrown during this
                invocation");
        else
            System.out.println(" An exception was raised during this invoke
                with message " + ex.toString());
    }

}
```

The methods pre_method(...) and post_method(...) are called in that order. The parameters to pre_method(...) include the operation (name of method being called), target (the object, remote or not, being targeted), and a Closure object. The Closure object allows the wrapper to store information away for later retrieval in post_method(...). In a multithreaded environment, this is the only approach for maintaining the correlation between several pre and post calls.

post_method(...) has the same parameters as pre_method(...) with the same purposes. The difference with post_method(...) is that it also presents an Environment object. The Environment object is necessary because the loose typing on your class doesn't allow for exceptions to be detected. If the Client calls the implementation and the implementation throws an exception, "who does the Untyped Wrapper know?", it is the Environment class that holds any exception information propagated during the call chain.

Installing Untyped Object Wrappers is similar to Typed Object Wrappers in that they must be installed before binding to any remote objects. They are different in that there is a single chain to join for Untyped Object Wrappers. The chain can be obtained by binding to the ChainClientUntypedObjectWrapper and adding a factory for your Untyped Wrapper to the chain. As a factory, your factory is responsible for returning an implementation of an Untyped Object Wrapper on demand. Listing 16.12 shows a factory for our SimpleUntypedObjectWrapper.

LISTING 16.12 UNTYPED OBJECT WRAPPER FACTORY

```
/*
 * Implementation of the Factory for our
 * simple UntypedObjectWrappers
 */
public class SimpleUntypedObjectWrapperFactory
implements com.visigenic.vbroker.interceptor.UntypedObjectWrapperFactory
{

    //Method required for the UntypedObjectWrapperFactory interface.
    //We return from this method the desired implementation of the
    //UntypedObjectWrapper interface
    public com.visigenic.vbroker.interceptor.UntypedObjectWrapper create(
        org.omg.CORBA.Object target)
    {
        //Print a message to the console for observation of process
        System.out.println("Factory has been requested to create Untyped" +
            " wrapper for target " + target.toString());
        //Return our "simple" implementation
        return new SimpleUntypedObjectWrapper();
    }
}
```

Why do Untyped Object Wrappers not use the `class.newInstance()` method of creation instead of the Factory pattern? One use of the Factory pattern over the mandatory creation of a new instance for each remote reference can be observed in the possible uses of Untyped Object Wrappers. Untyped Wrappers can be used for application-level instrumentation information like round-trip time or generic logging. If instrumentation is being written to a common log file, we don't want to have several instances writing to the same file. The factory gives the flexibility of returning the same object upon each `create()` call (the Singleton Pattern), or a new instance each time. Listing 16.13 shows a Client installing the Untyped Object Wrapper Factory before binding to any remote instances.

LISTING 16.13 INSTALLING UNTYPED OBJECT WRAPPER FACTORY ON CLIENT

```
/*
 * Client to test using an Untyped Object Wrapper
 */
public class Client
{
    public static void main(String[] args)
    {
        try
        {
            //Initialize the ORB
            org.omg.CORBA.ORB orb = org.omg.CORBA.ORB.init();

            //Obtain a reference to the chainUntypedObjectWrapperFactory.
            //It is through this object that we will add our own untyped
            //object wrapper.  We obtain this object first through the
            //resolve_initial_references call then we will narrow with the
            //helper
            org.omg.CORBA.Object rawChainFactory =
                orb.resolve_initial_references(
                "ChainClientUntypedObjectWrapperFactory");

            //Narrow the raw reference to our chainUntypedWrapperFactory
            com.visigenic.vbroker.interceptor.ChainUntypedObjectWrapperFactory
                chainFactory =
com.visigenic.vbroker.interceptor.ChainUntypedObjectWrapperFactoryHelper.narrow
                (rawChainFactory);

            //Add our SimpleUntypedObjectWrapperFactory to the chain
            chainFactory.add(
                new SimpleUntypedObjectWrapperFactory());

            //Bind to the Implementation of our StringManipulator
            generated.StringManipulator stringManipulator =
                generated.StringManipulatorHelper.bind
                (orb, "StringManipulator");

            //Call the two methods to show the untyped wrapper being called
            String aString = "VisiBroker";
            System.out.println("Within client, about to call
                countCharacters() ");
            int length = stringManipulator.countCharacters(aString);
            System.out.println("Within client, just after calling
                countCharacters() ");

            System.out.println("Within client, about to call toUpperCase() ");
            String upper = stringManipulator.toUpperCase(aString);
            System.out.println("Within client, just after calling
```

continues

LISTING 16.13   CONTINUED

```
                toUpperCase() ");
        }
        catch(Exception ex)
        {
            ex.printStackTrace();
        }
    }
}
```

Although we will not provide a code sample to demonstrate, the installation of Untyped Wrapper Factories on the Server uses the same techniques, except the `ChainServerUntypedObjectWrapperFactory` is bound instead of the `ChainClientUntypedObjectWrapperFactory`. The same type of object, however, is returned.

Combining Typed and Untyped Object Wrappers

Combining Typed and Untyped Object Wrappers doesn't impose any special coding considerations. Both work together to perform their functions, and don't interfere with one another. The only important point to make is that the `pre_method(...)` calls on Untyped Wrappers are called before any Typed Wrappers, and the `post_method(...)` call is made after all Typed Wrappers in the chain have been called.

SUMMARY

In this chapter we dealt with three technologies, Smart Stubs, Callbacks, and Object Wrappers. Smart Stubs offer the server developer a chance to alter the behavior of the stubs executing on the client. It is convenient in situations where features are required on the client, but such features aren't the domain of the client-side developer.

One example of behavior to place into a Smart Stub involves caching of data. If a client is making frequent calls to retrieve data that hasn't changed, caching that data on the client removes a potentially expensive network round trip. However, caches can become stale; that is why callbacks offer a technique for keeping client caches current. Callbacks allow the client process to host implementations that can be invoked by the server. An example of such an invoke is the call to refresh a cache.

Object Wrappers are an alternative to Smart Stubs. Both Smart Stubs and Object Wrappers allow logic to be inserted under the application level code on the client. Object Wrappers differ from Smart Stubs in that they are inserted into the call sequence not using inheritance (as with Smart Stubs) but with chaining.

EVENT HANDLERS AND PRINCIPAL AUTHENTICATION

CHAPTER 17

IN THIS CHAPTER

- THE PRINCIPAL *384*
- SERVER-SIDE EVENT HANDLERS *390*
- CLIENT-SIDE EVENT HANDLERS *399*
- HandlerRegistry *401*

In this chapter, we focus on how to customize VisiBroker so that the Client and Server implementations you write can be automatically notified when certain system level events occur. In other words, when a Client has an active connection to a Server Object, what default behavior would you like to see occur if this connection is abnormally terminated?

We will also examine the role of the Principal within CORBA. The Principal data structure was designed to provide a generic byte stream that is implicitly passed with every method invocation. The data that is written to the stream is entirely up to the application developer. In today's chapter we will demonstrate how the Principal type can be used as a means to pass some type of Client identity to the Server for authorization. By combining the Principal type and Event Handlers, you can very quickly set up your own access control to your Server Objects.

> **NOTE**
>
> The Principal data type has been deprecated in the latest CORBA specification. Although this feature is still useful in VisiBroker 3.x, it is uncertain if future versions of VisiBroker will continue to have support for this type.

THE PRINCIPAL

The Principal is a CORBA-defined data structure designed to allow application developers the ability to pass an identity to the Server. The Principal is defined in IDL as shown in Listing 17.1.

LISTING 17.1 THE IDL MAPPING FOR THE CORBA::Principal

```
sequence <octet>
```

From the IDL to Java language mapping discussed in Chapters 2–4, you should remember that an octet is mapped to a Java byte array. Thus, you see that the CORBA Principal is a Java byte array that can contain any data relevant to the application's authentication scheme. VisiBroker implements the Principal type as a Java class with a name attribute, providing an accessor and modifier method. The Principal class is shown in Listing 17.2.

LISTING 17.2 THE PRINCIPAL CLASS

```
public abstract synchronized class org.omg.CORBA.Principal extends
↪java.lang.Object
{
    public abstract void name(byte[]);
    public abstract byte name()[];
    public org.omg.CORBA.Principal();
}
```

Obtaining the Principal

There are two methods for obtaining a `CORBA::Principal`. The first is on the `org.omg.CORBA.ORB` class as shown in Listing 17.3.

LISTING 17.3 THE AVAILABLE METHODS ON THE `org.omg.CORBA.ORB` CLASS FOR OBTAINING A `CORBA::Principal`

```
public abstract synchronized class org.omg.CORBA.ORB extends java.lang.Object
{
    .........
public org.omg.CORBA.Principal default_principal();
        public void default_principal(org.omg.CORBA.Principal);
    .........
}
```

> **NOTE**
>
> Although this method appears on the `org.omg.CORBA.ORB` interface, it isn't an Object Management Group (OMG) method.

From Listing 17.3, you can see that the `org.omg.CORBA.ORB` class defines an attribute called `default_principal`, providing an accessor and modifier method for the default Principal value for the given Object Request Broker (ORB) handle. It is important to note that the Principal value is unique for each ORB reference you have. Thus, every separate process you have, which initializes its own ORB instance, has its own unique Principal value associated with that particular ORB.

After the Principal has been set, it can be obtained in the same process space by using the `default_principal()` method shown in Listing 17.3.

The second way of obtaining the Principal is by calling `get_principal(...)` on the `org.omg.CORBA.BOA` class. This is shown as follows in Listing 17.4.

LISTING 17.4 THE AVAILABLE METHOD ON THE `org.omg.CORBA.BOA` CLASS THAT PROVIDES THE CURRENT `CORBA::Principal` VALUE

```
public abstract synchronized class org.omg.CORBA.BOA extends java.lang.Object
{
.........
public abstract org.omg.CORBA.Principal get_principal(org.omg.CORBA.Object);
.........
}
```

The get_principal(...) method, as shown in Listings 17.4, is designed to return the Principal that has been passed as part of a method request to a given object. Remember that the Principal is an implicit parameter that is sent on every CORBA method invocation, whether you choose to set it or not. Thus, within any method implementation in your Server Object, you can call get_principal(...) to get the Principal value that was sent from the Client. It is through this mechanism that your method implementation can obtain the Principal value set on the Client.

An Example Using the Principal

Now take a look at an example in Listing 17.5. Using one of the basic IDL files from Chapter 2, "Introduction to IDL," we will modify this example to have the Client set a value in the Principal object and have the Server Object obtain this value as shown in Listing 17.4.

LISTING 17.5 THE MODIFIED VERSION OF THE SIMPLE IDL AND CLIENT ORIGINALLY SHOWN IN CHAPTER 2, INCORPORATING THE CORBA::Principal

```
module PrincipalExample
{

    interface LongTest
    {
        long testLong(
            in long inLongVal,
            inout long inoutLongVal,
            out long outLongVal);
    };
};
public class Client
{

public static void main(String[] args)
    {
        try
        {
            //Initialize the ORB
            org.omg.CORBA.ORB orb = org.omg.CORBA.ORB.init();

            //Bind to the Implementation
            PrincipalExample.LongTest longTest =
                PrincipalExample.LongTestHelper.bind(orb, "Long Sample");


            //Initialize the three parameters
            //    Create the int for the in value
```

```java
            int inLongVal = 5;

            //    Create the holder for the inout value
            org.omg.CORBA.IntHolder inoutLongVal =
                new org.omg.CORBA.IntHolder(5);

            //    Create the holder for the out value
            org.omg.CORBA.IntHolder outLongVal =
                new org.omg.CORBA.IntHolder();


            //For the purposes of observation, let's set the value on the
            //out parameter.  Note that on the server, this value is lost.
            outLongVal.value = 5;

            //For observation, print out the parameters
            //before making the call
            System.out.println("About to call testLong() method\n" +
                "\tin parameter" + inLongVal + "\n" +
                "\tinout parameter " + inoutLongVal.value + "\n" +
                "\tout parameter " + outLongVal.value);

            // Notice, these are the only lines that are added to "set" the
                // Principal value on the Client side.
                String user_name = new String("Ralph");
                byte[] byte_name = user_name.getBytes();
            org.omg.CORBA.Principal principal = orb.default_principal();
            principal.name(byte_name);
            orb.default_principal(principal);

            //Call the remote method with the in, inout, and out parameters
            int returnValue = longTest.testLong(
                inLongVal,
                inoutLongVal,
                outLongVal);

            //For observation, print out the parameters after making the call
            System.out.println("After calling testLong() method\n" +
                "\tin parameter" + inLongVal + "\n" +
                "\tinout parameter " + inoutLongVal.value + "\n" +
                "\tout parameter " + outLongVal.value);
        }
        catch(org.omg.CORBA.SystemException ex)
        {
            ex.printStackTrace();
        }
    }
}
```

It is important to note that the previous Client code is absolutely identical to our listings from Chapter 2, with the exception of the following lines of code:

```
String user_name = new String("CRalph ");
byte[] byte_name = user_name.getBytes();
org.omg.CORBA.Principal principal =
        orb.default_principal();
principal.name(byte_name);
orb.default_principal(principal);
```

From Listing 17.5, you see that the following sequence of steps are needed in order to set the default Principal value to pass to the Server Object.

Steps Needed in Client to Set the Default Principal and Pass This Value to the Server Object

1. Determine the identity value you want to store in the Principal data type. Copy this value into a byte array.

2. Obtain an `org.omg.CORBA.Principal` object by calling `default_principal()` on your ORB handle.

3. Call the `name(...)` method on the Principal object to set the Principal value with the byte array.

4. Set the newly initialized Principal object as the default Principal to be passed on all method invocations by calling `default_principal()` passing in the Principal object.

LISTING 17.6 THE SERVER IMPLEMENTATION FOR THE CLIENT SHOWN IN LISTING 17.5, WHICH IS A MODIFIED VERSION OF THE SERVER ORIGINALLY SHOWN IN CHAPTER 2 TO DEMONSTRATE THE USE OF THE CORBA::Principal

```
public class LongTestImpl extends PrincipalExample._LongTestImplBase
{
    //Constructor for transient object
    public LongTestImpl()
    {
    }

    //Constructor for persistent object
    public LongTestImpl(String name)
    {
        super(name);
    }

    public int testLong(
        int inLongVal,
        org.omg.CORBA.IntHolder inoutLongVal,
        org.omg.CORBA.IntHolder outLongVal)
```

```java
{
    // Notice that these are the only lines that must be added in order
        // to obtain the Principal passed to the Server from the Client.
        org.omg.CORBA.Principal p = _boa().get_principal
            ( (org.omg.CORBA.Object) this);
    String principal = new String(p.name());
    System.out.println(principal);

    //For observation, print out the parameters
    //before as passed to this method
    System.out.println("Beginning testLong() method\n" +
        "\tin parameter" + inLongVal + "\n" +
        "\tinout parameter " + inoutLongVal.value + "\n" +
        "\tout parameter " + outLongVal.value);

    //Change the value of the in parameter.  Note that
    //this is done to show that this new value is
    //NOT carried back to the client
    inLongVal = 6;

    //Change value of inout parameter
    inoutLongVal.value = 6;

    //Set value of the out parameter
    outLongVal.value = 6;

    //For observation, print out the parameters
    //before the return
    System.out.println("About to return from testLong() method\n" +
        "\tin parameter" + inLongVal + "\n" +
        "\tinout parameter " + inoutLongVal.value + "\n" +
        "\tout parameter " + outLongVal.value);

    return 0;
}

//Put registration code here in a main for convenience
public static void main(String[] args)
{
    try
    {
        // Initialize the ORB.
        org.omg.CORBA.ORB orb = org.omg.CORBA.ORB.init();

        // Initialize the BOA.
        org.omg.CORBA.BOA boa = orb.BOA_init();

        // Create the Principal objects.
        LongTestImpl longTest=
        new LongTestImpl("Long Sample");
```

continues

LISTING 17.6 CONTINUED

```
        // Export the newly create object.
        boa.obj_is_ready(longTest);

        System.out.println(longTest + " is ready.");

        // Wait for incoming requests
        boa.impl_is_ready();
    }
    catch(org.omg.CORBA.SystemException ex)
    {
        ex.printStackTrace();
    }
  }
}
```

Obtaining the Principal value that was passed to the Server can be done by calling the `get_principal(...)` method on the Basic Object Adapter (BOA). Remember, the Principal is simply a Java byte array that will need to be converted back into its original type before it can be used. In our example this involves converting a Java byte array into a Java String for validation. The following segment of the Server from Listing 17.6 does this:

```
org.omg.CORBA.Principal p = _boa().get_principal((org.omg.CORBA.Object) this);
        String principal = new String(p.name());
        System.out.println(principal);
```

The Server in Listing 17.6 demonstrates the basic steps needed to obtain the Principal value so that you can develop your own method-level access control. You will see in the following pages that using Server-side Event Handlers can allow you to implement connection-level access control. In other words, Server-Side Event Handlers will actually allow you to control which Clients are allowed to bind to the Server and which Clients are rejected. This is the focus of our next section on the Server-side Event Handler interface.

> **NOTE**
>
> The `org.omg.CORBA.Principal` is the only parameter passed as part of a CORBA method invocation that is not marshaled. The Principal byte stream isn't translated, interpreted, or modified in any way.

SERVER-SIDE EVENT HANDLERS

As mentioned briefly in the chapter introduction, the Client-side and Server-side Event Handlers are designed to give the application developer the opportunity to write his own custom code that gets invoked whenever certain system events occur. In other words, it allows the developer to define the default behavior if the network crashes or if a Client or Server crashes in the middle of a method request. In both the Client and Server Event Handlers, a series of predefined callback methods can be implemented that will get called by the ORB runtime around binding and method invocations. We will take a look at the Server-side interface as shown in Listing 17.7.

LISTING 17.7 THE IDL FOR THE `ConnectionInfo` STRUCTURE AND THE SERVER-SIDE EVENT HANDLER INTERFACE

```
struct ConnectionInfo {
    string hostname;
    long port;
};

interface ImplEventHandler {
void bind(in ConnectionInfo info, in Principal princ, in CORBA::Object obj);
void unbind(in ConnectionInfo info, in Principal princ, in CORBA::Object obj);
void client_aborted(in ConnectionInfo info, in CORBA::Object obj);
void pre_method(in ConnectionInfo info, in Principal princ, in
➥string operation_name, in CORBA::Object obj);
void post_method(in ConnectionInfo info, in Principal princ,
➥in string operation_name, in CORBA::Object obj);
void post_method_exception(in ConnectionInfo info, in Principal princ,
in string operation_name, in string exception_rep_id, in CORBA::Object obj);
};
```

A sample implementation of the `ImplEventHandler` is shown in Listing 17.8.

LISTING 17.8 A SAMPLE IMPLEMENTATION OF THE `ImplEventHandler` INTERFACE

```
/**
 * Server-side event handler.  Doesn't do very much, but does show
 * where calls are intercepted.
 */
public class MyImplEventHandler
  implements com.visigenic.vbroker.interceptor.ImplEventHandler
{

  private String name;
  private java.util.Hashtable clientsConnected =
    new java.util.Hashtable();

  public MyImplEventHandler(String name)
  {
    this.name = name;
  }
```

continues

LISTING 17.8   CONTINUED

```
  public void bind(
    com.visigenic.vbroker.interceptor.ConnectionInfo info,
    org.omg.CORBA.Principal princ,
    org.omg.CORBA.Object obj)
    throws org.omg.CORBA.NO_PERMISSION
  {
    System.out.println(name + " Event Handler: bind() for " + obj);
    System.out.println("from Client: ["
      + info.hostname + ":" + info.port + "]");
    System.out.println("Here is where we can develop some Basic
    ➥Authentication using Principal");
    String principal = new String(princ.name());
    System.out.println("The calling principal contained the name " + principal);
//      if (principal.compareTo("PASSWORD")!=0)
//      {
//          System.out.println ("Invalid Principal....");
//            throw (new org.omg.CORBA.NO_PERMISSION());
//      }

    System.out.println ("Principal is OK");
    clientsConnected.put(princ, info);
    System.out.println();
  }

  public void unbind(
    com.visigenic.vbroker.interceptor.ConnectionInfo info,
    org.omg.CORBA.Principal princ,
    org.omg.CORBA.Object obj)
  {
    System.out.println(name +
      " Event Handler: unbind() for " + obj);
    System.out.println("from Client: ["
      + info.hostname + ":" + info.port + "]");
    System.out.println("About to remove from hashtable");
    clientsConnected.remove(princ);
    System.out.println();
  }

  public void client_aborted(
    com.visigenic.vbroker.interceptor.ConnectionInfo info,
    org.omg.CORBA.Object obj)
  {
    System.out.println(name
      + " Event Handler: client_aborted() for " + obj);
    System.out.println("from Client: ["
      + info.hostname + ":" + info.port + "]");

    //Remove client from connected list
    clientsConnected.remove(info);
```

```
    System.out.println();
  }

  public void pre_method(
    com.visigenic.vbroker.interceptor.ConnectionInfo info,
    org.omg.CORBA.Principal princ,
    String   operationName,
    org.omg.CORBA.Object obj)
  {
    System.out.println(name +
      " Event Handler: pre_method() for " + obj);
    System.out.println("Right before the Server method: " + operationName);
    System.out.println("from Client: ["
      + info.hostname + ":" + info.port + "]");
    System.out.println();
  }

  public void post_method(
    com.visigenic.vbroker.interceptor.ConnectionInfo info,
    org.omg.CORBA.Principal princ,
    String   operationName,
    org.omg.CORBA.Object obj)
  {
    System.out.println(name
      + " Event Handler: post_method() for " + obj);
    System.out.println("Right after the Server method: " + operationName);
    System.out.println("from Client: ["
      + info.hostname + ":" + info.port + "]");
    System.out.println();
  }

  public void post_method_exception(
    com.visigenic.vbroker.interceptor.ConnectionInfo info,
    org.omg.CORBA.Principal princ,
    String   operationName,
    String   exceptionRepId,
    org.omg.CORBA.Object obj)
  {
    System.out.println(name
      + " Event Handler: pre_method() for " + obj);
    System.out.println("Exception occurred in the following Server method: "
      + operationName);
    System.out.println("Exception is: " + exceptionRepId);
    System.out.println("from Client: [" + info.hostname + ":" + info.port + "]");
    System.out.println();
  }
}
```

It is important to understand when Event Handlers are invoked. Client Event Handlers are executed after the call has left the client, but before the call reaches the Client stub.

`ImplEventHandlers` are executed before the call is made from the skeleton into the Server Object, as shown in Figure 17.1.

FIGURE 17.1
When Event Handler classes are invoked.

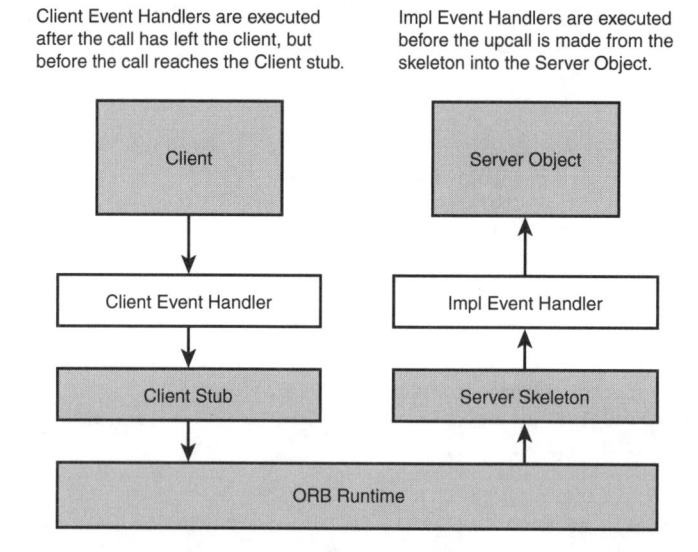

Client Event Handlers are executed after the call has left the client, but before the call reaches the Client stub.

Impl Event Handlers are executed before the upcall is made from the skeleton into the Server Object.

```
         Client                            Server Object
           │                                     ▲
           ▼                                     │
   Client Event Handler              Impl Event Handler
           │                                     ▲
           ▼                                     │
      Client Stub                       Server Skeleton
           │                                     ▲
           ▼                                     │
                      ORB Runtime
```

We will now discuss each of these methods in detail.

bind(in ConnectionInfo, in Principal, in CORBA::Object)

This method should look very familiar because this method is used on the Client to communicate with the Smart Agent and to get the reference to the Server Object. When the `bind()` method is called on the Client side, this `ImplEventHandler bind()` method will be the first method invoked on the Server side when the Server actually receives the `bind()` request. An example of this method is demonstrated in Listing 17.9.

LISTING 17.9 AN EXAMPLE OF HOW TO IMPLEMENT THE bind(...) METHOD OF THE `ImplEventHandler` INTERFACE TO MAKE USE OF THE CORBA::Principal IN ORDER TO PROVIDE ACCESS CONTROL TO THE OBJECT IMPLEMENTATION

```
public void bind(
    com.visigenic.vbroker.interceptor.ConnectionInfo info,
    org.omg.CORBA.Principal princ,
    org.omg.CORBA.Object obj)
    throws org.omg.CORBA.NO_PERMISSION
{
    System.out.println(name + " Event Handler: bind() for " + obj);
    System.out.println("from Client: ["
      + info.hostname + ":" + info.port + "]");
```

```
        System.out.println("Here is where we can develop some Basic
     ↪Authentication using Principal");
        String principal = new String(princ.name());
    System.out.println("The calling principal contained the name " + principal);
//      if (principal.compareTo("PASSWORD")!=0)
//      {
//          System.out.println ("Invalid Principal....");
//              throw (new org.omg.CORBA.NO_PERMISSION());
//      }

        System.out.println ("Principal is OK");
        clientsConnected.put(info, princ);
    System.out.println();
    }
```

The first parameter, the `ConnectionInfo` object, provides the important host and port socket information from the Client. This gives the Server the capability to keep track of all the Clients that are currently connected to the Server implementation. Moreover, the second parameter provides you with the Principal value for the Client. Here, a Server Object can maintain its own private access control list in order to decide which Clients are allowed access to the Server, and which ones don't have the necessary permissions. The third parameter indicates which Object the `bind()` method is attempting to bind to. This is very necessary in Servers that have several object implementations.

Listing 17.9 demonstrates the broad strokes of how you can use the Principal object and the `bind(...)` method within the `ImplEventHandler` to create your own list of all the Clients that have connected to the Server Object and to use the value passed in the Principal to determine which Clients have authorization to access this given Server Object. Thus when a Client calls `bind(...)` targeted at your Server, the previous Event Handler class is the first code to be executed when the request is received by the ORB and passed up to the Server Implementation. The first thing that happens is the `bind(...)` method shown in Listing 17.9 executes, providing the `ConnectionInfo` of the Client, the unique Principal value of the Client, and the Object implementation in which the Client is attempting to connect to. In this method, you can set up your own validation rules to determine which Clients are allowed to connect and which ones don't have adequate permission. If the Clients have permission, their `ConnectionInfo` can be stored in a local Hashtable.

unbind(in ConnectionInfo, in Principal, in CORBA::Object)

The unbind method is triggered when the Client gracefully disconnects from the Server. A *graceful* shutdown is defined as a deliberate call by the client telling the server it is going away. An ungraceful shutdown would result from an abnormal termination of the client because of some system failure. When the Server recognizes that the Client disconnects from the Server socket, the `unbind(...)` method is called so that the Server can be informed when Clients are no longer using the Server.

This method can be used in conjunction with the `bind(...)` event handler so that the Server Object can maintain an accurate list of all the Clients that have active connections to it. When a Client does a graceful shutdown, the Client ConnectionInfo and Principal information can be removed from the active list. The code in Listing 17.10 demonstrates using the Principal as the unique identifier with which to remove Clients from the Server's active clients list.

LISTING 17.10   A SAMPLE IMPLEMENTATION OF THE `unbind(...)` METHOD ON THE `ImplEventHandler` INTERFACE TO KEEP TRACK OF WHEN CLIENTS GRACEFULLY DISCONNECT FROM THE SERVER OBJECT

```
public void unbind(
    com.visigenic.vbroker.interceptor.ConnectionInfo info,
    org.omg.CORBA.Principal princ,
    org.omg.CORBA.Object obj)
{
   System.out.println(name +
      " Event Handler: unbind() for " + obj);
   System.out.println("from Client: ["
      + info.hostname + ":" + info.port + "]");
      System.out.println("About to remove from hashtable");
      clientsConnected.remove(info);
   System.out.println();
 }
```

client_aborted(in ConnectionInfo, in org.omg.CORBA.Object)

For unbind, we took into consideration the case of when a Client disconnects gracefully from the Server. However, this doesn't take into consideration situations in which the connection is closed because of some type of network communication failure. This situation is covered by the `client_aborted(...)` method. This method is triggered if the Client crashes unexpectedly or the network suddenly fails. An example implementation of the `client_aborted(...)` method is shown in Listing 17.11.

LISTING 17.11   A SAMPLE IMPLEMENTATION OF THE `client_aborted(...)` METHOD ON THE `ImplEventHandler` INTERFACE TO KEEP TRACK OF WHEN CLIENTS DISCONNECT BECAUSE OF SOME TYPE OF NETWORK FAILURE

```
public void client_aborted(
    com.visigenic.vbroker.interceptor.ConnectionInfo info,
```

```
    org.omg.CORBA.Object obj)
{
  System.out.println(name
    + " Event Handler: client_aborted() for " + obj);
  System.out.println("from Client: ["
    + info.hostname + ":" + info.port + "]");

  //Remove client from connected list
  clientsConnected.remove(info);
  System.out.println();
}
```

We won't search our Hashtable with the Principal as the key; rather, we will simply search on the `ConnectionInfo` object. This is sufficient because all Client connections from the same host are disconnected if the client host experienced some type of hardware or network failure.

pre_method(in ConnectionInfo, in org.omg.CORBA.Principal, in String operation_name, in org.omg.CORBA.Object)

The `pre_method(...)` method is designed to be triggered and executed as the last code segment called prior to the method code itself being executed. An example implementation of the `pre_method()` method is shown in Listing 17.12. It can be extremely useful for debugging, auditing, and timing purposes. As such, you can track which Client is making the invocation through the `ConnectionInfo` object, the unique Principal value of the Client, the actual method on the Server Object being invoked, and the Server Object being called.

LISTING 17.12 A SAMPLE IMPLEMENTATION OF THE pre_method(...) METHOD ON THE `ImplEventHandler`

```
public void pre_method(
    com.visigenic.vbroker.interceptor.ConnectionInfo info,
    org.omg.CORBA.Principal princ,
    String  operationName,
    org.omg.CORBA.Object obj)
{
  System.out.println(name +
    " Event Handler: pre_method() for " + obj);
  System.out.println("Right before the Server method: " + operationName);
  System.out.println("from Client: ["
    + info.hostname + ":" + info.port + "]");
  System.out.println();
}
```

post_method(in `ConnectionInfo`, in `org.omg.CORBA.Principal`, in String `operation_name`, in `org.omg.CORBA.Object`)

The `post_method()` method is designed to be triggered and executed as the first code segment called immediately after the method has returned. This too is very useful for debugging, auditing, and timing. Using a combination of both `pre_method()` and `post_method()`, you can isolate the precise timing for a certain operation. An example implementation of the `post_method()` method is shown in Listing 17.13.

LISTING 17.13 A SAMPLE IMPLEMENTATION OF THE post_method(...) METHOD ON THE ImplEventHandler

```
public void post_method(
   com.visigenic.vbroker.interceptor.ConnectionInfo info,
   org.omg.CORBA.Principal princ,
   String  operationName,
   org.omg.CORBA.Object obj)
{
   System.out.println(name
     + " Event Handler: post_method() for " + obj);
   System.out.println("Right after the Server method: " + operationName);
   System.out.println("from Client: ["
     + info.hostname + ":" + info.port + "]");
   System.out.println();
}
```

post_method_exception(in `ConnectionInfo`, in `org.omg.CORBA.Principal`, in String `operation_name`, in String `exception`, `org.omg.CORBA.Object`)

The `post_method_exception(...)` method is invoked if an exception was raised within the method itself. This is shown in Listing 17.14.

LISTING 17.14 A SAMPLE IMPLEMENTATION OF THE post_method_exception(...) METHOD ON THE ImplEventHandler

```
public void post_method_exception(
   com.visigenic.vbroker.interceptor.ConnectionInfo info,
   org.omg.CORBA.Principal princ,
   String  operationName,
   String exceptionRepId,
   org.omg.CORBA.Object obj)
{
   System.out.println(name
     + " Event Handler: pre_method() for " + obj);
```

```
    System.out.println("Exception occurred in the following Server method: "
      + operationName);
    System.out.println("Exception is: " + exceptionRepId);
    System.out.println("from Client:
➥[" + info.hostname + ":" + info.port + "]");
    System.out.println();
  }
```

CLIENT-SIDE EVENT HANDLERS

A similar interface is available on the Client side in order to handle specific client-side events as shown in Listing 17.15.

LISTING 17.15   THE IDL FOR THE ClientEventHandler INTERFACE

```
interface ClientEventHandler {
    void bind_succeeded(in CORBA::Object obj, in ConnectionInfo info);
    void bind_failed(in CORBA::Object obj);
    void server_aborted(in CORBA::Object obj);
    void rebind_succeeded(in CORBA::Object obj, in ConnectionInfo info);
    void rebind_failed(in CORBA::Object obj);
};
```

As you can see from the methods available on the `ClientEventHandler` interface, this interface provides useful methods for tracing, debugging, and auditing. Now, we will take an in-depth look at each of the methods in the `ClientEventHandler` interface.

- `bind_succeeded(...)`—Invoked if the Client is successful in binding to the Server Object.
- `bind_failed(...)`—Invoked if the Client is unsuccessful in binding to the Server Object. It can be very useful in overriding the default behavior of the ORB with the Smart Agent. If you recall from our discussion in Chapter 6 regarding the Smart Agent, the default behavior of the Client is to attempt to go back to the Smart Agent for another Server Object reference if the initial `bind(...)` call fails.
- `server_aborted(...)`—Indicates an unexpected closure of communication from the Server. It is analogous to the `client_aborted(...)` method on the `ImplEventHandler` interface, indicating that some type of program crash or network failure has occurred. The default behavior in this situation is for the Client to attempt to rebind to the same Server Object. If this rebind fails, the Client makes another call to the Smart Agent to get another instance of the same interface to connect to.

This behavior can be altered through the use of the `org.omg.CORBA.BindOptions` object when the `bind(...)` is issued. The `BindOptions` class was discussed initially in Chapter 6 with the Smart Agent, but we will quickly review in Listing 17.16.

LISTING 17.16 THE org.omg.CORBA.BindOptions CLASS

```
public final synchronized class org.omg.CORBA.BindOptions
↪extends java.lang.Object
{
    public Boolean defer_bind;
    public Boolean enable_rebind;
    public org.omg.CORBA.BindOptions();
    public org.omg.CORBA.BindOptions(Boolean,Boolean);
    public java.lang.String toString();
}
```

The `BindOptions` class provides two public Boolean data members that can be set to override the default ORB behavior when the `bind(...)` call is issued. The data member that is relevant to us here is the `enable_rebind` value. The default value for this member is true; thus when a Client detects some type of network failure or Server crash, the Client automatically attempts to rebind to the same Server instance. If you would like to prevent this behavior, you should set this value to false and put your own logic in the `server_aborted(...)` method to indicate what action you would like your Client to take.

- `rebind_succeeded(...)`—Invoked if the Client is able to successfully rebind to the same Server instance after an initial failure or server abort. This method is only called if the `enable_rebind` value discussed in the last section is set to true, otherwise a rebind would never be attempted.

- `rebind_failed(...)`—Invoked if the Client's attempt to rebind to the same Server instance was unsuccessful. The default behavior if the rebind fails is for the Client to make another call to the Smart Agent to get another instance of the Server that it can communicate with. If you would like to override this behavior, you can put logic within this method directing the Client how to proceed.

A full example of an implementation of the `ClientEventHandler` interface is shown in Listing 17.17.

LISTING 17.17 A SAMPLE IMPLEMENTATION OF THE ClientEventHandler INTERFACE

```
/**
 * Sample event handler for the client.  Doesn't do much
 * functionally, but shows where events can be intercepted
 */
public class MyClientEventHandler
    implements com.visigenic.vbroker.interceptor.ClientEventHandler
{

    private String name;

    public MyClientEventHandler(String name)
```

```
{
  this.name = name;
}

public void bind_succeeded(
  org.omg.CORBA.Object obj,
  com.visigenic.vbroker.interceptor.ConnectionInfo info)
{
  System.out.println(name +
    " Event Handler: bind_succeeded() for " + obj);
  System.out.println("from Client: ["
    + info.hostname + ":" + info.port + "]");
}

public void bind_failed(org.omg.CORBA.Object obj)
{
  System.out.println(name +
    " Event Handler: bind_failed() for " + obj);
}

public void server_aborted(org.omg.CORBA.Object obj)
{
  System.out.println(name +
    " Event Handler: server_aborted() for " + obj);
}

public void rebind_succeeded(
  org.omg.CORBA.Object obj,
  com.visigenic.vbroker.interceptor.ConnectionInfo info)
{
  System.out.println(name + " Event Handler: rebind_succeeded() for " + obj);
  System.out.println("from Client:
➥[" + info.hostname + ":" + info.port + "]");
}

public void rebind_failed(org.omg.CORBA.Object obj)
{
  System.out.println(name + " Event Handler: rebind_failed() for " + obj);
}
}
```

HandlerRegistry

After you have developed a Client or Impl Event Handler implementation, you must register it with the ORB. Registration of Event Handlers can be done in one of two ways: per-object or global. A per-object Event Handler means that each Client or each Server Implementation has its own unique Event Handler implementation. In contrast, a global Event Handler refers to a single Event Handler implementation that applies to all object implementations within a given Server instance.

Registration with the ORB is done through the use of the `HandlerRegistry` interface as shown in Listing 17.18.

LISTING 17.18 THE IDL FOR THE `HandlerRegistry`

```
interface HandlerRegistry
{
        HandlerRegistry instance();
        void reg_obj_client_handler(in CORBA::Object obj, in ClientEventHandler
                handler) raises (HandlerExists, InvalidObject);
        void reg_glob_client_handler(in ClientEventHandler handler) raises
        ➥(HandlerExists);
    void reg_obj_impl_handler(in CORBA::Object obj, in ImplEventHandler
    ➥handler) raises (HandlerExists, InvalidObject);
    void reg_glob_impl_handler(in ImplEventHandler handler) raises
    ➥(HandlerExists);
    void unreg_obj_client_handler(in CORBA::Object obj) raises
    ➥(NoHandler, InvalidObject);
    void unreg_glob_client_handler(in CORBA::Object obj) raises (NoHandler);
    void unreg_obj_impl_handler(in CORBA::Object obj) raises
    ➥(NoHandler, InvalidObject);
    void unreg_glob_impl_handler(in CORBA::Object obj) raises (NoHandler);
};
```

In order to use the `HandlerRegistry` to register your EventHandlers, you must first obtain a reference to the `HandlerRegistry`. This is done through the `resolve_initial_references(...)` method as shown in Listing 17.19.

LISTING 17.19 HOW TO OBTAIN A REFERENCE TO THE `HandlerRegistry` TO REGISTER YOUR CUSTOM EVENTHANDLER CLASSES

```
import com.visigenic.vbroker.interceptor.*;
.........
org.omg.CORBA.ORB orb = org.omg.CORBA.ORB.init();
org.omg.CORBA.Object obj = orb.resolve_initial_references("HandlerRegistry");
HandlerRegistry registry = HandlerRegistryHelper.narrow(obj);
.........
```

After a reference to the `HandlerRegistry` has been obtained, simply make use of the methods on the `HandlerRegistry` in order to register and unregister Event Handlers with the ORB.

To register a `ClientEventHandler`, use one of the following methods:

- `reg_obj_client_handler(...)`—Registers the given `ClientEventHandler` implementation associating it with the specific Server Object instance that the Client communicates with. Thus, it is possible for a Client to have a different EventHandler for every Server Object it communicates with.

- `reg_glob_client_handler(...)`—Registers the given `ClientEventHandler` implementation and uses this implementation for communication to all Server Objects.

To unregister a `ClientEventHandler`, use one of the following methods:

- `unreg_obj_client_handler(...)`—Unregisters the given `ClientEventHandler` from its association with the specified Server Object instance.
- `unreg_glob_client_handler(...)`—Unregisters the given global `ClientEventHandler`.

To register an `ImplEventHandler`, use one of the following methods:

- `reg_obj_impl_handler(...)`—Registers the given `ServerEventHandler` implementation associating it with a specific Server Object implementation. This allows every Server Object to have its own unique `ImplEventHandler` implementation.
- `reg_glob_impl_handler(...)`—Registers a single ImplEventHandler that is used for all Server Objects.

To unregister an `ImplEventHandler`, use one of the following methods:

- `unreg_obj_impl_handler(...)`—Unregisters the given `ImplEventHandler` from its association with the specified Server Object.
- `unreg_glob_client_handler(...)`—Unregisters the given global `ImplEventHandler`.

Now, we will take a look at a full example of using the Event Handlers and the Principal. For this example, we will use the `ClientEventHandler` and `ImplEventHandler` implementations described earlier in this chapter.

LISTING 17.20 A SAMPLE IDL AND CLIENT DEMONSTRATING USE OF THE PRINCIPAL WITH CLIENT-SIDE EVENTHANDLERS

```
// IDL
module EventHandlers
{
    interface LongTest
    {
        long testLong(
            in long inLongVal,
            inout long inoutLongVal,
            out long outLongVal);
    };
};

public class Client
{
```

continues

LISTING 17.20 CONTINUED

```java
public static void main(String[] args)
{
    try
    {
        String userName = "RALPH";

        //Initialize the ORB
        org.omg.CORBA.ORB orb = org.omg.CORBA.ORB.init();

        // Register the ClientEventHandler with the ORB
        org.omg.CORBA.Object obj =
                orb.resolve_initial_references("HandlerRegistry");
        com.visigenic.vbroker.interceptor.HandlerRegistry registry =
        com.visigenic.vbroker.interceptor.HandlerRegistryHelper.narrow(obj);
        registry.reg_glob_client_handler(new MyClientEventHandler("global"));

        byte[] byteName = userName.getBytes();
        org.omg.CORBA.Principal principal = orb.default_principal();
        principal.name(byteName);
        orb.default_principal(principal);

        //Bind to the Implementation
        chapter17.eventHandler.generated.LongTest longTest =
                chapter17.eventHandler.generated.LongTestHelper.bind
                (orb, "Long Sample");

        //Initialize the three parameters
        //    Create the int for the in value
        int inLongVal = 5;

        //    Create the holder for the inout value
        org.omg.CORBA.IntHolder inoutLongVal =
        new org.omg.CORBA.IntHolder(5);

        //    Create the holder for the out value
        org.omg.CORBA.IntHolder outLongVal =
        new org.omg.CORBA.IntHolder();


        //For the purposes of observation, let's set the value on the
        //out parameter.  Note that on the server, this value is lost.
        outLongVal.value = 5;

        //For observation, print out the parameters
        //before making the call
        System.out.println("About to call testLong() method\n" +
                "\tin parameter" + inLongVal + "\n" +
                "\tinout parameter " + inoutLongVal.value + "\n" +
                "\tout parameter " + outLongVal.value);
```

```
            //Call the remote method with the in, inout, and out parameters
            int returnValue = longTest.testLong(
                    inLongVal,
                    inoutLongVal,
                    outLongVal);

            //For observation, print out the parameters after making the call
            System.out.println("After calling testLong() method\n" +
                    "\tin parameter" + inLongVal + "\n" +
                    "\tinout parameter " + inoutLongVal.value + "\n" +
                    "\tout parameter " + outLongVal.value);
        }
        catch(Exception ex)
        {
            ex.printStackTrace();
        }
    }
}
```

In the Client implementation shown in Listing 17.20, notice that the only difference between this example and the Client examples used in previous chapters is the addition of the following lines:

```
// Register the ClientEventHandler with the ORB
org.omg.CORBA.Object obj = orb.resolve_initial_references
        ("HandlerRegistry");
HandlerRegistry registry = HandlerRegistryHelper.narrow
        (obj);
registry.reg_glob_client_handler(new MyClientEventHandler
        ("global"));

byte[] byte_name = user_name.getBytes();
Principal principal = orb.default_principal();
principal.name(byte_name);
orb.default_principal(principal);
```

The previous code is responsible for registering our `ClientEventHandler` with the ORB and setting the Principal value representing the Client identity. The Principal is implicitly passed to the Server with each remote method invocation and is checked on the Server for authentication (using the `EventHandler` defined in Listings 17.21 and 17.22).

LISTING 17.21 AN `ImplEventHandler` IMPLEMENTATION TO DEMONSTRATE HOW TO CHECK THE INCOMING PRINCIPAL VALUE

```
import java.util.*;
import java.text.*;
import org.omg.CORBA.*;
```

continues

LISTING 17.21 CONTINUED

```java
import com.visigenic.vbroker.interceptor.*;


class MyImplEventHandler implements ImplEventHandler {

  private String _name;
  private Hashtable clients_connected = new Hashtable();

  MyImplEventHandler(String name) {
    _name = name;
  }

  public void bind(ConnectionInfo info, org.omg.CORBA.Principal princ,
       org.omg.CORBA.Object obj) throws org.omg.CORBA.NO_PERMISSION
  {
      System.out.println(_name + " Event Handler: bind() to the following
            ➥object: ");
      System.out.println(obj);
      System.out.println("from Client: [" + info.hostname + ":" + info.port + "]
            ➥at: " + getDate());
      System.out.println();
      System.out.println("Here is where we can develop some Basic
            ➥Authentication using Principal");
      String principal = new String(princ.name());
      if (principal.compareTo("PASSWORD")!=0)
      {
            System.out.println ("Invalid Principal....");
            throw (new org.omg.CORBA.NO_PERMISSION());
      }

      System.out.println ("Principal is OK");
      clients_connected.put(info princ);
  }

  public void unbind(ConnectionInfo info, org.omg.CORBA.Principal princ,
  ➥org.omg.CORBA.Object obj)
  {
      System.out.println(_name + " Event Handler: unbind() to the following
            ➥object: ");
      System.out.println(obj);
      System.out.println("from Client: [" + info.hostname + ":" + info.port + "]
            ➥at: " + getDate());
      System.out.println();
      System.out.println("About to remove from hashtable");
      clients_connected.remove(info);
  }

  public void client_aborted(ConnectionInfo info, org.omg.CORBA.Object obj)
  {
```

```
        System.out.println(_name + " Event Handler: client_aborted() to the
                ➥following object: ");
        System.out.println(obj);
        System.out.println("from Client: [" + info.hostname + ":" + info.port + "]
                ➥at: " + getDate());
        System.out.println();

        for(int i=0; i< clients_connected.size(); i++)
        {
         clients_connected.remove(info);
        }

}
public void pre_method(ConnectionInfo info, org.omg.CORBA.Principal princ,
➥String   operation_name, org.omg.CORBA.Object obj)
{
        System.out.println(_name + " Event Handler: pre_method() to the following
                ➥object: ");
        System.out.println(obj);
        System.out.println("Right before the Server method: " + operation_name);
        System.out.println("from Client: [" + info.hostname + ":" + info.port + "]
                ➥at: " + getDate());
        System.out.println();
}

public void post_method(ConnectionInfo info, org.omg.CORBA.Principal princ,
➥String   operation_name, org.omg.CORBA.Object obj)
{
        System.out.println(_name + " Event Handler: post_method() to the following
                ➥object: ");
        System.out.println(obj);
        System.out.println("Right after the Server method: " + operation_name);
        System.out.println("from Client: [" + info.hostname + ":" + info.port + "]
                ➥at: " + getDate());
        System.out.println();
}

public void post_method_exception(ConnectionInfo info,
➥org.omg.CORBA.Principal princ, String   operation_name,
➥String exception_rep_id, org.omg.CORBA.Object obj)
{
        System.out.println(_name + " Event Handler: pre_method() to the following
                ➥object: ");
        System.out.println(obj);
        System.out.println("Exception occurred in the following Server method: " +
                ➥operation_name);
        System.out.println("Exception is: " + exception_rep_id);
        System.out.println("from Client: [" + info.hostname + ":" + info.port + "]
```

continues

LISTING 17.21   CONTINUED

```
                 at: " + getDate());
        System.out.println();
    }

    private String getDate()
        {
            SimpleDateFormat formatter = new SimpleDateFormat
                    ("dd/MMM/yyyyy:HH:mm:ss");
            formatter.setTimeZone(TimeZone.getDefault());
            Date currentTime = new Date();
            String dateString = ("["+ formatter.format(currentTime) + "]");
            return dateString;
        }

}
```

LISTING 17.22   A SERVER IMPLEMENTATION USING THE ImplEventHandler SHOWN IN LISTING 17.21 TO CHECK THE PRINCIPAL VALUE BEING PASSED WITH EACH METHOD INVOCATION

```
import com.visigenic.vbroker.interceptor.*;

public class LongTestImpl extends EventHandlers._LongTestImplBase
{

    //Constructor for transient object
    public LongTestImpl()
    {
    }

    //Constructor for persistent object
    public LongTestImpl(String name)
    {
        super(name);
    }

    public int testLong(
        int inLongVal,
        org.omg.CORBA.IntHolder inoutLongVal,
        org.omg.CORBA.IntHolder outLongVal)
    {
        //For observation, print out the parameters
        //before as passed to this method
        System.out.println("Beginning testLong() method\n" +
            "\tin parameter" + inLongVal + "\n" +
            "\tinout parameter " + inoutLongVal.value + "\n" +
            "\tout parameter " + outLongVal.value);

        //Change the value of the in parameter.  Note that
```

```java
        //this is done to show that this new value is
        //NOT carried back to the client
        inLongVal = 6;

        //Change value of inout parameter
        inoutLongVal.value = 6;

        //Set value of the out parameter
        outLongVal.value = 6;

        //For observation, print out the parameters
        //before the return
        System.out.println("About to return from testLong() method\n" +
            "\tin parameter" + inLongVal + "\n" +
            "\tinout parameter " + inoutLongVal.value + "\n" +
            "\tout parameter " + outLongVal.value);

        return 0;
    }

    //Put registration code here in a main for convenience
    public static void main(String[] args)
    {
        try
        {
            // Initialize the ORB.
            org.omg.CORBA.ORB orb = org.omg.CORBA.ORB.init();

            // Initialize the BOA.
            org.omg.CORBA.BOA boa = orb.BOA_init();

            org.omg.CORBA.Object obj = orb.resolve_initial_references
                ("HandlerRegistry");
            HandlerRegistry registry = HandlerRegistryHelper.narrow(obj);

            registry.reg_glob_impl_handler(new MyImplEventHandler("global"));

            // Create the LongTestImpl objects.
            LongTestImpl longTest= new LongTestImpl("Long Sample");

            // Export the newly create object.
            boa.obj_is_ready(longTest);

            System.out.println(longTest + " is ready.");

            // Wait for incoming requests
            boa.impl_is_ready();
        }
        catch(Exception ex)
        {
            ex.printStackTrace();
```

continues

LISTING 17.22   CONTINUED
```
        }
    }
}
```

Notice that the Server Object implementation hasn't changed. The only difference is the `ImplEventHandler` registration in the Server `main()`.

SUMMARY

In this chapter, we examined the `org.omg.CORBA.Principal` object and how it acts as the building block for an authentication mechanism within VisiBroker when used in conjunction with the Event Handler interfaces. The Principal object is defined by the CORBA specification as an octet sequence that is implicitly passed with every remote method invocation. The data that is contained within this byte array is entirely up to the application developer. In our examples in this chapter, we demonstrated a very simple example of passing some type of password string in the Principal object for validation and authentication on the Server.

The Event Handler interfaces are VisiBroker specific extensions and aren't defined by the CORBA specification. VisiBroker provides both a `ClientEventHandler` interface and an `ImplEventHandler` in order to allow the developer to override the default ORB behavior when certain events occur. Thus, on the Client side, the `ClientEventHandler` interface allows you to provide custom implementations for each of the following events:

- bind_succeeded
- bind_failed
- server_aborted
- rebind_succeeded
- rebind_failed

The `ImplEventHandler` interface provides the following events:

- bind
- unbind
- client_aborted
- pre_method
- post_method

Event Handlers must be registered with the ORB by using the `HandlerRegistry` interface. This interface provides methods for registering and unregistering both Client and `ImplEventHandlers`. Event Handlers can be registered as either per-object, in which you can write a custom Event Handler for each individual Server Object, or you can write a single Event Handler and register it as global, serving all Server Objects.

UNDERSTANDING THE GIOP PROTOCOL AND MESSAGE INTERCEPTORS

CHAPTER

18

IN THIS CHAPTER

- GIOP AND IIOP *412*
- INTERCEPTORS *420*

In this chapter, we will take an in-depth look at the underlying network protocol used by CORBA, the Internet Inter-ORB Protocol (IIOP). We will take a look at how IIOP packets are constructed on the Client side, and how they are interpreted when received by the Server. Within our understanding of IIOP, we will explore a very powerful feature within VisiBroker called Interceptors, which allow you to intercept IIOP messages before they ever reach the stubs and skeletons. Interceptors can be very powerful in their ability to allow you to see exactly what input streams and output streams are sent across the wire. The purpose of Interceptors is to allow you to develop your own sophisticated debugging, auditing, and timing capabilities into your application.

GIOP AND IIOP

Before we dive into our discussion of VisiBroker Interceptors, you must learn about the underlying network protocol that is used within VisiBroker. Interceptors work directly at the protocol layer and give you the ability to read and modify values being sent or received on the network. Thus, in order to make effective use of VisiBroker Interceptors, you must become familiar with the message structures used to pass information across the network. This section serves as a valuable reference as you begin to make use of Interceptors.

The CORBA 2.x specification defined the General Inter-ORB Protocol (GIOP) as the wire level protocol with which different vendors' ORBs would interoperate. The CORBA specification further defined a mapping for the GIOP protocol implementation over TCP/IP based networks, called the Internet Inter-ORB Protocol (IIOP). It wasn't mandatory that vendors make this their native protocol for communication between objects in their system. However, VisiBroker for Java was designed from the beginning with the IIOP protocol as its only native transport.

GIOP 1.0 supports only seven different types of messages. These are shown in Table 18.1. Listing 18.1 shows the GIOP IDL.

TABLE 18.1 GIOP 1.0 MESSAGE TYPES

MsgType	Originator	Value to Identify the Message in GIOP Header
Request	Client	0
Reply	Server	1
CancelRequest	Client	2
LocateRequest	Client	3
LocateReply	Server	4
CloseConnection	Server	5
MessageError	Both	6

> At the time of this writing, the latest version of GIOP was 1.1. However, VisiBroker for Java 3.x supports only GIOP 1.0. As such, this chapter focuses only on the constructs of GIOP 1.0 and VisiBroker for Java 3.x, not on the latest GIOP 1.1 specification. This is scheduled to be supported as part of VisiBroker for Java 4.0.
>
> GIOP 1.1 introduces a new IIOP type called Fragment, which isn't currently supported in VisiBroker 3.x.

LISTING 18.1 THE IDL MAPPING FOR GIOP 1.0

```
module GIOP
{
        enum MsgType {Request, Reply, CancelRequest, LocateRequest, LocateReply,
                      CloseConnection, MessageError};

        struct MessageHeader {char magic [4];
                              Version GIOP_version;
                              Boolean byte_order;
                              octet message_type;
                              unsigned long message_size;
                              };
};
```

In analyzing the GIOP IDL in Listing 18.1, we see the seven different types of GIOP messages all contained within an enumeration called `MsgType`. The next item is the standard Header structure for all GIOP messages. We will take a look at each item within the `MessageHeader` structure in the following list:

- `magic`—A basic identifier indicating it is the GIOP message protocol. As such, this is always the following four upper case letters: G, I, O, P.
- `GIOP_version`—A GIOP version that consists of a major and minor number. The Version struct is defined in Listing 18.2:

LISTING 18.2 THE GIOP::Version STRUCT

```
struct Version
{
        char major;
        char minor;
};
```

- byte_order—Indicates the byte ordering scheme for the given message. A Boolean value of `True` indicates the message is using little endian byte ordering. A Boolean value of `False` indicates the message is using big endian byte ordering.

- **message_type**—Indicates the type of message, providing the integer value for the corresponding message type contained in the `MsgType` enumeration.
- **message_size**—The size of the GIOP message in bytes after the message header.

The Request Message

The first message type we will take a look at is the Request message, which is sent from the Client to Server when it is making any type of method invocation.

A Request message contains three components:

- The GIOP `MessageHeader`
- `RequestHeader`
- `RequestBody`

The GIOP `MessageHeader` was discussed in the previous section, so we will examine the contents of the `RequestHeader` and the `RequestBody` in Listing 18.3.

LISTING 18.3 THE GIOP:RequestHeader STRUCT

```
module GIOP
{
        struct RequestHeader
        {
                IOP::ServiceContextList service_context;
                unsigned long request_id;
                Boolean response_expected;
                sequence <octet> object_key;
                string operation;
                Principal requesting_principal;
        };
};
```

The `RequestHeader` contains the following information:

ServiceContextList—This is a general field that can be filled by the application programmer with any application specific data. It is analogous to the Principal and Context types within IDL that might be filled with any data specific to an application. The structure for the `IOP::ServiceContextList` is defined in the IDL in Listing 18.4.

LISTING 18.4 THE IOP MODULE, WITH THE DEFINITION OF THE IOP::ServiceContext

```
module IOP
{
        typedef unsigned long ServiceID;
        struct ServiceContext
        {
```

```
            ServiceID context_id;
            sequence <octet>context_data;
    };

    typedef sequence <ServiceContext>ServiceContextList;
    const ServiceID TransactionService = 0;
};
```

- `request_id`—A unique value identifying a request from the Client. It is the responsibility of the Client to ensure that `request_ids` are unique and that no two outstanding requests share the same `request_id`.

- `repsonse_expected`—A Boolean value simply indicating whether an immediate response is expected. This is True unless the method is marked as a `oneway` or as a Dynamic Invocation Interface (DII) `send_deferred` method invocation.

- `object_key`—A byte value that identifies the Server Object being invoked. This is valuable for the Server, but should not be modified at all by the Client application. This field is appropriately filled by the Object Request Broker (ORB) runtime.

- `operation`—The Server Object method that is being invoked.

- `requesting_principal`—The Client's `Principal` value sent as an implicit argument. The value contained in this field will be made available through the `BOA::get_principal` method. For more details on the `Principal`, refer to Chapter 17, "Event Handlers and Principal Authentication."

The `RequestBody` consists of adding all the defined `in` and `inout` arguments into an IDL struct, building the struct as described in the following paragraph.

All `in` and `inout` arguments are encoded in the order in which they are defined by the IDL, starting from the left most argument and continuing to the right. If an IDL Context is defined, it is added as the last component. For example, the following method invocation

```
TestLong( in     long inLong,
      inout long inoutLong,
      out    long outLong);
```

will be constructed into the IIOP `RequestBody` found in Listing 18.5.

LISTING 18.5 A SAMPLE GIOP ENCODING OF THE SIMPLE IDL ORIGINALLY SHOWN IN CHAPTER 2, "INTRODUCTION TO IDL"

```
    struct TestLong_body
    {
        long inLong;
        long inoutLong;
    };
```

Notice that the Request message doesn't take into account out arguments because these are handled specifically in the Reply message.

The Reply Message

The Reply message is initiated from a Server Object to a Client. It includes any inout and out arguments, return values, exceptions, and object forwarding information.

The Reply message, like the Request message, is comprised of three components:

- A GIOP MessageHeader
- A ReplyHeader
- A ReplyBody

The ReplyHeader is shown in Listing 18.6.

LISTING 18.6   THE GIOP::ReplyStatusType AND GIOP::ReplyHeader

```
module GIOP
{
        enum ReplyStatusType
        {
                NO_EXCEPTION,
                USER_EXCEPTION,
                SYSTEM_EXCEPTION,
                LOCATION_FORWARD
        };

        struct ReplyHeader
        {
                IOP::ServiceContextList service_context;
                unsigned long request_id;
                ReplyStatusType reply_status;
        };
};
```

The first two elements of the ReplyHeader were introduced in the previous section on the RequestHeader. The ServiceContextList can contain any application specific data you want to include. The request_id is the same request_id that is passed from the Client Request message. The final argument is the reply_status that indicates how the actual ReplyBody is constructed. The ReplyBody is constructed in the following manner, based on the ReplyStatusType.

NO_EXCEPTION

The `ReplyBody` is constructed in exactly the same manner as `RequestBody`. It constructs a struct to hold all the `inout` and `out` arguments, adding each argument starting at the far left of its IDL definition.

USER_EXCEPTION or SYSTEM_EXCEPTION

The `ReplyBody` is constructed as an Exception. Exceptions are constructed as IDL strings. For User Exceptions, any exception members will follow the User Exception name encoded in the order in which they are defined in the IDL definition.

LOCATION_FORWARD

The `ReplyBody` contains an Interoperable Object Reference (IOR) to the actual Server Object location. It is the responsibility of the Client ORB runtime to transparently resend the operation to the new Server location.

As we start to look at the VisiBroker Interceptors later in the chapter, the Request and Reply message structures will be very important. The VisiBroker Interceptors actually allow you to implement code to interpret and modify the Request and Reply headers and bodies we just discussed.

The `CancelRequest` Message

The `CancelRequest` message is initiated from Clients to Servers in order to notify the Server that the Client is no longer interested in the results of a previously sent operation.

The `CancelRequest` message is comprised of only two elements:

- A GIOP `MessageHeader`
- A `CancelRequestHeader`

The `CancelRequestHeader` is defined in Listing 18.7.

LISTING 18.7 THE `GIOP::CancelRequestHeader` IDL

```
    module GIOP
{
        struct CancelRequestHeader
        {
                unsigned long request_id;
        };
};
```

The `request_id` is the unique identifier for the Request message to be cancelled. The Server isn't obligated to acknowledge this cancellation and might decide to send a Reply message back to the Client. This message won't be intercepted by the VisiBroker Interceptors.

The `LocateRequest` Message

The `LocateRequest` message is sent from the Client to the Server in an effort to determine if the Server is capable of servicing the request or if the Server has a forwarding IOR for the actual Server implementation.

A `LocateRequest` message is comprised of the following elements:

- A GIOP `MessageHeader`
- A `LocateRequestHeader`

The `LocateRequestHeader` is defined as shown in Listing 18.8.

LISTING 18.8 THE `GIOP::LocateRequestHeader` IDL

```
module GIOP
{
        struct LocateRequestHeader
        {
                unsigned long request_id;
                sequence <octet> object_key;
        };
};
```

The two elements include the `request_id`, uniquely identifying the Client request, and the Server `object_key` to be examined. The `object_key` is the value contained in the Server's IOR that the ORB uses to map Requests to the appropriate Server Object implementations. The following code in Listing 18.9 shows the IDL for an IIOP IOR.

LISTING 18.9 THE `IIOP::Version` AND `IIOP::ProfileBody` IDL, THE KEY ELEMENTS THAT MAKE UP A SERVER OBJECT'S IOR

```
module IIOP
{
        struct Version
        {
                char major;
                char minor;
        };

        struct ProfileBody
        {
```

```
                Version iiop_version;
                string host;
                unsigned short port;
                sequence <octet>object_key;
        };
};
```

The Server sends an appropriate `LocateReply` message to the Client, based on whether the `object_key` is provided within this Server or whether it provides a forwarding IOR to the actual Server implementation.

The `LocateReply` Message

`LocateReply` messages are sent from the Server to the Client in response to `LocateRequest` messages. `LocateRequest` messages contain the following three components:

- A GIOP `MessageHeader`
- A `LocateReplyHeader`
- A `LocateReply` Body

The `LocateReplyHeader` is defined in Listing 18.10.

LISTING 18.10   THE GIOP::LocateStatusType AND GIOP::LocateReplyHeader IDL

```
module GIOP
{
        enum LocateStatusType
        {
                UNKNOWN_OBJECT,
                OBJECT_HERE,
                OBJECT_FORWARD
        };

        struct LocateReplyHeader
        {
                unsigned long request_id;
                LocateStatusType locate_status;
        };
};
```

We once again see the familiar `request_id` uniquely identifying the `LocateRequest`. This is followed by a `LocateStatusType`. The construct of the `LocateReply` body will be based on the value returned in the `locate_status` field. We see from the IDL in Listing 18.10 that the `LocateStatusType` is one of the following three values:

- UNKNOWN_OBJECT—This returns a blank `LocateReply` body.
- OBJECT_HERE—The Client can use the existing reference it had, no `LocateReply` body is constructed.
- OBJECT_FORWARD—A `LocateReply` body is constructed in the Server IOR containing the actual Object implementation for the Client to call directly.

The `CloseConnection` Message

The `CloseConnection` message is sent only by the Server indicating it is dropping the connection to the Client. It doesn't provide any further information to the Client, and only returns a GIOP `MessageHeader` indicating that a `CloseConnection` message has been issued. Typically when a `CloseConnection` message has been issued to the Client, it receives the `COMM_FAILURE` System Exception.

The last message worth mentioning is the `MessageError` message. This message is passed at any point where the GIOP version or message type is unknown to the ORB.

INTERCEPTORS

VisiBroker provides three different interfaces that can be implemented to intercept different GIOP messages. This can be useful for debugging exactly what information the client stubs are marshaling on the wire and exactly what information the server skeletons are receiving on the server side. VisiBroker provides three different Interceptor interfaces that can be implemented by the application developer. They are

- `BindInterceptor`
- `ClientInterceptor`
- `ServerInterceptor`

You can either implement each of the preceding interfaces, or you can extend the default Interceptor classes. This allows you the option of only overriding the particular methods you choose. VisiBroker provides the following default classes that can be extended:

- `DefaultBindInterceptor`
- `DefaultClientInterceptor`
- `DefaultServerInterceptor`

Bind Interceptors

Bind Interceptors allow you to control how Server Objects are located by Clients. Rather than depending on the use of the default `bind()` implementation to the VisiBroker Smart Agent, you can intercept this `bind` call and implement your own Object Location strategy. We will take a look at the `BindInterceptor` interface in Listing 18.11, and we will examine each of the methods in the following sections.

LISTING 18.11 THE VISIBROKER `BindInterceptor` INTERFACE

```
interface BindInterceptor
{
        Boolean bind(inout IOR ior,
                     in Object object,
                     in Closure closure);

        Boolean bind_failed(inout IOR ior,
                     in Object object,
                     in Closure closure);

        void bind_succeeded(in IOR ior,
                     in Object object,
                     in Closure closure);

        Boolean rebind(inout IOR ior,
                     in Object object,
                     in Closure closure);

        Boolean rebind_failed(inout IOR ior,
                     in Object object,
                     in Closure closure);

        void rebind_succeeded(in IOR ior,
                     in Object object,
                     in Closure closure);

        void exception_occurred(in IOR ior,
                     in Object object,
                     in Closure closure);
};
```

bind(...)

This method is called before the ORB runtime attempts to establish a connection to the Server Object returned from the Smart Agent. This could allow the Client to use its own load balancing logic to determine which Server is to be contacted. The `bind(...)` method returns True if the IOR has been changed from that which is returned by the ORB.

The first argument is a holder for the IOR. The definition for the `IORHolder` class is shown in Listing 18.12.

LISTING 18.12 THE HOLDER CLASS FOR THE SERVER IOR

```
public final synchronized class com.visigenic.vbroker.IOP.IORHolder extends
java.lang.Object implements org.omg.CORBA.portable.Streamable
{
    public com.visigenic.vbroker.IOP.IOR value;
    public com.visigenic.vbroker.IOP.IORHolder();
    public com.visigenic.vbroker.IOP.IORHolder(com.visigenic.vbroker.IOP.IOR);
    public void _read(org.omg.CORBA.portable.InputStream);
    public void _write(org.omg.CORBA.portable.OutputStream);
    public org.omg.CORBA.TypeCode _type();
}
```

This holds the IOR of the Server Object that is returned from the `bind(...)` call to the Smart Agent. Because this object is an `inout` argument, the IOR can be modified so that the ORB will attempt to bind to another Server Object.

The second argument to the `ServerInterceptor bind(...)` call is the Server Object the Client is attempting to bind to. It is important to note that the Client proxy to the Server Object has not been initialized at this point, so it isn't legal to invoke remote methods on the Server Object.

The third argument is a Closure object as shown in Listing 18.13.

LISTING 18.13 THE CLOSURE CLASS

```
public synchronized class com.visigenic.vbroker.interceptor.Closure extends
java.lang.Object
{
    public java.lang.Object object;
    public com.visigenic.vbroker.interceptor.Closure();
}
```

Closure objects are designed to maintain application specific state information between sequences of Interceptor calls. With `BindInterceptor` interfaces, the Closure object that is created during the `bind(...)` method is the same Closure object that is returned in either the `bind_succeeded(...)` call or the `bind_failed(...)` call.

bind_failed(...)

This method is called automatically if the `bind(...)` call wasn't successful. Once this method is triggered, the application can attempt to override the default behavior in case of a `bind(...)` failure. For example, the developer can attempt to rebind to another Server IOR it has stored in a local cache.

The arguments for the `bind_failed(...)` are the exact same as that of the `bind(...)` Interceptor method. It contains the IOR that failed, which can thus be modified in a rebind attempt. It also contains the Client proxy that has failed in binding to the Server. The final argument is the same Closure object initialized in the `bind(...)` Interceptor method. This method returns True if the IOR in the `IORHolder` was modified and a rebind should be attempted.

bind_succeeded(...)

This method is called automatically if the `bind(...)` call was successful. It contains the same arguments as the `bind(...)` and the `bind_failed(...)` Interceptor methods. The first argument is the IOR of the Server Object to which the Client has successfully bound. The second argument is the Client Proxy that has established a successful connection to the Server Object. The third argument is the same Closure object initialized in the `bind(...)` Interceptor method. There is no return type to this particular method.

rebind(...)

This method is called by the ORB prior to its attempt to `rebind(...)` to the Server Object. This method is only invoked if the ORB `enable_rebinds` option is enabled. If you have forgotten about the default bind options of the ORB, refer to the `BindOptions` class discussed in Chapter 6.

The `rebind(...)` method contains the same arguments as the `bind(...)` Interceptor method. It allows a new Closure object to be created and initialized that can be accessed by both the `rebind_failed(...)` and `rebind_succeeded(...)` methods. The return value is True if the IOR in the `IORHolder` has changed.

rebind_failed(...)

This method is called automatically if the `rebind(...)` method wasn't successful. When this method is triggered, the application can attempt to override the default behavior in case of a `rebind(...)` failure.

The arguments for the `rebind_failed(...)` are the same as that of the `rebind(...)` Interceptor method. It contains the IOR that failed, which can thus be modified in another rebind attempt. It also contains the Client proxy that has failed in binding to the Server. The final argument is the same Closure object initialized in the `rebind(...)` Interceptor method. This method should return True if the IOR in the `IORHolder` was modified and another rebind should be attempted.

rebind_succeeded(...)

This method is called automatically if the `rebind(...)` call was successful. It contains the same arguments as the `rebind(...)` and the `rebind_failed(...)` Interceptor methods. The first argument is the IOR of the Server Object that the Client successfully bound to. The second argument is the Client Proxy that has established a successful connection to the Server Object. The third argument is the same Closure object initialized in the `rebind(...)` Interceptor method. There is no return type for this method.

exception_occurred(...)

This method is invoked if an exception occurred in one of the `BindInterceptor` methods. This method contains the same arguments as each of the other methods within the `BindInterceptor` interface. The first argument is the IOR of the Server in which the Client was attempting a connection. The second argument is the Client Proxy that attempted to connect to the Server Object. The Closure object is that which was previously initialized in either the `bind(...)` or `rebind(...)` call.

Listing 18.14 contains a sample `BindInterceptor` implementation.

LISTING 18.14 A SAMPLE `BindInterceptor` IMPLEMENTATION

```
package chapter18.bindInterceptor;

/*
 * A Simple implementation of the BindInterceptor so we can
 * observe the sequence of calls made through the ORB layer
 */

public class SimpleBindInterceptor
implements com.visigenic.vbroker.interceptor.BindInterceptor
{
  public SimpleBindInterceptor()
  {
  }

  public Boolean bind(com.visigenic.vbroker.IOP.IORHolder ior,
    org.omg.CORBA.Object object,
    com.visigenic.vbroker.interceptor.Closure closure)
  {
    System.out.println("BindInterceptor: bind(...)");
    return false;
  }

  public Boolean bind_failed(com.visigenic.vbroker.IOP.IORHolder ior,
    org.omg.CORBA.Object object,
    com.visigenic.vbroker.interceptor.Closure closure)
  {
    System.out.println("BindInterceptor: bind_failed(...)");
    return false;
```

```
        }
        public void bind_succeeded(com.visigenic.vbroker.IOP.IOR ior,
          org.omg.CORBA.Object object,
          com.visigenic.vbroker.interceptor.Closure closure)
        {
          System.out.println("BindInterceptor: bind_succeeded(...)");
        }

        public Boolean rebind(com.visigenic.vbroker.IOP.IORHolder ior,
          org.omg.CORBA.Object object,
          com.visigenic.vbroker.interceptor.Closure closure)
        {
          System.out.println("BindInterceptor: rebind(...)");
          return false;
        }

        public Boolean rebind_failed(com.visigenic.vbroker.IOP.IORHolder ior,
          org.omg.CORBA.Object object,
          com.visigenic.vbroker.interceptor.Closure closure)
        {
          System.out.println("BindInterceptor: rebind_failed(...)");
          return false;
        }

        public void rebind_succeeded(com.visigenic.vbroker.IOP.IOR ior,
          org.omg.CORBA.Object object,
          com.visigenic.vbroker.interceptor.Closure closure)
        {
          System.out.println("BindInterceptor: rebind_succeeded(...)");
        }

        public void exception_occurred(com.visigenic.vbroker.IOP.IOR ior,
          org.omg.CORBA.Object object,
          org.omg.CORBA.Environment env,
          com.visigenic.vbroker.interceptor.Closure closure)
        {
          System.out.println("BindInterceptor: exception_occurred(...)");
        }
}
```

Client Interceptors

The `ClientInterceptor` interface provides the ability to view and modify the GIOP Request messages being put on the wire to be sent to the Server Object. The interface for the `ClientInterceptor` is shown in Listing 18.15.

LISTING 18.15 THE `ClientInterceptor` INTERFACE

```
interface ClientInterceptor
{
        void prepare_request(inout RequestHeader hdr,
                             in Closure closure);

        OutputStream send_request(in RequestHeader hdr,
                             in OutputStream buf,
                             in Closure closure);

        void send_request_failed(in RequestHeader hdr,
                             in Environment env,
                             in Closure closure);

        void send_request_succeeded(in RequestHeader hdr,
                             in Closure closure);

        void receive_reply(in ReplyHeader hdr,
                             in InputStream buf,
                             in Environment env,
                             in Closure closure);

        void receive_reply_failed(in unsigned long req_id,
                             in Environment env,
                             in Closure closure);

        void exception_occurred(in unsigned long req_id,
                             in Environment env,
                             in Closure closure);
};
```

We will take an in-depth look at each method in the following sections.

prepare_request(...)

This method is called while the ORB runtime is preparing the contents of the `RequestBody`. At this point, the interceptor code can view and modify any of the contents of the `RequestHeader`. It also allows you to create a Closure object to hold state information before sending the request to the Server.

send_request(...)

This method allows you to view and modify the contents of the `RequestBody` before it is sent across the wire to the Server Object. The first argument is the same `RequestHeader` from the `prepare_request(...)` method. Any of the information contained within the `RequestHeader` can be modified. The second argument is the Request data being passed to the Server. You have the ability to view or modify this data. However, use caution when modifying these values and ensure that you are using the proper encoding for your changes so that the Server knows how to interpret the data when it is received. If the return value of this method isn't a null, the ORB will use the modified `OutputStream` as the contents of the `RequestBody`. Otherwise, if the return value is null, the ORB will use the original contents of the `OutputStream` that was passed in as the second argument.

send_request_failed(...)

This method is invoked as a result of a failure of the `send_request(...)` method. It contains the same `RequestHeader` that was sent in the `send_request(...)` method as its first argument. Its second argument is an Environment object. You might remember the Environment object from our work with the Dynamic Interface discussed in Chapters 12–14. The purpose of the Environment object is to contain the exception that prevented the Request from properly being sent. The Environment class is shown in Listing 18.16.

LISTING 18.16 THE ENVIRONMENT CLASS

```
public abstract synchronized class org.omg.CORBA.Environment extends
java.lang.Object
{
    public abstract void exception(java.lang.Exception);
    public abstract java.lang.Exception exception();
    public abstract void clear();
    public org.omg.CORBA.Environment();
}
```

Calling the `exception()` method on the Environment object will provide either the CORBA `SystemException` or `UserException` that prevented the request from being sent properly. The final argument is the Closure Object that was initialized in the `send_request(...)` method.

send_request_succeeded(...)

This method is invoked as a result of a successful `send_request(...)` method. It contains the same `RequestHeader` that was passed to the `send_request(...)` method, as well as the Closure object that was initialized by the `send_request(...)` method.

The following methods are called when the results of the request have been returned to the Client. These methods are invoked before the Client stubs receive the results.

receive_reply(...)

This method is called when the Server sends a GIOP Reply message back to the Client. The first argument is that of a GIOP `ReplyHeader`. The second argument contains a GIOP `ReplyBody`, consisting of the marshaled `inout`, `out`, and `return` values from the method request. For more details on the GIOP `ReplyBody`, refer to the first section of this chapter. The third argument is an Environment object that contains any exceptions that were thrown on the Server. The final argument is a Closure object that was initialized as part of the `prepare_request(...)` method.

`receive_reply_failed(...)`

This method is invoked as a result of a failure in the `receive_reply(...)` method. The first argument is the `request_id`, identifying the exact method request that failed. The second argument is the Environment object that contains the Exceptions that caused the failure. The final argument is the Closure object that was initialized for the corresponding `prepare_request(...)` method.

`exception_occurred(...)`

This method is invoked if there is an exception thrown by one of the `ClientInterceptor` methods themselves. The arguments here are the same as that of `receive_reply_failed(...)`, a `request_id`, an Environment object containing the Exception itself, as well as the Closure object that was initialized in the `prepare_request(...)` method. Listing 18.17 shows an implementation of the Client Interceptor that uses the `DefaultClientInterceptor` class.

LISTING 18.17 A SAMPLE IMPLEMENTATION OF A `ClientInterceptor` THAT EXTENDS THE `DefaultClientInterceptor` CLASS

```
package chapter18.chainedInterceptor;

/*
 * An implementation of the ClientInterceptor that adds
 * information into the Request header
 */

public class HeaderClientInterceptor
extends com.visigenic.vbroker.interceptor.DefaultClientInterceptor
{
  public HeaderClientInterceptor()
  {
  }

  public void prepare_request(
    com.visigenic.vbroker.GIOP.RequestHeaderHolder hdr,
    com.visigenic.vbroker.interceptor.Closure closure)
  {
    //Get the existing contexts from the holder.  Note that other
    //Interceptors could have added headers, so we need to retain the
    //existing value
    com.visigenic.vbroker.IOP.ServiceContext[] oldServiceContexts =
      hdr.value.service_context;
```

```
    //Create a new array of headers.  We will be adding one
    //more to the list
    com.visigenic.vbroker.IOP.ServiceContext[] newContexts =
      new com.visigenic.vbroker.IOP.ServiceContext
      ↪[oldServiceContexts.length + 1];

    //Copy any existing headers
    System.arraycopy(oldServiceContexts, 0, newContexts, 0,
    ↪oldServiceContexts.length);

    //Create a new header.  Note that this is only a small
    //example, so we've chosen to just write some bytes.
    byte[] theBytes = new String("Hello, World").getBytes();

    System.out.println("HeaderClientInterceptor: prepare_request(...)\n\t" +
      " Add header from the bytes of String Hello, World");

    //Add our new context to the end of the list
    newContexts[newContexts.length - 1] =
      new com.visigenic.vbroker.IOP.ServiceContext(1521, theBytes);

    //Reset the value of the holder
    hdr.value.service_context = newContexts;
  }
}
```

Server Interceptors

The `ServerInterface` gives you the ability to view and modify the GIOP Request messages from the Client, as well as the GIOP Reply messages that are constructed to be sent back to the Client. The `ServerInterceptor` provides methods for receiving GIOP Request messages, GIOP `CancelRequest` messages, or GIOP `LocateRequest` messages from the Client. The `ServerInterceptor` interface is shown in Listing 18.18.

LISTING 18.18 THE `ServerInterceptor` INTERFACE

```
interface ServerInterceptor
{
        IOR locate(in unsigned long req_id,
                    in OctetSequence object_key,
                    in Closure closure);

        void locate_succeeded(in unsigned long req_id,
                    in Closure closure);

        void locate_forwarded(in unsigned long req_id,
                    inout IOR forward_ior,
```

continues

LISTING 18.18   CONTINUED

```
                    in Closure closure);

        IOR locate_failed(in unsigned long req_id,
                    in OctetSequence object_key,
                    in Closure closure);

        InputStream receive_request(in RequestHeader hdr,
                    inout Object target,
                    in InputStream buf,
                    in Closure closure);

        void prepare_reply(in RequestHeader hdr,
                    inout ReplyHeader reply,
                    in Object target,
                    in Closure closure);

        OutputStream send_reply(RequestHeader reqHdr,
                    in ReplyHeader hdr,
                    in CORBA::Object target,
                    in OutputStream buf,
                    in string exception_rep_id,
                    in Closure closure);

        void send_reply_failed(in RequestHeader reqHdr,
                    in ReplyHeader replyHdr,
                    in Object target,
                    in Environment env,
                    in Closure closure);

        void request_completed(in RequestHeader reqHdr,
                    in Object target,
                    in Closure closure);

        enum ShutdownReason
        {
                    CLIENT_ABORTED,
                    SERVER_RESOURCES_EXCEEDED
        };

        void shutdown(in ServerInterceptor::ShutdownReason reason);

        void exception_occurred(in RequestHeader reqHdr,
                    in Closure closure);
};
```

We will examine each of the `ServerInterceptor` methods in the following sections. The first four methods are invoked if the Server receives a GIOP `LocateRequest` method.

locate(...)

This method is called when a Server receives a `LocateRequest` message. The first argument is the `request_id` that uniquely identifies the `LocateRequest`. The second argument is the `object_key` that is part of the `LocateRequest` method. The `object_key` is the value contained in the Server's IOR that the ORB uses to map `Requests` to the appropriate Server Object implementations. The final argument is a new Closure object that needs to be initialized to hold state information throughout each of the calls to the various location methods. If you wish to modify the location the Client goes to in order to contact the actual Server Object, this new IOR is returned as the return value. Otherwise, if you want to use the default value of the ORB, a null value should be returned. It is important to recall the various `LocateStatusTypes` possible when a `LocateRequest` message is sent.

```
enum LocateStatusType
{
        UNKNOWN_OBJECT,
        OBJECT_HERE,
        OBJECT_FORWARD
};
```

This is important as we look at the three possible follow-up methods that are called after `locate(...)`.

locate_failed(...)

This method is called if the `locate(...)` method wasn't successful, indicating that this particular Server Object isn't able to answer the message, nor does it have any forwarding information to another Server Object. This method can be implemented to return an alternative IOR to allow another `locate(...)` request to be made. If the IOR is unchanged or a null is returned, another `locate(...)` method won't get invoked. The method has the same arguments as the `locate(...)` method.

locate_succeeded(...)

This method is called if the `locate(...)` method was successful, indicating that this particular Server can answer the message and the request doesn't need to be forwarded to another Server Object. The `LocateStatusType` is `OBJECT_HERE`. This method has the same `request_id` and the same Closure object as the `locate(...)` method.

locate_forwarded(...)

This method is called if the `locate(...)` method was able to successfully forward the request to the actual Server Object. The LocateStatusType is `OBJECT_FORWARD`. The first argument is the same `request_id` from the `locate(...)` method. The second argument is the new IOR of the Server Object that the Client is looking to bind to. The final argument is the Closure object that was initialized in the `locate(...)` method. The following methods are invoked when the Client is issuing a GIOP Request message.

`receive_request(...)`

This method is called when a GIOP Request message is received from the Client. The first argument is the GIOP `RequestHeader`. The second argument is the Server Object for which the request is designated. The third argument is the GIOP `RequestBody`, containing all the marshaled `in` and `inout` parameters. If this buffer is modified in any way, it will need to be set as the return value for the ORB to use it. Otherwise, if the buffer is not modified or a null value is returned, the ORB uses the default GIOP `RequestBody` it received from the Client. The final argument is a new Closure object, which is the same Closure object constructed on the Client for this given `request_id`.

`prepare_reply(...)`

This method is invoked when the Server skeleton is preparing the GIOP Reply message to send to the Client. The first argument is the GIOP `RequestHeader` received in the `receive_request(...)` method. The second argument is a `HolderObject` for the GIOP `ReplyHeader`. The third argument is the Server Object in which the GIOP Reply is from. The final argument is a new Closure object that is used for the remainder of the calls used to construct a GIOP Reply back to the Client.

`send_reply(...)`

This method is invoked just prior to the Server sending the GIOP Reply to the Client. The first argument is the initial GIOP `RequestHeader` that came from the Client. The second argument is the GIOP `ReplyHeader` that was constructed from the Server in response to the initial request. The third argument is the Server Object that has initiated the GIOP Reply to the Client. The fourth argument is the GIOP `ReplyBody` containing all the marshaled `inout` parameters, `out` parameters, and return values. If you would like to modify this buffer, the revised buffer must follow all GIOP encoding rules and be passed as the return value of the method. Otherwise, if this buffer isn't modified or the return value is explicitly set to null, the ORB uses the original GIOP `ReplyBody` it constructed. The fifth argument is a `UserException` thrown, if any. The final argument is the Closure object that was initialized in the `prepare_reply(...)` method.

`send_reply_failed(...)`

This method is called as a direct result of a failure in the `send_reply(...)` method. It contains the same arguments as the `send_reply(...)` method.

request_completed(...)

This method is called as a direct result of a successful `send_reply(...)` call. This indicates that the Reply message was successfully sent to the Client. Alternatively, if the method invocation is a oneway, this method is invoked if the `receive_request` method was successful.

shutdown(...)

This method is called for one of two reasons, as indicated by the `ShutdownReason` enumeration shown in the following:

```
enum ShutdownReason
{
        CLIENT_ABORTED,
        SERVER_RESOURCES_EXCEEDED
};
```

The `shutdown(...)` method is called if the Client disconnects from the Server, either gracefully by sending a GIOP `CancelRequest` message or through an unexpected network failure. The other reason for a shutdown would be if the VisiBroker Connection Management has hit its maximum number of available socket connections. The VisiBroker Connection Management is discussed in detail in Chapter 5, "Server Essentials."

exception_occurred()

This method is called if there is an exception that has occurred within the `ServerInterceptor` methods themselves. This is also invoked if you have several `ServerInterceptors` chained together, which we will discuss later in this chapter. The first argument to this method is the GIOP `RequestHeader` that was received by the `ServerInterceptor`. The second argument is the Closure Object that was initialized in the `prepare_request(...)` method of the `ClientInterceptor` interface. Listing 18.19 is an example of a `ServerInterceptor`.

LISTING 18.19 A SAMPLE `ServerInterceptor` IMPLEMENTATION THAT EXTENDS THE `DefaultServerInterceptor` CLASS

```
package chapter18.chainedInterceptor;

/*
 * An implementation of the ServerInterceptor so we can
 * affect a new header
 */

public class HeaderServerInterceptor
extends com.visigenic.vbroker.interceptor.DefaultServerInterceptor
{
```

continues

LISTING 18.19 CONTINUED

```java
public HeaderServerInterceptor()
{
}
public org.omg.CORBA.portable.InputStream receive_request(
  com.visigenic.vbroker.GIOP.RequestHeader hdr,
  org.omg.CORBA.ObjectHolder target,
  org.omg.CORBA.portable.InputStream buf,
  com.visigenic.vbroker.interceptor.Closure closure)
{
  System.out.println("HeaderServerInterceptor: receive_request(...) Called");

  //Get our header from the RequestHeader
  com.visigenic.vbroker.IOP.ServiceContext[] contexts =
    hdr.service_context;

  //Go through the list and look for one with our ID
  for(int i = 0; i<contexts.length; i++)
  {
    if(contexts[i].context_id == 1521)
    {
      System.out.println("\tWe've found our header and it contains data for
➥" +
        new String(contexts[i].context_data).toString());
    }
  }
  return super.receive_request(hdr, target, buf, closure);
}
}
```

As we have discussed, the Client and Server Interceptors work directly on the message buffers that are to be put on the network. This is shown in Figure 18.1.

Interceptor Factories

After you have created an implementation class for your `ClientInterceptor` interface and `ServerInterceptor` interface, you need to make use of a Factory class in order to let the VisiBroker runtime create these Interceptors as needed. Both `ClientInterceptorFactorys` and `ServerInterceptorFactorys` can be implemented in one of the following two ways:

1. The Factory can be designed to create a new Interceptor instance for each connection.

    A `ClientInterceptorFactory` creates a new `ClientInterceptor` for every different Server Object it establishes a connection with. Similarly, a `ServerInterceptorFactory` can create a new `ServerInterceptor` instance for each Client connection.

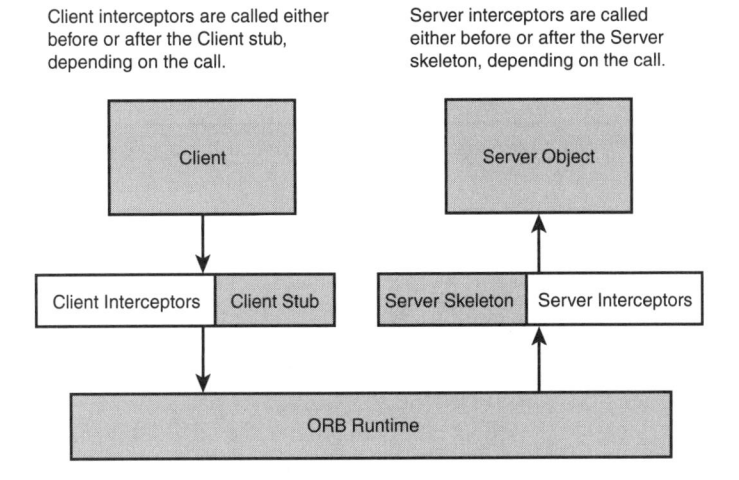

2. The Factory creates a single Interceptor instance that services all connections.

    A `ClientInterceptorFactory` creates a single `ClientInterceptor` regardless of how many Server Objects the Client has connections with. Similarly, a `ServerInterceptorFactory` can create a single `ServerInterceptor` instance to service all incoming Client connections.

FIGURE 18.1
Message Interceptors.

Client interceptors are called either before or after the Client stub, depending on the call.

Server interceptors are called either before or after the Server skeleton, depending on the call.

```
              Client                              Server Object
                |                                      ^
                v                                      |
    [Client Interceptors][Client Stub]    [Server Skeleton][Server Interceptors]
                |                                      ^
                v                                      |
                        ORB Runtime
```

> **NOTE**
>
> If you plan on using a `ServerInterceptor` for the GateKeeper, you must implement the `ServerInterceptorFactory` to only create a single Interceptor instance to handle all incoming connections. Otherwise, you will see erratic behavior and you will crash the GateKeeper.

The choice of whether to reuse the same object or create new objects from the factory method depends on your implementation of the interceptor. If server-state specific information is contained within the interceptor, separate instances must be used to avoid collisions. Your `ServerInterceptor` factory must implement the interface as shown in Listing 18.20.

LISTING 18.20 THE `ServerInterceptorFactory` INTERFACE

```
public interface com.visigenic.vbroker.interceptor.ServerInterceptorFactory
extends java.lang.Object
{
```

continues

LISTING 18.20 CONTINUED

```
            public abstract com.visigenic.vbroker.interceptor.
            ⮕ServerInterceptor create
(com.visigenic.vbroker.IOP.TaggedProfile);
}
```

The `create(...)` method introduces a new object of type `IOP::TaggedProfile`, as shown in Listing 18.21.

LISTING 18.21 THE `IOP::TaggedProfile` CLASS

```
public final synchronized class com.visigenic.vbroker.IOP.TaggedProfile extends
java.lang.Object
{
    public int tag;
    public byte profile_data[];
    public com.visigenic.vbroker.IOP.TaggedProfile();
    public com.visigenic.vbroker.IOP.TaggedProfile(int,byte[]);
    public java.lang.String toString();
}
```

The `TaggedProfile` object is used internally to provide the ORB all the necessary details it needs for identifying a Server Object. Your implementation of the `ServerInterceptorFactory` need not make use of this object. An example of a `ServerInterceptorFactory` is shown in Listing 18.22.

LISTING 18.22 A SAMPLE `ServerInterceptorFactory` IMPLEMENTATION

```
package chapter18.chainedInterceptor;

/*
 */

public class HeaderServerInterceptorFactory
implements com.visigenic.vbroker.interceptor.ServerInterceptorFactory
{
  public HeaderServerInterceptorFactory()
  {
  }

  public com.visigenic.vbroker.interceptor.ServerInterceptor create(
    com.visigenic.vbroker.IOP.TaggedProfile client_profile)
  {
    return new HeaderServerInterceptor();
  }

}
```

Your `ClientInterceptor` factory must implement the interface as shown in Listing 18.23.

LISTING 18.23 THE `ClientInterceptorFactory` INTERFACE

```
public interface com.visigenic.vbroker.interceptor.ClientInterceptorFactory
extends java.lang.Object
{
            public abstract com.visigenic.vbroker.interceptor.
            ➥ClientInterceptor create
                    (org.omg.CORBA.Object);
}
```

An example of a `ClientInterceptorFactory` is shown in Listing 18.24.

LISTING 18.24 A SAMPLE `ClientInterceptorFactory` IMPLEMENTATION

```
package chapter18.chainedInterceptor;

/*
 */
public class HeaderClientInterceptorFactory
implements com.visigenic.vbroker.interceptor.ClientInterceptorFactory
{
  public HeaderClientInterceptorFactory()
  {
  }
  public com.visigenic.vbroker.interceptor.ClientInterceptor create(
    org.omg.CORBA.Object object)
  {
    return new HeaderClientInterceptor();
  }
}
```

Chaining Interceptors

It is possible to register multiple Interceptors or to chain interceptor implementations together. This is useful if you would like to create several Interceptors with different jobs. For example, one might be responsible for tracking timing information and another might assist with load balancing. Rather than trying to combine these requirements into a single interceptor, they can remain discrete components and be chained together. In this case, if you register three `ServerInterceptor` classes to a given Server Implementation, the following happens.

When the Server receives a request from the Client, the `receive_request(...)` method in the first `ServerInterceptor` is invoked, the `receive_request(...)` method in the second `ServerInterceptor` is invoked, and so on. The methods are invoked in the order in which they were registered with the ORB.

It is important to understand the behavior of the chained Interceptors when an error occurs. In the previously described scenario, if there are three `ServerInterceptor` classes and an exception is raised in the second Interceptor during the `receive_request(...)` call, the `receive_request(...)` method in the third Interceptor will never get called. Rather, the `exception_occurred(...)` method will get invoked in the second Interceptor and will fire backwards, calling the `exception_occurred(...)` method from the first Interceptor.

We will walk through the steps needed to implement a chain of Server Interceptors.

1. First, you need several implementations of Server Interceptors with which to chain. A Simple Server Interceptor is shown in Listing 18.25.

LISTING 18.25 A SIMPLE `ServerInterceptor` IMPLEMENTATION

```java
package chapter18.chainedInterceptor;

/*
 * A Simple implementation of the ServerInterceptor so we can
 * observe the sequence of calls made through the ORB layer
 */

public class SimpleServerInterceptor
extends com.visigenic.vbroker.interceptor.DefaultServerInterceptor
{
  public SimpleServerInterceptor()
  {
  }
  public com.visigenic.vbroker.IOP.IOR locate(
    int req_id,
    byte[] object_key,
    com.visigenic.vbroker.interceptor.Closure closure)
  {
    System.out.println("SimpleServerInterceptor:
    ➥locate(...) Called");
    return super.locate(req_id, object_key, closure);
  }
  public void locate_succeeded(
    int req_id,
    com.visigenic.vbroker.interceptor.Closure closure)
  {
    System.out.println("SimpleServerInterceptor:
    ➥locate_succeeded(...) Called");
  }
  public void locate_forwarded(
    int req_id,
    com.visigenic.vbroker.IOP.IORHolder forward_ior,
    com.visigenic.vbroker.interceptor.Closure closure)
  {
```

```java
    System.out.println("SimpleServerInterceptor:
    ➥locate_forwarded(...) Called");
}
public com.visigenic.vbroker.IOP.IOR locate_failed(
  int req_id,
  byte[] object_key,
  com.visigenic.vbroker.interceptor.Closure closure)
{
  System.out.println("SimpleServerInterceptor:
  ➥locate_failed(...) Called");
  return super.locate_failed(req_id, object_key, closure);
}
public org.omg.CORBA.portable.InputStream receive_request(
  com.visigenic.vbroker.GIOP.RequestHeader hdr,
  org.omg.CORBA.ObjectHolder target,
  org.omg.CORBA.portable.InputStream buf,
  com.visigenic.vbroker.interceptor.Closure closure)
{
  System.out.println("SimpleServerInterceptor:
  ➥receive_request(...) Called");
  return super.receive_request(hdr, target, buf, closure);
}
public void prepare_reply(
  com.visigenic.vbroker.GIOP.RequestHeader hdr,
  com.visigenic.vbroker.GIOP.ReplyHeaderHolder reply,
  org.omg.CORBA.Object target,
  com.visigenic.vbroker.interceptor.Closure closure)
{
  System.out.println("SimpleServerInterceptor:
  ➥prepare_reply(...) Called");
}
public org.omg.CORBA.portable.OutputStream send_reply(
  com.visigenic.vbroker.GIOP.RequestHeader reqHdr,
  com.visigenic.vbroker.GIOP.ReplyHeader hdr,
  org.omg.CORBA.Object target,
  org.omg.CORBA.portable.OutputStream buf,
  org.omg.CORBA.Environment env,
  com.visigenic.vbroker.interceptor.Closure closure)
{
  System.out.println("SimpleServerInterceptor:
  ➥send_reply(...) Called");
  return super.send_reply(
    reqHdr,
    hdr,
    target,
    buf,
    env,
    closure);
}
```

continues

LISTING 18.25   CONTINUED

```
    public void send_reply_failed(
      com.visigenic.vbroker.GIOP.RequestHeader reqHdr,
      com.visigenic.vbroker.GIOP.ReplyHeader replyHdr,
      org.omg.CORBA.Object target,
      org.omg.CORBA.Environment env,
      com.visigenic.vbroker.interceptor.Closure closure)
    {
      System.out.println("SimpleServerInterceptor:
      ➥send_reply_failed(...) Called");
    }
    public void request_completed(
      com.visigenic.vbroker.GIOP.RequestHeader reqHdr,
      org.omg.CORBA.Object target,
      com.visigenic.vbroker.interceptor.Closure closure)
    {
      System.out.println("SimpleServerInterceptor:
      ➥request_completed(...) Called");
    }
    public void shutdown(
      com.visigenic.vbroker.interceptor.ServerInterceptorPackage.
      ➥ShutdownReason reason)
    {
      System.out.println("SimpleServerInterceptor:
      ➥shutdown(...) Called");
    }
    public void exception_occurred(
      com.visigenic.vbroker.GIOP.RequestHeader reqHdr,
      org.omg.CORBA.Environment env,
      com.visigenic.vbroker.interceptor.Closure closure)
    {
      System.out.println("SimpleServerInterceptor:
      ➥exception_occurred(...) Called");
    }
}
```

2. Now, we will chain Listing 18.25 with the `ServerInterceptor` implementation shown in Listing 18.19. As in our previous examples, each Interceptor is created by its own `ServerInterceptorFactory` implementation. After these factories are implemented, the Interceptors are added to the chain by adding another `ServerInterceptorFactory` to the chain as shown in Listing 18.26.

LISTING 18.26   STEPS NEEDED TO CHAIN INTERCEPTORS

```
.........
//Find the ChainServerInterceptorFactory
    org.omg.CORBA.Object rawServerChain =
      orb.resolve_initial_references("ChainServerInterceptorFactory");
```

Understanding the GIOP Protocol and Message Interceptors
CHAPTER 18

441

```
com.visigenic.vbroker.interceptor.
➥ChainServerInterceptorFactory serverChain =
  com.visigenic.vbroker.interceptor.
  ➥ChainServerInterceptorFactoryHelper.narrow
  ➥(rawServerChain);

//Add our simple factory to the chain
serverChain.add(new SimpleServerInterceptorFactory());

//Add our header factory to the chain
serverChain.add(new HeaderServerInterceptorFactory());
```
....

Thus, if you look at Figure 18.2, you can see the calling order as we chain more Interceptors on both the Client and Server side. Chaining Interceptors is no different from providing only one. Depending on the method, it will be called either before or after the stub/skeleton call. However, after the given method within the particular Interceptor is invoked, the same method will then be invoked in each of the remaining Interceptors in the chain.

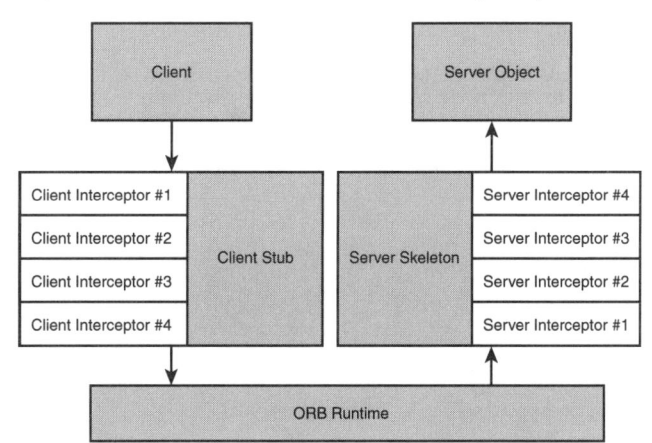

FIGURE 18.2
Chaining Interceptors.

Chaining Interceptors is no different than providing only one. Depending on the method, it will be called either before or after the stub/skeleton call. However, after the given method within the particular Interceptor is invoked, the same method will then be invoked in each of the remaining Interceptors in the chain.

The `ServiceInit` Class

After you create your `ClientInterceptorFactory` and `ServerInterceptorFactory`, you must register this factory class with one of the following VisiBroker classes:

- `ChainClientInterceptorFactory`
- `ChainServerInterceptorFactory`

This is done in one of two ways. You can write the code to do this registration server initialization code (usually called by the `main(...)` method or the constructor). The second option is to create your own class that extends the `com.visigenic.vbroker.orb.ServiceInit` class. The `ServiceInit` class is shown in Listing 18.26.

LISTING 18.26 THE `ServiceInit` CLASS

```
public synchronized class com.visigenic.vbroker.orb.ServiceInit extends
➥java.lang.Object
{
    public void init(org.omg.CORBA.ORB, java.util.Properties);
    public java.lang.String list_services()[];
    public org.omg.CORBA.Object resolve(java.lang.String);
    public com.visigenic.vbroker.orb.ServiceInit();
}
```

You must create your own subclass of the `ServiceInit` class previously described and override the `init(...)` method. This is necessary to register your `InterceptorFactories` and Interceptors with the ORB. It isn't necessary to override the `list_services()` and `resolve(...)` methods. Installing the interceptors used earlier in the chapter via a `ServiceInit` descendant is shown in Listing 18.27.

LISTING 18.27 A SAMPLE IMPLEMENTATION OF A `ServiceInit` CLASS

```
public class Init extends com.visigenic.vbroker.orb.ServiceInit
{
    public void init(org.omg.CORBA.ORB orb, Properties properties)
    {
        // Install SimpleBindInterceptor as shown in Listing 18.14
        try
        {
            com.visigenic.vbroker.interceptor.ChainBindInterceptor bind =
            com.visigenic.vbroker.interceptor.ChainBindInterceptorHelper.narrow
            ➥(orb.resolve_initial_references("ChainBindInterceptor"));
            bind.add(new SimpleBindInterceptor());
        }
        catch(org.omg.CORBA.ORBPackage.InvalidName e)
        {
            throw new org.omg.CORBA.INITIALIZE
            ➥("Bind interceptor failed: " + e);
        }

        // Install HeaderClientInterceptorFactory
        try
        {
            com.visigenic.vbroker.interceptor.
```

```
            ➥ChainClientInterceptorFactory clientFactory =
com.visigenic.vbroker.interceptor.ChainClientInterceptorFactoryHelper.narrow
➥(orb.resolve_initial_references("ChainClientInterceptorFactory"));
            clientFactory.add(new HeaderClientInterceptorFactory());
        }
        catch(org.omg.CORBA.ORBPackage.InvalidName e)
        {
            throw new org.omg.CORBA.INITIALIZE
              ➥("Client interceptor factory failed: " + e);
        }

        // install HeaderServerInterceptorFactory
        try
        {
            com.visigenic.vbroker.interceptor.ChainServerInterceptorFactory
              ➥serverFactory =
com.visigenic.vbroker.interceptor.ChainServerInterceptorFactoryHelper.narrow
➥(orb.resolve_initial_references("ChainServerInterceptorFactory"));
            serverFactory.add(new HeaderServerInterceptorFactory());
        }
        catch(org.omg.CORBA.ORBPackage.InvalidName e)
        {
            throw new org.omg.CORBA.INITIALIZE
              ➥("Server interceptor factory failed: " + e);
        }
    }
}
```

> **NOTE**
>
> Notice in Listing 18.27 that `BindInterceptors` aren't installed with Factories. Rather, they are installed with the `ChainBindInterceptor`. This is simply a difference in implementation from that of Client and Server Interceptors that use Factories.

The `ServiceInit` class allows you to create your own Services that can be made available to the rest of your VisiBroker environment through the standard `resolve_initial_references(...)` and `list_initial_services(...)` method calls. Thus, the following are the three methods that might be overridden in the `ServiceInit` class.

init(...)

This method is called when the ORB creates a new instance of the service and allows the object to perform any initialization.

`list_services(...)`

This method returns an array of names of the different services that are being made available through the instantiation of this class. It allows your services listed here to be added to the list that is returned from the general ORB invocation `list_initial_services(...)`.

`resolve(...)`

This method returns a reference to the specific service that is being requested. This is the method that is triggered when you call `resolve_initial_references(...)` to get a reference to the particular service.

Installing Interceptors and Interceptor Factories

The final step is to start either your Client or Server implementation with your new service. This is done as follows:

```
prompt> vbj -DORBservices=myService Client
```

To specify multiple services, you must comma delimit the property list:

```
prompt> vbj -DORBservices=myService1, myService2 Server
```

SUMMARY

In this chapter, we took a deep look into the specifics of the underlying network protocol of VisiBroker, the Internet Inter-ORB protocol (IIOP). It was important to lay this foundation of all the IIOP constructs, so we could make full use of the VisiBroker Interceptor interfaces. Interceptors provide developers a significant amount of control in terms of their ability to view and modify the bytes that are being passed from Client to Server. The idea here is to allow developers to develop sophisticated debugging and auditing logs, implement their own encryption schemes, provide their own load balancing and location strategies.

The CORBA 2.0 specification mandated the use of the General Inter-ORB Protocol (GIOP) as the protocol to be used when ORBs of different vendors are to communicate. The implementation of the GIOP over TCP/IP based networks was defined as the IIOP protocol. The GIOP protocol 1.0 has only seven general messages that are ever sent. They are `Request`, `Reply`, `CancelRequest`, `LocateRequest`, `LocateReply`, `CloseConnection`, and `MessageError`.

Through understanding each of the GIOP messages, VisiBroker's Interceptors can be useful on the Client and Server side in order to view and modify the headers and contents of the messages that are being put on the network. VisiBroker provides both a class that can be extended as well as an interface that you can implement in order to create your own Interceptors.

The default Interceptor classes that you can choose to subclass are `DefaultBindInterceptor`, `DefaultClientInterceptor`, and `DefaultServerInterceptor`.

The default Interceptor interfaces you can implement are `BindInterceptor`, `ClientInterceptor`, and `ServerInterceptor`.

After an Interceptor implementation has been designed, it must be created through the use of the following:

- `ChainBindInterceptor`—Add your `BindInterceptor` implementations here.
- `ChainClientInterceptorFactory`—Add your `ClientInterceptorFactory` implementations here.
- `ChainServerInterceptorFactory`—Add your `ServerInterceptorFactory` implementations here.

In order to instantiate your Interceptors and Interceptor Factories with the ORB, you must create your own subclass of the `com.visigenic.vbroker.orb.ServiceInit` class and override the `init()` method. Within the `init()` method, the `ChainBindInterceptor`, `ChainClientInterceptorFactory`, and `ChainServerInterceptorFactory` must all be created.

Finally, you must start your Client and Server implementations with pointing to your `ServiceInit` implementation using the `-DORBservices` option.

LOCATION SERVICE AND SMART AGENT TRIGGERS

CHAPTER 19

IN THIS CHAPTER

- LOCATION SERVICE AND SMART AGENTS *448*
- METHODS FOR QUERYING THE SMART AGENT *450*
- METHODS FOR USING SMART AGENT TRIGGERS *451*
- STARTING THE LOCATION SERVICE *454*

In this chapter we will take a look at an additional VisiBroker Service called the Location Service. No, it is not another Directory Service to find Server Objects. Rather, it is a Service that provides an Interface Definition Language (IDL) interface to query the information contained in memory by the Smart Agents. Thus, by using the IDL interfaces you can find all the information known by all the Smart Agents in your environment. This allows you to develop your own complex load balancing based on the number of Server instances available in the environment.

The Location Service also provides a dynamic trigger capability in which you can have the Smart Agent automatically notify your Load Balancing Service of when certain implementations are instantiated and others have gone down. This allows your load balancing Service the ability to automatically know which Server Implementations are available and which ones are no longer available to receive requests from Clients.

LOCATION SERVICE AND SMART AGENTS

If you recall our discussion on Smart Agents in Chapter 6, the Smart Agent maintains a local table of all available Server instances that have registered their location with the Agent. The Smart Agent never writes this information to disk; it is kept in in-memory tables. The Location Service provides an Application Programming Interface (API) to the Smart Agent tables throughout your environment. Thus, you need only run a single Location Service within your environment and it aggregates all the information known in each of the Smart Agent memory tables and provides this information through a single interface. Because the Smart Agent only knows about persistent object references, the Location Service is only able to provide information on persistent instances (you will recall that we discussed transient versus persistent object references in Chapter 6). It is important to remember that the sole purpose of the Location Service is to provide a programmable interface to the Smart Agent. The Location Service itself does not store Server location information because this information is already being stored within the Smart Agent in-memory tables. See Figure 19.1.

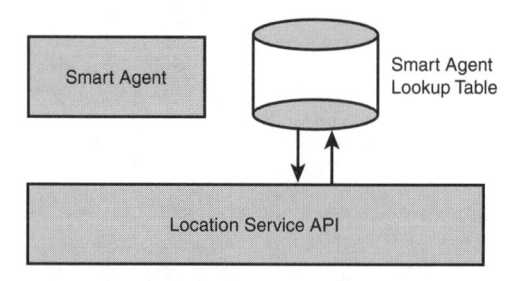

FIGURE 19.1
The Location Service API provides an ability to look up what Servers are registered in your environment.

The Location Service API provides an ability to look up what Servers are registered in your environment.

Before we examine the APIs to the Location Service, you need to fully understand what information the Smart Agent maintains in its local memory table. The structure in Listing 19.1 represents the information stored within the Smart Agent memory table.

LISTING 19.1 THE IDL FOR THE TABLE DESCRIPTIONS HELD BY THE SMART AGENTS

```
struct Desc {
    org.omg.CORBA.Object    ref;
    IIOP::ProfileBody    iiop_locator;
    string repository_id;
    string instance_name;
    Boolean activable;
    string agent_hostname;
};

typedef sequence<Desc>    DescSeq;

module IIOP
{                       // IDL extended for version 1.1
    struct Version
    {
        octet major;
        octet minor;
    };

    struct ProfileBody_1_0
    {                   // renamed from ProfileBody
        Version iiop_version;
        string host;
        unsigned short port;
        sequence <octet> object_key;
    };
};
```

We will take a closer look at each of the elements of the Desc structure, shown in the following:

- ref—This is the reference to the Server Object registered with the Smart Agent.
- iiop_locator—The IIOP::ProfileBody contains the necessary host and port information necessary to contact the Server Object.
- repository_id—The repository ID for the interface the given Server instance implements. If a Sever instance implements multiple IDL interfaces, there will be an entry for each interface supported.
- instance_name—The specific instance name for the Server. This is the specific string that is passed to the constructor of the Object when it is created, thus making it a persistent object.

- **activable**—A Boolean value that indicates whether the Server is registered to be activated by the oadj or if it is not registered with the oadj and must be activated manually.
- **agent_hostname**—The `host_name` of the Smart Agent for which the given Server instance is registered.

Now that we know what information is contained by the Smart Agent, we will examine the interface to the Location Service to understand how you can make use of this information. The Location Service interface is shown in Listing 19.2.

LISTING 19.2 THE LOCATION SERVICE INTERFACE

```
public interface com.visigenic.vbroker.ObjLocation.Agent extends
java.lang.Object implements org.omg.CORBA.Object
{
    public abstract java.lang.String all_agent_locations()[];
    public abstract java.lang.String all_repository_ids()[];
    public abstract org.omg.CORBA.Object all_instances(java.lang.String)[];
    public abstract org.omg.CORBA.Object all_replica(java.lang.String,
        java.lang.String)[];
    public abstract com.visigenic.vbroker.ObjLocation.Desc all_instances_descs
        (java.lang.String)[];
    public abstract com.visigenic.vbroker.ObjLocation.Desc all_replica_descs
        (java.lang.String, java.lang.String)[];
    public abstract void reg_trigger
        (com.visigenic.vbroker.ObjLocation.TriggerDesc,
        com.visigenic.vbroker.ObjLocation.TriggerHandler);
    public abstract void unreg_trigger
        (com.visigenic.vbroker.ObjLocation.Trigger Desc,
        com.visigenic.vbroker.ObjLocation.TriggerHandler);
}
```

There are two different types of methods on the Agent interface. They are

- Those that query for data held by the Smart Agents.
- Those that register and unregister triggers with the Smart Agent for automatic updates. Smart Agent Triggers can be set up to automatically notify one of your Servers if other Servers have been started (or have crashed).

METHODS FOR QUERYING THE SMART AGENT

We will examine in detail each of the methods used for querying the data held by the Smart Agents. The methods are

- `*) public abstract java.lang.String[] all_agent_locations();`

    This method returns an array of strings that list all the hostnames for which Smart Agents are running in your environment.

- *) `public abstract String[] all_repository_ids();`

    This method retrieves all interfaces, in the form of Repository IDs, available to every Smart Agent in the environment in an array of Strings.

- *) `public abstract org.omg.CORBA.Object[] all_instances`
    ➥`(java.lang.String repository_id);`

    After you have called `all_repository_ids()` to get a listing of every available interface known in your environment, you can use this method to get all the active instances of a given interface. This method returns an array of object references for active Server instances that support the interface in the `repository_id` argument.

    After this method is invoked, your Load Balancing Server can now determine which of the instances listed in this array has the least load. Thus, your Load Balancing Server can always maintain a listing of the average load on all Server instances for a given interface.

- *) `public abstract Desc[] all_instances_descs`
    ➥`(java.lang.String repository_id);`

    An alternative method to the `all_instances()` method previously described is the `all_instances_descs()` that also requires one of the `repository_ids` returned in the `all_repository_ids()` method. This method returns an array of `Desc` objects to describe each of the Server instances that support the interface in the `repository_id` argument.

- *) `public abstract Object[] all_replica(java.lang.String`
    ➥`repository_id, java.lang.String instance_name);`

    This method returns an array of `Object` references for active Server instances that support the interface in the `repository_id` argument and share the same instance name passed in as the second argument.

- *) `public abstract Desc[] all_replica_descs(java.lang.`
    ➥`String repository_id, java.lang.String instance_name);`

    This method returns an array of `Desc` objects for the active Server instances that support the interface in the `repository_id` argument and share the same instance name passed in as the second argument.

METHODS FOR USING SMART AGENT TRIGGERS

Through the Agent interface, it is possible to set up triggers within the Smart Agent. This simply involves creating your own local callback object that implements the `TriggerHandler` interface as shown in Listing 19.3.

LISTING 19.3 THE `TriggerHandler` INTERFACE

```
interface TriggerHandler
{
    void impl_is_ready(in Desc desc);
    void impl_is_down(in Desc desc);
};
```

Both methods have the same argument, a Desc object. You will recall from our earlier discussion that the Desc object represents an entry in the Smart Agent memory table. The triggers themselves need not be so exact as to match all items in the Desc object passed in with a corresponding entry in the Smart Agent memory table. Rather, the Desc object passed in for either method can contain any combination of the following instance information: `repository_id`, `instance_name`, and `host_name`. The more information you provide in your Desc object, the more specific your trigger notifications are. For example, if you simply create a Desc object that contains a particular `repository_id` and pass this to both the `impl_is_ready()` method and the `impl_is_down()` method, you will receive triggers for every Server instance that supports that particular `repository_id`. The runtime behavior of triggers is shown in Figure 19.2.

FIGURE 19.2
Location service triggers.

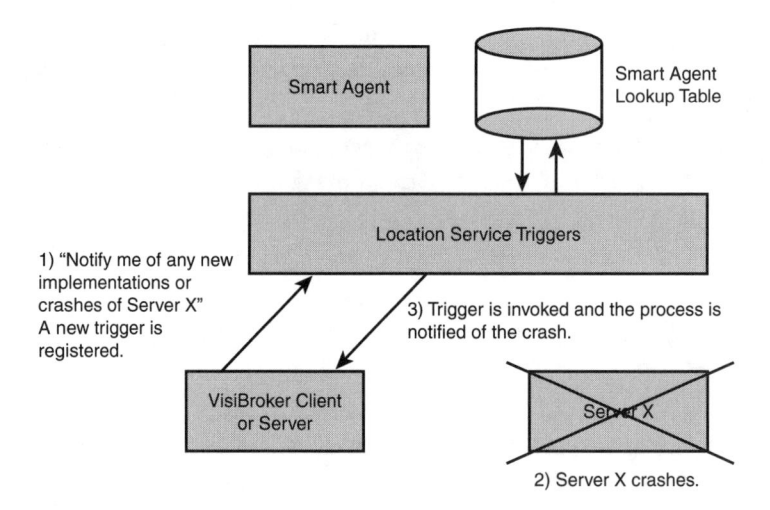

1) "Notify me of any new implementations or crashes of Server X" A new trigger is registered.

2) Server X crashes.

3) Trigger is invoked and the process is notified of the crash.

The two methods available on the Agent interface for registration and unregistration of triggers are

*) `public abstract void reg_trigger(TriggerDesc desc, TriggerHandler handler);`

This method registers a trigger with the Smart Agent.

The first argument is the `TriggerDesc` object. It can be defined as shown in Listing 19.4.

LISTING 19.4 THE `TriggerDesc` IDL

```
//IDL
struct TriggerDesc
{
    string repository_id;
    string instance_name;
    string host_name;
};
```

This object represents the trigger criteria. You might set up a trigger to send a notification for all instances of a given `repository_id`, or all instances of a given `repository_id` with a specific `instance_name`, or all instances of a given `repository_id` with a specific `instance_name` on a given host. You must provide a value for at least one of the elements in the `TriggerDesc` struct as a trigger criteria. It is not valid to pass an empty `TriggerDesc` object so that a notification is sent for all Server instances. This is simply unsupported functionality.

The second argument is your `TriggerHandler` callback object. This is the Server object that is called from the Smart Agent when there is a change in the status of the Server instances specified in the `TriggerDesc` object. Listing 19.5 shows registration for a trigger.

LISTING 19.5 SAMPLE CODE FOR SETTING UP A TRIGGER

```
            // Now let's set up our return trigger
            TriggerDesc desc = new TriggerDesc
                ➥("IDL:MY_MODULE/ExampleServer:1.0", "", "");
            MyTriggerImpl trig = new MyTriggerImpl();
            boa.obj_is_ready(trig);
            System.out.println(trig + "is ready");

              the_agent.reg_trigger(desc, trig);
```

In this example, we set up our trigger criteria in a new `TriggerDesc` object. We are looking for trigger notifications for all Server instances that implement the `ExampleServer` interface. Notice, we are not concerned about specific instance names or instances only running on specific hosts. The next thing to do is to instantiate our `TriggerHandler` callback object to receive the triggers from the Smart Agent. The final action is to register our trigger criteria `TriggerDesc` with our `TriggerHandler` callback object.

*) `public abstract void unreg_trigger(TriggerDesc desc, TriggerHandler handler);`

This method unregisters a given trigger from the Smart Agent. It takes the same arguments as the `reg_trigger()` method.

STARTING THE LOCATION SERVICE

As previously mentioned, the Location Service itself doesn't need to be started on every host in your environment. It need only be started once and it communicates to all Smart Agents, regardless of what host they are located on. Starting the Location Service is quite simple, as follows:

`prompt> locserv`

Alternatively, on Windows platforms the Location Service is started by clicking the icon within the VisiBroker Program Group.

The command-line options to the Location Service are as follows:

`-LOCverify`—Possible values are 0 or 1.

A 0 indicates disabling Server verification.

A 1 indicates enabling Server verification.

Server verification means that the LocationService actually checks to make sure that the Server instance listings it retrieves from the Smart Agent are active and running. This verification process has an impact on performance, but helps to ensure that the Server instances returned from the Smart Agent are valid.

Usage: `locserv—LOCverify 0`

`-LOCdebug`—Possible values are 0 or 1.

A 0 indicates to disable debugging info.

A 1 indicates to enable debugging info.

Usage: `locserv—LOCdebug 1`

`-LOCtimeout` time—The amount of time in seconds to wait for a response from a Server during verification. Only available when `-LOCverify` is set to 1. The default value is 1 second.

Obtaining a Reference to the Location Service

The first thing that must be done in order to make use of the Location Service API is to get a reference to the Location Service. This is done via the `resolve_initial_references(...)` call. Listing 19.6 demonstrates how to obtain the initial reference to the Location Service.

LISTING 19.6 How to Obtain a Reference to the Location Service

```
...
org.omg.CORBA.ORB orb = org.omg.CORBA.ORB.init();
com.visigenic.vbroker.ObjLocation.Agent the_agent = null;
```

```
try
{
        org.omg.CORBA.Object obj = orb.resolve_initial_references
        ➥("LocationService");
        the_agent = com.visigenic.vbroker.ObjLocation.AgentHelper.narrow(obj);
        ......
}
catch(Exception ex)
{
}
....
```

A Sample Load Balancer

Listings 19.7 and 19.8 demonstrate how you can use the Location Service API to create your own load balancing mechanisms.

LISTING 19.7 SAMPLE IDL FOR USE WITH LOCATION SERVICE

```
module chapter19Location
{
    interface StringCounter
    {
        long countString(in string aString);
    };
    interface StringCounterFactory
    {
        StringCounter findStringCounter();
    };
};
```

Our implementation of the `StringCounter` Server Object is shown in Listing 19.8.

LISTING 19.8 A SAMPLE IMPLEMENTATION OF `StringCounterImpl` AS DEFINED IN LISTING 19.7

```
package chapter19.location;

/*
 * A simple server that we will use to demonstrate the
 * Location service
 */
public class StringCounterImpl
extends chapter19.location.generated._StringCounterImplBase
{

    //Constructor for transient object
    public StringCounterImpl()
```

continues

LISTING 19.8 CONTINUED

```
    {
    }

    //Constructor for persistent object
    public StringCounterImpl(String name)
    {
        super(name);
    }

    public int countString(String aString)
    {
    System.out.println("countString() called");
    return aString.length();
    }
    //Put registration code here in a main for convenience
    public static void main(String[] args)
    {
        try
        {
            // Initialize the ORB.
            org.omg.CORBA.ORB orb = org.omg.CORBA.ORB.init();

            // Initialize the BOA.
            org.omg.CORBA.BOA boa = orb.BOA_init();

            // Create the object.
            StringCounterImpl counter =
            new StringCounterImpl("StringCounter");

            // Export the newly create object.
            boa.obj_is_ready(counter);

            System.out.println(counter + " is ready.");

            // Wait for incoming requests
            boa.impl_is_ready();
        }
        catch(org.omg.CORBA.SystemException ex)
        {
            ex.printStackTrace();
        }
    }
}
```

Now we will take a look at the implementation of the `StringCounterFactory`. The purpose of this interface is to use the API to the Location Service in order to get a listing of all available `StringCounter` Instances. It could then implement custom load balancing logic to determine which Instance is least used and should be connected to. In our example, we simplify this by using a round-robin load balancing, much like that of the default behavior of the Smart Agent. Round-robin load balancing basically means that the first Client gets the first Server reference in the list, the second Client gets the second Server reference. Server references are dispensed by continually looping through the list of implementations. The `StringCounterFactory` uses an inner class for the `TriggerImpl` object that is our trigger callback interface for the Smart Agent to send updates. This is demonstrated in Listing 19.9.

LISTING 19.9   StringCounterFactoryImpl AND TRIGGER CLASS IMPLEMENTATIONS

```
package chapter19.location;

/*
 * This server serves to act as a Home for finding
 * implementations of the "StringCounter" interface.  It
 * leverages the locator service to find an initial cache
 * of references then keeps the cache updated with
 * a "Trigger"
 *
 * To start this server, you must also use the ORBServices property
 * as follows
 *
 * prompt> java -DORBservices=com.visigenic.vbroker.ObjLocation
   ➥chapter19.location.StringCounterFactoryImpl
 */
public class StringCounterFactoryImpl
extends chapter19.location.generated._StringCounterFactoryImplBase
{
  //The list of servers
  protected java.util.Vector servers = null;
  //Our trigger for callbacks on the status
  //of servers
  private Trigger trigger = null;
  //A counter used for round-robin balancing
  private int count = 0;

  //Constructor for transient object
    public StringCounterFactoryImpl()
    {
    finishConstructor();
    }

    //Constructor for persistent object
    public StringCounterFactoryImpl(String name)
    {
        super(name);
    finishConstructor();
    }

  //In this method we do all the "real" work
  //of registering a trigger and assembling a cache
```

continues

LISTING 19.9 CONTINUED

```java
//of servers.
//We will try to locate and servers implementing the
//interface of interest.  We will also register a trigger
//so we can stay in sync with the state of the system over time.
private void finishConstructor()
{
  servers = new java.util.Vector();


  org.omg.CORBA.ORB orb = org.omg.CORBA.ORB.init();
      org.omg.CORBA.BOA boa = orb.BOA_init();

    try
    {
      //----------------------------------------
      // First, find the Location Service
      // and in initial list of servers

      //Get a reference to the Location Service
            org.omg.CORBA.Object rawLocator =
        orb.resolve_initial_references("LocationService");
      com.visigenic.vbroker.ObjLocation.Agent locator =
        com.visigenic.vbroker.ObjLocation.AgentHelper.narrow(rawLocator);

      //Assemble the Repository ID for the service
      //we are interested in locating
      String repositoryID =
        "IDL:chapter19Location/StringCounter:1.0";

      //Now find all instances of the interface
      org.omg.CORBA.Object[] allInstances =
        locator.all_instances(repositoryID);

      System.out.println("There are " + allInstances.length +
        " objects implementing the " +
        repositoryID +
        " interface");

      //Place each instance in the Vector.  Don't worry if
      //the instance is ready (or even dead).  We will determine
      //this upon callback and when we have to return instances
      for(int i = 0; i<allInstances.length; i++)
      {
        chapter19.location.generated.StringCounter counter =
          chapter19.location.generated.StringCounterHelper.narrow
            ↪(allInstances[i]);
        addServer(counter);

      }

      //----------------------------------------
      //Now, register our callback for the trigger.
```

```
      //First, create the description of the objects we
      //are interested in.  Because we only care about the interface
      //StringCounter, that is all the information we must provide
            com.visigenic.vbroker.ObjLocation.TriggerDesc desc =
        new com.visigenic.vbroker.ObjLocation.TriggerDesc(
        repositoryID, "", "");

      //Create an instance of our trigger
      trigger = new Trigger();

      //Export the object
      boa.obj_is_ready(trigger);

      //Register the trigger
      locator.reg_trigger(desc, trigger);

  }
  catch(Exception ex)
  {
    ex.printStackTrace();
  }
}

//This method implements a VERY primitive round-robin
//method of load balancing.  You should use a more sophisticated
//approach.  We have employed this method for simplicity of
//the example
public synchronized chapter19.location.generated.StringCounter
➥findStringCounter()
{
  System.out.println("findStringCounter() called");

  //Go through our vector of
  //StringCounters.  Choose the next one in our
  //list, but we must also check if the server
  //is active because there could be a lag between
  //the death of a server and the notification
  //from the trigger
  int startCount = count;
  chapter19.location.generated.StringCounter ret = null;
  do
  {
    if(count >= servers.size())
      count = 0;
    ret = (chapter19.location.generated.StringCounter)
      ➥servers.elementAt(count++);
    if(ret._non_existent())
      removeServer(ret);
    else
      return ret;
  }
  while(startCount != count);
```

continues

LISTING 19.9 CONTINUED

```java
      return ret;
  }

  protected synchronized void removeServer(org.omg.CORBA.Object deadObj)
  {
    System.out.println("RemoveServer");
    //Go through all servers and find the one
    //that matches the is_equivalent() method
    java.util.Enumeration en = servers.elements();
    while(en.hasMoreElements())
    {
      org.omg.CORBA.Object obj = (org.omg.CORBA.Object) en.nextElement();
      if(obj._is_equivalent(deadObj))
        servers.removeElement(obj);
    }
  }
  protected synchronized void addServer(
    chapter19.location.generated.StringCounter newServer)
  {
    System.out.println("Add Server");
    //Add a server to our list
    servers.addElement(newServer);
  }
    //Put registration code here in a main for convenience
    public static void main(String[] args)
    {
        try
        {
            // Initialize the ORB.
            org.omg.CORBA.ORB orb = org.omg.CORBA.ORB.init();

            // Initialize the BOA.
            org.omg.CORBA.BOA boa = orb.BOA_init();

            // Create the object.
            StringCounterFactoryImpl factory =
            new StringCounterFactoryImpl("StringConterFactory");

            // Export the newly create object.
            boa.obj_is_ready(factory);

            System.out.println(factory + " is ready.");

            // Wait for incoming requests
            boa.impl_is_ready();
        }
        catch(org.omg.CORBA.SystemException ex)
        {
            ex.printStackTrace();
        }
    }
  }

  //Use an inner-class as our implementation callback
```

```
class Trigger
  extends com.visigenic.vbroker.ObjLocation._TriggerHandlerImplBase
{
  //Method called when a new implementation of our
  //interface is ready
  public void impl_is_ready(
    com.visigenic.vbroker.ObjLocation.Desc desc)
  {
    try
    {
      //Call the addServer() method.  Note that
      //we narrow the reference before passing
      addServer(
        chapter19.location.generated.StringCounterHelper.narrow(desc.ref));
    }
    catch(Exception ex)
    {
      ex.printStackTrace();
    }
  }
  //This method is called when an instance of our interface goes down.
  public void impl_is_down(
    com.visigenic.vbroker.ObjLocation.Desc desc)
  {
    //Note that we use the .ref member of the
    //Desc.  This is the Object that we
    //will use for the is_equivalent() test
    removeServer(desc.ref);
  }
}
}
```

This example should serve as a good template to use in order to build your own custom load balancing servers. It provides a very flexible approach allowing you to determine what load criteria you want to use in order to return Server references to the Client. A simple Client implementation for the Server example shown in Listing 19.9 is shown in Listing 19.10.

LISTING 19.10 SAMPLE CLIENT IMPLEMENTING THE IDL IN LISTING 19.7

```
package chapter19.location;
/*
 * Client to test using the Location Service and a Factory
 * to do load balancing
 */
public class Client
{
    public static void main(String[] args)
    {
        try
        {
```

continues

LISTING 19.10 CONTINUED

```
        //Initialize the ORB
        org.omg.CORBA.ORB orb = org.omg.CORBA.ORB.init();

        //Find a reference to our factory
        chapter19.location.generated.StringCounterFactory factory =
                chapter19.location.generated.StringCounterFactoryHelper.bind
                (orb, "StringConterFactory");

        //Ask the factory for a StringCounter
        chapter19.location.generated.StringCounter counter =
                factory.findStringCounter();

        //Use the StringCounter to validate this operation worked
        //successfully.  Note that you might observe the load balancing
        //if you have several servers available
        System.out.println("The number of chars in VisiBroker is:
                " + counter.countString("VisiBroker"));

    }
    catch(Exception ex)
    {
        ex.printStackTrace();
    }
  }
}
```

SUMMARY

The Location Service provides a valuable interface into the information contained within the Smart Agents. The Location Service itself does not perform any part of the object location process, it simply provides an API that can be used to query the Smart Agents in your environment about what Server Objects they are aware of. The Location Service API is designed to allow you to build your own custom load balancing logic based on the Server Objects contained within the Smart Agent caches.

The Location Service interface also provides a trigger interface that allows your Load Balancing Service to be automatically updated whenever a new Server Object is started or whenever an existing Server Object crashes. These notifications allow your Load Balancing Server to maintain an up-to-date list of the currently available Servers.

THE COS EVENT SERVICE

CHAPTER 20

IN THIS CHAPTER

- EVENT BASICS *464*
- THE COS EVENT API *466*
- EVENTS AND THE ANY TYPE *471*
- IMPLEMENTING WITH THE PUSH MODEL *471*
- IMPLEMENTING WITH THE PULL MODEL *476*
- STARTING THE EVENT SERVICE *481*

As you might recall from our discussion of the COS Naming Service in Chapter 5, "Server Essentials", the Object Management Group (OMG) has defined several standard services for CORBA implementations. In this chapter we will be examining the OMG's mechanism for asynchronous, disconnected communications between one or more CORBA clients—the Event Service. We begin with a discussion of the principals of event-based programming. We will then introduce the four roles within the COS Event Service and the IDL that defines those roles. We will then demonstrate how to use Java API to the Event Service.

EVENT BASICS

Before introducing a new topic, it is best to build on familiar patterns in standard software. For the event service, we will discuss the two aspects of the event service—push and pull—in reference to two different software patterns.

In the case of the push model of events, we can start with the Observer/Observable Pattern that is seen throughout the JDK's Abstract Windowing Toolkit (AWT) package.

Although there are Observable and Observer interfaces defined in Java, the Listener Event pattern of the AWT 1.1 Event Model is the best place for demonstration.

If a programmer wants his application to react to the user pushing a button, he must create code to programmatically watch the button and wait for something to happen. A very inefficient way to do this would be to have some application code periodically ask the button, "have you been pushed?". This periodic asking is referred to as polling. Not only is this a bad way to service the user, but it also wouldn't be using the appropriate mechanism for Event-Driven Programming.

Instead of polling the button, the programmer adds an `ActionListener` callback to the button. `ActionListener` is a well-known interface with a callback method called `actionOccurred()`. The button maintains an internal list of listeners, and notifies those listeners when the button has been pushed.

Going back to our initial discussion of observers and observables, we can see that the Listener is observing the button, and the button is observable. Observables are the sources of events and Observers receive event notifications. Other systems use the terms source and sink or publisher and subscriber. Figure 20.1 shows the relationship between the event supplier and consumer with reference to the thread of execution.

Figure 20.1 shows a simple push model of events. The COS Event Service also supports a second event model—the pull model. To discuss a familiar example of the pull model, we will discuss one of the first Java programs you probably ever wrote, a simple console input program.

FIGURE 20.1
Simple Supplier Push Model.

Driving thread resides with supplier, calling consumer when events are available.

Consumer — Supplier

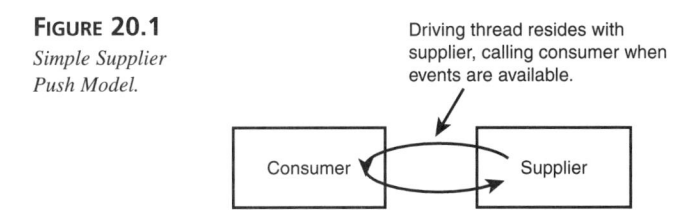

A simple command-line program in Java inevitably has a loop accepting input from standard in (what someone types at the command line). Within this loop is usually a call to read from standard in, and assign the byte(s) into a buffer. The call to read is a blocking call, very similar to the pull model of events.

FIGURE 20.2
Simple Consumer Pull Model.

Driving thread resides with consumer, who "pulls" events then ready.

Consumer — Supplier

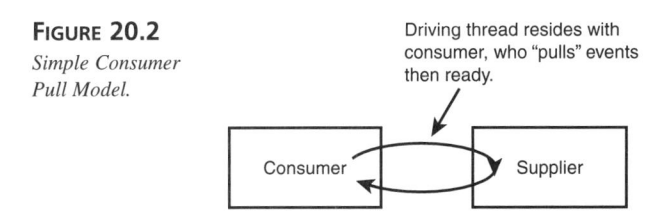

Figure 20.2 shows the consumer pulling an event from a supplier. In the case of your command-line program, the consumer is your input loop and the supplier is the operating system. We will begin to use the terms supplier as a source of information and the term consumer as a sink for that information. Although it looks different from our push model, it is still event driven. The system hangs indefinitely until an event (someone typing on the command line) triggers the system to continue.

Discussing events in the context of a single computer process is quite simple. What are the ramifications of distributing this type of pattern over a distributed system? Some of the issues involve locating each source of events. It is easy to find `System.in` or a button in a single program, but finding event sources across a network is a larger task. There is also the problem of timing. If a given supplier of events has three interested consumers, it is undesirable for the third consumer to wait until the first two have consumed the event.

To solve this problem, the COS Event Service has defined that there be a layer of abstraction between consumers and suppliers. A simple diagram of such an abstraction is seen in Figure 20.3.

By placing an intermediary between consumers and suppliers, we add several benefits. The rate of production can be different from production by placing a queue between the consumers and suppliers. The consumers also no longer have to be aware of the location of the suppliers. We have also added another constraint on the system—all consumers and suppliers must be of the same interface. Unlike AWT where there are typed events and callback interfaces, all interfaces are one of four types and all events are Any with the COS Event Service.

FIGURE 20.3
Separating Consumers from Suppliers with a Proxy.

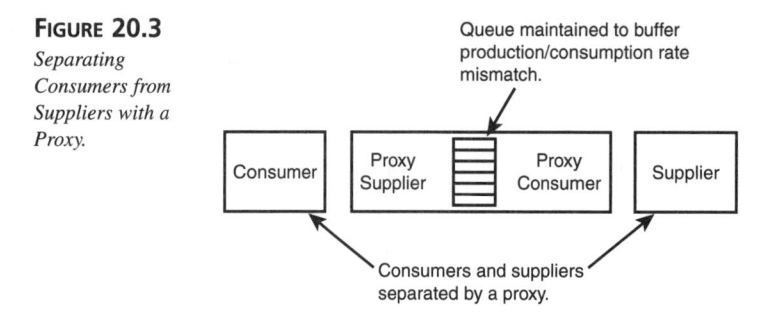

There are three primary participants in the COS event service: Consumer, Supplier, and Channel. The Consumer is defined as the element of the system who wishes to consume events. From the perspective of the consumer, they are observing the network for events. The Supplier is the analog of the observable or `System.in`. The Supplier sits on the network and allows the system to observe its state for events.

The EventChannel is the proxy that provides the de-coupling between consumers and suppliers. It allows the consumers and suppliers to rendezvous on a well-defined point known as a channel. To keep the model simple, consumers observe the channel and suppliers are observed by the channel. The Channel acts as a proxy for consumers and suppliers, allowing multiple instances of each to exist without knowledge of each other's location or implementation. This is shown in Figure 20.4.

FIGURE 20.4
Event Channel with Consumers and Suppliers.

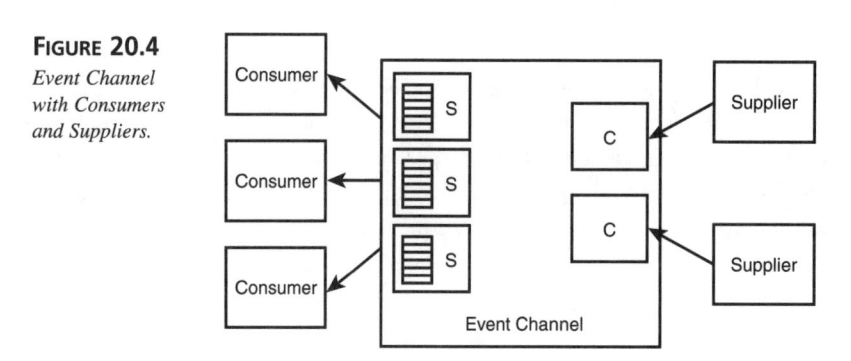

THE COS EVENT API

The COS Event API is split between two IDL modules (and thus two Java Packages). The first and simplest is the `CosEventComm` module. To the programmer this is the most important module in the COS Event Service because it contains one or more of the interfaces you will implement. The IDL for the `CosEventComm` module is shown in Listing 20.1.

LISTING 20.1 THE `CosEventComm` MODULE

```
module CosEventComm
{

  exception Disconnected {};

  interface PushConsumer
  {
    void push(in any data) raises(Disconnected);
    void disconnect_push_consumer();
  };

  interface PushSupplier
  {
    void disconnect_push_supplier();
  };

  interface PullSupplier
  {
    any pull() raises(Disconnected);
    any try_pull(out Boolean has_event) raises(Disconnected);
    void disconnect_pull_supplier();
  };

  interface PullConsumer
  {
    void disconnect_pull_consumer();
  };

};
```

Contained in the `CosEventComm` module are four interfaces and an exception. The exception should be fairly obvious by its name: `Disconnected`. This exception is thrown when one member of the system attempts to call a method on another that is now disconnected.

We will examine the four interfaces in detail in the following sections.

PushConsumer

The `PushConsumer` is the callback interface for objects wishing to be notified asynchronously with respect to events. The method `push(...)` is called by the ORB when events are made available on the channel. The method `disconnect_push_consumer(...)` is called when the channel wishes to disconnect the consumer because the channel is being destroyed. Note that one reason this is necessary is because any changes in the network must flow to the

PushConsumer asynchronously. If this method isn't available, the PushConsumer might wait forever if the server went down (as opposed to a request/reply implementation that would discover the failure upon the next call).

PushSupplier

The PushSupplier interface has only one method, disconnect_push_supplier(...). No other methods are necessary because a PushSupplier is driving and decides when to notify the channel of an event. By driving we are referring to the part of the system that triggers the system to go into action. The disconnect_push_supplier(...) method is called when the supplier's services in the system are no longer necessary (when the channel is being destroyed).

PullSupplier

The PullSupplier interface supports several methods for different types of polling. The method pull(...) is called by consumers (the proxy in the channel) to remove an event from the supplier. If the supplier doesn't have an event available, this call should be blocked.

The consumer can test the supplier for the availability of events by calling try_pull(...) that supports an out Boolean parameter indicating the availability of events. This method doesn't block. Although not defined by the simple IDL syntax, VisiBroker's implementation of the event service is constantly calling the pull(...) method and expecting the supplier to block until events are available.

PullConsumer

The PullConsumer interface, much like the PushSupplier, is implemented by an object that initiates actions. As such, there is only the disconnect_pull_consumer(...) interface, implemented for when the channel is being destroyed.

As previously stated, the four interfaces in the CosEventComm interface are to be implemented by the users of the COS Event Service. However, to join the system and use an event channel, we must examine the interfaces defined in the second COS Event Service Module—CosEventChannelAdmin.

CosEventChannelAdmin

The CosEventChannelAdmin interface is to be implemented by the ORB vendor (in this case, Inprise). The interfaces defined on the CosEventChannelAdmin interfaces are shown in Listing 20.2.

LISTING 20.2 THE CosEventChannelAdmin MODULE

```
module CosEventChannelAdmin
{

  exception AlreadyConnected {};
  exception TypeError {};

  interface ProxyPushConsumer : CosEventComm::PushConsumer
  {
    void connect_push_supplier(in CosEventComm::PushSupplier push_supplier)
      raises(AlreadyConnected);
  };

  interface ProxyPullSupplier : CosEventComm::PullSupplier
  {
    void connect_pull_consumer(in CosEventComm::PullConsumer pull_consumer)
      raises(AlreadyConnected);
  };

  interface ProxyPullConsumer : CosEventComm::PullConsumer
  {
    void connect_pull_supplier(in CosEventComm::PullSupplier pull_supplier)
      raises(AlreadyConnected);
  };

  interface ProxyPushSupplier : CosEventComm::PushSupplier
  {
    void connect_push_consumer(in CosEventComm::PushConsumer push_consumer)
      raises(AlreadyConnected);
  };

  interface ConsumerAdmin
  {
    ProxyPushSupplier obtain_push_supplier();
    ProxyPullSupplier obtain_pull_supplier();
  };

  interface SupplierAdmin
  {
    ProxyPushConsumer obtain_push_consumer();
    ProxyPullConsumer obtain_pull_consumer();
  };
```

continues

LISTING 20.2 CONTINUED

```
interface EventChannel
{
  ConsumerAdmin for_consumers();
  SupplierAdmin for_suppliers();
  void destroy();
};

interface EventChannelFactory
{

  exception AlreadyExists {};

  exception ChannelsExist {};

  EventChannel create();

  EventChannel create_by_name(in string name)
    raises(AlreadyExists);

  EventChannel lookup_by_name(in string name);

  void destroy()
    raises(ChannelsExist);

};
};
```

Unlike the CosEventComm module, we won't discuss each interface in detail. Instead, we will view the CosEventChannelAdmin module as two levels of factory and one level of proxies. At the top level of the CosEventChannelAdmin module is the EventChannel. Objects that implement the EventChannel interface should be obtained from the ORB (through one of several mechanisms discussed in Chapters 7–9). From the EventChannel, two factory objects can be accessed: the SupplierAdmin and the ConsumerAdmin. As the names suggest, user code acting as a Supplier would access the SupplierAdmin, and code acting as Consumers would access the ConsumerAdmin.

From these two factories (SupplierAdmin and ConsumerAdmin), we will obtain one of four interfaces. The interfaces are for the proxies for consumers, suppliers, push, and pull. The four Proxy interfaces are then used for runtime registration and notification. The relationship between objects in the CosEventChannelAdmin module is shown in Figure 20.5.

FIGURE 20.5
Factory Methods and Interfaces to obtain proxies within the Event Service API.

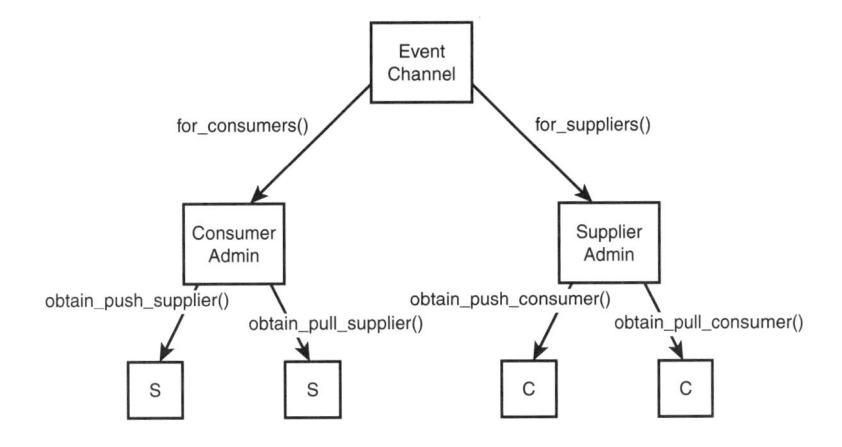

EVENTS AND THE Any TYPE

As can be observed from the IDL of the COS Event Service, the contents of events are of type Any. This provides a loosely typed interface between consumers and suppliers. Code can be written and compiled to only expect an object of type Any. Using standard interfaces and a single transport type makes for flexible code, but places the responsibility on both the consumer and supplier to agree upon a protocol for the Any's contents.

IMPLEMENTING WITH THE PUSH MODEL

Using the push model (as with the pull model) doesn't require you to create any IDL to take advantage of the service. For the consumer, you must create a class that implements the callback interface (extends the org.omg.CosEventComm._PushConsumerImplBase class). This provides the callback method push(). Listing 20.3 shows a client that is acting as a consumer on the event channel.

LISTING 20.3 PushConsumer CLIENT

```
/*
 * A client that will receive events
 * from a channel.
 * Note that before running this sample, the Channel
 * must be started as follows

        prompt>start vbj com.visigenic.vbroker.services.CosEvent.Channel Test
 */
```

continues

LISTING 20.3 CONTINUED

```java
public class SimplePushConsumer
extends org.omg.CosEventComm._PushConsumerImplBase
{
    public SimplePushConsumer()
    {
    }
  public void push(org.omg.CORBA.Any any)
  {
    System.out.println("push");
  }
  public void disconnect_push_consumer()
  {
    System.out.println("disconnect_push_consumer");
  }
    public static void main(String[] args)
    {
        try
        {
    //Initialize the ORB
            org.omg.CORBA.ORB orb = org.omg.CORBA.ORB.init();
    //Initialize the BOA
            org.omg.CORBA.BOA boa = orb.BOA_init();

    //Obtain a reference to the EventChannel.  Note that this is
    //just another CORBA server, so this pattern should look
    //familiar
    org.omg.CosEventChannelAdmin.EventChannel channel =
      org.omg.CosEventChannelAdmin.EventChannelHelper.bind(orb);

    //Use the channel admin as a factory for a ConsumerAdmin.  Note
    //that this method would likely be chained with the next call, but
    //we want our example to be explicit
    org.omg.CosEventChannelAdmin.ConsumerAdmin consumerAdmin =
      channel.for_consumers();

    //We now have a reference to the Admin for consumers (that's us!)
    //We will now obtain the proxy for this channel.  The proxy acts
    //like the single object we will be observing, although any number
    //of other objects can be "pushing" into the channel
    org.omg.CosEventChannelAdmin.ProxyPushSupplier observable =
      consumerAdmin.obtain_push_supplier();

    //Create a SimplePushConsumer, our object (this class) that
    //will receive the callbacks when events occur
    SimplePushConsumer observer = new SimplePushConsumer();

    //Because our callback is a CORBA server object, we must
    //initialize with the BOA
    boa.obj_is_ready(observer);
```

```
        //Add our observer to the observable
        observable.connect_push_consumer(observer);

            //wait till someone hits return then exit
            System.in.read();

        }
        catch(Exception ex)
        {
            ex.printStackTrace();
        }
    }
}
```

Implementing a Supplier in this situation goes through the same steps as shown in Listing 20.3 and Figure 20.5. Listing 20.4 shows a Supplier Client connecting to the Event Service and supplying events based on a thread.

LISTING 20.4 SUPPLIER CLIENT

```
/*
 * This "server" is just a process that periodically
 * wakes up and creates an event.  Note that because we are
 * creating a simple example based on a STANDARD CORBA service
 * we don't even need our own IDL
 * Note that before running this sample, the Channel
 * must be started as follows

            prompt>java com.visigenic.vbroker.services.CosEvent.Channel Test
 */
public class SimplePushSupplier
extends org.omg.CosEventComm._PushSupplierImplBase
implements Runnable
{
    /////////////////////////////////////////////////////
    //      Begin Data Member Declaration
    //

    //A number we will use to distinguish
    //between unique events
    private int theNumber = 0;
    //The proxy consumer for our events.  It must be an instance
    //member because we will be calling from another thread
    private org.omg.CosEventChannelAdmin.ProxyPushConsumer proxy = null;

    //The ORB must be an instance member because we will be calling
    //the push method from another thread
```

continues

LISTING 20.4 CONTINUED

```java
  private org.omg.CORBA.ORB orb = null;

  //      End Data Member Declaration
  //
  /////////////////////////////////////////////////////////////

  public SimplePushSupplier()
  {
    try
    {
      //Initialize the ORB
            orb = org.omg.CORBA.ORB.init();
      //Initialize the BOA
            org.omg.CORBA.BOA boa = orb.BOA_init();

      //Obtain a reference to the EventChannel.  Note that this is
      //just another CORBA server, so this pattern should look
      //familiar
      org.omg.CosEventChannelAdmin.EventChannel channel =
        org.omg.CosEventChannelAdmin.EventChannelHelper.bind(orb);

      //Use the channel admin as a factory for a SupplierAdmin.  Note
      //that this method would likely be chained with the next call, but
      //we want our example to be explicit
      org.omg.CosEventChannelAdmin.SupplierAdmin supplierAdmin =
        channel.for_suppliers();

      //We now have a reference to the Admin for suppliers (that's us!)
      //We will now obtain the proxy for this channel.  The proxy acts
      //like the one and only observer, although any number
      //of other objects can be observing into the channel
      proxy = supplierAdmin.obtain_push_consumer();

      //Declare our object ready
      boa.obj_is_ready(this);

      //Add ourselves to the event channel
      proxy.connect_push_supplier(this);

      //Begin the thread that pushes events
      new Thread(this).start();
        }
    catch(Exception ex)
    {
      ex.printStackTrace();
    }

  }
```

```java
//The disconnect method
  public void disconnect_push_supplier()
{
  System.out.println("Disconnect Push Supplier called");
}

//The run() method.  This is so we can create
//a "realistic" event system where events arrive
//at our client periodically
public void run()
{
  try
  {
    for(;;)
    {
      //Create the contents of our event
      org.omg.CORBA.Any event = orb.create_any();

      //Insert our number into the body of the event
      //Remember - A CORBA long is a Java int
      event.insert_long(++theNumber);

      //Push the event to our proxy observer
      proxy.push(event);

      //Let the console know what is going on
      System.out.println("Just pushed event with contents: " + theNumber);
      Thread.sleep(500);
    }
  }
  catch(Exception ex)
  {
    ex.printStackTrace();
  }
}

public static void main(String[] args)
  {
    new SimplePushSupplier();
  }
}
```

At runtime, our system consists of the consumer shown in Listing 20.3 and the supplier shown in Listing 20.4. Because this is the push model, the consumer is callback-driven. It is up to the supplier to determine when an event in available, and notify the channel. Because we have the channel separating the actual consumer from supplier, the channel can queue events should the production rate exceed that of consumption. Note that the size of this queue is configurable, and will be discussed when we introduce setting up the channel.

IMPLEMENTING WITH THE PULL MODEL

With the push sample we discussed earlier in the chapter, control resides with the supplier of events. With the pull model, control resides with the consumer. Setting up a simple pull system with a single consumer and supplier will now be introduced. Listing 20.5 shows our pull consumer.

LISTING 20.5 PullConsumer WITH DRIVING THREAD

```java
public class SimplePullConsumer
    extends org.omg.CosEventComm._PullConsumerImplBase
{
    //We will need to access this data member to poll
    //the supplier from our inner class, so it must
    //be of protected scope
    protected org.omg.CosEventChannelAdmin.ProxyPullSupplier proxy;

    public SimplePullConsumer()
    {
        try
        {
            //initialize the ORB
            org.omg.CORBA.ORB orb = org.omg.CORBA.ORB.init();

            //Initialize the BOA
            org.omg.CORBA.BOA boa = orb.BOA_init();

            //Obtain a reference to the event channel admin, our first entry
            //point into this system
            org.omg.CosEventChannelAdmin.EventChannel channelAdmin =
                org.omg.CosEventChannelAdmin.EventChannelHelper.bind(orb);

            //Use the channel admin as a factory for the ConsumerAdmin
            org.omg.CosEventChannelAdmin.ConsumerAdmin consumerAdmin =
                channelAdmin.for_consumers();

            //Use the ConsumerAdmin to obtain the proxy for pull
            //consumers
            proxy = consumerAdmin.obtain_pull_supplier();

            //Declare the object (this) ready
            boa.obj_is_ready(this);

            //Connect to the proxy
            proxy.connect_pull_consumer(this);

            //Start our polling thread
            new PullThread().start();

        }
```

```java
            catch(Exception ex)
            {
                ex.printStackTrace();
            }
        }

        public void disconnect_pull_consumer()
        {
            System.out.println("disconnect_pull_consumer");
        }

        public static void main(String[] args)
        {
            new SimplePullConsumer();
        }

        //Use an inner-class to drive the polling
        //of the supplier
        class PullThread extends Thread
        {
            public void run()
            {
                try
                {
                    while(true)
                    {
                        System.out.println("Poll the proxy");
                        //Create an out value for the Boolean, indicating
                        //if the channel has an event
                        org.omg.CORBA.BooleanHolder holder =
                            new org.omg.CORBA.BooleanHolder();
                        //Try polling the channel
                        org.omg.CORBA.Any any = proxy.try_pull(holder);
                        if(holder.value)
                        {
                          System.out.println("Just pulled event with contents " +
                                            any.extract_long());
                        }
                        else
                        {
                            System.out.println("No event was found while polling");
                        }
                        sleep(100);
                    }
                }
                catch(Exception ex)
                {
                    ex.printStackTrace();
                }
            }
        }
    }
```

Because control resides with the consumer, only one method, `disconnect_pull_consumer()` must be implemented. Note that although this example is considerably different from the push example, the same series of factory calls are used to initialize this client.

Listing 20.5 uses an inner-class to provide the thread to drive the system. Because we have used a thread on the consumer to initialize the pull, the supplier requires no such thread. The `EventChannel` polls the supplier on behalf of consumers. If the supplier is able to produce more events than a given consumer is able to consume, these are queued by the channel.

> ### REQUEST/REPLY VERSUS PULL
>
> It might seem to the reader that the Pull model is really just an extension of Request/Reply. Although true that pull is a prolonged request, the difference is not in the time but the actions between the request and the reply. The expectation with request/reply is that the server servicing the request is working on the response as soon as you request. Although some systems might have a long delay between the request and the reply (as with a long database query), the server is still working synchronously with respect to the request. A pull model doesn't have any such expectations, and the server is free to respond asynchronously with respect to receiving the request.

Listing 20.6 shows the corresponding supplier to the consumer introduced in Listing 20.5.

LISTING 20.6 PULL SUPPLIER

```
/*
 * Simple class to demonstrate the pull model
 * of events
 */
public class SimplePullSupplier
   extends org.omg.CosEventComm._PullSupplierImplBase
{

    //Keep a reference to the ORB so we can create Anys
    org.omg.CORBA.ORB orb = null;

    //A number we will increment to show the system working
    int theNumber = 1;

    public SimplePullSupplier(org.omg.CORBA.ORB orb)
    {
        this.orb = orb;
    }
```

```java
public org.omg.CORBA.Any pull()
{
    System.out.println("pull (but pause first)");
    //So the system doesn't clobber this process, choose
    //an arbitrary time to wait.  There would normally
    //be other application-factors limiting this call
    try
    {
        synchronized(this)
        {
            wait(1000);
        }
    }
    catch(Exception ex)
    {
        ex.printStackTrace();
    }
    //Create an any and insert our number
    org.omg.CORBA.Any ret = orb.create_any();
    ret.insert_long(theNumber++);
    //Return the any
    return ret;
}

public org.omg.CORBA.Any try_pull(org.omg.CORBA.BooleanHolder hasEvent)
{
    System.out.println("try_pull");
    hasEvent.value = true;
    return pull();
}
public void disconnect_pull_supplier()
{
    System.out.println("disconnect_pull_supplier");
}

public static void main(String[] args)
{
    try
    {
        //initialize the ORB
        org.omg.CORBA.ORB orb = org.omg.CORBA.ORB.init();

        //Initialize the BOA
        org.omg.CORBA.BOA boa = orb.BOA_init();

        //Obtain a reference to the event channel admin, our first entry
        //point into this system
        org.omg.CosEventChannelAdmin.EventChannel channelAdmin =
            org.omg.CosEventChannelAdmin.EventChannelHelper.bind(orb);
```

continues

LISTING 20.6 CONTINUED

```
        //Use the channel admin as a factory for the SupplierAdmin
        org.omg.CosEventChannelAdmin.SupplierAdmin supplierAdmin =
            channelAdmin.for_suppliers();

        //Use the SupplierAdmin to obtain the proxy for pull
        //consumers
        org.omg.CosEventChannelAdmin.ProxyPullConsumer proxy =
            supplierAdmin.obtain_pull_consumer();

        //Create an instance of our PullSupplier (this class)
        SimplePullSupplier supplier = new SimplePullSupplier(orb);

        //Declare the object ready
        boa.obj_is_ready(supplier);

        //Connect to the proxy
        proxy.connect_pull_supplier(supplier);

        //This is kind-of a kludge.  Because this "program"
        //is so simple, there are no threads to keep it alive
        //to be polled by the system.  To work around this, we'll
        //simple hang the main thread forever
        Object obj = new Object();
        synchronized(obj)
        {
            obj.wait();
        }

    }
    catch(Exception ex)
    {
        ex.printStackTrace();
    }
    }
}
```

Listings 20.6 showed a simple implementation of a pull supplier. The methods in which we are most interested are pull() and try_pull(...) as they will be called the most often. Only pull() is called by the Event Channel on the supplier. If no events are available at the time pull() is called, it is the responsibility of the supplier to block the incoming call. To demonstrate this, the pull supplier example paused for 1 second during the pull() call. Blocking the incoming thread is the only alternative if a new event is not available: returning null causes an exception.

STARTING THE EVENT SERVICE

Earlier in the chapter, we mentioned that the Service took the form of an Event Channel Server somewhere in your system. We will now take a closer look at this server.

The Event Channel is a server written by the developers of VisiBroker in the same way we've created servers throughout this book. Therefore, starting this server should seem familiar because it requires the same steps as our examples. The fully-qualified name of the server is

```
com.visigenic.vbroker.services.CosEvent.Channel
```

There is one argument required by this application—a name for the server. There are also several system properties that can be set for the server (you might recall that we discussed VisiBroker's heavy use of Java System Properties in Chapter 10, "Applets and the GateKeeper"). We won't cover all possible variables here. However, two very useful properties are as follows:

- `DDEBUG`—This flag enables debugging messages from the server to standard out.
- `DMAX_QUEUE_LENGTH=<length>`—This sets the size of a consumer's queue. Without this parameter, an unbounded condition could occur where producers produce information faster than a consumer might consume. The result would be that the server runs out of memory. To prevent this condition, a cap can be placed on the queue size. When the maximum length is reached, the oldest messages are removed (First In, First Out).

An example command line for starting the server would appear as follows:

```
prompt> vbj -DDEBUG com.visigenic.vbroker.services.CosEvent.Channel
```

SUMMARY

The COS Event Service provides a mechanism for one or more applications to communicate in an asynchronous, event-driven manner. This is accomplished through two models: the push model and the pull model.

The push model (the most common) follows closely to Java GUI programming. Applications register objects of a known interface for callbacks. The pull model, although less common, again supports the notion of a client program waiting for external input.

Both the push and pull model require the same registration process. The Event Channel must be obtained, and from the channel one of two factories must be obtained. From the factories the application's consumers and suppliers can join the system.

MONITORING AND DEBUGGING

CHAPTER 21

IN THIS CHAPTER

- **INTRODUCTION TO THE VISIBROKER MANAGEMENT API** *484*
- **THE ORB MANAGEMENT INTERFACE** *484*
- **THE VISIBROKER GRAPHICAL DEBUGGER** *493*

INTRODUCTION TO THE VISIBROKER MANAGEMENT API

This chapter finishes our discussion of VisiBroker for Java with a topic that is critical for large deployment: the ability to dynamically monitor and modify ORB- and BOA-level parameters, as well as debug requests from Client to Server.

VisiBroker provides an ORB Management interface that allows Server parameters to be queried and changed at runtime. VisiBroker has two interfaces that can be implemented by Server Objects to allow them to be monitored and configured at runtime, the Server interface and the Adapter interface. The Server interface allows the ORB attributes to be viewed and modified at runtime. The Adapter interface allows BOA attributes to be viewed and modified at runtime.

These interfaces will become increasingly important when developing your own performance monitors and load balancing Servers. From these interfaces you will be able to determine critical system level information, such as:

- Number of Clients actively connected to a given Server Object.
- Number of method requests the Server Object is actively working on.
- Number of active threads the Server Object currently has in use.
- A Server Object's activation policy.

Thus, based on the current load of a Server, you can dynamically change key parameters such as

- Increase or decrease the number of available connections to Clients.
- Increase or decrease the number of available threads the Server can use to service Client requests.
- Increase or decrease the number of cached connections.
- Increase or decrease connection idle times to ensure that all connections are used efficiently.

VisiBroker also provides a graphical Object Request Debugger to track method requests from Client to Server. It is implemented using the VisiBroker interceptor classes described in Chapter 18.

THE ORB MANAGEMENT INTERFACE

As you start to understand the ORB Management APIs, you must understand the notion of an Attribute and the different interfaces used as part of the Management API. We will first look at what an Attribute is and how it provides access to information within the ORB. Next, we will go into detail on the two different interfaces that provide the VisiBroker Management APIs: the Server interface, and the Adapter interface. The Server interface provides methods for querying and modifying the ORB parameters. The Adapter interface provides methods for querying and modifying the BOA parameters. For a better explanation of the various ORB and BOA parameters, refer to Chapter 5.

Attributes

When trying to understand how to make use of the ORB Management interfaces, it is important to understand that all the information about the ORB and BOA parameters is retrieved as an Attribute. An Attribute is an object that represents the property for a given Server Object. These properties can either by read-only or have both read and write capabilities. The ORB and BOA Attributes have the structure as shown in Listing 21.1.

LISTING 21.1 IDL FOR THE ORB MANAGEMENT ATTRIBUTE STRUCTURE

```
struct Attribute
{
    string id;
    any value;
    Boolean is_readonly;
};
```

The following bulleted list offers a description of each of the elements of the Attribute structure found in Listing 21.1:

- id—Represents the name of the ORB or BOA parameter.
- value—Represents the value of the parameter.
- is_readonly—A Boolean value indicating whether the parameter value is read-only or can be modified.

The base interface for both the Server and Adapter interface is the AttributeSet interface. This is defined in Listing 21.2.

LISTING 21.2 INTERFACE FOR THE AttributeSet WHICH IS THE BASE INTERFACE FOR BOTH SERVER AND ADAPTER INTERFACES

```
public interface com.visigenic.vbroker.services.ORBManager.AttributeSet
↪extends java.lang.Object
        implements org.omg.CORBA.Object
{
    public abstract org.omg.CORBA.Any get_attribute(java.lang.String);
    public abstract void set_attribute(java.lang.String, org.omg.CORBA.Any);
    public abstract com.visigenic.vbroker.services.ORBManager.
        AttributeSetPackage.Attribute get_all_attributes()[];
}
```

You will notice that the purpose of this interface is to provide a general accessor and modifier method that is used to get and set the ORB and BOA parameters. It also contains a method that gives you an entire listing of all the current parameter settings for either the ORB or the BOA.

You will never have to implement this interface directly; it is already done for you by both the Server and Adapter interface. Your Server Object implementation automatically implements these interfaces when your Server is started with the following ORBservice attached:

prompt>vbj -DORBservices=ORBManager Server

A key thing to note is that you don't need to write any special code to make use of the Management interfaces as shown in Figure 21.1.

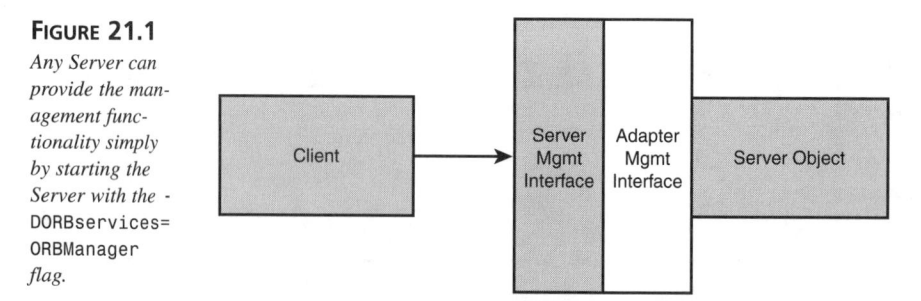

FIGURE 21.1
Any Server can provide the management functionality simply by starting the Server with the -DORBservices= ORBManager flag.

Any Server can provide the management functionality simply by starting the Server with the -DORBservices=ORBManager flag.

Server Interface

Through implementing the Server interface, a given Server Object can be queried for its current ORB settings. The Server interface is shown in Listing 21.3.

LISTING 21.3 THE ORB MANAGEMENT SERVER INTERFACE WHICH IS USED TO READ AND MODIFY ORB PARAMETERS

```
public interface com.visigenic.vbroker.services.ORBManager.Server extends
➥java.lang.Object implements
➥com.visigenic.vbroker.services.ORBManager.AttributeSet
{
    public abstract int process_id();
    public abstract int activation_policy();
    public abstract com.visigenic.vbroker.services.ORBManager.Adapter
    ➥get_adapter(java.lang.String);
    public abstract com.visigenic.vbroker.services.ORBManager.Adapter
    ➥get_all_adapters()[];
    public abstract void shutdown();
}
```

Notice that Server implements the `AttributeSet` interface, thus providing the `get_attribute()` and `set_attribute()` methods as well as the `get_all_attributes()` method. We will review the additional methods implemented by the Server interface in the following list:

- `process_id()`—Returns the process id for the process that was used to start your Server implementation.
- `activation_policy()`—Returns an integer for the activation policy of the Server. The possible values are

    0 = Shared Server Policy

    1 = Unshared Server Policy

    2 = Server-per-method Policy

- `get_adapter()`—Returns an Object Adapter (OA) reference with the specified argument. The OA reference is needed to `get` and `set` attributes on the Adapter interface. The possible values that can be passed in as arguments are
    - TPool
    - TSession
- `get_all_adapters()`—Returns an array of all Object Adapters currently initialized for a given Server. It is possible that a Server could have several Object Adapters initialized, each with different thread policies (that is, `TPool` or `TSession`).
- `shutdown()`—Causes the Server process to terminate gracefully and shut down.

Server Attributes

Table 21.1 summarizes the ORB attributes that might be obtained by calling `get_attribute()` or `get_all_attributes()` on the Server interface. Read/Write ORB attributes are shown in Table 21.2.

TABLE 21.1 READ-ONLY ORB ATTRIBUTES

Attribute	Description
ORBagentAddr	The IP address or hostname of the host that is running the Smart Agent. It returns a blank string if this parameter isn't explicitly set by the Server.
ORBagentPort	The port that the Server is using to broadcast to Smart Agents.
ORBbackCompat	A Boolean value indicating whether the Server is running in backward compatible mode.
ORBdisableAgentCache	A Boolean value indicating whether Smart Agent caching is enabled or disabled.

continues

TABLE 21.1 CONTINUED

Attribute	Description
ORBdisableLocator	A Boolean value indicating whether or not the Smart Agent and GateKeeper are enabled or disabled.
ORBgatekeeperIOR	The URL string that points to the location of the GateKeeper IOR file.
ORBnullString	A Boolean value indicating whether the ability to pass null strings is enabled or disabled. The IIOP specification doesn't allow null strings to be passed, throwing a CORBA::BAD_PARAM exception. However, VisiBroker allows you to set this option to allow null strings to be passed. If this value is set to true, null strings aren't allowed and a CORBA::BAD_PARAM exception is thrown.
ORBprocId	The process identifier of the Server.
ORBsecureShutdown	A Boolean value indicating whether the Server can be stopped using the shutdown() method on the ORBManager Server interface. If set to true, the Server cannot be stopped with the shutdown() method.
ORBsyncGC	A Boolean value indicating whether the Server will perform synchronous garbage collection. A value of true indicates that the server will perform synchronous garbage collection.

TABLE 21.2 READ/WRITE ORB ATTRIBUTES

Attribute	Description
ORBagentAddrFile	Name of file containing the IP addresses of Smart Agents.
ORBalwaysProxy	A Boolean value indicating whether a client will automatically attempt to connect to the Server via the GateKeeper.
ORBagentNoFailOver	A Boolean value indicating whether the Server will automatically rebind to another Smart Agent if its current Smart Agent becomes unavailable. The automatic rebind is the default behavior of VisiBroker, and is only disabled if this option is set to false.
ORBconnectionCacheMax	Maximum number of connections that the Server can cache.
ORBconnectionMaxIdle	Maximum number of seconds a Client connection can be idle before it will automatically be shutdown by the Server. A value of zero indicates that the connection will never time-out.
ORBdebug	A Boolean value that indicates whether debugging is enabled.
ORBdebugDir	The directory where debugging information is written.

Attribute	Description
ORBdisableGateKeeperCallbacks	A Boolean value that indicates whether GateKeeper callbacks are disabled or not.
ORBgcTimeout	The interval in seconds in which the garbage collection thread will be activated.
ORBmbufsize	The buffer size used on the Server side when processing method requests.
ORBtcpNoDelay	A Boolean value indicating whether the Server immediately sends all data written to the socket, rather than waiting for the buffer to fill before sending the request.
ORBtcpTimeout	Time in milliseconds that a socket waits to send data back to the Client before timing out. A value of `zero` disables the time-out.
ORBsendBindfalse	A Boolean value used for backward compatibility with VisiBroker for Java 2.5. If set to `false`, backward compatibility is enabled.
ORBservices	Any VisiBroker services that are installed on the Server. This could include the COS Naming Service, the Location Service, or any user-created Interceptors.
ORBwarn	The level of warning messages to be printed on the Server. The value, if one of the following: 0—Default setting, no warning. 1—Prints non-CORBA exceptions and their associated Java stack trace. 2—Prints the same information as level 1, plus any CORBA exceptions thrown as well.

Obtaining a Reference to the Server Interface

When your Server Implementation has been started with the `-DORBservices=ORBManager` argument, your Client has to obtain a reference to the `ORBManager` Server object in order to make use of the methods described in the previous section.

We will walk through an example. Suppose that you have the IDL shown in Listing 21.4.

LISTING 21.4 SAMPLE IDL FOR DEMONSTRATION WITH THE ORB MANAGEMENT INTERFACE

```
//IDL
module MyModule
{
```

continues

LISTING 21.4 CONTINUED

```
    interface MyInterface
    {
    };
};
```

Assume that you have a persistent implementation of this interface called `MyInterfaceImpl` with an instance name of `ORBMgrExample`. If you wanted to ensure that `MyInterfaceImpl` could be monitored for its ORB and BOA parameters, you would start this Server as follows:

`prompt> vbj -DORBservices=ORBManager MyModule.MyInterfaceImpl`

Now, within your Client that wants to query the `MyInterfaceImpl` for its ORB and BOA parameters, it must obtain a reference to the `ORBManager` Server interface. This can be done as shown in Listing 21.5.

LISTING 21.5 OBTAINING A REFERENCE TO THE ORB MANAGER SERVER INTERFACE

```
.........
org.omg.CORBA.ORB orb = org.omg.CORBA.ORB.init();
org.omg.CORBA.Object ORBMgrServer = orb.bind("IDL:MyModule/MyInterface:1.0",
➥"ORBMgrExample", null, null);
org.omg.CORBA.Object serverInt = ORBMgrServer._resolve_reference("ORBManager");
com.visigenic.vbroker.services.ORBManager.Server server =
com.visigenic.vbroker.services.ORBManager.ServerHelper.narrow(serverInt);
.........
```

Examine what Listing 21.5 does. First, obtain a reference to the local ORB. You will next use a `bind(...)` method that is on the ORB interface itself in order to obtain a generic root level object reference. The signature for this method is very similar to the different `bind()` signatures on the IDL generated Helper classes that you looked at in Chapter 6, shown below for reference.

```
public org.omg.CORBA.Object bind(java.lang.String repository_id,
                java.lang.String object_name,
                java.lang.String host_name,
                org.omg.CORBA.BindOptions bind_options);
```

Notice the difference here is that the first argument used in the connection is the IDL Repository ID, not the ORB parameter used with the Helper defined `bind()` methods. However, arguments 2–4 are exactly the same: the Server instance name, the specific host name, and a `BindOptions` object if you want to override the default settings.

Now that you have a root level CORBA Object, you will use the `_resolve_reference()` method to resolve the server-side interface with the constant identifier `ORBManager`. Now that you have a reference to the `ORBManager`, narrow to the `ORBManager` Server interface. At this point you can use your `ORBManager` Server reference to get and set attributes on the `MyInterfaceImpl` Server.

Getting Server attributes is done via calling `get_attribute` on your `ORBManager` Server object. Listing 21.6 is an example of how to obtain the Smart Agent's address.

LISTING 21.6 GETTING THE VALUE FOR A PARTICULAR ORB ATTRIBUTE

```
.........
org.omg.CORBA.Any attr_value = server.get_attribute("ORBagentAddr");
java.lang.String osagent_addr = value.extract_string();
.........
```

Setting the Server attributes is done in a similar fashion (see Listing 21.7).

LISTING 21.7 SETTING THE VALUE FOR A PARTICULAR ORB ATTRIBUTE

```
.........
    org.omg.CORBA.Any attr_value = orb.create_any();
    attr_value.insert_string("299.89.76.4");
    server.set_attribute("ORBAagentAddr", attr_value);
.........
```

Adapter Interface

Similar to the Server interface that returns the current parameters for the ORB, there is an Adapter interface that returns all the attributes for the BOA. You will notice in Listing 21.8 that the Adapter interface also implements the `AttributeSet` interface, providing the `get_attribute()` and `set_attribute()` methods for the BOA.

LISTING 21.8 THE ORB MANAGEMENT ADAPTER INTERFACE FOR READING AND MODIFYING BOA SETTINGS

```
public interface com.visigenic.vbroker.services.ORBManager.Adapter
extends java.lang.Object
implements com.visigenic.vbroker.services.ORBManager.AttributeSet
{
    public abstract java.lang.String adapter_id();
    public abstract org.omg.CORBA.Object[] persistent_objects();
}
```

The Adapter interface adds two more methods. They are

- `adapter_id()`—Returns the type of Object Adapter that the Server was started with. The two possible values are `TPool` and `TSession`.
- `persistent_objects()`—Returns an array of all persistent Server Objects that are currently registered with this Object Adapter.

Obtaining a Reference to the Adapter Interface

In order to get a reference to the Adapter, simply call the `get_adapter()` method on the `ORBManager` Server interface. You must specify which Object Adapter within the Server Implementation you want a connection to. The two options for this method are either `TPool` or `TSession`. This is shown in Listing 21.9. These BOA options are described in detail in Chapter 5.

LISTING 21.9 OBTAINING A REFERENCE TO THE ORB MANAGER ADAPTER INTERFACE

```
.........
com.visigenic.vbroker.services.ORBManager.Adapter   adapter =
➥server.get_adapter("TSession");
.........
```

> **NOTE**
>
> This operation fails if you attempt to get an adapter that wasn't initialized by the Server implementation. In other words, if you attempt to get a `TSession` Adapter reference for a Server Implementation that was initialized with a `TPool` Object Adapter, an Exception is thrown.

Adapter Attributes

Table 21.3 summarizes the BOA attributes that might be obtained by calling `get_attribute()` or `get_all_attributes()` on the Adapter interface.

TABLE 21.3 READ-ONLY BOA ATTRIBUTES

Attribute	Description
OAactivatedConnections	Current number of active Client socket connections.
OAactivatedRequests	Current number of outstanding requests.
OAallocatedThreads	Current number of allocated threads.

The preceding attributes are extremely useful when building your own load balancing mechanism. They provide very useful metrics for determining how busy the current Server Object is. Read/Write Attributes are shown in Table 21.4.

TABLE 21.4 READ/WRITE BOA ATTRIBUTES

Attribute	Description
OAconnectionMax	Maximum number of incoming Client connections allowed.
OAconnectionMaxIdle	Maximum number of seconds Client connections can be idle before the Server automatically disconnects them. A value of zero disables this option, no connections will ever time-out.
OAthreadMax	Maximum number of threads allowed to be created.
OAthreadMaxIdle	Maximum number of seconds a thread can sit idle before the thread is removed.
OAthreadMin	Minimum number of threads allowed.

THE VISIBROKER GRAPHICAL DEBUGGER

The VisiBroker debugger is designed to allow you to track the status of method invocations from the Client to the Server. It is important to note that it isn't designed to debug the VisiBroker runtime classes, just your Client and Server Object implementations.

The debugger is built using the VisiBroker Interceptors and Interface Repository in order to provide information on when method requests are sent and when method requests are received. By making use of the Interface Repository, the Debugger can dynamically return specific information about the Server Object being communicated with, such as their method names, argument lists, and possible exceptions.

Using the Debugger

The VisiBroker Debugger is just another VisiBroker Server process that is implemented as a special ORB service. As such, it requires the following:

- The Smart Agent to be running. Just like with any other VisiBroker Server, it registers with the Smart Agent.
- The Interface Repository must be running. It should load all the IDL of all the backend Server Objects that will be debugged. This is optional and not required to simply debug the messages sent from Client to Server. However, this limits the amount of information about the Server Object that the Debugger will be able to display, such as argument names, types, and any user exceptions.

Starting the Debugger

The VisiBroker Debugger is started with the following command:

```
prompt> vbdebug Debugger
```

This presents the following GUI:

<insert Debugger.pcx here>

In order for your Client and Server communication to be analyzed through this Debugger, you must start each process with the following:

`-DORBservices=com.visigenic.vbroker.debug`

Thus,

```
prompt> vbj -DORBservices=com.visigenic.vbroker.debug Server
prompt> vbj -DORBservices=com.visigenic.vbroker.debug Client
```

Options on the Debugger

When using the Debugger GUI, notice that all messages are displayed in the console window. The first messages that appear are the registrations of the Client and Server Processes that use the Debugger. The following lines show the critical information that is being sent as part of the Send and Receive messages from Client to Server. You should recognize the format of the information displayed in the Send and Receive entries because they are all from arguments contained within the `send_request()`, `receive_request()`, `send_reply()`, and `receive_reply()` methods on the Client and Server Interceptors. If the role of the Interceptors isn't as clear to you, refer to the discussion of Interceptors in Chapter 18.

The button functions are as follows:

- Continue Processes —This continues the execution of a process that has been suspended through a breakpoint. It can refer to either a Client process or a Server process that has registered with the Debugger.

- Stop All Processes—Stops execution of all Client and Server Processes that are registered with the Debugger.

- Step One Process—Similar to the notion of stepping through one line of code in traditional debuggers. This button allows you to isolate the execution of a single process.

- List All Processes—Lists all processes by name that are currently running.

- List Objects—This button requires that you specify a particular process in the text field at the top of the GUI. After this has been specified, this button lists all the objects within this process. In the case of listing a Client process, the Debugger lists all the objects used by the Client process.

- List Methods—This button requires that you specify an Interface name in the form of an IDL Repository ID in the text field at the top of the GUI. Given this interface, the button lists all the available methods.

- Set Breakpoint—This sets a breakpoint by specifying the following information in the text field at the top of the GUI:

    <process>¦<interface>¦<object>¦<operation>

    Any of the preceding can be made into a wild-card (*) indicating everything.
- Clear Breakpoint—Clears the Breakpoint
- List Breakpoints—Lists all current Breakpoints. They are listed in a numbered list. You can specify a particular number in order to have that specific breakpoint cleared.
- Set Verbose—Turns on verbose output.
- Clear Verbose—Clears verbose mode

SUMMARY

In our final chapter, we examine how to use two interfaces, the Server interface and the Adapter interface, in order to dynamically query and modify ORB and BOA parameters. This is very valuable when implementing your own Load Balancer or Performance Monitor. You can have a Monitor Server simply check to see how many connections and threads are being used within a given Server Implementation relative to the number of outstanding requests it is attempting to service. Based on these numbers, the Monitor Server can choose to increase either connections or threads, or decrease the connection idle time to allow new connections for new Clients.

You don't need to write any special code in your Server applications in order for their ORB and BOA parameters to be monitored. Moreover, you don't need to explicitly implement the Server and Adapter interfaces for your Server Implementation to support their methods. All that needs to be done for your Server Implementation is to start it with the following:

-DORBservices=ORBManager

After this has been done, your Server Implementation can now be monitored using the Server and Adapter interfaces.

INDEX

SYMBOLS

: (colon), 84
_ (underscore), 22
#include directive, 95-96
#pragma directive, 96-97

A

-a option (oadutil command), 354
abstract methods, 82
accessors, 32
activate() method, 355
activating objects
    Activators
        Activator interface, 354-355
        client implementation, 358-360
        custom classes, 356-357
        server implementation, 355-357
    BOA (Basic Object Adapter), 118
    oadj (Object Activation Daemon)
        activation policies, 348-349
        command-line options, 346-347
        environment variables, 347
        oadutil tool, 353-354
        object registration, 349-353
        querying, 351-352
        starting, 346
activation_policy() method, 487
Activator interface, 354-355
Activators
    Activator interface, 354-355
    client implementation, 358-360
    custom classes, 356-357
    server implementation, 355-357

Adapter interface
    attributes
        OAactivatedConnections, 492
        OAactivatedRequests, 492
        OAallocatedThreads, 492
        OAconnectionMax, 493
        OAconnectionMaxIdle, 493
        OAthreadMax, 493
        OAthreadMaxIdle, 493
        OAthreadMin, 493
    code listing, 491
    methods, 491
    referencing, 492
adapter_id() method, 491
addresses (IP), GateKeeper settings
    exterior addresses, 226-227
    interior addresses, 227-228
Agent interface, 450
agentaddr files (Smart Agent), 162
AliasDef object, 298
all_agent_locations() method, 450
all_instances() method, 451
all_instances_descs() method, 451
all_replica() method, 451
all_replica_descs() method, 451
all_repository_ids() method, 451
-all_serializable option
    idl2java compiler, 102
    java2idl compiler, 252
AlreadyExists exception, 205
Any event type, 471
Any type, 62-63, 259. *See also* Typecodes
    DynAnys
        client implementation, 334-338
        creating, 327-328
        DynAny interface, 328-331

DynArray interface, 331
DynEnum interface, 331-332
DynSequence interface, 332
DynStruct interface, 332-333
DynUnion interface, 333
IDL (Interface Definition Language), 318, 333-334
mapping, 327
passing, 321-323
server implementation, 318-321, 339-342
structures
    extracting, 321
    inserting, 323-324
TCKind enumeration, 324-325
types, passing
    complex types, 69-75
    primitive values, 63-68
applets, 212
    digital signatures, 233-234
        creating, 236
        Netscape pre-install, 234-238
    GateKeeper
        chaining, 232
        firewalls, 232
        gkconfig tool, 224-232
        HTTP (Hypertext Transport Protocol) tunneling proxy, 214
        HTTPd, 216
        Sandbox proxy, 213-214
        security, 232-233
        starting, 224
    HTML (Hypertext Markup Language) parameters, 221
        ORBalwaysProxy, 223
        ORBalwaysTunnel, 223
        ORBdisableGatekeeper Callbacks, 224
        ORBdisableLocator, 223
        ORBgatekeeperIOR, 222

org.omg.CORBA.ORB Class, 222
USE_ORB_LOCATOR, 222
initializing as Visibroker clients, 217-220
Sandbox security model, 212-213
ARG_IN class, 263
ARG_INOUT class, 263
arg_list
  parameter(create_request() method), 269
ARG_OUT class, 263
ArrayDef object, 299
arrays
  compared to bounded sequences, 57
  creating, 57
  language mapping
    IDL-to-Java, 58
    Java-to-IDL, 247
  ParameterDescription, creating
    ParameterDescription class, 304-305
    ParameterMode class, 305
AttributeDef object, 297
attributes
  Adapter interface
    OAactivatedConnections, 492
    OAactivatedRequests, 492
    OAallocatedThreads, 492
    OAconnectionMax, 493
    OAconnectionMaxIdle, 493
    OAthreadMax, 493
    OAthreadMaxIdle, 493
    OAthreadMin, 493
  defining, 31-32
  ORB Management attribute structure, 485-486
  Server interface
    accessing, 491
    ORBagentAddr, 487
    ORBagentAddrFile, 488
    ORBagentNoFailOver, 488
    ORBagentPort, 487
    ORBalwaysProxy, 488
    ORBbackCompat, 487
    ORBconnectionCacheMax, 488
    ORBconnectionMaxIdle, 488
    ORBdebug, 488
    ORBdebugDir, 488
    ORBdisableAgentCache, 487
    ORBdisableGateKeeper Callbacks, 489
    ORBdisableLocator, 488
    ORBgatekeeperIOR, 488
    ORBgcTimeout, 489
    ORBmbufsize, 489
    ORBnullString, 488
    ORBprocId, 488
    ORBsecureShutdown, 488
    ORBsendBindfalse, 489
    ORBservices, 489
    ORBsyncGC, 488
    ORBtcpNoDelay, 489
    ORBtcpTimeout, 489
    ORBwarn, 489
    setting, 491
AttributeSet interface, 485
automatic smart binding, 160

B

BAD_CONTEXT exception, 89
BAD_INV_ORDER exception, 89
BAD_OPERATION exception, 89
BAD_PARAM exception, 89
BAD_TYPECODE exception, 89
Basic Object Adapter. *See* **BOA**

BasicStructs
  extracting from Any types, 321
  inserting from Any types, 323-324
bind() method, 107, 193, 206-207, 296
  BindInterceptor interface, 421-422
  BindOptions
    defer_bind, 156
    enable_rebind, 157
  CORBA (Common Object Request Broker Architecture) compliancy, 158
  example, 394-395
  multiple object implementations, 158-160
  parameters, 395
  signatures, 154-156
  static, 266-267
binding
  COS Naming Service, 195
  defined, 186
  Interface Repository, 296, 301-302
  Smart Agents
    automatic smart binding, 160
    bind() method, 154-156
    defer_bind option, 156
    enable_rebind option, 157
    load balancing, 155-156
    multiple object implementations, 158-160
  smart binding, 10
BindingIterator enumeration, 197-198
BindingType enumeration, 196-197
BindInterceptor interface, 420
  code listing, 421
  methods
    bind( ), 421-422
    bind_failed( ), 422-423
    bind_succeeded( ), 423
    exception_occurred( ), 424

BindInterceptor interface

rebind( ), 423
rebind_failed( ), 423
rebind_succeeded( ), 423
sample implementation, 424-425
BindIterator objects, 197-198
BindList objects, 197
BindOptions (bind method)
defer_bind, 156
enable_rebind, 157
BindOptions class, 399-400
bind_context() method, 194
bind_failed() method, 399, 422-423
bind_new_context() method, 194
bind_succeeded() method, 399, 423
BOA (Basic Object Adapter)
initializing, 116
method invocation, 118-119
object activation/deactivation, 118
object registration, 118
thread policies, 120-121
boa( ) method, 133
Boolean data type, 38
bootstrapping, 141, 187-190.
See also **location strategies**
business methods, 129
buttons (Debugger)
Clear Breakpoint, 495
Clear Verbose, 495
Continue Processes, 494
List All Processes, 494
List Breakpoints, 495
List Methods, 494
List Objects, 494
Set Breakpoint, 495
Set Verbose, 495
Step One Process, 494
Stop All Processes, 494
byte_order value (GIOP messages), 413

C

-C option
asagent command, 146
idl2java command, 97
C++ command (Language menu), 314
Caffeine compilers, 11
advantages, 240-241
exceptions
IDL (Interface Definition Language), 254-255
implementing, 253
throwing, 253-254
extensible structs, 247-248
defining in IDL (Interface Definition Language), 252-253
example, 248-249
mapping with java2idl, 249-252
idl2java, 94
command-line options, 97-103
DII (Dynamic Invocation Interface) clients, 280-282
DSI (Dynamic Skeleton Interface) servers, 288-291
generated files, 103-110, 129-130
name collisions, 22-23
-portable option, 280-281, 288, 291
preprocessor directives, 95-97
java2idl, 244-247
command-line options, 245-246
development steps, 244-245
java2iiop
command-line options, 243-244
development steps, 241-243
sample Caffeine interface, 242
Callbacks, 366-367. *See also* **Smart Stubs**
clients, 368-369
IDL (Interface Definition Language) definition, 367-368
servers, 370-372
CancelRequest messages (GIOP), 417-418
CancelRequestHeader structure (CancelRequest messages), 417
chaining
GateKeeper, 232
interceptors, 437-441
Object Wrappers, 373
channels (COS Event Service), 466
char data type, 38
classes
ARG_IN, 263
ARG_INOUT, 263
ARG_OUT, 263
BindOptions, 399-400
Context, 259
defined, 82
DynamicImplementation, 283
Holder, 37
ImplementationStatus, 351-352
inheritance, 82
Java-to-IDL language mapping, 247
naming conventions, 87
ObjectStatus, 352
ParameterDescription, 304-305
ParameterMode, 305
Principal, 384
referencing, 365
Request, 267
ServerRequest, 283-284
ServiceInit, 441
code listing, 442
methods, 443-444
sample implementation, 442-443
State, 352

TaggedProfile, 436
Timer, 127
TypeCode
 code listing, 325
 methods, 326
CLASSPATH environment variable, 15
Clear Breakpoint button (Debugger), 495
Clear Verbose button (Debugger), 495
client stubs. *See* stubs
client-side event handlers
 ClientEventHander interface
  IDL (Interface Definition Language), 399
  methods, 399
  sample implementation, 400-405
 HandlerRegistry interface, 402
 registering
  HandlerRegistry interface, 401-402
  methods, 402-403
 unregistering, 403
ClientEventHandler interface
 IDL (Interface Definition Language), 399
 methods, 399
 sample implementation, 400-405
ClientInterceptor interface
 code listing, 425-426
 methods
  exception_occurred( ), 428
  prepare_request( ), 426
  receive_reply( ), 427
  receive_reply_failed( ), 428
  send_request( ), 426
  send_request_failed( ), 427
  send_request_succeeded( ), 427
 sample implementation, 428-429
ClientInterceptorFactory interface, 437

clients
 applets
  HTML parameters, 221-224
  initializing, 217-220
 Callback client, 368-369
 ComplexAnyTest, 69-72
 DII (Dynamic Invocation Interface)
  generating with idl2java, 280-282
  IDL (Interface Definition Language), 305-306
  Interface Repository, calling, 306-312
 DynAny client implementation, 334-338
 executing, 175
 factory client, 179-180
 locating servers, *see* location strategies
 Object Wrappers
  chaining, 373
  Typed, 376-377
  Untyped, 380-382
 PrimitiveAnyTest, 64-66
 PushConsumer client, 471-473
 PushSupplier client, 473-475
 Smart Agents, binding
  automatic smart binding, 160
  bind( ) method, 154-156
  defer_bind option, 156
  enable_rebind option, 157
  load balancing, 155-156
  multiple object implementations, 158-160
client_aborted( ) method, 396-397
clone( ) method, 160
CloseConnection messages (GIOP), 420
code listings
 Activators
  Activator interface, 355
  custom class, 356-357
  LongTest interface client, 359-360
  Register interface client, 358
  sample IDL (Interface Definition Language), 355
  server implementation, 356
  server mainline for RegImpl object, 357
 Any type
  extracting structures from, 321
  inserting structures into, 324
  TCKind enumeration, 325
 applets
  HTML (Hypertext Markup Language) page, 221
  IDL (Interface Definition Language), 217
  initialization code, 217
  server, 218
  Visibroker client, 219-220
 ARG_IN, ARG_INOUT, and ARG_OUT classes, 263
 arrays
  creating, 57
  declaring, 58
 attributes
  defining, 32
  generated interface, 32
 BOA (Basic Object Adapter)
  initializing, 116
  method invocation, 119
  object registration, 118
  specific parameter settings, 120
  thread policy, 120
 Caffeine sample interface, 242
 Callbacks
  client, 368-369
  IDL (Interface Definition Language), 368
  server, 370-372

code listings

client-side event handlers
  BindOptions class, 400
  ClientEventHandler IDL (Interface Definition Language), 399
  ClientEventHandler implementation, 400-401
  sample implementation, 403-405
comments, 22
ComplexAnyTest
  client, 69-72
  interface, 69
  server, 72-75
constants
  defining outside interfaces, 31
  defining within interfaces, 30-31
constructed data types, passing
  client, 59-60
  interface, 58
  server, 60-62
Contexts
  client/server sample application, 76-78
  Context class, 76, 259
  data types creating, 259
  generated code, 75-76
  values, 75
COS Event Service
  CosEventChannelAdmin module, 469-470
  CosEventComm module, 467
  PullConsumer implementation, 476-477
  PullSupplier implementation, 478-480
  PushConsumer client, 471-473
  PushSupplier client, 473-475

COS Naming Service
  binding, 195
  client resolving reference, 190
  IDL (Interface Definition Language), 191-192, 196
  list( ) iterator, 199
  list_initial_services( ) method, 189
  ORB (Object Request Broker) interface, 188
  outputting initial references, 189
  resolution, 195-196
DII (Dynamic Invocation Interface)
  client, 281-282
  exceptions, 280
DSI (Dynamic Skeleton Interface) server, 284-287*
DynamicImplementation class, 283
DynAnys
  client implementation, 334-338
  creating, 327
  DynAny interface, 328
  DynArray interface, 331
  DynEnum interface, 332
  DynSequence interface, 332
  DynStruct interface, 332
  DynUnion interface, 333
  IDL (Interface Definition Language), 318, 333-334
  passing, 321-323
  server implementation, 319-321, 339-342
enumerations
  Car Rental application, 47
  declaring, 47
  example, 45
  generated class, 46
Environment class, 265
Environment objects, 265

extensible structs
  client, 251-252
  HasAFrame interface definition, 248-249
  HasAFrame interface IDL (Interface Definition Language), 249
  HasAFrameImple interface, 250
  server mainline, 250-251
factories
  client implementation, 174-175, 179-180
  referencing, 171-173
  server IDL (Interface Definition Language), 176
  server implementation, 177-179
forward referencing, 30
GIOP (General Inter-ORB Protocol)
  CancelRequestHeader structure, 417
  IDL (Interface Definition Language) mapping, 413
  IOP::ServiceContext, 414
  LocateRequestHeader structure, 418
  LocateStatusType and LocateReplyHeader structures, 419
  ReplyStatusType and ReplyHeader structures, 416
  RequestHeader structure, 414
  sample encoding, 415
  Version structure, 413
HandlerRegistry
  IDL (Interface Definition Language), 402
  referencing, 402

code listings

IDL (Interface Definition Language) definition without modules, 28
IDL-to-Java language mapping, 22-23
idl2java
  example<IDL Interface Name>.java file, 110
  <IDL Interface Name>.java file, 104
  <IDL Interface Name>ImplBase.java file, 108-109
  <IDL Type Name>Helper.java file, 105-106
  -portable option, 280, 289-291
  sample IDL (Interface Definition Language) interface, 103
  st_<IDL Interface Name>.java file, 108
  <Type Name>Holder.java file, 104-105
IIOP (Internet Inter-ORB Protocol) Version and ProfileBody structures, 418
insert method, 324
interceptors
  BindInterceptor code, 421
  BindInterceptor implementation, 424-425
  chaining, 440-441
  ClientInterceptor code, 426
  ClientInterceptor implementation, 428-429
  ClientInterceptorFactory implementation, 437
  ClientInterceptorFactory interface, 437
  Closure class, 422
  Holder class, 422
  ServerInterceptor code, 429-430
  ServerInterceptor implementation, 433-434, 438-440
  ServerInterceptorFactory implementation, 436
  ServiceInit class, 442-443
interface inheritance
  ChildInterface implementation, 86
  example, 85-86
  IDL (Interface Definition Language), 84
  multiple inheritance, 83-85
  polymorphism, 87-88
  type safety, 84
Interface Repository
  binding, 296
  binding to, 302
  DII (Dynamic Invocation Interface) client application, 305-312
  initial container type, determining, 302-303
  IRObject interface, 300
  OperationDef interface, 297, 304
  ParameterDescription class, 304
  ParameterMode class, 305
  referencing, 301
  Repository object, 295-296
  sample IDL (Interface Definition Language), 294
interfaces
  example, 29
  implementing, 83
IORs (Interoperable Object References), 175
  contents of, 141, 169
  example, 140
  printIOR tool, 169-170, 174
java2idl, 244
java2iiop, 245

Location Service, referencing, 454-455
LongTest
  client, 41-42
  interface, 41
  server, 43-44
NamedValues
  creating, 262
  NamedValue interface, 262-263
nested module
  example, 25
  generated files, 26
  generated interface, 26
  IDL (Interface Definition Language) containing nested modules, 26-27
Netscape pre-install
  HTML (Hypertext Markup Language) page, 236-237
  pre-install script, 234-235
NVLists
  methods, 264
  NVList interface, 264
oadj (Object Activation Daemon)
  CreationImplDef class, 350
  ImplementationStatus class, 351-352
  OAD interface, 349
  ObjectStatus class, 352
  Policy class, 350-351
  State class, 352
object implementation, 134
operations
  example, 33
  oneway calls, 34
ORB (Object Request Broker) initialization
  command-line arguments, 115
  custom options, 114
  default options, 114

code listings

ORB Management APIs
  accessing attributes, 491
  Adapter interface code, 491
  Adapter interface references, 492
  attribute structure, 485
  AttributeSet interface, 485
  sample IDL (Interface Definition Language), 489-490
  Server interface code, 486
  Server interface references, 490
  setting attributes, 491
persistent objects, 148-149
preprocessor directives
  #include, 95
  #pragma, 96
PrimitiveAnyTest
  client, 64-66
  interface, 63
  server, 66-68
Principal type
  client implementation, 386-387
  get_principal( ) methods, 385
  IDL (Interface Definition Language), 384
  org.omg.CORBA.ORB class methods, 385
  Principal class, 384
  server implementation, 388-390
Request class, 267
Request objects, creating, 267-268
  create_request( ) method, 270-272
  LongTestImpl server object subset, 272-273
  request( ) method, 268-269
  sample interface, 268

Request objects, sending, 273
  invoke( ) method, 274-275
  multiple requests, 278
  send_deferred( ) and get_response( ) methods, 276-277
Runnable interface, 127-128
runtime exceptions, 91
sequences
  creating, 57
  defining, 56
server-side event handlers
  bind( ) method, 394-395
  client_aborted( ) method, 396-397
  ConnectionInfo structure, 391
  ImplEventHandler interface, 391-393
  post_method( ) method, 398
  post_method_exception( ) method, 398-399
  pre_method( ) method, 397
  sample implementation, 405-410
  unbind( ) method, 396
ServerRequest class, 283
servers, starting, 173
simple module
  example, 24-25
  generated files, 25
skeleton approach (object development)
  class definitions, 125
  example, 126
  IDL (Interface Definition Language) interface, 124
Smart Agents
  Agent interface, 450
  agentaddr file, 162
  bind( ) method signatures, 154
  broadcasts, turning off, 165
  clone( ) method, 160
  disabling, 182

memory tables, 449
multiple bind( ) calls, 158-159
multiple object instantiation, 158-159
sample IDL (Interface Definition Language), 143, 154
UNIX hosts, 163
Smart Stubs
  client application, 365
  IDL (Interface Definition Language), 363
  sample implementation, 363-364
structures
  constructor, 55
  example, 53
  generated myStruct class, 53
  instantiating, 54
TaggedProfile class, 436
Tie mechanism, 130-132
Timer class, 127
transient objects, 149-150
triggers
  registering, 453
  TriggerDesc object, 453
  TriggerHandler interface, 452
Typecodes
  code, 260
  creation methods, 260-261
  TCKind enumeration, 260
  TypeCode class, 325
  user-defined types, 261-262
Typed Object Wrappers
  client installation, 376
  IDL (Interface Definition Language) interface, 374
  sample implementation, 375
  server installation, 377-378
typedefs, 56

unions
    default( ) accessor method,
        51-52
    example, 48
    multiple union fields, 50
    name collision, 48
Untyped Object Wrappers
    client installation, 381-382
    factory, 380
    sample implementation,
        378-379
URLNaming service
    bind( ) method, 206-207
    IDL (Interface Definition
        Language), 202-203
    resolve_initial_references( )
        method, 203, 208-209
    server registration, 204
user-defined exceptions
    declaring, 92
    generated class file, 93
    generated interface, 94
    throwing, 94
**code suppression options
(idl2java compiler), 103**
collisions (name)
    compiler-generated files, 22-23
    IDL-to-Java language mapping,
        22
    reserved words, 23-24
colon (:), 84
command-line utilities
    idl2ir, 313
    idl2java
        -all_serializable option,
            102
        -C option, 97
        -d option, 97
        -deprecated option, 102
        -H option, 97
        -I option, 97
        -idl2package option, 100
        -incl_files option, 102
        -map_keyword option, 102
        -no_bind option, 103

-no_comments option, 103
-no_examples option, 103
-no_skel option, 103
-no_stub option, 103
-no_tie option, 103
-no_toString option, 103
-obj_wrapper option, 102
-P option, 97
-package option, 98-99
-portable option, 101,
    280-281, 288-291
-root_dir option, 100
-serializable option, 102
-smart_ proxy option, 101
-strict option, 101
-U option, 97
-verbose option, 101
-version option, 101
irep, 312-313
java2idl command, 245-246
java2iiop command
    -no_bind option, 244
    -no_comments option, 244
    -no_examples option, 244
    -no_tie option, 244
    -portable option, 244
    -root_dir option, 243
    -smart_stub option, 243
    -strict option, 243
    -version option, 244
    -W option, 244
    -wide option, 244
locserv, 454
oadj
    filename option, 346
    kill option, 346
    no_verify option, 347
    path option, 346
    timeout option, 346
    verbose option, 346
    version option, 346
oadutil
    reg argument, 353-354
    unreg argument, 354

osagent, 146
vbj, 115
vbjc, 115
commands (menu)
File menu (Interface
    Repository)
        Exit, 314
        Load, 313
        Save, 314
        Save As, 314
Language menu (Interface
    Repository)
        C++, 314
        IDL, 314
        Java, 314
comments (IDL), 21-22
CommFailure exception, 205
**Common Object Request
Broker Architecture (CORBA)
architecture, 4-6**
Common Object Services, 13
COMM_FAILURE exception, 89
Caffeine compilers, 11
    advantages, 240-241
    exceptions
        IDL (Interface Definition
            Language), 254-255
        implementing, 253
        throwing, 253-254
    extensible structs, 247-248
        defining in IDL (Interface
            Definition Language),
            252-253
        example, 248-249
        mapping with java2idl,
            249-252
    idl2java, 94
        command-line options,
            97-103
        DII (Dynamic Invocation
            Interface) clients,
            280-282
        DSI (Dynamic Skeleton
            Interface) servers,
            288-291

generated files, 103-110, 129-130
name collisions, 22-23
-portable option, 280-281, 288, 291
preprocessor directives, 95-97
java2idl, 244-247
  command-line options, 245-246
  development steps, 244-245
java2iiop
  command-line options, 243-244
  development steps, 241-243
  sample Caffeine interface, 242
configuring environment variables, 14-15
conflicts. *See* **collisions**
Connection Management, 10, 123-124
ConnectionInfo structure, 391
ConstantDef object, 298
constants
  defining
    outside interfaces, 31
    within interfaces, 30-31
  dk_Alias, 300
  dk_any, 300
  dk_Array, 300
  dk_Attribute, 300
  dk_Constant, 300
  dk_Enum, 300
  dk_Estruct, 300
  dk_Exception, 300
  dk_Interface, 300
  dk_Module, 300
  dk_none, 300
  dk_Operation, 300
  dk_Primitive, 300
  dk_Repository, 301
  dk_Sequence, 301
  dk_String, 301
  dk_Struct, 301
  dk_Typedef, 300

dk_Union, 300
dk_Wstring, 301
consumers (COS Event Service), 466
  PullConsumer implementation, 476-477
  PushConsumer client, 471-473
contained objects, 294
containers, 294
contents method, 303
Context types
  defining, 75-76
  strings, passing, 76-78
contexts
  Context class, 259
  creating, 258
  initial contexts, obtaining, 187-190
Continue Processes button (Debugger), 494
conversational state, 157
CORBA (Common Object Request Broker Architecture) architecture, 4-6
COS Event Service
  Any event type, 471
  channels, 466
  consumers, 466
  CosEventChannelAdmin module, 468-470
  CosEventComm module
    IDL (Interface Definition Langage), 466-467
    PullConsumer interface, 468
    PullSupplier interface, 468
    PushConsumer interface, 467
    PushSupplier interface, 468
  pull model
    compared to request/reply model, 478
    consumers, 476-477
    suppliers, 478-480

push model, 464
  consumer client, 471-473
  supplier client, 473-475
  starting, 481
  suppliers, 466
COS Naming Service, 186-187
  binding, 195
  compared to Smart Agent, 187
  IDL (Interface Definition Language), 191-192
  inital contexts, obtaining, 187
    list_initial_services( ) method, 189
    resolve_initial_references( ) method, 189-190
  Name arrays, 193
  name structure, navigating
    BindingIterator objects, 197-198
    BindingList objects, 197
    BindingType enumeration, 196
    list( ) iterator, 198-199
  NameComponents, 192
  NamingContext interface
    bind( ) method, 193
    bind_context( ) method, 194
    bind_new_context( ) method, 194
    destroy( ) method, 195
    new_context( ) method, 194
    rebind( ) method, 194
    rebind_context( ) method, 194
    resolve( ) method, 194
    unbind( ) method, 194
  resolution, 195-196
CosEventChannelAdmin module, 468-470
CosEventComm module
  IDL (Interface Definition Langage), 466-467
  PullConsumer interface, 468
  PullSupplier interface, 468
  PushConsumer interface, 467
  PushSupplier interface, 468

-cpp option (oadutil command), 353
create_CreationImplDef() method, 350
create_dyn_enum() method, 331
create_dyn_sequence() method, 332
create_dyn_struct() method, 332
create_dyn_union() method, 333
create_request() method
  client application, 270-272
  parameters, 269
  server application, 272-273
ctx parameter(create_request method), 269
custom Activator classes, 356-357

D

-D option (idl2java command), 97
-d option (oadutil command), 354
daemons. *See also* GateKeeper
  GateKeeper, 11, 16
    chaining, 232
    firewalls, 232
    gkconfig tool, 224-232
    HTTP (Hypertext Transport Protocol) tunneling proxy, 214
    Sandbox proxy, 213-214
    security, 232-233
    starting, 224
  HTTPd, 216
  oadj (Object Activation Daemon), 11
    activation policies, 348-349
    command-line options, 346-347

environment variables, 347
oadutil tool, 353-354
object registration, 349-353
querying, 351-352
starting, 346
data types. *See* types
DATA_CONVERSION exception, 89
deactivate() method, 355
deactivating objects, 118, 355
Debugger, 12, 493
  buttons
    Clear Breakpoint, 495
    Clear Verbose, 495
    Continue Processes, 494
    List All Processes, 494
    List Breakpoints, 495
    List Methods, 494
    List Objects, 494
    Set Breakpoint, 495
    Set Verbose, 495
    Step One Process, 494
    Stop All Processes, 494
  console window, 494
  requirements, 493
  starting, 493-494
declaring. *See* defining
default() method, 50-53
default_principal() method, 385
defer_bind option (bind method), 156
defining
  attributes, 31-32
  constants
    outside interfaces, 31
    within interfaces, 30-31
  enumerations, 47
  extensible structs, 252-253
  methods (operations)
    example, 33
    names, 32
    oneway calls, 33-34
    parameters, 33
    return types, 33

unions, 48
user-defined exceptions, 92
DefinitionKind values (Interface Repository), 300-301
def_kind method, 300
delegation
  Runnable interface, 127-128
  Tie mechanism, 128-132
deployment tools
  GateKeeper, 11, 16
    chaining, 232
    firewalls, 232
    gkconfig tool, 224-232
    HTTP (Hypertext Transport Protocol) tunneling proxy, 214
    Sandbox proxy, 213-214
    security, 232-233
    starting, 224
  gkconfig, 16, 224
    Exterior tab, 226-227
    General tab, 225-226
    HTTP tab, 230-231
    Interior tab, 227-228
    Properties tab, 231-232
    SSL tab, 228
  irep, 312-313
  locserv, 16, 454
  oadj (Object Activation Daemon), 11
    activation policies, 348-349
    command-line options, 346-347
    environment variables, 347
    oadutil tool, 353-354
    object registration, 349-353
    querying, 351-352
    starting, 346
  oadutil, 16
    reg argument, 353-354
    unreg argument, 354
  osagent, 16, 146
  osfind, 16
-deprecated option (idl2java command), 102

Desc structure, 449-450
destroy() method, 195
developing server objects
    skeleton approach, 124-126
    Tie delegation approach, 126-128
development tools, 15. *See also* compilers
digital signatures, 233-234
    creating, 236
    Netscape pre-install, 234-238
        HTML (Hypertext Markup Language) page, 236-237
        pre-install script, 234-235
DII (Dynamic Invocation Interface), 8-9, 265
    clients
        generating with idl2java, 280-282
        IDL (Interface Definition Language), 305-306
        Interface Repository, 306-312
    exceptions, 280
    requests
        creating, 267-273
        sending, 273-278
    return types, 279-280
    server object references, 266-267
directives (preprocessor)
    #include, 95-96
    #pragma prefix, 96-97
disabling Smart Agents, 182
disconnect_pull_consumer() method, 468
disconnect_push_consumer() method, 467
disconnect_push_supplier() method, 468
discriminants, 49
dk_Alias constant, 300
dk_any constant, 300
dk_Array constant, 300
dk_Attribute constant, 300
dk_Constant constant, 300

dk_Enum constant, 300
dk_Estruct constant, 300
dk_Exception constant, 300
dk_Interface constant, 300
dk_Module constant, 300
dk_none constant, 300
dk_Operation constant, 300
dk_Primitive constant, 300
dk_Repository constant, 301
dk_Sequence constant, 301
dk_String constant, 301
dk_Struct constant, 301
dk_Typedef constant, 300
dk_Union constant, 300
dk_Wstring constant, 301
DNS (Domain Name System), 163
DORBdisableLocator flag, 182
double data type, 40
DSI (Dynamic Skeleton Interface), 8-9, 282
    DynamicImplementation class, 283
    ServerRequest class, 283-284
    servers
        generating with idl2java, 288-291
        sample implementation, 284-288
duplicate() method, 181
Dynamic Invocation Interface. *See* DII
Dynamic Skeleton Interface. *See* DSI
DynamicImplementation class, 283
DynAny interface
    code listing, 328
    methods, 328-331
DynAnys
    client implementation, 334-338
    creating, 327-328
    DynAny interface
        code listing, 328
        methods, 328-331
    DynArray interface, 331

    DynEnum interface, 331-332
    DynSequence interface, 332
    DynStruct interface, 332-333
    DynUnion interface, 333
    IDL (Interface Definition Language), 318, 333-334
    mapping, 327
    passing, 321-323
    server implementation, 318-321, 339-342
DynArray interface, 331
DynEnum interface, 331-332
DynSequence interface, 332
DynStruct interface, 332-333
DynUnion interface, 333

E

-e option (oadutil command), 354
enable_rebind option (bind method), 157
enum type. *See* enumerations
EnumDef object, 298
enumerations
    BindingIterator objects, 197-198
    BindingList objects, 197
    BindingType, 196
    declaring, 47
    defined, 45
    example, 45
    IDL-to-Java language mapping, 45-46
    sample application, 47
    TCKind, 260, 324-325
Environment interface, 265
environment variables, 14
    ASAGENT_PORT, 162
    CLASSPATH, 15
    OSAGENT_LOCAL_FILE, 163
    OSAGENT_PORT, 146, 161, 164
    PATH, 15

VBROKER_ADM, 162, 347
VBROKER_IMPL_NAME, 347
VBROKER_IMPL_PATH, 347
VISIBROKER_ADM, 15
errors. *See* **exceptions**
event handlers, 12
   ClientEventHandler interface, 399-405
   HandlerRegistry interface, 402
   registering, 401-403
   server-side, 390
      bind( ) method, 394-395
      client_aborted( ) method, 396-397
      ConnectionInfo structure, 391
      ImplEventHandler implementation, 391-393, 405-410
      post_method( ) method, 398
      post_method_exception( ) method, 398-399
      pre_method( ) method, 397
      unbind( ) method, 395-396
   unregistering, 403
Event Service. *See* **COS Event Service**
_example files, 110
except( ) method, 284
ExceptionDef object, 298
exceptions
   DII (Dynamic Invocation Interface), 280
   Environment interface, 265
   IDL (Interface Definition Language), 254-255
   implementing, 253
   NullPointerException, 54
   runtime
      defined, 90
      throwing, 91-92
   system, 88-89
      BAD_CONTEXT, 89
      BAD_INV_ORDER, 89

      BAD_OPERATION, 89
      BAD_PARAM, 89
      BAD_TYPECODE, 89
      COMM_FAILURE, 89
      DATA_CONVERSION, 89
      FREE_MEM, 89
      IMP_LIMIT, 89
      inheritance hierarchy, 90
      INITIALIZE, 89
      INTERNAL, 89
      INTF_REPOS, 89
      INV_FLAG, 89
      INV_INDENT, 89
      INV_OBJREF, 89
      MARSHAL, 89
      NO_IMPLEMENT, 89
      NO_MEMORY, 90
      NO_PERMISSION, 90
      NO_RESOURCES, 90
      NO_RESPONSE, 90
      OBJ_ADAPTER, 90
      OBJ_NOT_EXIST, 90
      PERSIST_STORE, 90
      TRANSIENT, 90
      UNKNOWN, 90
   throwing, 253-254
   URLNaming service, 205
   user-defined
      declaring, 92
      generated class files, 93
      generated interfaces, 93
      throwing, 94
exception_occurred( ) method, 428
   BindInterceptor interface, 424
   ServerInterceptor interface, 433
executing clients, 175
Exit command (File menu), 314
extensible structs, 247-248
   defining, 252-253
   example, 248-249

   mapping with java2idl, 249-252
Exterior tab (gkconfig tool)
   Exterior Address and Exterior Port values, 226
   Exterior Callback Port values, 227
   Exterior Callback Proxy Port values, 227
   Exterior Proxy Address and Exterior Proxy Port values, 226
extract( ) method, 107
   Any class, 63-68
   Helper classes, 69-72
extraction methods (DynAnys), 330

F

factories
   client implementation, 179-180
   factory pattern, 168
   interceptor factories, 434-435
      ClientInterceptorFactory interface, 437
      installing, 444
      ServerInterceptorFactory interface, 435-436
   referencing, 171-173
   server implementation
      IDL (Interface Definition Language), 176
      program listing, 177-179
File menu commands (Interface Repository)
   Exit, 314
   Load, 313
   Save, 314
   Save As, 314
-filename option (oadj command), 346

files
   agentaddr, 162
   idl2java generated files, 103-104
      <IDL Interface Name>.java, 104, 110
      <IDL Interface Name>ImplBase.java, 108-109
      <IDL Interface Name>Operations.java, 109
      <IDL Type Name>Helper.java, 105-106
      st_<IDL Interface Name>.java, 107-108
      #tie#<IDL Interface Name>.java, 109
      <Type Name>Holder.java, 104-105
   localaddr, 163-164
   skeletons, 7-8
   stubs, 7-8
finalize() method, 181
firewalls, 232
forward declarations, 29-30
FREE_MEM exception, 89

G

garbage collection, 181
GateKeeper, 11, 16
   chaining, 232
   firewalls, 232
   gkconfig tool, 224
      Exterior tab, 226-227
      General tab, 225-226
      HTTP tab, 230-231
      Interior tab, 227-228
      Properties tab, 231-232
      SSL tab, 228
   HTTP (Hypertext Transfer Protocol) tunneling proxy, 214
   HTTPd, 216
   Sandbox proxy, 213-214
   security, 232-233
   starting, 224
General Inter-ORB Protocol. *See* GIOP
General tab (gkconfig tool)
   Clone Connection option, 225
   Disable Location Service option, 225
   Enable Callbacks option, 225
   IOR File field, 226
   Log File field, 226
   Log Level field, 226
getTheNumber() method, 364
get_adapter() method, 487
get_all_adapters() method, 487
get_implementation() method, 351
get_next_response() method, 278
get_principal() method, 385-386
get_response() method, 276-277
get_status() method, 351
get_status_all() method, 352
get_status_interface() method, 352
GIOP (General Inter-ORB Protocol), 412. *See also* interceptors
   CancelRequest messages, 417-418
   CloseConnection messages, 420
   headers
      byte_order value, 413
      magic identifier, 413
      message_size value, 414
      message_type value, 414
      version structure, 413
   IDL (Interface Definition Language) mapping, 413
   LocateReply messages
      LocateReplyHeader, 419
      LocateStatusType, 419-420
   LocateRequest messages, 418-419
   MessageError messages, 420
   Reply messages
      ReplyBody, 417
      ReplyHeader, 416
   Request messages
      RequestBody, 415-416
      RequestHeader, 414-415
gkconfig tool, 16, 224
   Exterior tab
      Exterior Address and Exterior Port values, 226
      Exterior Callback Port values, 227
      Exterior Callback Proxy Port values, 227
      Exterior Proxy Address and Exterior Proxy Port values, 226
   General tab
      Clone Connection option, 225
      Disable Location Service option, 225
      Enable Callbacks option, 225
      IOR File field, 226
      Log File field, 226
      Log Level field, 226
   HTTP tab, 230-231
   Interior tab, 227-228
   Properties tab, 231-232
   SSL tab, 228
graceful shutdowns, 395
graphical debugger. *See* Debugger

H

-H option (idl2java command), 97
HandlerRegistry interface, 401-402
handling events. *See* event handlers

HasAFrame interface, 248-249
HasAFrameImple interface, 250
hash() method, 133
headers (GIOP)
    byte_order value, 413
    magic identifier, 413
    message_size value, 414
    message_type value, 414
    version structure, 413
helper classes, 105-106
holder classes, 37, 104-105
-host option (oadutil command), 354
HTML (Hypertext Markup Language), applet markup, 221
    ORBalwaysProxy parameter, 223
    ORBalwaysTunnel parameter, 223
    ORBdisableGatekeeperCallbacks parameter, 224
    ORBdisableLocator parameter, 223
    ORBgatekeeperIOR parameter, 222
    org.omg.CORBA.ORBClass parameter, 222
    USE_ORB_LOCATOR parameter, 222
HTTP (Hypertext Transfer Protocol)
    GateKeeper settings, 230-231
    gkconfig settings, 230-231
    Tunneling, 214
HTTP tab (gkconfig tool), 230-231

I

-I option (idl2java command), 97
-i option (oadutil command), 353-354
id() method, 107

IDL (Interface Definition Language), 6, 20
    attributes, 31-32
    comments, 21-22
    constants
        defining outside interfaces, 31
        defining within interfaces, 30-31
    data passing
        constructed data types, 58-62
        direction, 36-37
        primitive data types, 40-44
    data types, *see* types
    extensible structs, 252-253
    inheritance, 82-83
        IDL-to-Java mapping, 85-86
        multiple inheritance, 83-85
        polymorphism, 87-88
        syntax, 84
        type safety, 84
    interfaces, 28-29
        definition files, 6-7
        example, 29
        forward declarations, 29-30
        implementing, 83
        arrays, 247
        classes, 247
        data types, 246
        interfaces, 247
    language mappings, 20-21
        IDL to Java, 22
        Java-to-IDL, 246-247
    modules
        avoiding, 27-28
        name scoping, 24-25
        nesting, 25-27
    name collisions, 22-23
    operations
        defined, 32
        example, 33
        names, 32
        oneway calls, 33-34

        parameters, 33
        return types, 33
    reserved words, 23-24
IDL command (Language menu), 314
IDL-to-Java language mapping. *See also* types; idl2java compiler
    data passing
        constructed data types, 58-62
        direction, 36-37
        primitive data types, 40-44
    interface inheritance, 85-86
idl2ir tool, 15, 313
idl2java compiler, 15, 94
    command-line options
        -all_serializable, 102
        -C, 97
        -d, 97
        -deprecated, 102
        -H, 97
        -I, 97
        -idl2package, 100
        -incl_files, 102
        -map_keyword, 102
        -no_bind, 103
        -no_comments, 103
        -no_examples, 103
        -no_skel, 103
        -no_stub, 103
        -no_tie, 103
        -no_toString, 103
        -obj_wrapper, 102
        -P, 97
        -package, 98-99
        -portable, 101, 280-281, 288, 291
        -root_dir, 100
        -serializable, 102
        -smart_proxy, 101
        -strict, 101
        -U, 97
        -verbose, 101
        -version, 101

DII (Dynamic Invocation
   Interface) clients, 280-282
DSI (Dynamic Invocation
   Interface) servers, 288-291
generated files, 103-104,
   129-130
   *_example_<IDL Interface
      Name>.java, 110*
   *<IDL Interface
      Name>.java, 104*
   *<IDL Interface
      Name>ImplBase.java,
      108-109*
   *<IDL Interface
      Name>Operations.java,
      109*
   *<IDL Type
      Name>Helper.java,
      105-106*
   *<Type Name>Holder.java,
      104-105*
   *st_<IDL Interface
      Name>.java, 107-108*
name collisions, 22-23
preprocessor directives
   #include, 95-96
   #pragma prefix, 96-97
**IIOP (Internet Inter-ORB
   Protocol), 412**
**ImplementationStatus class,
   351-352**
ImplEventHandler interface
   methods
      bind( ), 394-395
      client_aborted( ), 396-397
      post_method( ), 398
      *post_method_exception( ),
         398-399*
      pre_method( ), 397
      unbind( ), 395-396
   sample implementation,
      391-393, 405-410
impl_is_ready() method, 118
IMP_LIMIT exception, 89

in parameter (passing direction), 36
**-incl_files option (idl2java
   command), 102**
#include directive, 95-96
inheritance
   class, 82
   interface, 82-83
      *IDL-to-Java mapping,
         85-86*
      multiple inheritance, 83-85
      polymorphism, 87-88
      syntax, 84
      type safety, 84
   system exceptions, 90
init() method, 443
**initial contexts, obtaining,
   187**
   list_initial_services() method,
      189
   resolve_initial_references()
      method, 189-190
INITIALIZE exception, 89
initializing
   applets, 217-220
   BOA (Basic Object Adapter),
      116, 120-121
   ORB (Object Request Broker),
      114-115
**inout parameter (passing
   direction), 36-37**
Inprise Web site, 13
insert() method, 107, 324
   Any class, 63-68
   Helper classes, 69-72
**inserting BasicStructs,
   323-324**
**insertion methods (DynAnys),
   330**
installing
   interceptors, 444
   Object Wrappers
      clients, 376-377
      servers, 377-378
   Untyped Object Wrappers
      clients, 380-382
      servers, 382
   VisiBroker
      deployment tools, 16
      development tools, 15
      *environment variables,
         14-15*
      system requirements, 13-14
instantiating
   persistent objects, 148-149
   transient objects, 149-150
Interceptors, 12, 420
interceptors
   BindInterceptor interface,
      420-421
      code listing, 421
      methods, 421-424
      *sample implementation,
         424-425*
   chaining, 437-441
   ClientInterceptor interface
      code listing, 425-426
      methods, 426-428
      *sample implementation,
         428-429*
   factories, 434-435
      *ClientInterceptorFactory
         interface, 437*
      *ServerInterceptorFactory
         interface, 435-436*
   installing, 444
   ServerInterceptor interface
      code listing, 429-430
      methods, 431-433
      *sample implementation,
         433-434*
   ServiceInit class, 441
      code listing, 442
      methods, 443-444
**Interface Definition
   Language.** *See* **IDL**
Interface Repository
   binding, 296, 301-302
   containment structure, 294-295

interfaces

DII (Dynamic Invocation
  Interface) client application
    code listing, 306-312
    *IDL (Interface Definition
      Language), 305-306*
    requests, 306
GUI (graphical user interface),
  313-314
initial container type, determining, 302-303
objects
  AliasDef, 298
  ArrayDef, 299
  AttributeDef, 297
  ConstantDef, 298
  *DefinitionKind values,
    300-301*
  EnumDef, 298
  ExceptionDef, 298
  InterfaceDef, 296-297
  IRObject interface, 300
  ModuleDef, 296
  OperationDef, 297, 304
  PrimitiveDef, 299
  Repository, 295-296
  SequenceDef, 299
  StringDef, 298
  StructDef, 298
  UnionDef, 298
ParameterDescription arrays,
  creating
  *ParameterDescription
    class, 304-305*
  ParameterMode class, 305
populating
  *File menu commands,
    313-314*
  idl2ir command, 313
  *Language menu commands,
    314*
referencing, 301
starting, 312-313

InterfaceDef object, 296-297
**[InterfaceName]Operations
  files, 130**
interfaces, 28-29. *See also* **IDL
  (Interface Definition
  Language); Interface
  Repository**
  Activator, 354-355
  Adapter
    attributes, 492-493
    code listing, 491
    methods, 491
    referencing, 492
  Agent, 450
  AttributeSet, 485
  BindInterceptor, 420
    code listing, 421
    methods, 421-424
    *sample implementation,
      424-425*
  ClientEventHandler
    *IDL (Interface Definition
      Language), 399*
    methods, 399
    *sample implementation,
      400-405*
  ClientInterceptor
    code listing, 425-426
    methods, 426-428
    *sample implementation,
      428-429*
  ClientInterceptorFactory, 437
  constants, defining within,
    30-31
  defining, 6-7
  DII (Dynamic Invocation
    Interface), 8-9, 265
    clients, 280-282, 305-312
    exceptions, 280
    requests, 267-278
    return types, 279-280
    *server object references,
      266-267*

DSI (Dynamic Skeleton
  Interface), 8-9, 282
  *DynamicImplementation
    class, 283*
  *ServerRequest class,
    283-284*
  servers, 284-291
DynAny
  code listing, 328
  methods, 328-331
DynArray, 331
DynEnum, 331-332
DynSequence, 332
DynStruct, 332-333
DynUnion, 333
Environment, 265
forward declarations, 29-30
HandlerRegistry, 401-402
HasAFrame, 248-249
HasAFrameImple, 250
implementing, 83
ImplEventHandler
  methods, 394-398
  *sample implementation,
    391-393, 405-410*
inheritance, 82-83
  *IDL-to-Java mapping,
    85-86*
  multiple inheritance, 83-85
  polymorphism, 87-88
  syntax, 84
  type safety, 84
IRObject, 300
Java-to-IDL language mapping,
  247
NamedValue, 262-263
naming conventions, 87
NamingContext, 193-195
NVList, 263-264
PullConsumer, 468
PullSupplier, 468
PushConsumer, 467
PushSupplier, 468
Runnable, 127-128

Server
   attributes, 487-489
   code listing, 486
   methods, 487
   referencing, 489-491
ServerInterceptor
   code listing, 429-430
   methods, 431-434
ServerInterceptorFactory
   code listing, 435
   sample implementation, 436
TriggerHandler, 451-452
Interior tab (gkconfig tool), 227-228
   Interior Address and Interior Port values, 228
   Interior Proxy Address and Interior Proxy Port values, 228
   Min/Max Forwarding Port values, 228
INTERNAL exception, 89
Internet Inter-ORB Protocol (IIOP), 412
Interoperable Object References. *See* **IORs**
INTF_REPOS exception, 89
InvalidURL exception, 205
invoke() method, 273-275
invoking methods, 118-119
INV_FLAG exception, 89
INV_INDENT exception, 89
INV_OBJREF exception, 89
IORs (Interoperable Object References), 9, 168-169
   contents of, 116-118, 140-141, 169
   example, 140
   obtaining, *see* location strategies
   printIOR tool, 169-170, 174
   stringifying, 171-173
IP (Internet Protocol) addresses, GateKeeper settings
   exterior addresses, 226-227
   interior addresses, 227-228

-ir option (idl2ir command), 313
IR. *See* Interface Repository
irep command, 16, 312-313
IRObject interface, 300
is_a() method, 133
is_bound() method, 133
is_local() method, 133
is_persistent() method, 133
is_remote() method, 133

J

Java command (Language menu), 314
Java-to-IDL language mapping. *See also* java2idl compiler
   arrays, 247
   classes, 247
   data types, 246
   interfaces, 247
java2idl compiler, 15
   command-line options, 245-246
   development steps, 244-245
   extensible structs, mapping, 249-252
java2iiop compiler, 15
   command-line options
      -no_bind, 244
      -no_comments, 244
      -no_examples, 244
      -no_tie, 244
      -portable, 244
      -root_dir, 243
      -smart_stub, 243
      -strict, 243
      -version, 244
      -W, 244
      -wide, 244
   development steps, 241-243
   sample Caffeine interface, 242

K-L

keywords
   oneway, 33-34
   reserved words, 23-24
-kill option (oadj command), 346

language mapping. *See* Java-to-IDL language mapping; IDL-to-Java language mapping
Language menu commands (Interface Repository)
   C++, 314
   IDL, 314
   Java, 314
List All Processes button (Debugger), 494
List Breakpoints button (Debugger), 495
List Methods button (Debugger), 494
List Objects button (Debugger), 494
list() method, 198-199
list_initial_services() method, 189
list_services() method, 444
listings. *See* **code listings**
load balancing
   Location Service
      client implementation, 461-462
      sample IDL (Interface Definition Language), 455
      StringCounterFactoryImpl implementation, 457-461
      StringCounterImpl implementation, 455-456
   Smart Agents, 155-156
Load command (File menu), 313
localaddr files, 163-164
locate() method, 431

LocateReply messages (GIOP)
  LocateReplyHeader, 419
  LocateStatusType, 419-420
LocateReplyHeader structure (LocateReply messages), 419
LocateRequest messages (GIOP), 418-419
LocateRequestHeader structure (LocateRequest messages), 418
LocateStatusType structure (LocateReply messages), 419-420
locate_failed() method, 431
locate_forwarded() method, 431
Location Service, 12, 448. *See also* **Smart Agents**
  command-line options, 454
  load balancing
    client implementation, 461-462
    sample IDL (Interface Definition Language), 455
    StringCounterFactoryImpl implementation, 457-461
    StringCounterImpl implementation, 455-456
  referencing, 454-455
  starting, 454
location strategies, 140-141. *See also* **Location Service**
  COS Naming Service, 186-187
    binding, 195
    compared to Smart Agents, 187
    IDL (Interface Definition Language), 191-192
    initial contexts, 187-190
    Name arrays, 193
    name structure, navigating, 196-199
    NameComponents, 192

  NamingContext interface, 193-195
  resolution, 195-196
  factories
    client implementation, 179-180
    factory pattern, 168
    referencing, 171-173
    server implementation, 176-179
  Smart Agents, 142-146
    Agent interface, 450
    Agent-to-Agent communication, 147-148
    agentaddr files, 162
    binding, 154-160
    cloning, 160
    disabling, 182
    DNS (Domain Name Service) lookups, 163
    load balancing, 155-156
    memory tables, 449-450
    multihomed hosts, 163-164
    multiple domains, 161
    persistent objects, 148-153
    platform dependence, 142
    querying, 450-451
    starting, 146
    triggers, 451-453
    UDP (Unreliable Datagram Protocol) broadcasts, 146, 164-165
  URLNaming service
    bind( ) method, 206-207
    exceptions, 205
    IDL (Interface Definition Language), 202-203
    narrow( ) method, 208-209
    resolve_initial_references( ) method, 208-209
    server registration, 203-205
-LOCdebug option (locserv command), 454
locserv command, 16, 454

-LOCtimeout option (locserv command), 454
-LOCverify option (locserv command), 454
log files (GateKeeper), 226
long type, 40
long long type, 40
LongTestImpl object, 359-360

M

magic identifier (GIOP messages), 413
Management APIs (application programming interfaces), 484
  Adapter interface
    attributes, 492-493
    code listing, 491
    methods, 491
    referencing, 492
  attributes, 485-486
  Server interface
    attributes, 487-489
    code listing, 486
    methods, 487
    referencing, 489-491
mapping. *See* **Java-to-IDL language mapping; IDL-to-Java language mapping**
-map_keyword option (idl2java command), 102
MARSHAL exception, 89
member_count() method, 326
member_type() method, 326
memory, garbage collection, 181
MessageError messages (GIOP), 420
messages (GIOP), 412. *See also* **interceptors**
  CancelRequest, 417-418
  CloseConnection, 420

messages

headers
   byte_order value, 413
   magic identifier, 413
   message_size value, 414
   message_type value, 414
   version structure, 413
IDL (Interface Definition Language) mapping, 413
LocateReply
   LocateReplyHeader, 419
   LocateStatusType, 419-420
LocateRequest, 418-419
MessageError, 420
Reply
   ReplyBody, 417
   ReplyHeader, 416
Request
   RequestBody, 415-416
   RequestHeader, 414-415

methods

activate(), 355
activation_policy(), 487
adapter_id(), 491
all_agent_locations(), 450
all_instances(), 451
all_instances_descs(), 451
all_replica(), 451
all_replica_descs(), 451
all_repository_ids(), 451
bind(), 107, 193, 206-207, 296
   BindInterceptor interface, 421-422
   BindOptions, 156-157
   CORBA (Common Object Request Broker Architecture) compliancy, 158
   example, 394-395
   multiple object implementations, 158-160
   parameters, 395
   signatures, 154-156
   static, 266-267
bind_context(), 194
bind_failed(), 399, 422-423
bind_new_context(), 194
bind_succeeded(), 399, 423
boa(), 133
client_aborted(), 396-397
clone(), 160
create_CreationImplDef(), 350
create_dyn_enum(), 331
create_dyn_sequence(), 332
create_dyn_struct(), 332
create_dyn_union(), 333
create_request()
   client application, 270-272
   parameters, 269
   server application, 272-273
deactivate(), 355
default(), 50-53
default_principal(), 385
definitions (operations)
   example, 33
   names, 32
   oneway calls, 33-34
   parameters, 33
   return types, 33
def_kind(), 300
destroy(), 195
disconnect_pull_consumer(), 468
disconnect_push_consumer(), 467
disconnect_push_supplier(), 468
duplicate(), 181
except(), 284
exception_occurred(), 424, 428, 433
extract(), 107
   Any class, 63-68
   Helper classes, 69-72
finalize(), 181
getTheNumber(), 364
get_adapter(), 487
get_all_adapters(), 487
get_implementation(), 351
get_next_response(), 278
get_principal(), 385-386
get_response(), 276-277
get_status(), 351
get_status_all(), 352
get_status_interface(), 352
hash(), 133
id(), 107
impl_is_ready(), 118
init(), 443
insert(), 107, 324
   Any class, 63-68
   Helper classes, 69-72
invoke(), 273-275
invoking, 118-119
is_a(), 133
is_bound(), 133
is_equivalent(), 133
is_local(), 133
is_persistent(), 133
is_remote(), 133
list(), 198-199
list_initial_services(), 189
list_services(), 444
locate(), 431
locate_failed(), 431
locate_forwarded(), 431
member_count(), 326
member_type(), 326
naming conventions, 87
narrow(), 106, 208-209
new_context(), 194
next_n(), 199
next_one(), 199
non_existent(), 133
object_name(), 133
orb(), 133
param(), 287, 304
params(), 284
persistent_objects(), 491
poll_next_response(, 278
post_method(), 379, 398
post_method_exception(), 398-399
prepare_reply(), 432
prepare_request(), 426
pre_method(), 379, 397

process_id( ), 487
pull( ), 468
rebind( ), 194, 423
rebind_context( ), 194
rebind_failed( ), 423
rebind_succeeded( ), 400, 423
receive_reply( ), 427
receive_reply_failed( ), 428
receive_request( ), 432
reg_glob_client_handler( ), 403
reg_glob_impl_handler( ), 403
reg_implementation( ), 349
reg_obj_client_handler( ), 402
reg_obj_impl_handler( ), 403
release( ), 181
repository_id( ), 133
request( ), 268-269
request_completed( ), 433
resolve( ), 194, 444
resolve_initial_references( ),
 189-190, 208-209
result( ), 284, 305
return_value( ), 279
send_deferred( ), 276-277
send_reply( ), 432
send_reply_failed( ), 432
send_request( ), 426
send_request_failed( ), 427
send_request_succeeded( ), 427
server_aborted( ), 399
setSmartStub( ), 364
set_return_type( ), 279
shutdown( ), 433, 487
testLong( ), 357
testShort( ), 7
try_pull( ), 468
type( ), 107
unbind( ), 194, 395-396
unregister_all( ), 353
unreg_glob_client_handler( ),
 403
unreg_implementation( ), 353
unreg_interface( ), 353
unreg_obj_client_handler( ),
 403

unreg_obj_impl_handler( ), 403
value( ), 305
modifiers, 32
ModuleDef object, 296
modules
 avoiding, 27-28
 CosEventChannelAdmin,
  468-470
 CosEventComm
  IDL (Interface Definition
   Langage), 466-467
  PullConsumer interface,
   468
  PullSupplier interface, 468
  PushConsumer interface,
   467
  PushSupplier interface, 468
 name scoping, 24-25
 nesting, 25-27
multihomed hosts
 UNIX, 163-164
 Windows NT, 164
multiple inheritance, 83-85
multithreading, 119
 BOA (Basic Object Adapter)
  initialization, 120-121
 Connection Management, 10
 Thread Pool model, 121-123
 Thread-per-Session model, 121

N

Name arrays, 193
name collisions
 compiler-generated files, 22-23
 IDL-to-Java language mapping,
  22
 reserved words, 23-24
 unions, 48-49
name scoping, 24-25
NameComponents, 192
NamedValues
 creating, 262
 NamedValue interface,
  262-263

naming operations, 32
naming services
 COS Naming Service, 13,
  186-187
  binding, 195
  compared to Smart Agent,
   187
  IDL (Interface Definition
   Language), 191-192
  initial contexts, 187-190
  Name arrays, 193
  name structure, navigating,
   196-199
  NameComponents, 192
  NamingContext interface,
   193-195
  resolution, 195-196
 URLNaming, 202
  bind( ) method, 206-207
  exceptions, 205
  IDL (Interface Definition
   Language), 202-203
  narrow( ) method, 208-209
  resolve_initial_references( )
   method, 208
  server registration, 203-205
NamingContext interface
 bind( ) method, 193
 bind_context( ) method, 194
 bind_new_context( ) method,
  194
 destroy( ) method, 195
 new_context( ) method, 194
 rebind( ) method, 194
 rebind_context( ) method, 194
 resolve( ) method, 194
 unbind( ) method, 194
**narrow() method, 106,
 208-209**
**navigating name structures,
 196-199**
nesting modules, 25-27
Netcaster, 238
new_context() method, 194
next_n() method, 199

next_one() method, 199
non_existent() method, 133
-no_bind option
    idl2java command, 103
    java2iiop command, 244
-no_comments option
    idl2java command, 103
    java2iiop command, 244
-no_examples option
    idl2java command, 103
    java2iiop command, 244
NO_IMPLEMENT exception, 89
NO_MEMORY exception, 90
NO_PERMISSION exception, 90
NO_RESOURCES exception, 90
NO_RESPONSE exception, 90
-no_skel option (idl2java command), 103
-no_stub option (idl2java command), 103
-no_tie option
    idl2java command, 103
    java2iiop command, 244
-no_toString option (idl2java command), 103
-no_verify option (oadj command), 347
null vales, passing, 55
NullPointerExceptions, 54
NVList interface, 263-264

O

-o option (java2idl compiler), 246
OA (Object Adapter), 9-10
OAactivatedConnections attribute (Adapter interface), 492
OAactivatedRequests attribute (Adapter interface), 492
OAallocatedThreads attribute (Adapter interface), 492
OAconnectionMax attribute (Adapter interface), 493
OAconnectionMaxIdle attribute (Adapter interface), 493
oadj(Object Activation Daemon), 16
    activation policies
        Persistent Server, 348
        Server-per-method, 349
        Shared Server, 348
        Unshared Server, 348
    command-line options, 346-347
    environment variables, 347
    oadutil tool
        reg argument, 353-354
        unreg argument, 354
    objects
        registering, 349-351
        unregistering, 353
    querying
        get_implementation() method, 351
        get_status() method, 351
        get_status_all() method, 352
        get_status_interface() method, 352
    starting, 346
oadutil tool, 16
    reg argument, 353-354
    unreg argument, 354
OAthreadMax attribute (Adapter interface), 493
OAthreadMaxIdle attribute (Adapter interface), 493
OAthreadMin attribute (Adapter interface), 493
Object Activation Daemon. See oadj
Object Adapter (OA), 9-10
Object Management Group (OMG), 4-5
Object Request Broker. See ORB
Object Request Debugger, 12
Object Wrappers, 372-373. See also Smart Stubs
    chaining, 373
    combining, 382
    Typed, 373-374
        IDL interface, 374
        installation, 376-378
        sample implementation, 375
    Untyped
        factories, 380
        installation, 380-382
        sample implementation, 378-380
objectifying IOR (Interoperable Object Reference) strings, 171
objects. See also interfaces
    Activators, 118
        Activator interface, 354-355
        client implementation, 358-360
        custom classes, 356-357
        server implementation, 355-357
    AliasDef, 298
    ArrayDef, 299
    AttributeDef, 297
    BindingIterator, 197-198
    BindingList, 197
    ConstantDef, 298
    core operations, 132-133
    deactivating, 118
    DefinitionKind values, 300-301
    development
        skeleton approach, 124-126
        Tie delegation approach, 126-128

EnumDef, 298
ExceptionDef, 298
  implementing, 134-137
InterfaceDef, 296-297
IORs (Interoperable Object References)
  contents, 169
  contents of, 116-118, 140-141
  example, 140
  obtaining, see location strategies
  printIOR tool, 169-170, 174
  stringifying, 171-173
LongTestImpl, 359-360
ModuleDef, 296
NamedValue, 262
oadj (Object Activation Daemon)
  activation policies, 348-349
  command-line options, 346-347
  environment variables, 347
  oadutil tool, 353-354
  object registration, 349-353
  querying, 351-352
  starting, 346
OperationDef, 297, 304
passing by value, *see* extensible structs
persistent
  instantiating, 148-149
  pring messages, 150-153
PrimitiveDef, 299
RegImpl, 357
registering, 118
Repository, 295-296
Request
  creating, 267-273
  sending, 273-278
SequenceDef, 299
serialization, 241
StringCounter, 455-456
StringCounterFactory, 457-461

StringDef, 298
StructDef, 298
transient, 149-150
TriggerDesc, 452-453
UnionDef, 298
ObjectStatus class, 352
OBJECT_FORWARD value (LocationStatusType), 420
OBJECT_HERE value (LocationStatusType), 420
object_key value (RequestHeader structure), 415
OBJ_ADAPTER exception, 90
OBJ_NOT_EXIST exception, 90
-obj_wrapper option (idl2java command), 102
octet type, 38
OMG (Object Management Group), 4-5
oneway operations, 33-34
operation parameter (create_request method), 269
operation value (RequestHeader structure), 415
OperationDef object, 297, 304
operations
  defined, 32
  example, 33
  names, 32
  oneway calls, 33-34
  parameters, 33
  return types, 33
ORB (Object Request Broker), 4-5, 10
  initializing, 114-115
    custom options, 114
    default options, 114
  Management APIs, 484
    Adapter interface, 491-493
    attributes, 485-486
    Server interface, 486-491
orb() method, 133

ORBagentAddr attribute (Server interface), 487
ORBagentAddrFile attribute (Server interface), 488
ORBagentNoFailOver attribute (Server interface), 488
ORBagentPort attribute (Server interface), 487
ORBalwaysProxy attribute (Server interface), 488
ORBalwaysProxy parameter, 223
ORBalwaysTunnel parameter, 223
ORBbackCompat attribute (Server interface), 487
ORBconnectionCacheMax attribute (Server interface), 488
ORBconnectionMaxIdle attribute (Server interface), 488
ORBdebug attribute (Server interface), 488
ORBdebugDir attribute (Server interface), 488
ORBdisableAgentCache attribute (Server interface), 487
ORBdisableGateKeeperCallbacks attribute (Server interface), 489
ORBdisableGatekeeperCallbacks parameter, 224
ORBdisableLocator attribute (Server interface), 222, 488
ORBgatekeeperIOR attribute (Server interface), 222, 488
ORBgcTimeout attribute (Server interface), 489
ORBmbufsize attribute (Server interface), 489
ORBnullString attribute (Server interface), 488

ORBprocId attribute (Server interface), 488
ORBsecureShutdown attribute (Server interface), 488
ORBsendBindfalse attribute (Server interface), 489
ORBservices attribute (Server interface), 489
ORBsyncGC attribute (Server interface), 488
ORBtcpNoDelay attribute (Server interface), 489
ORBtcpTimeout attribute (Server interface), 489
ORBwarn attribute (Server interface), 489
osagent command, 16, 146
OSAGENT_LOCAL_FILE environment variable, 163
OSAGENT_PORT environment variable, 146, 161-164
osfind tool, 16
out parameter (passing direction), 36

P

-P option (idl2java command), 97
-p option (oadutil command), 354
-package option (idl2java command), 98-99
param() method, 287
ParameterDescription arrays, creating
 ParameterDescription class, 304-305
 ParameterMode class, 305
ParameterDescription class, 304-305
ParameterMode class, 305

parameters
 applets
  ORBalwaysProxy, 223
  ORBalwaysTunnel, 223
  ORBdisableGatekeeper Callbacks, 224
  ORBdisableLocator, 223
  ORBgatekeeperIOR, 222
  org.omg.CORBA.ORBClass, 222
  USE_ORB_LOCATOR, 222
 operations, 33
params() method, 284, 304
passing
 direction
  in, 36
  inout, 36-37
  out, 36
 DynAnys, 321-323
 null values, 55
PATH environment variable, 15
-path option (oadj command), 346
persistent objects
 instantiating, 148-149
 Smart Agents, communicating with, 150-153
Persistent Server policy, 348
persistent state, 157
persistent_objects() method, 491
PERSIST_STORE exception, 90
ping messages, 150-153
platform dependence (Smart Agents), 142
platforms
 UNIX, 163-164
 Windows NT, 164
policies, activation
 Persistent Server, 348
 Server-per-method, 349
 Shared Server, 348
 Unshared Server, 348

poll_next_response() method, 278
polymorphism, 87-88
populating Interface Repository
 File menu commands, 313-314
 idl2ir command, 313
 Language menu commands, 314
-portable option
 idl2java compiler, 101, 280-281, 288, 291
 java2iiop compiler, 244
ports, GateKeeper settings
 exterior ports, 226-227
 interior ports, 227-228
post_method() method, 379, 398
post_method_exception() method, 398-399
#pragma directive, 96-97
prepare_reply() method, 432
prepare_request() method, 426
preprocessor directives
 #include, 95-96
 #pragma prefix, 96-97
pre_method() method, 379, 397
primitive types. *See* types
PrimitiveDef object, 299
Principal class, 384
Principal type
 client implementation, 386-388
 IDL (Interface Definition Language), 384
 obtaining
  get_principal() method, 385-386
  org.omg.CORBA.ORB class, 385
 Principal class, 384
 server implementation, 388-390

printIOR tool, 169-170, 174
process_id( ) method, 487
program listings. *See* **code listings**
properties, GateKeeper, 224, 231-232
    exterior IP (Internet Protocol) address/port values, 226-227
    general properties, 225-226
    HTTP (Hypertext Transport Protocol), 230-231
    interior IP address/port values, 227-228
    SSL (Secure Sockets Layer), 228
Properties tab (gkconfig tool), 231-232
protocols
    DNS (Domain Name Service), 163
    GIOP (General Inter-ORB Protocol), 412
        CancelRequest messages, 417-418
        CloseConnection messages, 420
        headers, 413-414
        IDL (Interface Definition Language) mapping, 413
        LocateReply messages, 419-420
        LocateRequest messages, 418-419
        MessageError messages, 420
        Reply messages, 416-417
        Request messages, 414-416
    HTTP (Hypertext Transfer Protocol), 214
    IIOP (Internet Inter-ORB Protocols), 412
    UDP (Unreliable Datagram Protocol), 146, 164-165

pull model (events)
    compared to request/reply model, 478
    consumers, 476-477
    suppliers, 478-480
pull( ) method, 468
PullConsumer interface, 468
PullSupplier interface, 468
push model (events), 464
    consumer client, 471-473
    supplier client, 473-475
PushConsumer, 476-477
    client, 471-473
    interface, 467
PushSupplier application
    client, 473-475
    implementation, 478-480
    interface, 468

Q-R

querying
    oadj (Object Activation Daemon)
        get_implementation( ) method, 351
        get_status( ) method, 351
        get_status_all( ) method, 352
        get_status_interface( ) method, 352
    Smart Agents
        all_agent_locations( ) method, 450
        all_instances( ) method, 451
        all_instances_descs( ) method, 451
        all_replica( ) method, 451
        all_replica_descs( ) method, 451
        all_repository_ids( ) method, 451

-r option (oadutil command), 353-354
read-only attributes
    Adapter interface
        OAactiveConnections, 492
        OAactiveRequests, 492
        OAallocatedThreads, 492
        OAconnectionMax, 493
        OAconnectionMaxIdle, 493
        OAthreadMax, 493
        OAthreadMaxIdle, 493
        OAthreadMin, 493
    Server interface
        ORBagentAddr, 487
        ORBagentPort, 487
        ORBbackCompat, 487
        ORBdisableAgentCache, 487
        ORBdisableLocator, 488
        ORBgatekeeperIOR, 488
        ORBnullString, 488
        ORBprocId, 488
        ORBsecureShutdown, 488
        ORBsyncGC, 488
read/write attributes (Server interface)
    ORBagentAddrFile, 488
    ORBagentNoFailOver, 488
    ORBalwaysProxy, 488
    ORBconnectionCacheMax, 488
    ORBconnectionMaxIdle, 488
    ORBdebug, 488
    ORBdebugDir, 488
    ORBdisableGateKeeperCallbacks, 489
    ORBgcTimeout, 489
    ORBmbufsize, 489
    ORBsendBindfalse, 489
    ORBservices, 489
    ORBtcpNoDelay, 489
    ORBtcpTimeout, 489
    ORBwarn, 489
rebind( ) method, 194, 423

rebind_context() method, 194
rebind_failed() method 423
rebind_succeeded() method, 400, 423
receive_reply() method, 427
receive_reply_failed() method, 428
receive_request() method, 432
references
    forward declarations, 29-30
    server references, obtaining, 205-206
        bind( ) method, 206-207
        narrow( ) method, 208-209
        resolve_initial_references( ) method, 208-209
referencing
    Adapter interface, 492
    classes, 365
    factories, 171-173
    HandlerRegistry, 402
    Interface Repository, 301
    Location Service, 454-455
    Server interface, 489-491
reg argument (oadutil tool), 353-354
RegImpl object, 357
registering
    event handlers
        HandlerRegistry interface, 401-402
        methods, 402-403
    objects
        BOA (Basic Object Adapter), 118
        oadj (Object Activation Daemon), 349-351
    servers, 203-205
    triggers, 452-453
reg_glob_client_handler() method, 403
reg_glob_impl_handler() method, 403

reg_implementation() method, 349
reg_obj_client_handler() method, 402
reg_obj_impl_handler() method, 403
release() method, 181
remote objects, locating. *See* location strategies
replace option (idl2ir command), 313
Reply messages (GIOP)
    ReplyBody, 417
    ReplyHeader, 416
ReplyBody structure (Reply messages), 417
ReplyHeader structure (Reply messages), 416
Repository. *See* Interface Repository
repository_id() method, 133
ReqFailure exception, 205
Request class, 267
Request message (GIOP)
    RequestBody, 415-416
    RequestHeader
        code listing, 414
        object_key value, 415
        operation value, 415
        requesting_ principal value, 415
        request_id value, 415
        response_expected value, 415
        ServiceContextList field, 414-415
Request objects
    creating, 267-268
        create_request( ) method, 269-273
        request( ) method, 268-269
    Request class, 267
    sending
        multiple requests, 278
        send( ) method, 273-275

        send_deferred( ) method, 276-277
        send_response( ) method, 276-277
request() method, 268-269
request/reply model, 478
RequestBody structure (Request messages), 415-416
RequestHeader structure (Request messages)
    code listing, 414
    object_key value, 415
    operation value, 415
    requesting_principal value, 415
    request_id value, 415
    response_expected value, 415
    ServiceContextList field, 414-415
requesting_principal value (RequestHeader structure), 415
request_completed() method, 433
request_id value (RequestHeader structure), 415
reserved words, 23-24. *See also* keywords
resolution, 195-196
resolve() method, 194, 444
resolve_initial_references() method, 189-190, 208-209
response_expected value (RequestHeader structure), 415
result() method, 305
result parameter (create_request method), 269
result() method, 284
return types
    DII (Dynamic Invocation Interface)), 279-280
    operations, 33

return_value() method, 279
-root_dir option
    idl2java compiler, 100
    java2iiop compiler, 243
Runnable interface, 127-128
runtime exceptions
    defined, 90
    throwing, 91-92

S

-s option (oadutil command), 353-354
Sandbox security model (applets), 212-213
Save As command (File menu), 314
Save command (File menu), 314
scoped names, 24-25
Secure Sockets Layer. *See* SSL
security, 233-238
    GateKeeper, 232-233
    Sandbox model, 212-213
sending Request objects
    methods
        send(), 273-275
        send_deferred(), 276-277
        send_response(), 276-277
    multiple requests, 278
send_deferred() method, 276-277
send_reply() method, 432
send_reply_failed() method, 432
send_request() method, 426
send_request_failed() method, 427
send_request_succeeded() method, 427
SequenceDef object, 299
sequences, 56-57
-serializable option (idl2java command), 102

serialization, 241
Server interface
    attributes
        accessing, 491
        ORBagentAddr, 487
        ORBagentAddrFile, 488
        ORBagentNoFailOver, 488
        ORBagentPort, 487
        ORBalwaysProxy, 488
        ORBbackCompat, 487
        ORBconnectionCacheMax, 488
        ORBconnectionMaxIdle, 488
        ORBdebug, 488
        ORBdebugDir, 488
        ORBdisableAgentCache, 487
        ORBdisableGateKeeper Callbacks, 489
        ORBdisableLocator, 488
        ORBgatekeeperIOR, 488
        ORBgcTimeout, 489
        ORBmbufsize, 489
        ORBnullString, 488
        ORBprocId, 488
        ORBsecureShotdown, 488
        ORBsendBindfalse, 489
        ORBservices, 489
        ORBsyncGC, 488
        ORBtcpNoDelay, 489
        ORBtcpTimeout, 489
        ORBwarn, 489
        setting, 491
    code listing, 486
    methods, 487
    referencing, 489-491
server objects. *See* **objects**
server skeletons. *See* **skeletons**
Server-per-method policy, 349
server-side event handlers, 390
    bind() method, 394-395
    client_aborted() method, 396-397

ConnectionInfo structure, 391
ImplEventHandler implementation, 391-393, 405-410
post_method() method, 398
post_method_exception() method, 398-399
pre_method() method, 397
registering
    HandlerRegistry interface, 401-402
    methods, 403
unbind() method, 395-396
unregistering, 403
ServerInterceptor interface
    code listing, 429-430
    methods
        exception_occurred(), 433
        locate(), 431
        locate_failed(), 431
        locate_forwarded(), 431
        prepare_reply(), 432
        receive_request(), 432
        request_completed(), 433
        send_reply(), 432
        send_reply_failed(), 432
        shutdown(), 433
    sample implementation, 433-434
ServerInterceptorFactory interface
    code listing, 435
    sample implementation, 436
ServerRequest class, 283-284
servers. *See also* **ORB (Object Request Broker)**
    BOA (Basic Object Adapter)
        initializing, 116
        method invocation, 118-119
        object activation/deactivation, 118
        object registration, 118
    Caffeine-created interfaces, 250-252
    Callback server, 370-372
    ComplexAnyTest, 72-75

connection management, 123-124
DSI (Dynamic Skeleton Interface)
  generating with idl2java, 288-291
  sample implementation, 284-288
DynAny server implementation, 339-342
factory server
  IDL (Interface Definition Language), 176
  program listing, 177-179
locating, *see* location strategies
Object Wrappers
  chaining, 373
  Typed, 377-378
  Untyped, 382
PrimitiveAnyTest, 66-68
registering, 203-205
starting, 173
threading models, 119-121
  Thread Pool, 121-123
  Thread-per-Session, 121
server_aborted() method, 399
service activators
  Activator interface, 354-355
  client implementation, 358-360
  custom classes, 356-357
  server implementation, 355-357
ServiceContextList field (RequestHeader structure), 414-415
ServiceInit class, 441
  code listing, 442
  methods
    init(), 443
    list_services(), 444
    resolve(), 444
  sample implementation, 442-443

services
Common Object Services, 13
COS Event Service
  Any event type, 471
  channels, 466
  consumers, 466
  CosEventChannelAdmin module, 468-470
  CosEventComm module, 466-468
  pull model, 476-480
  push model, 464, 471-475
  starting, 481
  suppliers, 466
COS Naming Service, 13, 186-187
  binding, 195
  IDL (Interface Definition Language), 191-192
  initial contexts, 187-190
  Name arrays, 193
  name structure, navigating, 196-199
  NameComponents, 192
  NamingContext interface, 193-195
  resolution, 195-196
  Smart Agent, compared, 187
Events Service, 13
Location Service, 448
  command-line options, 454
  load balancing, 455-462
  referencing, 454-455
  starting, 454
URLNaming, 11
  bind() method, 206-207
  exceptions, 205
  IDL (Interface Definition Language), 202-203
  narrow() method, 208-209
  resolve_initial_references() method, 208

server references, obtaining, 205
server registration, 203-205
Set Breakpoint button (Debugger), 495
Set Verbose button (Debugger), 495
setSmartStub() method, 364
set_return_type() method, 279
Shared Server policy, 348
short data type, 39
shutdown() method, 433, 487
shutdowns, graceful, 395
signatures (digital), 233-234
  creating, 236
  Netscape pre-install, 234-238
    HTML (Hypertext Markup Language) page, 236-237
    pre-install script, 234-235
signed applets, 233-234
  creating, 236
  Netscape pre-install, 234-238
    HTML (Hypertext Markup Language) page, 236-237
    pre-install script, 234-235
sites (Web). *See* **Web sites**
skeletons, 7-8
  DSI (Dynamic Skeleton Interface), 8-9, 282
    DynamicImplementation class, 283
    ServerRequest class, 283-284
    servers, 284-291
  generating, 108-109
  object development
    class definitions, 125
    example, 126
    IDL (Interface Definition Language) interface, 124

Smart Agents, 10, 142-146, 448. *See also* **Location Service**
  Agent interface, 450
  Agent-to-Agent communications, 147-148
  agentaddr files, 162
  binding
    automatic smart binding, 160
    bind() method, 154-156
    defer_bind option, 156
    enable_rebind option, 157
    multiple object implementations, 158-160
  cloning, 160
  compared to COS Naming Service, 187
  disabling, 182
  DNS (Domain Name Service) lookups, 163
  load balancing, 155-156
  memory tables, 449-450
  multihomed hosts
    UNIX, 163-164
    Windows NT, 164
  multiple domains, 161
  persistent objects
    communication, 150-153
    instantiating, 148-149
  platform dependence, 142
  querying
    all_agent_locations() method, 450
    all_instances() method, 451
    all_instances_descs() method, 451
    all_replica() method, 451
    all_replica_descs() method, 451
    all_repository_ids() method, 451
  starting, 146
  triggers
    registering, 452-453
    TriggerDesc object, 452
    TriggerHandler interface, 451-452
    unregistering, 453
  UDP (Unreliable Datagram Protocol) broadcasts, 146, 164-165
smart binding, 10
Smart Stubs, 12, 362-366. *See also* **Callbacks**
  client applications, 364-365
  creating, 362-363
  limitations, 366
  sample implementation, 363-364
-smart_proxy option (idl2java command), 101
-smart_stub option (java2iiop compiler), 243
source code listings. *See* **code listings**
SSL (Secure Sockets Layer), 228
starting
  COS Event Service, 481
  Debugger, 493-494
  GateKeeper, 224
  Interface Repository, 312-313
  Location Service, 454
  oadj (Object Activation Daemon), 346
  servers, 173
  Smart Agents, 146
state, conversational/persistent, 157
State class, 352
static bind() method, 266-267
Step One Process button (Debugger), 494
Stop All Processes button (Debugger), 494
-strict option
  idl2java command, 101
  java2iiop compiler, 243
string data type, 39
StringCounter object, 455-456
StringCounterFactory object, 457-461
StringDef object, 298
stringifying IORs (Interoperable Object References), 171-173
StructDef object, 298
structures
  ConnectionInfo, 391
  constructors, 54-55
  defined, 53
  Desc, 449-450
  example, 53
  extensible, 247-248
    defining in IDL (Interface Definition Language), 252-253
    example, 248-249
    mapping with java2idl, 249-252
  extracting from Any types, 321
  IDL-to-Java language mapping, 53
  inserting into Any types, 323-324
  Principal
    client implementation, 386-388
    IDL (Interface Definition Language), 384
    obtaining, 385-386
    Principal class, 384
    server implementation, 388-390
stubs, 7-8
  generating, 107-108
  Smart Stubs, 12, 362-366
    client applications, 364-365
    creating, 362-363

stubs

    limitations, 366
    sample implementation, 363-364
supplier push model, 464
    consumer client, 471-473
    supplier client, 473-475
suppliers (COS Event Service), 466
    PullSupplier implementation, 478-480
    PushSupplier client, 473-475
system exceptions, 88-89
    BAD_CONTEXT, 89
    BAD_INV_ORDER, 89
    BAD_OPERATION, 89
    BAD_PARAM, 89
    BAD_TYPECODE, 89
    COMM_FAILURE, 89
    DATA_CONVERSION, 89
    FREE_MEM, 89
    IMP_LIMIT, 89
    inheritance hierarchy, 90
    INITIALIZE, 89
    INTERNAL, 89
    INTF_REPOS, 89
    INV_FLAG, 89
    INV_INDENT, 89
    INV_OBJREF, 89
    MARSHAL, 89
    NO_IMPLEMENT, 89
    NO_MEMORY, 90
    NO_PERMISSION, 90
    NO_RESOURCES, 90
    NO_RESPONSE, 90
    OBJ_ADAPTER, 90
    OBJ_NOT_EXIST, 90
    PERSIST_STORE, 90
    TRANSIENT, 90
    UNKNOWN, 90

T

tables (Smart Agent) 449-450
TaggedProfile class, 436
TCKind enumeration, 260, 324-325
testLong() method, 357
testShort() method, 7
Thread Pool model, 121-123
Thread-per-Session model, 121
threading models, 119
    BOA (Basic Object Adapter) initialization, 120-121
    Thread Pool model, 121-123
    Thread-per-Session, 121
threads, 10
throwing exceptions
    Caffeine, 253-254
    runtime exceptions, 91-92
    user-defined exceptions, 94
Tie mechanism, 128-130
    object development
        example, 127
        Runnable interface, 127-128
    server implementation
        binding, 131-132
        code listing, 130-131
        creating, 131-132
tie_[InterfaceName].java files, 130
-timeout option (oadj command), 346
Timer class, 127
tools. *See* **command-line utilities**
TRANSIENT exception, 90
transient objects, 149-150
TriggerDesc object, 452-453
TriggerHandler interface, 451-452
triggers
    registering, 452-453
    TriggerDesc object, 452
    TriggerHandler interface, 451-452
    unregistering, 453
troubleshooting. *See* **Debugger; exceptions**
try_pull() method, 468
Tunneling (HTTP), 214
type() method, 107

Typecodes
    code listing, 260
    creating, 260-261
    TCKind enumeration, 260
    TypeCode class, 325-326
    user-defined types, 261-262
Typed Object Wrappers, 373-374
    IDL interface, 374
    installation
        clients, 376-377
        servers, 377-378
    sample implementation, 375
typedef type, 55-56
types
    Any, 62-63, 259. *See also* Typecodes
        extracting structures, 321
        inserting structures, 323-324
        passing values, 63-75
        TCKind enumeration, 324-325
    arrays, 57-58
    Boolean, 38
    char, 38
    Context, 258-259
        defining, 75-76
        strings, passing, 76-78
    double, 40
    DynAny
        client implementation, 334-338
        creating, 327-328
        DynAny interface, 328-331
        DynArray interface, 331
        DynEnum interface, 331-332
        DynSequence interface, 332
        DynStruct interface, 332-333
        DynUnion interface, 333
        IDL (Interface Definition Language), 318, 333-334
        mapping, 327

passing, 321-323
server implementation, 318-321, 339-342
enum, 45-47
  declaring, 47
  defined, 45
  example, 45
  sample application, 47
language mapping
  IDL-to-Java, 37-38
  Java-to-IDL, 246
long, 40
long long, 40
octet, 38
passing
  constructed data types, 58-62
  primitive data types, 40-44
Principal
  client implementation, 386-388
  IDL (Interface Definition Language), 384
  obtaining, 385-386
  Principal class, 384
  server implementation, 388-390
sequences, 56-57
short, 39
string, 39
struct
  constructors, 54-55
  defined, 53
  example, 53
type safety, 84
typedef, 55-56
union, 47
  declaring, 48
  default( ) accessor method, 50-53
  example, 48
  finding value of, 49
  IDL-to-Java language mapping, 48
  multiple, 49-50
  name collisions, 48-49

unsigned long, 40
unsigned long long, 40
unsigned short, 39
wchar, 38
wstring, 39

U

-U option (idl2java command), 97
UDP (Unreliable Datagram Protocol), 146, 164-165
unbind( ) method, 194, 395-396
underscore(_), 22
UnionDef object, 298
unions, 47
  declaring, 48
  default( ) accessor method, 50-53
  example, 48
  finding value of, 49
  IDL-to-Java language mapping, 48
  multiple, 49-50
  name collisions, 48-49
UNKNOWN exception, 90
UNKNOWN_OBJECT value (LocationStatusType), 420
unreg argument (oadutil tool), 354
unregistering
  event handlers, 403
  objects, 353
  triggers, 453
unregister_all( ) method, 353
unreg_glob_client_handler( ) method, 403
unreg_implementation( ) method, 353
unreg_interface( ) method, 353
unreg_obj_client_handler( ) method, 403

unreg_obj_impl_handler( ) method, 403
Unreliable Datagram Protocol (UDP), 146, 164-165
Unshared Server policy, 348
unsigned long type, 40
unsigned long long type, 40
unsigned short type, 39
Untyped Object Wrappers
  combining, 382
  factories, 380
  installation
    clients, 380-382
    servers, 382
  sample implementation, 378-380
URLNaming service, 11
  exceptions, 205
  IDL (Interface Definition Language), 202-203
  server references, obtaining, 205-206
    bind( ) method, 206-207
    narrow( ) method, 208-209
    resolve_initial_references( ) method, 208-209
  server registration, 203-205
user-defined exceptions
  declaring, 92
  generated class files, 93
  generated interfaces, 93
  throwing, 94
USE_ORB_LOCATOR parameter, 222

V

value method, 305
value, passing by, 255. *See also* **extensible structs**
variables
  environment, 14
    ASAGENT_PORT, 162
    CLASSPATH, 15

variables

OSAGENT_LOCAL_FILE, *163*
OSAGENT_PORT, *146, 161, 164*
PATH, *15*
VBROKER_ADM, *162, 347*
VBROKER_IMPL_NAME, *347*
VBROKER_IMPL_PATH, *347*
VISIBROKER_ADM, *15*
naming conventions, 87
vbj tool, 115
vbjc tool, 115
VBROKER_ADM environment variable, 162, 347
VBROKER_IMPL_NAME environment variable, 347
VBROKER_IMPL_PATH environment variable, 347
verbose option
idl2java command, 101
oadj command, 346
oadutil command, 354
verbose option (java2idl compiler), 246
version option
idl2java command, 101
oadj command, 346
oadutil command, 354
version option (java2idl compiler), 246
version option (java2iiop compiler), 244
Version structure (GIOP messages), 413
VisiBroker installation, 13-15
deployment tools, 16
development tools, 15
environment variables, 14
CLASSPATH, *15*
PATH, *15*
VISIBROKER_ADM, *15*
system requirements, 13-14
VISIBROKER_ADM environment variable, 15

W-Z

-W option (java2iiop compiler), 244
wchar type, 38
Web servers. *See* servers
Web sites
Inprise, 13
OMG (Object Management Group), 5
wide option
java2idl compiler, 246
java2iiop compiler, 244
wrappers. *See* Object Wrappers
wstring data type, 39

mcp.com
The Authoritative Encyclopedia of Computing

Resource Centers
Books & Software
Personal Bookshelf
WWW Yellow Pages
Online Learning
Special Offers
Site Search
Industry News

▶ Choose the online ebooks that you can view from your personal workspace on our site.

About MCP   Site Map   Product Support

Turn to the *Authoritative* Encyclopedia of Computing

You'll find over 150 full text books online, hundreds of shareware/freeware applications, online computing classes and 10 computing resource centers full of expert advice from the editors and publishers of:

- Adobe Press
- BradyGAMES
- Cisco Press
- Hayden Books
- Lycos Press
- New Riders

- Que
- Que Education & Training
- Sams Publishing
- Waite Group Press
- Ziff-Davis Press

mcp.com
The Authoritative Encyclopedia of Computing

Get the best information and learn about latest developments in:

- Design
- Graphics and Multimedia
- Enterprise Computing and DBMS
- General Internet Information
- Operating Systems
- Networking and Hardware
- PC and Video Gaming
- Productivity Applications
- Programming
- Web Programming and Administration
- Web Publishing

When you're looking for computing information, consult the authority. The Authoritative Encyclopedia of Computing at mcp.com.

WHAT'S ON THE CD-ROM

WHAT'S ON THE CD

The companion CD-ROM contains VisiBroker for Java trial edition and the sample code from the book.

WINDOWS 95 INSTALLATION INSTRUCTIONS

1. Insert the CD-ROM disc into your CD-ROM drive.
2. From the Windows 95 desktop, double-click the My Computer icon.
3. Double-click the icon representing your CD-ROM drive.
4. Double-click the icon titled START.EXE to run the CD-ROM interface. You can install the Visual Basic 6.0 Working Model Edition software from the interface.

> **NOTE**
>
> If Windows 95 is installed on your computer, and you have the AutoPlay feature enabled, the START.EXE program starts automatically whenever you insert the disc into your CD-ROM drive.

WINDOWS NT INSTALLATION INSTRUCTIONS

1. Insert the CD-ROM disc into your CD-ROM drive.
2. From File Manager or Program Manager, choose Run from the File menu.
3. Type `<drive>\START.EXE` and press Enter, where `<drive>` corresponds to the drive letter of your CD-ROM. For example, if your CD-ROM is drive D:, type `D:\START.EXE` and press Enter. This will run the CD-ROM interface. You can install the Visual Basic 6.0 Working Model Edition software from the interface.

By opening this package, you are agreeing to be bound by the following agreement:

You may not copy or redistribute the entire CD-ROM as a whole. Copying and redistribution of individual software programs on the CD-ROM is governed by terms set by individual copyright holders.

The installer and code from the author(s) are copyrighted by the publisher and the author(s). Individual programs and other items on the CD-ROM are copyrighted by their various authors or other copyright holders.

This software is sold as-is, without warranty of any kind, either express or implied, including but not limited to the implied warranties of merchantability and fitness for a particular purpose. Neither the publisher nor its dealers or distributors assumes any liability for any alleged or actual damages arising from the use of this program. (Some states do not allow for the exclusion of implied warranties, so the exclusion might not apply to you.)

NOTE: This CD-ROM uses long and mixed-case filenames requiring the use of a protected-mode CD-ROM Driver.